William Penn's 'Holy Experiment': Quaker Truth in Pennsylvania, 1682–1781

James Proud

Inner Light Books
San Francisco, California
2019

William Penn's 'Holy Experiment':
Quaker Truth in Pennsylvania, 1682–1781

© 2019 James Proud

All rights reserved

Except for brief quotations, no part of this publication may be reproduced, stored in a retrieval system, or transmitted in any form or by any means, electronic, mechanical, photocopy, recorded, or otherwise, without prior written permission.

Editor: Charles Martin
Copy editor: Kathy McKay
Layout and design: Matt Kelsey
Maps: David Toliver

Published by Inner Light Books

San Francisco, California

www.innerlightbooks.com

editor@innerlightbooks.com

Library of Congress Control Number: 2019940896

ISBN 978-0-9998332-9-2 (hardcover)
ISBN 978-1-7328239-3-8 (paperback)

For Kathleen

Contents

FOREWORD i

1. ENGLAND (CA. 1350–1682): "THE SUFFERINGS OF THE
   PEOPLE OF GOD CALLED QUAKERS" 1
   Of George Fox (1624–1691) and his vocation to "walk cheerfully
      over the world, answering that of God in everyone" 1
   "The very ocean of darkness and death" 8
   Gathering the Religious Society of Friends 35
   In the twilight of the Restoration, the royal grant of
      Pennsylvania's charter 74
   Embarking on the 'holy experiment' 97

2. PLANTING PENNSYLVANIA (1682–1718): WILLIAM PENN'S
   GOVERNANCE OF "MY COUNTRY" 105
   Penn comes into his province for the first of two periods (1682–
      1684); Harrison and Pemberton settle their new lives 105
   Penn returns to England (1684–1699) but meets new major
      challenges 118
   Penn visits his province for the second and last time
      (1699–1701) 138
   Penn in England for his final years (1701–1718) 158
   The state of the holy experiment at Penn's death 199

3. UNBINDING THE TIES BETWEEN THE QUAKER CHURCH
   AND THE STATE IN PENNSYLVANIA (1719–1750) 205
   Hannah Penn's caretaker administration of the proprietorship
      and government of the colony (1719–1726) 205
   An era of laissez faire expansion in the province and of
      worldly leadership in PYM (1727–1750) 221
   Embracing, then deceiving, the "nations of Indians" 237
   The state of the holy experiment on the eve of its reform 293

4. ENDING THE HOLY EXPERIMENT: QUAKER TRUTH IN
   PENNSYLVANIA AT THE CLOSE OF AMERICA'S COLONIAL
   AGE (1750–1781) 301
   Condemning the inhumanity of enslavement (1750–1781) 301
   Disaffection among Pennsylvania's "One People":
      The French and Indian War (1756–1763) 316
   Teedyuscung at Easton: An American Tragedy in Six Acts 350
   Separation and revolution: End times (1764–1781) 404

APPENDICES
    1. Glossary   426
    2. The Statutory Oaths Demanded of Early Quakers in
        England   432
    3. Glossary of Religious Sects Referred to in Chapter 1   436
    4. Phineas Pemberton's Prefatory Epistle in the First
        Philadelphia Yearly Meeting Minute Book, ca. 1700   439
    5. Penn's Disposition of His Proprietary Interests in the
        Province under His Several Last Wills and Testaments   442
    6. Opinion of Sir Edward Northey, Counsel to Hannah Penn,
        in Penn v. Penn (December 11, 1719)   444
    7. Israel Pemberton Jr.'s Letter of April 29, 1749, to His
        Brother James   446
    8. Chronology of Events   448
    9. Biographical Information on Europeans   471
    10. Native Americans: Nations and Leaders,
        Alliance Systems, and the Walking Purchase   476
    11. Church and State Leadership in Colonial Pennsylvania
        (1682–1781)   490

BIBLIOGRAPHY AND ABBREVIATIONS   494

INDEX   500

LIST OF MAPS
England's Counties in the Period of George Fox and
    William Penn   xii
Southeastern Pennsylvania in the Period of William Penn
    and James Logan   104
Pennsylvania in the Period of the French and Indian War   204
The Southern Tier of New York and the Northern Tier of
    Pennsylvania in the Period of the American Revolution   300

FOREWORD

William Penn's life was, at its core, a search for peace. This study concentrates attention on his greatest effort to secure true peace for all—his undertaking to populate and cultivate that region of North America granted him by the English Crown in March 1681.[1] Viewed as "wilderness" by Penn and his fellow planters, the land was given the name 'Pensilvania' (Penn's woods) by the man who wore the crown, Charles II, in tribute to his friend, Penn's deceased father, a naval hero. Penn's historic undertaking has earned the honorific 'holy experiment.'

Penn is known to have used the phrase 'holy experiment' at least once. Writing a letter to James Harrison, a fellow Quaker living near Manchester, England, in August 1681, Penn appointed Harrison as an agent to sell land in Penn's newly acquired province. Penn intended that Pennsylvania should be a haven for seekers of religious freedom and liberty of conscience, especially those who, for the sake of faith and principle, had suffered property forfeiture or bodily imprisonment during the persecutions of the English Civil War, Commonwealth, Protectorate, and Restoration. In commenting on how he had acquired Pennsylvania and what ends it might serve, Penn wrote to Harrison:

> For my country, [I eyed] the Lord in the obtaining of it; and more was I drawn inward to look to Him, and to o[we it] to His hand and power, than to any ot[her way]. I have so obtained it and desire that I may not be unworthy of His love, but do that which may answer yet His kind providence and serve His Truth and people; that an example may be set up to the nations. There may be room there, though not here, for such a holy experiment.[2]

---

[1] The extent to which the region granted Penn was already inhabited and settled, especially in and around its eastern waterways, by Lenapes and Susquehannocks, Swedes and Finns, and Dutch and English as well as others is described in Jean R. Soderlund's study *Lenape Country: Delaware Valley Society before William Penn* (Philadelphia: University of Pennsylvania Press, 2015).

[2] William Penn to James Harrison, dated "25th 6 mo 81," in Mary Maples Dunn and Richard S. Dunn, *The Papers of William Penn*, 5 vols. (Philadelphia:

William Penn's 'Holy Experiment'

Whether Penn later remembered having described his vast and daring enterprise 'beyond the seas' as a holy experiment is uncertain, but history has judged it to have been so, even though the unfolding of the experiment, the people and events by which it proceeded, are now nearly forgotten. The holy experiment, like Penn himself, is far distant from our time and so blurred in the details that the honorific may seem ironic considering that era's serious political and moral problems.

This book tracks the historical progress of the foremost themes of the holy experiment from 1681, when Penn wrote the above letter to Harrison, through the era of several Quaker meeting clerkships under the Pembertons, Harrison's direct descendants. These themes were most fully realized by the 1750s, but the holy experiment continued until 1781, when the experiment was finally laid down. The great themes of the experiment, in addition to the founding principles of peace grounded in religious freedom and liberty of conscience, were public education, preserving friendship with the Native Americans, and abolishing the obscene evil of slavery. By the end of the experiment in 1781, both successes and failures had been realized, successes and failures that continue to underlie the society America has become since those days of its birthing at Philadelphia when the founding fathers gave order to the United States.

Never intended to be an unattainable ideal or utopia, the province of Pennsylvania (given the name that the king Latinized out of *Penn's woods*), from its capital of Philadelphia (given the name that Penn Latinized out of *city of brotherly love*), placed religious toleration and the welfare of all at the center of its common life. Uniformity and conformity in matters of faith and belief throughout the province were antithetical to that life. Penn intended that ties of mutual respect and interdependence should bind the populace that, in self-interest, would resist conflict and confrontation and renounce violence in all its forms.

History gives only rare examples of earlier successful experiments in preserving peace amidst diversity and in promoting the general good of all. Especially notable were the reigns of Ashoka (304–232 BCE), the third emperor of the Mauryan dynasty, whose edicts promoted the way of peace for the welfare of all in the Indian subcontinent, and of Abd-ar-

---

University of Pennsylvania Press, 1981–), 2:108 (hereafter cited as *PWP*).
Missing material that has been reconstructed is in brackets.

Foreword

Rahman III (891–961 CE), the first caliph of Córdoba, who, on behalf of the Umayyad family, reclaimed the caliphate, or rulership, of Islam and shared peace and prosperity within the borders of al-Andalus (Spain) with Jews and Christians.[3] Penn was kindred to these notable predecessors in his large embrace of the general population dwelling in well-being and harmony. The Quakers of Pennsylvania were only later seen as sectarian when others in the free society that Penn had planted no longer practiced 'brotherly love' and became intolerant of pacifist Friends.

Penn, in his letter to Harrison, set forth another core principle of his undertaking—the desire to serve not only the Lord's people but His Truth. For Quakers, the Truth is the mystery of God's being and purposes as revealed in the creation, salvation, and sanctification of the world and made manifest in human affairs through social justice, peace, and equity. In a profound and living sense, Truth and God are synonymous.

My purpose in these pages is to present an historical survey of the struggles that formed and then challenged the principles of Penn's 'holy experiment' from as early as the 1350s and onward to 1781. In most of those years, conflicts abounded. They arose among Quakers as well as between Quakers and others, such as the Crown and its ministers, Parliament, the Penn proprietorship (Penn himself and then those sons and grandsons of Penn who were his successors at law), its agents, and the antiproprietary and other political factions in the colony. The conflicts also involved adjoining colonies, the French, the Native Americans, and the flood of immigrants, to name only the major antagonists. The issues were manifold, and the records are complex and scattered. I have sought to present the challenges to the holy experiment and to identify and locate the preserved record, giving context to the most significant of the underlying issues. Although I have my own views and judgments on many of the issues, some of which I express herein, I have not attempted a

---

[3] For more on Ashoka, see John Keay, *India: A History* (New York: Atlantic Monthly Press, 2000), 88–100; Mortimer Wheeler, *Early India and Pakistan to Ashoka* (London: Thames and Hudson), 1959, 170–80. For more on Abd-ar-Rahman III (sometimes Abd-al-Rahman III), see *The New Cambridge History of Islam*, 6 vols., ed. Michael Cook (Cambridge: Cambridge University Press, 2010), 1:581–621; Albert Hourani, *A History of the Arab Peoples* (New York: Warner Books, 1991), 41–43, 187–98.

probing commentary or modern analysis of the holy experiment itself other than to explain the history of its principal elements. By presenting the totality of the problems and by locating the record, I trust the interested reader will have the tools with which to make an independent judgment on the overriding dilemma: can a peaceable society be created in a pluralistic, conflicted world? In the end, the question may be humanly unanswerable.

The four chapters of this book span the more than 430 years from the Black Death and the age of Wycliffe and the Lollards, the English Civil War and the accompanying sufferings endured by religious nonconformists in the British Isles and the settling of Pennsylvania to the American Revolution. Penn's experiment in peace took place in the context of far-reaching historical events.

Chapter 1 covers the period from 1643 to 1682. Here will be found accounts of George Fox's journeys of spiritual searching and of the 'openings' or revelations that came to him; of the conviction or 'convincement' of believers drawn to his message as they grew in numbers to become the Religious Society of Friends; and of the Friends' or Quakers' sufferings for their faith through such penalties as imprisonment, fines, and property forfeiture imposed on them by the government. The early sufferers and their sufferings were memorialized in detail by Joseph Besse in his *A Collection of the Sufferings of the People called Quakers for the Testimony of a Good Conscience*.[4] Here also will be found the details of the imprisonments of George Fox and William Penn for their beliefs; the legal schemes of England's transitioning national authorities desperate to maintain order; and the royal grant to Penn of his province. Out of all the openings, convincements, and sufferings of "the people called Quakers," the seed for planting Penn's holy experiment in his American colony found life. The essential sources I used for this narrative were *The Journal of George Fox* and *The Papers of William Penn* as well as the official *Statutes of the Realm* and the *Acts and Ordinances of the Interregnum*.[5] The state's official

---

[4] Joseph Besse, *A Collection of the Sufferings of the People called Quakers for the Testimony of a Good Conscience*, 2 vols. (London: Luke Hinde, 1753). The classic formulation of "the sufferings of the people called Quakers" is sometimes rendered "the sufferings of the people of God in scorn called Quakers."

[5] George Fox, *The Journal of George Fox with an Epilogue by Henry J. Cadbury and an Introduction by Geoffrey F. Nuttall*, rev. ed. by John L. Nickalls (Philadelphia: Religious Society of Friends, 1997) (hereafter cited as Fox, *Journal*); PWP; *The Statutes of the Realm ... from original records and authentic manuscripts*, 10 vols. (London: 1810–1828); and C. H. Firth and R. S.

Foreword

documents are complemented by the vast treasure of public and private papers and journals carefully preserved from their inception by all branches of the Religious Society of Friends.

Chapter 2 sketches the governing of Pennsylvania by Penn himself during his first visit (1682–1684), his prolonged stay back in England (1684–1699), his second visit to the province (1699–1701), and then his final years back in England, when he managed from afar until mentally incapacitated in 1712 and then lived until his death in 1718 under the care of his wife, who administered the province from England through the agency of James Logan in Philadelphia. *The Papers of William Penn* again provide the source materials for this period, together with the extensive collection of documents held by the Historical Society of Pennsylvania and other institutions as custodians of the records of the Penn, Logan, and other families of colonial Pennsylvania.

Chapter 3 opens in a dark period in the history of the holy experiment (1719–1750), dark in that the record is so (intentionally) thin and because the issues presented were so antithetical to the moral precepts and professed discipline of the Quakers. The issues concerned the practices of Friends who traded in or owned slaves and of all persons who acquired the lands of Native Americans by fraud (as alleged in the case of the Walking Purchase of 1737) or through illegal occupation. The source materials for the contest over Quakers' participation in the evil of slavery are the cited printed literature of abolitionist authors and the measures reported in the Philadelphia Yearly Meeting (hereafter cited as PYM) minute books to punish any who broke the unity of Friends. The wrongful taking of the native peoples' lands, however, was under the purview of the government, not of the Quaker community, and records of those transactions were secreted from the public eye. First James Logan hid the records, even from the proprietors, and after Logan was replaced as secretary of the Proprietary Land Office in April 1733 for irregularities, they were accessible only to the proprietors and their agents. The late Francis Jennings carried out exhaustive research on this topic beginning in the 1960s, and in his scholarly articles and books he detailed many lapses if not wrongs in the administration of the Proprietary Land Office.

Rait, eds., *Acts and Ordinances of the Interregnum*, 3 vols. (London: H. M. Stationery Office, 1911).

Jennings's published work cited herein, secondary though it is, exposes the record of the deteriorating relationship between Pennsylvania and the Indian nations at that time.

Chapter 4 brings resolution to these besetting issues by describing how Israel Pemberton Jr., upon becoming clerk of PYM in 1750, managed to forge a consensus in the Quaker community that resulted in the condemnation of slave trading and owning. Simultaneously with that axial moment in 1754, early skirmishes of the French and Indian War broke the peace of the province and soon brought Pennsylvania to the brink of war with the Lenapes[6] and other native peoples of the province. Pemberton and his Quaker colleagues then battled with colonial authorities in trying to aid the Lenapes, first to gain redress for the injustice of the Walking Purchase through a series of six treaties at Easton and then to escape destitution and death in their former homelands. In the ensuing American Revolution, Pemberton and fellow PYM activists were interned in Virginia as enemies of the American cause from September 1777 to April 1778. This was followed in 1779 by ruinous conflict between the colonists and the Iroquois in regions of the upper Susquehanna River and on into New York. The retirement of James Pemberton from the PYM clerkship marked the end of the holy experiment. At the same time, the American Revolution came to a successful conclusion, bringing with it the beginnings of the American union. The principal sources for this history are the PYM minute books and ancillary documents; the records of the Quakers' "Friendly Association for regaining and preserving peace with the Indians by pacific measures"; the treaties involving the native peoples and Pennsylvania between 1736 and 1762;[7] and contemporaneous writings, especially those of Charles Thomson[8] and Benjamin Franklin as well as the later studies of Jennings.

---

[6] Going against the mainstream and even several of the quotations in these pages, I refer to the Native Americans occupying the lands of the Delaware River and its tributaries as 'Lenapes,' not the usual 'Delawares,' and I distinguish them by their various locations along the river as well as their inland and western settlements in the Ohio country. For example, I refer to the Lenapes living at the Falls of the Delaware River as the "Falls Lenapes," those at the confluence of the Delaware and Lehigh Rivers as the "Forks Lenapes," and those on Brandywine Creek as the "Brandywine Lenapes."

[7] For the full citation of these treaties, see Susan Kalter, ed., *Benjamin Franklin, Pennsylvania and the First Nations: The Treaties of 1736–62* (Urbana: University of Illinois Press, 2006).

[8] Thomson's study of the Proprietary Land Office deeds underlying his work for Israel Pemberton Jr. and the "Friendly Association" in supporting the

Foreword

An additional bibliographical note is necessary. The leadership of PYM had long been concerned with preserving the history of Penn's experiment in the province, and the ongoing search for a historian from within that body is shown in PYM's earliest minute books. Some of those approached, themselves principal actors in the events laid out in the pages that follow, could have revealed much that remains hidden to this day. We can only imagine how Caleb Pusey, David Lloyd, Isaac Norris I, James Logan, or John Kinsey—each sounded out about writing the first history of the province and of Penn's founding labors—might have viewed and analyzed the experiment up to their own times. Great hope was placed in Samuel Smith, an active member of PYM and the author of colonial New Jersey's published history, who agreed to draft a history of Pennsylvania and its "first colonists and early settlers," but none of his history was published until 1913, long after his death.

At last, Israel Pemberton Jr. found the author in Robert Proud,[9] an instructor in the Latin division of the Philadelphia Friends Public School. Proud was under the charge of Pemberton, clerk of the school's overseers, who had asked John Fothergill in London to recommend such an instructor. Proud, a Quaker born in England and related to Fothergill, taught in the Friends Public School from 1761 to 1770 and again from 1780 to 1790. He spent the decade between his two teaching periods engaged in business with his brother in Philadelphia and, as stated on the title page of his *History of Pennsylvania*, wrote that work "principally between the years 1776 and 1780."[10] Because the American Revolution and its aftermath interrupted the life of the land, Robert Proud's work was not printed until 1797, requiring him to carry the history beyond 1742 and end it instead at 1770. He wrote with the benefit of the documents assembled by those before him who had considered but declined undertaking this important labor, and he had the additional

---

Lenapes' claim at the Easton treaties is invaluable. See [Charles Thomson], *An Enquiry into the Causes of the Alienation of the Delaware and Shawanese Indians from the British Interest* (1759; repr., St. Claire Shores, MI: Scholarly Press, 1970).

[9] No relation to the author.

[10] Robert Proud, *The History of Pennsylvania in North America, from the Original Institution and Settlement of that Province under the first Proprietor and Governor William Penn, in 1681, till after the Year 1742*, 2 vols. (Philadelphia: Z. Poulson, 1797).

benefit of their notes and comments. Proud was a bachelor, often ill and always on the economic margins, and he found the years of the American Revolution trying and the populace "strangely disposed for revolution, rebellion, and destruction under the name and pretense of liberty."[11] It was an unforgiving time for any Quaker to be writing such a study, and he judged his history of Pennsylvania "imperfect and deficient."[12]

In studying the documents of this period, the reader needs to keep in mind the great calendar change of 1752 made in the English-speaking world, an interesting historical anomaly.[13] For immediate purposes it means that Old Style (Julian calendar) dates are used herein for identifying times prior to September 14, 1752, and that New Style (Gregorian calendar) dates are used for identifying times on or after September 14, 1752. That change means that there is no written record for the eleven days that would have fallen between September 2 and 14, 1752, under the Julian calendar. Another change was to move the first day of

---

[11] Robert Proud, "Autobiography of Robert Proud, the Historian," *The Pennsylvania Magazine of History and Biography* 13 (1889): 43 (this journal is hereafter cited as *PMHB*).

[12] Ibid., 437.

[13] Historical note: On September 2, 1752, Britain and its dominions (including the American colonies) ceased following the Old Style (or Julian) calendar (in use since 45 BCE) and, on the following day, accounted as September 14, began using the New Style (or Gregorian) calendar, which was already being followed in Scotland and most other nations of Europe. This complex adjustment was made pursuant to the British government's Calendar (New Style) Act of 1750, formally captioned "An act for regulating the commencement of the year, and for correcting the calendar now in use" (24 Geo. 2, c. 23).

The conversion from the Julian calendar, introduced by and named for Julius Caesar, to the Gregorian calendar was introduced by and named for Pope Gregory XIII in a papal bull issued February 24, 1582. The change was made to correct a date drift by calculating the time between vernal equinoxes as 365.2425 days instead of 365.25 days. The countries in western Europe touched by the Protestant Reformation variously delayed accepting this directive of the Roman Church and put off changing their civil calendars. Britain, one of the last to do so, found it necessary to skip eleven days in order to restore March 21 as the spring equinox, which was of great concern to the Council of Nicaea in 325 CE in order to fix the date of Easter. The skip was made by having Wednesday, September 2, 1752, succeeded by Thursday, September 14, 1752.

In addition, the English enabling act changed the commencement of the new year from March 25 (the Feast of the Annunciation and close to the spring equinox) to January 1 (which was the day Janus, the god of gates, doors, and beginnings, was honored by the Romans).

Foreword

each year (New Year's Day) from March 25 to January 1. In this volume, all years are shown as under the Gregorian calendar.

For the sake of clarity, I have edited most of the spelling, capitalization, and punctuation that I judged would hinder the modern reader. I use square brackets to signify editorial matter such as reconstructions of missing words or definitions of archaic terms.

Appendices 1 to 3 in this book are designed to assist the reader in navigating the unfamiliar legal terms, archaic statutes, test oaths, Quaker terminology, and disparate religious bodies that drive the narrative. Pertinent to chapter 2 are the prefatory essay of Phineas Pemberton inscribed in the first PYM minute book and a summary of Penn's changing plans for disposing of his proprietorship of Pennsylvania in his successive wills (appendices 4 and 5). For chapter 3, appendix 6 contains the opinion of Hannah Penn's legal adviser that guided the final adjudication placing Penn's proprietary rights to Pennsylvania in the hands of the sons of his second marriage. Also for chapter 3, appendix 7 offers a glimpse of the very private Israel Pemberton Jr. through a self-revealing moment in a letter to his brother James, the last PYM clerk of the holy experiment era.

Appendices 8 to 11 provide a chronology of the flow of events in the book as well as brief biographies of the actors upon this historical stage (European and Native American). Appendix 11 is a table that charts the leaders of the Quaker community and the leaders of the provincial government in colonial Pennsylvania up to the time that the holy experiment was laid down.

I have received much kind and generous assistance along the way from individuals and from institutions where this work was prepared. I would especially like to thank Ann Upton, Chris Densmore, Pat O'Donnell, Susanna Morikowa, and Clifford Pemberton. To Jean Soderlund I owe special thanks for reading an early draft and making invaluable suggestions for its improvement. The steady editorial guidance of Charles Martin, the exacting copyediting of Kathy McKay, the production expertise of Matt Kelsey, and the cartographic and other skills of Dave Toliver have put the finishing touches on my labors. I bear all responsibility for all errors herein.

There would be little scholarship if learned institutions did not preserve and make available for modern study the primary and secondary materials of history past and present. I have been fortunate to have free access to such institutions in preparing this book and am particularly grateful to the libraries and librarians at Haverford College, Swarthmore College, Bryn Mawr College, the Historical Society of Pennsylvania, Germantown Friends School, St. Charles Borromeo Seminary in Philadelphia, Friends House London, and Woodbrooke College in Birmingham, England.

This work was written with the invaluable support and scholarly help I have received from all these individuals and institutional libraries, but it also owes much to the lands and places named within its pages where I have been able to walk historic ground and feel the past. I have had occasion to reflect in places where I know that principals upon this stage such as George Fox and William Penn, John Woolman and Israel Pemberton Jr., Teedyuscung and Charles Thomson have been before me. And I have been at sites where those without voice in this narrative were heard in their day and can yet be encountered. Visits at two such sites are unforgettable. One, at Birmingham Meetinghouse in the Brandywine Valley, is described on the text's final page. The other visit occurred on a Sunday afternoon during Independence Day celebrations in Philadelphia a few years ago. My wife and I had gone to visit the Penn Treaty Park on the Delaware River where the Lenape village of Shackamaxon (now part of Philadelphia) may once have stood. In the car park we heard the musical sounds of what seemed a culture more recently added to American life coming from the distant corner diagonally across the open green field. As we walked past the woods and riverside edging the field, we came to the place of the music makers. They were Native Americans, dancing and chanting an outdoor prayer service with pipes, hand drums, and gentle rattles, making water offerings out of a gourd to the earth and sky, scattering seeds, and smoking a shared pipe. I felt a moment of streaming peace as if from the ancient peoples who had welcomed Penn into their homelands, ancient peoples whose descendants have not been allowed even one reservation in Pennsylvania. Yet in that moment an ageless, gentle spirit proved to be still alive.

Above all, I am grateful to Kathleen, my wife, for her constant support and encouragement to pursue this search for Truth in the founding years of Pennsylvania. Thus, from my heart to hers, the dedication.

England's Counties in the Period of George Fox and William Penn

Key to Numbers

1. Bedfordshire
2. Berkshire
3. Buckinghamshire
4. Cambridgeshire
5. Cheshire
6. Cornwall
7. Cumberland
8. Derbyshire
9. Devon
10. Dorset
11. County Durham
12. Essex
13. Gloucestershire
14. Hampshire
15. Herefordshire
16. Hertfordshire
17. Huntingdonshire
18. Kent
19. Lancashire
20. Leicestershire
21. Lincolnshire
22. Middlesex
23. Norfolk
24. Northamptonshire
25. Northumberland
26. Nottinghamshire
27. Oxfordshire
28. Rutland
29. Shropshire
30. Somerset
31. Staffordshire
32. Suffolk
33. Surrey
34. Sussex
35. Warwickshire
36. Westmorland
37. Wiltshire
38. Worcestershire
39. Yorkshire

CHAPTER 1

ENGLAND (CA. 1350–1682): "THE SUFFERINGS OF THE PEOPLE OF GOD CALLED QUAKERS"

Before the 'holy experiment' of William Penn were the sufferings, and before the sufferings were the convincements, and before the convincements were those 'openings' to George Fox so boldly described in the first pages of his *Journal*.[1] The openings—received as divine insights or revelations—were held by Fox with a firmness from which he never retreated and were thereafter maintained by his faithful followers with convictions strong enough to found—and even suffer for—the Religious Society of Friends, also known as Quakers.

Of George Fox (1624–1691) and his vocation to "walk cheerfully over the world, answering that of God in everyone"

In September 1643, the third month in his twentieth year of life, Fox set out from Drayton-in-the-Clay, his Leicestershire birthplace and parental home (later renamed Fenny Drayton), to be, at God's command, "as a stranger unto all."[2] He was on a journey of spiritual wrestling. Although the journey ultimately took him to London before he returned home the following year, his first outbound stop was in Lutterworth, near his starting place. Although he records nothing of the Lutterworth sojourn other than that he remained there "some time,"[3] symbolically it marked his being in the place where, almost 260 years earlier,

---

[1] The early Quakers used the term 'openings' to refer to believers' "transformative and perfecting conversion (metanoia) in which the old self... was stripped away so that the new person could willingly submit to divine Love (God).... The Day of the Lord, now dawning through convincement, anticipated the victory of God's love over 'Satan's kingdom'—the empire of evil—both within and in the 'carnal' world." Gerard Guiton, *The Early Quakers and the 'Kingdom of God': Peace, Testimony and Revolution* (San Francisco: Inner Light Books, 2014), 5. For definitions of early Quaker terms as well as of other terminology from this period, see appendix 1.

[2] Fox, *Journal*, 3.

[3] Ibid.

John Wycliffe (ca. 1328/31–1384), the 'morning star of the Reformation,' had completed his public career, lived out his final days, and been laid to rest.

Communing with the spirit of John Wycliffe

Fox's impressionable spirit in his time of searching for guidance would have been open to Wycliffe's work and legacy as it abided in Lutterworth.[4] Wycliffe began his adult career in and near Oxford University, where he achieved academic mastery in "logic, philosophy, divinity, morality, and the speculative art without peer,"[5] according to the university's testimonial of 1406. For a period, he was Master of Balliol College. After earning a doctorate in divinity, he became a lecturer in the university and commenced speaking and writing with authority on the urgent issues of his day.

The pandemic known as the Black Death, which ravaged England in its course across Europe, had a searing influence on Wycliffe and his generation.[6] It might well have seemed to be an invasion by the pale horse of the apocalypse, carrying its rider Death to scourge the earth with sword, famine, pestilence, and wild beasts.[7] Indeed, the first biblical commentary Wycliffe wrote may have been his work on the apocalypse as described in the Revelation to John, the final book of the Bible:

> It seems probable that Wycliffe's first attempt at the interpretation of Scripture was his commentary on the Apocalypse. The fearful pestilence which between 1345 and 1349 swept away a large portion of the human race, and other calamities, arising as well from the strife of

---

[4] For the closeness of Wycliffe's and Fox's views regarding Christ, the church, Scripture, and social reform, see Daniel Staley Zemaitis, *Convergent Paths: The Correspondence between Wycliffe, Hus and the Early Quakers* (PhD diss., University of Birmingham, 2012).

[5] As quoted in John Foxe, *The Book of Martyrs*, ed. and abr. G. A. Williamson (Boston: Little, Brown & Co., 1965), 18.

[6] See G. M. Trevelyan, *History of England* (London: Longmans, Green & Co., 1926); Colin Platt, *King Death: The Black Plague and Its Aftermath in Late-Medieval England* (London: UCL Press, 1996); John Aberth, *The Black Death: The Great Mortality of 1348–1350: A Brief History with Documents* (New York: Palgrave Macmillan, 2005).

[7] Revelation 6:8.

nations and parties as from the discord of the natural elements, cast a general gloom over society.[8]

In the years that followed, Wycliffe wrote commentaries on the gospels. Finally, by the early 1380s, the Wycliffe circle, which was composed of some of his learned associates from the Oxford community, had completed the translation of the Vulgate, the official Latin Bible of Western Christianity, into the language of the English nation, thereby presenting the English people for the first time with the gift of being able to read and interpret their holy scriptures for themselves. That unique achievement has survived in over 250 manuscript copies.

John Purvey, one of Wycliffe's foremost learned associates, in his prologue to a ca. 1395 revision of the English Bible, wrote:

> And we English people, descended from heathens, are meant through our Christian faith, to proclaim holy scripture. . . . Yet failing so, the common people of our realm who belong to Christ, the great cornerstone, are rightly identified as stones set firmly in His foundation, for though our covetous clergy are altogether carried away by bribery, heresy, and many other sins, and though they despise and hate holy scripture as much as they can, yet the common people cry out for that scripture, to know and obey it, with great cost and peril to their lives. For these reasons and others, and with the loving purpose of saving all people in our realm whom God would save, a simple creature has translated the Bible out of Latin into English.[9]

The church's official judgment fell heavily on this first English Bible that ever since has been called the Wycliffe Bible, even though the extent, if any, of Wycliffe's contributions to the text has never been determined. In November 1407, the Council of Oxford prohibited

> anyone from translating on his own authority any book of Scripture into English, or reading any book, booklet, or treatise of this nature composed in the time of the said John Wycliffe or later, unless the translation had been

---

[8] *The Holy Bible . . . made from the Latin Vulgate by John Wycliffe and his followers*, ed. J. Forshall and F. Madden, 4 vols. (Oxford: 1850), 1:vii.

[9] Ibid., 56–57 [modernized from 1382 vernacular English by the author].

approved by the diocesan [bishop] or by a provincial [church] council.[10]

Posterity has been kinder. A nineteenth-century British historian noted that Wycliffe's "exertions in translating the Bible into the vulgar tongue deserve unqualified praise, and might alone entitle him to immortality."[11]

Wycliffe's concerns, however, were much larger than giving the English people the Bible in their common language. He increasingly took the measure of the worldliness of the established church in his day. He questioned the historical justification for claims of papal supremacy, and he saw corruption in the monasteries and moral failures among the clergy. He disputed sacramental doctrines. And by encouraging his partisans and supporters at Oxford—who were silenced or purged from the university when its liberties were withdrawn by the king and the Archbishop of Canterbury—he helped spread the influence in the land of his teachings (known as 'Wycliffism'), which were promoted by the populist political and reforming Lollard movement.

> This purge, which had to be repeated in the reign of Henry IV, cut off Lollardry from its roots in the best culture of the day [Oxford], and helped to turn it into popular evangelicalism, hiding from authority and propagating itself among the poor.[12]

The authorities repeatedly acted upon the perceived threat of Wycliffism and Lollardry. Wycliffe's writings and beliefs were condemned in his lifetime by Pope Gregory XI in May 1377, who sent five bulls (edicts) to Richard II of England, the Archbishop of Canterbury, the Bishop of London, and the chancellor of Oxford University directing Wycliffe to be arrested, imprisoned, and examined, for having

> rashly broken forth into such detestable madness that he does not fear to assert, profess, and publicly proclaim . . . certain propositions and conclusions, erroneous and

---

[10] As quoted by W. A. Craigie, "The English Versions to Wyclif," in *The Bible and Its Ancient and English Versions,* ed. H. Wheeler Robinson (Oxford: Clarendon Press, 1940), 142–43.

[11] Jeremy Collier, *An Ecclesiastical History of Great Britain,* ed. Francis Barham, 9 vols. (London: Wm. Straker, 1840), 3:189n.

[12] See Trevelyan, *History of England,* 249.

false, and discordant with the faith, which endeavour to subvert and weaken the stability of the entire Church.[13]

Further condemnation came when Oxford University in 1381, through the authority of its chancellor and thirteen learned doctors, censured Wycliffe for his eucharistic teaching that Christ was only present "figuratively and emblematically" in the bread and wine of the altar, whereupon Wycliffe left Oxford and took up residence in his rectory at Lutterworth.[14] Then in 1382 the Convocation of Canterbury, at its meeting at Blackfriars, London, found Wycliffe chargeable with ten "heretical conclusions" and fourteen "erroneous conclusions."[15]

The authorities continued their attacks on Wycliffe's ideas even after his death in 1384 following a stroke, beginning with the Convocation of Canterbury meeting in London in 1397 that condemned Wycliffe on eighteen articles brought by "the canonists and civilians of Oxford."[16] The next attack came from Oxford University, which in 1410 censured Wycliffe's opinions.

> And here about eighty, or, as some report, two hundred conclusions in Wycliffe's books, were publically condemned by the university; and all members of that society forbidden to teach, preach, or maintain, any of those censured propositions, under the penalty of losing their respective degrees. And to make this order the more regarded, the censured books were burnt at the same time. But, as it happened, these opinions of Wycliffe, instead of being stifled, gained ground by this opposition, and his books were more valued than before.[17]

Another assault was launched by the Council at Rome in 1412–1413. And then in 1415, the Council of Constance, the fifteenth ecumenical council recognized by the Roman Catholic Church, condemned Wycliffe as well as his follower John Hus, rector of the University of Prague, and also deposed Pope John XXIII, the convener of the Council. An active participant in the proceeding,

---

[13] Henry Gee and William John Hardy, *Documents Illustrative of English Church History* (London: Macmillan & Co., 1896), 106.

[14] Collier, *An Ecclesiastical History of Great Britain*, 3:152.

[15] Ibid., 108–10.

[16] Ibid., 221–22.

[17] Ibid., 287.

Cardinal Guillaume Fillastre of St. Mark, Paris, wrote in his diary:

> [Session XV.] On the following Saturday, which was the 6th of July, the Council held a session to deal with the errors of Master John Wyclif of England, deceased, condemn his memory, and pass sentence on Master John [Hus] of Bohemia. The following sentences were passed. First, as regards Wyclif, the Council condemned the forty-five articles [previously condemned by the Universities of Paris and Prague] . . . , on the one hand, and the 260 articles [previously condemned by Oxford University] on the other hand, and approved the sentence of the last Roman council, which had condemned his books and his memory. The same day it passed sentence on Master John Hus, who was present, condemned and degraded him for heresy, and delivered him to the secular court. For he persisted in his errors and when urged in the Council to repent, recant, and abjure, stood up and declared in a loud voice that he would not recant, because he believed that by so doing he would displease God and the saints; nor would he be a scandal to the multitude to whom he had preached his doctrines in Bohemia. So that very day he was conducted by the secular court and burned, impenitent.[18]

Further, the Council sought to exterminate by fire whatever might be left of the mortal remains of Wycliffe and thus decreed

> that the body and bones of the said John Wycliffe, if they might be discerned from the bodies of other, faithful people, be taken out of the ground and thrown away far from the burial of any church, according unto the canon laws and decrees.[19]

Almost thirteen years later, this official act of the Council of Constance was carried out on the orders of the Bishop of Lincoln acting pursuant to the instructions of Pope Martin V. In the springtime of 1428, Wycliffe's bones were removed from the Lutterworth church cemetery and burned, and the ashes were cast into the River Swift.

---

[18] Quoted in Louise Ropes Loomis, *The Council of Constance: The Unification of the Church,* ed. and ann. J. H. Mundy and K. M. Woody (New York: Columbia University Press, 1961), 256.

[19] As quoted in Foxe, *The Book of Martyrs,* 18–19.

Wycliffe's ideas and teachings must have remained vital in England even during the lifetime of George Fox, and Fox, on his soul-despairing pilgrimage, could well have realized that he, too, was on a quest for spiritual liberty similar to the one Wycliffe had undertaken. Wycliffe's teachings that "religion was overcharged with ceremonies"[20] and that "oaths" were not lawful[21] surely had resonance for Fox. So also did the following Lollard Conclusion of 1394 addressing the issue of war:

> 10. That manslaughter in war, or by pretended law of justice for a temporal cause, without spiritual revelation, is expressly contrary to the New Testament, which indeed is the law of grace and full of mercies. This conclusion is openly proved by the examples of Christ's preaching here on earth, for he specially taught a man to love his enemies, and to show them pity, and not to slay them. The reason is this, that for the most part, when men fight, after the first blow, charity is broken. . . . The law of mercy, which is the New Testament, prohibits all manner of manslaughter, for in the Gospel: 'It was said unto them of old time, Thou shalt not kill.' . . . Christ Jesus hates and threatens men who fight and kill, when He says: 'He who smites with the sword shall perish by the sword.'[22]

In November 1644, some months after Fox had returned home from his initial journey, his near contemporary John Milton (1608–1674) published the *Areopagitica*, an appeal to Parliament on behalf of a free press, in which he lauded Wycliffe as the herald of change and reform:

> Why else was this Nation chos'n before any other, that out of her as out of *Sion*, should be proclaimed and sounded forth the first tidings and trumpet of Reformation to all *Europ*? And had it not bin the obstinate perversnes of our Prelats against the divine and admirable spirit of *Wicklif*, to suppresse him as a schismatic and *innovator*, perhaps neither the *Bohemian Husse* and *Jerom* [of Prague], no, nor the

---

[20] Collier, *An Ecclesiastical History of Great Britain*, 3:180.

[21] Henry Bettenson, *Documents of the Christian Church*, 2nd ed. (London: Oxford University Press, 1963), 245.

[22] Ibid., 249–50.

name of *Luther* or of *Calvin* had bin ever known; the glory of reforming all our neighbors had bin compleatly ours.[23]

"The very ocean of darkness and death"

Before and during the time Fox traveled through central England undergoing his spiritual exercises and trials, England itself was being tried by countervailing forces threatening to tear apart the nation's state and church and social order. It was to be the worst of conflicts—civil war. Whereas Charles I (r. 1625–1649) maintained his belief that the monarchy's rights were divine, his Houses of Parliament asserted their obligation to protect the subjects' rights. As in Wycliffe's age, suddenly there loomed in the land the specter of apocalypse, this time manifested by the red horse carrying a rider wielding a great sword who "was permitted to take peace from the earth, so that men should slay one another."[24] In October 1642, almost eleven months before Fox left home to travel in Leicestershire and its neighboring counties, an early engagement of the war was fought to a draw between the royal and the parliamentary forces at Edgehill in Warwickshire, on the southwestern flank of Leicestershire. A month later the king, prevented by arms from entering London, retreated to Oxford in Oxfordshire, lying on the southeastern side of Warwickshire, and established his new base there. In July 1644, the year Fox returned home from his initial journey, three armies fielded by Parliament met two royal armies in an inconclusive engagement at Marston Moor near York. Later in the same year, the parties confronted each other at Newbury in Berkshire (stretching across the southern border of Oxfordshire). Here again, nothing was resolved.

Although Fox records no personal travel in 1645, other than taking "a chamber for a while at a professor's house"[25] in Coventry (Warwickshire), back home he continued "in great sorrows and troubles"; he sought spiritual counsel from four priests in the area but found no solace. That year, the war entered a decisive phase. Following the standoff at Newbury in

---

[23] John Milton, *Areopagitica*, ed. John W. Hales (Oxford, England: 1917), 45, spelling and italicization as in original.

[24] Revelation 6:4.

[25] Fox, *Journal*, 5. Fox used 'professor' here and elsewhere to refer to a person who openly asserted or affirmed his or her religion.

1644, Parliament enacted reforms that resulted in the creation of the "New Model Army," which was both national, rather than county or regional, and subject to central command and control. Further, to secure competent commanders and to minimize political interference, the "Self-Denying Ordinance" barred all members of either House of Parliament from holding any military or civil office under parliamentary appointment. After being initially unprepared in the 1645 campaign season, during which Leicester, the county town of Leicestershire, was besieged, captured, and plundered in May by the Royalist army, in June the New Model Army demonstrated its effectiveness in the field by destroying the king's forces at the battle of Naseby (Northamptonshire), within twenty miles of Leicester. By September the New Model Army had overcome the besieged forces of the king at Bristol and thus sealed the defeat of the royal cause in the west of England.

Without referring in his *Journal* to the nation's turmoil, Fox records that at the beginning of 1646 he left home again on his second journey to find the Lord's will in his life. As he was "going to Coventry,"[26] a series of important revelations from the Lord came to him. These 'openings' showed that the true believers are all those who are born of God and have passed from death to life;[27] that a university education is not enough to fit and qualify people to be ministers of Christ;[28] that God dwells on earth in people's hearts, not in buildings made with hands;[29] and that regarding the scriptures, within each person is an anointing to teach, and the Lord will teach his people himself.[30]

Fox continued his journey of wrestlings and 'openings' into 1647, traveling "up and down as a stranger in the earth."[31] Finally, after he "had forsaken all the priests . . . and left the separate preachers also,"[32] he heard a voice which further opened to him that:

'There is one, even Christ Jesus, that can speak to thy condition', and when I heard it my heart did leap for joy.

---

[26] Ibid., 7.
[27] Ibid.
[28] Ibid.
[29] Ibid., 8.
[30] Ibid.
[31] Ibid., 10.
[32] Ibid., 11.

Then the Lord did let me see why there was none upon the earth that could speak to my condition, namely, that I might give him all the glory; for all are concluded under sin, and shut up in unbelief as I had been, that Jesus Christ might have the pre-eminence. . . . My desires after the Lord grew stronger, and zeal in the pure knowledge of God and of Christ alone, without the help of any man, book, or writing. For though I read the Scriptures that spoke of Christ and God, yet I knew him not but by revelation, as he who hath the key did open, and as the Father of life drew me to his Son by his spirit.[33]

Then came the final 'openings' showing that Christ himself had been tempted and had overcome the same devil; that Fox would overcome also through Christ "and his power, light, grace, and spirit";[34] that all in Fox's life was done "in and by Christ"; and all the troubles he faced "were good for me, and temptations for the trial of my faith which Christ had given me."[35] Later that year near Manchester and Dukinfield (Lancashire), Fox records that he declared "Truth" among the people and that "the Lord's power was over all."[36]

At last, Fox's spiritual trials in "the very ocean of darkness and death" were over and he could write that "by the eternal power of God I was come out of it, and was brought over it and the power of it, into the power of Christ."[37]

At that time, it seemed that the nation had also survived its ordeal. The first Civil War came to a close in June 1646 when Oxford surrendered to the New Model Army (Charles having become a prisoner of the Scots the previous month); a year later, Charles was in the custody of the army.[38]

---

[33] Ibid.
[34] Ibid., 12.
[35] Ibid., 14.
[36] Ibid., 18.
[37] Ibid., 21.
[38] See Austin Woolrych, *Britain in Revolution 1625–1660* (Oxford: Oxford University Press, 2002).

Fox's sufferings and imprisonments under the interregnum: 1649–1656

Fox's *Journal* records that he began his mission to the nation in 1648. In his account, commencing on the first page of chapter 2, he definitively speaks of "Friends," "meetings," and the power of the Lord to "shake." He was embarking upon what would be a decade-long journey of witnessing to and suffering for the Truth as revealed to him in his 'openings.'

As Fox set out that year into England's central counties, what had seemed in 1647 to be a land at peace following civil war proved to be an illusion. The king had escaped the custody of the New Model Army (which had seized him from Parliament after that body proposed to disband the army), then had negotiated with both Parliament and the Scots for support, and finally had made an arrangement with the Scots as uprisings in Wales, Essex, and Kent grew. At the end, however, the king saw all his hopes dashed when Oliver Cromwell defeated the Scots army at Preston (Lancashire) on August 17, 1648. When Parliament then attempted an arrangement with Charles, it was purged by order of the Army Council (carried out by troops under the command of Colonel Thomas Pride), resulting in the expulsion of a number of its members (mostly Presbyterians) accused of being Royalist sympathizers. The New Model-dominated remnant of Parliament, called the 'Rump,' on January 4, 1649, declared that "the people are, under God, the original of all just power; that the Commons of England, in parliament assembled, being chosen by and representing the people, have the supreme power in this nation."[39] Thereafter the House of Commons legislated alone for the nation, without either the concurrence of the House of Lords or a royal assent. The Rump forthwith used its supreme power to order the trial of Charles by a high court of justice that it created for the purpose. After his conviction for treason, on January 30, 1649, the king was beheaded. To complete the national reordering, the Rump enacted the abolition of the monarchy on March 17, the abolition of the House of Lords on March 19, and the creation of England as a commonwealth, governed by the Rump together with its appointed officers and ministers, on May 29.

---

[39] Ibid., 431.

England's national life was now thrust into radical change. So, too, its religious life was cut loose from conformity and set astir by Anglicans, Puritans (seeking to reform what had been the established church), Presbyterians, and Roman Catholics (whom Fox calls 'papists'). In his *Journal*, Fox refers as well to Independents, Seekers, Baptists, Socinians, Brownists, Lutherans, Calvinists, Arians, Familists, Muggletonians, Ranters, and Fifth Monarchy Men (see appendix 3).[40] Among these "jangling"[41] religious believers, who would provide direction? And what would that direction be? Could England face the challenge of continuing the reform of its spiritual life begun in the days of John Wycliffe and the Lollards? Might there be freedom of religion, or would there be conformity to a state church? What of liberty of individual conscience? And by what agencies might a wounded nation find healing after spilling royal blood and being made, by fiat, a "commonwealth" governed by a rump legislative body, popularly elected in another era now nine years gone, and by an unelected army council giving itself executive leadership in a civil state? These issues would continue to vex and roil the nation over the next forty years until they were settled by the Glorious Revolution of 1688. Across that time span and even beyond, until his death in 1691—and in every English county as well as in parts of North America and continental Europe—George Fox's message would be heard: 'the power of the Lord was over all.'

Fox embarked on his mission to the nation in 1648 with all the boldness and certainty of an Old Testament prophet. He sought those of tender conscience, and, as one reads in the *Journal*, he taught and preached to them with exceptional power and authority. He looked for that of God in everyone and shared with all who would receive it the Truth that had been opened to him in his earlier journeys of spiritual wrestling. In the public square he directly confronted not only the 'jangling' and 'chaffy' debaters but the opponents who defended the array of religious beliefs then sweeping the land, from the reforming Puritans to the Calvinist Presbyterians to the Baptists to a wide variety of Independents and other nonconformists. He personally took the message he had for the established Church of England into its Sunday services of worship and there, within its 'steeplehouses,'

---

[40] Fox, *Journal*, 419.

[41] 'Jangling' is an archaic word frequently found in the *Journal*; it refers to discourse that is idle, discordant, or quarrelsome.

gave rebuttal to the sermons he heard. In the face of rising opposition from law enforcement officials, clergymen, other Christian 'professors,' the general population, and especially members of Parliament, he heroically persisted and steadfastly continued to teach and preach.

The price Fox paid for his resolve in teaching and preaching the Truth during his missions and travels was to bear abuse and scorn, beatings and stonings, and imprisonments—sometimes in 'close,' or solitary, confinement and sometimes in dungeons. He was imprisoned eight times: four during the interregnum and four during the Restoration. The more sufferings Fox endured, the greater strength and determination he manifested. To control, if not correct, his public activities on behalf of the Truth, the authorities imposed various statutory and other legal restraints.

Fox's first confrontation with the keepers of public order—and the first imprisonment of the eight he was to suffer in his ministry—came in Nottingham (Nottinghamshire) in 1649 when, on arriving at the top of a hill one Sunday morning, "as I looked upon the town the great steeplehouse [the Church of St. Mary] struck at my life when I spied it, a great and idolatrous temple."[42] Fox went in while the service was in progress, heard part of the sermon, and found "I could not hold, but was made to cry out," so he publicly corrected the preacher.[43] He was arrested, presumably for disturbing the public peace; examined before the mayor, aldermen, and sheriffs of Nottingham; and held, first in a sheriff's house, then in the common prison. Official delay kept his case from being heard in the assize, so he was put in the common gaol [jail], where his imprisonment caused enough public disorder that troops were required to disperse the "very rude" people. Fox was set free after being "kept prisoner a pretty long time."[44] Immediately resuming his mission, he traveled north to Mansfield-Woodhouse (Nottinghamshire), where again he went to the steeplehouse service on Sunday, "and when the priest had done I declared the Truth to the priest and people."[45] On this occasion he was assaulted within the building, "almost smothered," "sorely" bruised, then thrown into the yard, set in

---

[42] Ibid., 39.
[43] Ibid., 40.
[44] Ibid., 43.
[45] Ibid., 44.

the stocks, and "mazed and dazed" as he was pelted and struck by stones. After being questioned by a magistrate, he was released and left the town under orders never to return.[46] Still later in 1649, on market day at Market Bosworth (Leicestershire)—and for the third time that year—Fox both in and outside the church publicly corrected the preacher, someone he had known in his home town. Thereupon hundreds of the town's and market's people "fell upon us and stoned us very sore and abused us . . . a great way out of the town, [so] that it was a wonder that we escaped with our lives."[47] Nowhere does Fox ever record any attempt by magistrates to protect either himself or other Friends when they were being set upon or abused by 'rude' local people.

Because of the need to control religious extremism in the land, on August 9, 1650, the Rump Parliament passed an "act against several atheistical, blasphemous and execrable opinions derogatory to the honour of God, and destructive to human society" known as the Blasphemy Act.[48] Fox's second imprisonment occurred in late October 1650 when he came into the net of the Blasphemy Act by attending "a great lecture" in Derby (Derbyshire) given by Colonel Nathaniel Barton—a public preacher, an officer in the New Model Army, and a local justice of the peace—before army officers and "priests and preachers." After the lecture, Fox declared to them the Truth, the day of the Lord, "and the light within them, and the spirit to teach and lead them to God."[49] An officer then took him by the hand and led him to the magistrates, who examined him at length. He was convicted of "uttering and broaching of divers blasphemous opinions contrary to a late Act of Parliament."[50] The preacher, Colonel Barton, was one of the two magistrates who examined, convicted, and then committed Fox to a six-month sentence in Derby's House of Correction. The other magistrate was Gervase Bennet, a justice of the peace, who, as Fox noted, was the "first [who] called us Quakers because we bid them tremble at the word of God, and this was in the year 1650."[51] From his detention

---

[46] Ibid., 44–45.
[47] Ibid., 48.
[48] See appendix 1.
[49] Fox, *Journal*, 51.
[50] Ibid., 52.
[51] Ibid., 58.

England 1350–1682

Fox wrote a profusion of letters of protest, including at least six to Colonel Barton.

Fox's six-month commitment in Derby was extended in April 1651 to a forty-nine week imprisonment when he refused the offer of a captaincy in the New Model Army, then seeking reinforcements after the discovery of a plot to restore Charles II to the throne. Fox's rejection of the military commission inspired him to write this peace statement:

> I told them I lived in the virtue of that life and power that took away the occasion of all wars, and I knew from whence all wars did rise. . . . I told them I was come into the covenant of peace which was before wars and strife were.[52]

For his refusal to take up arms, he was put "into the dungeon amongst thirty felons in a lousy, stinking low place in the ground without any bed. Here they kept me a close prisoner almost a half year."[53] Again in August that year, as the New Model Army marched close to Derby on its way to engage the Scottish army at the Battle of Worcester (September 3, 1651), Fox was pressured to join the ranks, being twice offered press-money.

> I told them I was brought off from outward wars. . . . They said I should go for a soldier, but I told them I was dead to it. They said I was alive. I told them, 'Where envy and hatred are there is confusion.'[54]

In his ordeal, Fox uttered a poignant lament over Derby, including this:

> O Derby! . . . Look where thou art, and how thou art grounded; and consider, before thou art utterly forsaken . . . it doth break my heart to see how God is dishonoured in thee, O Derby![55]

The magistrates of Derby were uncertain how to resolve their George Fox 'problem.' They considered having him "up before the Parliament" or banished to Ireland. In the end, about

---

[52] Ibid., 65.
[53] Ibid.
[54] Ibid., 67.
[55] Ibid., 69.

October 8, 1651, after being "kept a year, within three weeks, in four prisons," he "was set freely at liberty."[56]

For the rest of 1651, Fox records that he visited in Nottinghamshire and Derbyshire before leaving the midlands and moving his mission into England's northern counties. In 1652 he was assaulted at Warmsworth (Yorkshire), Wakefield (Yorkshire), Staveley (Lancashire), Lancaster, Ulverston (Lancashire), Walney Island (Westmorland), and Cartmel (Lancashire).[57]

During late spring, after the Wakefield assault, as if a door to the wider world had opened, a succession of three events occurred, reported in the *Journal*, that would soon lead to the transformation of Fox's mission into a movement. The first came when Fox, inspired by the Lord, made a steep climb "with much ado" to the top of "great high" Pendle Hill (Lancashire) where, after sounding the day of the Lord, he was shown by God "in what places he had a great people to be gathered."[58]

The second event came shortly later, in the week following Whitsunday, when Fox came to Firbank Fell (Westmorland) where, at the chapel,

> Francis Howgill and John Audland preached in the forenoon to a seeking and religious people there separated from the common way of national worship. The said George Fox bore [refrained] till they had done, walking about the chapel door, and when the meeting broke up, gave notice of a meeting afternoon the same day intended, hard by the said chapel; whither many did resort, and then and there the said George Fox was opened in a living testimony by the word of life to the reaching God's witness in many hearts, and the said John Audland was then fully convinced of Truth, with many more.[59]

---

[56] Ibid., 70.

[57] Ibid., 97, 101, 112, 120, 127, 130, and 146, respectively.

[58] Ibid., 103–4. The "day of the Lord" refers to the end time when all unfaithful souls will be brought to God for judgment. See Isaiah 13:6–8; Ezekiel 7:5–12; Joel 2:1–2; Amos 5:18.

[59] Norman Penney, ed., *"The First Publishers of Truth": being early records (now first printed) of the introduction of Quakerism into the counties of England and Wales* (London: Headley Brothers, 1907), 243.

On the three hundredth anniversary of that day, a tablet was secured to the rock from which the seated Fox preached, now known as Fox's Pulpit. The tablet reads in part:

> Here or near this rock George Fox preached to about one thousand Seekers for three hours. . . . Great power inspired his message and the meeting proved of first importance in gathering the Society of Friends known as Quakers. Many men and women convinced of the truth on this fell and in other parts of the northern counties went forth through the land and over the seas with the living word of the Lord enduring great hardships and winning multitudes to Christ.[60]

Many of those convinced of the Truth at Firbank Fell who then "went forth through the land and over the seas with the living word of the Lord" are known as the Valiant Sixty and remembered as leading apostles and missionaries of the Religious Society of Friends. Their number was probably greater than sixty, and some of their names remain unknown. These men and women, also honored as the First Publishers of Truth, carried the "living word" far afield as itinerant preachers and as authors of tracts and pamphlets.

The third event happened after the Staveley assault, when Fox for the first time came to Swarthmoor Hall, the home of Judge Thomas Fell, chancellor of the Duchy of Lancaster, and his wife Margaret. By 1655, Margaret Fell had established at Swarthmoor the first organizational and communications center of the Religious Society of Friends, and Fox returned to Swarthmoor many times during his life.

In 1653 Fox again suffered assaults for his preaching, at Bootle (Lancashire) and Carlisle (Cumberland).[61] The Carlisle incident, which began on market day, Saturday, and continued into the following Monday, resulted in a warrant for Fox's arrest issued by "the officers and justices and magistrates of the town" who, after examining Fox, ordered his third imprisonment, beginning August 1, 1653, "as a blasphemer, a heretic, and a seducer."[62] For the second time he was being charged under the Blasphemy Act. Even though there was "a cry in the country that

---

[60] "Fox's Pulpit," *Visit Cumbria*, www.visitcumbria.com/yd/foxs-pulpit/#.
[61] Penney, *"The First Publishers of Truth,"* 148, 158.
[62] Ibid., 159.

I was to be hanged,"[63] and even though during his imprisonment the assizes came to Carlisle, the county seat of Cumberland, the circuit-riding assize judges of the Court of King's Bench avoided hearing his case, choosing to leave the matter by default to the disposition of the local officials. Anthony Pearson, a Friend as well as a justice of the peace in three other counties (presumably Yorkshire, Northumberland, and Bishoprick), was moved to write "to the Judges of Assize and Jail-delivery for the Northern Parts sitting at Carlisle" this appeal:

> I am moved to lay before you the condition of George Fox, whom the magistrates of this city have cast into prison for words that he is accused to have spoken, which they call blasphemy. He was sent to the gaol till he should be delivered by due course of law; and it was expected that he should have been proceeded against . . . at this Assize. . . . To my knowledge, he utterly abhors and detests every particular, which, by the Act against blasphemous opinions, is appointed to be punished. . . .
>
> Though he be committed, judgement is not given against him, nor have his accusers been face to face to affirm before him what they have informed against him, nor was he heard as to the particulars of their accusations, nor doth it appear that any word they charge against him is within the Act. Indeed I could not yet so much as see the information, no, not in court, though I desired it. . . . That his friends may not speak with him I know no law nor reason for. I do therefore claim for him a due and lawful hearing, and that he may have a copy of his charge, and freedom to answer for himself, and that rather before you than to be left to the rulers of this town who are not competent judges of blasphemy.[64]

The unintended results of this professional advocacy to the court were twofold: the assize judges ignored the matter and simply left town, and Fox was moved into a dungeon "where men and women were put together and never a house of office [toilet], in a nasty and very uncivil manner which was a shame to Christianity. And the prisoners were exceeding lousy; and there

---

[63] Ibid., 160.
[64] Ibid., 161.

was one woman almost eaten to death with lice."[65] A letter-writing campaign to Carlisle ensued, with Fox writing to the two justices of the peace; Anthony Pearson and another writing to the magistrates, priests, and people; and Parliament writing to the sheriff and magistrates. The governor and Anthony Pearson came down to examine the dungeon. In time, Fox was "set at liberty by the justices and the Lord's power came over them all."[66] He had been incarcerated for seven weeks. Later that year, while still in Cumberland, Fox was assaulted by guards with pitchforks near Wigton and stoned and abused by "rude fellows" near Caldbeck.[67]

On December 15, 1653, England settled the constitution of the Commonwealth by adopting the *Instrument of Government* under which Oliver Cromwell was made the lord protector of England. Although articles 35 and 36 of the *Instrument* provided that Christianity would be "held forth . . . as the public profession" of the nation's faith, articles 37 and 38 introduced a limited liberty of conscience to those Christians who differed from the "Doctrine, Worship, or Discipline" of the public profession, as follows:

> Art. 37. That such as profess Faith in God by Jesus Christ, (though differing in Judgment from the Doctrine, Worship, or Discipline publickly held forth) shall not be restrained from, but shall be protected in the Profession of their Faith, and Exercise of their Religion, so as they abuse not this Liberty to the Civil Injury of others, and to the actual Disturbance of the publick Peace. Provided this Liberty be not extended to *Popery* or *Prelacy*, or to such, as under the Profession of Christ, hold forth and practice Licentiousness.
>
> Art. 38. That all Laws, Statutes, Ordinances, and Clauses in any Law, Statute or Ordinance, to the contrary of the aforesaid Liberty, shall be esteemed null and void.[68]

---

[65] Fox, *Journal*, 162.

[66] Fox, *Journal*, 164.

[67] Fox, *Journal*, 165–66.

[68] As quoted in Besse, *A Collection of the Sufferings of the People Called Quakers*, 1:vi–vii, capitalization as in original.

In a speech made to Parliament on September 12, 1654, Oliver Cromwell set forth his own generous view of liberty of conscience as a natural right.

> Is not Liberty of Conscience a Fundamental? So long as there is Liberty for the supreme Magistrate to exercise his Conscience in erecting what form of Church-Government he is satisfied he should set up, why should he not give it to others? Liberty of Conscience is a natural Right, and he that would have it, ought to give it, having Liberty to settle what he likes for the Publick. Indeed that hath been the Vanity of our Contests. Every Sect saith, *Give me Liberty:* But give it him, and to this Power he will not yield it to any Body else. Where is our Ingenuity? Truly that is a Thing that ought to be very reciprocal. The Magistrate hath his Supremacy, and he may settle Religion according to his Conscience: And I may say it to you, I can say it: All the Money in the Nation would not have tempted Men to fight upon such an Account as they have engaged, if they had not had Hopes of Liberty better than they had from *Episcopacy*, or than would have been afforded them from a *Scottish Presbytery*, or an *English* either, if it had made such Steps, or been as sharp and rigid as it threatened when it first set up. This I say is a Fundamental, it ought to be so, it is for us and the Generations to come.[69]

During 1654 Fox concluded his initial work in the northern counties before returning to the central counties from where, in 1655, he carried the mission into the rest of England. His next arrest (but without imprisonment) took place near Leicester, the seat of his home county of Leicestershire, where, on February 11, 1655, as Friends were about to meet, Fox was "taken up" by seventeen troopers and delivered to their commander, Colonel Francis Hacker, and his major and captains, "for at this time there was a noise of a plot against Oliver Cromwell."[70] Several times Fox was offered his liberty if he promised to go home and stay there and not go out to meetings. But Fox refused those conditions, insisting he was innocent of all plots and that to make himself a prisoner at home "would manifest that I was guilty of something. . . . I told them I should go to meetings as

---

[69] Quoted in ibid., 1:vii.
[70] Fox, *Journal*, 191.

the Lord ordered me, and therefore could not submit to that, but said we were a peaceable people."[71] In the face of such resolve, Colonel Hacker ordered that Fox be escorted to London to appear before the lord protector. En route, Fox wrote Cromwell a loving letter of advice, commencing: "Dear Friend, Be still, and in the counsel of God stand, and that will give thee wisdom." On the day before their London meeting on March 6, 1655, Fox wrote Cromwell again, as follows:

> I, who am of the world called George Fox, do deny that the carrying or drawing of any carnal sword against any, or against thee, Oliver Cromwell, or any man. In the presence of the Lord God I declare it. . . .
>
> From under the occasion of [the magistrate's] sword I do seek to bring people. My weapons are not carnal but spiritual, and 'my kingdom is not of this world', therefore with a carnal weapon I do not fight, but am of those things dead. . . .
>
> This I am moved to give forth for the Truth's sake, who a witness stand against all unrighteousness and all ungodliness, who a sufferer am for the righteous Seed's sake, waiting for the redemption of it, who a crown that is mortal seek not, for that fadeth away, but in the light dwell, which comprehends that crown, which light is the condemnation of all such; in which light I witness the crown that is immortal, that fades not away.[72]

As their interview in Cromwell's home ended, Cromwell "catched me by the hand and said these words with tears in his eyes, 'Come again to my house; for if thou and I were but an hour in a day together we should be nearer one to the other', and that he wished me no more ill than he did to his own soul."[73]

Notwithstanding these hopeful signs of a more tolerant policy toward Fox and the Friends, fifty-two days later, on April 26, Cromwell's Protectorate issued a proclamation requiring all those suspected of being Roman Catholics to abjure and renounce, under oath, the Pope's authority over "the Catholic

---

[71] Ibid., 192.
[72] Ibid., 197–98.
[73] Ibid., 199.

Church in General and over myself in particular."[74] Anyone refusing the oath was to be adjudged a "papist." Fox noted that rather than toleration, there was an increase of the sufferings "upon Friends by reason that envious magistrates made use of that oath as a snare to catch Friends in, who they knew could not swear at all."[75] As Fox in his earlier letter to Cromwell had used the metaphor of the magistrate's sword, so he used it again when he wrote the following:[76]

> A Paper of George Fox's to Oliver Protector concerning his making people to suffer for not taking the Oath of Abjuration. 1655.
>
> The magistrate is not to bear the sword in vain, which is a terror to the evil doers, but the magistrates bearing the sword in vain, are not a terror to evil doers, so they are not a praise to them that do well. So God hath raised up a people with his spirit, whom people and priests and magistrates without the fear of God scornfully call Quakers, which . . . do cry against oaths, for because of such the land mourns, and they we see are at liberty, to which the sword should be a terror; and for crying against such are many cast into prison. . . .
>
> To the measure of God in thee I speak, to consider . . . for whom thou dost rule, that thou mayest receive power from God for him to rule, and all that is contrary to God may be with his light condemned.
>
> From a lover of thy soul and eternal good,   GF

Despite the Protector's word at their first meeting that Fox had his liberty to go "whither I would," that liberty was short-lived. He was arrested again on January 18, 1656, while on mission in Cornwall. Prior to his arrest he had written "a little paper to the conditions of that dark people [of Cornwall] to be sent to the seven parishes at the Land's End."[77] In it he announced the coming of the day of the Lord and the consequent punishment and condemnation of those who neglect their salvation. After examination by the justice of the peace, Fox

---

[74] For the text of the Oath of Abjuration and its legislative history, see appendix 2.

[75] Fox, *Journal*, 220.

[76] Ibid., 220–21.

[77] Ibid., 236.

admitted he had written the paper and then was presented with the Oath of Abjuration, an oath required to be taken by individuals, pursuant to the 1655 act of Parliament, renouncing "the pope's supremacy and authority over the Catholic Church in general, and over my self in particular." For protesting the oath, Fox was ordered into his fourth imprisonment at Launceston (Cornwall) under a mittimus that charged Fox and two Friends with having "spread several papers tending to the disturbance of the public peace" as well as having no cause to come into Cornwall, traveling up and down without passes, refusing to give surety for good behavior, and refusing to take the Oath of Abjuration.[78] He awaited the assizes for over two months. When his case was called in late March, the sitting judge was John Glynne (1603–1666), lord chief justice of England. The trial proceeded with fits and starts, Fox being brought into and then ordered out of the courtroom until his fourth entrance, when a hearing was held—on the belated and spurious charge of inciting treason. This time Judge Glynne sent Fox back to prison for the sole offense of refusing to honor the court's dignity by removing his hat, a judicial irritation from the outset of his several appearances. Fox unsuccessfully argued against the hat honor on biblical grounds, and he was ordered held until he paid the fine. Fox further aggravated the situation by refusing to pay both the fine and the prison charges for his own care and that of his horse. As punishment for this additional defiance, Fox was put for the next thirteen days into the dungeon called Doomsdale, "a nasty stinking place where they said few people came out alive; where they used to put witches and murderers before their execution; where the prisoners' excrements had not been carried out for scores of years."[79]

Fox protested these sufferings in writing to the Sessions court at Bodmin (Cornwall) and to Oliver Cromwell. The court's justices ordered the dungeon door opened and gave the prisoners liberty both to clean the place and to buy their food in town. Cromwell ordered an examination into prisoner abuse.[80] In time, Fox wore out all of the authorities who were keeping him in prison. Cromwell had deputized his commander of the western counties, Major General John Desborough, to arrange Fox's

---

[78] Ibid., 247.
[79] Ibid., 252.
[80] Ibid., 254.

liberty, but Fox declined the offer of release because it was conditioned on a promise of going home and preaching no more. Desborough left the matter to Colonel Robert Bennet, the gaol commander, who, after making several unsuccessful requests for his gaoler's fees, set Fox and his two companions at liberty on September 9, 1656. They had been imprisoned more than eight months.

Another legal strategy put in effect at this time (and alluded to in the mittimus to Launceston) for the purpose of breaking Quakers and other nonconformists was the revived enforcement of an Elizabethan law "against sturdy vagrants and beggars going up and down."[81] Road watches and checkpoints were established to discourage Friends from traveling in the ministry. To protest this intimidation, Fox had written from prison *An Exhortation and Warning to the Magistrates* as well as an answer to the Sessions' justices at Exeter (Devonshire) who had issued a warrant "for the apprehending of all Quakers."[82]

Five weeks after his release from prison in Launceston, Fox had his second meeting with Oliver Cromwell. It began with a chance encounter when the protector was riding through Hyde Park to St. James's Park gate in London, and it was later continued in Whitehall. On these occasions, Fox reported to Cromwell about the sufferings of Friends in the nation, disputed with him about the light of Christ, and "bid him lay down his crown at the feet of Jesus."[83]

In early 1657 Fox went to London and there wrote to Cromwell, placing before him the sufferings of Friends not only in the nation but in Ireland as well. They had their third meeting, on March 24 and 25, in the "Park" and later at Cromwell's house. Fox warned Cromwell against accepting the hereditary monarchy that Parliament had offered him in February, telling him that receiving an earthly crown would take away his life and bring shame and ruin upon him and his posterity as well as darkness upon the nation.[84] Cromwell subsequently refused the crown and on May 25 ratified the *Humble Petition and Advice*, the constitutional replacement for the *Instrument of Government*.

---

[81] Ibid., 258. Fox is referring to *An Act for punishment of rogues, vagabonds and sturdy beggars* (39 Eliz. I. c. 4). *The Statutes of the Realm*, vol. 4:899–902.

[82] Fox, *Journal*, 260.

[83] Ibid., 274.

[84] Ibid., 289.

After his time with Cromwell, Fox took his mission into Wales and then traveled again through England's central and northern counties. During a meeting in Manchester, he was assaulted "with coals, clots, stones, water" by "many rude people out of the town."[85] Although Fox had twice in the past been arrested for interrupting a sermon and later a lecture, this time the authorities ignored the assailants and instead "plucked down and haled" Fox before the local Sessions court, which was then sitting. Fox successfully defended himself before the justices of the peace, citing the *Instrument of Government* protection "that none should be molested in their meetings that professed God and owned the Lord Jesus Christ, which I did."[86] It was his last journaled encounter with keepers of the public peace before Charles II ascended the throne. Upon leaving Manchester, Fox commented that "the Lord has raised up a people to stand for his name and Truth in that town over those chaffy professors."[87]

Later in 1657, Fox felt "drawings in my spirit to go into Scotland,"[88] where he remained on mission until the following year. When he returned to England in 1658, he once more worked his way through the northern and central counties, attended a General Yearly Meeting of Friends held in Bedfordshire for the whole nation over three days sometime in May–June,[89] and then went to London. There he saw Oliver Cromwell for the fourth and last time to address again the problem of the sufferings of Friends. They met in Hampton Court Park and arranged to speak the next day in Cromwell's house, but when Fox arrived for the interview Cromwell was too ill to see him, "so I passed away, and never saw him no more."[90]

Cromwell died on September 3, 1658, and was succeeded by the protector he had chosen, his son Richard. During Richard's brief tenure the apparatus of the Protectorate itself was disabled as the New Model Army's influence rose and Parliament's power sank. On May 25, 1659, Richard was forced to resign as protector, but not before he had acceded to demands to dissolve the Protectorate Parliament and recall the Rump. In the short

---

[85] Ibid., 307–8.
[86] Ibid., 308.
[87] Ibid.
[88] Ibid., 315.
[89] Ibid., 339.
[90] Ibid., 350.

ensuing second period of the Commonwealth, the national situation grew increasingly chaotic while a consensus emerged that a path toward stability might be found by restoring the monarchy and bringing back from exile the claimant to the throne, Charles II.

At the end of England's revolution and experiment with republican government, Fox could reflect upon his five arrests, four imprisonments, and four meetings with Cromwell. He could also ponder the results of his personal attempts to test the constitutional boundaries of liberty of conscience and to give expression to the ideals of peace (and the futility of war) and of personal integrity (and the meaninglessness of oaths), not only in his visible witness but in his writings. Regarding war, he admonished:

> Keep yourselves clear of the blood of all men, either by word, or writing, or speaking.[91]

And concerning oaths, he wrote:

> Take heed of giving people oaths to swear, for Christ our Lord and master saith, 'Swear not at all, but let your communications be yea, yea, and nay, nay, for whatsoever is more than these cometh of evil.'[92]

Fox's sufferings and imprisonments under the Restoration: 1660–1675

The invitation on May 2, 1660, from Parliament to Charles II—that he return to England and receive the crown that had devolved upon him at the beheading of his father in January 1649—was preceded by his promises made in the Declaration of Breda (the Netherlands) on April 4. Those promises related to crimes committed and property transferred during the years of the interregnum, the army's pay arrears and future service, and religious toleration. Regarding toleration, Charles stated:

> And because the passions and uncharitableness of the times have produced several opinions in religion, by which men are engaged in parties and animosities against each other, which when they shall hereafter unite

---

[91] Ibid., 263.

[92] Ibid., 244. Fox is quoting Matthew 5:34 and 37 in the King James Version of the Bible.

in a freedom of conversation, will be composed or better understood: We do declare a liberty to tender consciences, and that no man shall be disquieted or called in question for difference of opinion in matters of religion, which do not disturb the peace of the kingdom, and that we shall be ready to consent to such an Act of Parliament, as upon mature deliberation shall be offered to us for the full granting that indulgence.[93]

It seemed the dawn of a new era after more than a decade of unrest and—for many—of suffering.

Charles landed in England on May 25 and entered a jubilant London on May 29. As for Fox, his liberty was shortly thereafter denied him, the promise of Breda notwithstanding. On the warrant of five or six magistrates, he was seized while visiting Swarthmoor and then examined at Lancaster by Major Henry Porter (1613–1666), who was a justice of the peace, member of Parliament, the constable of Lancaster Castle, and sometime mayor of Lancaster. Porter claimed he had an order from the sheriff of Middlesex (London), which he would not let Fox see, and on June 5, 1660, he committed Fox to his fifth imprisonment—his first under the Restoration—commanding the gaoler, as Fox reported, "to keep me a close prisoner and to let none come at me and there to keep me till delivered by the King or Parliament."[94] He was held until October 25 under a mittimus alleging that he was "suspected to be a disturber of the peace of the nation, a common enemy to His Majesty our lord the King, a chief upholder of the Quakers' sect," who with fellow sectarians "had of late endeavoured to raise insurrections in this part of the country to the imbrueing the nation in blood."[95] Fox answered the mittimus (which had been summarized for him by Friends permitted only to scan it) in a written statement to Charles reviewing and denying in detail all the charges. He restated his peace testimony:

> My weapons are spiritual, that take away the occasion of war and which lead into peace. . . . For the peace of this nation I am not a disturber of, but seek the peace of it and of all men, and stand for all nations' and men's

---

[93] As quoted in Besse, *Sufferings of the People Called Quakers*, 1:viii.
[94] Fox, *Journal*, 378.
[95] Ibid., 379.

peace upon the earth, and wish that all nations and men knew my innocency in these things.[96]

Margaret Fell of Swarthmoor Hall, a widow since the death in 1658 of her husband, Judge Thomas Fell, went to London and spoke with the king on Fox's behalf, offering her own life "to the King to stand as a pledge for the peace and quietness of all Friends and for their faith."[97] On July 17 she saw Charles a second time and presented Fox's answer to the mittimus. With her was Ann Curtis, daughter of the sheriff of Bristol whom Parliament had hanged for his Royalist action in 1643, and Curtis requested the king to have Fox and his accusers brought before him to judge the matter. The king's secretary insisted the matter must proceed by law and advised giving an order of habeas corpus to remove Fox from Lancaster to the Court of King's Bench, London. After the order's procedural errors were resolved, Fox went to London, at his own expense and accompanied only by two Friends, and appeared at the appointed time before the Court of King's Bench in Westminster Hall. The hearing was held in front of a panel of several judges and was presided over by the lord chief justice of England, Robert Foster (1589–1663). No accuser appeared. Fox responded to the charges of inciting new war and of being an enemy to the king by declaring, "I never learned the postures of war, and I loved all men; I was an enemy to no man."[98] The chief justice and another judge said they neither accused nor had anything against Fox, and because Fox's liberty was at the king's pleasure, they referred the matter to king and council. Shortly after came the king's warrant setting Fox free.

Fox's sixth imprisonment—his second in the reign of Charles—occurred on September 2, 1662, at Swannington in the northwestern part of his home county of Leicestershire. Apprehended while talking with a poor widow and her daughter, he was nevertheless charged with "meeting contrary to the Act" and committed to the gaol in Leicester.[99]

The law referred to was the Quaker Act, which had become effective less than six months earlier on March 24 and had made it unlawful for anyone either to refuse to take an oath required by

---

[96] Ibid., 379–80.
[97] Ibid., 383.
[98] Ibid., 389.
[99] Ibid., 431.

the laws of the realm or for five or more adult Quakers to assemble outside their homes under the pretense of joining in religious worship. The Act's introductory "whereas" recitals summarily dismissed Fox's principled defense that the New Testament prohibited the swearing of oaths.

> Whereas of late times certain persons under the name of Quakers, and other names of separation, have taken up and maintained sundry dangerous opinions and tenets, and (among others) that the taking of an oath in any case whatsoever, although before a lawful magistrate, is altogether unlawful and contrary to the word of God; and the said persons do daily refuse to take an oath, though lawfully tendered, whereby it often happens that the Truth is wholly suppressed and the administration of justice much obstructed: and

> Whereas the said persons under a pretence of religious worship do often assemble themselves in great numbers in several parts of this realm to the endangering of the public peace and safety, and to the terror of the people, by maintaining a secret and strict correspondence amongst themselves, and in the mean time separating and dividing themselves from the rest of his majesty's good and loyal subjects, and from the public congregations, and usual places of divine worship.

> For the redressing therefore, and better preventing the many mischiefs and dangers that do and may arise by such dangerous tenets, and such unlawful assemblies: be it Enacted . . .[100]

At Fox's appearance before the Court of Quarter Sessions, the justices of the peace declined to hear the charge in the mittimus concerning "a meeting"; instead, they indicted him for refusing to take the Oath of Allegiance and the Oath of Supremacy, of which the jury found him guilty.[101] Those two oaths[102]—as well as the Oath of Abjuration[103]—had precedents with long, separate histories of their own in the nation, reaching

---

[100] Besse, *Sufferings of the People Called Quakers*, 1:xi.
[101] Fox, *Journal*, 434–35.
[102] For the texts, see appendix 2.
[103] Fox, *Journal*, 238.

back to the Magna Carta of 1215. The Oath of Allegiance tendered Fox was that of James I under the Popish Recusants Act of 1605 enacted after the Gunpowder Plot (an attempt by some English Roman Catholics to assassinate the king and others by blowing up the House of Lords at the State Opening of Parliament); the Oath of Supremacy tendered Fox was that of Elizabeth at her accession just after the religious persecutions and martyrdoms suffered in the restoration of Roman Catholicism ordered by her predecessor, Mary I; and the Oath of Abjuration tendered Fox was that of the Protectorate in 1655 (then nullified and reenacted in 1657) ordered to be taken by suspected Roman Catholics to compel their renunciation of obedience to papal authority and teaching. Each of these oaths in Fox's time was intended to meet the 'Papist problem,' but the state found that requiring sworn oaths of Friends gave it a legal solution to the 'Quaker problem.'

The end of Fox's time in Leicester prison was anticlimactic. Upon being returned to gaol, he was offered his liberty by the gaoler if he would pay any tithes that were due together with the gaoler's fees, "but I shall leave it to you to give me what you will."[104] Fox simply took his liberty, having been held about one month.

Fox's seventh imprisonment—his third during the Restoration era—was the longest he would ever suffer. It began in early January 1664 when, upon returning to Swarthmoor after completing his third national mission, he learned soldiers had been searching for him. He set off to the home of their colonel five miles away to inquire about the search. Although he was assured there was nothing against him, the colonel warned Fox that Margaret Fell "could not keep great meetings at her house for they met contrary to the Act"[105] (presumably a reference to the Quaker Act of 1662). Later arrested upon a warrant, Fox was examined by the justices of the peace, ensnared on his principled refusal to take any oaths, and dismissed subject to his engagement to appear at the Lancaster Sessions, which he did on January 12.[106] Before the Sessions' justices, Fox eloquently defended the Quaker principles of holding Truth and loving all people and of being neither a terror to the king's subjects nor an enemy to any, as premised in the Act's introduction and implied in the justices' questions. Upon being asked to take the Oath of

---

[104] Ibid., 435.

[105] Ibid., 456.

[106] Ibid., 460–61.

Allegiance, his response that Quaker "allegiance did not lie in oaths but in truth and faithfulness"[107] made inevitable his commitment to prison to await the assizes. On March 14 and 16, Assize Judge Thomas Twysden (1602–1683) heard Fox's defense regarding the oath: that in obedience to Christ he did not swear, that he was a man of tender conscience, and that he had both the king's word and his declaration at Breda promising protection to those of tender consciences. He was found guilty and denied the verdict, which required his being remanded to jail to await the next assizes. In the meantime, Fox directed Friends to inscribe an account of their sufferings and put them before the Sessions' justices. "For Friends had suffered deeply by fines and distresses, the bailiffs and officers making great havoc and spoil of their goods, but no redress was made."[108]

On August 29, Fox appeared before Turner, another assize trial judge, and so vigorously pointed out to judge and jury a number of technical errors in the indictment that it was thrown out and he was made free "from all that has been done against you."[109] Whereupon there was laughter in the courtroom and Fox rebuked them, declaring it was apparent "how the justices and jury were forsworn men."[110] The enraged Judge Turner then called a grand jury and again unsuccessfully tendered the Oath of Allegiance to Fox who, after a new indictment was laid against him, pleaded not guilty and was again committed to "close prison" to await the next assizes.

The next assizes were held in Lancaster on March 22, 1665, with Judge Twysden presiding over Fox's third appearance before that court. And though Fox found and tried to point out errors in the indictment, Twysden would hear no argument. Instead, the judge had Fox taken out of the courtroom, heard the jury's verdict of guilty, and "reckoned [Fox] as a praemunired person."[111] In early May, the king and council ordered Fox removed from Lancaster Castle. Fox protested that he was the sheriff's, not the king's, prisoner, there being no sentence—and certainly no praemunire sentence—laid upon him of which he

---

[107] Ibid., 463.
[108] Ibid., 473.
[109] Ibid., 480.
[110] Ibid. "Forsworn men" here means that the men had sworn falsely.
[111] Ibid., 487.

knew. He was transferred to Scarborough Castle (Yorkshire).[112] In July the Great Plague broke out in London, and with it an apocalyptic vision seemed to return, as in Wycliffe's time, but now it was under the sign of the pale horse that left behind a misery of sickness, pestilence, and death.[113]

Sometime in 1666, after Fox had been held at Scarborough "above a year," he wrote Charles II regarding his imprisonment and mistreatment. The king granted this release:

> That the King, being certainly informed that George Fox is a man against all plotting and fighting, and one that is ready at all times to discover plots rather than to make them, and was an instrument of discovering a plot in Yorkshire, orders that he should be discharged of his imprisonment, giving security for to live peaceable.[114]

On September 1, the governor of Scarborough Castle signed a permit allowing Fox "quietly to pass about his lawful occasions, without any molestation,"[115] thus ending almost thirty-two months of an incarceration that had begun January 12, 1664. On September 2, the day Fox left prison, the Great Fire of London erupted.[116] Yet again, there seemed to be an apocalyptic vision in the land.

The eighth imprisonment—the fourth under the Restoration and the final such suffering of Fox's life—began with his arrest on December 17, 1673, after a meeting held at Armscote in Tredington (Worcestershire). He was sent to Worcester gaol by a mittimus alleging his attendance as teacher or speaker at a meeting of about 200 persons "which tends to the prejudice of the reformed and established religion and may prove prejudicial to the public peace . . . to appear at the next Sessions of the peace . . . to answer the breach of the common-laws of England."[117] Fox noted in his records that at the time of the arrest he was traveling to visit his dying mother, then over seventy years of age, and "when she heard that he was stopped and sent to prison it struck

---

[112] Ibid., 490.
[113] Revelation 6:8.
[114] Fox, *Journal*, 502.
[115] Ibid.
[116] Ibid., 503.
[117] Ibid., 671.

her to her heart and killed her, as he received [in] a letter from a doctor of that country [Leicestershire]."[118]

At the January 12, 1674, Quarter Sessions of the Peace, the justices accepted Fox's account of events, received no evidence of a breach of the common laws, yet for their better satisfaction asked Fox to take the Oath of Allegiance and Oath of Supremacy. Upon his refusal to take the oaths for conscience's sake, he was held in prison until by a writ of habeas corpus he was removed between January 29 and February 2 to the Court of King's Bench in London. There he appeared before a panel of three judges presided over by the chief justice but was remanded to Worcester after, Fox suspected, false information was given to the court by the justice of the peace who had issued the original mittimus. Back in Worcester, the assize court sent him in April to the Sessions court for a second trial regarding the oath. Fox denied the jury verdict of guilty and for the second time was removed by habeas corpus to the Court of King's Bench, London. He was remanded to Worcester for the second time where, in July, at the third proceeding in the Sessions court, Fox again was put on trial before a judge and jury. The judge, Thomas Street (1626–1696), a member of Parliament for Worcester as well as a judge in the Welsh circuit, ruled that Fox could not argue about errors in the indictment. As Street ordered Fox taken from the courtroom, Fox wrote, "He told me what a sad sentence a praemunire was, that I must forfeit my liberty and all my goods and chattels and endure imprisonment for term of life."[119] Fox then asked Street whether praemunire was the sentence, but Street said it was not. After Fox left, the judge told the clerk that praemunire "was his sentence and should stand."

From his Worcester prison, it "came upon" Fox to write to the king, not about his own sufferings but about "our principle, and us as a people." What followed was a classic statement regarding the Friends' concern for keeping the king's peace as well as peace itself and for preserving godliness in the land and easing the burden on magistrates in punishing sin. And he explained why, in tenderness of conscience to the biblical commands, Friends could not take oaths.

To the King.

---

[118] Ibid., 673.
[119] Ibid., 697.

The principle of the Quakers is the Spirit of Christ, who died for us, and is risen for our justification; by which we know that we are his. He dwelleth in us by his Spirit; and by the Spirit of Christ we are led out of unrighteousness and ungodliness. It brings us to deny all plottings and contrivings against the King, or any man. . . . The Spirit of Christ brings us to seek the peace and good of all men, and to live peaceably; and leads us from such evil works and actions as the magistrates' sword takes hold upon. . . .

For as people are led by the good Spirit of Christ, it leads them out of sin and evil, which the magistrates' sword takes hold upon, and so would be an ease to the magistrates. . . .

Now we are a people, who, in tenderness of conscience to the command of Christ and his Apostle, cannot swear; for we are commanded in Matt. v. and James v. to keep to 'Yea' and 'Nay', and not to swear at all; neither by heaven, nor by the earth, nor by any other oath, lest we go into evil, and fall into condemnation. . . .

If we could take any oath at all, we could take the oath of allegiance, as knowing that King Charles was by the power of God brought into England, and set up King of England, etc., over the heads of our old persecutors; and as for the Pope's supremacy, we do utterly deny it. But Christ and the apostle having commanded us not to swear, . . . we desire, therefore, that the King would take this into consideration, and how long we have suffered in this case. This is from one who desires the eternal good and prosperity of the King and of all his subjects in the Lord Jesus Christ.   G.F.[120]

Then Margaret Fell, Thomas Fell's widow and, since October 1669, Fox's wife, met with the king in London to discuss Fox's conviction for refusing the oath and his sentence of praemunire. Because the sentence made Fox his prisoner, the king was willing to grant a pardon, but Fox would not accept a pardon as it was not "agreeable with the innocency of my cause."[121] It would have been "dishonorable to truth," and he still sought a trial of the

---

[120] Fox, *Journal*, 699-700.
[121] Ibid., 701.

errors in the indictment.[122] Thereupon he was brought on the third writ of habeas corpus to the Court of King's Bench, London, where, on February 11, 1675, after a trial held before four judges, Lord Chief Justice Matthew Hale presiding, it was determined that there were errors in the indictment and the sentence of praemunire had to be annulled. Fox at last was restored to the liberty taken from him almost fourteen months earlier, on December 17, 1673.

Gathering the Religious Society of Friends

Although George Fox's *Journal* speaks to many leading themes in his ministry and witness, no theme is more overarching than his missions, undertaken 'in the power of the Lord' to the English nation and beyond. His life was essentially defined by the missions he ceaselessly traveled, missions wherein he gathered and formed the Religious Society of Friends. Indeed, due to this journeying it is difficult to identify a single resting place he made for himself in his adult years. Although he had "homes" and "haunts" and "retreats"[123] in and around London where he spent his later years, and although he frequently was in his wife's home at Swarthmoor Hall in Lancashire, he seems never to have made a domicile, or even a residence, of his own.

Fox's first national mission—conducted against the background of the Civil War, regicide, Commonwealth, and Protectorate—began in 1648 and lasted through early 1657. Spanning nearly ten full years of preaching and teaching, interrupted only by his first four imprisonments that took up the equivalent of almost two years of his life, Fox's first journey carried him through every county of England. Looking back over that accomplishment, he wrote of the General Meeting of Friends out of Cornwall and Devonshire held on March 8, 1657, in Exeter (Devonshire):

> I saw and said that the Lord's power had surrounded this nation round about, as with a wall and bulwark, and his Seed reached from sea unto sea, and Friends were

---

[122] Ibid., 702.

[123] These terms are used by Henry J. Cadbury in his epilogue to Fox's journal. Ibid., 742, 747.

established in the everlasting Seed of life, Christ Jesus, their life, rock, teacher, and shepherd."[124]

That first mission was the longest Fox would ever conduct. From 1648 to 1651 he had remained in and traveled through the seventeen central counties of Bedfordshire, Berkshire, Buckinghamshire, Cheshire, Derbyshire, Gloucestershire, Herefordshire, Hertfordshire, Leicestershire, Northamptonshire, Nottinghamshire, Oxfordshire, Rutland, Shropshire, Staffordshire, Warwickshire, and Worcestershire. From later in 1651 to 1654, he was in the six northern counties of Cumberland, Durham (sometimes Bishoprick), Lancashire, Northumberland, Westmorland, and Yorkshire. He returned to the central counties in 1654 and left them again in 1655 to missionize until early 1657, first in London (Middlesex County); then in the four southeastern counties of Hampshire, Kent, Surrey, and Sussex; then in the six eastern counties of Cambridgeshire, Essex, Huntingdonshire, Lincolnshire, Norfolk, and Suffolk; and finally in the five southwestern counties of Cornwall, Devon, Dorset, Somerset, and Wiltshire.

Upon completion of the initial English mission, Fox made the first of his several visits to Wales and, later in 1657, began his only journey to Scotland. At the end of the Scottish journey in 1658, he then undertook his second national mission to England that ended—again after he had visited all the English counties—almost simultaneously with the restoration of Charles II to the throne in May 1660.[125]

Ten days after Charles landed in England, Fox was committed to his fifth imprisonment, which lasted nearly five months. Thereafter, he appears to have remained in London until the middle of 1662, when he began his third national mission, which concluded at the end of 1663. The *Journal* records that in the span of eighteen months, Fox visited all but seven of the English counties and went into Wales as well.

The next thirty-two months—from January 12, 1664 to September 2, 1666—were lost to the mission enterprise while Fox suffered his seventh imprisonment. Upon regaining his liberty, he embarked on the fourth national mission, which ended in 1670. From its inception, an important purpose of this mission

---

[124] Ibid., 288.

[125] Despite Fox's observation in the *Journal* that "this was the third time I had been most part about the nation" (p. 374), the record indicates it was only his second time.

was to "settle in good order" the Society's structure of meetings for business:

> And the Lord opened to me and let me see what I must do, and how I must order and establish the Men's and Women's Monthly and Quarterly Meetings in all the nation, and write to other nations, where I came not, to do the same.[126]

After establishing monthly meetings in London he went through all the counties of England (except Rutland, which is not named in the *Journal* in this period, and four of the northern counties—Cumberland, Durham, Northumberland, and Westmorland; to each of these counties, as well as to Scotland, he "sent papers . . . for them to settle the Monthly Meetings in the Lord's power, which they did").[127] In 1668, Fox observed that "after I had settled the Monthly Meetings throughout the nation I stayed in London a time and visited Friends' meetings."[128] Additionally in this period, he made further orders regarding marriages (first regularized for Friends in 1653) by requiring that proposed unions be considered by the men's monthly and quarterly meetings "so that all things might be kept clean and pure and done in righteousness to the glory of God" and also so that if any "came out of another county or nation," they must bring a certificate from the meeting where they belonged to the meeting "where they took their wife or husband."[129] And he now records for the first time the establishment of schools, one at Waltham for the "teaching of boys" and one at Shacklewell for instructing "young lasses and maidens in whatsoever things were civil and useful in the creation."[130]

---

[126] Fox, *Journal*, 511. As Fox notes, "And about this time [1657] I was moved to set up the men's Quarterly Meetings throughout the nation, though in the North they were settled before." Ibid., 285. Over the centuries, Quakers have maintained essentially this same organizational structure for worship, making decisions, and providing guidance. 'Monthly meeting' is the term for the local congregation, which meets once a month for business; the 'quarterly meeting' is a regional gathering of monthly meetings held four times a year; and the 'yearly meeting' is an annual gathering that draws Friends from a larger geographic area than the quarterly meetings.

[127] Ibid., 514.
[128] Ibid., 528.
[129] Ibid., 519.
[130] Ibid., 520.

Between May and August 1669, Fox "was moved of the Lord to go over into Ireland, to visit the Seed of God in that nation."[131] And then on October 27 that year, he and Margaret Fell were married "at a large meeting appointed of purpose in the meeting house at Broad Mead in Bristol." This was after they had obtained the approval not only of her children but of the Bristol Men's Meeting on October 18, a joint men's and women's meeting on the 21st, and a public meeting on the 22nd, William Penn being one of the speakers on the 18th and again on the 22nd.[132] The certificate of the marriage was signed by the family members present as well as "by most of the ancient Friends of that city, besides many other Friends from divers parts of the nation."[133] Husband and wife remained together a brief time until she returned home to Swarthmoor and he resumed his mission, going as far as London.

Early in 1670 Fox wrote an epistle to all the quarterly meetings describing his plan to help poor Friends by establishing an apprenticeship program in which their children would receive instruction in a trade under the guidance of a suitable master, "whereby they that are decaying in their families, in seven years time they be rearing them up, and preserving of them."[134] Then, over the next eighteen months the newly married couple was buffeted by severe challenges. First, Margaret was arrested in her home and cast again, by an order of king and council, into Lancaster prison upon an old praemunire charge, one from which she had been discharged the prior year, also by an order of king and council. By diligent efforts, her freedom and property were regained through a new order from the king, but not until April 4, 1671, and only after a fresh tide of persecutions and sufferings had arisen nationwide. On May 10, 1670, the amended Conventicle Act went into effect, which prohibited meetings for unauthorized worship of five or more persons not of the same household. Five days later, it being First Day (Sunday), Fox passed through London streets filled with local militia and expectant throngs on his way to meeting for worship, where he intended to speak, certain to invite his own arrest. While preaching, he was "plucked down" and "pulled out" by a "constable with an informer, and an officer with a file of

---

[131] Ibid., 536.
[132] Fox, *Journal*, 555; Penn's *My Irish Journal*, PWP, 1:103, 105, 132n24.
[133] Fox, *Journal*, 555.
[134] Ibid., 556.

musketeers" and taken to the lord mayor's court, where he successfully defended himself. After the informer had slipped away without being identified or giving testimony, the sympathetic magistrate set Fox free.[135]

In the following months, however, while completing his fourth national mission in the southeastern and eastern counties, Fox became gravely ill, and as his health steadily deteriorated he lost his hearing and sight. "And it was a cruel bloody persecuting time, but the Lord's power went over all, and his everlasting Seed. And as persecution began to cease I began to arise out of my sufferings."[136] A sense of new mission opportunities arose in Fox, "for it was upon me to go beyond the seas into America and Barbados. . . . I began to prepare to go beyond sea after I had finished my service here in England for the Lord." [137]

"Beyond the seas into America and Barbados"

Testifying to the success of Fox's English missions, persons were so convinced of the Truth he preached that they individually felt a vocation to undertake their own mission journeys, some even "beyond the seas." In 1656 Mary Fisher and Ann Austin, arriving in Barbados from England, became the first Quakers to set foot in the New World. From there they went on to the Massachusetts Bay Colony, where they were met with persecution and imprisonment. In 1657 the British agent in Jamaica requested policy instructions from the London government regarding "some people lately come hither called Quakers. . . . Now my education and judgment prompting me to an owning of all, that pretend any way to godliness and righteousness . . . hath put me to some stand how to carry myself towards them . . . being desirous to steer my course to the interest I serve."[138]

That same year, the first monthly meeting of Quakers in America was held at Sandwich, Massachusetts, but it was followed in 1659 by a wave of persecutions against Friends in

---

[135] Ibid., 560–65.

[136] Ibid., 572.

[137] *Journal*, 579.

[138] Edward D'Oyley to John Thurloe, secretary of state, February 28, 1657, in John Thurloe, *A Collection of the State Papers: containing authentic memorials of the English affairs from the year 1638 to the restoration of King Charles II*, 7 vols. (London: 1742), 6:834.

New England, resulting in the deaths that year of William Robinson and Marmaduke Stevenson, of Mary Dyer in 1660, and of William Leddra in 1661. By 1661 the New England sufferings had drawn Fox's attention, which he sets out in the *Journal*,[139] as well as the intervention of Edward Burrough (1634–1662), a prominent Quaker minister, who went directly to the king and obtained a royal warrant dated September 9, 1661, addressed to the governors "of our plantations of New England, and of all the colonies thereunto belonging," requiring them,

> if there be any of those people called Quakers amongst you, now already condemned to suffer death or other corporal punishment, or that are imprisoned, . . . you are to forbear to proceed any further therein; but that you forthwith send the said persons (whether condemned or imprisoned) over into this our kingdom of England, together with the respective crimes or offences laid to their charge; to the end such course may be taken with them here, as shall be agreeable to our laws and their demerits.[140]

Charles II's ready concern for the Quaker sufferings in New England is not surprising. He had, in the days preceding his return to England and the restoration to his throne, laid the foundation of a religious toleration policy for all Christians, both conformist and nonconformist. At Breda (Netherlands) he offered 'a liberty to tender consciences' to all, even dissenters and separatists, 'for differences of opinion in matters of religion which do not disturb the peace of the kingdom.' Then, months after the Restoration, on October 25, 1660, the king repeated that policy in his first royal Declaration of Indulgence (to be reiterated again in December 1662 and yet again in March 1672 in the third Declaration of Indulgence for Tender Consciences). It was Charles who, in late 1660, concerned himself in Fox's fifth imprisonment and ordered the warrant setting him free.[141] It was also Charles who ordered the discharge of Fox from his seventh imprisonment in 1666, ending nearly thirty-two months of incarceration. In the release, the king noted he was informed that Fox was "a man against all plotting and fighting, and one that is

---

[139] Fox, *Journal*, 411–15.
[140] Ibid., 413–14.
[141] See p. 28 above.

ready at all times to discover plots rather than to make them."[142] And it would be Charles again, in 1675, who used his good offices to facilitate the trial that resulted in the lifting of Fox's sentence of praemunire and ended his eighth, and final, imprisonment.[143]

There is no evidence that either Charles's Breda promise or his offered indulgence of liberty to those of tender consciences was hypocritical, dissembling, or politically duplicitous. Nor is there any such evidence for Oliver Cromwell's proclaimed view of liberty of conscience as a natural right. But each of these heads of the British state faced parliamentary forces opposing any policy other than the re-establishment of religious peace by means of enforced unity and conformity in the land. Leading causes of the Quaker sufferings were parliamentary statutes readily enforced by a judiciary and squirearchy wielding local power. As noted above, in Cromwell's time such statutes were the Blasphemy Act of 1650 and the requirement of the Oath of Abjuration in 1655. Upending Charles's policy, beginning in 1661 Parliament put in place the four enactments that came to be known collectively as the Clarendon Code: the Corporation Act of 1661, the Uniformity Act of 1662, the Conventicle Act of 1664, and the Five Mile Act of 1665.

Most threatening to the Quakers were the Conventicle Act (which prohibited five or more persons, not of the same household, from gathering or assembling for a religious meeting unless in accord with the liturgy and practice of the Church of England) and the Five Mile Act (which barred any clergyman not subscribing to the Church of England's Book of Common Prayer, as well as any lay preacher, from coming or being within five miles of any city or incorporated town or of any borough that sent burgesses to Parliament or of any parish church where the clergy might have served). As already noted, the Quaker Act of 1662, entitled "An Act for preventing the Mischiefs and Dangers that may arise by certain Persons called Quakers and others refusing to take lawfull Oaths," was a legislative prohibition against Fox's fundamental claim of the biblical—and divine—injunction against swearing oaths. Later, Parliament would pass the Test Act of 1673, "An act for preventing dangers which may happen from popish recusants," expanding a penal law from James I's time to include nonconformists and requiring them, as

---

[142] See p. 32 above.

[143] See pp. 34–35 above.

a condition for holding public office, to take the Oaths of Supremacy and Allegiance, to subscribe to a declaration against transubstantiation, and to receive Holy Communion.

Fortuitously for the Quakers, in March 1664 Charles granted to his brother James, the Duke of York, a royal patent for territory along America's Atlantic seaboard, land included within the Republic of the United Netherlands' colonial province in America newly won by English arms. In June the same year, James transferred a portion of the territory "hereafter to be called Nova Caesarea, or New Jersey" to Sir George Carteret and John Lord Berkeley, two courtiers of the royal family, as joint proprietors. In time their interests, which were partitioned into East and West Jersey, were conveyed to English Quakers. But before those conveyances were set in motion, George Fox in 1672 made his epic journey "beyond the seas" in which he traveled through Barbados and Jamaica and traversed the province of New Jersey as he missionized in America between Rhode Island and Carolina.

Fox's decision to undertake his first international mission begs an explanation, but the historical record—and George Fox—are both silent, Fox simply stating in the *Journal* that "it was upon me to go."[144] As with all his English missions, he expresses no doubts or wrestlings about what he should do, or where he should travel, or even whether he should go. But then, after his initial soul struggles and 'openings,' there seemed to be few, if any, vocational doubts in his life. His guidance and course, he undoubtedly would say, were from God. Just as Paul had written in his epistle to the church at Rome of his hope to carry his mission out of the eastern and into the western Mediterranean, "since I no longer have any room for work in these regions, and since I have longed for many years to come to you,"[145] Fox may have understood his work in England to be finished, and he yearned to see the New World where some convinced Friends had already preceded him.

Fox's journal account of the transatlantic mission begins:

> About the 6th month [August 1671] I went down with Margaret [Fell Fox] and William Penn and Mary Penington and her daughter Guli, and we got the King's barge, and they carried us down from Wapping to the

---

[144] Fox, *Journal*, 579.
[145] Romans 15:23 RSV.

ship which lay three miles below Gravesend. And they went with me to the Downs [a sheltered stretch of water in the North Sea near the English Channel and the Straits of Dover].[146]

The ship that Fox boarded was the ketch *Industry*, which sailed from England on August 14. "We were in number of passengers about fifty."[147] Other than an earlier reference to William Penn's book of trials, this is the first mention of Penn in the *Journal*. Also in the party were Gulielma Maria Springett (1644–1694), known as Guli, and her mother, Mary Penington. Mary, the daughter of Sir John Proude, was first married to William Springett, who died before the birth of their daughter Gulielma. Mary's second husband (and Guli's stepfather) was Isaac Penington (1616–1679), son of a former lord mayor of London who, with Mary, had become a convinced Friend and member of the Society in 1657 or 1658, earning renown as a Quaker witness through his published testimonies.[148] About the time that Fox first stepped onto the American continent—near West River, Maryland, in April 1672—Penn and Guli became husband and wife, fulfilling their lengthy engagement.

Of the convincement and sufferings of William Penn (1644–1718)

William Penn, born in London (and baptized at the Church of All Hallows by the Tower), was the elder son of Admiral Sir William Penn (1621–1670) who, during the years of the civil war and the republic, had served Parliament and Oliver Cromwell but on the approach of the Restoration became a Royalist. It was Admiral Penn who commanded the ship bringing Charles II from exile in the Netherlands back to his throne in Britain. The senior Penn's rewards from the interregnum government included appointment as rear admiral in 1648 (with further advancements thereafter) and estates in Ireland, whereas those from the Stuarts included a knighthood in 1660 and later appointment as a commissioner of the Royal Navy. In the younger William Penn's account of his own convincement, which he "delivered by himself

---

[146] Fox, *Journal*, 579–80.

[147] Ibid., 581–82.

[148] See *Works of Isaac Penington*, 4 vols. (Glenside, PA: Quaker Heritage Press, 1995–1997).

to Thomas Harvey" in about 1699, he said his father, who was a celebrity in national life, "had train'd him up in Learning and other accomplishments for a courtier—as for an Ambassador or other Minister."[149] The father gave his son educational opportunities meant to fulfill his paternal expectations and develop his son's natural gifts, first at Chigwell School near London and then at Christ Church, Oxford. The father's plans began to derail when his son was expelled from Oxford in the winter of 1661/1662 for his public criticism of church ceremonials. Penn was next sent to Paris but chose to go on from there and undertake studies in 1663/1664 at the Protestant Academy of Saumur, a Huguenot university in western France founded in 1591 (and closed when toleration of French Protestantism ended with the revocation of the Edict of Nantes in 1685). At Saumur, Penn studied Christian humanism, including religious toleration. After returning to England, in February 1665 he began preparing for a law career at Lincoln's Inn, one of the four Inns of Court in London in which British barristers, solicitors, and judges were trained.[150] During this time, he also attended the royal court to represent his father in both professional naval matters and personal business affairs, such as claims to land in County Cork, Ireland.

Although the admiral was religiously committed to the Church of England, he unintentionally planted the seed that ultimately led his son to grow away from his own churchmanship and into the embrace of the Religious Society of Friends (and thus into the doctrinal controversies of the day). The Christian faith as 'opened' to George Fox was twice witnessed to young William Penn through the ministry of Thomas Loe of Oxford, a Quaker missionary and "the Apostle of Ireland."[151] On the first occasion, Penn was "but a child living at Cork [Ireland] with his Father"[152] when the admiral invited Loe to conduct a meeting in the Penn home for the family. There the impressionable son, about twelve years of age, witnessed both his father and one of

---

[149] "The Convincement of William Penn," *Journal of Friends Historical Society* 32 (1935):24.

[150] Inns of Court are professional associations of lawyers in London where attorneys are prepared in the law and then maintain their chambers or offices and work together in communal precincts. Today's four principal Inns of Court, which originated in the medieval period, are Lincoln's Inn, the Inner Temple, the Middle Temple, and Gray's Inn.

[151] *PWP*, 1:68n2.

[152] *PWP*, 1:22.

his father's "Blacks" moved to tears. Then in late summer or early autumn 1667, while Penn was in Cork on his father's business, he again heard Loe[153] in a meeting and "was exceedingly reach'd so that he wept much and it seemed to him as if a Voice sayd stand on thy feet How dost know but somebody may be reach'd by thy tears so he stood up that he might be seen."[154] Thereafter, Penn began attending meetings in Cork and grew convinced that he had found his spiritual home in the Religious Society of Friends. With his convincement came his sufferings for conscience's sake—sufferings not only of arrest and imprisonment but of estrangement from his father. By the time three years had elapsed from his standing on his feet to weep as Loe preached, Penn was to suffer the anguish of death's untimely removal first of Loe the spiritual mentor and then of his earthly father.

Penn's first arrest occurred in Cork on November 3, 1667, when, with eighteen others (for whom he acted as advocate and spokesman), he was taken from a Quaker meeting to a hearing before the mayor of Cork and charged with "being present at a riotous and tumultuary assembly."[155] When Penn asked by what legal authority the mayor acted, both a January 1661 proclamation, which prohibited meetings of Quakers, Fifth Monarchy Men, and Anabaptists and required the Oath of Allegiance, and the Conventicle Act of 1664 were cited.[156] Penn's forensic arguments for all of the accused failed, and the Quakers were jailed. However, within days they were released upon the advice given the mayor by the Earl of Orrery, lord president of the province (Munster), who trusted that "mildness may operate on such offenders" after they were reproved and admonished "not to hold meetings against the law."[157] In the meantime, Penn had written the earl protesting his innocence on the grounds of freedom of conscience and presuming the earl shared with him "this infallible observation that diversity of faith and worship contribute not to the disturbance of any place where moral

---

[153] *PWP*, 1:49, 68n2.

[154] "The Convincement of William Penn," 23.

[155] *PWP*, 1:51.

[156] *PWP*, 1:51. See also William C. Braithwaite, *The Second Period of Quakerism*, 2nd ed. (Cambridge: University Press, 1961), 9.

[157] *PWP*, 1:53.

uniformity is barely requisite to preserve the peace."[158] The presumption misfired. Orrery wrote back to Penn stating he "could not but approve what he [the mayor of Cork] did" and adding, "I confess I was surprised and sorry to see you thus associated; and apprehending what I should say unto you (seeing you now joined with the Quakers) would be of little validity with you, I sent this day by the post to your father a copy of Mayor's letter to me with my opinion on it to him."[159] Even before this contretemps, Admiral Penn had ordered his son to return home without delay.

By the time the twenty-three year-old Penn, filled with his fresh-found convincement, finally did get back to London and meet his father in December, their respective resolves were already fixed in opposition. Even though they entreated each other for understanding and forbearance, there was to be none. The son was expelled from the father's home and disowned. In the internal exile that followed, Penn sought to justify himself to his father in writing and to make a new home for himself within the Religious Society of Friends by becoming acquainted with Quakers in the capital as well as by committing his rhetorical skills to the Society's polemical battles with its foes and to his own advocacy for liberty of conscience.

In the time between Penn's estrangement from his father and his commitment to the Tower of London in December 1668, he wrote the following paper to his father—notwithstanding the admiral's "high wrath against me." Although filial respect might have been intended in offering this studied explanation, its title, introductory letter, and content no doubt only increased the paternal wrath.

> A Relation, & Description of the Nature & Fruits of the two kingdoms of darkness & light, as they were collected out of the holy truths declared in scripture, as the requirings of the Lord to be presented to my father, who at that time was in high wrath against me because of my separation from the world, & testimony against it, that the deeds thereof were evil.
>
> Dear Father,

---

[158] *PWP*, 1:51.
[159] *PWP*, 1:53.

Fearing that words may create wrath, and that reasons or citations, though most true in themselves may lose much of their native force, and usual success, when by a child alleged unto his parent, it seems good unto the Lord (who first put it into my heart) that I should only offer unto thee, a few words out of his own written will, as discovering the most inward qualifications, as well as external garb and appearance of those two spirits, that act or lead the sons and daughters of men, either to serve the god of this world, or the God of heaven.[160]

Penn then provided quotations from the Bible in two columns captioned "The Spirit and Practice of the World" and "The Spirit and Doctrine of Christ" and under the subheadings of Persecution vs. Love; Mocking vs. Silence; and Profaneness, Swearing, Uncleanness, Drunkenness, Blood, Wantonness, and Pleasure vs. Holiness, Reverence, Chastity, Temperance, Forbearance, Modesty, and Moderation. After citing the last worldly sin, Penn wrote that "there might be more instances of the genius, temper, and complexion of the worldly spirit, but it would be too large and prolix."[161] In his conclusion, Penn told the admiral he had "been made daily desirous of dying to all the sin, pomp, and vain fashions of this world that I might be found in a continual beholding of the Lord's glory."[162] It was the end of any plans the father had to make his son a courtier serving his nation in the favor of his sovereign and remaining in the prestigious favor of his prince, the heir apparent. How and when—or even if—the breach was ever healed is not clear, but the next documented record shows that Penn's release from the Tower (about July 28, 1669) ordered that he "be forthwith set at liberty and delivered to his father."[163] Once again the father sent the son from London to be his business agent in Ireland. Penn left on this assignment on September 15.

Between early 1668, the time of his expulsion from home and disownment by his father, and the end of the year, Penn also committed his considerable spiritual energies and well-trained advocacy skills to the doctrinal controversies of the day as a

---

[160] *PWP*, 1:60.
[161] *PWP*, 1:65.
[162] *PWP*, 1:67.
[163] *PWP*, 1:97.

Quaker polemicist and pamphleteer. That year he wrote and saw into print three short works. The full title of each gives, in the style of the day, a précis of the work. Each was printed in London in 1668, but there is no more specific dating; hence, their sequence is not now known. The various ways in which the author identifies himself in the titles of these pamphlets are revealing. The titles (in italics) of each of these three 1668 works are given below, plus those of later works by Penn, and are followed by brief discussions of each pamphlet.

Truth Exalted; in a short, but sure, testimony against all those religions, faiths, and worships that have been formed and followed in the darkness of apostacy.—And for that glorious light which is now risen, and shines forth in the life and doctrine of the despised Quakers, as the alone good old way of life and salvation. Presented to princes, priests, and people, that they may repent, believe, and obey. By William Penn the Younger, whom divine love constrains in a holy contempt to trample on Egypt's glory, not fearing the king's wrath, having beheld the majesty of him who is invisible

This work was a proclamation lifting up the Quakers' understanding of Christ and calling to repentance "ye dark and idolatrous papists, ye superstitious and loose protestants, ye zealous and carnal professors. . . . You are altogether strangers to the yoke, to the daily cross, and self-denying life, but are yet the corrupt ground, and evil tree, which bring forth evil fruits, thorns, briers, and sour grapes."[164] This title reveals the youthful author's temerity, both in trading upon his wrathful father's reputation and in his "holy contempt to trample on Egypts [read England's] glory, not fearing the kings wrath."

The Guide Mistaken, and Temporizing Rebuked: Or, a brief reply to Jonathan Clapham's book, intituled A Guide to the True Religion. *By W. P. A friend to the true religion*

This pamphlet of sixty-three pages was Penn's rebuttal to Jonathan Clapham, a priest of the Church of England whose work referred to in the title had been printed earlier in 1668. In 1656 Clapham had published *A Full Discovery and Confutation of the Wicked and Damnable Doctrines of the Quakers*, and now

---

[164] William Penn, *Truth Exalted* . . . , London: n.p., 1668, 16–17.

in 1668 he argued that Quakers and certain others were outside salvation and "in total apostasy from Christianity." Penn's rebuttal detailed the false arguments, hypocrisies, aspersions, and contradictions contained in Clapham's *A Guide to the True Religion* and raised up the Quakers' principles which, with attendance on "its holy motions entirely resigned unto, with that noble, but necessary resolution, of despising the shame, and patiently enduring the cross, shall make thee a righteous magistrate, a reformed priest, or a holy citizen of the New Jerusalem."[165]

The Sandy Foundation Shaken: Or, those so generally believed and applauded doctrines, of one God, subsisting in three distinct and separate persons, the impossibility of God's pardoning sinners without a plenary satisfaction, the justification of impure persons by an imputative righteousness, refuted. From the authority of scripture testimonies, and right reason. By W. P. j. A builder on that foundation which cannot be moved

Penn's activities in 1668 also included the lively public advocacy of Quaker doctrine. When two Presbyterian women attended a meeting for worship in London, thereafter becoming convinced Friends and enraging their church's pastor, conflict was set in motion between the two church bodies. As the Presbyterians cast insults upon the Quakers, Penn and his colleague George Whitehead asked for and were given the opportunity to respond to the issues in face-to-face debate. The parties joined their issues in the Spitalfields home of the outraged Presbyterian clergyman, Thomas Vincent, attended by several of his fellow clergy as well as members of his congregation. Their disagreement came into focus on the theological definitions of the Trinity and the atonement. According to Penn, the unruly meeting was abruptly terminated by Vincent after he had made his own presentation but before the Quakers had had a full opportunity to respond. When denied another public debate, Penn wrote this thirty-one-page rebuttal. Condemned as a "Blasphemous Booke" by the state authorities, the rebuttal earned for Penn an imprisonment lasting more than eight months.

---

[165] William Penn, *The guide mistaken, and temporizing rebuked* ... London: 1668.

Before that blow struck him, however, there came the death on October 6 of Thomas Loe, Penn's spiritual mentor. The following day Penn wrote to "Dr. G.S." ["Dear Gulielma Springett," a Quaker since ca. 1659 whom he would marry in 1672], informing her of Loe's death and burial and of his own heavy sense of loss:

> Whom my soul loved, whilst alive; and bemoans, now dead, and yet have pure fellowship with that which lives forever. This day we lay the body in the ground, as having done its Maker's work, and well. And being it's thus, let us all press after the inheritance he hath obtained, through travels, trials, perils, temptations, afflictions, cruel mockings, and what not; so shall it be well with us.[166]

Penn's second arrest came on December 16, 1668, and was made pursuant to the Privy Council's peremptory order that he be indefinitely committed to the Tower of London (where his father had also been committed from September 20 to October 25, 1655, upon his return from the West Indies as general and commander-in-chief of an English fleet).[167] The son's commitment was for having authored the "Blasphemous Booke" *The Sandy Foundation Shaken*. Not only was the printer, John Derby, simultaneously imprisoned in the Gate House, London, but both men were held under close, virtually solitary confinement.

These recent 'trials' and 'perils' endured by Penn formed the background of the two new works he wrote while in the Tower. The first had this title:

No Cross, No Crown: Or several sober reasons against hat-honour, titular-respects, you to a single person, with the apparel and recreations of the times. . . . With sixty eight testimonies of the most famous persons, of both former and latter ages for further confirmation. In defence of the poor despised Quakers . . . By W. Pennj.

This pamphlet of 105 pages, printed in London in the fall of 1669, was later heavily edited by Penn, and the revised edition was

---

[166] *PWP*, 1:68.

[167] Leslie Stephen and Sydney Lee, eds., *The Dictionary of National Biography: From the Earliest Times to 1900*, 22 vols. (London: Oxford University Press, 1921–22), 15:754.

printed in 1682. The extent and purpose of the revision are shown in the enlargement to 592 pages and in the new subtitle: *A discourse shewing the nature and discipline of the holy cross of Christ, and that the denyal of self, and daily bearing of Christ's cross, is alone the way to the rest and kingdom of God. To which are added, the living and dying testimonies of divers persons of fame and learning, in favour of this treatise.* In its second edition, *No Cross, No Crown* became the most widely known of the author's religious writings. Penn, in his October 17, 1668, letter to Isaac Penington reporting on Thomas Loe's death, indicates that the title was inspired by Loe himself. Undoubtedly, Penn intended the book to be a memorial to Loe.

> When I came in and had set myself upon the bedside, several heavenly expressions fell from his mouth, and so shook was he by the power of the Lord, and overcome by the ravishing glory of his presence, that it was wonderful to all friends, whose testimony concerning his departure was that they judged it impossible for any to have lain so long with more patience, resignation, and lamb-like innocency than he did, yet truly bold and courageous. His expressions as I wrote them down were these: Glory, glory, for thy powers known—Good is the Lord—then taking me by the hand, he spake thus, Dear heart, bear thy cross, stand faithful for God, and bear thy testimony in thy day and generation, and God will give thee an eternal crown of glory that none shall ever take from thee. There is not another way; this is the way the holy men of old walked in; and it shall prosper.[168]

Innocency with Her Open Face Presented by Way of Apology for the Book Entituled The Sandy Foundation Shaken, *to all serious and enquiring persons, particularly the inhabitants of the city of London: By W. P. j*

Printed in 1669, this pamphlet earned for Penn his release from the Tower. In the thirty-one pages of the document that Penn certainly wrote, what he presented "by way of apology" was not intended as a confession of error but as a restatement of belief. Nor was he here writing a direct plea for freedom but rather a

---

[168] *PWP*, 1:70.

defense of the faith he owned. The additional pages of argument following Penn's farewell were probably written by friends concerned that Penn's words of vindication would not earn his liberty. Penn's own closing words were:

> Choose by fair and moderate debates (not penalties ratified by imperial decrees) to determine religious differences; so will you at least obtain tranquility which may be called a civil unity. But if you are resolved severity shall take its course in this, our case can never change, nor happiness abate, that no humane edict can possibly deprive us of his glorious presence, who is able to make the dismal'st prison so many receptacles of pleasure, and whose heavenly fellowship doth unspeakably replenish our solitary souls with divine consolation, by whose holy, meek, and harmless Spirit I have been taught most freely to forgive, and not less earnestly to solicit the temporal and eternal good of all my adversaries. Farewell.
>
> William Penn, jun.

And here ended the youthful Penn's earliest salvos in the pamphleteering word wars.

Penn was released from the Tower of London by order of the Privy Council dated July 28, 1669, the order noting that he was "sensible of the impiety and blasphemy" of his heretical opinions and that "he doth recant and retract the same."[169] As the parties adroitly spoke past each other, the Council's direction that the imprisoned son "be forthwith set at liberty and delivered to his father" was carried into effect. Once reunited with his father, Penn again was sent to Ireland on family business, leaving London on September 15 and finishing his affairs in Ireland on July 1 the following year. On the outward journey, he arrived in Bristol on September 22, 1669, remaining there until October 23 when he sailed to the Irish port of Cork. During the month in Bristol, Penn spent time with George Fox as he prepared for his marriage there to Margaret Fell. Penn wrote in *My Irish Journal*: "I was moved among others to testify to George Fox's marriage."[170] He did so in the Bristol Men's Meeting on October 18 and in a public meeting on October 22. He sailed for Ireland

---

[169] *PWP*, 1:97.
[170] *PWP*, 1:105.

on October 23 and so was away before the wedding four days later.[171]

While Penn served his father's business—as well as attending to Quaker matters—in Ireland, the admiral, in his forty-eighth year, was dying at his country home in Wanstead (Essex), north of London. On April 29, 1670, he had written to his son, "I wish you had well done all your business there and that you were here, for I find myself to decline. . . . Pray keep out of harm's way and the God of mercy direct and preserve you. I am your very affectionate father, W Penn."[172]

Yet when the son did return to London in early summer, he soon plunged into harm's way. His third arrest for conscience's sake was made while he was openly preaching outdoors to a congregation of Friends while "soldiers by force of arms" were barring them from entering their meeting house (place of worship) on Gracechurch Street (also known as Gracious Street), London. This seizure, on August 14, 1670, differed sharply from the two previous experiences. During the first arrest, at Cork in November 1667, Penn had needed to persuade the authorities that notwithstanding his father's status as an eminent member of the landed gentry, the son was indeed a Friend, worthy (and desirous) of incarceration with his fellow Quakers. At his second arrest, in December 1668, he was peremptorily ordered without trial to be confined in the Tower of London "until farther Order." At this third arrest, he was seized and sent to the City of London's Newgate Prison upon the order of the lord mayor of London, Sir Samuel Starling, there to await trial with another Friend, William Mead, for "preaching seditiously."[173] The trial, held September 1–5 at the Old Bailey, gave Penn the occasion to exhibit his skills as legal advocate.

Counterbalancing what Penn described as his suffering for living "godly in Christ Jesus" was his filial love and concern for his father, who was then upon his deathbed. The pain of their separation at this time was a trial to both. Writing to his father on August 15, the day after his arrest, Penn minimized his imprisonment as a matter of having "my hat pulled off," asked that his father "be not displeased nor grieved," and assured him

---

[171] *PWP*, 1:132n24.
[172] PWP, 1:152–53.
[173] PWP, 1:172.

that "I was never better: and what they have to charge me with is harmless." He then concluded:

> Well, eternity, which is at the door, (for he that shall come, will come, and will not tarry.) that shall make amends for all. The Lord God grant everlasting consolate and support thee, by his holy power and presence, to his eternal rest and glory. Amen.

Thy faithful and obedient son,

My duty to my mother.   William Penn[174]

Penn and his fellow defendant Mead were tried together in early September by the Court of Quarter Sessions. The bench was composed of ten justices (London's mayor, a recorder who acted as prosecutor, six aldermen, and two sheriffs) and a jury of twelve male citizens of London. The indictment charged that the defendants and some three hundred other persons

> with force and arms . . . unlawfully and tumultuously did assemble and congregate themselves together to the disturbance of the peace . . . by reason whereof a great concourse and tumult of people in the street aforesaid, then and there a long time did remain and continue, in contempt of the said Lord the King, and of his law, to the great disturbance of his peace, to the great terror and disturbance of many of his liege people and subjects, to the ill example of all others in the like case offending, and against the peace of the said Lord the King, his crown and dignity.[175]

As scholars have noted,[176] Mayor Starling overreached in charging Penn and Mead with breach of the peace and tumultuous assembly rather than with demonstrable violations under the several acts of the Clarendon Code (particularly the Conventicle Act as revised in 1670). If Penn had only been tendered the praemunire loyalty oath, he would have refused, thereby ensuring his conviction and severe punishment. Instead, the prosecution grounded the indictment on a charge of breach of the peace which, as Penn successfully showed the jury, could not be sustained by the evidence.

---

[174] William Penn to Sir William Penn, August 15, 1670, *PWP*, 1:173–74.
[175] Besse, *Sufferings of the People Called Quakers*, 1:417.
[176] *PWP*, 1:171–72.

England 1350–1682

On September 1 the jury was impaneled, the indictment was read, and each defendant pleaded not guilty. The court continued the matter on September 3, beginning with a wrangle over 'hat-honour,' Penn and Mead having this time come to the bar with their hats off and the mayor directing a court officer to place their hats back on their heads and then ordering Penn to remove his while standing at the bar. Penn's failure to take off his hat was ruled to be contempt of the court (notwithstanding, as Penn argued, that the hats had been placed on their heads by court order), and Penn and Mead were each fined forty marks.[177] Then, the witnesses' testimony was heard and Penn made the following arguments:

> We confess ourselves to be so far from recanting, or declining to vindicate the assembling of ourselves, to preach, pray, or worship the eternal, holy, just God, that we declare to all the world, that we believe it to be our indispensible duty to meet incessantly upon so good an account, nor shall all the powers upon earth be able to divert us from reverencing and adoring our God who made us. . . .
>
> I affirm I have broken no law, nor am guilty of the indictment that is laid to my charge, and to the end the bench, the jury, and myself, with those that hear us, may have a more direct understanding of this procedure, I desire you would let me know, by what law it is you prosecute me, and upon what law you ground my indictment. . . .
>
> Shall I plead to an indictment that hath no foundation in law? If it contain the law you say I have broken, why should you decline to produce that law, since it will be impossible for the jury to determine, or to agree to bring in their verdict, who have not the law produced by which they should measure the truth of this indictment, and the guilt, or contrary, of my fact. . . .

---

[177] At this time, the English mark was worth 160 pence and unskilled rural laborers earned about 8 pence a day. Thus, forty marks represented a significant fine. *Oxford English Dictionary*, 2nd ed., ed. J. A. Simpson and E. S. C. Weiner (Oxford: Clarendon Press, 1989), 9:380; Jeffrey L. Forgeng, *Daily Life in Stuart England* (Westport, CT: Greenwood, 2007), 82.

> The question is not, whether I am guilty of this indictment, but, whether this indictment be legal. It is too general an answer to say, *It is the common law*, unless we know both when, where, and what it is. For where there is no law, there is no transgression; and that law which is not in being, is so far from being common, that it is no law at all.[178]

When Penn was silenced and removed to the bale-dock at the court's order, Mead declared:

> You men of the jury, here I do now stand to answer to an indictment against me, which is a bundle of stuff full of lies and falsehood; for therein I am accused that I met *vi & armis, illicité & tumultuosé*. Time was, when I had freedom to use a carnal weapon, and then I thought I feared no man, but now I fear the living God, and dare not make use thereof, nor hurt any man; nor do I know I demeaned myself as a tumultuous person. I say, I am a peaceable man, therefore it is a very proper question, what William Penn demanded in this case, an *Oyer* of the law on which our indictment is grounded.
>
> *Recorder*. I have made answer to that already.
>
> *Mead*, turning his face to the jury, said, You men of the jury, who are my judges, if the Recorder will not tell you what makes a riot, a rout, or an unlawful assembly, Cook [Coke], he that once they called the Lord Cook, tells us what makes a riot, a rout, or an unlawful assembly.—A riot is when three or more are met together to beat a man, or to enter forcibly into another man's land, to cut down his grass, his wood, or break down his pales.[179]

Mead was then ordered to the bale-dock with Penn, from which Penn was heard to say in a loud voice that charging the jury in the absence of the prisoners was "directly opposite to and destructive of the undoubted right of every English prisoner," citing Lord Coke and his commentaries on the Magna Carta. Then Mead and Penn were sent to solitary confinement as the jury deliberated, having been instructed to reach a unanimous

---

[178] Besse, *Sufferings of the People Called Quakers*, 1:419.
[179] Ibid., 420.

verdict that found Penn guilty of preaching to the people and drawing a tumultuous company and Mead guilty of aiding him.

As only eight jurors agreed to the directed verdict and four dissented, the frustrated justices berated the dissenters, trying to force the verdict they had insisted upon. The dissenters were unmoved. The foreman reported that unanimity in the jury could be reached only on the single fact that Penn was "guilty of speaking in Gracious-street"; there was no agreement that he was speaking to an "unlawful assembly" or to a "tumult of people." The court refused the verdict and would not let the jury depart. Ordered back to their deliberations, the jurors asked for pen, ink, and paper, and when they returned, they handed in their signed verdict, finding, as first delivered, Penn guilty of speaking or preaching to an assembly in Gracious Street. They found Mead to be not guilty.

The court, again insisting upon its directed verdict, ordered the jury held overnight and the defendants back to jail. The order followed this exchange:

Recorder. You shall not be dismissed, till we have a verdict that the court will accept, and you shall be locked up without meat, drink, fire, and tobacco. You shall not think to abuse the court. We will have a verdict by the help of God, or you shall starve for it.

Penn. My jury, who are my judges, ought not to be thus menaced; their verdict should be free, and not compelled. The bench ought to wait upon them, but not forestall them. I do desire that justice may be done me, and that the arbitrary resolves of the bench may not be made the measure of my juries verdict...

It is a great mistake. We did not make the tumult, but they that interrupted us. The jury cannot be so ignorant, as to think that we met there with a design to disturb the civil peace; since, first, we were by force of arms kept out of our lawful house, and met as near it in the street as their soldiers would give us leave; and secondly, because it was no new thing, nor with the circumstances expressed in the indictment, but what was usual and customary with us. 'Tis very well known, that we are a peaceable people, and cannot offer violence to any man.
...

The agreement of twelve men is a verdict in law, and such an one being given by the jury, I require the clerk of the peace to record it, as will answer it at his peril. And if the jury bring in another verdict contradictory to this, I affirm, they are perjured men in law. (And looking upon the jury, said) You are Englishmen; mind your privilege; give not away your right.[180]

On Sunday, September 4, at 7 a.m., the justices, defendants, and jurors were all back in court. Again the jurors were asked for their verdict, and again the foreman reported they could agree only that Penn was guilty of speaking in Gracious Street. For yet the fourth time, the court again demanded its directed verdict. Failing to obtain it, all were ordered to return the next morning.

On September 5, at 7 a.m., the case continued. Now, on the fifth—and final—demand, when asked if Penn and Mead were guilty as formally charged in their indictments, the foreman declared each had been found not guilty. For this, the court fined the jurors "forty Marks a man, and imprisonment till paid."[181] Penn and Mead were to be kept in prison until payment of their contempt fines imposed on the first day of the trial. As Penn was being ordered away, he addressed the recorder with the last word:

Penn. I can never urge the fundamental laws of England, but you cry, Take him away, take him away. But it is no wonder since the Spanish Inquisition hath so great a place in the Recorder's heart.[182]

Observer. They haled the prisoners into the baledock, and from thence they were sent to Newgate for non-payment of their fines, and so were their jury.[183]

Author. Thus ended that memorable trial, wherein the ancient and just liberties of the people were notably

---

[180] Ibid., 423.

[181] Ibid., 426.

[182] On the previous day, the recorder had admitted that this case had given him an understanding of the "policy and prudence of the Spaniards in suffering the Inquisition among them" and why something similar was necessary in England.

[183] Edward Bushell, one of the original four dissenting jurors, refused to pay the fine and petitioned the Court of Common Pleas for a writ of habeas corpus. It was granted and resulted in that court's landmark opinion, written by Chief Justice John Vaughan, that a jury cannot be punished for its verdict.

asserted against the arbitrary proceedings of men in power, who would have made their wills a law, according to that saying of Juvenal,

Sic volo, sic jubeo, stat pro Ratione voluntas.[184]

Later that day, Penn wrote his dying father that "because I cannot come, I write." He reported on the conclusion of the case, and added: "The circumstances I shall personally relate if the Lord will. I am more concerned at thy distemper and the pains that attend it than at my own mere imprisonment which works for the best."[185]

On September 6 the son again wrote his father:

I desire thee not to be troubled at my present confinement. I could scarce suffer upon a better account, nor by a worse hand: & the will of God be done. It is more grievous & uneasy to me that thou shouldst be so heavily exercised (God almighty knows) than any living worldly concernment. I am clear by the jury, and they in my place. . . . I entreat thee not to purchase my liberty. They will repent them of their proceedings. I am now a prisoner notoriously against law. I desire the Lord God, in fervent prayers, to strengthen and support thee and anchor thy mind in the thoughts of the immutable blessed state which is over all visible perishing concerns.[186]

On September 7—from Newgate Prison—the son wrote his last letter to his father:

If God in his holy will did see it meet that I should be freed, I could heartily embrace it; yet considering I cannot be free, but upon such terms as strengthening their arbitrary and base proceedings, I shall rather choose to suffer any hardship. I am persuaded some clearer way will suddenly be found out to obtain my liberty, which is no way so desirable to me, as on the account of being with thee. . . . Solace thy mind in the thoughts of better things, dear father. Let not this wicked world disturb thy mind, and whatever shall come to pass,

---

[184] From Juvenal's *Satire VI*: Let the fact that I wish it be sufficient reason.
[185] William Penn to Sir William Penn, September 5, 1670, *PWP*, 1:177.
[186] William Penn to Sir William Penn, September 6, 1670, *PWP*, 1:179.

William Penn's 'Holy Experiment'

I hope, in all conditions to approve myself, thy obedient son,

William Penn[187]

Shortly after writing this letter, Penn was released from Newgate. Presumably the admiral had arranged for the fine to be paid so that he might see his son for the last time. And presumably the son accepted the liberty his father had purchased so that he could be at the deathbed.

Admiral Sir William Penn died on September 16, 1670, in his forty-eighth year. The final duties that he laid upon William, his elder son, were to serve as the sole executor of his last will and testament that had been made on January 20, 1670; to "give mourning" at the funeral; and to be the heir of the entire estate after satisfying the provisions in the will for the specific bequests to his wife (who also was to have the use during her life of some personal conveniences and property), his younger son Richard (who was to have annual support until reaching the age of twenty-one), his granddaughter (the daughter of the admiral's only other child, Margaret), four nephews, two cousins, two servants, and the "Poor" of two Bristol parishes—Redclyffe (where the admiral's body was to be interred near his deceased mother) and St. Thomas (where he had been baptized).

The last echo of the sometime estrangement between father and son could be heard in a final provision of the will regarding any differences that might arise after the admiral's decease between William and his mother, in which case "I do hereby request and desire . . . require, conjure, and direct my said dear wife and my said son William by all the obligations of duty, affection, and respect which they have and ought to have to me and my memory" to refer them to "the arbitration and final judgment and determination of my worthy friend, Sir William Coventry . . . for the total prevention of all suits in law or equity which upon any occasion or misunderstanding might otherwise happen between them."[188] Coventry had been an esteemed colleague of the admiral on the Navy Board. There is no record that this provision of the will was ever invoked or that the administration of the estate was not successfully fulfilled.

The fourth arrest of William Penn took place on February 5, 1671, as he preached in the Wheeler Street meeting house in

---

[187] William Penn to Sir William Penn, September 7, 1670, *PWP*, 1:180.
[188] Admiral William Penn's last will and testament, *PWP*, 1:150.

Spitalfields, London. Thence he was taken to the Tower, where he was examined by its lieutenant, Sir John Robinson. Robinson was also a London alderman and one of the ten justices who had been on the bench at the Penn-Mead trial five months earlier. Among those attending this Tower hearing was Samuel Starling, the presiding justice at that trial. This time Robinson sought not another trial but a quick and easy verdict of guilty and the imposition of a prison sentence for Penn. Accordingly, he charged Penn under the Clarendon Code's Five Mile Act, which mandated an oath forswearing the taking of arms against the king. Penn admitted he was speaking to an assembly of people but argued, unsuccessfully, that this act was explicitly directed against ordained clergy and that it was well known the Friends did not take up arms. When he refused the oath on established Quaker principles, Robinson summarily pronounced his conviction and sentenced Penn to Newgate Prison for six months. Then came this exchange:

> J.R. I vow, Mr. Penn, I am sorry for you. You are an ingenious gentleman, all the world must allow you that, and you have a plentiful estate. Why would you render yourself unhappy by associating with such a simple people?
>
> W.P. I confess I have made it my choice to relinquish the company of those that are ingeniously wicked to converse with those that are more honestly simple.
>
> J.R. I wish you wiser.
>
> W.P. And I wish thee better.[189]

At the end of the hearing, Penn had these last words:

> W.P. I would have thee and all men to know that I scorn that religion which is not worth suffering for, and able to sustain them that are afflicted for it. Mine is. And whatever may be my lot for my constant profession of it, I am no ways careful, but resigned to answer the will of God, by the loss of goods, liberty, and life itself. When you have all, you can have no more, and then perhaps you will be contented, and by that you will be better informed of our innocency. Thy religion persecutes, and

---

[189] Besse, *Sufferings of the People Called Quakers*, 1:433.

mine forgives. And I desire my God to forgive you all that are concerned in my commitment, and I leave you in perfect charity, wishing your everlasting salvation.

J.R. Send a corporal with a file of musketeers, along with him.

W.P. No, no. Send thy lackey. I know the way to Newgate.[190]

During his incarceration in Newgate Prison, Penn busied himself with writing, just as he had done in the Tower of London. Now, however, he was more circumspect and self-protective in distributing his words.

Injustice Detected or a brief relation of the illegal commitment of William Penn by him called Sir J R, Lieutenant of the Tower, from an Eye- & Ear-Witness is a detailed account of the examination of Penn by Sir John Robinson, the lieutenant of the Tower of London, in a hearing here reported to have been held late at night and from which anyone "unconcerned in the business" was barred. The colloquy, written as if verbatim, is finely crafted and invariably shows Penn in command. There is no reason to doubt either that Penn himself prepared the work or that his reason for then withholding it from the printer was because its publication would give the authorities pretext for extending his confinement. Joseph Besse included it in abbreviated form in his two-volume edition entitled *A Collection of the Works of William Penn* published in London in 1726. Besse also incorporated the edited version in *A Collection of the sufferings of the people called Quakers . . .*, which he edited in two volumes and which was printed by Luke Hinde in London in 1753 (and from which the extract above was taken).

A serious apology for the principles & practices of the people called Quakers, against the malicious aspersions, erroneous doctrines, and horrid blasphemies of Thomas Jenner and Timothy Taylor, in their book, entitled, Quakerism anatomized and confuted, divided into two parts is a tract written by George Whitehead and Penn (Penn wrote part 2). It was printed in 1671. Concerned with the persecution of Irish Quakers at the hands of the government and religious critics such as Jenner, it was addressed to the king's lieutenant-general, the general-governor, and the Council of Ireland.

---

[190] Ibid., 1:435.

In addition to tracts and religious testimonies, Penn prepared legal instruments to help Friends in their struggle for liberty of conscience. In April he drafted a petition on behalf of himself and four other Quakers, then prisoners with him in Newgate, addressed to Parliament because that body was considering yet further legislation against "seditious conventicles," meetings for worship suspected of conspiring insurrection. The 1664 Conventicle Act had been amended in 1670. Now the House of Commons had passed tougher proposals, which had been sent to the House of Lords, for strengthening even more the state's authority against dissenters and nonconformists. Speaking for Friends everywhere, Penn wrote in part:

> As we have ever lived most peaceably under all the various governments that have been since our first appearance (*notwithstanding we have been as their anvil to smite upon*), so we do thereby signify that it is our fixed resolution to continue the same, that where we cannot actually obey, we patiently shall suffer (thereby manifesting to the whole world that we love God above all, and our neighbors as ourselves).[191]

Upon his release from Newgate about August 5, 1671, William Penn—now at age twenty-six the heir of his deceased father's estate and the executor of his will—appears to have embarked upon a plan for reordering the course of his life. As noted earlier, one of the first times Penn is mentioned in the pages of Fox's *Journal* concerns his joining Fox and his wife in the barge that carried them from Wapping, London, down to Gravesend, where Fox boarded the ship departing on August 14 for the voyage across the Atlantic. With Penn on that occasion were Gulielma Maria Springett and her mother, Mary Penington, the wife of Isaac Penington, himself a Quaker who had suffered for refusing to take oaths and was the author of works of spiritual direction. On February 7, 1672, William and Gulielma declared to Friends their intention to marry, and on April 4, 1672, "Guli" became the wife of William Penn. In addition, after leaving Newgate Penn had begun to take a larger role in the Religious Society of Friends, not only through growing contact with George Fox but also by undertaking missionary travel to the Netherlands and Germany in August-October, through Essex and Suffolk in

---

[191] *PWP*, 1:206-7, emphasis in original.

October-November, and, a year later, into Kent, Sussex, and Surrey. Continuing to provide legal counsel, in November Penn corresponded at large to "beloved Friends and Brethren" advising against "endeavors, earnest and pressing" to bring a legal action against the king "for the delivery of our dear Friends that are sufferers upon the oaths."[192] The legal action he advised against was to attack "the oaths running in the name of King James and he dead,"[193] Penn arguing, in part, that to invalidate the oaths would absolve the people from all allegiance, whereas the Quaker objection, based on Christ's admonition, was against swearing, there being no admonition against loyalty.

When Fox safely came back to England from his voyage to America, landing on June 28, 1673, at Bristol—where he and Margaret Fell had been married and where Admiral Penn had grown up—Guli and Penn came from London to welcome him.[194] Later in that same year, George and Margaret Fox with her daughter Rachel Fell were house guests of the Penns at Rickmansworth (Hertfordshire).[195] Thereafter, a closer working relationship developed between Fox and Penn regarding such issues facing Friends as relief from persecution, governance of the Society, and answering attacks from religious opponents. Curiously, whatever discussions or exchanges the two might have had about the New World, and especially America—from which Fox had just returned and in which Penn was about to be deeply involved—are not known.

Planting a free society in a new world

Penn's direct involvement with America, first evidenced in a letter of January 20, 1675, finds him trying to resolve a dispute arising in London between two Quakers over their claims to the proprietorship of West Jersey. The English Crown had by this time granted to favored persons certain American colonies, e.g., Maryland, New Jersey, and New York, under proprietary (in contrast to royal or otherwise special) charters. Each of these grantees, who were referred to as "proprietors" or "proprietaries," had the right to govern and distribute the land within his colony, subject to the unique terms of its particular

---

[192] *PWP*, 1:219–21.
[193] *PWP*, 1:220.
[194] Fox, *Journal*, 665.
[195] Ibid., 670.

royal charter and to changing English law and royal policy. On March 12, 1664, the king had granted land in North America to his brother James, the duke of York, who on June 24 the same year transferred a portion, "hereafter to be called Nova Caesarea, or New Jersey," to Sir George Carteret and John Lord Berkeley as joint proprietors. Both had been loyal supporters of the Crown during the interregnum. Ten years later (and two years after Fox had traveled through the area), on March 18, 1674, Berkeley sold his undivided one-half interest to John Fenwick. Fenwick, a convinced Quaker, had been an officer in Cromwell's army where he may have met Edward Byllynge, a fellow officer, who had become a convinced Quaker during Fox's mission to Scotland in 1657. In reality, the sale was intended by Berkeley to be for the benefit of his bankrupt friend Byllynge, who needed to mend his finances and hoped to do so through further land transfers. To avoid problems with Byllynge's creditors, Berkeley made the grant to Fenwick, who was understood to be acting as trustee or agent for Byllynge. Afterwards, Fenwick, a trained lawyer, and Byllynge argued over their arrangement, Fenwick demanding a share of the undivided one-half interest as well as reimbursement for his cash outlay of the purchase price. Failing satisfaction, he threatened to take the matter into the royal Court of Chancery. Friends were appalled at the prospect of public trials over members' disagreements and in this case prevailed upon Penn to arbitrate the dispute.

> John Fenwick The present difference betwixt thee & E.B. fills the hearts of Friends with grief. . . . As oppressed as I am with business I will give an afternoon tomorrow or next day to determine, and so prevent the mischief that will certainly follow divulging it in Westminster Hall. . . . O John, let truth and the honor of it in this day prevail, woe be to him that causeth offences. I am an impartial man.
>
> W Penn.[196]

As Fenwick continued to haggle over the settlement, Penn protested: "John I am sorry that a toy, a trifle should thus rob men of time, quiet, and a more profitable employ. I have had a good conscience in what I have done in this affair."[197] In the end,

---

[196] Penn to John Fenwick, January 20, 1675, *PWP*, 1:384.
[197] Penn to John Fenwick, February 13, 1675, *PWP*, 1:386.

Penn awarded ninety of one hundred shares in the proprietorship to Byllynge and the remaining ten shares and £400 to Fenwick. The settlement was formally agreed upon in an indenture reciting this history dated February 10, 1675, and duly executed by Fenwick, Byllynge, Penn, and two other Quakers, Gawen Lawrie and Nicholas Lucas, who were creditors of Byllynge[198] and who, with Penn, were made trustees of Byllynge's shares.[199]

Thereafter, the trustees set about selling shares in the West Jersey proprietorship, Penn finding himself increasingly engaged in this venture of marketing the American wilderness among suffering Quakers in England and beyond. He was not, however, without experience in matters of real estate, having trained in the law at Lincoln's Inn; having been the agent for managing his father's tenanted farms and estates in Ireland, including making leases and collecting rents; having the fiduciary responsibilities for settling his father's testamentary estate; and having assisted his wife in administering the real estate she had received from her own father, who died before she was born. Yet nothing could have prepared him for the vast undertaking now ahead of surveying and settling boundaries for an unfamiliar land "beyond the seas," of securing title to property from an indigenous people unaccustomed—and for lands never before made subject—to English property law, of defining and separating the province of New Jersey into East and West Jersey, and, above all, of creating a government that could maintain security, peace, and civil order especially for 'sufferers' who had experienced harsh, arbitrary, and novel homeland statutes and judicial proceedings intended to bring them not only into conformity with but also allegiance to a state that refused them religious liberty or freedom of conscience. It was a monumental task.

On July 1, 1676, an indenture was executed among Sir George Carteret, Byllynge, and Penn with the two other trustees, Lawrie and Lucas, fixing the partition line between East and West Jersey—the land east of the line going to Carteret and that west of the line to Byllynge's trustees.[200] By the middle of August 1676, a plan had been prepared and signed in London for this new province of West Jersey that established and regulated private ownership of its land, determined the fundamental laws

---

[198] *PWP*, 1:383.
[199] *PWP*, 1:649–51.
[200] *PWP*, 1:654.

of its civil order, and structured its political governance. For Friends, this venture provided a unique creative moment for building a new home free from the oppressions so many of them had been made to suffer in England and elsewhere, starting in the 1640s with the chaos of the Civil War. The whole of this ambitious plan was entitled *The Concessions and Agreements of the Proprietors, Freeholders and Inhabitants of the Province of West New Jersey in America*.[201] The *Concessions* were divided into forty-four brief chapters, the first twelve being concerned with surveying, dividing, conveying, and registering the West Jersey land acquired by the first purchasers of the 100 full shares created and marketed by Byllynge's trustees and the buyers of the fractions of any shares then sold by first purchasers. All such full and fractional shares were to be converted into land when it was laid out, surveyed, and ready for possession.[202] After the initial twelve chapters, another caption—*The Charter or fundamental Laws of West Jersey agreed upon*—is followed by chapters 13 through 31. Then comes another caption—*The General Assembly and their Power*—followed by chapters 32 through 44 that give order to a plan of republican government under an annually elected legislature. The legislature in turn both elects, as the executive body, twelve commissioners each year to manage the province during adjournments and dissolutions of the assembly (chapter 37) and "constitute[s] all courts . . . as also the several judges" with the direction that no person in the province shall "sustain or bear two offices . . . at one and at the same time" (chapter 40). The *testimonium* clause after the final chapter and above the signatures cites "these present Laws [which word is omitted from the title] Concessions and Agreements."[203] Of the 151 signatories, most of the initial thirty-one executed the document in London in July or August, the rest doing so in West Jersey following its arrival there in the winter of 1676/1677.[204]

The authorship of the *Concessions* has never been determined. It is a safe assumption that the substance was

---

[201] For the full text, see *PWP*, 1:388–408.

[202] See John E. Pomfret, "The Proprietors of the Province of West New Jersey, 1674–1702," *The Pennsylvania Magazine of History and Biography* 75 (1951): 118–23.

[203] *PWP*, 1:406.

[204] See *PWP*, 1:410n16.

largely the work, by consensus, of Byllynge and his three trustees, Penn, Lawrie, and Lucas, all of whose signatures appear at or near the top of the two columns of London signatories. A further safe assumption is that the drafting may have involved others, undoubtedly Friends, who had legal skills. Byllynge himself was a London Quaker and a successful brewer by occupation. He worked with his trustees to promote the planting of the province and by 1682 was out of debt and a proprietor, with Penn and others, of East Jersey as well as West Jersey. Of the trustees, Penn alone was a trained lawyer, Lawrie being a London merchant and Lucas a maker of malt (used in brewing and distilling) in Hertford. In addition, Lawrie purchased two proprietary shares in West Jersey and later became a proprietor and deputy governor of East Jersey, where he died in 1687. Another London signer of the *Concessions,* Thomas Rudyard—a proprietor of both West and East Jersey, a Quaker activist who traveled with Penn on missions to the Netherlands and Germany in 1671 and 1677, a lawyer who had interceded on behalf of George Fox during his Worcester imprisonment, and the trustees' agent in George Yard on Lombard Street, London, whom potential purchasers were directed to contact—would have had a sufficient interest in the experiment to offer his services in drafting the foundational instrument.

The second major section of *The Concessions and Agreements,* captioned *The Charter or fundamental Laws of West Jersey agreed upon* (chapters 13 through 31), set down a template for an inscribed constitution intended to be as inviolable as—but more certain and fixed than—England's unwritten organic law. It declared that the "common law or fundamental rights" and the unalterable "foundation of the government" were to be maintained by the legislature, which is "to make no laws that in the least contradict, differ, or vary" therefrom (chapter 13); if any assembly man or men design to subvert any fundamental of the constitution, he or they "shall be proceeded against as traitors" (chapter 14); and "these concessions, law, or great charter of fundamentals" are to be written on tablets and read by the local chief magistrate in the presence of the people at the beginning and dissolving of every general free assembly and four times every year "in every common hall of justice within this province" (chapter 15).

This section is followed by the particular fundamental laws that not only gave order to this free society from its inception but also catalogued and gave constitutional protection against some of the tribulations and trials through which the Quakers newly inhabiting West Jersey had already passed.

[Freedom of religion and conscience]

That no Men nor number of Men upon Earth hath power or Authority to rule over mens consciences in religious matters therefore it is consented agreed and ordained that no person or persons whatsoever within the said Province at any time or times hereafter shall be any waies upon any pretence whatsoever called in question or in the least punished or hurt either in Person Estate or Priveledge for the sake of his opinion Judgment faith or worship towards God in matters of Religion but that all and every such person and persons may from time to time and at all times freely and fully have and enjoy his and their Judgments and the exercise of their consciences in matters of religious worship throughout all the said Province. (chapter 16; quoted without alteration of the text)

The document ensured that a "due trial and judgment passed by twelve good and lawful men of his neighborhood" would be conducted before any inhabitant would be denied "life, limb, liberty, estate, property, or any ways hurt in his or their privileges, freedoms, or franchises" (chapter 17). Further, no one was to be "attached, arrested, or imprisoned," except for felonies, crimes, or treason, without a judicial hearing (chapter 18), and three justices were to sit with every jury to pronounce the judgment received from and directed by the jury (chapter 19).

No one who was unable to pay and satisfy a judgment or other debt should be imprisoned, provided they solemnly declared they had no further assets and three reputable witnesses testified they conscientiously believed the "condemned has not wherewith further to pay" the debt (chapter 18).

All trials of civil and criminal matters were freely open to inhabitants "that justice may not be done in a corner nor in any covert manner" and so that every inhabitant "shall as far as in us lies be free from oppression and slavery" (chapter 23).

In addition, acknowledging at least the conflicts of laws and cultures if not the moral dilemmas and ethical issues involved with taking possession and 'ownership' of a territory occupied over centuries by ancient peoples, provisions were made for doing justice with "Indian natives" regarding wrongs or injuries between them and the new inhabitants (chapter 25) and for appropriating the natives' land before surveying it (chapter 26).

Shortly before *The Concessions and Agreements* were settled, the trustees proceeded with marketing West Jersey in a broadside entitled *The Description of the Province of West-Jersey in America: as also, Proposals to such who desire to have any Propriety therein.* At the conclusion of this sales promotion, they emphasized their essential concern with religion, conscience, and property:

> Being resolved (by the help of God) that every individuals Property, as also Liberty of Conscience; both as Men, and Christians, shall be inviolably preserved (to all Intents and Purposes) from all manner of Invasions, and Violations whatsoever, THE END[205]

Through his role in the successful launching of the colonization of New Jersey—and thereby in providing a refuge "beyond the seas" for England's suffering Quakers—Penn was becoming a rising figure not only within the Religious Society of Friends but also in the English nation. The son and heir of an illustrious father, he was now gaining recognition in his own right.

Within the Society, Penn was emerging as a counselor to George Fox on major legal and other issues, with whom he could readily confer whenever both were in London. He was with Fox on the mission to the Netherlands and Germany in 1677. Not only had Penn suffered imprisonments after his convincement, he had also steadily been engaged in the doctrinal wars with the Friends' religious opponents and their pamphleteers.[206] Penn was also familiar with the leading Quakers of his time. Because of his happy marriage to Gulielma Springett, he moved in the company of her stepfather Isaac Penington, who became a convinced Friend about 1658 and who from his day to ours has, through his extensive writings,[207] remained a revered guide to

---

[205] The full text is in "English Publicity Broadsides for West Jersey, 1675–1676," *Proceedings of the New Jersey Historical Society* 54 no. 1 (1936): 8–11.

[206] In the years 1672–1674, for example, Penn saw into print at least twenty-one works addressed to various adversaries of Quakerism, taking on Socinians, Muggletonians, Baptists, nonconformists, Quaker schismatics, and Anglicans in broadsheets, pamphlets, and books. For a list and summary of these works, see *PWP*, 5:137–91.

[207] See Isaac Penington, *The works of the long-mournful and sorely-distressed Isaac Penington, whom the Lord in His tender mercy, at length visited and relieved by the ministry of that despised people, called Quakers; and*

the Quaker interior spiritual life. Penn was close to his own contemporary Robert Barclay (1648–1690), who remains even now a major Quaker systematic theologian.[208] Barclay traveled with Fox, Penn, and others on the 1677 mission to the Netherlands and Germany. In 1683, Penn and his fellow proprietors appointed this Scottish theologian governor of East Jersey.

Within the English nation, the 1670s were still times of political testing and transformation—ongoing since the 1640s—in which religious freedom and liberty of conscience were often at the crux of the conflict. In March 1672, Charles II for the third time issued a royal Declaration of Indulgence for those of tender consciences in which he suspended the execution of penal laws against nonconformists and dissenters. As we have seen, he had originally promised this at Breda (Netherlands) on the eve of the Restoration, before sailing home to England aboard the newly named *Royal Charles* commanded by admiral Sir William Penn. He again issued such royal declarations in October 1660 and in December 1662. Each time, the king was forestalled by Parliament, which was seeking to root out nonconformity. As before, the king was checkmated when, in March 1673, Parliament forced him to revoke the Declaration of Indulgence and accept another new statute, the Test Act, that required any officeholder, civil or military, to take the Oaths of Supremacy and Allegiance and sign a declaration against transubstantiation (a denial that there was any elemental change made by the consecration of the altar bread and wine used in observing the Lord's Supper).

Penn was no stranger to this struggle over religious liberty and freedom of conscience. In 1670, while employed on his

---

in the springings of that light, life and holy power in him, which they had truly and faithfully testified of, and directed his mind to, were these things written, and are now published as a thankful testimony of the goodness of the Lord unto him, and for the benefit of others. In two parts (London: B. Clark, 1681). Penn's testimony is on pp. v–viii.

[208] See Robert Barclay, *An apology for the true Christian divinity, as the same is held forth, and preached by the people, called, in scorn, Quakers: being a full explanation and vindication of their principles and doctrines, by many arguments . . . presented to the King/Written and published in Latine, for the information of strangers, by Robert Barclay. And now put into our own language, for the benefit of his countrey-men* (Aberdeen: John Forbes, 1678). This work was originally published in Latin at Amsterdam in 1676; the translation into English was by Barclay.

father's business in Ireland, he had witnessed the sufferings of Quakers and feared worse to come as Parliament set about revising the provisions of the Conventicle Act of 1664, that part of the Clarendon Code barring meetings for nonconformist worship by more than five people who were not members of the same household. The 1670 revision imposed a fine upon attenders of five shillings for a first-time offense and ten shillings for a second. The fines on the householder hosting the assembly were twenty and forty shillings, respectively. Penn addressed a pamphlet to the king asking that the new legislation be set aside. Entitled *The Great Case of Liberty of Conscience once more debated and defended with some brief observations on the late act, presented to the king's consideration*, it was printed in Dublin in March 1670. The work was a plea against persecution and for toleration as an English birthright. By the time it was revised and printed in London in the second edition dated February 7, 1671, the infamous Penn-Mead trial had been in the public eye and had exposed the overreaching of the presiding magistrate, the mayor of London, for proceeding against—and failing to convict—the defendants, not under the revised Conventicle Act but rather for breach of the peace and tumultuous assembly. On February 5, 1671, Penn had been arrested again and this time quickly convicted of a violation under the Five Mile Act of the Clarendon Code, and he was sentenced to a six-month term in Newgate Prison. From prison, he signed the introduction to the English edition of *The Great Case of Liberty* "From a Prisoner for Conscience Sake, W.P." and promised to suffer persecution so long as unjust laws were enforced against nonconformists.[209]

Next, when in March 1673 Parliament compelled the king to renounce his Declaration of Indulgence of the prior year—under which, for example, in October Charles had pardoned 491 Quakers held in English jails[210]—and passed the Test Act ("for preventing dangers which may happen from popish recusants") that required all officeholders to take the Oath of Allegiance and make a declaration denying transubstantiation, Penn authored a petition "To the Commons of England assembled in Parliament/the request of the people called Quakers."[211] In it, he asked the House of Commons to accept any Friend's solemn *Yea*

---

[209] *PWP*, 5:113.
[210] *PWP*, 1:259.
[211] *PWP*, 1:260–61.

or *Nay* in lieu of an oath. Pointing out that Quakers were not 'popish recusants' and that the law was not directed against them or their peaceful principles, he argued that because oaths were prohibited by Christ, the Quakers were unable to deny satisfactorily what they did not believe without violating their consciences unless Parliament allowed their simple affirmations. Penn suggested "that our Word may be taken instead of an Oath." Although the Commons ignored the petition, it did settle, also in March 1673, on a bill for the relief of Protestant dissenters that, after failing to pass the House of Lords, was not enacted and was never reconsidered.[212]

As the indulgence of nonconformity faded and the execution of ecclesiastical penal laws increased, Penn in 1674 sent a statement directly to Charles regarding "very severe" prosecutions in Somersetshire, entreating Charles to check the zealous enforcers "that not only defy the Kings Clemency, & his well known purpose of Liberty, but the wholesome Laws of England that are both Jealous & Lawfull of the Property of Englishmen."[213]

Then, in May 1675, Penn wrote his major work on oaths that was endorsed and signed by leading Quakers in London Yearly Meeting. Entitled *A Treatise of Oaths containing several weighty reasons why the people called Quakers refuse to swear . . . presented to the King and Great Council of England assembled in Parliament,* this was a carefully prepared, lawyer-like brief (in fact, a book of 168 pages) citing many authorities and coming back to a central Quaker tenet: swear not at all but suffer the same penalties for perjury as the oath-takers.

Also in 1675, Penn carefully argued the case for religious toleration in *England's Present Interest Discovered with honor to the prince and safety to the people . . .*[214] Here Penn, who was not identified until the second edition (also printed in 1675), enumerated the fundamental rights of Englishmen as property, personal liberty, citizenship, government by elected legislative representatives, just laws, and trial by jury. In his view, neither was religion properly a part of government nor should citizens be denied their civil rights on religious grounds. He argued that government should strive for equilibrium regarding religious

---

[212] See *PWP*, 1:277n4, 284n1.
[213] *PWP*, 1:283–84.
[214] William Penn, *A Treatise of Oaths* . . . ([London: Andrew Sowle], 1675).

affairs and thereby bring tolerance and forbearance to the body politic.

In the twilight of the Restoration, the royal grant of Pennsylvania's charter

When, in October 1677, the fifty-three-year-old George Fox and the thirty-three-year-old William Penn, with fellow influential Quakers, returned to England from the religious mission into the Netherlands and Germany, they found the nation still locked in its divisions born of conflicting claims between monarchical supremacy and parliamentary prerogatives and between religious conformity and freedom of conscience. The sufferings of Friends continued, notwithstanding the king's good-faith attempts to lift from them the rigors of the several statutes and oaths laid on Quakers and others by Parliament.

But in the summer of 1678, the nation lurched into the hysteria of the Popish Plot, a spurious crisis invented by Titus Oates alleging that there was a broad Roman Catholic conspiracy in England to assassinate Charles II and thereby bring his brother the Duke of York, a known Catholic, to the throne as James II. Fear-mongering and witch-hunts followed. Evidence of the fictitious scheme ultimately fell apart, but only after a number of alleged conspirators were executed, one of them Edward Colman, a Catholic courtier, who was not only close to the Duke of York but in fact had maintained treasonable correspondence with French agents in a plan to obtain financial assistance for Charles from Louis XIV. Such assistance was sought to lessen the controls of the anti-Catholic English Parliament.[215] In reaction, the House of Commons passed the Test Act of 1678, extending the 1673 act to require that the declaration against transubstantiation be taken by all peers sitting in the House of Lords and by all members of the House of Commons, thus excluding Roman Catholics from Parliament. Because the Duke of York had revealed himself to be a Catholic by refusing to make the declaration in 1673 under the first Test Act, a bill was now introduced excluding him from the succession to the thrones of England, Ireland, and Scotland. This led to the exclusion crisis, which continued for several years. Although the

---

[215] The correspondence was seized and, in Colman's letters to the French king's confessor, revealed "plans for the forcible reconversion of Great Britain." Trevelyan, *History of England*, 462.

exclusion bill failed, it did spur into being the Whigs (Scots, from *whiggamor*, 'cattle driver') and Tories (Irish, *torai*, 'outlaw'), England's two major political parties thereafter. At their inception, the Whigs supported James's exclusion from the throne, whereas the Tories supported his succession to the throne.

Fox and Penn both addressed the crises brought on by the Popish Plot and the exclusion proposal—Fox indirectly and discreetly (his eighth imprisonment, lasting almost fourteen months, had ended as recently as February 1675) in several epistles of general biblical exhortations and in a political tract concerning persecuting governors of New England and Penn with energetic directness in an epistle to Friends' meetings, a major work on the evils in state and church then prevailing in the nation, and a pair of political pamphlets. Of the two leaders, Penn was the first in print.

Shortly after the Popish Plot erupted, Penn authored a seven-page epistle entitled *To the Children of Light in this Generation, called of God to be partakers of eternal life in Jesus Christ, the Lamb of God & Light of the World*,[216] addressed to "My Endeared Friends and Brethren" with a request that it be read in the meetings.[217] Noting the deplorable "abominations and gross impieties" breaking out in the nation, he had "a deep sense, that the overflowing scourge of God's wrath and indignation was just ready to break out upon the people, confusion, amazement and misery!"[218] Then, in early 1679 Penn brought forth a major book, *An Address to Protestants upon the Present Conjuncture, In II Parts, by a Protestant, W.P.*"[219] The first part considered the besetting sins in the state and secular society, the second part those in the church.

The Parliament[220] was dissolved by the king in January 1679, and for the election campaign that followed Penn contributed, under a nom de plume, a four-page pamphlet outlining criteria for the matters to be considered by the new

---

[216] William Penn, *To the Children of Light in this Generation* . . . (London: Andrew Sowle [?], 1678).

[217] *PWP*, 5:236.

[218] Ibid., 235.

[219] William Penn, *An Address to Protestants* . . . (London: Andrew Sowle, 1678).

[220] This was the Cavalier Parliament, which had been elected in 1661.

Parliament, for electors' rights and duties, and for worthy candidates. In conclusion, he asked for religious toleration. The work, *England's Great Interest in the choice of this new parliament; dedicated to all her freeholders and electors*,[221] cited in its preamble "that universal agitation, that is now upon the spirit of the nation . . . there seems never to have been a time, wherein this kingdom ought to show itself more serious and diligent in the business of its own safety." It was signed at the end by "your honest monitor and old England's true friend, Philanglus," presumably because at the time Penn was rumored to be too close to the Duke of York and thus a closet papist.[222] A second "Philanglus" pamphlet followed after the election: *One Project for the good of England: that is, our civil union is our civil safety. Humbly dedicated to the Great Council, The Parliament of England*.[223] Here Penn addressed the need for religious toleration generally and asked Parliament, as well as all Protestants, to grant it to nonconformists and dissenters. (In the concluding pages Penn proposed a declaration in lieu of an oath for dissenters that, slightly altered, was printed in 1680 in a half broadsheet as *A Declaration or Test to distinguish Protestant Dissenters from Papists and Popish Recusants*.[224] Although no authorship is claimed for *A Declaration*, some authorities have attributed it to Penn.)

In contrast to Penn, Fox wrote confidently not of England's political disorder but of the sovereign power of God to override all the troubles of this world and to secure in God's truth the peace and well-being of Friends, even as they were beset by temporal crises. In *An Epistle to Friends, to keep in the power of God in their peaceable habitations, over all the troubles of the world*, written at Swarthmoor on December 6, 1678, Fox made a general allusion to shedding "men's blood concerning religion, church, and worship." With his usual power, he wrote of

> Christ the rock and foundation, that cannot be shaken, though the rocks and foundations of the world may be shaken, and cloven in pieces, and the pillars of the earth may reel and stagger, and all hypocrites and sinners may fear; but they that fear the Lord, and wait upon him,

---

[221] William Penn, *England's Great Interest* (London: Andrew Sowle, 1679).

[222] *PWP*, 5:245–47.

[223] William Penn, *One Project for the good of England* (London: Andrew Sowle, 1679).

[224] *PWP*, 5:251.

shall be as Mount Zion, that cannot be removed; for the Lord's power is over all, by which he keeps his people to the day of salvation....

And the Lord did not build his Zion, and outward Jerusalem, with blood, in the old covenant; for they that did build their Zion and Jerusalem with blood, made their Zion a field, and their Jerusalem a heap; so if this practice was forbidden in the old covenant, much more in the new, who think to build Zion and Jerusalem with blood and iniquity; for such have not been Zion's children, nor Jerusalem's, that is from above, who shed men's blood concerning religion, church, and worship; for Christ rebuked such that would have had men's lives destroyed, and told them, 'they knew not what spirit they were of;' so they that do not know what spirit they are of, they are not like to build up God's Zion and Jerusalem.[225]

In a lengthy epistle written in early 1680 and addressed to "Dear Friends every where," Fox encouraged the faithful to stand fast in the truth and in "that liberty wherewith Christ hath made you free ... which is an everlasting freedom and liberty above all bondage and false fallen liberties and freedoms." He continued:

Love the word, and keep the word of patience, and the Lord will keep you, for it is a tried word, and it will keep you in all trials, which shall come upon all the world to try them. For the word was before the world was, and will be when the world is gone....

If the world do hate you, it hated Christ your Lord and master also; if they do mock, and reproach, and defame, and buffet you, they did so to your Lord and master also. ...

If the world do persecute you, and take away your goods or clothes, was not your Lord and master so served? Did not they cast lots for his garments? Was not he haled from the priests to Herod, and before Pontius Pilate, and spit upon? And if they hate thee, and spit upon thee, he

---

[225] *The Works of George Fox*, ed. & biblio. T. H. S. Wallace, 8 vols. (1831; repr., State College, PA: New Foundation Publication, George Fox Fund, 1990), 8:150, 152.

was hated and spit upon for thee. Did he not go to prison for thee? And was he not mocked and scourged for thee? Did not he bow to the cross and grave for thee, he who had no sin, neither was guile found in his mouth? And did he not bear thy sins in his own body upon the tree? And was he not scourged for thee, by whose stripes we are healed? Did not he suffer the contradiction of sinners, who died for sinners, and went into the grave for sinners, and died for the ungodly, yea, tasted death for every man, who through death destroyed death, and the devil, the power of death, and is risen?. . .

The eternal living God of truth, he is a God of order, and is not the author of confusion, but of peace in all the churches of the saints. . . .

And they that follow the world's god, that are out of truth, and disobey their Creator, the God of truth, and the Lord Jesus Christ; I say, all such obey and follow him in whom there is no truth; and such cannot endure to hear talk of the order of truth, and of the gospel, or the law, or order of the spirit of life which is in Christ Jesus.[226]

Fox's other works in this period were a tract, *Caesar's due rendred unto him according to his image and superscription: and God's & Christ's due rendred*, written in response to an attack made on him by Roger Williams of Rhode Island, and an epistle, *To Friends in America, concerning their Negroes, and Indians*. Both writings were dated 1679 and evidenced Fox's focus on America even as the crises in England were increasing in gravity.

Those crises did not abate. A new Parliament was elected in March 1679, but because of the renewed demand for exclusion, it was prorogued by the Crown in May and dissolved in July. Yet another Parliament was summoned but, delayed by Charles's illness in August, did not assemble until October 1680. The political turmoil roiling the centers of authority in London and elsewhere in the nation continued.

---

[226] Ibid., 8:181, 182, 184.

England 1350–1682

Penn at home: A landed gentleman securing his family and estates

After his return in October 1777 from the continental mission with Fox, Penn needed both to spend time at home with his family and to focus attention on his own business affairs. Shortly after his marriage in April 1672 to Gulielma Springett, they became the owners of a country estate some twenty-five miles northwest of London at Rickmansworth (Hertfordshire). They took up residence there together, he moving from Wanstead (Essex) and Guli moving from her stepfather and mother's home in nearby Penn (Buckinghamshire). While living in Rickmansworth, the Penns marked the births of their first four children—and suffered the deaths of three of them. Only the fourth, their son Springett (1675–1696), survived those years. In 1676 Penn decided to buy a larger, 300-acre country home at Warminghurst (Sussex), over forty miles southwest of London. The family relocated there in September, and Penn owned and occupied this home until 1707. At Warminghurst Guli gave birth to four more children, but only the first two, Letitia (1678–1746) and William Jr. (1681–1720), survived childhood. The third and fourth, both daughters, lived three weeks and four years, respectively. In addition to the deaths of five of their eight children, other family losses were to follow with the deaths in 1679 of Guli's beloved stepfather Isaac Penington and in 1682 of both Penn's mother Margaret and Guli's mother Mary Penington. Additional burdens were to come to Penn with the deaths in 1694 of Guli and in 1696 of Springett.

Having married and started raising his family, Penn settled into the life and responsibilities of the landed gentry, wherein he was challenged to succeed as the custodian and manager not only of the wealth he had received from his father but also of the estate Guli had received from her natural father. Sir William Springett had died before the birth of Guli, his only child, and she was the sole heir of his lands in Kent, Sussex, and Surrey. Penn undertook the challenges and responsibilities presented to him, armed not only with an excellent education but also with experience in managing family wealth. Trained as a lawyer, he was familiar with the extensive body of English land law. Twice— in 1666–1667 and in 1669–1670—he had been in Ireland serving as agent for his father's estates in County Cork (some twelve thousand English acres meant to provide £1,000 annual rental income).[227] After their April 1672 wedding, William and Guli began taking active measures for their own economic well-being. In July they raised cash by selling some of Guli's lands in Kent,[228] and in October William went into Kent and Sussex to collect rents from Guli's tenants.[229]

Penn knew from experience that he could not manage such extensive family business affairs without assistance. Throughout *My Irish Journal*,[230] the account that Penn kept during all but the final weeks of his 1669–1670 trip attending to his father's land affairs in Ireland, he mentions Philip Ford (ca. 1631–1702),[231] who accompanied Penn there as steward. Ford, a Quaker, had suffered imprisonment in 1665 with Isaac Penington, now his neighbor in Buckinghamshire. For years thereafter, Ford would continue to serve Penn as steward in collecting his revenues and paying his debts, ordering his supplies, and even serving him as private banker through the advancement of monies Penn never repaid in full. Ford's preserved accounts with Penn begin in April 1672 and end in March 1680, but there are gaps in the records during those years,[232] and his stewardship may have continued thereafter. When Ford died in 1702, Penn was still in his debt for borrowed money, and Ford's widow proceeded for its recovery in the courts.

Penn also knew the necessity of having wise legal counsel in order to preserve the wealth that he and his wife had separately inherited. He continued to engage the services of Richard Langhorne (d. 1679), a witness to, and probably the draftsman of, Admiral Penn's last will and testament.[233] Langhorne was a lawyer, a member of the Inner Temple, and a Roman Catholic, being the Jesuits' attorney in England.[234] Continuing to represent Penn interests, several months before William and Gulielma married in 1672, Langhorne was appointed under a premarital trusteeship agreement as one of the five trustees empowered to approve the sale of Guli's real estate whenever she

---

[227] *PWP*, 1:570.

[228] They did so again in 1676 and 1678. See *PWP*, 1:646.

[229] *PWP*, 1:241

[230] For the full text, see *PWP*, 1:103–31.

[231] *PWP*, 1:131–32n9.

[232] See discussion in *PWP*, 1:574–77.

[233] *PWP*, 1:148–51.

[234] See Stephen and Lee, *The Dictionary of National Biography*, 11:543–44.

and William had critical need of money. (At least one other trustee, James Master of Gray's Inn, was also a lawyer; another, Sir Henry Oxenden, had been an overseer under Guli's father's will.) Indentures from 1672 and 1676 are preserved, signed by William and Guli as grantors together with all five trustees, that convey her properties in Kent and Sussex.[235] Disbursement entries in Ford's accounts for 1673, 1674, and 1678 show continuing business activity between William and Langhorne. And on July 1, 1676, Langhorne was one of six witnesses to the agreement settling the boundary between East and West Jersey, a resolution sought by Penn, one of the parties to the agreement, in advancing the Quaker colonization of West Jersey.[236]

Langhorne, a prominent Catholic, was the first person accused by Titus Oates of involvement in the infamous but counterfeit Popish Plot. Although innocent, he was arrested in October 1678 and held in Newgate Prison where Penn, twice himself a prisoner there, visited on June 9, 1679. Less than a week later, Langhorne was tried, found guilty, and, on July 14, executed.[237] During April that year Penn had petitioned the Privy Council for permission to repossess "some writings (which concern his estate and with which he was entrusted) and were left in the custody of Mr. Richard Langhorne, delivered to him out of the said Langhorne's chamber." On April 16, 1679, "His Majesty was pleased to order ... that ... the writings that really concern the said William Penn, and with which he was entrusted, and were by him, or his order, delivered to the said Langhorne" be taken from Langhorne's chamber and delivered to Penn.[238] In addition to papers regarding Penn's own affairs, there likely would have been papers not only concerning Guli's matters but also ones pertaining to the further administration of Admiral Penn's estate, upon which William was soon to act.

Fox at Swarthmoor: A working sojourner

George Fox was not of the landed gentry. He was an artisan, and although his father was a weaver, the son had learned the craft of a leatherworker. He had no estates, although he married

---

[235] See abstracts, *PWP*, 1:647–48.
[236] See abstract, *PWP*, 1:654.
[237] Stephen and Lee, *The Dictionary of National Biography*, 11:544.
[238] *PWP*, 1:550–51.

an eminent landed gentleman's widow, herself the mistress of a distinguished seat, Swarthmoor Hall. He had no children of his own, yet his wife's three sons and six daughters and their families gave him genuine love and service. In these circumstances, Fox during his adult years was able to devote himself solely to his vocation of speaking God's truth throughout a troubled land. He made a rare break in his travels when, from September 1678 until March 1680, he remained at Swarthmoor with his wife Margaret.

Theirs was a loving marriage, but it was marked by frequent separations, the result of imprisonments, missionary journeys at home and abroad, Margaret's need to be at Swarthmoor with her family, and George's need to be in London for the work of building up the Religious Society of Friends. They were apart from each other more than they were together. Margaret explained it thus:

> And though the Lord had provided an outward habitation for him yet he was not willing to stay at it, because it was so remote and far from London, where his service most lay. And my concern for God, and his holy eternal Truth, was then in the north, where God had placed and set me, and likewise for the ordering and governing of my children and family: so that we were very willing, both of us, to live apart for some years upon God's account and his Truth's service, and to deny ourselves of that comfort which we might have had in being together, for the sake and service of the Lord and his Truth.[239]

Prior to their wedding in October 1669, Margaret had suffered her first imprisonment—for refusal to swear the oath of allegiance and for holding meetings in her home. She was arrested at Swarthmoor in 1663 and held in Lancaster Castle until her trial in August 1664, at which she was found guilty, and the sentence of praemunire was imposed on her. That sentence was, in her own words (as quoted in Besse), "that she should be out of the King's Protection, and forfeit all her estate, real and personal, to the King, and suffer imprisonment during life."[240] Her account continues: "So then I remained in prison twenty

---

[239] Fox, *Journal*, 742–43.

[240] Besse, *Sufferings of the People Called Quakers*, 1:312–14 (quotation is from p. 314).

months before I could get so much favor from the sheriff, as to go to my own house, which then I had for a little time, and returned to prison again." Margaret remained in prison about four years until her release by an order of the king and Council.[241] Her release came in 1668, but it seemed transitory when in 1670, a year after their marriage, Margaret was arrested at Swarthmoor and returned to Lancaster prison "upon her old praemunire."[242] Not until April 1671 was she freed again under another order of the king and Council (which granted her estate to Susannah and Rachel, two of her daughters). Upon her release, Fox left for his journey to the New World (August 1671 to June 1673) and then shortly after his return was committed to his eighth imprisonment (from December 1673 to February 1675). Not until June 1675 through March 1677 did Fox take extended time with his wife in her northern home. After that he was away again, principally on the mission to the Netherlands and Germany from July to October 1677. Following that trip, he returned to Margaret and her home at Swarthmoor for his second extended stay, both times being employed to oversee administrative matters and, especially, to advance the print and epistolary ministry of a host of itinerant Quaker preachers, with support from a central communications facility.[243] When Fox left in early March 1680, it was, as Henry Cadbury notes, "for the last time."[244]

Penn's petition to Charles II for land in America

As Fox ended his northern working sojourn and began to visit Quakers and attend their meetings while progressing through the counties on his way to London, there to resume ongoing participation in the leadership of the Religious Society of Friends,[245] Penn was embarking upon the major venture of his life. His family was continuing to increase—during his recent

---

[241] Ibid.

[242] Fox, *Journal*, 557.

[243] See Kate Peters, *Print Culture and the Early Quakers* (Cambridge: Cambridge University Press, 2005).

[244] Fox, *Journal*, 730.

[245] Fox did so chiefly by attending weekly sessions of the Meeting for Sufferings and of the Second Day's Morning Meeting (of men ministers). See Fox, *Journal*, 732.

time at Warminghurst, Letitia had been born (March 6, 1678),[246] and she was healthy. Along with the joys of his marriage to Guli and of their surviving two children—soon to be three with the birth of William Jr. in March 1681—Penn carried heavy responsibilities. He carried the financial obligation of supporting the family household at Warminghurst out of the rents he had to collect from his Irish tenants and from those tenants Guli still had in England following the sales at the time of their marriage of "well over 1250 acres of productive land" in Kent and Sussex. He carried a growing burden of debt (estimated to have been, by June 1678, £6,231 in principal and interest owing on property he had mortgaged and £3,256 in unsecured loans). [247] Additionally, Penn had the steadily increasing balance due for monies advanced to him over many years by Philip Ford, as discussed above. Still unpaid at Ford's death in 1702 and thereafter pursued in the courts by Ford's widow and children, in 1708— after judgment was found against him in the Court of Common Pleas, after Warminghurst was sold to satisfy mortgaged indebtedness, and after he spent three-quarters of that year in the Fleet, London's prison for debtors, for his refusal to pay the Fords—Penn settled and discharged their claim for £7600.[248]

Another burden Penn carried was his moral battle against both religious intolerance in England and the consequent suffering of Quakers who for conscience's sake would not swear to oaths, pay tithes, deny their beliefs, cease attending meetings for worship, or otherwise comply with whatever legal stratagems the state might enact to break their nonconformity. Penn, himself a sufferer, had written often in protest against such violations of the freedom of religion.

At this moment, as the persecution of those outside the walls of the established church intensified in the wake of the Popish Plot and as the heat of countrywide political debate related to parliamentary elections mounted, Penn authored a written request to Charles II for the settlement of a debt owed his father by the Crown in which he asked the Crown to grant land in America to Penn. At the admiral's death, the debt had passed through his estate to Penn, the principal heir. Although the

---

[246] *PWP*, 1:519n4. Because of a threat of schism within the Religious Society of Friends, Penn had to be away from home and in Bristol for a period before the birth. See *PWP*, 1:328–29, 531n1.

[247] *PWP*, 1:646–47.

[248] *PWP*, 4:569–71; see also *PWP*, 1:574–77.

details and proof concerning the debt are not now certain, Penn later wrote in a 1704 letter to Robert Harley that he "had a debt upon the Crown of about £16,000 of money lent by my father for the victualling of the Navy 1667, which was shut up in the Exchequer."[249] What is certain is that the admiral ended his service at sea following the victory of the English fleet against the Dutch in the Battle of Lowestoft, fought in June 1665 forty miles off the Suffolk coast in the North Sea. In this, the opening engagement of the Second Anglo-Dutch War, Admiral Penn was serving as chief-of-staff to James, the Duke of York, the lord high admiral of the fleet. After that victory, Admiral Penn served ashore in the government as a commissioner of the navy until his death. The war, at least in part an English attempt to wrest trade routes and colonies from the Dutch, continued for the next two years, but the English fortunes sank with the catastrophic disasters of the Great Plague (striking London in July 1665) and the Great Fire of London (September 1666) and the looming economic collapse of the nation. By early 1667, the Crown could not pay its debts or keep its fleet seaworthy, and it is credible that Admiral Penn, a commissioner of—and a hero in—the naval service, would advance his own monies for "victualling" or providing food for his comrade officers and men. By midyear, both the war and the English fleet were lost in the Dutch raid on the Medway, a tributary at the mouth of the Thames.

Note the following circumstances of the documentary evidence for Penn's petition:

Original documents. Penn's working copies of his original petition for payment are now lost. In 1735 there remained, in the records of the Board of Trade, a committee of the Privy Council, only the left side of the original written sheet. Both that fragment and a scholarly conjectural reconstruction of the whole are reproduced below.[250]

Date. As presently documented, the request is undated. Because the king in his minute of June 1, 1680, writes that he favorably read "the petition" and is referring it for consideration to the "Committee of Council for Trade and Foreign Plantations" for

---

[249] *PWP*, 2:30–31. For text of this letter to Robert Harley dated February 9, 1704, see The Papers of William Penn, Historical Society of Pennsylvania, Philadelphia (hereafter cited as *Microfilm*), 2:793.

[250] *PWP*, 2:32–33, with the suggested reconstruction by the *PWP* editors.

advice on how to proceed, it is generally assumed that Penn's request was made in May the same year.

Title. The document has no title. Whereas Penn framed his request as "The Humble Ad[dress]," the king in his Minute of June 1 referred to it as a "petition," by which description it is today generally known.

The parties. The petition is from William Penn, "Son to Sir W[illiam Penn, deceased]." Unstated are the known facts that the admiral had died ten years earlier and that the son is both the executor of his father's last will and testament and the residuary heir of his estate. Stated, and possibly unknown to the king, are that Penn and his mother have "[great debts and otherwise certain] ruin." The petition is addressed to the "King's Majesty," and so also is the later humble prayer. Presumably, it is upon the sovereign's "Royal Grace" and his personal "Princely Respect" for the admiral, rather than the state's discretionary largesse, that the desired relief is grounded. Here Penn may have been artfully invoking the Stuarts' belief in the divine right of their kingship.

The boundaries of the land sought in America. The boundaries of the sought-for land in the reconstructed petition follow those in the king's minute of June 1 and in the minute of the Committee of Trade of June 14, both minutes presumably having copied Penn's description verbatim from his petition. Penn's concern must have been how to describe land neither he nor the king had ever seen that would fit exactly within the territories previously granted by the Crown to the colony of Maryland on the South, to the colony of New Jersey on the East, and to the colony of New York on the North and would have western limits similar to Maryland. There were no scruples as to how the "King's Majesty" might presume to grant ownership in lands that had been occupied by indigenous peoples for unknown generations.

   William Penn's Petition for Royal Charter:
  Original Fragment [with reconstructed text in brackets]

For the [King's Majesty]
The Humble Ad[dress of William Penn]
Son to Sir W[illiam Penn, deceased.]
Sheweth,
That having [sought payment for debts due to his father]
in *Ireland* by the oppression of the Lord [Treasurer
  this account was not settled at his father's]

decease (though most of it remitted by [order of the Ordnance Office) he was forced]
to borrow every penny of it, by reason [that since the year 1672 His Majesty's Treasury of]
England was under the Stop of the Ex[chequer, so that the debt now amounts to £16,000]
with the growing interest of it, and 9 ye[ars having passed, the petitioner humbly prays]
for the relief of his own, and his mother's [great debts and otherwise certain]
ruin.
He humbly prays that [the King's Majesty, out of His Royal Grace and]
that princely respect he of [old has shown to the petitioner's father, and from]
his compassion to the afflicte[d, will grant him letters patent for a tract of land in]
America, lying *north* of *M*[*aryland*, on the east bounded with Delaware]
River, on the west, limit[ed as Maryland is, and northward to]
extend as far as plantable, [which is altogether Indian. And]
he doubts not by his intere[st that he will undertake to render it a]
profitable plantation to the [crown. And the petitioner further promises]
to raise that speedy and sufficient [sum of money from this grant to satisfy his]
encumbrances, that he may [settle his accounts and extinguish his]
debt of at least £11,000 and be [of such service to His Majesty in this place]
and time as shall be most [beneficial to the Kingdom.]
And [he in duty prays, etc.]

The grant of the royal charter of Pennsylvania

On March 4, 1681, less than a year after receiving Penn's "Humble Address" to the "King's Majesty," Charles II, "of our special grace, certain knowledge, and mere motion, have given and granted . . . this our present charter . . . unto . . . William

Penn, his heirs and assigns,"[251] creating and constituting him "the true and absolute proprietary" of the province "to be called by the name of Pensilvania,"[252] a word Charles himself invented out of "regard to the memory and merits" of Admiral Penn. A lengthy and complex document in twenty-three sections, the charter set land boundaries adjusted after comments solicited from the agents of Lord Baltimore, the proprietor of Maryland, and the Duke of York (the royal grantee of New York), and it allowed powers of government generous in their reach at a time the Crown was trying to take more control over the trade and plantations supervised by the Privy Council through the Lords of Trade. The charter was, however, silent on Penn's paramount issues of religious liberty and freedom of conscience. Since his working papers, including a draft charter, are lost, it is now unknown what Penn may have requested regarding these issues, but religious liberty and freedom of conscience are not addressed in the draft outline prepared for him by John Darnall, an attorney whom he consulted.[253] Penn's lost draft charter was, however, reviewed on behalf of the Crown by Lord Chief Justice Francis North, who amended the final instrument at the request of the Bishop of London to make provision for a preacher to be sent by the bishop when requested by twenty inhabitants. North's suggestion that the charter should also include a provision that "concerning matters . . . ecclesiastical [it] be subordinate and subject to the power and regulation of the Lords of the Privy Council"[254] was not accepted.

To the overarching question of why Charles was "graciously disposed to gratify the petitioner in his humble suit,"[255] notwithstanding Penn's being known to be a supporter of the Crown's political opponents and, worse, a religious nonconformist, the general record supports two probable reasons. One can be conveniently labeled 'the camaraderie of the *Royal Charles*' and the other 'the promise of Breda.'

Regarding the camaraderie of the *Royal Charles*, both Charles II and his brother James, the Duke of York, had lasting

---

[251] Jean R. Soderlund, ed., *William Penn and the Founding of Pennsylvania 1680–1684: A Documentary History* (Philadelphia: University of Pennsylvania Press, 1983), 41–50 (document 11).

[252] *PWP*, 2:77.

[253] *PWP*, 2:40.

[254] *PWP*, 2:58.

[255] *PWP*, 2:34.

personal associations with Admiral Penn in connection with the naval vessel of that name. The admiral had originally offered his services to the exiled king in 1654, but at that time Charles was unable to accept his help. When, in 1660, the king was brought home from exile, an English fleet came for him, led by an eighty-gun first-rate three-deck naval ship of the line built earlier at the direction of Parliament and named *Naseby* (to honor the decisive military victory over Charles I on June 14, 1645, in Northamptonshire). When Charles II boarded the ship at Scheveningen in the southern Netherlands, she was renamed the *Royal Charles*, and Admiral Penn, who had boarded in England, was then knighted and became a member of the king's party for the triumphant voyage back to Dover. In June 1665 the admiral had command of the now flagship *Royal Charles*, with the Duke of York aboard, at the head of an accompanying fleet about to engage the enemy in the Second Anglo-Dutch War. The admiral was also serving as chief of staff under the duke who, without naval experience, was lord high admiral at the beginning of the war. He needed and relied on Penn's experience and skill to guide him. The notable English victory of that war at the naval Battle of Lowestoft came on June 13. By 1667, however, English affairs had fallen to such a disastrous low that the Crown, unable to pay its debts—because of which, as noted earlier, the admiral had advanced funds for victualling the crews—ordered the fleet decommissioned and anchored on the Medway near the mouth of the Thames, where, except for the *Royal Charles*, it was destroyed by the Dutch. The Dutch took the *Royal Charles* as a prize to the Netherlands, where she was later sold for scrap.

In the legal preamble of section I of the charter, which describes the grant of Pennsylvania, the king in effect acknowledged the special bonds both he and his brother had formed with Admiral Penn, giving testimony also to the admiral's loyalty, honor, valor, and extraordinary services with these words:

> having regard to the memory and merits of his [Penn's] late father, in diverse services, and particularly to his conduct, courage, and discretion, under our dearest brother James, Duke of York, in that signal battle and

victory fought against the Dutch fleet . . . in the year 1665.[256]

This "gift and grant" of land named for a national hero and conveyed to his heir surely was intended as a grateful gesture from a sovereign who had not, during the admiral's lifetime, rewarded him with the expected titles and honors.

The promise of Breda, the other probable reason motivating Charles to grant the charter, refers to his long-held willingness and policy to

> declare a liberty to tender consciences, and that no man shall be disquieted or called in question for difference of opinion in matters of religion, which do not disturb the peace of the kingdom; and that we shall be ready to consent to such an Act of Parliament, as, upon mature deliberation, shall be offered to us, for the full granting that indulgence.[257]

As discussed above, this promise was first made at Breda, the city in the southern Netherlands where Charles resided in the last days of his exile. There, on April 4, 1660, the eve of his return to England, he issued the Declaration of Breda proclaiming his four pillars for "a full and entire administration of justice throughout the [wounded] land." In addition to "liberty to tender consciences" (the second pillar), he granted a free and general pardon to all who declared "that they return to the loyalty and obedience of good subjects," excluding those excepted by Parliament; he allowed Parliament to determine all issues relating to grants, sales, and purchases of estates during the interregnum; and he declared his ready consent to any parliamentary act for the full satisfaction of all arrears due the officers and men of General George Monck's parliamentary army as well as their reception into the king's service.

The recognition of "liberty to all tender consciences," as promised at Breda, had long been sought by William Penn. It was a cause the king did not forsake, even when thwarted or countermanded by Parliament. On October 25, 1660, the restored king had issued a royal Declaration on Ecclesiastical

---

[256] Soderlund, *William Penn*, 41.
[257] Besse, *Sufferings of the People Called Quakers*, 1:viii.

England 1350–1682

Affairs[258] reaffirming a policy of toleration. Parliament considered it but took no action until 1661, when it passed the Corporation Act effectively barring nonconformists from public office. And then in 1662 Parliament passed the Act of Uniformity, which made use of the Book of Common Prayer compulsory in public worship services. These were the first two of the four penal laws that became known as the Clarendon Code. Also in 1662, Parliament passed the Quaker Act to prevent Friends' "mischiefs and dangers . . . [in] refusing to take lawful oaths."

Then, on December 26, 1662, Charles again issued a royal declaration, renewing the promise of Breda and stating he would seek from Parliament its legislative concurrence in granting toleration for nonconformists.[259] Rather than concur, Parliament in 1664 passed an act to "prevent and suppress seditious Conventicles" intended to stop the meetings of dissenting religious groups, and then in 1665 it passed the Five Mile Act to prevent nonconformists from living in incorporated towns. These were the third and fourth, the last, of the Clarendon Code's penal laws.

Seven years later, on March 15, 1672, the king issued yet another royal declaration of indulgence, this time asserting his supreme ecclesiastical authority and decreeing the suspension of the penal laws against nonconformists and popish recusants. Unfortunately, at the same time Charles was sorely in need of a parliamentary grant to build up the Royal Navy then preparing for the Third Anglo-Dutch War. His declaration was met with implacable opposition. So resolved was the Commons and so financially strapped was Charles that, one year after declaring the indulgence, he was forced to cancel it to obtain money for the fleet. Moreover, he had to accept the Test Act of 1673 requiring all persons in Crown offices to take the Oath of Supremacy and Oath of Allegiance, sign the declaration against transubstantiation, and receive the sacrament of Holy Communion according to the rites of the Church of England. Of the Test Act of 1673, historian David Ogg has written:

> It was the clearest possible repudiation of the tentative efforts at toleration which, with fluctuations, had

---

[258] William Cobbett and T. C. Hansard, eds., *The Parliamentary History of England from the earliest period to the year 1803*, 36 vols. (London: T. C. Hansard [etc.], 1806–1820), 4:131–41.

[259] Ibid., 4:257.

influenced Charles's policy ever since the Declaration of Breda. . . . Its strength lay in its intolerance and exclusiveness, a fact which came to be appreciated by English Catholics and Dissenters; because, in place of the shifting sands of latitude and compromise, it substituted the rock of rigid dogma, and transformed a Reformation doctrine from a spiritual conviction into a national safeguard.[260]

If Charles's political efforts to make his policy of toleration a national reality failed, it was not because of a feeble will. His perseverance against parliamentary opposition on this issue never wavered, even though it was costly to him. In that perseverance he may well have admired the same quality in William Penn, who had not only suffered estrangement from his father for a time but had endured imprisonments for his Quaker convictions. Because Charles was a fellow but secret religious dissenter with Penn—revealing on his deathbed his own religious nonconformity by professing obedience to the Roman Church— his prerogative grant of Pennsylvania may have been his final courageous act of perseverance intended to fulfill his promise of Breda.

Ten days after Penn received the charter, his third child to survive infancy, William Jr., was born. Filled with that joy and care, the new father undertook his responsibilities as proprietor of Pennsylvania "to transport an ample colony unto . . . parts of America not yet cultivated and planted."[261] Penn immediately commenced work on many tasks, which included making appointments to assist in the initial governing; promoting land sales among prospective settlers; drafting a constitution and laws as well as planning land distribution; opening communications with the indigenous peoples and with authorities and other interested parties in Maryland, Delaware, and New York; and readying himself and his affairs to leave England for life in the New World. He probably had little time to concern himself with the indictment "for absence from the National Worship" voted against him at the assizes at Horsham (Sussex) that same year.[262]

---

[260] David Ogg, *England in the Reign of Charles II*, 2 vols., 2nd ed. (Oxford: Clarendon Press, 1955), 1:369.

[261] Charter preamble, as quoted in Soderlund, *William Penn*, 41.

[262] Besse, *Sufferings of the People Called Quakers*, 1:723.

"I shall have a tender care to the government that it be well laid at first"[263]

The drafting in England of a constitutional framework for Pennsylvania began in earnest on March 4, 1681, with the grant of the royal charter. After a number of reworkings, the foundational document was finished in two parts on April 25 and May 5, 1682. To his task of settling the governance for a fresh province to be planted overseas in an unknown tract of a new world, Penn came supplied with an excellent legal education, experience in helping prepare *The Concessions and Agreements . . . of the Province of West New Jersey in America*, and extensive reading in political theory and constitutional law. In addition, he was known among Quakers in England, Ireland, and Scotland; had traveled on two religious missions in the Netherlands and Germany; and was a fellow among suffering Friends who had been imprisoned for their religious convictions. Penn expected to find many of his new planters and freemen from among Quakers, and his constitutional principles would instinctively have been sensitive to their values and needs.

In the summer of 1681, Penn completed one of the earliest, if not the first, of the several known drafts of the constitutional structure for Pennsylvania. It is likely that he alone wrote the document entitled *The Fundamental Constitutions of Pennsylvania as they were drawn up, settled, and signed by William Penn, Proprietary and Governor, and consented to and subscribed by all the first adventurers and freeholders of that province, as the ground and rule of all future government.*[264] The draft, neither signed nor published in Penn's lifetime, proposed in twenty-four articles (each called a "fundamental constitution") a government centered on an assembly elected annually (article 3) that in turn chose from its members a council to advise and assist the governor in the business of government in the "intervals of the Assembly" (article 7). He introduced the whole work with a preamble that was theological in nature and also included commentaries at the head of the individual articles revealing the theological and constitutional considerations he had weighed. Thus, he opened the preamble as follows:

---

[263] William Penn to Robert Turner, March 5, 1681, *PWP*, 2:83–84.
[264] For the text, see Soderlund, *William Penn*, 96–111.

> When it pleased Almighty God, the creator and upholder of all things, to make man His great governor of the world, He did not only endue him with excellent knowledge but an upright mind, so that his power over the creation was balanced by an inward uprightness, that he might use it justly. Then was the law of light and truth writ in his heart, and that was the guide and keeper of his innocence; there was not need of any external precepts to direct or terrify him.[265]

Penn fixed at the outset, as the first "fundamental constitution," his long-sought principle of religious toleration, here balanced with due reverence to God and respect for authority:

> Considering that it is impossible that any people or government should ever prosper where men render not unto God that which is God's, as well as to Caesar that which is Caesar's; and also perceiving the disorders and mischiefs that attend those places where [there is] force in matters of faith and worship; . . . and further weighing that this unpeopled country can never be planted if there be not due encouragement given to sober people of all sorts to plant, and that they will not esteem anything a sufficient encouragement where they are not assured, but that after all the hazards of the sea and the troubles of a wilderness, the labor of their hands and sweat of their brows may be made the forfeit of their conscience, and they and their wives and children ruined because they worship God in some different way from that which may be more generally owned. Therefore, in reverence to God the Father of lights and spirits, the author as well as object of all divine knowledge, faith, and worship, I do declare for me and mine and establish it for the First Fundamental of the government of my country, that every person that does or shall reside therein shall have and enjoy the free possession of his or her faith and exercise of worship towards God, in such way and manner as every person shall in conscience believe is most acceptable to God, and so long as every such person uses not this Christian liberty to licentiousness (that is to say, to speak loosely and profanely of God, Christ, or religion, or to commit any evil in their conversation), he

---

[265] Ibid., 97.

or she shall be protected in the enjoyment of the aforesaid Christian liberty by the civil magistrate.[266]

Having lived in England under its unwritten constitution, where he experienced the oppression of conflicting royal and legislative policies struggling with each other to exact obedience in an age of dynamic change, Penn wanted a written constitutional plan that would fasten, as securely as an architectural framework, provisions to establish the peace and stability of an open society for free citizens. Penn had begun his task alone but in time came to seek comments and assistance from others, especially from Thomas Rudyard (d. 1692), a Quaker attorney of London who had assisted in the Penn-Mead trial of 1670 and who, with Penn and ten others, purchased East Jersey in 1682[267] and served as its deputy governor until 1684. The foundational document being crafted was renamed the Frame of the Government, and it went through at least ten drafts, Rudyard assisting with the final six. The completed work was formally titled the Frame of the Government of the Province of Pennsylvania in America: together with certain laws agreed upon in England by the governor and divers freemen of the aforesaid province.[268] Penn signed the Frame of the Government, which he also called "this present Charter of Liberties," on April 20, 1682, and its annexed Laws Agreed upon in England on the following May 5. In this final version, the principle of religious toleration, which had been the first of the Fundamental Constitutions, was stated more directly, but it was relegated to the thirty-fifth of the forty Laws Agreed upon in England:

> That all persons living in this province who confess and acknowledge the one almighty and eternal God to be the creator, upholder, and ruler of the world, and that hold themselves obliged in conscience to live peaceably and justly in civil society, shall in no ways be molested or prejudiced for their religious persuasion or practice in matters of faith and worship, nor shall they be compelled

---

[266] Ibid., 98–99.

[267] In addition to his involvement in settling West Jersey (see pp. 64–70), Penn in February 1682, with eleven others, acquired the proprietary interests to East Jersey; he later sold 11/12 of his share to Robert Barclay. See *PWP*, 2:295n8.

[268] For the full texts of these documents see *PWP*, 2:211–27; Soderlund, *William Penn*, 120–33.

at any time to frequent or maintain any religious worship, place, or ministry whatever.

Also noteworthy was the enlarged theological preamble to the Frame of the Government that, after months of critical comments and advice from Penn's friends such as Algernon Sydney, Benjamin Furley, and even Rudyard, reflected a change from man's relative innocence in the Fundamental Constitutions to an acknowledgment of man's instinct to corrupt his "native goodness" so that "lust prevailing against duty made a lamentable breach upon it,"[269] with the result that "men side with their passions against their reason." Although the government Penn structured in the Frame of the Government was meant to serve free citizens in a democratic, not a theocratic, state, Penn could honestly say that "government seems to me a part of religion itself, a thing sacred in its institution and end." How that government operates, nevertheless, depends upon men.

> But lastly, when all is said, there is hardly one frame of government in the world so ill designed by its first founders, that in good hands would not do well enough; and history tells us, the best in ill ones can do nothing that is great or good . . . wherefore governments rather depend upon men, than men upon governments. Let men be good, and the government cannot be bad; if it be ill, they will cure it. But if men be bad, let the government be never so good; they will endeavor to warp and spoil it to their turn.[270]

The Frame of the Government and the Laws Agreed upon in England were printed in London and made available, shortly after they were signed by Penn, for wide distribution among prospective colonists. This constitutional settlement served as the governance of the province for almost one year. After Penn arrived in Pennsylvania and the government had come into being, the two houses of the legislature, the Provincial Council and the General Assembly, sought substantial changes, to which Penn agreed, and on April 2, 1683, a second Frame of the Government went into effect.

---

[269] *PWP*, 2:211.
[270] Soderlund, *William Penn*, 122.

Embarking on the 'holy experiment'

For the peopling of his new province, Penn reached out through his wide network of friends for help in selling land in the New World. He made such an overture to James Harrison (ca. 1628–1687), a Quaker of Bolton (Lancashire), in a letter dated August 25, 1681, appointing him an agent for the sale of "any parcel of land in Pennsylvania (not below 250 acres to any one person) from time to time."[271] In the letter, Penn indicates his recruitment is reaching beyond England and that "many flock in to be concerned with me. I am like to have many from France, some from Holland, and I hear some Scots will go." He continues:

> I have so obtained [my country] and desire that I may not be unworthy of His love, but do that which may answer yet His kind providence and serve His Truth and people; that an example may be set up to the nations. There may be room there, though not here, for such a holy experiment.[272]

The effect of this letter was momentous and twofold. First, Harrison himself decided to buy five thousand acres of Pennsylvania land and to relocate there with his family in order to settle in a new home. A little more than one year after the date of the letter, on September 5, 1682, Harrison and family sailed for America from England, never to return. (Penn left England one week before them, on August 30, 1682, for the first of his two visits to America.)

The other consequence of Penn's letter to Harrison was that in his characterization of the plantation in Pennsylvania as 'a holy experiment,' he gave to the ages, once the letter became known to the public, a term of semi-reverence exceeding any significance Penn may have foreseen by his one-time usage. So far as is known, Penn never again made that reference in writing. It is an ironic twist of history that the holy experiment was ultimately guided by Harrison's descendants, not Penn's.

---

[271] *PWP*, 2:109.

[272] *PWP*, 2:108.

Of the convincements and sufferings of James Harrison (1628–1687) and Phineas Pemberton (1650–1702)

George Fox, giving an account in his *Journal* "of Friends going forth out of the north into the service of the Lord and to preach the gospel in this nation and other nations," recorded that James Harrison with others "past uppe into Scotlande to preach ye gospel this yeere: about ye 10th month 1655."[273] The editor adds that Harrison was born near Kendal (Westmorland); a shoemaker by trade, he was called into the public ministry, traveling "in many parts of this nation . . . and particularly in the lower parts of Lancashire, where he married, and he and his family settled for several years" before departing for Pennsylvania.[274] After his death, Harrison's memorialists (Phineas Pemberton, his son-in-law, and William Yardley, a brother-in-law) wrote of his beginnings in Westmorland, stating that "in the breaking forth of the truth in those parts he was early convinced thereof, and in a short time after, came forth in a public testimony for the same." As a consequence, the enemies of truth "often raged forth against him, so that his sufferings were very great, both by imprisonment, and by spoil of goods."[275] Because the date of 1655 is fixed for his public ministry in Scotland, it is probable that Harrison's convincement as a Quaker occurred during Fox's first mission to the northern counties between 1651 and 1654.

His family remembered the following imprisonments Harrison suffered for conscience's sake:

> In this year, 1660, James Harrison . . . and several others, were imprisoned for their testimony, at Burgasgate in Shrewsbury. . . . From this prison, James Harrison and his friends were released in consequence of a royal proclamation, dated at Whitehall, May 11th, 1661. James Harrison was also confined in prison in 1663, in

---

[273] George Fox, *The Journal of George Fox*, ed. Norman Penney, with an introduction by T. Edmund Harvey, 2 vols. (Cambridge: Cambridge University Press, 1911), 2:325, 326.

[274] Ibid., 2:326n12. Also see Penney, "The First Publishers of Truth," 258.

[275] *A Collection of Memorials concerning divers deceased ministers and others of the people called Quakers, in Pennsylvania, New-Jersey, and parts adjacent, from nearly the first settlement thereof to the year 1787* (Philadelphia: Crukshank, 1787), 8–10.

the county jail of Worcester; and in 1664, 65, and 66, at Chester castle.[276]

In 1668 Harrison moved with his family from Cheshire to Bolton (Lancashire), near Manchester. In a Manchester grocery, Harrison's young daughter Phoebe (1660–1696), while shopping with her mother, encountered Phineas Pemberton, a Friend born in Wigan (Lancashire). He had been apprenticed in 1665 for seven years to the store's owner, John Abraham, a local Quaker.[277] When his service ended, Phineas went into business for himself in Bolton. In 1677, their mutual attraction having endured, Phoebe and Phineas were married[278] in Hardshaw (Lancashire) Monthly Meeting.

Phineas' imprisonments for conscience's sake were also remembered by his descendants:

> He became a mark for those in power, even while he was an apprentice, and was several times imprisoned in Chester and Lancaster castles, for his attendance of the religious meetings of Friends. . . . In the 11th month, 1669, Phineas Pemberton and . . . some others, were carried before three justices, for holding a meeting at Nehemiah Pool's house; and on the 1st of 2d month, he was imprisoned; remaining nineteen weeks and five days in Lancaster castle. . . . [He] was imprisoned in 1670, for going towards his own place of worship; and he was also frequently exposed to vexatious interruptions, while transacting his master's business.[279]

Not only were Friends punished by imprisonments, often repeatedly, as well as by threats of imprisonment, but they were

---

[276] These imprisonments are given in "The Annals of the Pemberton Family," which consists of extractions made by Harrison's great-grandson John Pemberton from the narrative written by his grandfather (and Harrison's son-in-law) Phineas Pemberton describing Harrison's and his own early sufferings in England. The original document was later lost. John Pemberton, "The Annals of the Pemberton Family," in *Friends' Miscellany*, edited by John and Isaac Comly, 12 vols. (Philadelphia: William Sharpless, printer, 1831–1839), 7:10. See also John W. Jordan, ed., *Colonial Families of Philadelphia*, 2 vols. (New York: Lewis Publishing 1911), 1:282–83.

[277] George Williams Brown, *Historical Sketches, chiefly relating to the early settlement of Friends at Falls, in Bucks County, Pennsylvania* (Philadelphia: J. P. Murphy, 1882), 4–5.

[278] Pemberton, "The Annals of the Pemberton Family," 7:18–19.

[279] Ibid., 7:4, 15.

also subject to economic sanctions in which they were stripped, robbed, plundered—despoiled—of their personal property, or "distressed of their goods." Besse reports the "spoil of goods" that befell Harrison as well as Pemberton and his wife in 1679:

> On the 31st of the month called March this year was a Meeting at Macclesfield in Cheshire to which the Mayor and two other justices came, and took what names they pleased. After a short time, the meeting still continuing, they came again. At their first coming they found James Harrison, of Bolton in Lancashire, preaching, for which they fined him £20 and at their coming again, he still preaching, they called that a second offence and fined him £40 which convictions and fines they certified to John Hartley, a justice near Manchester in Lancashire, who issued his warrant to the constables of Bolton to levy the fines. They made distress of the said Harrison's household goods of about £40 value, taking all they could find, not leaving so much as a skillet to boil the children's milk in. . . . But before they proceeded to any farther seizure, an appeal was entered on his behalf to the Quarter Sessions, where the conviction was adjudged illegal, for they had made two offences of once preaching. But though the conviction was set aside, yet he could not obtain the restitution of his goods. . . .
>
> On the 9th of November, as James Harrison was preaching at a meeting in his own house, the constables came and pluckt him away. They caused him to be fined, and by a warrant . . . made a seizure of leather and other goods to the value of £10 19s. Phineas Pemberton, for himself and wife being at the said meeting, had goods taken from him to the value of £4 15s 4d. In order to convict the persons met at Bolton, the justices, informers and witnesses, with the attendants, ate and drank in one afternoon as much as cost 50s which the constable engaged to pay for. Thomas Russel, an under-bailiff, was so drunk, that he was found in the street wallowing in his vomit about three in the morning, and some time after died suddenly.[280]

---

[280] Besse, *Sufferings of the People Called Quakers*, 1:323–24.

England 1350–1682

At some point, the Harrison and Pemberton families decided they had suffered enough in England and could better entrust their futures to Penn's holy experiment in the wilderness of Pennsylvania. They could also hope to have a bond with the proprietor and governor of the province who, in his August 1681 letter to James Harrison, had addressed him: "Dear J. Harrison: In the fellowship of the Gospel of love, life, and peace, which God our Father that has brought with Jesus from the dead, do I tenderly salute thee, owning thy love and kindness to me." The letter warmly concluded with "and in the love and fellowship of the Truth, I end Thy friend and brother, Wm Penn." Harrison and Pemberton, being resolved to go to America, made their arrangements to depart England and did so on September 5, 1682, aboard the *Submission*, sailing from Liverpool (Lancashire). Their party included Harrison, his wife, his mother, his daughter Phoebe and her husband Phineas Pemberton and their children, Phineas's father, a housekeeper, and a young lad who was under James's care. Their intended destination was near the Falls of the Delaware River, in present-day Bucks County, Pennsylvania.

Meanwhile, Penn had sailed just days before, on August 30, from Deal (Kent) aboard the *Welcome*. The final months before his departure were marked by a crush of business details, which included planning for the settlement and economic vitality of the new colony, resolving boundary questions with the adjacent northern and southern provincial proprietors, and establishing peaceful and honest relations with the native peoples. During this time, Penn chose to rewrite *No Cross, No Crown*, transforming his pamphlet of 1669 into the classic 592-page book that had three printings in 1682 and "has been kept in print ever since."[281]

These final months were also marked by crises in Penn's private life. He had hoped through the proprietorship of Pennsylvania to find financial relief from the growing debt he was incurring due to the costs of maintaining his family and estates—and now of planting a colony in the New World—that were not matched with sufficient rental income. On the eve of his departure, he learned that his indebtedness to his agent Philip Ford was much greater than previously known and that it needed

---

[281] *PWP*, 2:289.

to be secured before Penn's departure. The mortgage and bond he gave would be harshly reckoned with years later.

Penn was also beset with cares and losses in his personal life at this time. His mother, Lady Margaret Penn, died around March 1 that year. When he sailed, Guli's mother, Mary Penington, was nearing death. With her daughter caring for her, she died several weeks after Penn had started across the Atlantic. The greatest void was created when it was decided that Guli, who was never of robust health and was again pregnant, needed to remain at home in Warminghurst with Springett, Letitia, and William Jr. What might have been a relocation to Pennsylvania for Penn and his family became for him an abbreviated visit only. (In fact, Guli and Springett never set foot in Pennsylvania.) And once more death visited the Penns. In a letter to Penn dated August 21, 1683, Guli wrote: "it pleased the Lord to take away my little one when it was about 3 weeks old. It was a mighty great child and it was near dead when it was born, which I think it never got over."[282] The infant girl, the Penns' seventh child, was born in early March 1683. Her name and dates are not known. During one of the three weeks of the child's life, Guli had house guests: George Fox; Philip Ford's wife, Bridget; and James and Helena Claypoole, a Quaker couple. In her letter to Margaret, Guli had written: "Dear G[eorge] F[ox] came a purpose to see me, which I took very kindly and was truly refreshed in his company."[283]

In Penn's final days at home, he had written a lengthy letter of tender love to Guli and his children, which included the following passages:

> My dear wife, remember thou was the love of my youth, and much the joy of my life, the most beloved, as well as most worthy, of all my earthly comforts. And the reason of that love was more thy inward than thy outward excellences (which yet were many). God knows, and thou knows it. I can say it was a match of providence's making, and God's image in us both was the first thing and the most amiable and engaging ornament in our eyes. Now I am to leave thee, and that without knowing whether I shall ever see thee more in this world. Take my

---

[282] Gulielma Maria Penn to Margaret Fox, August 21, 1683, *PWP*, 2:460. See also Soderlund, *William Penn*, 324.

[283] Gulielma Maria Penn to Margaret Fox, August 21, 1683, *PWP*, 2:460. See also Soderlund, *William Penn*, 324.

counsel into thy bosom and let it dwell with thee in my stead while thou lives. . . .

So farewell to my thrice dearly beloved wife and children. Yours, as God pleases, in that which no waters can quench, no time forget, nor distance wear away, but remains forever,

William Penn[284]

---

[284] *PWP*, 2:270, 275; Soderlund, *William Penn*, 165, 170.

Southeastern Pennsylvania in the Period of William Penn and James Logan

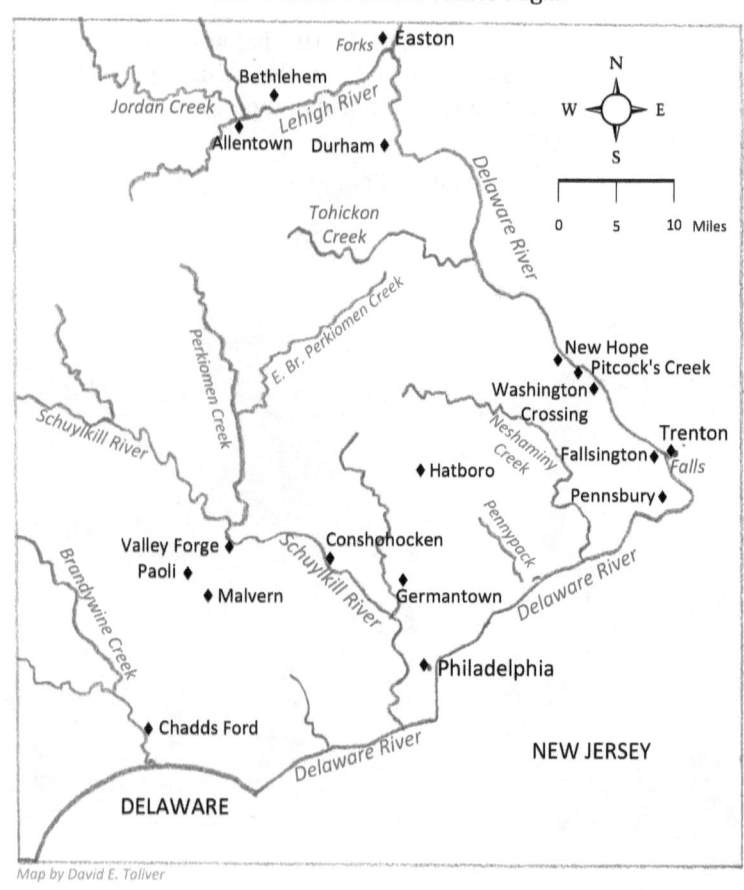

Map by David E. Toliver

CHAPTER 2

PLANTING PENNSYLVANIA (1682–1718): WILLIAM PENN'S GOVERNANCE OF "MY COUNTRY"

Penn comes into his province for the first of two periods (1682–1684); Harrison and Pemberton settle their new lives

When Penn arrived as one of his new colony's first English settlers on October 28, 1682, separated from his beloved wife and children at home in England and now beyond the seas he had spent two months crossing, he found himself coming into a land that was unknown to him. He arrived not only as one of the Delaware Valley's first English settlers but as its sole proprietor and governor. He had known of this region intellectually, having written promotional sales literature for West Jersey and his own plantation of Pennsylvania. But this merely intellectual understanding could not prepare him for the challenges and problems lying ahead.

To order a quiet and peaceable plantation

Before leaving the *Welcome* at New Castle, Penn called aboard the commissioners stationed there by the governor of New York who, under James, Duke of York, had authority over this colony of Delaware so critically situated on the west side of the lower Delaware River and on the western shore of Delaware Bay, south of its opening onto the Atlantic Ocean and extending even farther down the seacoast for several miles. The first Europeans to enter the Delaware area were Dutch traders, who came about 1615. Subsequently, the Dutch attempted to plant, and the Lenapes soon uprooted, an agricultural settlement in 1631, one year before Charles I's patent for Maryland was granted to Lord Baltimore. By the time of Penn's arrival, Swedish, Finnish, and English as well as Dutch settlers were living in the Delaware colony. Because of the critical need to provide free access to the sea for his plantation in Pennsylvania, Penn had worked for more than a year in England to secure his legal position in these Delaware waters. He began receiving the fruits of his labors only shortly before his departure for America. On August 24, "the Most Illustrious Prince His Royal Highness James Duke of York and Albany Earl of Ulster &c." executed four instruments conveying his interests in the Delaware colony and its sea access to Penn. He conveyed two deeds of title—one for New Castle and the Twelve Mile Circle area and the other for the area south of it—and also two leases for ten thousand years, one each for the same areas, possibly given in case the duke's right to convey land granted him in 1664 by Charles II was disputed. Such a dispute was certain to be raised by Lord Baltimore, who claimed that the area was included within the boundaries described in the Maryland charter of 1632 even though that charter excluded lands occupied by Europeans.[1]

When the commissioners were received aboard the *Welcome*, Penn presented the two deeds for their examination. The report written years later by John Moll, "being then left the first in commission by Sir Edmund Andros governor general under his Royal Highness James Duke of York,"[2] recited that the commissioners, after a period of study, had unanimously agreed to comply with the duke's orders and "did give and surrender in the name of his Royal Highness . . . actual and peaceable possession of the fort at New Castle" by giving Penn the key to the fort, some turf with a twig in it, and a small bowl of river water. A few days later, the ritual was repeated farther south to symbolize the conveyance to Penn of the two lower counties of Kent and Sussex as well.[3] The response in the colony to these conveyances was so positive that in early December, when the Pennsylvania Assembly held its first meeting at Chester, freeholders of the three lower counties comprising Delaware petitioned for an act of union and "their incorporation in and with the province of Pennsylvania in order to their enjoyment of all the rights and privileges of the aforesaid province and that

---

[1] *PWP*, 2:281–84.

[2] *PWP*, 2:305–6. Andros served James as governor of New York from 1674 to 1681; Moll was also named by James in the two Delaware deeds as one of two attorneys-in-fact, each of whom was empowered to deliver "quiet and peaceable possession" to Penn.

[3] Penn renamed the existing two southernmost lower counties in 1682, giving them the same names as the two southeasternmost English counties, Kent and Sussex. See *PWP*, 2:310nn2, 3.

they might be forever after esteemed and accounted as free men of the before named province."[4] Penn and the assembly granted the petition.[5]

Before leaving England, Penn had also worked to acquire the eastern shores of the lower Delaware River and of the Delaware Bay down to the Atlantic. This was completed in September by the purchase, made through the agency of his attorney in London, of the Salem Colony in West Jersey.[6] Penn took possession in December,[7] thereby securing for Pennsylvania the right of unhindered passage to and from the Atlantic over the waters of the Delaware River and Bay.

Penn reached his province of Pennsylvania shortly after going ashore at New Castle in late October. In those first days of actually planting the community—determining and bounding the first counties, which were Chester, Philadelphia, and Bucks; ordering the administration of all governments and choosing their administrators; selecting the site for Philadelphia, the provincial capital, and planning its construction; allotting land to and meeting the concerns of the first purchasers of Pennsylvania—the tasks already begun in England would now seem myriad and the time for execution all too finite. Penn began with some able assistance but had to make quick decisions as he recruited more counselors and entrusted his enterprise to others, many of whom, other than being Friends, were strangers to him. He gave one of the earliest commissions to his cousin William Markham (ca. 1635–1704), whom Penn appointed (even though he was not a Quaker) his deputy governor in April 1681, a month after receiving the charter. Markham had left England for New York, where the acting governor there gave him a proclamation ordering the people of Pennsylvania to transfer their allegiance to Penn. Penn soon proceeded from New Castle to Chester, arriving by August 3.[8] As directed, Markham had selected a provincial council of nine members over which he presided, and this council undertook the initial work of determining

---

[4] *PWP*, 2:318–20.

[5] *PWP*, 2:300.

[6] *PWP*, 2:300–302. To remove any doubt as to his title, in March 1683 Penn purchased from John Fenwick, his predecessor in title, whatever remaining interest or claims he might have. See *PWP*, 2:355–57.

[7] *PWP*, 2:316–18.

[8] *PWP*, 2:85–87.

boundaries with neighboring provinces, surveying, creating courts and appointing lesser officials, and enacting ordinances for preserving peace and safety.[9]

Penn gave another commission of critical importance one year later, in April 1682, to Thomas Holme (1624–1695), a Friend and first purchaser. Holme became surveyor general of Pennsylvania, in which office Penn confirmed him for life in 1688. Holme's achievement over the years is attested in his plan of Philadelphia and map of Pennsylvania.[10]

Although Penn did not leave a journal of his time during these early months in America, some of his activities can be reconstructed from other sources. On November 21, 1682, he was in New York, "where I last night persuaded all parties to let fall their animosities, which they promised," according to his letter of that date to the secretary of the Lords of Trade and to a clerk of the Privy Council in London.[11] (The parties referred to were local officials in the Duke of York's government; Penn was undoubtedly serving the interests of his friend the duke as well as introducing himself on a neighborly political visit.)

From December 4 to 7, he was known to be engaged at Upland (which Penn about this time renamed Chester),[12] meeting with the duly elected representatives of the General Assembly of the province of Pennsylvania along with representatives of the adjacent lower counties of Delaware,[13] recently purchased by Penn from the Duke of York. There he met a major disappointment: the refusal of the Assembly to ratify his Frame of the Government (his draft constitution for Pennsylvania) without modifications. He had noted a concern over the possibility of just such interference or obstruction in his preface to the Frame, issued the previous April in England, writing that it was

> uneasie to me to think of publishing the ensuing *Frame* and *Conditional Laws*, foreseeing, both the censures

---

[9] Markham served as deputy governor until Penn's arrival in Pennsylvania in late 1682. Thereafter, he served as provincial secretary 1685–1691 and as deputy governor of the lower counties (Delaware) 1691–1699 and of Pennsylvania 1693–1699. See *PWP*, 2:86n2.

[10] For the plan, see *A Portraiture of the City of Philadelphia*, *PWP*, 2:515; for the map, see *A Map of the Improved Part of Pennsilvania*, *PWP*, 3:644–49.

[11] *PWP*, 2:311–12.

[12] *PWP*, 2:121–22n5.

[13] *PWP*, 2:309–11.

they will meet from men of differing humors and engagements, and the occasion they may give of discourse beyond my design.¹⁴

It would not be until April 2, 1683, that the changes were agreed upon and the second Frame of the Government became Pennsylvania's first working constitution.¹⁵

The Assembly also dealt Penn a major defeat by refusing to confirm the charter for the Free Society of Traders in Pennsylvania, which he had granted March 24, 1682. This was an enterprise intended to promote and exploit the province's economic potential and resources and to build its markets. Quaker merchants in England invested in this corporation of venture capitalists and received from Penn the use of twenty thousand acres known as the Manor of Frank, along with certain rights, including that of holding their own independent court. This was an anachronistic echo of feudal times. But the Assembly would not then, or ever, confirm the charter, and the project eventually collapsed.¹⁶

Between December 11 and 13, Penn met with Charles Calvert (1637–1715), the third Lord Baltimore, in an attempt to resolve the newly discovered problem of determining the border between Maryland and Pennsylvania.¹⁷ This was but the beginning of his search for a solution to this vexing issue that would, in its course, compel Penn to make his first return to England, disturb his colonists in Pennsylvania and Delaware for decades, and keep land titles in a state of uncertainty until almost the eve of the Revolutionary War, when the Mason-Dixon survey settled the matter.

Harrison and Pemberton take up their duties

Meanwhile, the Harrison and Pemberton families were facing their own challenges as they crossed the Atlantic to the New World, arriving not in the province of Pennsylvania on or near the Delaware River as intended but in Lord Baltimore's

---

[14] *PWP*, 2:214.

[15] *PWP*, 2:226n11, 362–67. For the text, see 265–73.

[16] *PWP*, 2:246–56. See Gary B. Nash, "The Free Society of Traders and the Early Politics of Pennsylvania," *PMHB*, 89 (1965): 147–73.

[17] See *PWP*, 2:37n2, 258, 381–82. See also Hazel S. Garrison, "Cartography of Pennsylvania before 1800," *PMHB*, 59:259–63.

Maryland, at Choptank on the Eastern Shore of Chesapeake Bay. The voyage had begun on September 5; it ended on October 30. In his log, the captain of their ship, the *Submission* out of Liverpool, noted the three days when the vessel was becalmed, some days of "very cold" and some of "extraordinary hot" weather, as well as two great storms, one of which caused considerable damage to the lifeboat, main hatches, and rudder. The travelers experienced the joys of whale and porpoise sightings and the grief over the death on the day of the most punishing storm of a ten-year-old boy, a passenger, who died for reasons not given.[18] Most inexplicable was the failure of the captain to record in the log the last nine days of the crossing, leading one commentator to observe:

> As Captain Settle was bound for another port, and the weather being overcast, it is highly probable that upon the twenty-first day of the seventh month [October is intended here] he did not know where he was, and therefore did not complete the log.[19]

The Pembertons later attributed the great inconvenience of being put ashore in Maryland rather than in Pennsylvania to the captain's "dishonesty," inasmuch as he had been paid £4.5s for each of them (except for two children who were each charged half fares), as well as 30s per ton for their possessions, to take them to "Delaware River, or elsewhere in Pennsylvania, to the best conveniency of freighters."[20] The entire Harrison-Pemberton party consisted of thirteen souls: James Harrison; Ann, his wife; Agnes, his mother; the Harrisons' servants Alice Dickerson and Jane Lyon; Robert Bond, Harrison's ward; Phoebe Pemberton, the Harrisons' daughter; Phineas Pemberton, Phoebe's husband, with their children Abigail and Joseph; Ralph Pemberton, Phineas's father; and the Pembertons' servants Joseph Mather and Elizabeth Bradley.[21]

---

[18] L. Taylor Dickson, "The Sailing of the Ship 'Submission' in the Year 1682, with a True Copy of the Vessel's Log," *Publications of the Genealogical Society of Pennsylvania* 1, no. 1 (1895): 7–13.

[19] Ibid., 7.

[20] Pemberton, "The Annals of the Pemberton Family," 7:26.

[21] See "A Partial List of the Families Who Resided in Bucks County, Pennsylvania, Prior to 1687, with the Date of Their Arrival," *PMHB*, 9:230–31. It is noted in the abstract that each servant was to serve four years and to have fifty acres of land, "being the Governor's allowance." Also noted was the arrival of the Pembertons' two other servants aboard the *Friend's Adventure*, which arrived September 28 that year.

Harrison and Pemberton arranged for the care of the others in their party with the local community of Friends that had been forming since the 1650s and had been visited by George Fox in 1672 and 1673. They then proceeded overland to their original destination, the Falls of the Delaware River above the future site of Philadelphia in what would become Bucks County. On the way, they stopped in New Castle to confer with Penn, only to find that he had left, some said for New York. Next, stopping in the "wilderness" of what then was Philadelphia, their horses disappeared for some days, compelling them to finish the journey up the Delaware by boat.[22]

Upon their arrival at the Falls, Harrison and Pemberton were reunited with Harrison's brother-in-law, William Yardley, who had preceded them by several weeks and was already constructing his home. Harrison and Pemberton each chose a site for their new family estates. Pemberton's selection was noted in the Pemberton family annals, although not in Penn's land records:

> Near the same spot, on the banks of the Delaware, opposite to Oreclan's island, Phineas determined to settle, and purchased a tract of three hundred acres of land, which he named 'Grove Place.'[23]

Harrison, a first purchaser by his April 1682 investment in five thousand acres in Bucks County (entitling him also to a lot in Philadelphia),[24] chose property "on the main river called Sepasse."[25] Penn refers to this in his own last will and testament of August 1684, made before his return to England, but "The Annals of the Pemberton Family" are silent on this estate.[26]

Having resolved where their families would reside, Harrison and Pemberton set out to rejoin their families in Maryland. Public duty, however, intervened, and Harrison went to Upland

---

[22] Ibid.

[23] Pemberton, "The Annals of the Pemberton Family," 27. The island name Oreclan probably derives from Oreckton (Aurickton), a Native American who sold land at the Falls several times beginning in 1675 (see *PWP*, 2:266n5). In a deed executed July 15, 1682, Oreckton conveyed to Penn, "Chief Proprietor of the Province of Pennsylvania," Oreckton's island (*PWP*, 2:261–69). This island in the Delaware near Trenton is now known as Biles Island.

[24] *PWP*, 2:645.

[25] Sepassinck, near the Falls of the Delaware.

[26] *PWP*, 2:585.

(Chester) for the first meeting of the provincial General Assembly, held December 4–7. The official records are incomplete for this session,[27] but the Pemberton Annals state that Harrison was chosen a member of the Assembly (which seems likely) and "speaker of the house of Provincial representatives" (which does not).[28] By April or May 1683, the two families at last completed their move to Pennsylvania.[29] Even then, the Pembertons were guests in the home of Lyonel Britain until their own house at Grove Place was built.[30]

On May 2, 1683, these newly arrived Friends joined with others of their religious society already residing in the Falls area in organizing a monthly meeting and made this minute of their formal decision:

> At a meeting at William Biles's house, the second day of the third month [May], 1683, then held to wait upon the Lord for his wisdom, to hear what should be offered, in order to inspect into the affairs of the church, that all things may be kept therein sweet and savory to the Lord, and, by our care over the church, helpful in the work of God; and we whose names are as follows, being then present, thought it fit and necessary that a Monthly Meeting should be set up, both men and women, for that purpose; and that this meeting to be the first of the men's meetings after our arrival into these parts. The Friends present, —
>
> William Yardley, James Harrison, Phineas Pemberton, William Biles, William Dark, Lyonell Brittanie, William Beaks.[31]

Also in 1683, Pemberton—aged thirty-three years and with experience as a grocer in Bolton (Lancashire)—began receiving requests to enter public service. The first came from Penn's provincial register-general, Christopher Taylor (d. 1686), who appointed Pemberton to be his deputy as register for Bucks County. The provincial enrollment office or registry, as described in the proprietor's Laws Agreed upon in England, was charged

---

[27] Soderlund, *William Penn*, 192.

[28] Pemberton, "The Annals of the Pemberton Family," 27.

[29] Ibid., 28; "A Partial List," 230.

[30] Pemberton, "The Annals of the Pemberton Family," 28.

[31] William Wade Hinshaw, *Encyclopedia of American Quaker Genealogy*, 6 vols. (Ann Arbor, MI: Edwards Bros., 1936–1950), 2:951.

with registering all forms of land conveyances, whether executed within or outside the province; all promissory instruments "above five pounds and not under three months"; and the "names, time, wages, and days of payment" for all servants.[32] That same year Penn appointed Pemberton as "clerk of the court"[33] in Bucks County. The Laws Agreed upon in England also mandated a separate enrollment, "distinct from the other registry," for "births, marriages, burials, wills, and letters of administration,"[34] and in 1684 Pemberton was appointed by Taylor as the register of wills for Bucks County. On February 20 that same year, Phineas's son Israel (1685–1754) was born.

In these first appointments to new offices in a new government in a new province, a major challenge would have been to devise and put in place the filing systems and registry books necessary to effect the orderly function of the office. Pemberton's initial success was attested by his later commissions as the deputy master of the rolls (1686), receiver of proprietary quitrents (1689), registrar general (1691), and master of the rolls (1696), all in Bucks County.[35]

In 1683, between March 10 and April 4, James Harrison was fully engaged at Philadelphia with the Provincial Council in its proceedings with the General Assembly to resolve their differences over the organic law of the province. The first Frame of the Government had been written by Penn and then signed solely by him in London on April 25, 1682. However, the General Assembly at its first meeting the following December at Chester had declined to approve it without major changes. At the March–April 1683 meeting in Philadelphia, meant to resolve the disagreements, Penn, as proprietor and governor, presided over the Council, of which Harrison was now one of its sixteen elected members.[36] The most significant changes made in the Frame were to enlarge its extent beyond the province of Pennsylvania to the three lower counties on the Delaware (called "the territories thereunto annexed") and to reduce the size of the Council from

---

[32] Laws XX and XXIII, *PWP*, 2:223.

[33] Brown, *Early settlement of Friends at Falls*, 79; Pemberton, "The Annals of the Pemberton Family," 28.

[34] Law XXII, *PWP*, 2:223.

[35] Brown, *Early Settlement of Friends at Falls*, 79.

[36] For the minutes of both the council and assembly, see Soderlund, *William Penn*, 226–65.

seventy-two to eighteen members and of the Assembly from two hundred to thirty-six, the membership to be proportionately increased with population growth up to the limits of seventy-two in the Council and two hundred in the Assembly. But not until 1701 would Penn concede the right of the Assembly to initiate legislation. In all these proceedings and negotiations, Harrison took an active part—serving on Council committees; conveying the position of the Council to the Assembly; conferring with the Assembly on behalf of the Council; and with four other Councilors preparing, "by 8 of the clock tomorrow morning,"[37] the second Frame of the Government of the Province of Pennsylvania in America (also referred to internally as "this present Charter of Liberties").[38] Penn, twelve members of the Council (including Harrison), the governor's secretary, and the Council's clerk, twenty-one members of the Assembly and its clerk, and four "inhabitants of Philadelphia present" signed, on April 2, 1683, the governing document for the province and "the territories thereunto annexed."

Appointing agents to manage the proprietor's affairs in Pennsylvania as Penn prepares for an early return to England

During the long weeks spent guiding the second Frame to completion and final adoption, Penn had the opportunity to closely observe the talents of his associates, talents he would need to draw on for assistance in the many challenges lying ahead. He soon commissioned Harrison—aged fifty-five years and experienced as a shoemaker and shopkeeper in Bolton (Lancashire)—to serve with various other Council members on three missions, all concerned with Penn's two persistent southern boundary problems with Lord Baltimore: (1) whether or not Lord Baltimore's 1632 patent included the lower counties of Delaware and (2) the location of the 40th degree of latitude. Years after these issues were finally resolved, historian Walter B. Scaife described these two disputes:

> One of the most important points of Pennsylvania colonial history, and the one perhaps least generally understood, is that of the true grounds of the dispute between the Penns and the Lords Baltimore in regard to

---

[37] Ibid., 256.

[38] For the text of the second Frame of the Government, see ibid., 265–73.

their respective boundaries. This notable quarrel continued more than eighty years; was the cause of endless trouble between individuals; occupied the attention not only of the proprietors of the respective provinces, but of the Lords of Trade and Plantations, of the High Court of Chancery, and of the Privy Councils of at least three monarchs; it greatly retarded the settlement and development of a beautiful and fertile country, and brought about numerous tumults which sometimes ended in bloodshed. The ultimate cause of the difficulty is to be found in the lack of exact information on the part of Europeans generally in respect to the topography of America, and the reckless extravagance of European monarchs in parcelling out a continent to their subjects. Immediate survey and complete possession of these immense tracts were alike impossible, so that the fixing of definite, certainly known boundary-lines was impracticable. The consequence was that the grants of different monarchs often conveyed a paper title to the same region, while the same sovereign not unfrequently granted to a later favorite a part of a former gift. The practical result was that possession gave title, which title, however, had sometimes to yield to the power of might over right.[39]

The first commission involving Harrison with the Penn-Baltimore boundary issues was issued June 11, 1683, after a rumor originating in West Jersey had distressed Penn's land sales in England with word that Lord Baltimore had claimed the Delaware River, as Penn put it, "from Upland to the Falls of Delaware . . . I had no place where ship or boat could come."[40] On that date, Penn wrote a formal protest letter to his friends and allies (and sometime political associates) the governor and Council of West Jersey, describing the "Provincial Wrong" done him and demanding redress. In a simultaneous letter of instructions to his commissioners—Harrison and his fellow councilors Christopher Taylor and Thomas Holme together with Thomas Wynne, speaker of the Assembly—Penn instructed them

---

[39] Walter B. Scaife, "The Boundary Dispute between Maryland and Pennsylvania," *PMHB*, 9:241–42.

[40] William Penn to the governor and council of West Jersey, June 11, 1683, *PWP*, 2:391.

to deliver his protest letter, present the evidence of the charge, obtain satisfaction, and "insist upon my title to the river, soil, and islands" of the Delaware.[41]

On July 1, Harrison was again commissioned by Penn, along with fellow councilors William Markham and William Clarke. This time they were charged to deliver to Lord Baltimore in person Penn's protest over Baltimore's May 15 proclamation setting new and lower rates for those taking up land in the lower Delaware counties of Kent and Sussex.[42]

Then in March 1684, after Lord Baltimore had directed George Talbot, his cousin who was also a member of the Maryland Council, to claim for him the area south of the 40th degree of latitude and to build a fort near Christiana Creek in central New Castle County, Penn signed a commission to Harrison and his fellow councilors John Simcock, William Welch, and John Cann, instructing them to proceed to the lower counties; contact and, if necessary, apprehend several of their colleagues there resident who had failed to attend recent Pennsylvania Council meetings; assess the extent to which Baltimore's emissaries did "seduce the people from their obedience" to Penn; dismiss unfaithful magistrates and appoint new ones who were more trustworthy; and generally settle the tumult and bring the disaffection to an end.[43]

What the meetings between Penn and Lord Baltimore on December 6, 1682, and May 29, 1683, could not accomplish, neither could the three embassies—Harrison being their one constant member—sent out by Penn. By April 1684, Lord Baltimore had determined that his redress lay in England, and in May he sailed for London to resolve the matter.[44] Penn followed him in August to protect his own interests at the seat of power.[45]

Despite the ongoing distractions of the controversies concerning Maryland, Penn addressed many other concerns at this time, including the advancement in America of the Religious Society of Friends. At the yearly meeting of Quakers for the provinces of West and East Jersey held in Burlington in September 1683, it was judged "requisite for the benefit and advantage of Truth that a General Yearly Meeting might be

---

[41] *PWP*, 2:391, 393.
[42] *PWP*, 2: 400–404, 410–11.
[43] *PWP*, 2:543–45.
[44] *PWP*, 2:554, 556.
[45] *PWP*, 2:581–82.

established in these parts," covering New England to Carolina.[46] Penn and Harrison with Christopher Taylor from Pennsylvania and three Friends from West Jersey, all known to Penn, were appointed to write and speak to Quakers in the other American provinces in furtherance of this ambitious plan and to report on these matters to the yearly meeting of Friends in England. Although the Burlington Yearly Meeting minutes do not name the attendees, a fair assumption can be made that Penn, the former trustee of West Jersey and now an owner of certain proprietary (governing) rights in both West and East Jersey as well as the owner of property in West Jersey, was present at the meeting, along with Harrison and Taylor. The establishment of a continental general meeting or synod of Friends would be a vision worthy of Penn, as would his corresponding hope that it would, in time, become a sister institution to London Yearly Meeting.

In the meantime, Penn was settling his personal affairs in the province and by July 1683 had acquired his own manorial seat on the Delaware River in Bucks County, which he named Pennsbury. His near neighbors were Pemberton and Harrison, and in February 1684 the latter wrote Penn concerning several injurious trespasses on the fields and buildings at Pennsbury being made by the person who had sold the property to Penn. Harrison even refers in his letter to damage in Penn's fields where Harrison, presumably with Penn's permission, had sown "some thousands, wheat clover, and other seeds."[47]

As Penn began preparations for his return to England in search of a royal resolution of the boundary controversies with Lord Baltimore, his foremost concerns were to select worthy stewards for the daily administration of his province and to settle his personal affairs. In these concerns, Penn entrusted Harrison with significant responsibilities. Penn wrote to Harrison in July 1684 asking that he and his wife "shouldest be the Steward of my household to oversee servants, building, and what relates to the place where I live."[48] Harrison accepted and was commissioned steward of Pennsbury by Penn on the eve of Penn's departure aboard the *Endeavour*. In the administration of provincial matters, Penn appointed as the commissioners of estate and

---

[46] *PWP*, 2:480–81.
[47] *PWP*, 2:524–26.
[48] *PWP*, 2:568–69.

revenue, charged with collecting his proprietary revenues, Harrison (who continued on the Provincial Council); Thomas Holme (the surveyor general); Robert Turner (the registrar general, provincial treasurer, as well as a supreme court justice); Samuel Carpenter (a rising merchant trader also holding public office); and Philip Lehnmann (Penn's secretary).[49]

Then on August 6, Harrison, Holme, Thomas Lloyd (newly appointed president of the Provincial Council), and William Clarke (an attorney and justice in the lower counties) witnessed Penn's execution of his last will and testament, which concluded with his prayer:

> The Lord bless my dear family and keep them and the people of this province and territories in his fear, that in love and concord they may live together while the sun and moon endureth. Amen. Amen.[50]

Finally, on August 7, Penn, "not knowing how it may please almighty God to deal with me in this voyage and of how great moment it is that the administration of the government be carefully provided for in case of my decease," executed a declaration appointing Thomas Lloyd, James Harrison, and John Simcock, in that order, to be, successively, the individual "commissioners and guardians in government to my dear heir Springett Penn" during his minority or, in case of his early death, then to Penn's next successive heir.[51] On August 18, Penn sailed from Lewes, on the Delaware below Philadelphia, aboard the *Endeavour* bound for Worthing (Sussex) near the South Downs of England. He had been in America almost one year and ten months.

Penn returns to England (1684–1699) but meets new major challenges

When Penn, the proprietor and governor of the province of Pennsylvania as well as one of the preeminent leaders in the Quaker world, departed for England, both Pennsylvania's head of state and leading Friend were gone—but neither its government nor its ongoing life had left. What had been virtually unified in

---

[49] *PWP*, 2:581; also see the Instructions to the Commissioners, *Microfilm*, 4:018.

[50] *PWP*, 2:585–87.

[51] *PWP*, 2:588–89.

his person now became divided into three parts: the church and the state, which remained in the province, and the founder, now in England, who tried the best he could to deal with leadership issues as they arose in Pennsylvania. Penn had intended his absence from the province—and his restricted ability to direct its administration and be its leading citizen—to be brief. It turned out otherwise.

Before 1685 was over, there began a seemingly unending succession of unfortunate and untimely events: Penn's arrest in London for public preaching; months of delay arising from the mishap of leaving behind in Pennsylvania the documents necessary to prove his case for establishing the boundary he sought with Maryland; and the death in February 1685 of Charles II and the accession of the Duke of York to the throne of England as James II. James was Penn's good friend, and now this friend and patron had need of the proprietor's time and talents. Although the Privy Council did resolve the boundary dispute with Lord Baltimore in Penn's favor thirteen months after his arrival in England, Penn stayed away from his province for a full fifteen years. Governing Pennsylvania from afar was not a success.

At the Stuart court prior to the Glorious Revolution

Penn was reunited with Gulielma and their children in early October, and later in the month he met with Charles II, who was in failing health, and the Duke of York.[52] In November Penn, an advocate of freedom of religion and liberty of conscience, was arrested and fined £20 for preaching at a meeting of Friends in Westminster.[53] After the king's death and James's accession to the throne, in February Penn was still waiting for his files in order to proceed with his case against Lord Baltimore. As he had in the past, he used the waiting time to write pamphlets and other pieces that were mostly concerned with the polemical controversies of the day, Penn himself sometimes being the issue. James II, a Roman Catholic, at his accession had a concern that toleration be extended to all dissenters, including Catholics and Quakers, and the polemics against him brought his friend Penn under suspicion as a 'Jesuit in disguise.' Penn responded

---

[52] *PWP*, 2:607n10.
[53] *PWP*, 3:26.

with, first, a broadsheet, followed by three pamphlets on religious toleration.[54] Then in December, following the decision by the Privy Council the previous month in Penn's favor resolving the Maryland boundary dispute, the proprietor wrote another pamphlet,[55] this one promoting settlement in the province. In it, Penn advised prospective land purchasers that the Lords of Trade had rejected Lord Baltimore's claim in Delaware and that Penn intended to expand development in his province into the Susquehanna region of western Pennsylvania. He also wrote of his planned return to Pennsylvania in the summer of 1686. But once again, he was delayed in England by other concerns.

By 1686, there was rising opposition in England to James's reordering of the religious landscape through his policy of accepting Roman Catholics and other dissenters into the national life. He evidenced his open toleration on March 9 by granting a general pardon to Penn, "his family and servants," discharging them from all prosecution related to a vast array of punitive legal procedures recited in the preamble of the pardon, including "refusing to take the oaths of allegiance and supremacy."[56] Days later, on March 15, James granted a general pardon to the Quakers and thereafter ordered the suspension of legal proceedings against all Friends and their release from prison.[57] That summer, Penn traveled to the Netherlands and Germany to meet with Friends but also secretly conferred on James's behalf with James's son-in-law, William of Orange, at The Hague to seek support for the king's promotion of general religious toleration.[58]

On April 4, 1687, James issued his prerogative grant of toleration, the Declaration of Indulgence, which was similar to

---

[54] William Penn, *Fiction found out* [London?: n.p., 1685]; *A defence of the Duke of Buckingham's book of religion and worship, from the exceptions of a nameless author* (London: printed for A. Banks, 1685); William Penn, *Animadversions on the apology of the clamorous squire against the Duke of Buckingham's seconds, as men of no conscience* [London: 1685]; and William Penn, *A perswasive to moderation to dissenting Christians, in prudence and conscience: humbly submitted to the King and his great council* [London: Andrew Sowle, 1685]. See *PWP*, 5:311–17.

[55] William Penn, *Further Account of Pennsylvania* (London: Andrew Sowle, 1685). See *PWP*, 5:320–23.

[56] *PWP*, 3:83–84.

[57] *PWP*, 3:73, 156n11.

[58] *PWP*, 3:97–99.

that granted by Charles in 1672, "suspending the Test Acts and all the penal laws against Protestant Dissenters as well as Catholics."[59] Parliament never gave its approval. The hoped-for support from William of Orange, a champion of the Protestant cause, never appeared. But Penn, being grateful, loyal, and a longtime champion of the precious liberty of religious toleration, obtained from London Yearly Meeting its address to the king, adopted on May 19, expressing its gratitude to God "that he hath inclined the King to hear the cries of his suffering subjects for conscience sake." Penn delivered the address along with his own speech to the king on May 24 and heard the king's answer:[60]

> There are some here present, and I am sure you Mr. Penn have heard me say, that it was always my principle that conscience ought not to be forced, and it was always my judgment men ought to have the liberty of their consciences, and as I have promised it in my declaration, I am resolved it shall continue as long as I live, and before I die I hope to settle it so, that it shall not be in the power of after ages to alter it.[61]

James stayed his course and in late summer that year made a royal progress, accompanied by William Penn, through nine counties of central England,[62] promoting his policy of toleration and the repeal of punitive laws against nonconformists. But, increasingly, king and people were becoming estranged from each other. In that struggle, Penn, ever firmly the king's friend and supporter, brought into print in June the same year his book supporting the royal policy of religious toleration: *Good Advice to the Church of England, Roman Catholic, and Protestant Dissenter, in which it is endeavoured to be made appear that it is their duty, principles and interest to abolish the penal laws and tests.*[63]

That same summer, James's first son was born, thereby making likely the succession to the throne of another Roman

---

[59] J. P. Kenyon, *Stuart England*, 2nd ed. (London: Penguin Books, 1985), 252. In April 1688, James reissued the declaration. Ibid., 258.

[60] *PWP*, 3:154-57.

[61] *PWP*, 3:156.

[62] This is referred to in a letter from William Penn to James Harrison dated September 8, 1687, *PWP*, 3:163.

[63] This was published in 1687 in London by Andrew Sowle. See *PWP*, 5:347-52.

Catholic instead of James's Protestant daughter, Mary, the wife of William of Orange. Fears of resurgent Catholicism in England were widespread, and gossip even circulated that Penn was a Jesuit, ordained to the priesthood in Rome but with a papal dispensation to marry, and that he held significant influence at court. When Penn received a letter from William Popple reciting these charges, he met the calumny by publishing Popple's letter together with his own refutation of the rumors.[64]

The ultimate confrontation for James was reached when William of Orange landed his army on the Devonshire coast at Brixham on November 5, 1688, and then advanced to London. William entered London on December 17, but James had already started his flight to France five days earlier (and thrown the Great Seal of England into the Thames), where he finally settled by December 22.

The Glorious Revolution had begun, and England's throne was empty. Whether the event that emptied the throne was to be deemed a forfeiture or abdication or lapse or deposition or desertion or vacancy or something else was a contentious issue for the legislative authority to resolve as it sought to find a way forward to secure the stability of the realm. Even determining what properly constituted the legislature at that moment was a problem; it was politically and constitutionally unclear whether it was the Loyal Parliament, the only one elected during the reign of James II, or its predecessor, the Oxford Parliament, the last to be elected in Charles II's reign. In the end, on the recommendation of an assembly of peers, William, who declined to take the crown by conquest, summoned a convention that began meeting on January 22, 1689. By February 14 the convention had settled the matter and by proclamation brought William III and Mary II to two thrones of England as joint monarchs.[65]

During its deliberations, the convention had also resolved that England was to be a Protestant nation and that only a Protestant could henceforth be its monarch. In addition, the

---

[64] William Penn, *A Letter to Mr. Penn: with his answer* (London: printed for Andrew Wilson, 1688). See *PWP*, 5:356–61.

[65] The recitals of the Declaration of Rights, later inscribed in the Bill of Rights, were that "King James the Second having abdicated the government and the throne being thereby vacant," the throne was given to William, the Prince of Orange, "whom it hath pleased Almighty God to make the glorious Instrument of delivering this kingdom from popery and arbitrary power." 1 W. & M. Sess. 2. c. 2, in *The Statutes of the Realm*, 6:142

convention drew up a Declaration of Rights in which it described the alleged misrule of James and declared the various rights of Parliament and of Protestant subjects. The convention, having brought the Glorious Revolution to this conclusion, declared itself a regular Parliament, lawfully constituted,[66] and it was thereafter known as the Convention Parliament.[67] On May 24 it passed the Toleration Act,[68] which allowed Quakers to declare their fidelity to the sovereigns and their rejection of foreign powers rather than swearing oaths, and also to subscribe to a profession of Christian faith. Then, on December 16, Parliament passed a Bill of Rights that restated its Declaration of Rights presented to William and Mary before they had been made the English sovereigns.[69]

The Glorious Revolution effectively committed James II to exile for the rest of his days; his abortive attempt at a return was defeated at the Battle of the Boyne in Ireland on July 1, 1690. Jacobite support for the royal pretensions of his son and grandson into the next century eventually collapsed.

The reign of Mary, James's daughter, and William, who was both James's son-in-law and nephew (William's mother was James's sister Mary), ushered in a new constitutional era in which parliamentary freedoms could no longer be subverted by royal prerogatives and claims of divine right. England began a peaceful transition into a constitutionally secured Protestantism as the nation began to accept a degree of pluralism in religious matters and a toleration for dissent previously unknown.

---

[66] "An act for removing and preventing all questions and disputes concerning the assembling and sitting of this present parliament." 1 W. & M. c. 1, in ibid., 6:23–24.

[67] When the first parliament summoned by William and Mary assembled in March 1690, it initially passed "an act for recognizing King William and Queen Mary and for avoiding all questions touching the acts made in the parliament assembled at Westminster the thirteenth day of February 1689." 2 W. & M. c. 1, in ibid., 6:15.

[68] "An act exempting their majesties Protestant subjects dissenting from the Church of England from the penalties of certain laws." 1 W. & M. c. 18, in ibid., 6:74–76.

[69] "An act declaring the rights and liberties of the subject and settling the succession of the crown." 1 W. & M. Sess. 2. c. 2, in ibid., 6:142–45.

Penn under suspicion of treason

William Penn paid a high price for his known friendship with James II. Their association now kept Penn under ongoing suspicion, with both voluntary and involuntary seclusion through November 1693. These new troubles commenced in December 1688 when Penn stood before the Privy Council, "where no order or matter appeared against me," and was required to post "an excessive bail," which was discharged the following May.[70] On February 27, 1689, a warrant was issued for his arrest on charges of treason, but no action was then taken.[71]

On June 22, 1689, a warrant was issued at Whitehall for Penn's arrest "on suspicion of high treason or treasonable practices." By June 29 he was arrested, in July he was bailed and released, on September 27 he was back in custody, on October 25 released again on bail, and on November 28 discharged.[72] The arrest charges were based on a letter from James that was intercepted en route to Penn. Penn's successful defense was that he had had no correspondence with his exiled friend, but he remained under suspicion of involvement in Jacobite plots.[73] Later that same year, he wrote *An Epistle General to the people of God called Quakers* in which he gave testimony to the Truth, exhorting the Friends and brethren in England to walk in that Truth. To vindicate himself from the recent "slanders of wicked men," he wrote:

> I acknowledge I was an instrument to break the jaws of persecution, and to that end I did take the freedom to remember [remind] King James of his frequent assurances in favor of liberty of conscience, and with much zeal used my small interest with him to gain that point upon his ministers, that he told me were against it.[74]

---

[70] William Penn to the Earl of Shrewsbury (Charles Talbot), March 7, 1689, *PWP*, 3:235–36. Talbot was made a secretary of state on the accession of William and Mary.

[71] Ibid.

[72] Warrant dated June 22, 1689, and letter from Penn to the Marquis of Halifax (George Savile) dated June 28, 1689, *PWP*, 3:251–52. Halifax had been lord president of the Privy Council under Charles II; he served until he was dismissed by James II in 1685.

[73] *PWP*, 3:663.

[74] *PWP*, 3:269.

On July 14, 1690, Queen Mary issued a proclamation for the arrest of Penn, along with eighteen others, on charges of conspiring to commit high treason. He surrendered himself at Whitehall and was denied bail, imprisoned for a month, and discharged by order of the Court of King's Bench late in November that year.[75]

Great personal loss through death now resumed its painful march through Penn's life. On January 13, 1691, George Fox died in London at the age of 67. Among his last words were: "All is well. The Seed of God reigns over all, and over death itself. And though I am weak in body, yet the power of God is over all, and the Seed reigns over all disorderly spirits."[76] On June 14 of that year, Penn, in a letter to Thomas Lloyd in Philadelphia "and the friends and family of God in those parts," described Fox's death followed by the public meeting and committal at Friends' Burial Ground near Bunhill Fields, London:

> I was with him, he earnestly recommended to me, his love to you all, and said William, mind poor friends in America. He died triumphantly over death, very easily, foresaw his change. He was buried on the sixth day [of the week] like a general meeting, 2000 people at his burial, friends and others. I was never more public than that day. I felt myself easy he was got into his inn, before the storm that is coming overtook him, and that night, very providentially as ever since, I escaped the messengers' hands.[77]

Penn had serious cause for concern about being seen in public and escaping the messengers' hands. He had been accused by Viscount Preston (Richard Graham) of being involved in an active Jacobite conspiracy to restore James to the throne, a conspiracy Preston himself participated in and for which he was found carrying letters to James from the conspirators when apprehended on January 1. Two of the letters may have been written by Penn, and for self-protection Preston named Penn a conspirator.[78] Instead of surrendering himself, Penn remained out of public sight, thus the above comments at the end of the

---

[75] Ibid., 283–84nn1, 3.
[76] Thomas Ellwood, Epilogue, in Fox, *Journal*, 760.
[77] Penn to Thomas Lloyd, June 14, 1691, *PWP*, 3:327.
[78] See *PWP*, 3:294nn2, 3, 6 and 351n14.

passage from his letter to Thomas Lloyd regarding his open visibility at George Fox's burial and "that night" having "escaped the messengers' hands." On February 5, 1691, yet another proclamation was issued for the arrest of Penn on charges involving high treason. Not until the end of 1693, however, did Penn regain his freedom, and then only because Preston refused to corroborate in court the charges brought against Penn, "forcing the government to drop the matter."[79]

The known record sheds little if any light on Penn's whereabouts during much of the period from 1690 through 1693. If the government had seriously sought his custody after the February 1691 proclamation ordering his apprehension, undoubtedly he would have been found. Following the long absence from his family during his first visit to Pennsylvania, at this time he most likely would have wanted to be either with or near Gulielma and their children, if not in the Warminghurst manor in Sussex then in another English residence suitable for his or their needs. Closeness to the family would also have been imperative because of Gulielma's failing health and apparent coming death. The government's restraint in its search for Penn may have been compassionate. And Penn, as in past retirements and seclusions, could not be idle. Thus, he turned his time and energy to authoring books and pamphlets as well as contributing to others' works, focusing his considerable intellectual skills on pressing concerns in business and church affairs.

Ever the planner, and now in greater need of income as the revenue streams from his Irish properties and American plantation had nearly dried up due to his distraction by issues more pressing than governing the province, Penn conceived the expansion of Pennsylvania into its western Susquehanna Valley and authored a broadside announcement in 1690. *Some Proposals for a Second Settlement in the Province of Pennsylvania*[80] also announced that the land would be sold until the spring of 1691, when Penn and the first purchasers would sail to America. But the Crown's proclamation in February 1691 calling for Penn's arrest halted Penn's immediate prospects for the Susquehanna project.

Penn's next writings were tributes to two of his colleagues, both leaders within the Religious Society of Friends, who had died the year before George Fox's own passing. The first was a

---

[79] *PWP*, 3:663.

[80] This was printed in London by Andrew Sowle. See *PWP*, 5:367–69.

tribute to John Burnyeat (1631–1690), one of the First Publishers of Truth and an itinerant minister out of Cumberland whose missions for Truth's sake had twice taken him to America. Penn wrote the preface to his memorial volume and also signed a testimonial with others.[81] The second was a tribute to the Scottish academic Robert Barclay (1648–1690), who not only was the leading theologian of the Quakers but also was both a developer of East Jersey along with Penn and its nonresident governor. Penn wrote the preface, testimony, and commentary for the fourteen writings of Barclay contained in the tribute.[82] Two years later, in April 1694, Penn would see into print his preface to the journal of George Fox entitled "A Brief Account of the Rise and Progress of the People Called Quakers," which was edited following Fox's death by Thomas Ellwood. As some Friends were apprehensive of Penn's reputation at that time, especially because of his loyalty to the king in exile, the preface was not included in all copies of the *Journal* but appeared instead as a separate publication. Later in 1692, Penn engaged in the polemical wars by writing several tracts before preparing a short handbook setting forth the essentials of Quaker belief entitled *A Key opening the way to every common understanding*.[83]

In the year 1693, Penn brought into print two works, one his proposal for advancing peace in Europe and the other on human solitude, two seemingly disparate concerns yet fundamentally connected through the search for both outward and inward stability. Because war had broken out in Europe and spread to theaters in northernmost America, Penn, ever an advocate of the Quaker principle of nonviolence, had concern for peace in general but particularly within his province of Pennsylvania. The conflict was known in Europe as the War of the League of Augsburg (sometimes the War of the Grand Alliance or the Nine Years' War) and in America as King William's War. It was one of the several major wars Louis XIV of France undertook to expand his territories, and it was fought against European forces led by England's William III (who was also the stadtholder of the

---

[81] John Burnyeat, *The Truth Exalted in the Writings of that eminent and faithful servant of Christ, John Burnyeat* (London: for Thomas Northcott, 1691).

[82] Robert Barclay, *Truth Triumphant through the spiritual warfare, Christian labours, and writings of that able and faithful servant of Jesus Christ, Robert Barclay* (London: for Thomas Northcott, 1692).

[83] This was printed in 1693 in London for Thomas Northcott.

United Provinces of the Netherlands), the Holy Roman Emperor, and the kings of Spain and of Savoy as well as others. Penn's peace proposal appeared in a small book, *An Essay towards the present and future peace of Europe, by the establishment of an European dyet, parliament, or estates*,[84] in which he discussed the benefits of permanent peace and proposed an international body to regulate and maintain peace in Europe.

Then, later in 1693 Penn prepared *Some Fruits of Solitude: in reflections and maxims relating to the conduct of human life*,[85] which, as stated in his preface, he "writ for private satisfaction, and now published for an help to human conduct." It is a wisdom book that offers guidance on how to live a life grounded in the virtues of patience, honesty, truth-telling, forbearance, justice, integrity, generosity, sound labor, and learning. Solitude, he noted in the preface, is "a school few care to learn in, tho' none instructs us better."

In December that year, Penn wrote to Friends in Pennsylvania that his retirement from public life had formally ended in late November when William III granted him his freedom and the Privy Council acquitted him of treason charges.[86] In his letter, he noted that on the day he obtained his release he had gone to a meeting for worship in London, "thence to visit the sanctuary of my solitude [possibly Hoddesdon, Hertfordshire] and after to see my poor wife and children, my eldest [Springett] being with me all this while. My wife is yet weakly but I am not without hopes of her recovery who is the best of wives and women."[87]

The proprietor remotely governs the state while the church grows organically

Once declared innocent of the highest crime against the state and thus freed from an involuntary retirement, Penn came under pressing need to repair his financial fortunes and see to the management of his affairs in Pennsylvania. The province had already suffered badly from his nine-year absence, an absence originally intended to last but one year and which even then was

---

[84] This was printed in 1693 in London.

[85] This was printed in 1693 in London for Thomas Northcott.

[86] See Penn's letter to Friends in Pennsylvania dated December 11, 1693, *PWP*, 3:382–85nn5, 15.

[87] *PWP*, 3:383.

to stretch on for another six. Without the founder's firm, ongoing control and vision, it had declined into factionalism among disparate ethnic, religious, political, and geographic groups. And without Penn, the provincial center could not hold.

At the time of his departure for England, Penn had set the resident executive authority of Pennsylvania in the Provincial Council under the presidency of Thomas Lloyd, trusting in the collective talent of eighteen freemen "of most note for their virtue, wisdom, and ability"[88] to "maintain and exercise government for the good of the province and territories."[89] Twenty-nine months later, on February 1, 1687, he restricted that authority to five members of the Provincial Council named as commissioners of state, any three of them to constitute a quorum: Thomas Lloyd, Nicholas More, James Claypoole, Robert Turner, and James Eccle.[90] When their factionalism doomed that plan, Penn decided to place the authority in one person and, after Lloyd declined the position, in July 1688 offered the post of deputy governor of Pennsylvania to John Blackwell, a Puritan from New England who had served in Cromwell's Army, then later in his Parliament, and most recently had been living in Boston, where he served as a magistrate.[91]

Blackwell accepted the appointment and arrived in Philadelphia in December 1688 to take up his duties. The relations between the Quaker councilors and their absent executive grew so contentious, however, that Blackwell was removed in January 1690 upon receipt of Penn's instructions in August to return the executive authority to the Provincial Council acting collectively under Thomas Lloyd, its president.[92] The arrangement Penn had made at the outset of his absence from the province was now reinstated. Earlier, it had lasted thirty-one months. On this second attempt it lasted thirteen months, until it was undone not by Penn but by the Provincial Council itself when, on April 2, 1691, it proclaimed Lloyd the deputy governor,

---

[88] The second Frame of the Government, Art. 1. Soderlund, *William Penn*, 267.

[89] Commission of Penn to President Thomas Lloyd and the Provincial Council dated August 6, 1684, *PWP*, 2:583.

[90] Instructions of Penn to commissioners of state dated February 1, 1687, *PWP*, 3:144–46.

[91] Commission of Penn to John Blackwell dated July 12, 1688, *PWP*, 3:194–95 (see also discussion on p. 183).

[92] *PWP*, 3:218, 246, 253–61.

thereby provoking the councilors from Delaware's lower counties to withdraw from their union with Pennsylvania.[93] This usurpation of the proprietor's authority was also a short-lived experiment, for on October 21, 1692, the supervening authority of William III and Mary II, seeing "great miscarriages in the government of our province of Pennsylvania, in America, and the absence of the proprietor, the fabric was fallen into disorder and confusion,"[94] asserted the sovereign power of England, Scotland, France, and Ireland to appoint the royal governor of New York, Benjamin Fletcher, "to be our Captain General, and Governor in Chief, in and over our province of Pennsylvania, and in the country of New-Castle, and all the tracts of land depending thereon in America."[95]

Fletcher, like Blackwell before him a former army officer and non-Quaker, was sure to meet opposition from Penn's adherents on the Council and elsewhere in the provincial government, especially as he set about obtaining Pennsylvania's contribution to the frontier defense needs against the French and their Native American allies around Albany and elsewhere in the province of New York during King William's War (1688–1697). But Fletcher's service was relatively brief. One year after July 1693, when the new royal governor had arrived to undertake the governing of Pennsylvania, Penn exercised his newly restored freedom and petitioned Queen Mary and the Privy Council to vacate Fletcher's commission and let Penn himself be "suffered to enjoy his said province as entirely as heretofore."[96] Fletcher's commission was revoked by order of the Queen on August 20, 1694.[97] After being reinstated in his own government, Penn commissioned another non-Friend, his cousin William Markham, to again be the deputy, or lieutenant, governor.[98]

Although the civil administration of Pennsylvania may have, in their majesties' words, "fallen into disorder and confusion; by means whereof not only the public peace, and administration of justice was broken and violated, but there was also great want of provision for the guard and defence of our said province against

---

[93] Council of the Lower Counties to Penn, April 6, 1691, *PWP*, 3:299.

[94] Proud, *History of Pennsylvania*, 1:377n.

[95] Ibid., 379.

[96] Breviate of petition to Queen Mary and the Privy Council from Penn dated ca. July 4, 1694, *PWP*, 3:395–96.

[97] Proud, *History of Pennsylvania*, 1:403; *PWP*, 3:393.

[98] Proud, *History of Pennsylvania*, 1:404.

our enemies,"[99] the administration of the planted church had endured, its system of meetings secure and functioning, Penn's absence notwithstanding. He alone had planned and ordered the state from the beginning. On the other hand, Friends, including Penn, had brought with them from England the familiar organizational structure of their religious society, and this they put in place in the Delaware Valley. Indeed, monthly and yearly meetings had already been instituted across the river in West and East Jersey and even in Pennsylvania by the time of Penn's arrival in America in 1682.

In early September 1681, the monthly meetings in the Jerseys of Burlington and Salem (to be increased by the meeting at Shrewsbury, whose transfer from the jurisdiction of the Long Island yearly meeting was requested at that time) met, together with the monthly meetings of Marcus Hook, Upland (Chester), and Falls in Penn's new province. This constituted the first meeting of Burlington Yearly Meeting.[100] As already discussed, in 1683, Penn and James Harrison attended the Burlington Yearly Meeting, where it was proposed that a general yearly meeting for Friends in all the provinces on the Atlantic seaboard between New England and Carolina be established. Penn, Harrison, and four others were instructed to communicate with these more distant American Friends for advancing the proposal and to inform and take the advice of London Yearly Meeting.[101] The minutes for the Burlington Yearly Meeting of 1684 are lost, but those of the meeting in September 1685, the first to be held in Philadelphia, record agreement that there should be one yearly meeting for Pennsylvania and West Jersey that would alternate annually between Philadelphia and Burlington as the place of gathering. That meeting also passed the first of a series of annual resolutions of concern regarding profiteering from the sale of rum to Native Americans.[102] The 1686 yearly meeting settled the

---

[99] Ibid., 403n. The quoted passage is from the first "whereas" clause of the royal grant dated August 20, 1694, restoring Penn to his government.

[100] Philadelphia Yearly Meeting of the Religious Society of Friends (Quakers), Minute Book 1681–1746, pp. 1–2, Haverford College Quaker Collection, Haverford College, Haverford, Pennsylvania (hereafter cited as PYM Min Bk B).

[101] PYM Min Bk B 4, pp. 1–2; see also *PWP*, 2:480–81.

[102] "This meeting doth unanimously agree, and give as their judgment, that it is not consistent with the honor of Truth, for any that make profession thereof, to sell rum or other strong liquors to the Indians, because they use them not to moderation, but to excess and drunkenness." Ezra Michener, *A Retrospect of Early Quakerism; being extracts from the Records of Philadelphia Yearly*

all-encompassing name of the meeting as Friends of "Pennsylvania, East and West Jerseys and of the Adjacent Provinces," and the minutes noted that Virginia and Carolina were "to attend this General Yearly Meeting."[103]

In 1687, the PYM minutes began to record the names of delegates attending the meeting and to give an occasional indication of who the presiding officer, or clerk, might be. That year, the epistle of PYM to its subordinate quarterly meetings "was signed by order of the meeting by Anthony Morris,"[104] who possibly served as clerk for all or some of the meetings through 1695. The 1688 meeting of PYM officially considered the confounding moral dilemma "of buying and keeping of negroes," which the Friends of Germantown presented in a paper. Thus was raised for the first time the issue that, when resolved in 1754, would become a foundational precept of Penn's holy experiment. That resolution was not reached, however, until after sixty-six years of struggle within the ranks of Friends. The 1688 meeting decided to "forbear"[105] after determining it was not proper to give judgment on the issue. The 1688 meeting also was the first to record the attendance of Phineas Pemberton for Bucks Quarterly Meeting. The 1689 meeting noted its concern for education and appointed a committee to prepare a study of "keeping discipline and instructing children," which soon led to the founding of the Friends Public School in Philadelphia.

Starting in 1692, the Friends of Pennsylvania were battered by a storm named George Keith (ca. 1639–1716). Keith was the son of a Scottish Presbyterian family. He had graduated in 1657 with a master of arts degree from Marischal College, Aberdeen, where he had been immersed in Calvinist learning and biblical studies and had refined his literary and mathematical skills.[106] A seeker of religious truth, he became associated with the Quakers in Aberdeen, for which he was disowned by his family, and during the persecution of Friends following the Restoration was imprisoned several times. In 1670 he left Scotland for London,

---

Meeting and the meetings composing it (Philadelphia: T. Ellwood Zell, 1860), 308.

[103] PYM Min Bk B, p. 12.

[104] PYM Min Bk B, p. 15.

[105] PYM Min Bk B, pp. 19–20.

[106] See H. C. G. Matthew and Brian Harrison, *Oxford Dictionary of National Biography*, 60 vols. (Oxford: Oxford University Press, 2004), 31:63–69; Ethyn Williams Kirby, *George Keith (1638–1716)* (New York: Appleton-Century, 1942).

where he became esteemed for his speaking and writings as a Public Friend (an itinerant preacher). Accepted within the Quaker leadership, he journeyed with George Fox, Robert Barclay, Penn, and others on the 1677 mission to the Netherlands and Germany. Keith also suffered for his faith in England, a tyranny he finally escaped when, upon his 1684 discharge from Newgate Prison in London, he departed for America to serve as the surveyor general of East Jersey, having been appointed by Barclay, its nonresident governor. In that post, he was involved in surveying and determining the boundary lines between West Jersey and New York and between East and West Jersey.

Seeking to improve his circumstances, Keith obtained in July 1689 the new position as master of the Friends Public School in Philadelphia, then about to open.[107] Effective both as a preacher and writer, Keith began to advocate tightening the doctrine and discipline of Friends, beginning with the need for a confession of faith. His "relentless forwardness" came in the aftermath of other recent turbulence between Governor Blackwell and the Quakers over politics. PYM rejected the proposed credal confession in 1690 and again in 1691.[108] Keith persisted in the standoff, leading some Friends into separation, until June 30, 1692, in Philadelphia when the meeting of Public Friends issued its Declaration, or Testimony, of Denial against George Keith which PYM in September confirmed, condemning the "mischievous and hurtful separation" and declaring "we have not, nor can have, unity, in spirit, with any of them, until they return and repent of their evils aforesaid."[109] Keith carried his cause to England, where London Yearly Meeting in May 1695 confirmed his disownment and declared he "ought not to preach or pray in any of Friends' meetings, nor be owned or received as one of us" until

---

[107] Proud, *History of Pennsylvania*, 1:343–45. The PYM minutes for the September 1689 meeting record that Keith, Samuel Carpenter, Thomas Lloyd, and six others were instructed to prepare a paper on keeping discipline and instructing children. PYM Min Bk B, p. 22.

[108] In 1691, Keith enlarged his attack on the Quakers by going beyond criticizing their worship and doctrine to faulting their exercise of civil government, accusing Quaker magistrates of violating the peace principle, and reviling Thomas Lloyd, then deputy governor, as impudent and unfit for office. See Proud, *History of Pennsylvania*, 1:371–76.

[109] Ibid., 368n. The minutes of the PYM September 1692 meeting record its epistle to London Yearly Meeting, with commentary on the Keith separation, as well as Bucks Quarterly Meeting's findings against Keith at its meeting the prior June. PYM Min Bk B, pp. 34–37.

he publically acknowledged his "great offence" and gave proof of "his unfeigned repentance."[110] Keith made no such acknowledgment and, unrepentant, continued to be a public enemy of the Quakers. He remained in London long enough to be received into the ministry of the Church of England, in which he served both in England and in America. On his deathbed, he is reputed to have said, "I wish I had died when I was a Quaker, for then I am sure it would have been well with my soul."[111]

Despite the eruption flowing from the separation of Keith and his followers, the work and witness of PYM moved forward. And, increasingly, Phineas Pemberton was an important mover in its affairs. A mark of his ascendancy in yearly meeting appears in the appointments he received to the all-important and prestigious committee for preparing the annual epistle to London Yearly Meeting: in 1692 he was one of its signers; again, in 1693 he was a, if not the only, signer; and in both 1695 and 1696 he and one other were the epistle's authors. Then in 1696 the yearly meeting entrusted its ultimate oversight to Pemberton and agreed he should "be clerk of this meeting." The significance of his appointment was heightened by its being the first time ever that PYM's clerk was clearly identified in its minutes.[112] His clerkship of the institution came with an instruction that he "get the books and papers relating to the same, and record all minutes not recorded, or so many of the minutes and papers as are fit to be recorded and can be had."[113]

Phineas Pemberton sets the template for Philadelphia Yearly Meeting

Pemberton came to his new responsibilities after a dozen years of dedicated service establishing the records and procedures of the civil government in Bucks County. There he was clerk of all the courts, register of wills, and recorder. From the founding of Bucks County until his death, "The records of the county were written wholly by his hand; and in them he left a memorial of himself that will not be lost so long as the history of

---

[110] Proud, *History of Pennsylvania*, 1:368–69nn.

[111] Ibid., 1:370.

[112] Philadelphia Yearly Meeting of the Religious Society of Friends (Quakers), Minute Book 1681–1710, pp. 20–36, Haverford College Quaker Collection, Haverford College, Haverford, Pennsylvania (hereafter cited as PYM Min Bk A).

[113] PYM Min Bk A, p. 34.

the commonwealth which he helped to establish shall be read."[114] In the government of the commonwealth, he had been a member of the Provincial Council from 1685 to 1687 and again in 1695 as well as of the Provincial Assembly in 1689 and 1694. In his lifetime, he also served the province as master of the rolls, registrar general, and recorder of proprietary quitrents.[115]

All of Pemberton's public service was performed during the time he was securing his young family in their new home on the 300-acre tract he had purchased along the banks of the Delaware River close to its Falls. His near neighbor there was William Penn, whose country estate, Pennsbury Manor, had, in its first years, been under the stewardship of James Harrison, Pemberton's father-in-law. Pemberton named his own estate Grove Place, and there seven of his nine children were born and five were buried, all at young ages. Only one son, Israel, born in 1685, survived to marry and continue the family tradition of public service.

Mortality frequently stalked the extended Harrison-Pemberton families after their arrival in Pennsylvania. The most severe test struck in May 1687, when

> 'there was a great land flood'; and . . . a 'rupture.' It is probable that the river overflowed its banks to a great extent; and that on its subsiding it left a vast quantity of vegetable matter, which, being decomposed by a hot sun, the miasmata thence exhaled, together with an unusual quantity of rain, became the cause of much sickness in the neighborhood near the river and Falls, and a number of the settlers were removed by death.[116]

Fatally stricken by the miasma were Phineas's father Ralph (age seventy-seven years), who was laid to rest in July in a burial ground the son dedicated in Grove Place. Although Phineas, his wife, and their children were also sickened, they survived. Not so James Harrison's mother Agnes (age eighty-six years), who was buried in August. Then in October James Harrison, Penn's friend, counselor, and the steward of Pennsbury, succumbed to the plague at the age of sixty. It fell to Phineas in his official

---

[114] W. W. H. Davis, *History of Bucks County, Pennsylvania*, 3 vols. (New York, Chicago: Lewis Publishing, 1905), 3:4.

[115] Ibid.

[116] Pemberton, "The Annals of the Pemberton Family," 30–31.

capacity as register of wills in Bucks County to issue letters of administration to his widowed mother-in-law for the settlement of her late husband's estate. This was done in December 1688, "being the fourth year of the king's reign and eighth of the proprietaries' government."[117] Included in the estate were three tracts of land in Bucks County identified as belonging to Harrison on *A Map of the Improved Part of the Province of Pennsilvania in America* prepared by the surveyor general Thomas Holme and finished in early 1687.[118] Presumably, these non-contiguous lots comprised the five thousand acres that Harrison had purchased for £100 in England in June 1682, entitling him to a bonus of one hundred one-acre lots in Philadelphia.[119] And finally, as 1690 began, Harrison's widow, Anne, weakened from her own illness and grieving the loss of family members, joined her husband in death.[120] All of these departed were buried in Pemberton's Grove Place cemetery, which in the twentieth century was relocated to Pennsbury Manor.

In 1696 Pemberton began exercising his responsibilities as clerk of PYM, a role for which he was eminently well prepared. He not only had established the protocols for keeping the records of government in Bucks County, records he himself maintained for almost two decades, he had also been active in and the record keeper for both the Falls Monthly Meeting of Friends from its inception in 1683 and the Bucks Quarterly Meeting from its first meeting in 1684. In Pemberton's first year as its clerk, PYM heard again several papers on the keeping and importing of enslaved people from Africa. In 1697 the meeting agreed to provide relief for Friends in New England who were suffering from crop failures, a concern also recorded by Falls Monthly Meeting several months earlier.

In these first years of his clerkship, Pemberton continued fulfilling his responsibilities in the county government and also took on provincial obligations as an elected member of the Assembly in 1698 (for which year he was called by his peers to be their speaker) and again in 1700 and of the Council in 1697 and

---

[117] Will Book A, p. 38, File #24, 1688, Office of Register of Wills, Bucks County, Doylestown, Pennsylvania.

[118] The three tracts are keyed to the map grid as 22H, 24–25 FG, and 25B. See *PWP*, 3:649, 652.

[119] *PWP*, 2:97.

[120] Pemberton, "The Annals of the Pemberton Family," 31–33.

1699. In the midst of these time-consuming public duties, mortality struck once more when Pemberton's wife Phoebe died in October 1696. She was then but thirty-six years old, the mother not only of their six surviving children but of three they had previously buried.[121] In 1699 Phineas married Alice Hodgson of Burlington at the Falls Meeting House and shortly afterwards relocated with his children and new wife from Grove Place on the Delaware River to an estate on higher, presumably healthier, ground five miles inland, which he named "Pemberton." His son Israel would later inherit Pemberton and divide it into two parts called Wigan and Bolton in honor of his father's home communities in England.

Meanwhile, Penn's return to Pennsylvania, an event that had seemed imminent after his acquittal on treason charges in November 1693, met repeated and indefinite delays that kept him in England for another five and a half years. First, death struck down Penn's beloved wife Gulielma in February 1694 after a long illness. Then, as he parented his young children at home, he was drawn again into active participation in Quaker leadership, and he wrote extensively on religious issues of the day, including the Keithian controversy. He made ministerial tours with his son Springett; repaired his finances, particularly the revenues from his Irish estates; married again in March 1696 to Hannah Callowhill of Bristol; and suffered again in April 1696 when Springett, the elder son of whom the father had had great expectations, died.

Through all this, Penn remained distantly engaged with the affairs of his province as its government was restored to him by the Privy Council in 1694, as the Crown began tightening its control over colonial administration in 1696, as he dealt with his creditor Philip Ford who exacted more security in the form of Pennsylvania property interests, as he responded to the Provincial Assembly's demand for more independence from the proprietor, and as the proprietor himself was adding to his responsibilities by marketing his Susquehanna Valley project. Penn's Pennsylvania plantation was increasingly put at risk as his absence continued and his connection with the planters was all but lost. Even the reception he would find among them on his return was uncertain.

---

[121] Jordan, *Colonial Families of Philadelphia*, 1:285–86.

William Penn's 'Holy Experiment'

Penn visits his province for the second and last time (1699–1701)

On December 3, 1699, William Penn traveled for the second time to America. He arrived aboard the *Canterbury*, which had sailed from the Isle of Wight on September 3. With him were Hannah, his new wife then pregnant with their first child who would be named John at his birth on January 28, 1700 (and, as Penn's only child born in the New World, would also be known later as "the American"); his unmarried daughter Letitia; and his newly appointed secretary James Logan (1674–1751), a Quaker born in Ireland of Scottish descent and most recently engaged as the master of a school in Bristol. Logan would reside for the rest of his life in Pennsylvania, where, under the proprietor's early patronage and by virtue of his own merits, he became, in the judgment of one historian, the province's "most influential statesman, most distinguished scholar, and most respected citizen."[122]

Although Penn was not a stranger to the provincial topography itself, he no longer knew many of the people now living on the land, some even in leadership positions, most of them stirred by social, political, and economic dynamics working at cross purposes and many of them quite indifferent, if not hostile, to his proprietary concerns. His return after a fifteen-year absence found him a virtual stranger in his own colony. At his first coming he had been a vigorous thirty-eight-year-old man of wealth and the beneficiary of the royal grant of this bountiful region of the North American wilderness, educated and experienced in law and theology, actively championing—even having suffered punishment for—his beliefs during a time of revolutionary fervor in England. Now Penn was an aging fifty-five-year-old widower with young children, recently remarried and beginning a new family, burdened with mounting debts, and under instructions of an invigorated English government that was exerting tighter control over its international trade as a means of increasing the state's revenues. Thus it was that Penn came back to Pennsylvania as a man in the middle—pressed by his principal creditor in England; under orders from the royal Board of Trade in matters of provincial governance; and

---

[122] Frederick B. Tolles, *James Logan and the Culture of Provincial America*, ed. Oscar Handlin (Boston: Little, Brown, 1957), 6.

perceived by many of the planters and merchants, freeholders, and other citizens in his province of Pennsylvania as an intruder if not a threat who was set on oppressing them through taxation and tighter oversight.

Penn's slow Atlantic crossing in late 1699 did save him from one danger, however, that being the "sickness and mortality from Barbadoes" that "extremely afflicted" Philadelphia.[123] The first historian of colonial Pennsylvania later wrote that by the time of Penn's arrival,

> a dangerous and contagious distemper, called the Yellow Fever, having raged in the province, and carried off great numbers of people, had ceased. This remarkable sickness, which, in the latter part of this year, had caused a great mortality in Philadelphia, had, for some time before, been very fatal in some parts of the West India islands.[124]

England's mercantilist policy and colonial system: The Navigation Acts and administration of "trade and plantations"

The immediate cause of Penn's long-delayed return to America was the looming certainty that the English Crown was about to take legal action to divest not only Penn but all other proprietors of English colonies in America of their powers as 'chief governor' in their respective jurisdictions, powers originally granted under royal patent. Such a proposal had been formally presented to the House of Lords in February 1697 by Edward Randolph, the Crown's surveyor general of the plantations in America, who made detailed charges against the several proprietary governments under his oversight, including not only Pennsylvania but Delaware as well as East and West Jersey, in which Penn also had proprietary governmental interests.[125] Randolph's charges focused on the several governments' failure to enforce England's mercantile policy—the creation and securing of a favorable balance of trade between and among the mother country and its colonies through

---

[123] See letter from Penn to the Board of Trade, *PWP*, 3:589.

[124] Proud, *History of Pennsylvania*, 1:421.

[125] *The Manuscripts of the House of Lords, 1695–1697* (London: 1903), 440–44.

developing agriculture and manufactories, expanding the merchant marine, and controlling trade monopolies. The mercantile policy was planned as a system of commercial interdependency and managed through a series of Navigation Acts, the first having been passed at the Restoration in 1660 after the nullification of the earlier, and similar, Commonwealth legislation.

In March 1696, Parliament had passed another in its series of Navigation Acts, to be effective in March 1698.[126] This act required that goods in the colonial trade were to be moved only within the system and by ships built and owned in England, Ireland, or the plantations ("in Asia, Africa, or America"). All the officers of each ship and three-quarters of each crew were to be from those places (section I). The past torment regarding 'oaths' was renewed for the Quakers because the act required all governors of English plantations to "take a solemn oath to do their utmost" to "punctually and bona fide" observe all provisions of the several Navigation Acts (section III) and, further, that every English- or plantation-built ship was to be registered by proof "made upon oath" by one or more of a ship's owners (section XVI).

Then, in May 1696 William III created the Lords Commissioners of Trade and Foreign Plantations (commonly known as the Board of Trade) to administer and enforce his tightening mercantilist policy.[127] The first instance of such executive oversight had occurred in 1621 when James I created a temporary committee of the Privy Council to investigate trade problems and their relationship to declining Crown revenues. Later, in 1660 Charles II appointed a Committee for Foreign Plantations, and thereafter such a body, variously called a committee or board or council or "the Lords of Trade," operated under the aegis of the Privy Council in administering the colonial system.[128] Sometimes its administration was effective and energetic; at other times—such as the period prior to 1696 when the oversight was given to the Privy Council acting as a

---

[126] "An Act for preventing frauds and regulating abuses in the plantation trade" (commonly known as the Navigation Act of 1696), 7 & 8 Gul. III, c. 22, *The Statutes of the Realm*, 7:103–7. This act in the reign of William III followed four prior enactments (cited in the 1696 preamble) made under Charles II for encouraging English navigation and regulating its plantation trade.

[127] See discussion in *PWP*, 3:441–42.

[128] See Winfred T. Root, "The Lords of Trade and Plantations, 1675–1696," *American Historical Review* 23 (October 1917): 20–41.

committee of the whole known as the Lords of Trade—it was lax. William III, seeking strong policy-making and administrative oversight to improve England's mercantile enterprise, decided to commission a board separate from the Privy Council that was composed of sixteen members, eight of whom were permanent salaried administrators and the other eight of whom were Privy councilors sitting ex officio.

One of the first problems presented to the new Board of Trade in the year of its creation was to repair the defect in that year's Navigation Act: the failure to provide for maritime, or admiralty, courts in the proprietary colonies for enforcing the Crown's rights against infringements of its mercantile laws. Absent such courts, in proprietary colonies such as Pennsylvania, actions to enforce the navigation laws had to be initiated by the Crown in colonial common law courts sitting with juries rather than in admiralty courts where there were no juries. Edward Randolph proposed to remedy this defect by having the Crown both create separate admiralty courts in the colonies and then appoint judges and prosecutors to serve on them. Penn knew of this by year's end and mounted a vigorous defense of his proprietary rights. In a letter to Sir William Trumbull, the English secretary of state for the Northern Department (responsible for home affairs as well as the Protestant states of northern Europe), Penn wrote in January 1697:

> Here is a breach like to be made upon us in our colonies in America, by an *imperium in imperio*; two independent deputations, powers, courts, and administrations in the same province; one by proprietaries, the other by a court of admiralty to be set up by the king's immediate authority, among our own tenants and people, which will so alarum and balk the people and planters, that they will halt, both in their trade and improvements and ruin me, that have spent and lost above £30,000 already, and extremely pinch the rest in my circumstances. . . . Let me beg of thee to dispose the king, not to discourage and bruise us, who make colonies at our charge to his advantage; every man there being worth three times more to him, at the year's end, than to us. We venture lives and fortunes upon public faith and protection, and hope not to be shaken in

them by lawyers' niceties. The equity, the necessity, and nature of the thing is for us.[129]

As noted above, in February 1697 the House of Lords had heard a proposal that would divest Penn and others of their governing powers in proprietary colonies in America. The proposal was made by Edward Randolph, the surveyor general of the American plantations since 1691 who was serving under the Commissioners of Customs, an arm of the Lords of the Treasury. He had proven himself a vigorous enforcer for his masters in collecting the customs due under the trade laws and now, after an inspection of the customs offices in the American proprietary colonies, had returned to London resolved to correct the mismanagement and lax performance he had found in those offices.[130] His report on affairs in Pennsylvania found much fault:

> Mr. Penn is the sole proprietor, and has the right to the soil and government thereof. Mr. William Markham is by Mr. Penn's commission the present governor, to whom Samuel Carpenter and John Goodson (both Quakers) were, by another commission from Mr. Penn, joined in the government with him, but refused to act. . . . The Acts of Trade are not observed in this Province. The judges in the courts of judicature are not legally qualified, neither can the officers of the customs obtain justice for his majesty. One vessel with Scotch goods came last year from Scotland, and was admitted to entry at Philadelphia; another about the same time with wine and brandy from Norway, a Dutchman being her master. The governor is a favorer of the pirates, which came from the South and the Red Sea about three or four years ago, and several Scotchmen are traders there. He desired me to make him Collector of the Customs in Philadelphia, having (as he wrote me) but a small maintenance; by which your Lordships may please to take notice that governors under such necessities will be easily tempted to do and connive at unlawful things. Pennsylvania lies in the centre between Maryland and New York, most commodiously for the illegal trade. It will soon become a staple of Scotch and Holland goods. No place has in so

---

[129] *PWP*, 3:475–76.

[130] Winfred Trexler Root, *The Relations of Pennsylvania with the British Government, 1696–1765* (New York: D. Appleton, 1912), 46–48.

short a time been by such ways so greatly improved. The Commissioners of the Customs have appointed a Collector to reside at Philadelphia, but to little purpose till the government be duly regulated in relation to trade.[131]

Randolph summarized his review of all the proprietary colonies in America by observing that

> great numbers of people are now settled in some of these Proprieties, but have been long endeavoring to break loose and set up for themselves, having no sort of regard to the Acts of Trade, and discountenancing appeals to his Majesty in Council. The persons appointed by the Proprieties to be their governors are generally men of very indifferent qualifications for parts and estate; their maintenance is inconsiderable, which renders their governments precarious also.[132]

His recommendations were to require the royal commissioning of all governors, such as Markham, who until then had been appointed to act by colonial proprietors, not by the Crown. Randolph saw this as the best means of bringing 'illegal trade' under control, by which he meant all pirates and the nations not within the closed commercial system created by the Navigation Acts (sometimes called the Acts of Trade):

> By which and by no other methods the many pirates so long and so generally complained of to be harbored and countenanced in some of the Proprieties, and their piracies will be effectually suppressed, the Acts of Trade hitherto eluded will be vigorously executed, the officers of the Customs assisted and encouraged, and the inhabitants, being always secured in their properties, will be happy and secure from all spoil and rapine.[133]

---

[131] *The Manuscripts of the House of Lords, 1695–1697*, 441–42. Scotland was outside England's mercantile system prior to the political union of the kingdoms of England and Scotland in 1707. Piracy is criminal activity, usually robbery, on the seas or other navigable waters. It is related to privateering, the official licensing of private vessels to prey upon an enemy's commerce, but has no regard to a vessel's flag.

[132] Ibid., 444.

[133] Ibid.

He concluded his report to the House of Lords as follows:

> It is therefore humbly proposed that a clause be brought in to invest the government of all the Proprieties in his Majesty, with a saving to the owners and the inhabitants the properties to their lands and possessions.[134]

Randolph's proposal lapsed with the dissolution of Parliament in July 1698, but English faultfinding regarding Pennsylvania's proprietary government continued. A persistent official critic was Robert Quary, sometime acting governor of South Carolina, who in the summer of 1698 accepted the commission to be the judge of the new vice admiralty court for Pennsylvania, West Jersey, and Maryland. In letters to the Board of Trade, Judge Quary charged that David Lloyd, the attorney general of Pennsylvania, had affronted the king's dignity in open session of a local court; that Anthony Morris, while a justice of the peace (he also was a sometime judge and was soon to be mayor of Philadelphia), had ordered the release of allegedly illegal goods taken into custody by the Admiralty Court; and that William Markham, the provincial governor in Penn's absence, had ordered the seizure of a vessel for illicit loading of tobacco and then taken a bribe to release it. Penn knew of these charges, having been at the Board of Trade on August 3, 1699, one month before he sailed from England for America. He also knew beforehand of the actions the Board would formally require of him in their letter of September 12 and took action accordingly upon his arrival in Pennsylvania even though the letter did not reach him until the following April.

The Board of Trade ordered Penn to remove from office Lieutenant Governor Markham (and to recommend for the king's approval a "duly qualified" replacement), Attorney General David Lloyd (and to discharge him as well "from all other public employments whatsoever"), and Justice of the Peace Anthony Morris. Penn was additionally charged to see that "all due obedience" was given to the vice admiralty court as well as encouragement to its officials and those of the customs office and that those "turbulent and busy in opposing the proceedings of the said Court" were duly punished. Further, he was made responsible to see to the punctual observance of the six Navigation Acts (referred to as the Acts of Trade) passed between 1660 and 1696. Finally, he was charged to provide laws against

---

[134] Ibid.

piracy, "settle and establish" a militia for the defense and security of the province, govern and regulate all public proceedings to prevent any prejudice to the king or England, and, speedily after his arrival, give the king a report on the state of the province.[135]

On February 9, 1700, Pennsylvania's General Assembly addressed Governor Penn regarding the concerns of the Board of Trade and declared its abhorrence of piracy, its care to prevent forbidden trade that was "not only prejudicial to the king's revenues but injurious to lawful traders," and its innocence of any wrongdoing in the government which, if there were any, it was hoped "our accusers may be put upon proof thereof, that the innocent may not stand charged with the guilty as criminals." It also asked Penn to represent to the king that not only was the royal interest injured but trade was discouraged in the province unless Quaker ship owners there were allowed to register their vessels upon "attest or solemn affirmation" instead of oath, as was allowed in England and Maryland.[136]

Another grave concern of the Board of Trade had previously been resolved. In May 1698, the Pennsylvania Assembly had passed "an act for preventing frauds & regulating abuses in trade within the Province of Pennsylvania & counties annexed."[137] The provision of the act allowing jury trials in provincial courts for violations of the trade laws was especially offensive to the English authorities as it was in derogation of the exclusive jurisdiction of the juryless vice admiralty courts. On August 31, 1699, the lord justices of the Board had declared the act to be "null, void and of no effect" from its inception.[138] This was after Penn had given the act his "negative" in 1698.[139]

Penn's compliant answers to the Board of Trade's written demands of September 12, 1699, were made, first, in his brief letter of February 27, 1700, and then two months later on April

---

[135] Board of Trade to Penn, September 12, 1699, *PWP*, 3:576–78. The letter was signed by four members of the Board of Trade, one of whom was the political philosopher, liberal theorist, and physician John Locke, a board member from 1696 to 1700, who had served as secretary to the lords and proprietors of the Carolinas.

[136] "The humble address of the ... General Assembly," *PWP*, 3:584–87.

[137] *PWP*, 3:562n1. Its title paralleled that of England's Navigation Act of 1696: "An act for preventing frauds and regulating abuses in the plantation trade."

[138] *PWP*, 3:576.

[139] *PWP*, 3:561.

28,[140] after he had at last received the Board's September letter. As ordered, the lieutenant governor (his cousin William Markham) "is of course laid aside," and "the Offensive Justice," Anthony Morris, was "displaced," as was also the attorney general, David Lloyd whose prosecution was being delayed by Quary, his accuser. Penn submitted for approval new acts dealing with piracy and illegal trading. And he also voiced his frustration with the entire enterprise:

> You cannot easily imagine the difficulties I lie under, what with the king's affairs, those of the government, and my proprietary ones. No king's governor, without vanity, has had more care and vexation, though I receive nothing from the crown to support me under it. . . . As for the people here they are soured to see their accusers believed, and think themselves both innocent and meritorious. However 'tis I that pay the reckoning, for instead of a free and flowing regard to my long expensive circumstances, both in beginning and in preserving this colony and government . . . besides the loss of time, hazards run, interest employed, and fatigues endured nineteen years, they are very cool in considering my circumstances, thinking themselves injured in their reputation, and unsafe in their interests. . . . That they came hither to have more and not less freedom than at home.[141]

The royal threat to take back the governing rights in proprietary colonies did not go away in 1698; it only lay dormant. On April 24, 1701, it reappeared in a new Parliament with the introduction of a reunification bill in the House of Lords sponsored by the Board of Trade. When Penn learned of it in August, he angrily wrote to his London agent, denouncing "such vigorous attacks made against proprietary governments at large and mine in particular," and, continuing, marveled that

> beggars, fools, and knaves are in good governments marked not to be trusted; must they here be rewarded as well as employed merely for the sake of mischief? But if the Parliament can be so imposed upon as to think it is not best for the crown to settle colonies at the cost of

---

[140] *PWP*, 3:592–99.
[141] *PWP*, 3:595.

others, and direct the governors of them as materially as if it paid them, I have done.[142]

Some of the same heat is found in Penn's letter eight days later to the Board of Trade defending his government in Pennsylvania generally (its major faults, he protested, occurred in the administration of Benjamin Fletcher as provincial governor, serving by Crown appointment during Penn's suspension from October 1692 to August 1694) and specifically (regarding the appointment of water bailiffs to police the Delaware River, an alleged secret trade with Curacao, and removing pirates at the capes of Delaware Bay).[143] In between those two August letters, however, Penn had resolved that unless he personally attended to his own proprietary interests in England, he could not effectively protect his rights and reputation, his family's future well-being and security, and his colonists' liberties and privileges. He had little time to settle his affairs in Pennsylvania before leaving the province forever on November 3.

Penn's final days in his province: Repairing the body politic, tending the 'holy experiment'

Although Penn's external provincial problems with England were of paramount concern to him, difficult internal issues were demanding his attention as well. Among them was the need for a new fundamental law (the 1683 Frame of the Government had been superseded in 1696), and this at a moment when the disunion of Pennsylvania "and the adjacent counties" was threatened. Penn's time for dealing with these and other critical issues was severely constrained, the more so because of the colonists' increasing independence and factionalization compounded by their disaffection toward the proprietor; few had sympathy with either his political or financial problems. Yet in the time remaining to him in Pennsylvania, Penn found occasions to enjoy family life at Pennsbury, share his concerns in Quaker councils, and bear a singular witness by deed and action to what he once in the past had termed 'a holy experiment.'

In late January 1700, eight weeks after William and Hannah Penn's arrival in Philadelphia, she gave birth to the first of their seven children. Given the name John (1700–1746), he was the

---

[142] Penn to Charlwood Lawton, August 18, 1701, *PWP*, 4:66–67.
[143] Penn to Board of Trade, August 26, 1701, *PWP*, 4:76–80.

only one of William's fifteen children to be born in America. Although he inherited half of his father's proprietary interest, John Penn returned to the province only once, in 1734–1735. During the summers of his infancy in 1700 and 1701, the family took respite at Pennsbury Manor, its estate in Bucks County on the Delaware River just below the Falls, far enough away from the capitol in Philadelphia to escape the city's seasonal heat as well as the endless pressures and politics of administering a fractious government.

In the beginning of January, Penn brought the issue of a new fundamental law to the Council.[144] From the time he had received his province of Pennsylvania from Charles II by letters patent under the Great Seal of England, Penn as constitutional lawyer had labored to bring forth a model instrument of government. After numerous drafts and consultations, the final instrument, known as the second Frame of the Government, "with the assent and approbation of the freemen in Provincial Council and Assembly met," had become the basic law in 1683, not only of the province but of the three annexed Delaware counties purchased by Penn from the Duke of York. It served until a hiatus was created in 1692 when the Crown first transferred the provincial governing power from Penn to Benjamin Fletcher and then in August 1694, upon Penn's restoration, returned the power to Penn with the condition, one of several, that Pennsylvania contribute "eighty men or the value of the charge thereof" for the defense of New York.[145] Penn in England commissioned William Markham in Pennsylvania to continue acting as deputy governor there until his return. Markham found that the military condition would not be met by the Assembly unless the Frame of 1683 was revised in a manner Penn had long opposed—by granting the Assembly the power to prepare and propose to the governor and Council "all such bills as the major part of them shall at any time see needful to be passed into laws." The Assembly also demanded control of its adjournments. In November 1696 the impasse was resolved, the defense requirement approved, and Markham and the Assembly enacted the Frame of the Government of 1696, which would remain in effect until the proprietor "shall signify his pleasure to

---

[144] *PWP*, 3:581n1.
[145] *PWP*, 398, 458.

the contrary by some instrument under his hand and seal in that behalf."[146]

After his arrival in Philadelphia, the compliant Penn could report to the Board of Trade that he had carried out its instructions and removed Markham, the deputy governor (Penn's Anglican cousin who in the beginning had preceded him by fourteen months to first administer affairs in Pennsylvania).[147] On April 1 he addressed the Provincial Council on the need for charter reform with these words:

> I advise you not to trifle with government. I wish there were no need of any, but since crimes prevail government is made necessary by man's degeneration. It's not an end but a means. He that thinks it an end aims at profit to make a trade on it. He who thinks it to be a means understands the true end of government. Friends, away with all parties and look on yourselves and what is good for all as a body politic.[148]

In May 1700 the Assembly considered a new charter, but no action was taken[149] other than the surrender of the Frame of 1683 to Penn "with the understanding that he would govern under his royal patent and the Act of Union in the mean time."[150] In the fall of 1700, Penn met with the Assembly at New Castle and urged on them the need to resolve constitutional as well as legal and proprietary tax issues, but the contentious spirit of the body and the growing dissension between Pennsylvania's representatives and those of the lower counties frustrated his efforts to bring others to share his understanding of the "true end of government."[151] Resolution of the constitutional issue did not

---

[146] The Frame of the Government was signed in Philadelphia by "Order of the House" by Assembly Speaker John Simcock on November 7, 1696. The text is given in *PWP*, 3:457–64, where it is run together without paragraphs and the sections (some twenty-four) are unnumbered. The section granting the assembly power to initiate bills is at the bottom of p. 462, and that giving Penn power to veto the Frame of the Government is in the middle of p. 464.

[147] *PWP*, 3:587.

[148] Penn's speech to the Provincial Council, dated April 1, 1700, *PWP*, 3:591.

[149] See *Votes and Proceedings of the House of Representatives of the Province of Pennsylvania, Dec. 4, 1682–June 11, 1707, Vol. 1, with Preface and Appendix* (Philadelphia: B. Franklin and D. Hall, 1752), 119–22.

[150] *PWP*, 4:109–10n4. For the Act of Union of December 1682 by which the three lower counties (of Delaware) were annexed into the province of Pennsylvania, see Soderlund, *William Penn*, 192–93.

[151] See discussion in *PWP*, 3:567.

come until a year later, on the eve of Penn's leave-taking from Pennsylvania.

One significant indicator of the Assembly's differences with Penn was its insistence that protection of property rights took precedence over the liberties threatened by a royal takeover of proprietary governing rights. So resolute was the Assembly that when it met in September 1701, Penn, with seven weeks left to him before departing from America, was compelled by the necessity of time to negotiate and execute two separate basic laws, the first being the Charter of Property that had been drafted by David Lloyd.[152] (On returning from England, Penn had dismissed Lloyd, pursuant to an order of the Board of Trade, from his position as attorney general of the province, thereby creating the leader of the antiproprietary faction in Pennsylvania.) The other was the Charter of Privileges, which in its preamble set out Penn's account of the constitutional history to date.[153] There, in a series of "whereas" clauses, Penn recited the 1681 grant of Pennsylvania from Charles II to Penn and his heirs, the 1682 deeds for the lower counties of Delaware from the Duke of York to Penn, the 1683 grant of the Frame of the Government by Penn to the province's "freemen, planters, and adventurers," and, finally, the Assembly's delivery back to Penn of the Frame in 1700 because it was

> found in some parts of it not so suitable to the present circumstances of the inhabitants . . . [and] I was then pleased to promise that I would restore the said charter to them again with necessary alterations or in lieu thereof give them another better adapted to answer the present circumstances and conditions of the said inhabitants which they have now by their representatives in a general assembly met at Philadelphia requested me to grant.[154]

Absent was any reference to the Fletcher-Markham hiatus of 1692–1694 or the Frame of 1696. The new Charter of Privileges being "approved of and agreed to" by the Assembly and ordered to be signed by the speaker, it was "thankfully received" by the

---

[152] See *PWP*, 4:115–16.
[153] For the text, see *PWP*, 4:104–10.
[154] *PWP*, 4:105–6.

Assembly and filed.[155] Penn had also signed it along with six other officials witnessing, as the "Proprietary and Governor's Council," the artifact of what had been a bicameral legislature. Now the sole legislative body, the Assembly could sit with full powers to prepare bills, judge the qualifications of its members, and "sit upon their own adjournments." The Council's only function now was to advise the executive. In an addendum ("I think fit to add this following proviso . . ."), Penn allowed for the separation of the province and lower counties within three years, preserving to the separated peoples the "liberties, privileges, and benefits" granted in the charter.[156] The complete separation came in 1704.

Penn, however, placed his most distinctive mark upon the Charter of Privileges by restoring to it provisions for the basic freedom of conscience and of religious profession and worship that had inspired the holy experiment from its inception. Had there been no persecution of dissenters in England, had Quakers and others not been made to suffer condemnation, scorn, and imprisonment for professing Christian beliefs other than those 'established' by the English state and its church, there might have been no need for a dissenters' refuge in the New World. The guarantee of religious freedom at the core of Penn's entire American enterprise that was set forth clearly in the Frame of 1683 had, however, been omitted from Markham's Frame of 1696, reason enough for that document not even to be acknowledged by Penn in his preamble to the Charter of Privileges. The restored freedom bookended the charter; it was highlighted in the first section (as the sole subject) and in the next-to-last section (where it was made inviolable forever).[157]

In his final American months, Penn bore witness to other issues affecting his experiment in the wilderness, issues beyond trade and governance concerned with shielding those persons in the growing colony who were not its "freemen, planters, and adventurers." In March 1700, Penn shared with Philadelphia Monthly Meeting the concerns with which

---

[155] Both charters were executed on October 28, 1701. The Charter of Privileges was, however, referred to as "this present Charter of Liberties" immediately following the concluding formulaic "In Witness Whereof . . . ," *PWP*, 4:108.

[156] *PWP*, 4:109.

[157] *PWP*, 4:106, 108.

his mind had long been engaged, for the benefit and welfare of the Negroes and Indians; exhorting and pressing them to the full discharge of their duty, every way, in reference to these people; but more especially in regard to their mental part; that they might as frequently as possible have the advantage of attending religious meetings, and the benefit of being duly informed in the Christian religion. Hence a meeting was appointed more particularly for the Negroes once every month; and means were used to have more frequent meetings with the Indians; William Penn taking part of the charge upon himself, particularly, the manner of it, and the procuring of interpreters.[158]

Then, in April 1701 Penn met a delegation of about forty Native American chiefs in Philadelphia to execute their Articles of Agreement relating to mutual concerns in the Susquehanna Valley. The parties pledged peace with each other, declaring "that they shall forever hereafter be as one head and one heart and live in true friendship and amity as one people."[159] The attending chiefs represented the Susquehannock Indians who had recently returned to their ancestral lands along the lower Susquehanna River, the Shawnees who had just relocated there from Maryland, and the Conoy Indians living farther to the south on the Potomac River. Another participant was a leader of the Onondaga Indians of New York, a brother of the emperor of the Iroquois.[160] In addition to pledging mutual peace and friendship between the colonists and indigenous peoples in their agreement, pledges Penn had exchanged with the natives of the Delaware Valley on his first visit to Pennsylvania, the proprietor was also furthering his ambitious plan of colonization in Susquehanna lands. For years, Penn had pursued this expansion of his real estate and financial interests, but he had been thwarted by interference from New York and its allies, the Iroquois Nation. The interference eased in January 1697 when Penn leased from Thomas Dongan, a former governor of New York, the lands adjacent to the Susquehanna River from the New York-Pennsylvania border to the mouth of Chesapeake Bay. Later, in September 1700 two Susquehannock chiefs had sold

---

[158] Proud, *History of Pennsylvania*, 1:423.
[159] Articles of Agreement dated April 23, 1701, *PWP*, 4:51–55.
[160] *PWP*, 4:54nn1–5.

him the natives' interests in Susquehanna River lands, and that sale was also being ratified in the Articles. Another concern was to prevent the abuses "too frequently put upon" the Indians by traders. For this purpose, the sixth of the unnumbered sections of the Articles called for trading with the Indians to be restricted to those traders duly granted licenses by Penn and his successors.[161]

The next month, Penn placed this concern before his Council to discuss the problem of "the great abuses committed in the Indian trade, with the dangers and disadvantages which might arise from thence to the province."[162] The abuses of concern were the sale of spirituous liquor to the Indians and the traders' sharp practices, such as price gouging. Particular attention was given to trade regulation and the promotion of Christian practices and instruction.

Amid the whirlwind of final legislative acts and official duties leading up to his departure, on October 25 Penn confirmed the charter of the Friends Public School by its corporate name of "The Overseers of the Public School founded in Philadelphia at the request and costs and charges of the people of God called Quakers."[163] The school had been established in May 1689 by Philadelphia Monthly Meeting and was, on the petition of that body in February 1698, incorporated by the then lieutenant governor and Provincial Council. Six of the original seven petitioners were still alive (those still living included Samuel Carpenter, Edward Shippen, Anthony Morris, and David Lloyd), and they applied to Penn to confirm the 1698 incorporation. In granting the request, Penn noted that "I greatly favor the good inclinations and just and laudable desires and conscientious regard of the said petitioners and people for the education, instruction, and literature of their children and posterity and more especially their care and concern for the poor." The document that Penn signed included statements from the original petition that a school (understood as a system with a number of sites) was desired "where poor children might be freely maintained, taught, and educated in good literature until they should be fit to put apprentices or capable to be masters or ushers in the said school." Additionally, the school was to be

---

[161] *PWP*, 4:52, 54n9.

[162] Proud, *History of Pennsylvania*, 1:432.

[163] For the text, see *Microfilm*, 9:703.

open to "all children and servants, male and female," and they were to be "received, admitted, taught, and instructed, the rich at reasonable rates and the poor to be maintained and schooled for nothing."[164]

Two days later, on October 27, Penn appointed Andrew Hamilton, a Scotsman then serving as the governor of East and West Jersey, to be "my Deputy in the government or my Lieutenant Governor" of Pennsylvania and the counties annexed, posts Hamilton held until his death in 1703.[165] At the same time, Penn appointed James Logan, who seven days earlier had celebrated his twenty-seventh birthday, the "Secretary of the State and Government and Clerk of the Council . . . [and] Secretary of Property for the said Province and Territories."[166]

The next day, October 28, Penn signed his commission to the newly created Council of State,[167] a ten-member advisory board to serve the proprietor as well as the governor or his lieutenant or deputy. This remnant of the legislative Provincial Council created in the Frame of 1683 was now transformed into a council of advice to the executive and began its official service when six of the ten councilors witnessed Penn's signing of the Charter of Privileges.[168] Phineas Pemberton, one of the witnessing councilors, had been described by Penn in a letter to Logan written from Pennsbury in early September as follows:

> Poor Phineas is a dying man . . . tho he crept, as I may say, to meeting yesterday. I am grieved at it, for he has not his fellow, and without him this is a poor County indeed.[169]

On October 30, while already at New Castle but before embarking on the voyage to England, acknowledging "because it is appointed for all men once to die, and that their days are in the hand of the almighty, their Creator," Penn executed a new will[170] in which he made generous provision for his family, relatives, friends, and servants. For these beneficiaries he was especially munificent in granting acreages of Pennsylvania land, which he

---

[164] *Microfilm*, 9:703.

[165] See Penn's commission to Hamilton, *Microfilm*, 9:716.

[166] See Penn's commission to Logan, *Microfilm*, 9:721.

[167] See *PWP*, 4:110–12.

[168] *PWP*, 4:109.

[169] Penn to James Logan, September 8, 1701, *PWP*, 4:88.

[170] For the text, see *PWP*, 4:112–15.

could well afford. He included in this will a provision to give to "my blacks their freedom, as under my hand already," a provision, however, not included in his subsequent will of 1705 nor his final will of 1712.[171]

Farewell to Pennsylvania

Because Penn's parting from Pennsylvania was hastened by political and economic pressures, he had little time left either for his own peace or spiritual reflection. The distractions were many, and so it seemed were his enemies. As one commentator notes, "The forces of discontent among various overlapping groups—Anglicans, landholders, taxpayers, Lower Counties settlers, royal officials, and Pennsylvania assemblymen—were too great for him to overcome."[172] Penn offered no valedictory words for Pennsylvania as he had done six days before boarding ship for his 1684 return to England. He had, however, attended Philadelphia Yearly Meeting in late September when Pemberton, for the last time, presided as clerk. Penn was appointed with three others to draw up an epistle rendering an account of the state of the meeting that, on completion, Pemberton signed "by order on behalf of the said meeting." The epistle was sent to the quarterly and monthly meetings in Pennsylvania and West and East Jersey, and in it Penn and his colleagues addressed such issues as godly humility, the care of families, and the profession and preservation of Truth and concluded with this exhortation for peace:

> And now, dear friends and brethren, we recommend to you peace and concord as the great fruits of charity without which we are nothing, and that we labor to approve ourselves men of peace and makers of peace which is our bounden duty and overarching ensign as the disciples of Jesus. But if any be otherwise minded, the churches of Christ have no such custom, nor can they therein be countenanced or suffered. But so it is to the grief of our hearts and scandal of our profession that some laying claim to the same (in divers provinces within the verge of this meeting) have been too factious

---

[171] For the text of the two wills, see *PWP*, 4:394–96 and *PWP*, 4:715–19, respectively.

[172] *PWP*, 4:86.

and troublesome in the governments under which they ought peaceably to live and have by their seditious words, insinuations, and practices disquieted the minds of others, to the making of parties and disturbances, and some under the fair color of law and privileges have promoted their sinister ends, when indeed it was but to take vengeance on those, against whom they had taken disgust; and this we cannot but declare our just abhorrence of, that any should sacrifice the peace of a province to private revenge, warning all to beware of such, and where ever they find them forthwith to deal with them and to acquit their holy profession of them in a gospel way, for by God's help we have now for many years approved ourselves peaceable subjects to those whom God by his providence hath set over us; first to the king as supreme, and next unto those in authority under him, being subject, not for wrath but conscience; Rom. 13 (for there is no power but of him) rendering unto all their dues, tribute to whom tribute, custom to whom custom, fear to whom fear, honor to whom honor, but when at any time it hath pleased God to suffer the rulers that have been over us to impose anything against our allegiance to God, we have patiently suffered under them 'til the Lord hath thought fit to open their understandings and mollify their hearts towards us, and this we also recommend to be continued amongst us.[173]

The 1701 PYM minutes record that Pemberton with fifteen other members "met with William Penn at whose request they discussed some 'weighty occasion.'"[174]

There were some, however, who expressed their own deep feelings and apprehensions concerning Penn's departure. In an address, the kings and sachems of the Susquehannock and Shawnee Indians told their "loving and good friend and brother" that although they understood he was obliged to go back to England to speak with the great king there, it was to "our great

---

[173] "An Epistle to the Quarterly and Monthly Meeting[s] of Friends in Pennsylvania and West and East Jersey, from our Yearly Meeting in Philadelphia held the 24th and 25th days of the 7th month [September], 1701," PYM Miscellaneous Records, Call #D1.1.1, Haverford College Quaker Collection, Haverford College, Haverford, Pennsylvania.

[174] Philadelphia Yearly Meeting of the Religious Society of Friends (Quakers), Minute Book 1747–1779, pp. 82–83, Haverford College Quaker Collection, Haverford College, Haverford, Pennsylvania (hereafter cited as PYM Min Bk C).

grief and the trouble of all the Indians of these parts." They acknowledged that "he has been not only always just but very kind to us . . ., careful to keep a good correspondence with us, not suffering us to receive any wrong from any of the people under his government. . . . He has paid us for our lands, which no governor ever did before him, and we hope and desire that the great king of the English will be good and kind to him and his children, and grant that they may always govern these parts, and then we shall have confidence" and keep the agreement "we have solemnly made for us and our posterity as long as the sun and the moon shall endure, one head, one mouth, and one heart."[175]

The monthly meeting of Friends near the Falls of Delaware in the county of Bucks prepared a certificate of removal from membership in the monthly meeting for William and Hannah Penn addressed to the several meetings in England where they might carry it. The certificate, a dutiful "compliance with the good order used amongst us," was written by Pemberton and three other meeting members and approved on October 8. It sheds some light on the conditions in the province and on Penn's state of mind that found expression in the PYM epistle he had written shortly before with others. Of Penn himself, the Falls Friends wrote:

His testimony hath been in the power and authority of Truth from time to time and at all times when amongst us hath labored to invite and persuade us to live the life of true religion and keep in the power thereof by an humble and close walking with the Lord and to beware of losing ourselves in the world and cares thereof lest deadness and dryness enter and only a form of religion remain. . . . His trials and exercises by false friends as well as open enemies have not been a few considering the time he hath been here, yet he hath borne over them with a steady mind knowing that it's for Truth's sake and its followers that such things happen to him otherwise generally loved and esteemed of most. For some of us have heard that some of his chiefest opposites have said he is too good a man to be governor and others of them they would never desire a better governor were he not a Quaker. It's wherefore not him but the Truth they strive

---

[175] The record of the address, delivered about October 7, 1701, was written by James Logan. For the text, see *PWP*, 4:98–100.

against and therefore the controversy not merely his own for it's very evident to us there is a spot of enmity greatly strives here as well as with you to bring these American Churches into a suffering state of which when you are made sensible we have hope that you will not stand unconcerned but assist him as much as in you lies, the which we shall be always ready to acknowledge as acts of brotherly kindness.[176]

Penn's second sojourn in America came to a close on November 3 when he and his family sailed for England aboard the *Dolmahoy*.

Penn in England for his final years (1701–1718)

The weeks and months after Penn's return to England must have been eerily discomforting for him, seeming to bring a revisitation of the trials endured during his first homecoming from America. Documents necessary to the presentation of his plea to the Crown for resolving the issue of whether to continue proprietary government, the very cause of his Atlantic crossing, had been left behind in Pennsylvania. Eminent individuals essential to the oversight and prospering of his provincial and financial ventures were felled by death in rapid succession: Philip Ford, Penn's English business agent, steward, and major creditor, died in January 1702; Phineas Pemberton, the civil administrator of Bucks County from its inception and the current clerk of PYM, died the first day of the following March; one week later, the sovereign William III was dead, succeeded to the throne by Anne, James II's second daughter, who would be the last Stuart monarch; and then in April 1703 Penn's deputy governor in Pennsylvania, Andrew Hamilton, died, barely eighteen months after his appointment by Penn and little more than three after his confirmation by the Crown, proof of which reached Philadelphia only after his death. Worse yet was the tragedy beginning to unfold in the life of William Penn Jr., upon whom rested the father's hopes of nurturing an heir apparent worthy of the proprietorship of Pennsylvania. The familiars of Penn's world were departing from his Pennsylvania experiment, and who their successors and what their qualities would be was not at all

---

[176] Certificate of Removal for William and Hannah Penn from Falls Monthly Meeting, October 8, 1701, *PWP*, 4:100–102.

certain. For some of them, the experiment itself was of little or no concern—possibly even an impediment to their own enrichment in the province.

A season of deaths and a birth

The Crown's proposed reunification bill for ending colonial proprietary rule, introduced in the House of Lords on April 24, 1701, with support from the Board of Trade, had failed to advance before the June 23 dissolution of Parliament, the fifth in the reign of William III and Mary II.[177] Notwithstanding, Penn returned to England, certain another such attempt would be made. He reported these developments in his ongoing correspondence with James Logan, urging also the dispatch of the documents left behind:

> Nothing yet done in my affairs, but my coming I do more and more see necessary, on divers accounts, though a troublesome and costly journey. . . . I am not without hopes of a tolerable conclusion, tho it will not be obtained without charge and pains. They that seek the ruin of proprietors, they say, will renew their Bill, but try the Commons first, this time. I shall say little of that affair, only pray fail not to send what I so much need, and was so indiscreetly disregarded, viz. all requisite certificates and affidavits that are yet behind, as to our conduct and our foolish knavish enemies also.[178]

The death in January 1702 of Philip Ford, for many years Penn's principal business agent and private banker in England, ushered in an ordeal of litigation and imprisonment that in the end cost Penn £7,600—mostly borrowed money—to settle with Ford's estate. The additional costs in time and energy of Penn's long-standing debt to Ford spanned nearly seven years after the proprietor's return to England.

Then, on March 1 Phineas Pemberton died. After foreseeing the approaching death of the "father of Bucks County"[179] the previous September when he wrote to Logan that "poor Phineas

---

[177] For the bill, see *The Manuscripts of the House of Lords, 1699–1702* (London, 1908), 314–15. In general, see *PWP*, 4:63–65.

[178] Penn to James Logan, January 4, 1702, *PWP*, 4:141–42.

[179] This is Logan's term, used in his letter to Penn dated July 4, 1705, *PWP*, 4:362–63.

is a dying man,"[180] Penn even then had further need of Pemberton's services and so in late October appointed him one of the ten members of the proprietor and governor's new Council of State. Upon learning of Pemberton's death, Penn wrote from London to Logan in 1702, "I mourn for poor Phineas Pemberton, the ablest as well as one of the best men in the province."[181] Samuel Carpenter had given the news to Penn, informing him that

> Phineas Pemberton died the 1st month last [March] and will be greatly missed, having left few or none in these parts or adjacent like him for wisdom, integrity and general service, and he was a true friend to thee and the government. It is a matter of sorrow when I call to mind and consider that the best of our men are taken away, and how many are gone and how few to supply their places.[182]

Samuel Carpenter himself was one of those "best of our men" whose service to Penn and the province was vital to the early stability of the new government. He had arrived in Philadelphia in July 1683, having prospered through business ventures in Barbados despite suffering penalties for refusing military service. Besse records that for his "defaults in appearing or sending men in arms," Carpenter was "distressed" (suffered the legal and forcible taking from him) of 1,110 pounds of sugar and that for the same offense he and one Henry Whearly were distressed of 6,673 pounds of sugar.[183] His departure from Barbados was also hastened by his repugnancy at the treatment and condition of enslaved Africans as well as at local legislation intended to prevent their attendance at Friends' meetings for worship. In Penn's province, Carpenter became an investor in wharves, mines, timber, mills, and plantations, holding properties in the city and in Bucks and Chester Counties as well as in West Jersey. Over time, he and Penn partnered in some ventures.

---

[180] Penn to James Logan, September 8, 1701, *PWP*, 4:88.

[181] As quoted in Jordan, *Colonial Families of Philadelphia*, 1:281.

[182] Ibid. Pemberton could well have been providing his own epitaph when he signed his prefatory epistle in the first PYM minute book as "a friend to Truth, and a lover of all those that sincerely love it" (see appendix 4).

[183] Besse, *Sufferings of the People Called Quakers*, 2:318, 330.

Carpenter was also a diligent servant in the affairs of church and state. Penn first called him to duty in August 1684 as one of the eleven colonists deputized to manage the affairs of the province during the proprietor's first return to England, naming Carpenter, James Harrison, and three others as his commissioners of estate and revenue, responsible for collecting the proprietary receipts. Carpenter was elected for various terms to both the Provincial Assembly and Council, and after October 1701 he served appointed terms to the latter when it became the Council of State serving the proprietor and governor. He served as deputy governor of the province from November 24, 1694, until September 3, 1698, and as the provincial treasurer between 1704 and 1713. And, just as he had served with James Harrison by Penn's appointment in governing the province during the proprietor's first return to England, so by similar appointment he served with Phineas Pemberton, Harrison's son-in-law, when Penn made his second (and last) journey across the Atlantic.

In Pemberton's final years, he and Carpenter had reason to bond even more closely. Pemberton's son Israel, born in 1685 at Grove Place in Bucks County, had been sent by his father to Philadelphia for his formal education at Friends Public School under the care of Philadelphia Monthly Meeting. There, in the summer of 1698, Francis Daniel Pastorius, the assistant school master, had beaten the thirteen-year-old Israel "in a fit of rage . . . with a stick for some perceived failing or infraction. The beating, about the head, was so severe that the boy's sister, with whom he was living, reported the incident to their father, Phineas, who withdrew the boy from the school."[184] Israel Pemberton never returned as a student. Rather, sometime after the incident he was bound as an apprentice to Samuel Carpenter to be instructed in mercantilism and domestic and foreign commercial trade practices and in political economy through the development of trading interests and partnerships. In these pursuits, Carpenter had achieved great success[185] and thus was an apt master for his apprentice, who served until reaching his majority in 1706, whereupon young Pemberton

---

[184] William Penn Charter School, *Better Than Riches: A Tricentennial History of the William Penn Charter School, 1689–1989* (Philadelphia: William Penn Charter School, 1988).

[185] Carpenter did suffer financially because of the depressed trade from 1702 to 1709 during Queen Anne's War.

entered into business for himself, and having an excellent talent for mercantile pursuits, and being industrious in his habits, he soon was extensively engaged in trade as was desirable. In the year 1708, he visited Barbadoes and other West India Islands for purposes of traffic, and doubtless to enter into business arrangements with men of standing there, as consignees or factors.[186]

In the time of his service as clerk of PYM and nearing the end of his life, the elder Pemberton wrote a "short testimony" in praise of God's "infinite goodness and good providence" in settling Quakers in the American wilderness, admonishing later generations of Friends neither to "trample under foot" their forefathers' work and sufferings nor "grow careless, slothful, and negligent" in God's work and service, for that will be "too heavy to be borne in the day of account." This testimony briefly reviewed the early life of the church in the Delaware Valley and served as Pemberton's own spiritual testament. It was placed in the opening pages of the first volume of PYM minutes after it passed from the hands of Phineas to his son Israel and then to Israel's son James during the latter's time as clerk of PYM.[187]

William III died one week after the death of Phineas Pemberton, on March 8, 1702. He had outlived his wife, Mary II, on the throne of England for eight years. Under the English Bill of Rights of 1689, Parliament invited Mary, the older daughter of James II, and her husband (and first cousin) William, the Stadtholder of Orange, both firm Protestants, to take the "crown and royal dignity" as king and queen of England, France, and Ireland "and the dominions thereunto belonging," noting that "it hath been found by experience that it is inconsistent with the safety and welfare of this Protestant kingdom to be governed by a popish prince, or by any king or queen marrying a papist." To secure Protestantism for the future, Parliament ordered the royal succession to be through Mary's heirs, then to her sister Anne or her heirs, and then through William's heirs. Mary and William being childless, Anne ascended the throne.[188]

---

[186] *The Friend* 31, 141–42 (January 7, 1858).

[187] For the text, see appendix 4.

[188] An act declaring the rights and liberties of the subject and settling the succession of the crown (commonly known as the Bill of Rights), 1 Gul. & Mar. Sess. 2 c. 2, in *The Statutes of the Realm*, 6:144.

Planting Pennsylvania 1682–1718

Providing a note of joy during this time of unrelenting dying was the birth of Hannah and William Penn's second son, Thomas, one day after the king's death. Thomas was born in Bristol, where his mother had gone to be with her parents for the birth. Penn himself was staying in London, where he remained most of the time on business and church concerns.

Although the reunification bill of 1701 failed to advance in the House of Lords that year, due in part to the active defense provided by William Penn Jr. on behalf of his father's proprietary interests—those interests also being his own as presumed heir of the province and its government—the bill's reintroduction was planned for early 1702 in the House of Commons. By that time, however, the Crown's attempt to compel the surrender of proprietary rights in colonial governments had been brought to an indefinite stop due to the royal transition. Instead, the initiative for change passed to Penn, who, in a radical turnabout, conceived his own plan of "resigning" to the Crown "upon a reasonable satisfaction" his governing rights in the colony. Increasingly discouraged by his ongoing battle with critics at the Board of Trade in London and with their allies and other factious Pennsylvanians in the province—as well as by a near-desperate need for both money and relief from expenses—as early as mid-1702 Penn began seriously considering the sale of the provincial government of Pennsylvania to the Crown.[189] In a letter of May 1703, he informed the Board of Trade of his intention, and one month later he submitted to the Lords Commissioners for Trade and Plantations a summary of his surrender proposals, asking £30,000 as the price for his government.[190]

Increasingly beset with financial problems, in January 1705 Penn tried to unclog the lethargic negotiations with the Board of Trade, offering in correspondence to modify his previously stated reservations and conditions but specifying a new requirement for preserving the colonials' liberty of conscience.[191] He pressed his initiative by presenting to the government, no later than the

---

[189] See Penn's letters to James Logan dated June 21 and July 28, 1702, *Microfilm*, 10:267, and *PWP*, 4:182n8, respectively. Generally, see Root, *Relations of Pennsylvania*, 343–56.

[190] For the texts of the May letter and of the June proposals, see *PWP*, 4:221–22 and 4:224–26, respectively.

[191] See Penn's letters to the Board of Trade, January 2, 3, and 11, 1705, and the Board's queries to Penn, January 11, 1705, *PWP*, 4:318–21. The reservation for liberty of conscience is made in the first letter, p. 319.

following April, a draft of his proposed deed for surrendering colonial governing powers.[192] Shortly after that he submitted his draft of a new royal patent[193] that included protective provisions for liberty of conscience, freedom of religion, affirmations rather than oaths, and Quaker marriages as well as "speech gesture or carriage," plus a provision against compulsory militia service. In addition, he made extensive provision for himself by proposing a grant of a "County Palatine or Palatinate" with the "regalities, powers, jurisdictions and authorities" as exercised in England's "County Palatine of Durham," that is, a county within a kingdom where the county owner held certain royal powers.[194] On June 6, 1705, Penn answered the objections of the Lords Commissioners to his draft of a new patent and then, in a further attempt to push forward, drastically reduced his requests and prayed the queen, in a letter received September 1, to grant upon the surrender to members of the Religious Society of Friends liberty of conscience, liberty of education "by schools of our own," exemption from militia service, and several other matters.[195]

Not until February 1707 did the Board of Trade conclude its study, finding it would be of "great use and benefit" if the colonial government were reunited with the Crown. Finally, or so it seemed, the official recommendation to proceed with the purchase of Pennsylvania's government was made to the Privy Council.[196] Of Penn himself the Board of Trade appreciatively wrote:

---

[192] For the text, see *PWP*, 4:344–45.

[193] For the text, see *PWP*, 4:353–58.

[194] The first county palatine or Palatinate in England was created by William of Normandy after the Norman Conquest of 1066. Borrowing a practice from continental Europe of settling a hereditary nobility to govern, with quasi-royal powers, a border county situated to act as a frontline defense for the kingdom, William granted such powers to the office of the bishop of Durham on England's Scottish border. The palatine powers were not completely lifted from Durham until 1836. In the meantime, other counties palatine had been created and terminated, such as for Chester on the Welsh border and for Lancaster on the Scottish marches. The charter of Maryland, granted by Charles I to Cecilius Calvert, second Baron Baltimore, on June 20, 1632, was with governing rights "as amply as any Bishop of Durham in our kingdom of England hath at any time heretofore had." Penn was requesting what Lord Baltimore had. C. C. Hall, *Narratives of Early Maryland 1633–1684* (New York: Charles Scribner's Sons, 1910), 103.

[195] *PWP*, 4:392–93.

[196] Board of Trade to the Earl of Sunderland, February 5, 1707, *PWP*, 4:571–73.

We take leave to represent, that upon consideration of his case, it appears to us that Mr. Penn with great expense, many risks and dangers, both to his person and fortune, with continued pains and industry, and by the help of his own personal interest, has in great part accomplished a very difficult undertaking, by cultivating and improving what before was a desolate wilderness into a well-peopled colony, which by an increase of trade, as appears by the accounts of the custom house, does yearly add a considerable revenue to Her Majesty; for effecting of which public work he has much impaired and diminished his own private fortune, not having had time enough hitherto to reap the profits of his forepast charge and labor, and the returns which have been made him not countervailing in any reasonable degree his many expenses.

But then in May the Board again asked Penn for financial information he had previously submitted. In July, he sharply responded that

I am extremely concerned that after almost six years' attendance and the necessary great expense thereof, with a family in town, that what has been done should be done over again, like a man that being ready to enter his port is blown back again to that he left.

His response also included a reduction in his asking price for the government of Pennsylvania to £20,000.[197]

Again, bureaucratic lethargy followed. Again, Penn sought to urge consideration of his proposal and wrote, in July 1710, a respectful memorial (statement of facts) to "the Queen and her ministry . . . for the more speedy dispatch of the affair."[198] He reminded her that "near thirty years ago" he had received from Charles II "an unhospitable wilderness" now raised "to a flourishing country . . . from whence considerable advantages have accrued to the kingdom, as well by the constant consumption of its manufactures, and improvement of navigation, as by the increase of duties paid here on goods from

---

[197] See William Popple Jr. to Penn, May 1707, and Penn to Popple, July 2, 1707, *PWP*, 4:583–84. Popple, having succeeded his father as secretary of the Board of Trade, served from May 1707 until his death in 1722.

[198] For the text, see *PWP*, 4:681–83.

thence." He also reminded her of the grant to him from James II, then Duke of York, of the land on the lower part of the Delaware now included in his colonial enterprise. The memorial seemed to make a gentle appeal to the camaraderie aboard the *Royal Charles* that Admiral Penn had once shared with Anne's royal uncle and father, men to whom both the writer and his father had been ever loyal. Back the matter went to the Board of Trade, which in November again asked Penn for financial data.[199] Answering in December that the information sought was already before them, on February 2, 1711, Penn submitted a memorial to the Board restating the justice of his offer.[200] Then, within only eleven days, the Board rendered its opinion "that the revesting the government of Pennsylvania in your majesty will be a benefit to the trade of this kingdom."[201] In the only reference to matters of conscience and religion, which for Penn made up the critical core of his 'experiment,' the Board reported only his limited but most diplomatically expressed hope that

> he should think himself obliged on surrendering his government to desire leave in all humility to recommend to your majesty's royal protection and favor the people called Quakers (who under him first settled, cultivated, and improved that colony) were he not so sensible of your majesty's great justice and goodness that he doubts not but they will be protected in a full enjoyment of that indulgence in religious matters, and of all those civil rights and privileges which by law they now enjoy.[202]

The mills of the bureaucracy continued to grind slowly. Not until February 1712 did the attorney general issue his official, and favorable, report to the lord treasurer,[203] and not until September 9 that year did Anne's warrant go forth to "our high treasurer" declaring her resolve to accept the surrender of Penn's governing rights in Pennsylvania for the price, which she reduced, of £12,000, stating it to be "our will and pleasure" that he should have a present advance of £1,000, with the balance to

---

[199] For the Board's letter, see *PWP*, 4:683–84.

[200] For the texts of Penn's letter dated December 7, 1710, and his memorial dated February 10, 1711, both to the Board of Trade, see *PWP*, 4: 684–86 and *Microfilm*, 14:209.

[201] For the full text of the report of the Board of Trade to Queen Anne dated February 13, 1711, see *PWP*, 4:689–92.

[202] *PWP*, 4:690.

[203] See *PWP*, 4:726n2; for the text, see *Microfilm*, 14:367.

be paid in four years from the execution of the deeds of surrender and conveyance yet to be prepared.[204] Within days, the advance payment was made to Penn,[205] but there the matter came to a complete end, for Penn soon became incapacitated by the last two of the debilitating strokes that he suffered in 1712. Thus it was that English bureaucratic lethargy ultimately defeated the transfer of Pennsylvania's government from William Penn back to the English Crown. As a result, colonial government remained in the hands of the Penn family until the American Revolution.

Finding direction for provincial affairs in state and church

Across the decade of Penn's unsuccessful attempt to sell his proprietary government to the English Crown for a fair consideration, he was beset with other major challenges. The series of deaths that had begun after his final voyage home to England included that, in April 1703, of Andrew Hamilton, his deputy governor in the colony. Hamilton was a Scottish merchant who, after immigrating to East Jersey in 1686, had served as governor there and later in both East and West Jersey until the government of the Jerseys was surrendered to the Crown in 1702.[206] Having found in Hamilton an experienced administrator whom Penn believed would be an able deputy governor for Pennsylvania during his own, hopefully brief, absence in England, the proprietor's commission was issued on October 27, 1701.[207] The Board of Trade's objection that this authority was not entrusted to an Englishman delayed Crown approval until January 21, 1703,[208] however, and even then it was granted for only a year. Further delay in delivery of the royal approbation resulted in Hamilton not knowing he had been confirmed in office at the time of his death on April 26, 1703.

Penn's search for Hamilton's replacement as deputy governor came at the same time that he initiated his approach to

---

[204] Warrant of Queen Anne to "our high treasurer," dated September 9, 1712. For the text, see *PWP*, 4:725–26.

[205] *PWP*, 4:726n4.

[206] *PWP*, 4:48n1; see also Proud, *History of Pennsylvania*, 1:452.

[207] *PWP*, 4:116n3. For the text of the commission, see *Microfilm*, 9:716.

[208] For the text of Queen Anne's approval of Andrew Hamilton as lieutenant governor, see *Microfilm*, 10:728.

the Crown for the sale of proprietary rights in the provincial government. Needing to cultivate better relations with the Board of Trade, he must have been especially careful about recommending a worthy and unobjectionable deputy governor. By early summer he had chosen John Evans (ca. 1678–ca. 1743), a twenty-six-year-old Welsh gentleman, for the post. Seeking the requisite Crown approval, on July 6, 1703, Penn petitioned the queen in a letter to the Board of Trade,[209] and the next day he wrote a second letter to the Board describing Evans' merits. He had received "a liberal education, been abroad and knows the world very well, is sober, discreet, and of a good understanding. No merchant and so no temptation that way. No soldier . . . is not in debt, but lives like a gentleman upon his estate here. He is a single man, neither voracious nor extravagant, and is a known zealous member of the Church of England."[210] Weeks later, in a letter to Logan, who was but four years older than Evans, Penn noted that the new deputy was "the son of an old friend of mine that valued me not a little."[211] These two youthful administrators of the colony were to be joined by an even younger agent for Penn, his own son William Jr., the twenty-two-year-old heir apparent to the proprietorship who was then being sent to the province by his father.

Evans arrived in Philadelphia in February 1704. Although he came without any administrative experience, he had the benefit of Penn's personal instructions laid out in a letter dated August 9, 1703, advising him under fourteen points, the first being,

> Take care in all things, to keep within the compass of and to keep up the powers of my grants from King Charles the Second and his brother the Duke of York; and the laws and constitutions of the country made in pursuance thereof by and with the early unanimity of the country; and in no wise suffer them to be broken in upon by any refractory or factious persons whatever; that as I would

---

[209] In a petition to Queen Anne (*Microfilm*, 10:1022) sent with a cover letter to the Board of Trade (*Microfilm*, 10:1024), both dated July 6, 1703, William Penn sought crown approval of John Evans as the new governor for the colony.

[210] Penn to Board of Trade, July 8, 1703, *PWP*, 4:227. The Board gave its approval July 9 (*PWP*, 4:244n6).

[211] Penn to James Logan, August 27, 1703, *PWP*, 4:240.

not have thee exert the rigor of thy authority, so neither to endure it to be condemned or encroached upon.[212]

In addition to Penn's written instructions on such other matters as the maintenance of strict compliance with the laws of trade and plantations, the administration of justice, and the keeping of public order, Evans was to have the advice and counsel of James Logan, who, probably better than any other person in the province, knew Penn's mind in the constant oversight of government affairs. Penn's tenth instruction was the recommendation that Evans seek the "esteem and conversation for knowledge and counsel" of five eminent Quakers in the community, and he named Samuel Carpenter, Edward Shippen, Richard Hill, Griffith Owen, and Isaac Norris as well as Logan. And, in a notable display of fairness, Penn also named seven men "that go to the Church of England" as being "moderate church men" worthy of cultivating.[213]

Shortly after arriving in the province, Evans vigorously attempted to head off the looming legislative separation of the province from those adjacent territories at the mouth of the Delaware River and along the Bay to the ocean that were known as the lower counties (then, as now, the Delaware counties of New Castle, Kent, and Sussex). In April, the new deputy governor convened a meeting of elected representatives from the province and territories in the Council chamber in Philadelphia and attempted to reunite them and "to bring about a coalition, so necessary for both."[214] He was, in fact, racing against the deadline of October 28, 1704, the third anniversary of the Charter of Privileges Penn had granted as "Proprietary and Governor of the Province of Pennsylvania and Territories belonging thereto," which, in its final addendum, provided for the "separation of the Province and Territories in respect of legislation" upon their failure to "agree to come together."[215] Although Evans acted with promising energy, his purpose failed. In response to his plea,

---

[212] Penn to John Evans, August 9, 1703, *PWP*, 4:230.

[213] The men Penn named were William Markham, Samuel Finney, Robert Assheton, John Bewly, Thomas Farmer, William Trent, and Charles Read.

[214] Proud, *History of Pennsylvania*, 1:458.

[215] See *PWP*, 4:150.

the members of the territories, who before appeared to have principally occasioned the division, now seemed willing to accede, to accept the charter on conditions, and to unite with the members of the province in legislation; but the latter, who had so long been hampered with the refractory behavior of the former, now, in their turn, absolutely refused to be connected with them, and adhered to their prior agreement for a separation.[216]

Penn wrote apprehensively to Logan on July 22:

> This business of the disunion sticks with me still. I fear 'twill lead to a worse thing.... What will the Queen think after all my memorials to preserve the government without a seam, to find, and that on our side, it is torn into. O the weakness of men![217]

The winner in this political theater was undoubtedly David Lloyd, former attorney general of Pennsylvania, who was radicalized into Penn's implacable political foe upon being dismissed from the provincial government by the proprietor himself at the order of the Board of Trade. Following his dismissal in early 1700, Lloyd set about organizing and leading an antiproprietary political force representing the interests of the provincial property owners. These owners came from many factious groups, and their interests spanned serious concerns, including those regarding local defense while colonial wars threatened to overflow from nearby provinces; the economic and legal constraints forced by England's regulation of colonial trade; the constant demands for payment of the proprietary quitrents; and the cloud of uncertainty raised by Penn's negotiations to sell his government to the Crown after hurrying back to England to prevent such a Crown takeover. Lloyd, a Quaker, because of his active presence in Pennsylvania had a decided advantage over Penn who, living in England, was always many months behind in receiving reliable news of developments in this explosive mix. Nor was the youthful and inexperienced Evans any match for Lloyd, who for twelve of the years between 1703 and 1728 was elected speaker of the Assembly that, because of Penn's grant in 1701 of the Charter of Privileges, had become the sole provincial

---

[216] Proud, *History of Pennsylvania*, 1:458.
[217] Penn to James Logan, July 22, 1704, *PWP*, 4:284.

legislative body. From that position of influence and control Lloyd could—and did—hamstring Penn's government.

Lloyd used his control as speaker in 1704 to have the Assembly authorize a committee of eight to draft an address of remonstrance to Penn detailing the grievances against the proprietor. Seizing the opportunity, Lloyd, according to Logan, wrote the remonstrance himself with only one other committee member and then signed it "by order of the House" at a date beyond his term of office. The impolitic intensity of Lloyd's anger toward the proprietor sounds in his words near the close:

> And we hope we need not be more express in charging thee as thou tenders thy own honor and honesty or the obligations thou art under to thy friends and particularly thy first purchasers and adventurers into this province that thou do not surrender the government [on] whatever terms thou may . . . make for thy self and family, which we shall deem no less than a betraying [of] us, and at best will look like first fleecing than selling. . . . And if after thy endeavors used to keep the government it be perforce taken from thee thou will be clearer in the sight of God and us the representatives of the people of this thy province who are thy real friends and well wishers, as we hope is evident in that we have dealt thus plainly with thee.[218]

Lloyd's campaign of confrontation continued when, in November 1706, the Assembly demanded the dismissal of James Logan and then, in December, of both Logan and Evans.[219] In February 1707 articles were drawn up for the impeachment of Logan,[220] and then in June the Assembly issued a further remonstrance to Penn for the dismissal of Evans and Logan.[221]

Evans, however, through his own misadventures, had rendered himself in Penn's judgment unfit for his administrative responsibilities, and the governor needed neither advice nor

---

[218] Address of Remonstrance from the Provincial Assembly to Penn dated August 25, 1704, *PWP*, 4:295–304, at p. 303.

[219] *PWP*, 4:563n14, 592n 2.

[220] *PWP*, 4:601n23. For the text, see State of Pennsylvania, *Minutes of the Provincial Council of Pennsylvania, from the Organization to the Termination of the Proprietary Government*, 17 vols. (Harrisburg, PA: 1851–1860), 2:344–47 (hereafter cited as *MPCP*).

[221] *PWP*, 4:600n5.

demands from the Assembly to replace his deputy. In his letter to Evans of May 15, 1707,[222] Penn observed that Evans was "disgraced" and that Penn had grave uneasiness concerning reports received of Evans' involvement in the hoax of reporting an approaching French naval invasion coming up the Delaware to Philadelphia and the deep confusion resulting from so malicious a false alarm;[223] of Evans's procuring passage by the Delaware Assembly of a militia act that penalized Quakers who would not serve in the militia; and of Evans's encouraging the growth of vice by failing to suppress it, citing David Lloyd's report of Evans beating a Philadelphia constable attempting to break up a tavern brawl in which Evans himself was involved. There being no satisfactory reply to this letter, on May 27, 1708, Penn again wrote Evans.[224] Now he added two new charges: of "an extreme false step" in allowing New Castle to impose a tonnage tax payable in gunpowder on vessels coming into the Delaware River and of "a lewd deportment at Conestoga" involving Evans's release of an absconding debtor. By now Penn had had enough, and he informed Evans, albeit gently, that, as it was time "to change hands," he had petitioned the queen for her approbation of "my choice and commission," not telling Evans in the letter that his selection as the new deputy was Charles Gookin.

If the state during these years seemed in search of direction, the church in the province appeared to be on a steady course. Despite the loss of leadership PYM suffered in 1702 with the death of Phineas Pemberton, other eminent Friends came forward to continue the meeting's growth. No clerk was again named in the minutes until 1711, but it appears from the appointments for signing various epistles during the intervening years that the clerk's duties were held by Griffith Owen in 1702, by Caleb Pusey and Anthony Morris in 1704, and by Morris again in 1710. The meeting's signal accomplishment during these years was the adoption in 1704 of the first *Book of Discipline*, a topical codification of its advices and testimonies[225] from earlier days

---

[222] *PWP*, 4:575–77.

[223] The invasion hoax was reported to Penn by Logan in his letter dated May 28, 1706, *PWP*, 4:534–35.

[224] *PWP*, 4:605–07.

[225] The advices and testimonies at this time were excerpts from the minutes and epistles of Quaker yearly and other meetings intended as guidance for the soul's inward journey to find God and for living in harmony with the Truth. They served as the chief means of establishing a "discipline" among the congregants.

concerning the church's discipline and organizational structure. It had been prepared by a committee of fifteen appointed at the meeting of 1703, whose members included Owen, Pusey, and Morris. This 1704 *Discipline*, as well as its 1719 revision titled *The Book of Discipline*, were published only in manuscript form as the works were meant to circulate within the Religious Society of Friends, not in society in general.[226] Other institutional foundations were laid with the appointment, in 1705, of a committee to correspond with other American yearly meetings "as there may be occasion," and, in 1709, of the initial Overseers of the Press, a body of eight members that included Owen, Pusey, Morris, and Isaac Norris.[227]

Although Penn's new deputy governor in the province, Charles Gookin, was an older person of good family, a soldier in the War of the Spanish Succession, bearer of the title of colonel, and initially believed by Penn to be possessed of "virtue, moderation, good humor,"[228] he, too, proved as unsatisfactory in the position as his predecessor. He was dismissed in 1717. Again, as with Evans before him, Gookin was an Anglican and a bachelor, but of Irish rather than Welsh descent. Again, as with Evans, Penn referred him to the wise guidance of Quakers such as Samuel Carpenter, Griffith Owen, Isaac Norris, and Richard Hill to "avoid the Rock the former governor split upon." In Penn's letter to these trusted Friends and allies in the province, he wrote:

> I have sent you a new governor of years and experience, of a quiet and easy temper, that will give offense to none, nor too easily put up [with] any if offered him. . . . He has promised me to avoid the Rock the former governor split upon, as much as he can. He is sober, understands to command and obey, moderate in his temper, and of what they call a good family, his grandfather Sir Vincent

---

[226] See R. W. Kelsey, "Early Books of Discipline of Philadelphia Yearly Meeting," *Bulletin of Friends Historical Association*, 24:12–23.

[227] The Overseers of the Press was a body of censors created by the following 1709 resolution of PYM: "The care of the Press being recommended to the care of Philadelphia Monthly Meeting, [to appoint] a committee of eight Friends, any five of whom are desired to take care to peruse all writings or manuscripts that are intended to be printed, before they go to the Press, with power to correct what may not be for the service of Truth; otherwise not to suffer anything to be printed." PYM Min Bk A, p. 90.

[228] Penn to James Logan, September 29, 1708, *PWP*, 4:619.

> Gookin having been an early great planter in Ireland in King James the First's time and the first King Charles's days, and intends if not ill treated to lay his bones as well as substance among you, having taken leave of the war and both Ireland and England to live among you. And as he is not voluptuous so he will be an example of thriftiness. In short, he has instructions as much to the virtue, justice, and peace of the country as I can express my self, or you desire for your comfortable living, I believe. Pray, therefore, receive him kindly.[229]

Gookin arrived in Philadelphia on January 31, 1709, having come, after his sea voyage, overland from Virginia through Maryland. He was proclaimed in his office on February 1 and the next day held a meeting of the Governor's Council. When, on February 3, Logan resumed his stream of written reports to Penn on affairs in the province,[230] he noted "the good news" of Gookin's arrival and then immediately set out the problem that would be a stumbling block for the duration of the new administration: the deputy governor's salary. By the time he came to Philadelphia, Gookin was aware that his official income in Pennsylvania compared unfavorably with equivalent offices in some of the other colonies. At the time, Penn was barely out of debtor's prison in London; he had never been able to either subsidize through his own resources or rely on the Assembly's commitment to authorize and supply an appropriate salary for the deputy governor. Logan understood from Gookin also that his expectation from Penn in London had been that the Assembly would provide him £400 annually but that Penn had obliged him at Portsmouth to agree to £200 annually, a salary that, at best, could be described as frugal. Most importantly, Logan found himself unable to pay Gookin anything, having only Penn's instructions to pay Gookin £100 against bills of exchange, bills that Gookin failed to produce. Further, Gookin claimed he had loaned Penn another £100 for the use of William Jr. and now wanted to be repaid, although he could not produce even those bills of exchange. Logan wrote:

> This makes both him and me uneasy, and indeed upon the small observations he has been able to make of the

---

[229] Penn to Samuel Carpenter and others, September 28, 1708, *PWP*, 4:616–17.

[230] James Logan to Penn, February 3, 1709, *PWP*, 4:629–34.

country, he is apprehensive that he has changed for the worse. . . . He seems to be a plain honest man and of a temper best suiting a soldier; but of prudence enough to consider as well how he himself is to live in the world, as how he shall be helpful to others in it, and therefore seems jealous, from the opportunities he has had of considering matters in passing through Virginia and Maryland, that he shall be far from being enabled by his new post to make any provision for a change if one should happen, that his whole allowance will scarce be a subsistence. . . . This is the substance of a discourse he had with me yesterday, and I cannot but think it will prove a great unhappiness to us if his reflections upon the disappointment he may think he meets with should discourage his zeal in the business he is engaged in, for were he a Solomon he will certainly meet with enough to try his temper. But we shall do our best.[231]

The next disappointment for Gookin, who had been a professional soldier, arose out of his concern for the security of the province in his charge. His arrival in the latter years of Queen Anne's War (1702–1713), the second of the four wars during the colonial period that spilled over from Europe's dynastic conflicts into North America, coincided with pressing defense issues, one in the lower counties and the other in a regional strategy contemplating armed invasion from New England into Canada. As Logan reported to Penn, an English naval vessel that had been captured and made into a French privateer landed a force of men at Lewes in the lower counties and plundered the town in early May.[232] Other enemy forces had also infested that coast. Further, the Crown had ordered the American colonies to make their several contributions in men or money to the proposed Canadian expedition, but the Assembly in peaceable Pennsylvania had deferred compliance. Logan's letter contrasts with the rising anxieties about security in the population and with the principles prevailing in the Assembly where Quakers held control. The situation along coastal Delaware, he wrote,

> has exceedingly alarmed the country beyond what could be easily imagined from no more pressing a danger. . . .

---

[231] *PWP*, 4:630–31.
[232] James Logan to Penn, June 14, 1709, *PWP*, 4:647–51.

This threw those who are always calling for a defense under the greatest uneasiness and has put them upon forming an address to the Queen or Lords which I believe no endeavors here will be sufficient to prevent. Friends are so tired out with the clamors and abuses of these men that the thoughts of government become very uncomfortable to them. And what heightens their uneasiness is the indignation of others at the Assembly's refusal to do any thing in obedience to the queen's commands towards the expedition against Canada. . . . [The deputy governor] must of necessity answer the queen's letter to him which is exceedingly positive in this business and for his answer must send a copy of the Assembly's proceedings, which I am sure will be of no service to thee, this place, or Friends of any other.[233]

Not only was the Pennsylvania Assembly a hindrance to Gookin in his oversight of provincial defense matters, but its interference in proprietary administration was another stumbling block. Since November 1706 the antiproprietary Assembly had been unsuccessfully seeking to get at Penn by demanding James Logan's dismissal from his offices as secretary of the province and member of the Proprietary and Governor's Council.[234] In February 1708, it voted articles of impeachment against Logan, but John Evans, then deputy governor, refused to judge the charges.[235] By 1709 Logan, who had served as Penn's eyes and ears in Pennsylvania for a decade, was resolved to return to England for consultations with Penn on the future course of the province while negotiations continued for the sale of the government to the Crown, dismaying many Friends in Philadelphia. Logan's impeachment had been at a standstill from the outset, and he wanted to resolve the matter; he demanded more specific charges, but the Assembly refused. There matters remained until the eve of his departure for England, when Logan petitioned the Assembly for a trial in order to clear himself. The response was a warrant issued by the Assembly for Logan's arrest, which was then trumped by a superseding order from Gookin to the sheriff of Philadelphia that Logan be protected

---

[233] *PWP*, 4:647–48.

[234] See James Logan to Penn, February 26, 1706, *PWP*, 4:562.

[235] See Penn to James Logan, May 3, 1708, *PWP*, 4:597–602 (see especially 4:601n23).

from such interference. In consequence, there was no trial of impeachment, and on December 3, 1709, Logan boarded Isaac Norris's ship *Hope Galley* to sail for England.[236] He was away for over two years. Gookin, meanwhile, was left to exercise the executive power of government without benefit of the experience and sagacity of Penn's agent in the province.[237]

While Penn pursued his plan to sell the proprietary governing rights to the Crown, he was concerned to protect the basic liberties upon which Pennsylvania had been founded. Of particular concern was the right to make an affirmation (solemnly declaring a matter to be true under penalty of perjury) in lieu of taking an oath (using the name of God to attest that one's word is true). This was a hard-won right for which Quakers had suffered in England. On March 14, 1711, Penn wrote to Gookin while Logan was still out of the province and expressed his wish that the Assembly "seriously and soberly consider what is fit for them in modesty to ask of the crown as well as me . . . for a fitting and requisite affirmation to be taken in evidence and for qualifying officers."[238] In 1696 the Assembly had passed an affirmation act for officials assuming office, but a similar law of 1700 had been disallowed by the Crown. And a 1694 law allowing witnesses to testify "by solemnly promising to speak the truth, the whole truth, and nothing but the truth" in all legal proceedings was approved, but later the Church of England complained that England's Quakers Act of 1695 only permitted affirmations in civil, not criminal, cases.[239] As Isaac Norris, on behalf of himself and the other stalwart Quaker loyalists on the Provincial Council, wrote in April to inform Penn, on February 28 Gookin and the Assembly had passed fourteen laws, including an affirmation act that was being actively opposed by the Church of England in Philadelphia through its vestry (presumably a reference to the board of trustees, so named, of Christ Church) in a letter to the Bishop of London with representations to the British Crown.[240] Norris's letter evidences both the growing

---

[236] Tolles, *James Logan and the Culture of Provincial America*, 75.

[237] See Wilson Armistead, *Memoirs of James Logan: A Distinguished Scholar and Christian Legislator* (London: C. Gilpin, 1851), 27–31.

[238] Penn to Charles Gookin, March 14, 1711, *PWP*, 4:694.

[239] *PWP*, 4:696n7.

[240] Provincial Council (signed by Isaac Norris) to Penn, April 10, 1711, *PWP*, 4:696–99.

sectarian discord in the province and Gookins's partisanship therein.[241]

> The affirmation act (of which enclosed is a copy) has stirred up great uneasiness and opposition in some men of the church and as we understand a vestry was called under color of augmenting the church . . . and a letter written to the Bishop of London and as we are also informed a representation to the queen against the said act . . . [we entreat] thy interest and care for a confirmation if possible. Otherwise our condition here as Friends will be very precarious and hard, as thou art fully sensible, and this being a law that was for the ease of our Society [of Friends] and to the general satisfaction of Friends here. . . . The [deputy] governor has used his endeavors to please and oblige the church men, has adapted his commissioners on our new constitutions of courts accordingly, putting in this county seven of them to five Quakers and in the other counties as many as could be got or by any means thought fit. . . . But now it is so managed and wrought up that not one of the church magistrates . . . did or would act, so that to disappoint the supposed design of bringing in oaths before Friends on the bench thereby to strengthen their complaint, the courts have only been called and adjourned, and thus matters now stand.[242]

The depth of the sectarian discord is revealed in these passages from the correspondence of the Anglicans in Philadelphia to the Bishop of London, which Norris attached to his letter.

> When the interest of our holy mother Church of England is attacked by her restless enemies the Quakers . . . we presume to enclose to your lordship an humble address to her majesty in behalf of this infant branch planted in the midst of a people dangerous to church and state, to one denying the benefit of the laws, to the other the use of arms. . . . We beg leave to lay before you the dangerous and pernicious effects of several other laws made this

---

[241] The act was titled "An act directing an affirmation to such who for conscience' sake cannot take an oath," in *The Statutes at Large of Pennsylvania from 1682–1801*, comp. James T. Mitchell and Henry Flanders (Harrisburg, PA: State Printer, 1896), 2:355–57.

[242] *PWP*, 4:697.

Assembly . . . but above all our present naked circumstances. . . . The naked circumstances is the want of defense expressing how open we lie to the enemy that the French have been several times up in the river and done mischief in the outskirts of the country. . . . [They] carry on their design of passing their law or act for affirmation or to that purpose and that the laws of this kind have been so often repealed or disliked by the queen yet nothing will obstruct them. Therefore we beg it may be put out of their power of doing the like hereafter, or to this purpose.[243]

Shortly after, Penn heard from nine of his loyal Philadelphia Friends, who included Isaac Norris, Samuel Carpenter, Griffith Owen, and Edward Shippen, commenting on the proposed surrender of "this large and fruitful country so commodiously situated on a noble capacious navigable river and bay, for trade as it were in the center of the English Empire on the main [the high sea]."[244] Noted were

the great difficulties which thou and Friends here lie under in the executive part of the government for want of a militia and defense and for not taking and administering oaths, without which some look upon themselves unsafe, which grows worse and worse and is come to that point by the refusal of the Church of England magistrates to sit in courts ever since the [deputy] governor passed the act for the affirmation, that a full stop is thereby put to our courts of justice and thereupon occasions are taken for complaints to the queen against Friends as being unfit to be concerned in government. The constant uneasiness of the Church of England party under the administration of Friends and the frequent attempts to wrest the government out of thy hands, and endeavors to deprive us of the affirmation acts and other laws most suited to our conscientious circumstances, to bring us under sufferings or render us obnoxious to our superiors and to make thee and Friends dissenters under thy own government and these bold attempts being made against thee and us while thou

---

[243] *PWP*, 4:698–99.
[244] Edward Shippen and others to Penn, May 23, 1711, *PWP*, 4:700.

sits at the helm, what may we expect when thou hast given up thy charge when it will be out of thy power to assist and defend us.... We put thee in mind of our laws and charters in general and particularly our laws for liberty of conscience and the affirmation act.[245]

In the end, the affirmation act of February 1711 was short-lived. It was repealed by order of the queen in Council on December 19, 1711. On receiving that news, the Provincial Assembly then passed, on June 7, 1712, "A supplementary act about the manner of giving evidence," which in turn was repealed on February 20, 1714.[246] The situation so deteriorated from there that James Logan wrote on March 2, 1715, "We have no courts, no judicial proceedings, these two years past," and Isaac Norris about the same time penned, "We have now no justice administered, and everybody does what is right in their own eyes."[247]

Gookin's administration drifted into a general malaise as he increased the time spent at his plantation in the lower counties, removing himself from Philadelphia's Quaker leadership while trying to secure through other political allies his appointment as royal governor in the event of the Crown's takeover of Pennsylvania's government.[248] Logan noted Gookin's refusal during this period to honor commissions to public office and his interest in the "raking in of money" for his own use.[249] Finally, on September 13, 1716, a petition was made to the new royal government in London of George I for the approval of William Keith (1680–1749) as governor.[250] Keith, then the surveyor general of customs in the colonies, was approved in November. His administration of Pennsylvania, beginning in May 1717 after the dismissal of Gookin, lasted about ten years.[251]

The Religious Society of Friends remained steadfast in Pennsylvania throughout the Gookin years. Beginning in 1711, the minutes of PYM resumed naming the clerk of the meeting,

---

[245] *PWP*, 4:701–2.

[246] See James Logan to Penn, June 12, 1712, *PWP*, 4:719–21n3.

[247] As quoted in Armistead, *Memoirs of James Logan*, 62.

[248] See Gary B. Nash, *Quakers and Politics: Pennsylvania, 1681–1726*, (Boston: Northeastern University Press, 1993), 314–15.

[249] *PWP*, 4:743nn13, 15.

[250] *Microfilm*, 14:578.

[251] *PWP*, 4:751n2.

and for nineteen consecutive years that clerk was Isaac Norris, a man already eminent in the affairs of PYM and active in the business community of Philadelphia as a venture merchant. He was a trusted adviser and confidant of Penn, having been away in England between 1706 and 1708 to help the proprietor defend himself in his worsening financial conflict with Philip Ford's heirs. Norris served in the Provincial Assembly for many years between 1699 and 1734, being elected its speaker in 1712 and 1720, and he also served on the Governor's Council from 1709 to 1735.[252] In the first decade of his leadership of PYM, he presided over the recurring discussions of the slavery issue brought to the meeting by Chester Quarterly Meeting and participated in revising the first discipline book into its successor, the 1719 *Book of Discipline*, which was published in manuscript form only.

Norris gave stability to the Quaker ecclesiastical structure through his leadership over nearly two decades as the affairs of state remained factional and adrift. Also during this period, the next generation of Quaker leaders was assuming positions of responsibility and bonding through family ties and community activities. Of significance was the marriage in 1710 of Israel Pemberton, son of the late Phineas Pemberton, to Rachel Read of Burlington, New Jersey, whose sister Sarah would marry James Logan in 1714. This was also the year of a historic dynastic shift in Great Britain as Anne, the last of the Stuart monarchs, died and George I, the first of the Hanoverian monarchs, came to the British throne. Whatever stability the province itself could find during the next decades would appear to be due more to the continuity in public service of Logan, a humanist and secular Quaker, and the steady hand of leaders in PYM such as Norris. Norris's son Isaac II married Logan's daughter Sarah in 1739. With the incapacity and then death of Penn, Logan and Norris became the chief representatives of the Penn family's proprietary interests in America.[253]

Penn's last crises

The force that drove William Penn across the Atlantic in 1701 was the need to be in England to protect his Pennsylvania

---

[252] American Council of Learned Societies, *Dictionary of American Biography*, 20 vols. (New York: Scribner's, 1928–36), 13:553–54.

[253] Ibid., 13:554.

investment, that investment principally being founded on the estate inherited from his father and the wealth borrowed from others whom he was obligated to repay. Other paramount concerns were the needs to protect the freedoms and fortunes of many venture planters already deeply committed in the province and to secure the fruits of his own dedicated labor over twenty years in shaping a new social order founded on liberty of conscience and freedom of religion. Penn, now fifty-seven years old, above all else was driven by the need to settle the well-being of his wife and children and their succeeding generations through careful stewardship of his proprietary interests in Pennsylvania, whether or not those included the right of government. Thwarting the compelling needs of Penn's later years were the three coming crises he was to endure.

The first crisis began with the death of Springett, his eldest son, at Lewes (Sussex) on April 10, 1696. The loss of Springett just two years after that of the young man's mother, Gulielma, dashed Penn's hopes of passing on his proprietorship to this promising heir. Penn memorialized the double deaths of "my excellent child, to my deepest grief"[254] and of his mother in his work *An Account of the Blessed End*.[255]

After the death of the twenty-year-old Springett, Springett's younger brother (and Gulielma's surviving son) William Jr. became Penn's presumed successor as the proprietor and governor of Pennsylvania. In January 1701, Penn wrote from the province to William Jr. in England with directions and advice regarding advocating for the proprietary (including governmental) rights with Parliament, the Board of Trade, and, if need be, the monarch.[256] The son, who in ten weeks' time would be twenty years old, was to act as Penn's agent in London together with the experienced Charlwood Lawton. Already married and the father of a daughter and soon to become the father of his first son, much was hoped for and needed from young Penn. After the father returned to England, he had expectations that William Jr. would travel to Pennsylvania for a closer experience of the place. In early 1703, before the death of

---

[254] Penn to Robert Turner, December 25, 1696, *PWP*, 3:472.

[255] This was privately printed in 1699 under the full title *An Account of the Blessed End of Gulielma Maria Penn, and of Springet* [sic] *Penn, the beloved wife and eldest son of William Penn*, "for the benefit of his family, relations, and particular friends, in memory of them, and the Lord's goodness to them."

[256] Penn to William Penn Jr., January 2, 1701, *PWP*, 4:27–30.

Planting Pennsylvania 1682–1718

Deputy Governor Andrew Hamilton, Penn had written Logan that his son was coming soon and, revealing his anxieties about what might happen, gave Logan these instructions:

> Immediately take him away to Pennsbury and there give him the true state of things, and weigh down his levities as well as temper his resentments, and inform his understanding, since all depends upon it as well for his future happiness as in measure the poor country's. . . . Watch him, outwit, and honestly overreach him—for his good. Fishing, little journeys, as to see the Indians, etc. will divert him, and pray Friends to bear all they can and melt towards him, that they may melt and gain him, at least civilly if not religiously. He will empty himself to thee. . . . Pennsylvania has cost me dearer in my poor child than all other considerations.[257]

The proprietor's heir apparent delayed his trip to Philadelphia until February 2, 1704, when he arrived with John Evans, who was taking up his duties as deputy governor following the untimely death of his predecessor, Andrew Hamilton. Evans was single and three years older than the young Penn, who had left his wife and three small children at home in Warminghurst. On February 15 Logan wrote Penn about the arrival, observing of the son:

> It is his stock of excellent good nature that in a great measure has led him out into his youthful sallies when too easily prevailed on, and the same I hope when seasoned with the influences of his prevailing better judgment, with which he is well stored, will happily conduct him into the channel of his duty to God, himself, and thee. He is very well received and seldom fails of drawing love where he comes and hope it will be increased. 'Tis his good fortune here to be withdrawn from those temptations that have been too successful over his natural sweetness and yielding temper with his associates.[258]

---

[257] Penn to James Logan, January 24, 1703, *PWP*, 4:208–9. The last sentence is an expression of Penn's concern that his preoccupation with Pennsylvania's affairs had kept him from guiding this immature and profligate son into responsible adulthood.

[258] James Logan to Penn, February 15, 1704, *PWP*, 4:263.

Writing to Penn on the same date, William Jr. reported only that he was at "Pennsbury and like it well," asking his father for a "good gardener" so that "I could make it one of the pleasantest places in the world" and begging both that he "may have some more hounds sent over" as well as the stallion "thee promised to get for me, he is a fine horse."[259] Nothing was written of the province or its people, not even that Evans had appointed him a member of the Proprietary and Governor's Council. The son asked his father to excuse him for not being "able to write much . . . for I suppose James Logan will supply my defect." It was Logan who told Penn of the Council appointment.

The events during William Jr.'s stay in the province were so unsettling that he fled the place in November of the year he arrived. During his nine months in Pennsylvania in 1704, he earned both in his public conduct and personal behavior the condemnation of the area's leading Quakers, his father's good friends, many of whom were meanwhile struggling in the general depression caused by the disruption of Pennsylvania's extensive mercantile trade in the Caribbean at the hands of French privateers in that theater of Queen Anne's War (1702–1713).[260] On May 25, deputy governor Evans issued a proclamation noting the queen's command that the colonial government make "due preparation . . . for the defense and security of the same," and ordering that all "inhabitants of this government . . . whose persuasion will, on any account, permit them to take up arms in their own defense, that forthwith they do provide themselves with a good firelock and ammunition, in order to enlist themselves in the militia."[261] Despite both the proclamation's exception for conscientious objectors and the professed adherence to the Friends' peace testimony shared by his father and leading Philadelphia Quakers, Penn Jr. took up arms and, for a while, the command of a militia unit. His fitness to be the proprietor's successor was put in jeopardy. Then in September he was involved in a Philadelphia tavern disturbance and charged to

---

[259] William Penn Jr. to William Penn, February 15, 1704, *PWP*, 4:261–62.

[260] One scholar has noted, concerning the economic situation when Penn Jr. and Evans arrived in February 1704, that "disheartening losses were suffered throughout the colony. Samuel Carpenter, whose mercantile success in the seventeenth century had been unequaled, went bankrupt. William Trent and Isaac Norris, Philadelphia's largest traders after Carpenter's retirement, lost one-third of their estates in 1704." Nash, *Quakers and Politics*, 253.

[261] Proud, *History of Pennsylvania*, 1:460.

appear before the mayor's court.[262] In October he sold, to Isaac Norris and William Trent, the gift he had received from his father of the 7,000-acre manor named Williamstadt near the Schuylkill River north of Philadelphia.[263] Shortly thereafter he left Pennsylvania, the province of which he might eventually have become the proprietor and governor. He never returned.

On his arrival in England in January 1705, William Jr. met with his father, as arranged by appointment, and conferred for three hours at a location somewhere between London and Warminghurst. The son dutifully delivered Logan's recent letters reporting the sad history of his own Pennsylvania sojourn. Penn's anguished, almost incoherent response to Logan reflected his near despair:

> A melancholy scene enough always; religiously upon my poor child: Pennsylvania began it by my absence here, and there it is accomplished, with expense, disappointment, ingratitude and poverty. The Lord uphold me under these sharp and heavy burdens. . . . He is my greatest affliction for his soul's and my posterity's and family's sake. . . . See, how much more the bad friends' treatment of him stumbled him from the blessed truth than those he acknowledges to be good ones could prevail to keep him in the profession of it, from the prevailing ground in himself to what is loose more than what is retired, circumspect, and virtuous.[264]

Back home in England, young Penn's career fared no better. In 1705 he lost an election for a seat in Parliament[265] and then unsuccessfully sought a position in the government through the Lord Treasurer.[266] Most devastating for the father was the son's renunciation that same year of the fellowship of the Quakers, the Religious Society of Friends, in which his father was a recognized leader and his deceased mother, as well as his own young wife, securely rooted. In writing to Samuel Carpenter and other Philadelphia friends, Penn thanked them for their letters of "comfort to me in the midst of my manifold afflictions, the

---

[262] *PWP*, 4:313n7, 328n33, 531n26.
[263] *PWP*, 4:387nn6–7, 532n27.
[264] Penn to James Logan, January 16, 1705, *PWP*, 4:322–23.
[265] Penn to James Logan, April 30, 1705, *PWP*, 4:346–52, 348n32.
[266] Penn to James Logan, December 28, 1705, *PWP*, 4:521–24, 523n17.

nearest, my poor son's going off from truth's way."[267] Penn's measured, practical response to the son's desertion of the Quakers for the Anglicans—thereby reversing the journey he himself had made to the despair of his own father—was to change his 1701 will, particularly the disposition of the "Province of Pennsylvania and Counties annexed." On October 20, 1705, Penn made a new will reducing William Jr.'s interests in Pennsylvania from that of governor and sole proprietor to proprietor of either two thirds or of one third, depending upon whether he would share his Irish estates with Hannah's children.[268]

By 1707 the financial straits of father and son necessitated the sale of Warminghurst, which they jointly owned and where the young Penns had been living since 1699. Reporting this in a June letter to Logan, the father observed:

> We are entering, or it seems likely we should, into nearer friendships than before, he knowing, I hope, the world and duty to a father better. For he has been of no use, but much expense and grief to me, many ways, and years too; losing him before I found him, being not of that service and benefit to me that some sons are, and 'tis well known I was to my father before I married. But O! if he will recommend himself and show himself a good child and a true friend, I shall be pleased and leave the world with less concern for him and the rest also.[269]

Penn was already nearing the climax of the second of the three crises in his final years when he made this confession to Logan of the prodigal son being of "no use, but much expense and grief to me, many ways, and years too." His words ring with a sense of a father's true pain and despair. It was not empty rhetoric.

The second crisis, also a cause of pain and despair for Penn and long in the making, had begun to unfold in 1702 following the death of Philip Ford, the steward and financial manager of Penn's English and Irish business affairs from 1669 onwards. Ford's surviving reckonings of Penn's account with him begin in April 1672 and run to March 1680 (all statements from July 8, 1674, to April 27, 1677, as well as all those after March 9, 1680, are missing). Statements of account probably received only

---

[267] Penn to Samuel Carpenter and others, November 18, 1705, *PWP*, 4:515.
[268] For the text, see *PWP*, 4:394–96. See also appendix 5.
[269] Penn to James Logan, June 10, 1707, *PWP*, 4: 580.

cursory attention from Penn, who had full confidence in Ford. As earlier noted, Ford was a Quaker who for conscience's sake had suffered the penalty of imprisonment with his neighbor and Penn's first father-in-law, Isaac Penington. Penn devoted his own business energies principally to building the Pennsylvania project rather than carefully supervising his capital. As a result, he overspent his account with Ford, who obligingly continued to advance credit to his patron, friend, and debtor. Thus their financial affairs continued for many years as Penn's debt grew larger. To protect himself, initially Ford required and received from Penn, in August 1682, a week before the debtor departed on his first voyage to America, both a bond obliging Penn to pay him £6,000 and a mortgage for three hundred thousand acres of land in Pennsylvania as security, together with a power of attorney granting Ford full authority to collect any and all manner of monies and credits due that Penn might have in England, Ireland, Jamaica, the Netherlands, or elsewhere and to dispose of his land in Pennsylvania, East and West Jersey, England, and Ireland.[270]

Penn's expenses in organizing and governing his American province and territories continued to exceed his income from the sale of land, quitrents, and various official fees there as well as from all his other resources. Thus, by the time of his second voyage to England the debt to Ford had grown much larger, and it continued to grow thereafter. In the years from 1684 to 1699, during which Penn stayed in England before returning to America for his second stay, he and Ford held to their pattern of the straitened principal, with Penn depending upon his business agent for credit. Ford allowed this to continue, but he protected himself by requiring Penn over those years to execute sixteen complex legal instruments evidencing the mounting indebtedness in several ways.[271] In brief, (1) in June 1685 for new debt set at £5,000, Penn leased from Ford for five thousand years the three hundred thousand acres in Pennsylvania already mortgaged in 1682, along with his manors of Pennsbury, Springettsbury, and Springfield and his Philadelphia city lot. (2) Then in April 1687, for more debt set at £6,000, Penn leased

---

[270] *PWP*, 2:290–95.

[271] Descriptions of those instruments are to be found in Document 211, "Calendar of Legal Transactions between William Penn and Philip Ford, 1685–1699," *PWP*, 2:3:656–63, items A to P (Penn was not a party to item Q).

from Ford, again for five thousand years, all of Pennsylvania. (3) Thereafter, in August and September 1690, Penn, having failed to make full payment on the 1687 bonded indebtedness due in 1688, forfeited his right to buy back the 1687 lease, which was then assigned in trust to a Friend close to Gulielma's family in England, Penn giving a new lease of Pennsylvania and the lower counties for one year to Ford, which secured additional indebtedness of £6,900. (4) In September 1696, Penn having failed to pay any amount on his debt and Ford having advanced a further £3,447, Penn and Ford executed five separate legal instruments, among them an accounting agreeing that Penn's debt to Ford totaled £10,347 15s 5½d. Another of the instruments made Ford the legal owner of Pennsylvania and the lower counties due to Penn's failure to make payment on the 1690 bond. (5) In April 1697 Penn confirmed Ford in his right to the province and the annexed counties; Ford empowered Penn to govern them for ten years with Samuel Carpenter, William Markham, and three others as his attorneys in Pennsylvania; and Ford granted Penn a three-year lease of Pennsylvania for an annual rent. (6) The final legal undertaking between Penn and Ford was Penn's power of attorney, dated two weeks before his second voyage to America, giving Ford authority to sell lands in Pennsylvania and East and West Jersey.

Ford's death on January 8, 1702, ended this bewildering dance of legal documents between debtor and creditor. The papers had been created to protect Ford's right to be repaid and Penn's equity, including the power to govern, in the province and territories. But they were also intended to obscure the true financial picture from investors, purchasers, and creditors generally and from the royal authorities in England and the settlers in America especially. This imposing volume of legalese mostly succeeded. The strategy even continued for three years and nine months following Ford's death because his widow and executor, Bridget Ford, was led to believe that Penn would pay his debt to the estate in order to avoid both revealing his true financial circumstances and bringing on the sale of Pennsylvania by trustees named in Ford's will. But when Penn continued to default, Bridget Ford lost patience, and on October 4, 1705, she filed the will for probate in the Prerogative Court of Canterbury, an ecclesiastical court representing the Crown's oversight authority for the proving of wills and confirming and holding fiduciaries accountable in the administration of estates involving property in several districts (dioceses) of the church.

And thus began three years of another bewildering dance, this time in the English Courts of Chancery, of Exchequer, and of Common Pleas, the documents now being formal pleadings such as complaints, cross-complaints, answers, replications, demurrers, and briefs. It started, four weeks after the will was filed, with an action in the equity Court of Chancery brought on October 31 by Philip Ford's son, married daughter and her husband, and two unmarried daughters against Penn, William Jr., and the three trustees[272] holding the legal ownership of Pennsylvania and the territories.[273] Then in early 1706 Bridget Ford sued Penn in the Court of Exchequer, demanding both his payment of the 1696 bond for £20,000 and his arrest. Penn had this action halted until the Chancery suit could be resolved.[274] In his cross-complaint against the Fords dated February 25, 1706, brought in the initial Chancery action, Penn described the Fords' four separate suits against him in the Court of Common Pleas,[275] in at least one of which the Fords won judgment in 1707 for nonpayment of the rent owed them for Pennsylvania.[276]

Then, after years of frustration and litigation, in January 1708 the Fords began to take stronger action. On January 7 they tried to have Penn arrested at the meeting house of Gracechurch Street Friends for nonpayment of the judgment in the Court of Common Pleas. Penn escaped that attempt by putting himself in the Fleet prison for debtors, later arranging for lodgings in the Old Bailey.[277] On January 22 a petition from the Fords to Queen Anne for royal letters affirming their ownership of Pennsylvania and the territories annexed and quieting the title of those who purchased from Penn who "hath no title"[278] was referred by the queen in Council to William Cowper, Great Britain's first lord chancellor after the union in 1707 of England and Scotland. In

---

[272] All three trustees—Bridget Ford (Philip's widow) and John Hall and Thomas Moss (London merchants)—were Quakers. See *PWP*, 4:413–14nn 16–18.

[273] For the text, see "The Fords' Bill of Complaint," *PWP*, 4:402–14.

[274] *PWP*, 4:444. 450n70.

[275] *PWP*, 4:417–52, particularly 451–52nn73–76.

[276] *PWP*, 4:494, 497n9.

[277] *PWP*, 4:497n10. Located next to Newgate prison, in 1708 the Old Bailey was used as a court, with accommodations available for London officials as well as others. By the nineteenth century it was made the Central Criminal Court and had jurisdiction throughout England for major criminal trials.

[278] For the text of the petition, see *PWP*, 4:493–97. The quotation concerning Penn is on p. 496.

March, the lord chancellor advised the queen that, because the Fords' original complaint in the Court of Chancery was still undecided, they "have craved your majesty's assistance too soon."[279]

With the Fords' prospect of certain expense and more delay as they awaited the uncertain outcome of these judicial proceedings; with Penn's lengthening separation from his family, his province, his Quaker faith community, and his ordinary life; and with the Religious Society of Friends increasingly subjected to new scorn as this tempest of litigation among Quakers gained wider public attention, the time for settling the Ford-Penn dispute seemed to be overdue. On September 16 that year, Penn wrote to Samuel Carpenter and his wife that "agreement is made with the Fords,"[280] and on the 28th of the same month he wrote to Carpenter, Isaac Norris, and five other Philadelphia Friends that the legal instruments resolving the dispute were nearly complete—"in seven days they will be executed."[281] The settlement was accomplished with a flurry of nine documents executed between October 2 and 8.[282] By these, Penn was freed from confinement and from obligation to the Fords but was still in debt, now for £6,600 to a consortium of thirty-eight English and Irish Friends; the Fords received £7,600 to satisfy all their claims regarding Pennsylvania and the territories; and the new creditors held, through the nine who were named trustees (including Thomas Callowhill, Penn's father-in-law), administrative authority over the province, pursuant to the mortgage securing their loan.

Penn in late 1708 was now entering his sixty-fifth year and just beginning the difficult tasks of resuming the rounds of his personal life and regaining some control over his business affairs. He was increasingly concerned with securing his young family's future. Planning and overseeing the assets of his estate until the next generation could assist in that responsibility required careful management and the assistance of trustworthy younger associates.

---

[279] For the text of the lord chancellor's report, see *PWP*, 4:500.

[280] Penn to Samuel and Hannah Carpenter, September 16, 1708, *PWP*, 4:614–16.

[281] Penn to Samuel Carpenter and others, September 28, 1708, *PWP*, 4:616–18.

[282] For a summary of these documents, see "The Settlement of the Ford Case, 1708," Document 211A-I, *PWP*, 4:769–73.

Penn had earlier considered two persons as essential aides if he were to meet the challenges facing the Penn family's business enterprise in Pennsylvania, which for simplicity I call "Penn Incorporated." One of them, William Jr., had been made in Penn's 1701 will the heir apparent of his father's American interests after the death of Springett, Penn's first-born son. As discussed above, the new heir apparent was proving himself so unsuited for the responsibilities and duties of the undertaking that Penn in his 1705 will reduced his son's inheritance from the entirety to a fraction. By 1712 Penn had lost hope of his son ever playing a role in the future of the American enterprise, and in the spring of that year he executed what would be his last will.[283] In it, stating that "my eldest son being well provided for by a settlement of his mother's and my father's estate[s]," he settled all of his own estate upon other heirs—even William Jr.'s children—to the exclusion of his eldest son.

Penn's other essential assistant in the ongoing operations of Penn Incorporated was James Logan, the Quaker schoolmaster whom he had employed in Bristol and brought to America in 1699 as his secretary. In that capacity, Logan well demonstrated his skill, diligence, and loyalty by engaging directly in proprietary and governmental matters. When, almost two years later, Penn decided to make what he intended to be a brief return to England to protect his powers of provincial government from being taken over by the British Parliament and Crown, he left Logan behind, serving in the offices of clerk of the Governor's Council, secretary of the province, a commissioner of property, and receiver general of the province. In effect, Logan was to be Penn's American agent and watchdog, even as deputy governors—and the then heir apparent—arrived and departed. It was also intended that Logan would be the principal informant and correspondent regarding all of Penn's interests in Pennsylvania and the territories. Again, Logan steadily served Penn, and provincial matters are documented by their many letters that ended in February 1713 when Penn could no longer formulate his instructions or understand Logan's responses.

Logan's spirits must have been raised when he received Penn's letter written to him on December 29, 1708, triumphantly announcing that "the Fords were paid and the country redeemed

---

[283] See appendix 5, section E.

to and by me, and I granted my assistants a fresh mortgage."[284] By June 1709, however, Logan was better informed through others of the true situation and knew that, although Penn had "redeemed" his province from the Fords, the "my assistants" now holding the "fresh mortgage" were thirty-eight Quaker investors. He also knew that these new mortgage holders, although sympathetic to Penn's situation, intended to be active in protecting their investment. In addition, Logan was now weary of his responsibilities as Penn's representative for the province, which included not only the duties of governmental and proprietary affairs but additional and burdensome concerns such as looking after the inexperienced John Evans and the immature William Jr.; protecting the proprietor in the malicious political arena churned by David Lloyd's animus in revenge for his dismissal by Penn as attorney general; and defending himself (as another target in Lloyd's campaign against Penn) from impeachment charges and trial at the hands of the General Assembly, the unicameral legislature created by the Charter of Privileges reluctantly granted by Penn in October 1701 and for some time under the control of David Lloyd, its elected speaker.

Logan's letter to Penn of June 14 reflected the situation:

> The settlement made upon the advance of the money paid the Fords making a great alteration in affairs of property here, the commissioners [of property] cannot well proceed by any powers they now have. I have received a letter from Thomas Callowhill [Penn's father-in-law] and others of Bristol informing me thou hast made over to them and others of London and Ireland not only the province but all thy debts [money owed to Penn by others] of whatever kind here and therefore they desire me to get in all I can to have it ready for their orders. [Here, Logan expresses his concern that Penn has transferred to his new creditors the funds meant to pay his other debts and obligations soon to be due.] Upon this I cannot but reflect upon the dangers I exposed myself to before, though unwittingly, from which through the good providence of God, I am now with thee and thine happily relieved, but must from thence take a caution for the future. However, I have

---

[284] *PWP*, 4:626–27.

adventured to pay the bills, at least the greatest part of them, and hope I shall be able to justify it, but think it unsafe to proceed much further until I have an opportunity of seeing thee. . . . I think this Fall to make a trip over without waiting any further advice. I have many things to induce me to this besides what I have here hinted, and particularly that 'tis impossible for me to be easy, or any way enjoy myself under such a load of confusion as oppresses me in matters of government. I resolved to be patient and sit quiet till the late threatening storms blew over, but since I have no prospect of a serenity under this constitution as now modeled [the Charter of Privileges of 1701], I must endeavor to breathe liberty again and taste freedom once more. I hope my voyage may prove of service to thee as I fully design it as far as it may lie in my power.[285]

On December 3, 1709, the tenth anniversary of his arrival in Philadelphia, Logan departed the city on his way to New Castle, where he boarded the *Hope Galley*, a newly launched vessel owned by Isaac Norris. After being honored at his leave-taking from the province by a distinguished escort to the ship made up of not only Norris but also the deputy governor of Pennsylvania and his predecessor, several fellow government officials, and other friends, Logan was finally away to England.[286] His arrival in London was delayed until late March 1710, however, due to storms at sea and then the task of cargo handling in Lisbon, where, after completing his duties as the owner's commercial agent aboard ship, Logan hurried ahead to London in a packet boat. More delay followed as that boat was seized by a French privateer in the waning days of the War of the Spanish Succession (which in America was known as Queen Anne's War), and Logan and the other captives were taken to France, where they were stranded for some days.[287]

During the more than twenty months of his English sojourn, Logan held steadily to the plan announced in his letter of June 14, 1709, for settling with the founder the future course of

---

[285] *PWP*, 4:648–49. Thomas Callowhill was one of the thirty-eight new mortgagees of Pennsylvania (along with the "others" of Bristol, London, and Ireland referred to above), as well as one of the nine mortgage trustees.

[286] Tolles, *James Logan and the Culture of Provincial America*, 75.

[287] Ibid., 79–81.

directing proprietary and governmental matters under his care as Penn's agent in the province. The first concern was to appoint and secure legal authority for new provincial property commissioners in Pennsylvania to sell tracts of land owned there by Penn as proprietor and to convey incontestable title to the purchasers. As that land was now subject to the new mortgage given by Penn, the Quaker trustees for the mortgagees needed to agree upon the commissioners' authority. These arrangements were completed in November 1711 when, on the 9th, Penn appointed Edward Shippen, Samuel Carpenter, Richard Hill, Isaac Norris, and Logan as his commissioners of property in Pennsylvania; on the 10th, Penn and the trustees for the mortgage holders signed a power of attorney to the new commissioners; and on the 30th, the trustees wrote to the commissioners informing them that "we have invested you with full authorities to sell and fully to confirm unto such purchasers that have or shall buy any tracts of land &c. belonging to the province or territories of Pennsylvania, for want of which instrument we perceive no persons there deem themselves sufficiently qualified to dispose of."[288]

Another major concern requiring attention was the stalemate in the government caused by the obduracy of the Assembly, the unicameral legislative chamber that Penn had established under the Charter of Privileges of October 1701. That body was the vehicle driven for many years by David Lloyd after he became Penn's nemesis upon being discharged as provincial attorney general in 1700. Lloyd had his revenge in the Assembly, where he spearheaded the antiproprietary forces in the colony. From 1702, when Lloyd first won a seat in the Assembly, and thereafter every year but one until 1718, the year of Penn's death, Lloyd was elected to that body, and in seven of those years he was voted by his colleagues as their speaker. He returned again after Penn's death and was a member of the Assembly, as well as its speaker, in 1723 and from 1725 to 1728.[289] In June 1710, Penn, in consultation with Logan, whom the 1709 Assembly under Lloyd had unsuccessfully sought to arrest before he embarked on his English visit, wrote to the people of his colony, "my old friends," appealing for moderation in a government that would promote peace and sound industry.[290] This was printed in

---

[288] *PWP*, 4:709–10nn1–3.

[289] See *Votes and Proceedings of the House of Representatives*.

[290] Penn to the people of Pennsylvania, June 29, 1710, *PWP*, 4:675–80.

Philadelphia as *A Serious Expostulation with the inhabitants of Pennsylvania, in a letter from the proprietor and governor*,[291] but it may not have been distributed until after the October 1710 election, which resulted in a defeat of the antiproprietary interests and a victory for moderation. Penn began his friendly protest:

> It is a mournful consideration and the cause of deep affliction to me that I am forced by the oppressions and disappointments which have fallen to my share in this life to speak to the people of that province in a language I once hoped I should never have occasion to use. But the many troubles and oppositions that I have met with from thence oblige me in plainness and freedom to expostulate with you concerning the cause of them.
>
> When it pleased God to open a way for me to settle that colony I had reason to expect a solid comfort from the services done to so many hundreds of people. And it is no small satisfaction to me that I have not been disappointed in seeing them prosper and grow up to a flourishing country blessed with liberty, ease, and plenty beyond what many of themselves could expect and wanting nothing to make themselves happy but what with a right temper of mind and prudent conduct they might give themselves.
>
> But alas! as to my part instead of reaping the like advantages some of the greatest of my troubles have arisen from thence, the many combats I have been engaged in, the great pains and incredible expenses for your welfare and ease to the decay of my former estate, of which (however some there would represent it) I too sensibly feel the effects with the undeserved oppositions I have met with from thence, sink me into a sorrow, that if not supported by a superior hand, might have overwhelmed me long ago. And I cannot but think it hard measure, that while that has proved a land of freedom and flourishing, it should become to me by whose means it was principally made a country the cause of grief, trouble, and poverty.[292]

---

[291] See *PWP*, 5:507–9.
[292] *PWP*, 4:675–76.

The third concern Logan came across the Atlantic to address with Penn was that of the proposed transfer of the proprietary government to the Crown. Because the issue had been pending for three years with no perceptible progress, Logan sought both to bring Penn out from under his oppressive burden of distant governance and to resolve the uncertainty created for the provincials by the want of resolution. Accordingly, to re-energize the negotiations, in late July 1710, Penn addressed a memorial to the "Queen and Her Ministry," noting that his own "fatigues and expense have become unsupportable to him [Penn]" and that he desired to "surrender those powers of government with which he [Penn] is invested, and deliver them entirely into the hands of the Queen," provided he received reasonable compensation for the surrender.[293] The new initiative set in motion a more expeditious review by the Crown, which in September 1712 resolved to accept Penn's surrender and conveyance of the government of Pennsylvania and to allow him £12,000, paid out over four years.[294] Sadly, that resolution came too late, for by then Penn was felled by the third, and last, crisis of his final years—his mental and physical incapacitation.

Beyond these consultations with Penn on official matters, Logan had also noted in his June 1709 letter that during his time in England he needed "to breathe liberty again and taste freedom once more."[295] This he did through his explorations of London's cultural and intellectual life, by his browsing in bookstores to build up his own scholarly library, and in setting a course for his own future in Pennsylvania. He wanted to be done with the burdens of his official responsibilities in the colony at the end of two more years and settle himself there with a family and comfortable living built upon opportunities he could venture for himself. While in England he bought up rights to purchase lands in Pennsylvania that English Quakers had acquired but never exercised, thus amassing, at minimal cost, claims to approximately seven thousand acres of land in the colony of which he was a property commissioner with invaluable knowledge.[296] Through a connection with the family of Isaac Norris, he met and courted a young Quaker woman who lived near Birmingham and experienced, for the second time in his

---

[293] *PWP*, 4:682.

[294] *PWP*, 4:725–26.

[295] *PWP*, 4:649.

[296] Tolles, *James Logan and the Culture of Provincial America*, 86–87.

life, the rejection of his proposal of marriage, each time because of objections to his circumstances made by the intended's family.[297] An unexpected consequence of his time in England was his evolving friendship with Hannah Penn and her children, which would continue the Penn family's interests in the affairs of the province until the American Revolution.

Logan left London on December 10, 1711, to board the *Mary Hope* at Gravesend and arrived back in Philadelphia on March 22, 1712. In the intervening days the third and last crisis of Penn's final years had begun its course. In February and again at the beginning of April 1712, Penn was so seriously ill that he prepared a new will, signing it about April 6,[298] in which he named Hannah the sole executrix of his estate and their children the ultimate heirs of all his Pennsylvania property except for the government, which he left to trustees to sell to the Crown "or any other person." Over the remainder of that year, Penn suffered three debilitating apoplectic strokes—the first later in April, the next on October 4 in Bristol where he had gone to settle the estates of Hannah's parents, who had died in April and June, and the last at home in late December. Thereafter, until his death on July 30, 1718, William Penn remained in the world but totally removed from the causes and concerns, the conflicts and controversies, in which he had so courageously invested his energies—and faith—to find just resolution.[299]

Penn's stroke on October 4 came as he was writing what would be his last letter to James Logan. Before the attack he had written:

> My recovery is perfecting through the Lord's goodness, that have been most dangerously ill at London. . . . I advise you to be discreet in those parts, and may the simplicity, humility, and serious sincerity of the Christian life and doctrine be your aim and attainment in the peace and plenty you are blessed withal.

He finished the letter on October 13:

---

[297] Ibid., 84–85.

[298] See appendix 5, section E.

[299] For a summary, see *PWP*, 4:708. Also see Proud, *History of Pennsylvania*, 2:105–13.

I am through the Lord's mercy pretty well. . . . So farewell, and pursue former, earnest orders and thou wilt oblige thy real Friend.

Wm Penn[300]

By the end of December 1712, Hannah Penn found that the calamitous old year had taken away not only both of her parents but the mental and physical health of her husband, who was now entirely dependent upon her. There were also in her daily care their five surviving, and very young, children—John, Thomas, Margaret, Richard, and Dennis. For some time, notwithstanding her limited means, she even contributed to the support of the wife and children of William Jr., who had abandoned his family and disappeared into Europe "to seek the lowest dregs of pleasure and dissipation."[301] And with all these cares and responsibilities came the necessity for her to remain constantly informed and vigilant regarding governmental and proprietary affairs in Pennsylvania. For the next years she managed those affairs on behalf of her husband with the experienced assistance of Logan in Pennsylvania through their ongoing correspondence concerning provincial matters.[302] The surrender to the Crown of the proprietary government, a slow bureaucratic grind, was never consummated, due in part to the death of Queen Anne in 1714. And the land title problems arising out of the uncertain location of the Pennsylvania-Maryland boundary were put in abeyance with the deaths of "the young and old Lords Baltimore" in 1715.[303] But the commissioning of William Keith as deputy governor and the dismissal of his predecessor, Charles Gookin, in late 1716 was a necessary task that she successfully undertook.

When he learned of the founder's final crisis, James Logan did not hesitate to put aside his plan to withdraw from service to the Penns. Knowing that the need for his services in the province was now greater than ever and that his duty to the proprietor and governor as well as his family would keep him engaged in Penn Incorporated indefinitely, he continued as their knowledgeable agent until the death of William Penn in 1718 and for years beyond. At the same time, however, he kept to his resolve to

---

[300] *PWP*, 4:729.

[301] Armistead, *Memoirs of James Logan*, 53. See also *PWP*, 4:752n3.

[302] For some of their letters until the death of Penn, see Armistead, *Memoirs of James Logan*, 41–70.

[303] See Hannah Penn to James Logan, June 2, 1715, ibid., 60.

make for himself a fulfilling personal life. On his return from England he began a profitable venture into the fur trade, building on the excellent relations Penn had always maintained with the Native Americans in the province. Then in December 1714 he married Sarah Read, whose sister Rachel had married Israel Pemberton Sr. in 1710. And he steadily continued to import from Europe scholarly books on such broad subjects as science, literature, history, and law, which in time grew into his well-used and renowned library.[304]

The state of the holy experiment at Penn's death

Whether William Penn ever recalled describing his great enterprise in North America as 'a holy experiment,' which he did only once, in his August 1681 letter to James Harrison, is doubtful or else he probably would have used the term more than that one time. It was a later generation that recovered his apt description and launched it over time into wide circulation, making it the sign and symbol of how Penn intended to answer God's "kind providence and serve His Truth and people"[305] after receiving the royal patent for Pennsylvania. But it cannot be questioned that Penn held fast for the rest of his life to nurturing the organic growth of the fundamental laws and institutions of the community he envisaged through the light of Quaker Truth.

The primary Truth for Penn from the inception of his experiment had been freedom of religion and liberty of conscience for all persons who "live peaceably and justly in civil society."[306] He never relented from the necessity of securing this keystone. Having himself suffered imprisonment for these human rights, he intended to establish them firmly in the refuge of religious freedom he was creating in the New World. They were cemented into the 1682 Frame of the Government but then, astoundingly, omitted from the 1696 revision of the Frame written and passed by the Provincial Assembly that, omitting these essential rights of the people, then arrogated to itself powers the absent Penn had long denied them. At the conclusion of his final visit to the province, Penn granted the Charter of

---

[304] See Tolles, *James Logan and the Culture of Provincial America*, 89–99.

[305] Penn to James Harrison, August 25, 1681, *PWP*, 2:108.

[306] Article XXXV of the Frame of the Government of the Province of Pennsylvania in America, signed by Penn on April 20, 1682, *PWP*, 2:225.

Privileges, which he signed and sealed October 28, 1701, supplanting without comment the 1696 Frame and restoring the peoples' "freedom of their consciences as to their religious profession and worship" as the first and foremost of their "liberties, franchises, and privileges."[307]

Penn also recognized that another basic requirement for the experiment to succeed was the "instruction and sober education of youth," which was first addressed for Philadelphia at his meeting with the Provincial Council in December 1683 by the order that a schoolmaster be hired.[308] At his first departure from the province in 1684, Penn made a will in which he gave "ten thousand acres of land in the County of Philadelphia towards the support of a school."[309] Then on October 25, 1701, ten days before his second and final departure from the province, Penn as "true and absolute Proprietary and Governor" granted and confirmed the charter for the Friends Public School. The school, established some years before by the Philadelphia Monthly Meeting, was to continue under that meeting's oversight and operate in a number of venues in the community.

A third pillar of Truth in Penn's experiment—the equality of all people in the sight of God and in civil society—moved slowly toward recognition in the Delaware Valley.[310] It grew from the 1688 protest of the Germantown Meeting "against the traffic in man body."[311] Thereafter, this antislavery cause was kept before PYM by Chester Quarterly Meeting. At last, with the 1719 *Book of Discipline*, PYM codified its evolving testimony against slavery, which would not significantly change until 1754, by advising

> that none among us be concerned in the fetching or importing Negro slaves from their own country or elsewhere. And it is the advice of this meeting that all

---

[307] Article First of the Charter of Privileges, signed by Penn on October 28, 1701, *PWP*, 4: 106.

[308] Michener, *A Retrospect of Early Quakerism*, 243–44.

[309] See Penn's last will and testament dated August 6, 1684, *PWP*, 2:585–87. This was revoked by a later will, and Penn never again made a testamentary gift of school land.

[310] In Penn's last will and testament dated October 30, 1701, made at his final departure from America, he gave to "my blacks their freedom as is under my hand already" (*PWP*, 4: 113). This was revoked by a later will, and Penn never again made the same gift.

[311] For the text of the Germantown Meeting protest dated April 18, 1688, see Michener, *A Retrospect of Early Quakerism*, 332–34.

friends who have any of them do treat them with humanity and in a Christian manner.[312]

Yet another pillar, and for some the preeminent of all the Quaker testimonies, was the preservation of peace. The peace of Penn's experiment, there to welcome all new arrivals in the colony, was being preserved through his vigilant policy of maintaining just relations with the Native Americans. Ironically, this son of an active-duty admiral in England's Civil War who had also served under the Restoration monarch was a tireless seeker of peaceful coexistence, as evidenced by his seventy-page work published in 1693 entitled *An Essay towards the present and future peace of Europe by the establishment of an European dyet, parliament, or estates*.[313] The core principle of the Quaker peace testimony, surely well known to Penn, had been expressed by George Fox in the declaration to Charles II given January 21, 1661, protesting the penalties laid on Quakers after other dissenters had caused a riot in London:

> Our principle is, and our practices have always been, to seek peace and ensue it and to follow after righteousness and the knowledge of God, seeking the good and welfare and doing that which tends to the peace of all. We know that wars and fightings proceed from the lusts of men (as James 4:1–3), out of which lusts the Lord hath redeemed us, and so out of the occasion of war. . . . All bloody principles and practices, we, as to our own particulars, do utterly deny, with all outward wars and strife and fightings with outward weapons, for any end or under any pretence whatsoever. And this is our testimony to the whole world.[314]

In 1695, however, Penn was caught in the vise of his moral commitment to this testimony and his need to accommodate the Crown's demand that Pennsylvania contribute a number of troops to the defense of New York. Although the colonial wars of North America did not touch the soil of his province until 1754,

---

[312] Collection 976, PYM Books of Discipline 1719, Cresson manuscript, pp. 14–15, Haverford College Quaker Collection, Haverford College, Haverford, Pennsylvania.

[313] This was printed in London in 1693. See also *PWP*, 5:396.

[314] Fox, *Journal*, 399. See William C. Braithwaite, *The Second Period of Quakerism* (London: Macmillan, 1919), 9–13.

in 1694 Penn knew that his being restored to the proprietary governance was conditioned upon Pennsylvania contributing to the military defense of New York. Penn met the Crown's condition, but this was at the cost of both his principles and his relations with Quakers in his government, especially in the Assembly, which, in exchange for these controversial military appropriations, enacted the Frame of 1696 and thereby obtained the power to propose legislation.[315] It was these legislators and other perceived internal political enemies, described as "too factious and troublesome in the governments under which they ought peaceably to live," whom Penn, the chief author, was undoubtedly addressing in the 'peace passage' of the 1701 epistle from PYM to its quarterly and monthly meetings.[316]

If at the end of his days it seemed to Penn that his experiment in civil government had been rendered more factious and distorted by the provincials' greed and self-interest than he could have foreseen, he nevertheless could take encouragement that the experiment still looked to a stable future because of the well-grounded presence of the American Quaker community, with its established organizational structure and its experience in reaching unity in resolving new problems and finding new testimonies in a new land. Its discipline and order, as set for the moment in PYM's 1719 edition of the *Book of Discipline,* were growing organically. Its leadership was able and extensive, well established in the community. He could also find comfort that his family affairs both at home and in the province were more than capably administered by his wife Hannah, who had the advice and services of trusted friends such as Logan and Norris in America.

But even in death the affairs of William Penn raised new controversy. After he died on July 30, 1718, at Ruscombe (Berkshire) following almost six years of being a home-bound invalid, his final will, executed in 1712, was offered in probate.[317] Upon examining the instrument, Logan commented that it "gives me some uneasiness as being drawn in haste I believe by himself only."[318] Under his 1701 will, Penn had given all his estate in America to William Jr. "as proprietary and governor"; under his

---

[315] See *PWP*, 3:393, 415–17.

[316] See more complete quotation on pp. 155–56 above.

[317] For the text of Penn's will of 1712, see *PWP*, 4:715–19. Also see the discussion of Penn's several wills in appendix 5.

[318] *PWP*, 4:715.

1705 will that son's share had been reduced to two thirds if he shared his Irish estates with his half-siblings and to one third if he did not; but under the 1712 instrument, William Jr. was entirely passed over because, as the father noted, he was already "well provided for" by provisions in the estates of his mother, Gulielma, and of Admiral Penn. William Jr. unsuccessfully challenged the 1712 will, of which Hannah was named the sole executrix.[319] Eight years later, William Jr. died of tuberculosis, alone in Belgium. In 1726, the year Hannah died, title to Pennsylvania vested in the three surviving sons of her marriage to William Penn: John, Thomas, and Richard.[320]

---

[319] *PWP*, 4:715
[320] See *PWP*, 4:718n7.

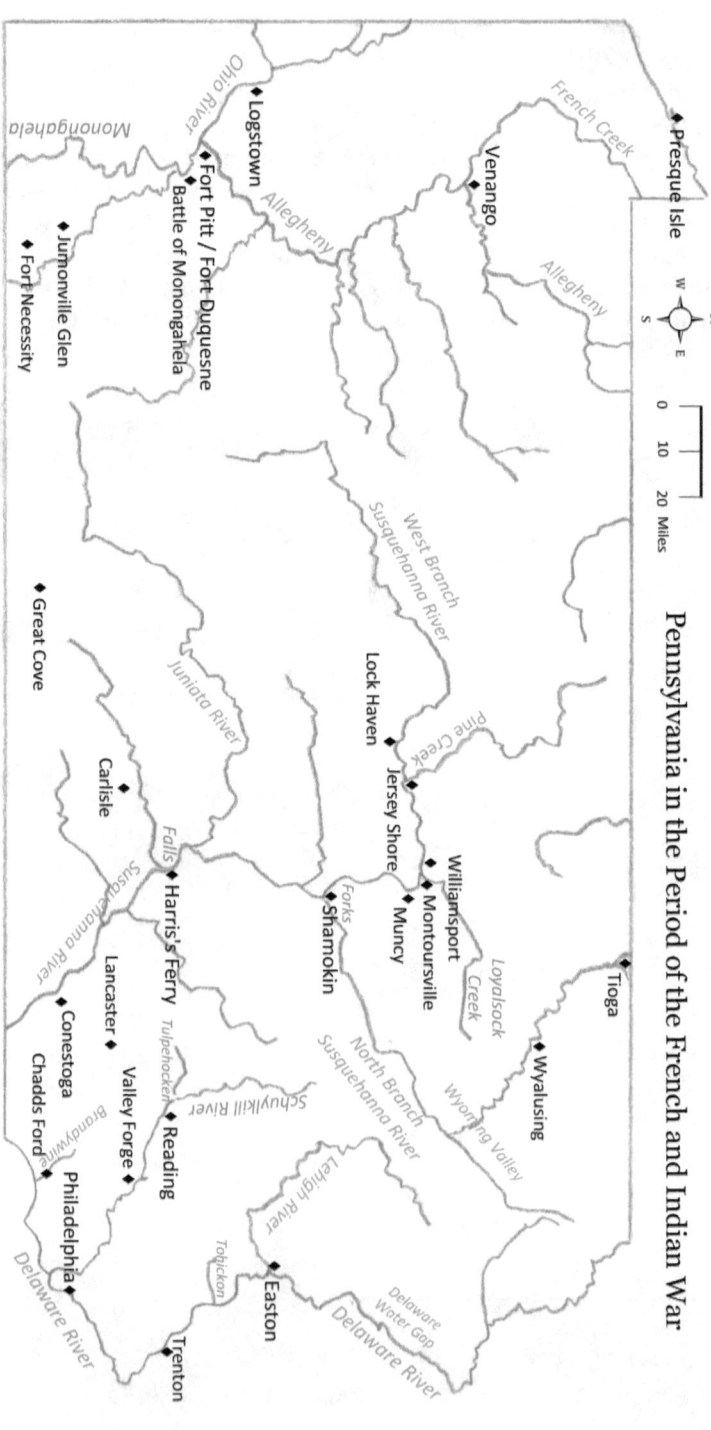

CHAPTER 3

UNBINDING THE TIES BETWEEN THE QUAKER CHURCH AND THE STATE IN PENNSYLVANIA (1719–1750)

Hannah Penn's caretaker administration of the proprietorship and government of the colony (1719–1726)

From the onset of the illness that seized control of William Penn's considerable gifts of mind, memory, and spirit, the responsibility for both his care and that of his family, together with the oversight of the affairs of Penn Incorporated—including the province of Pennsylvania and its territories in America—fell upon his second wife, Hannah Penn.

Hannah was less than half the age of William Penn when she married him on March 5, 1696. Born in Bristol, England, on February 11, 1671, to Thomas and Hannah Hollister Callowhill, she was the sixth of her parents' nine children and the only one to survive childhood. Her parents were Friends who belonged to Bristol's rising middle class, and they prospered in commerce at home and in international trade. Hannah grew up amid the Quaker values and teachings to which her loving parents were committed. Their church life was centered near home, at Friends' Friars Meeting House in Friars' Orchard, which stood on ground once owned by Hannah's maternal grandfather. Within the family, Hannah had frequent occasion to learn the ways of conducting business and managing financial resources in the world.[1]

On October 13, 1712, Hannah added a note to a business letter her husband had begun writing nine days earlier to James Logan in which she explained that Penn, mid-letter, had been "taken with a second fit of his lethargic illness, like as about six months ago at London."[2] From that point on, Hannah Penn and James Logan maintained a correspondence critical to the

---

[1] Sophie Hutchinson Drinker, *Hannah Penn and the Proprietorship of Pennsylvania* (Philadelphia: The National Society of the Colonial Dames of America in the Commonwealth of Pennyslvania, 1958), 1–4.

[2] Hannah Penn to James Logan, October 13, 1712, as quoted in ibid., 33.

preservation of the Penn family's interests in the province and to the administration of the proprietorship. Their correspondence continued for the remainder of Hannah's life and survived due to Logan's care in preserving her letters to him and his custom of keeping copies of his own letters.

The Hannah Penn-James Logan correspondence began on a foundation of friendship that over earlier years had developed into the esteem they had for each other by 1712. When Penn sailed in September 1699 from the Isle of Wight to make his second visit to Pennsylvania, there were in the company his wife Hannah of Bristol; his daughter from his first marriage Letitia, who was only seven years younger than Hannah; and Logan, the new secretary to the governor and proprietor, former head of Bristol's Friends School at the Friars Meeting House, himself only three years younger than Hannah. After the Penn family's departure from America in 1701, Logan had visited them in England during the years 1710 and 1711 to confer on proprietary and provincial matters, a necessity that again took him to England in 1723–1724 during Hannah's de facto administration of the province.

Hannah's letters to Logan over the years provide a rich source for understanding her management of the family's interests, including the burdens she carried and the challenges she faced in preserving the lives of the family members in her charge. Almost always addressing Logan as "Loving Friend" and signing as "Thy assured friend" or "Thy real friend," amid discussions of the business affairs of government and proprietorship, Hannah clearly portrayed her household concerns in her letters to Logan.

Under the matriarchal roof

Several letters Hannah wrote in 1715 reveal her husband's condition. They also indicate that the family members, whether at home or away at school, included the wife and three children of William Jr.[3] On January 22, 1715, she wrote:

> My poor husband has had two or three little returns of his paralytic disorder but I thank the Lord it went off and he

---

[3] Living in the family home at Ruscombe were William and Hannah Penn, their children John (b. 1700), Thomas (b. 1702), Margaret (b. 1704), Richard (b. 1706), and Dennis (b. 1707), as well as Mary Jones Penn (b. 1677), the wife of William Penn Jr., and their children Gulielma Maria (b. 1699), Springett (b. 1701), and William III (b. 1703).

is now in pretty good health, not worse in his speech than for some months past; nor can I say he's better, but when I keep the thoughts of business out of his head, he is very sweet, comfortable and easy, and is cheerfully resigned to the Lord's will, yet takes delight in his children. . . . My daughter Penn and Guly are now here and salute thee. The two boys at G. Thompson's, all under my care.[4]

On February 24, she explained more fully Penn's distress at seeing business conducted:

My poor husband's weakness continues and he is scarce ever easy (whether with or without company) unless I am at his elbow and to write in his sight does so much renew his cares and the thoughts of what he was wont to do himself which increasing his trouble and uneasiness I am forced to drop many things that should otherwise be minded, and is the reason that thou hast heard so little from me of late.[5]

And on April 2 she noted again that William Jr.'s wife and children were continuing in her care:

My children are, I bless God, all well at present as is my daughter Penn and Guly, now here, but we are placing her abroad to school, which she wants enough. I must not enlarge [write more], [it] being past midnight, for my writing time is generally when my poor husband is in bed to prevent his uneasiness thereat.[6]

She mentioned again the burden caused by William Jr. in a letter one year later:

I am but a woman and by the indisposedness of my husband have the whole load of a large family affairs, I may say that of a double family for so in reality it is, because the person thou mentioned in one of thine [William Jr.] as reformed is notwithstanding all their pretences but exactly ditto. I wish I could say otherwise, I

---

[4] Hannah Penn to James Logan, January 22, 1715, as quoted in Drinker, *Hannah Penn*, 62–63. The reference to "my daughter Penn and Guly" is to William Jr.'s wife and their daughter Gulielma; the reference to "the "two boys" is to their sons Springett and William III, then attending a boarding school in Lancashire.

[5] Hannah Penn to James Logan, February 24, 1715, as quoted in ibid., 65.

[6] Hannah Penn to James Logan, April 2, 1715, as quoted in ibid., 73.

might then have ease of my burdens which I now labor under in many respects for he has put himself out of the way of everything except the enjoyment of that which has brought him to where he is. My daughter Penn is here and gives her love to thee as does my husband.[7]

On March 2, 1717, writing another letter from Ruscombe (Berkshire), where the family had removed in 1710 after the sale of Warminghurst (Sussex), Hannah wrote to Logan:

My poor Dearest's life is yet continued to us, but I know not how long that may be, for he is very weakly. I have for this three or four years continued on this large house and expense only to keep him as comfortable as I can; for he has all along delighted in walking and taking the air here, and does still, when weather allows; and at other times, diverts himself from room to room; and the satisfaction he takes therein, is the greatest pleasure I have in enjoying so large a house, which I have (with the necessary expenses and loads I bear), long found too much for me and our shrunk income.[8]

Then a month later, on April 6, she wrote Logan from Bristol:

A few days past I left my dear husband as well as is now usual (in his weakly way) at Ruscombe, being hastened hither by my poor dear John's illness who I found full of the small-pox.... He has in some ways been much worse than Tomme, who is well recovered of his at London.... [At Ruscombe] I left both my daughters Aubrey and Penn to take care of their father and the family until my return; the latter to be pitied for, poor woman, her husband continues the same. She has placed Springett, her eldest son, with a Friend in Ireland—a merchant in Limerick ... and the place promises well.... But the cares I have had in bringing up and placing the three children, with their mother, and my own five, I have thought sometimes was enough to weigh me down; but hitherto I rest in hope and having now put my hand of help to change the governor for you and make you easy therein, I hope thou and those concerned will also think of ways to make us easy and let us see at last that my husband's affairs are the better for

---

[7] Hannah Penn to James Logan, April 2, 1716, as quoted in ibid., 91.
[8] Hannah Penn to James Logan, March 2, 1717, as quoted in ibid., 105.

his having that place [Pennsylvania] which to be sure hath given him and me likewise fatigue and trouble enough. I shall be glad to see it does in any measure answer the toil of our day.⁹

In the above letters, written between January 1715 and April 1717, we hear the concerns of a loving wife who bears the responsibilities of maintaining a large residence and grounds for the comfort of her husband in his declining days as well as providing for the care and well-being of not only their own five children but also of the abandoned wife and three children of William Jr., the surviving son of Penn's first marriage. She expresses her feelings to Logan about the need to stay at Penn's side and free him of business cares, about boarding school arrangements for her stepgrandchildren, and about the illnesses of John and Thomas, her two older sons. Hannah explains to Logan that her letter-writing time for official business is "past midnight" when her husband is in bed. She concludes with a gentle plea stating her need for Logan "and those concerned" to "think of ways to make us easy and let us see at last that my husband's affairs are the better for his having that place [Pennsylvania] which to be sure hath given him and me likewise fatigue and trouble enough. I shall be glad to see it does in any measure answer the toil of our day."¹⁰

Penn v. Penn

Early in September 1718, following her husband's death on July 30 at Ruscombe after almost six years of invalidism, Hannah went to London to initiate the official proceeding for probating his will and obtaining her own appointment as sole executrix empowered to administer his estate. Jurisdiction over English estates at the time was still vested in the Church of England (and remained there until the middle of the nineteenth century), where it was exercised either through the ecclesiastical court of the

---

⁹ Hannah Penn to James Logan, April 6, 1717, as quoted in ibid., 107–8. The references to "John" and "Tomme" are to Hannah's first and second sons, John and Thomas; to "daughters Aubrey and Penn" are to Letitia Penn Aubrey and to William Jr.'s wife, Mary Jones Penn; to "Springett" is to William Jr. and Mary's elder son Springett. The phrase "change the governor for you" refers to the dismissal of Lieutenant Governor William Keith and the commissioning of his successor, Patrick Gordon.

¹⁰ Drinker, *Hannah Penn*, 108.

diocese (district) where the decedent lived and where the property was located or in the highest such court, known as the Prerogative Court of the Archbishop of Canterbury, located in London, if the decedent had property in two or more dioceses. Hannah presented the 1712 will in the latter court for proving it was duly executed and having it admitted to probate. Immediately, the legal stumbling blocks in her way became apparent, and she noted them in her letter from London dated September 4, 1718, to Thomas Story, a close family friend, a sometime attorney who had been an official in the governments of Pennsylvania and Philadelphia, and a distinguished Quaker now living in England.

> Being here on purpose to have proved the will and finding at last a caveat entered against me I trouble thee this once to advise thee thereof, and also that, by applying to Counsel, the imperfections are more and more apprehended, and in short my troubles more and more apparent. The heir seems to think himself, or nobody, entitled to the government and with due therefrom. The intended provisions of three hundred pounds per annum is thought invalid for want of witnesses. The personal estate to pay debts but that hard to find; all which makes me thoughtful and on which I would beg thy advice but that being so hard to get I almost despair and am loath to trouble thee.[11]

One of Hannah Penn's many gifts was her ability to write clearly and succinctly. In this message to Story, she touches upon most of the issues that were to try her gifts of patience and persistence over the next years. The "caveat" she mentions was the legal strategy used at the time to prevent the administration of decedents' estates until formal objections were resolved. It was a caution or warning not to proceed in the exercise of an office until such challenges were settled.[12] The person warning Hannah not to proceed in administering Penn's estate was the self-proclaimed "heir"— William Penn's eldest son, William Jr. Challenging his father's 1712 will on various grounds, he sought to have it barred and himself declared the "heir at law" who, if his deceased father had died without a valid will, would be deemed to

---

[11] Hannah Penn to Thomas Story, September 4, 1718, as quoted in ibid., 119.

[12] William Blackstone, *Commentaries on the Laws of England: In four books* (Portland, [ME]: Thomas B. Wait & Co., 1807), 3:246; William Edward Baldwin, ed., *Bouvier's Law Dictionary* (Cleveland: Banks-Baldwin Law Publishing Co., 1940), 156.

have inherited all the paternal lands—together with the "government" and the "due therefrom"—pursuant to the law of primogeniture.

Notwithstanding the caveat, the Prerogative Court admitted the will to probate on November 4, 1718.[13] But the court was only an administrative office for processing estates, not a tribunal for the administration of justice with powers to settle issues of law; it did not resolve the dilemma of how to proceed in the face of the caveat.

Hannah, anticipating these problems, had already taken action. Being experienced in estate administration as the executrix under her father's will, she knew the value and necessity of receiving expert legal advice, and by the time of her letter to Story she had asked for the opinion of a "counsel" learned in the law, Sir Edward Northey, as to the validity of the 1712 will in the face of the unresolved challenge of the caveat.[14] In so doing, she had the trusted guidance of her uncle, Simon Clement, the husband of her mother's sister, who was both a Quaker wool merchant and a long-time acquaintance of William Penn. She also had the wise counsel of Herbert Springett, Penn's London solicitor and a cousin of Gulielma Penn, as well as of his law partner John Page. Although Northey did not render his opinion for another year, Hannah nevertheless in late 1718 began an action in the Court of Chancery, where both equity and the common law were applied to issues touching upon the "King's conscience," such as those in this probate.[15] The unique issues here, which were without precedent in the common law and required the ingenuity of equity to do justice in the case, were the faulty signing, witnessing, and dating of Penn's tripartite will and the inability to complete the transfer of Pennsylvania's proprietary government to the Crown due to Penn's death.

Further, on November 18, two weeks after the 1712 will was admitted to probate, Hannah exercised the power Penn had given her in the will to convey the American lands in the estate "among my children which I have by my present wife in such proportions and for such Estates as my said wife shall think fit."[16] By deed of appointment, Hannah proportioned one half of the founder's

---

[13] Drinker, *Hannah Penn*, 121.
[14] Ibid.
[15] Ibid., 121–22.
[16] *PWP*, 4:716.

Pennsylvania property to John, their eldest son,[17] and the other half to Thomas, Richard, and Dennis, their younger sons.

The "imperfections" of the 1712 will that Hannah refers to in the Story letter were indeed formidable. Although the will was considered a single instrument, it actually consisted of three separately executed sections, each signed at the end by Penn, the first being entitled "my last Will & Testament," the second untitled but in the form of a codicil, and the third entitled "Postscript in my own hand." The principal issue concerned whether the statutory formalities of execution[18] had been met by Penn and his witnesses, the first section being witnessed but not dated, the second being both witnessed and dated, and the third being neither witnessed nor dated. There were other problems, such as the misnaming of one of the two trustees for the government of Pennsylvania and the omission from the first section of any provision for payment of an annual sum to Hannah for the support and education of their children (such a provision was later placed in the unwitnessed, undated third section). Most damaging, perhaps, was Penn's statement in the second section concerning "some unworthy expressions" in the will he had made when ill in London "as if I knew not what I did I do now that I am recovered." Upon first seeing the will, Logan commented that it "gives me some uneasiness as being drawn in haste, I believe by

---

[17] John Penn also was the heir by will of all the lands in Pennsylvania owned by his maternal grandfather, Thomas Callowhill (consisting of 6,500 acres in the province, another 80 acres of liberty lands, and a Philadelphia town lot at Front and High Streets). *PWP*, 4:730n10. Historical note: Penn's marketing strategy for his province in 1681 was to give the first purchasers bonus or dividend acres in "town" (Philadelphia) in proportion (1:50, or 2 percent) to the acreage purchased for their "country lots"; these bonus acres were known as the "town lots." *Certaine Conditions or Concessions agreed upon by William Penn Proprietary & Governor of the Province of Pensilvania, & those who are the adventurers and purchasers in the same Province The 11 of July 1681*, *PWP*, 2:98, 101nn2, 3. By 1701, his personal economic needs required giving an additional inducement to potential buyers with a further gift of 2 percent acreage, this time in the "liberty lands" adjacent to Philadelphia. *Instructions To my Commissioners of Property to be observed by them in granting of Lotts and Lands in my Province of Pensilvania & Counties Annexed [1 November 1701]*, *PWP*, 4:117, 118n3.

[18] The Statute of Wills enacted and amended in the reign of Henry VIII (32 Hen. VIII. c. 1. and 34 & 35 Hen. VIII. c. 5.) was the first law granting an alternative to the law of primogeniture in England. The law was subject to rules for the proper execution of the instruments. See *The Statutes of the Realm*, 3:744, 901–4.

himself only, when such a settlement required a hand better acquainted with affairs of that nature."[19]

Hannah, meanwhile, persevered in her quest for a resolution of this family dispute. At some point she had met with William Jr. and come away believing they could proceed "in a friendly way." That meeting, however, was followed by a letter with threats from young Penn that stated he would cut off the provision for her support under the challenged will, which drove her to institute suit in the Court of Chancery. She next instructed attorney John Page to negotiate with her stepson's counsel, but the counsel remained unresponsive. All of this Hannah touched upon in her letter to William Jr. of January 13, 1719, addressed to "Sonn Penn" and signed "Thy Lo[ving] Mother, H. Penn."

> When I last parted from thee 'twas in hope that thou would, as thou then said, be best pleased to have all our matters settled in a friendly way, and to which I agreed as choosing to have it so. But thy mind soon altered, and in thy first letter I had threats instead of friendship and a stop to my income, before I had received even enough to pay for thy poor Father's funeral, a very aggravating circumstance after the regards I had shown, in a constant expense on thy family, and was a sufficient motive to make me look out for my own safety in time to come, and to seek relief from Chancery, if not else to be had, but as I only fled, or desire to fly to it, only for my own and children's safety, so left the matter with John Page to treat with thee upon, who wrote me word he had left the writings in thy lawyer's hands, since which I have heard little from him, but that the matter goes on in Chancery, which as far as my safety requires, I must assent to and shall pursue but have no desire of giving thee unnecessary trouble, nor, increasing unnecessary charge, and therefore if thou art of the same mind as Henry Gouldney gives me to expect I would have no longer time delayed. But on thy appointing two proper persons, I will also write to my Uncle Clement and John Page to meet them; and there to settle all our differences if may be ended

---

[19] James Logan to Simon Clement, November 4, 1718, as quoted in Drinker, *Hannah Penn*, 121. Apparently, Penn had been assisted in writing the will by Robert West (d. 1718), another of his London attorneys, who was then recovering from a stroke. See *PWP*, 4:715.

without Chancery, and to go on in that in a way of friendship, of which I desire thy answer by the next post.[20]

William Jr. did not answer this letter. It remained for a court of law to resolve the family dispute.

On December 11, 1719, Sir Edward Northey completed his opinion letter regarding the validity of Penn's 1712 will at issue in Penn v. Penn.[21] In preparing it, he was undoubtedly instructed by Herbert Springett and John Page, who, as solicitors for Hannah, had cited the facts they deemed relevant (and supportive of their client's position) from which they framed the questions in a document (written legibly but in an unknown hand) that was then submitted to Northey for his opinion. They described the critical—and well-documented—events upon which, they held, the matter for adjudication rested. In brief, these were: the 1680 letters patent from Charles II granting Penn and his heirs the province of Pennsylvania, making them the absolute proprietors of the country with full and absolute right to make laws "with the assent of the freemen" and with specified powers to govern, "saving the sovereignty of the king"; the 1682 lease from James, Duke of York, to Penn of the territory now known as Delaware; the 1708 mortgage given by Penn and William Jr.[22] conveying Pennsylvania and the adjacent territory of Delaware to "Henry Gouldney and others" for securing the repayment of Penn's £6,600 debt and interest; and the 1712 "treaty" Penn had with Queen Anne for the sale of the powers of government in the province and territories. The 1712 negotiation was interrupted, however, when Penn

---

[20] Hannah Penn to William Penn Jr., January 13, 1719, *PWP*, 4:751–52; also in Drinker, *Hannah Penn*, 122–23. The phrase "a constant expense on thy family" refers to Hannah's maintenance in her home from 1713 to 1718 of William Jr.'s wife and children after he had abandoned them, at a cost of almost £300. See *PWP*, 4:752n3. "Thy lawyer" refers to Grimble Pauncefort, a London attorney who had represented William Penn in the Ford lawsuit. Henry Gouldney was a trusted adviser of Penn; he was a Quaker merchant in London and a first purchaser in Pennsylvania, one of the nine mortgage trustees of the province and one of the twelve trustees of Penn's properties in Pennsylvania named in his 1712 will.

[21] The original document consisting of three unnumbered pages is in the Penn-Forbes papers, 1644–1744, vol. 1, p. 31, Collection 485C, Historical Society of Pennsylvania, Philadelphia (hereafter cited as HSP).

[22] The factual statement noted that "WPenn junior was not taken into this conveyance for any pretense he had to the government, but because of some title he had to some of the lands." Ibid.

was taken with an apoplectic fit, and upon his recovering out of it, did make his Will and execute it, at first without date, but did again execute the same Will in the presence of seven witnesses on the 27th of May 1712, and in September following he came to an agreement with the Queen to sell the government for £12000 and received £1000 in part thereof; and the Attorney General [Northey] was ordered to draw up an instrument for his resigning the same to the crown in due form; but before the Attorney General had finished that instrument he [Penn] was taken with another fit from which he never recovered so well as to be capable to make the said resignation.[23]

The letter as presented by solicitors Springett and Page to Northey for his expert opinion concludes the statement of facts by summarizing, in order, the provisions of Penn's 1712 will. The summary recites that William Jr. was otherwise provided for by settlements in his mother's estate and in Admiral Penn's will; that the government of Pennsylvania had been left in trust to the Earl of Oxford and Earl Poulett[24] to "dispose thereof to the Queen or any other person"; that all of Penn's lands in America were left to trustees (the will named seven in England and five "in or near Pennsylvania") to pay his debts, convey ten thousand acres each to Letitia Penn and the three children of William Jr., and all the rest to and among Penn's children by Hannah as she should appoint; and that all his personal estate and the arrears of Pennsylvania rents were to go to Hannah, who was made his sole executrix.

Then came the following carefully crafted preamble to the four questions Hannah's solicitors presented to Northey, in which the validity of the will is taken for granted and the sale of the provincial government is presumed, lacking only the completion of its formal surrender to the Crown in exchange for the balance of the purchase price due the estate, the balance being determined to be "personal" property due to Hannah as

---

[23] Ibid. Northey served as attorney general for England and Wales from June 1701 to April 1707 and again from October 1710 to March 1718.

[24] The Earl of Oxford, who was also Earl Mortimor (Robert Harley), had worked with William Penn in the fight for liberty of conscience; sometime speaker of the House of Commons, at the time of the execution of the 1712 will he was lord high treasurer of the realm. Earl (John) Poulett was a friend of Penn and a political associate of Harley.

executrix, not "real" property that might pass to William Jr., the heir by right of primogeniture:[25]

> It is to be noted, that this Will was made and twice published whilst the Testator was only in treaty for sale of the government, and before the contract was perfected and the thousand pounds received aforesaid so that this devise to the Earls was only designed for the investing them with power to complete the same and receive the money in case he [Penn] had then died, but as he recovered, and did himself perfect the contract, receive the sum paid in part thereof, and settle the terms for the payment of the rest; there wanted nothing but of formal surrendry [conveyance] to finish the whole transaction; and therefore it would be presumed that no further power remained in the Lords than to make the surrendry to the crown and to administer the government 'till that were performed; and that then the rest of the purchase money to be paid might be considered as a debt due from the crown, and so included in the Testator's personal estate.

Having considered these facts and accepted the premises of the queries put to him on behalf of Hannah and her children, Northey's expert responses to the technical legal questions put to him were that the power to convey the government was vested in the owners of the mortgage to whom Penn the debtor had pledged his proprietary rights in the province as security, thus making those owners necessary parties to the sale, and that the sale proceeds were personal property to be applied to pay off the mortgage debt, with the remainder belonging to the executrix. Consequently, the sale ["devise"] of the land to the Crown excluded the claim ["pretence"] of William Jr. as heir, and the will gave Lords Oxford and Poulett enabling powers to complete the surrender.[26]

A long wait for judicial resolution of the Penn family dispute then followed. In Pennsylvania, there was uncertainty in the administration of proprietary affairs, instructions being sent there by both Hannah and William Jr. For Hannah, 1720 brought major changes. During that year she moved out of the

---

[25] The legal term "real" property" was understood to be land "and generally whatever is erected or growing upon or affixed to land." Baldwin, *Bouvier's Law Dictionary*, 1021. "Personal property" was every other thing a person owned.

[26] A transcribed copy of the holographs of Springett and Page's queries and of Northey's answers are set forth in appendix 6.

Ruscombe estate into London lodgings.[27] Then, in June, William Jr. died, consumptive and alone in Belgium.[28] His elder son Springett, having succeeded to his father's claim to be the heir by right of primogeniture, then continued the family feud in his father's stead, against his stepgrandmother in whose home he had lived—and by whom he had been supported—for years. Also in 1720, Hannah petitioned the lord justices of Britain to urge action on the surrender of Pennsylvania's government to the Crown and on settling the boundary dispute with Maryland, the two seemingly insoluble problems with which Penn had long struggled and for which she now sought resolution.[29]

In 1721, Hannah took another bold initiative. Having in April successfully petitioned the Lords of the Treasury to allow her to bring her action for resolution of the estate controversy in the Court of Exchequer, in October she filed her complaint in Exchequer on behalf of herself and her children against Springett, his mother, his brother, his sister and her husband, his aunt Letitia and her husband, the Earl of Oxford and Earl Poulett, the twelve testamentary trustees of Pennsylvania, and a majority of the mortgage trustees. The defendants' refusals to join in proceeding as directed in the 1712 will were, she pleaded,

> contrary to equity and good conscience and tend to the great loss and prejudice of your orators and oratrixes and for that your orators and oratrixes are remediless in the premises at the common law but are properly relievable in a court of equity before your honors.[30]

Then, as the respondents prepared their answers to the complaint, the long wait for resolution in the Court of Exchequer began.

From Pennsylvania, James Logan reminded Hannah that "it will be absolutely necessary that some of the family should

---

[27] Drinker, *Hannah Penn*, 125.

[28] See Howard M. Jenkins, *The Family of William Penn, Founder of Pennsylvania: Ancestry and Descendants* (London: Hadley Bros., 1899), 126; Hannah Penn to James Logan, June 29, 1720, in Drinker, *Hannah Penn*, 137.

[29] See Drinker, *Hannah Penn*, 140–41, 196.

[30] Bill of complaint by Hannah Penn and children in the Court of Exchequer against Springett Penn et al., Penn family papers, 1592–1960, Series VIII, NV-079, Collection 485A, Ex. 1, pp. 50–51, HSP. The orators and oratrixes (the court's terminology for male and female plaintiffs or petitioners) were Hannah's then living sons John, Thomas, Richard, and Dennis (orators) and Hannah herself and her daughter Margaret (oratrixes).

come over to settle and manage your business here." He especially pressed for John to be "fixed" in the province and to "graft" himself into a leading family through marriage.[31] But Hannah was facing other burdens in England. In November or December 1721 she suffered a stroke, described by John in his letter to Logan in March 1722 as "a fit of the dead palsy, which though much gone off, has left her weakly."[32] During her illness, yet another great sorrow fell upon her—the death by "violent smallpox" of her youngest son Dennis, "a hopeful youth of about sixteen."[33] And of constant concern was the health of John himself, "suffering chronically from rheumatic fever."[34]

When an opening for the resolution of the Maryland boundary dispute with Lord Baltimore arose, Logan seized the moment to return to England for conferences with the Penn family. He left Pennsylvania aboard the *London Hope* in October 1723, not returning home until the following July. The boundary negotiations went so well that Hannah, Lord Baltimore, and two trustees of the Pennsylvania mortgage signed an agreement in London on February 17 resolving major issues.[35] At the same time, Logan and the Penns also discussed the increasingly unsatisfactory performance in office of the provincial lieutenant governor, William Keith, who was more and more at odds with Logan and was administering Pennsylvania independently of the Penns' interests. This was addressed by Hannah in a stern letter of instructions to Keith, which included strong support for Logan reinforced by other personal letters to Keith, one from some of the mortgage trustees and the others from John Penn and Springett Penn, all in unity with Hannah.[36] And, as a token of their esteem and gratitude for his years of faithful service to Penn Incorporated, James Logan received a deed to five thousand acres of land on Siccasarong Creek, a feeder stream of the Susquehanna River. The deed was signed by Hannah, John, Thomas, and Springett.[37]

---

[31] James Logan to Hannah Penn, May 28, 1721, as quoted in Drinker, *Hannah Penn*, 145.

[32] Drinker, *Hannah Penn*, 146.

[33] Ibid.

[34] Ibid., 124.

[35] Ibid., 197.

[36] Ibid., 151–62.

[37] Ibid., 164.

Church and State 1719–1750

By 1725 the fortunes of the Pennsylvania proprietorship had so improved that it appeared likely the mortgage debt could soon be paid in full and the powers of government as well as the proprietary lands, vested as security in the trustees, restored to the Penns. This led Hannah to reconsider the need for and advisability of the surrender of governmental powers to the Crown, and it also led Logan to remind her that Penn Incorporated needed to find a "person of skill, resolution, and true honor," preferably one of the Penn sons, to be sent to Pennsylvania to serve as proprietor and governor or else as lieutenant governor.[38] The bad news that year was Lieutenant Governor Keith's continuing insubordination to the Penns, particularly his disregard of Hannah's letter of instructions and his encouragement of antiproprietary partisanship in the Provincial Assembly.[39] Regarding the need to discharge Keith and appoint a new lieutenant governor, the Penn family was once more united; Hannah and Springett together took steps resulting in the removal of Keith and the nomination and royal approval of Major Patrick Gordon as lieutenant governor of the province.[40]

In early 1726, Hannah revised plans for distributing her own estate and securing her children's future. On January 7 she executed a new will as well as a new deed of appointment pursuant to Penn's will, the changes reflecting the earlier death of her son Dennis. The deed appointed one half of the Pennsylvania proprietorship to John and the other half to Thomas and Richard.[41] On February 9, she filed a memorial and petition on behalf of herself and her surviving children in the Court of Exchequer to revive the original action, now against Springett et al. and reflecting the intervening deaths of Dennis Penn, William Jr., and other named parties in the original proceeding.[42]

At long last, on December 13, the lord justices of the Court of Exchequer not only heard but decided in Hannah's favor the case of Penn v. Penn and

---

[38] Ibid., 170–71.
[39] Ibid., 167–68.
[40] Ibid., 172–74.
[41] Ibid., 177.
[42] Ibid., 185.

declared that the said Will and Declaration of the said Testator William Penn was duly proved and thereupon it was ordered, adjudged, and decreed by the court that the said Will and Declaration of the Testator William Penn the elder should be duly performed.[43]

The court thereupon proceeded to give directions on how the estate should be administered, including the transfer of the proprietary lands to Hannah's children as she should determine, paying off the mortgage, and adding the proceeds from the sale of the government to the personal estate. It also ordered that Springett Penn, who had absented himself from the court hearing in order to collect rents in Ireland, join in all conveyances of land as directed in the will.

This was a notable victory for the persevering Hannah, a victory that withstood all further judicial proceedings. Not only had she secured for her children the fruits of the labors underlying their father's investment in a New World refuge of peace and religious toleration, she had also vindicated her own father's investment as a leader and trustee among thirty-seven other Friends of London and Bristol who had rescued the founder's hopes with a fresh mortgage when the enterprise reached its nadir in the Ford debacle.

But it was a victory that Hannah did not long enjoy. On December 20, one week after the Court of Exchequer had given resolution to her problems, Hannah Penn died. Soon her remains were placed next to those of her husband and their youngest son in the burial ground of the Friends Meeting House in the village of Jordans, Chalfont St. Giles, Buckinghamshire. To their sons who survived, William and Hannah had given the proprietary lands and governing rights in Pennsylvania. They had also entrusted to John, Thomas, and Richard the skills of James Logan and, with it, his invaluable experience and knowledge gained over twenty-five years of steadfast service to the Penn family in the province.

---

[43] Penn family papers, 1592–1960, Ex. 11, p. 25, Series VIII, NV-079, Collection 485A, HSP.

Church and State 1719–1750

An era of laissez faire expansion in the province and of worldly leadership in PYM (1727–1750): Condoning enslavement and resisting abolition

The death of the widow of William Penn brought the founder's era to an end in the province that he had planned and, for most of its years, had tried to manage from afar. Although the Court of Exchequer had resolved the issue of the proprietary succession, there followed an extended period of uncertainty as to whether and how the three sons of William and Hannah would use their inheritance in the province to serve both their own interests and the people's welfare. John Penn, age twenty-six and the eldest of the sons, now owned half of the proprietorship. Born in America in 1700, he was an infant when his parents took him to England in 1701, where he thereafter resided. Never in robust health, John managed in later life to visit Pennsylvania only once (1734–1735). He died in 1746 at age forty-six, unmarried and without issue, leaving his share of the proprietorship to Thomas, the older of his two brothers. From 1726 onwards, James Logan wrote to the young proprietors stressing that one of them should be present in the province and involved in its affairs and governance. Not until 1732 with the arrival of Thomas Penn—almost thirty-one years after his father concluded his last visit—did a proprietor again live in Pennsylvania. Thomas stayed for nine years. In the meantime, responsibility for proprietary affairs in the province of Pennsylvania remained with Logan, who increasingly found counsel and support from Isaac Norris, with whom he was building a lasting friendship.

For many years prior to 1726, Logan had wanted to be released from his responsibilities to the proprietors in order to begin securing his own independent financial future and growing his own family. His unrivalled knowledge of Pennsylvania and his unique official experience in its affairs well equipped him to fulfill the first ambition. Of equal importance, from the time Penn had introduced him into the company of Philadelphia's Quaker venture merchants, Logan had had access not only to financial but to social networks with which he might build alliances. Soon after his coming, he had assisted in arranging Penn's participation in a partnership with Philadelphia's leading venturer, Samuel Carpenter (Penn's contemporary and good friend), Isaac Norris (Logan's contemporary), and several others involving international maritime trade—proprietary ships sailing secure routes for trade with credit-worthy customers.[44] That opportunity arose early in the time of Queen Anne's War (1702–1713), when the risks of losing any ship and its cargo to the elements, pirates, or the French enemy were high. The Philadelphians' venture was ill fated, and they lost all. As a result, Penn was further straitened financially as he neared his showdown with the Fords, who were trying through the courts to collect the debt he owed them, a debt secured by the mortgage upon Pennsylvania. The loss brought Carpenter's career in such ventures to an end. Norris, who was younger, withstood his losses and waited for better opportunities, which came in the economic boom beginning toward the war's end. In 1709 Logan, en route to England for his consultation with Penn, had sailed aboard the *Hope Galley*, a ship newly built for Norris, who sent it to Europe on a successful trading voyage laden with cargo under the supervision of Logan, who even ventured a small cargo of his own. Upon returning home from England in 1712, Logan then began to venture into the Indian trade on the frontiers of the province that he knew so well. The beginnings of his new life were settled in December 1714, when he at last married. By the 1720s, Logan and his wife were nurturing their three young children (his older daughter would in time marry Isaac Norris II). By this time, Logan had become affluent, primarily by becoming Pennsylvania's largest dealer in Indian trade goods and skins and furs.[45]

In 1711, when Isaac Norris I was appointed clerk of PYM, he was forty years old and already successful in business and politics. Born in London, he was the youngest child of Thomas Norris, a Quaker merchant who, to avoid religious persecution, around 1678 moved with his family to Jamaica. There Thomas again suffered for his Quaker beliefs.[46] In 1690 he was twice fined "for not appearing in Arms," the fine being paid by the seizure of goods. For the first incident, a gun that had cost £3 was taken for an 18 shilling demand. The following year three of his leather chairs were seized from him for his son's refusal to appear in arms.[47] To find safe refuge for the family, Thomas sent

---

[44] See Albright G. Zimmerman, "James Logan, Proprietary Agent," *PMHB* 78 (1954): 143–76.

[45] Ibid., 174.

[46] For more information on Norris, see Jordan, *Colonial Families of Philadelphia*, 1:82–83.

[47] Besse, *Sufferings of the People Called Quakers*, 2:391.

his son Isaac to Philadelphia to study the advisability of another move. Upon Isaac's return to Jamaica the next year, he discovered that during his absence the entire family except for one sister and his stepmother had perished in an earthquake and the ensuing pestilence in Port Royal, their home. In 1693 he moved to Philadelphia on his own, armed with a letter of introduction from Mordecai Lloyd to his father, Thomas Lloyd, who had been lieutenant governor of Pennsylvania from 1684 to 1688 and again from 1690 to 1691.

Norris was soon more than successful. In 1694 he married Lloyd's third daughter, Mary. Ten years later, in 1704, together with a partner, William Trent, he purchased from William Penn Jr. the 7,480-acre manor of Williamstadt on the Schuylkill River, which had been part of William Jr.'s patrimony. (In 1712 as he began his PYM clerkship, Norris would buy out Trent's interest, renaming the whole Norriton, which today includes Norristown, while Trent relocated to his own tract in New Jersey, which today includes Trenton.) In 1707, at William Penn's call, Norris went to England to assist Penn in the Ford litigation. He remained there two years, and upon his return to Philadelphia his public career rose meteorically. Before his English mission for Penn, he had, beginning in 1699, been elected to five terms in the Provincial Assembly; after his return home, he served nine more one-year terms, two of them as speaker (in 1712 and 1720). Also after his return, he was called into twenty-five years of service on the governor's Provincial Council. He began service as an alderman of the City of Philadelphia in 1708, served a term as mayor in 1724, and was a justice of its courts, declining an appointment as chief justice of the province to continue on the city court. In the service of the proprietary family, the Penns, he and Logan for years remained its chief representatives in the affairs of Pennsylvania.[48]

The era in Pennsylvania that began with the succession of John, Thomas, and Richard Penn to their father's proprietorship of the province was laid on the template of venturesome enterprise and arduous labor that Norris and Logan had begun to personify in the preceding fifteen years. It was a model based on the laissez-faire economics of the state and on the personal

---

[48] American Council of Learned Societies, *Dictionary of American Biography*, 13:553–54; see also John A. Garraty and Mark C. Carnes, eds., *American National Biography* (New York: Oxford University Press, 1999), 16:501–2.

ethical discipline of members of the Religious Society of Friends. But even though the Quaker leadership in the second quarter of the eighteenth century was officially silent regarding the holy experiment, serious problems were growing in church and state that by mid-century had seized the attention of reforming hearts and minds.

The PYM clerkship of Isaac Norris I (1711–1729): Condoning the evil of slavery

Norris took up his responsibilities as the clerk of PYM at a favorable time. In late 1711, the economic hardships brought on by Queen Anne's War, which had levied such a toll on Carpenter, Penn, and many other Quakers, were easing, and investment opportunities were reopening to those who had survived the war years with sufficient means and the necessary connections intact. Norris had survived—indeed, he was now the owner of that emblem of power and wealth, the slate-roof house that Carpenter had built for himself in 1698 and that Penn had made his Philadelphia residence during his second visit. And, importantly, Norris was trusted and respected for his service in both the provincial and municipal governments. Seen to be endowed with proven qualities that promised steady and able leadership for the Religious Society of Friends in the coming years, he was selected as the first clerk of PYM to be named in its minutes after the death of Phineas Pemberton in March 1702. However, the Friends who appointed Norris as their clerk were willing either to overlook or forgive his active participation in the slave trade, which he carried on as part of his profitable West Indian merchant ventures. Norris continued trading slaves until shortly before his death in 1735, even, according to one commentator, "in the face of an increasingly firm stand against the traffic by the Society of Friends." His protests against that traffic reportedly lacked "any vigorous or moral indignation."[49]

The significant accomplishment of PYM in the years between Pemberton's death and Norris's appointment had been the adoption in 1704 of the *Book of Discipline* and thereafter the enforcement of its provisions for personal ethical conduct.[50]

---

[49] Darold D. Wax, "Quaker Merchants and the Slave Trade in Colonial Pennsylvania," *PMHB* 87 (1962): 143–59 (quotes are from pp. 156 and 151).

[50] The discipline of American Quakers and its enforcement in their meetings are discussed at length in Jack D. Marietta, *The Reformation of American*

Church and State 1719–1750

PYM's minutes in later years reflect the Quaker leadership's ongoing concern for righteous living among its members, evidenced both in its hearing many appeals from monthly meeting judgments censuring or disowning fallen individuals and in the frequent epistles sent to the quarterly and monthly meetings exhorting all members to be faithful in attending meetings, to be moderate in alcohol consumption and in gaming, and to be diligent in the education of youth and in honoring marriage. The first revision of the *Discipline* was made in 1719 during Norris's tenure.

Not surprisingly, in light of Norris's own involvement in the slave trade, PYM evidenced less principled certitude and even less will to confront the hellish problem and its practitioners: the grim evil of bringing into Penn's province persons captured and enslaved in Africa, carried as cargo into a 'new world' and there sold into chattel servitude for life. This wickedness touching public ethics had first come to the official attention of PYM through the channels of Philadelphia Quarterly and Dublin Monthly Meetings. The concern had originated in Germantown Meeting in 1688, when the Quakers from the Rhineland formulated their objections to "the traffic in man body" and asked, "Is there any that would be done or handled in this manner, viz: to be sold, or made a slave, for all the time of his life?"

> And, in case you find it good to handle these blacks in this manner, we desire, and require you hereby, lovingly, that you may inform us herein; which, at this time, never was done, viz, that Christians have such a liberty to do so; to the end that we shall be satisfied in this point, and satisfy likewise our good Friends and acquaintances in our native country, to whom it is a terror, or fearful thing, that men should be handled so in Pennsylvania.[51]

The meeting at Dublin found the issue "so weighty" they would not "meddle" but committed the subject to Philadelphia Quarterly Meeting as "nearly [closely] related to the Truth." In turn, the quarterly meeting referred it to PYM as "a thing of too

---

Quakerism, 1748–1783 (Philadelphia: University of Pennsylvania Press, 1984), chaps. 1–5.

[51] Address of the Germantown Friends dated April 18, 1688, in Michener, *A Retrospect of Early Quakerism*, 332–34.

great weight for this meeting to determine." PYM, however, "adjudged [the slave trade] not to be so proper for this meeting to give a positive judgment in the case, it having so general a relation to many other parts; and, therefore, at present they forbear it."[52]

In the succeeding years, other voices—both individual and corporate, some within and others separated from the Religious Society of Friends—dissented from PYM's timid policy of forbearance concerning the traffic in slaves. The first dissenter was the schismatic George Keith, whom PYM had disowned in 1692 in a testimony signed by 151 of its members.[53] One of Keith's chief controversies with Quaker policy and practice concerned the enslavement and 'ownership' of Africans. One year after the disownment, Keith set forth his abhorrence of this evil in a six-page pamphlet entitled *An exhortation and caution to Friends concerning buying or keeping of Negroes*.[54] The premise of the pamphlet was announced in the declaration that Christ had come

> [not] to bring any part of mankind into outward bondage, slavery or misery, nor yet to detain them, or hold them therein, but to ease and deliver the oppressed and distressed, and bring into liberty both inward and outward.[55]

To end "these evil practices of man-stealing" that transgress the Golden Rule, readers were cautioned against buying any slaves "unless it were on purpose to set them free." Then followed "some reasons and causes of our being against keeping of Negroes for term of life," all biblically based and all embraced by PYM itself sixty-three years later.

Keith did not claim the authorship of his *Exhortation*. Instead, the colophon read: "Given forth by our monthly meeting in Philadelphia the 13th day of the 8th [October] month, 1693 and recommended to all our Friends and Brethren, who are one with us in our testimony for the Lord Jesus Christ, and all

---

[52] Extracts from the minutes of Dublin Monthly Meeting, Philadelphia Monthly Meeting, and PYM, as quoted in ibid., 334–35.

[53] See discussion of Keith on pp. 132–34 above.

[54] George Keith, *An exhortation & caution to Friends concerning buying or keeping of Negroes* (New York: William Bradford, 1693).

[55] This was printed for the "Monthly Meeting of Friends of Philadelphia" by William Bradford, PYM's own printer, to the great dismay of the leadership of PYM.

others professing Christianity." To the uninformed, the pamphlet would seem to be the work of the Philadelphia Monthly Meeting of the Religious Society of Friends and printed under its authority. In fact, it was from the "Monthly Meeting of Friends of Philadelphia," a meeting of the Keithian separation, self-styled 'Christian Quakers,' who adopted Keith's essay and published it through PYM's official printer. That it was the voice of Philadelphia's known schismatic Quaker may have given PYM's leaders some comfort and been answer enough to Keith's abolitionist message.

In 1696, grave concerns regarding the purchase or ownership of slaves were separately brought to PYM once again, this time by two ministers of the Religious Society of Friends, Cadwalader Morgan of Merion and William Southersby (sometimes Southeby) of Philadelphia. Morgan had sent the yearly meeting a letter observing that God had led him to understand that he "had no freedom to buy or take any of them upon any account."[56] Southersby presented his abolitionist views in a paper heard by Philadelphia Monthly Meeting, which referred the matter to Philadelphia Quarterly Meeting, which in turn passed it to the yearly meeting.[57] Responding to both Morgan and Southersby, in 1696 PYM advised Friends "not to encourage the bringing in any more negroes" and to be "careful" not to "bring them to meetings" or to "have meetings with them, in their families."[58] With that, Morgan seemed to rest his public case. For Southersby, however, who saw the "total incongruity" of slavery with Christ's teachings, the battle was only beginning. Raised and educated a Roman Catholic, he had grown up along the Sassafras River on Maryland's Eastern Shore. There, about 1671–1672, during the time George Fox was leading his mission through that province, Southersby heard and was convinced by the message of the Friends. Shortly after Penn gained the proprietorship of Pennsylvania, Southersby moved into the new

---

[56] Cadwalader Morgan, Letter, 1696 5th month 29th, Merion, Pa. to friends at Philadelphia Yearly Meeting, Haverford College Quaker Collection, Haverford College, Haverford, Pennsylvania; see also Thomas E. Drake, "Cadwalader Morgan, Antislavery Quaker of the Welsh Tract," *Friends Intelligencer* 98 (1941): 575–76.

[57] None of Southersby's writings appears to have survived to the present; see Thomas E. Drake, *Quakers and Slavery in America* (Gloucester, MA: P. Smith, 1965).

[58] Michener, *A Retrospect of Early Quakerism*, 335.

Quaker province, becoming in time a landholder, a member of the Provincial Council (holding office between 1684 and 1686),[59] and a recognized minister in the Religious Society of Friends.[60]

In 1700 another protesting voice, albeit mild, was heard in Philadelphia Monthly Meeting when William Penn expressed his concern for "the negroes and Indians," a concern duly recorded in the minutes.[61] The next year, at his departure from the province for England, he evidenced his concern by making a new will (later revoked) granting "my blacks their freedom as is under my hand already."[62]

Then in 1711, at the outset of Norris's clerkship, Chester Quarterly Meeting began a stream of complaints to PYM protesting the evil of slavery by declaring their "dissatisfaction with Friends buying and encouraging the bringing in of negroes, and [desiring] the care of this meeting concerning it."[63] PYM's reaction was to direct Chester Quarterly Meeting to the PYM 1696 minute and, in its 1712 epistle to London Yearly Meeting, to ask for its counsel and advice "touching the importing and having negro slaves, and detaining them and their posterity as such, without any limitation or time of redemption from that condition." London's advice to hold the status quo was not received until 1714, but William Southersby's response came in 1712: PYM "ought to do its own duty, and leave other bodies to perform their own."[64] Breaking unity with his brothers and sisters in the faith—in that era deemed a greater sin than owning slaves—Southersby, the elected provincial councilor, petitioned the Provincial Assembly to declare all slaves in the province to be free. The Assembly's answer was prompt and brusque: "It is neither just nor convenient to set them at liberty."[65] That answer was inevitable, Isaac Norris being at the time both clerk of PYM and speaker of the Assembly. At its 1714 session, PYM heard

---

[59] Southersby is recorded as having attended Council meetings between 12th day 3rd month 1684 and 17th day 9th month 1686 (*MPCP*, 1:105, 193). In addition, he and two fellow councilors were appointed commissioners in charge of the provincial office of the registrar general for over four months in 1686. *MPCP*, 1:185–86, 193.

[60] "William Southeby," *The Friend* 28 (1855): 293, 301–2, 309–10.

[61] Michener, *A Retrospect of Early Quakerism*, 336.

[62] *PWP*, 4:113.

[63] Michener, *A Retrospect of Early Quakerism*, 338.

[64] "William Southeby," 301.

[65] Ibid.

Church and State 1719–1750

London's answer that consultation among Friends in other American plantations was advisable before more guidance could be settled but that importing slaves from Africa by Friends "is not a commendable nor allowable practice," citing the Golden Rule.[66]

Southersby's passionate appeal on behalf of the enslaved was also heard in 1714, first in a paper (not included in the minutes) and then with these words spoken on the floor:

> You strive to discourage me for being so plain with you, but seeing it is really and truly for the promotion of Truth and Righteousness in the earth . . . I am not much concerned for the frowns or displeasure of any that may oppose it.[67]

The result of this standoff was twofold. PYM wrote another epistle to London Yearly Meeting that in effect agreed with the status quo.[68] And Southersby wrote an anti-slavery pamphlet that he had printed and distributed without the approval of the PYM Overseers of the Press. For this he was condemned by Philadelphia Monthly Meeting and ordered to withdraw the pamphlet from distribution and to recall the copies already circulating. Southersby apparently complied.[69]

Chester Quarterly Meeting, however, was not put off by the temporizing of the yearly or other meetings and persisted with its queries, writing next in 1715 and eliciting from PYM a reminder that all Friends should observe and put into practice the meeting's former guidance, with a caution that "Friends avoid judging one another in this matter publicly or otherwise."[70] The meeting distributed an epistle to the same effect.

Not to be deterred, Chester Quarterly Meeting put the question of the slave trade back before the meeting the next year for its consideration and heard again the former "judgment" with an additional word of circumspection:

> And yet in condescension to such Friends as are straitened in their minds against the holding them, it is

---

[66] Michener, *A Retrospect of Early Quakerism*, 338–39.

[67] "William Southeby," 301.

[68] Michener, *A Retrospect of Early Quakerism*, 339.

[69] "William Southeby," 309.

[70] PYM Min Bk B, p. 168. PYM's epistle to the same effect is on pp. 172–73.

desired that Friends generally do as much as may be [to] avoid buying such Negroes as shall hereafter be brought in, rather than offend any Friends who are against it. Yet this is only caution and not censure.[71]

In 1717 and again in 1718, William Southersby wrote abolitionist pamphlets, had them printed and distributed, and when they were condemned, withdrew them. His courageous anti-slavery voice fell silent after 1718, but other advocates were to follow where he had led.[72]

The next early abolitionist was John Farmer, a native of England.[73] After traveling through New England in the Quaker ministry, writing and preaching strongly against slavery, he was disowned by the Rhode Island Yearly Meeting of Ministers assembled at Newport in 1716. He carried his message to Philadelphia the next year, where, in various meetings, he read his papers and pamphlets opposing enslavement. Philadelphia Yearly Meeting refused him fellowship in the Truth until he should be reconciled with the Rhode Island meeting that had disowned him.[74] He died in Philadelphia, unreconciled with his church.

---

[71] Ibid., 176. "Caution and not censure" here addresses the concern of not intentionally offending a fellow believer's faith and practice regarding the purchase of a fellow creature. The concern is only for the fellow believer, not for the fellow creature being sold and bought. A caution is an advice, whereas a censure is a judgment after the breaking of a command or rule. If the offender disregarded the caution and willfully persisted, one of several punishments might be imposed, including disownment. The use of the term 'caution' suggests that the believer should carefully examine his or her own conscience.

[72] "William Southeby," 309.

[73] Farmer (1667–1725) was born near Taunton, Somersetshire, England. A woolcomber by trade, he joined the Friends in 1685, married a widow (like himself a traveling minister) in 1699, and made two journeys to America, the first described in his work *John Farmer's First American Journey, 1711–1714*, edited by Henry J. Cadbury (Worcester, MA: American Antiquarian Society, 1944), which recounts his experiences among Native Americans. His second journey to America, from which he never returned, began in 1715, took him into New England, and ended in Philadelphia. It was reported that at a Philadelphia meeting he was caused to "flinch" when "a great man who kept negroes asked Friends there to look on [Farmer] as an open enemy to the country." At those words, Farmer "sunk under it, declined in his gift, and never went back to England." *Friends' Miscellany* 4:274 (1833).

[74] "John Farmer," *The Friend* 28 (1855): 316–17. Farmer had been disowned by the Rhode Island Yearly Meeting of Ministers for his anti-enslavement views, which were found to be contrary to the mind of the Religious Society of Friends and thus a breach of its unity at that time. Even as a traveling minister, he could not have unity with Philadelphia Friends until he was restored to unity with Rhode Island Friends.

In 1729, Chester Quarterly Meeting complained that if the importation of slaves was restricted by the *Discipline*, why should not the buying of already imported slaves also be restricted? The answer to this complaint was left to Norris's successor to resolve at the next year's meeting since Norris had requested, as the final recorded matter considered by the 1729 PYM meeting, that he be discharged as clerk.[75] The assembled members proceeded to appoint John Kinsey his successor, to be assisted by Israel Pemberton Sr. In addition, Pemberton was requested to "provide a suitable fair [pleasing] book and therein to cause fairly and truly to be entered all the minutes of this meeting" from its inception.[76] Both men accepted their new responsibilities.

The PYM clerkship of John Kinsey (1730–1750): Resisting the abolitionists

John Kinsey's success as a lawyer had led to his rise to prominence in public life. For many years a member and speaker of the New Jersey Assembly, he moved his residence from New Jersey to Pennsylvania in 1730 when he began his PYM clerkship. He was elected to the Provincial Assembly each year from 1731 until his death and was its speaker for his last eleven years. In addition, he was Pennsylvania's attorney general from 1739 to 1741 and then its chief justice from 1743 to 1750.[77] The twenty years of Kinsey's PYM clerkship were momentous ones for the province and its people as well as for Britain's other American colonies. In Pennsylvania, the proprietary rule of Penn's sons proved indifferent to their father's Quaker principles as the local struggle intensified to comprehend and resolve both the issue of African enslavement and, as discussed below, the deterioration of Native American affairs. New colonists escaping hardship in their European homelands crowded into the province, settling farther westward on an unbounded frontier. Fatefully, the importation of Europe's wars into America provoked conflict among the British and French and their

---

[75] Michener, *A Retrospect of Early Quakerism*, 341. The distinction between importing (bringing in) slaves and buying and selling slaves once they were in Pennsylvania had not previously been made.

[76] PYM Min Bk B, pp. 339–40.

[77] See Proud, *History of Pennsylvania*, 2:231n; Marietta, *The Reformation of American Quakerism, 1748–1783*, 43.

respective Indian allies. A compelling voice of moral leadership—such as William Penn had had in his day—was sorely needed. Unfortunately, as one historian has commented, "Kinsey was only the most recent of a series of politician-clerks: Griffith Owen, Caleb Pusey, and Isaac Norris, Sr."[78]

Although PYM in the Kinsey years kept up its enforcement of the *Book of Discipline* in regulating the behavior of its members, it continued its policy of temporizing over the great catastrophe of enslavement. Chester Quarterly Meeting's renewed query on the issue had been carried over from Norris's final PYM meeting in 1729, to be answered in Kinsey's first PYM meeting. The other Pennsylvania quarterly meetings—Philadelphia and Bucks—each deferred to PYM, whereas the New Jersey quarterly meetings—Burlington, Gloucester, and Shrewsbury—were agreed that purchasing slaves was as wrong as importing them. After hearing the "mind" of each quarterly meeting, PYM concluded that "Friends ought to be very cautious of making any such purchases for the future. It being disagreeable to the sense of this meeting." The monthly meetings were to "admonish and caution" those "who offend herein."[79]

During Kinsey's PYM years, two lone souls used their voices and pens to argue against enslavement. Both were English-born Friends who put in print their charges against a complacent and complicit Quaker leadership, charges they steadfastly maintained in the face of opposition. The first to appear on the Philadelphia scene was Ralph Sandiford (1693–1733). Born in Liverpool and raised in the Church of England, sometime after his youthful convincement to become a Quaker he emigrated to Philadelphia, where he was engaged in the West Indies trade. Witnessing the cruelty of slavery in Philadelphia's slave market and in the islands, and holding it "inconsistent with the rights of man, and contrary to the precepts of the Author of Christianity," he began his career as a reformer.[80] In 1730 his book *The Mystery of Iniquity* was printed by Franklin and Meredith in Philadelphia. It was an expansion of his examination printed the prior year regarding the local slave trade. Addressed to London's

---

[78] Marietta, *The Reformation of American Quakerism, 1748–1783*, 43.

[79] PYM Min Bk B, pp. 346–47, 349.

[80] Roberts Vaux, *Memoirs of the Lives of Benjamin Lay and Ralph Sandiford: Two of the Earliest Public Advocates for the Emancipation of the Enslaved Africans* (London: William Phillips, 1816), 38.

Second-Day's Morning Meeting[81] and to the yearly meeting in London, the author dared state that

> the ruling part amongst us at this time, is so far gone from their first love, which could not touch with the least thing [whatever] the judgment of truth was against, who can now buy and sell mankind and their seed for evermore, and yet retain their unity with the church.[82]

At the end of his argument, Sandiford referred to "the seamen and merchants of Babylon who have by this trade corrupted this New World" and concluded that

> in tormenting the creature; the sight and sense thereof hath caused great suffering in me to behold the afflicted under such cruel bondage; and yet their masters in worse captivity than their bondslaves.[83]

For his boldness in rebuking Quaker leadership in Pennsylvania, Sandiford was threatened by the provincial chief justice David Lloyd "with severe penalties, if he permitted [his book] to be circulated." Despite the danger, Sandiford proceeded to distribute copies of his book free of charge.[84] However, the ensuing battle with his opponents so impaired his health, mentally and physically, that in 1732 Sandiford retired to Bustleton on the northern outskirts of Philadelphia. He died there on March 28, 1733, unmarried and childless, at the age of forty years. A man "small in stature, conscientiously opposed to luxury," the simple acknowledgment on his gravestone reads: "he bore a testimony against the negro trade."[85]

---

[81] Second-Day's Morning Meeting was established by George Fox in 1673 upon his return to England from the American mission. It was a committee of men ministers that met every Monday in London "chiefly for supervising books and for distributing the ministry in the London area." It met from September 1673 until 1901 and followed Fox's order that "two of a sort of all books written by Friends are to be procured and kept together, 'that, if any book be perverted by our adversaries, we may know where to find it,' and a copy is to be got of every book 'written against the Truth from the beginning.'" Braithwaite, *The Second Period of Quakerism* (1919), 279–80.

[82] Ralph Sandiford, *The Mystery of Iniquity: in a brief examination of the practice of the times. . . . Unto which is added in the postscript, the injury this trading in slaves doth the Commonwealth, humbly offer'd to all of a publick spirit* ([Philadelphia]: Printed for the author [by Franklin and Meredith], 1730), 3.

[83] Ibid., 108–9.

[84] Vaux, *Memoirs of the Lives of Benjamin Lay and Ralph Sandiford*, 40–41.

[85] Ibid., 42, 43–45.

Then, in the three successive years of 1735, 1736, and 1737, Chester Quarterly Meeting repeated its concern to PYM over the great evil of slavery, only to hear the same advices and cautions as before reiterated each time.

In 1731, the year after Sandiford's *The Mystery of Iniquity* was printed, there arrived in Philadelphia another ardent abolitionist English Friend, Benjamin Lay (1677–1759). Lay was born to Quaker parents in Colchester (Essex), England, and he soon became "intimately acquainted" with Sandiford. In addition to their anti-slavery passion, the two shared another common feature: each was small in stature. Lay stood less than five feet in height and had a large head and hunched back; in 1710 he had married Sarah, who also was of diminutive size and had a crooked back. Sarah was a recognized Quaker minister.[86] In his early years, Lay had had a varied career, spending some time at sea as a sailor, some time on land as a farmer.[87] Considered an eccentric, in 1717 he was disowned by Friends in England for causes unknown.[88] The next year the Lays moved to Barbados, and they remained there, exposed to the unchecked slave trade, until their 1731 relocation to Philadelphia's northern suburbs, where they settled on a small farm.

Lay expressed in print his outrage over slave-keeping, especially the owning of slaves by Quaker ministers, elders, and leaders, four years after the early death of Sandiford. Benjamin Franklin, with whom Lay kept up "uninterrupted intercourse,"[89] in 1737 printed a book by Lay without the approval of the Overseers of the Press, as required by the Quaker *Discipline*. The book is well summarized by its title:

> *All slave-keepers that keep the innocent in bondage, Apostates pretending to lay claim to the pure and holy Christian religion; of what congregation so ever; but especially in their ministers, by whose example the filthy leprosy and apostasy is spread far and near; it is a notorious sin, which many of the true Friends of Christ, and his pure Truth, called Quakers, has been for*

---

[86] Ibid., 14–15, 26

[87] William Bacon Evans, "The Dictionary of Quaker Biography," 124 vols., typescript ms., Haverford College Quaker Collection, Haverford College, Haverford, Pennsylvania.

[88] Vaux, *Memoirs of the Lives of Benjamin Lay and Ralph Sandiford*, 11.

[89] Ibid., 26.

> many years, and still are concerned to write and bear testimony against; as a practice so gross and hurtful to religion, and destructive to government, beyond what words can set forth, or can be declared of by men or angels, and yet lived in by ministers and magistrates in America.
> The leaders of the people cause them to err.
> Written for a general service, by him that truly and sincerely desires that the present and eternal welfare and happiness of all mankind, all the world over, of all colors, and nations, as his own soul;
> Benjamin Lay[90]

This publication offended and angered influential Friends in the province. Although Lay did not name specific offenders, few if any could remain unknown, including Isaac Norris, Kinsey's recently deceased predecessor in the clerk's chair. PYM took official action at its meeting in 1738 by ordering Kinsey to place an advertisement in the Philadelphia newspapers stating that Lay's book "was not published by the approbation of Friends, that he is not in unity with us, and that his book contains false charges as well against particular persons of our Society as against Friends in general."[91]

But the sixty-year-old author was both zealous and made of stern stuff, and he flinched from nothing, withdrawing not a word. As he had written:

> I know no worse or greater stumbling blocks the devil has to lay in the way of honest inquirers, than our ministers and elders keeping slaves; and by straining and perverting holy scriptures, preach more to hell than ever they will bring to heaven, by their feigned humility and hypocrisy.[92]

Vividly portraying the false Quaker leaders as apostates, he wrote:

> this monstrous, beastly spirit in men and women, rising up out of the sea ... and have got the dragons power and

---

[90] Benjamin Lay, *All Slave-keepers that keep the innocent in bondage...* (Philadelphia: 1737; repr., New York: Arno Press, 1969).
[91] PYM Min Bk B, p. 411.
[92] Lay, *All slave-keepers*, 85.

seat, and great authority, and the whole world wonders after the beast, the worldly mind, and dark earthly spirit among us.[93]

Three years after the publication of *All slave-keepers*, Lay and his wife moved from their small farm and became boarders near the Abington Friends Meeting House, living out the rest of their days active in the abolitionist cause. Sarah predeceased Benjamin by many years, leaving him without children or other relatives. Noting that Benjamin Lay was obstinate, ungracious, of violent temper, and eccentric, his memoirist wrote that he was also pious, benevolent, and generous, adding that "oppression will make a wise man mad." He died in his eighty-third year and was buried at Abington Meeting House on February 3, 1759, in the knowledge that PYM had, before his death, officially recognized that enslaving others has "a tendency to lessen our humanity."[94]

The issue of slavery remained before PYM in 1739, 1741, and 1742. Again, the old cautions and advices were repeated (with the addition in 1742 of the bureaucratic burden of requiring the quarterly meetings to "make report of their care herein" to the next yearly meeting).[95]

The seed of change leading to a way out of "the worldly mind and dark earthly spirit among us" that enslavement manifested was not planted until the 1746 meeting of PYM, where John Woolman and Israel Pemberton Jr. met for the first time and commenced their work together. Woolman, then twenty-six years old and a first-time representative to PYM from Burlington Quarterly Meeting, had renounced his birthright expectation as eldest son and thus his prospect of becoming in time the head of the family in his generation and principal owner of its plantation lands and other property. Instead, through apprenticeship he learned the occupations of keeping a general store and of tailoring, which he then followed together with that of orchardist, a skill learned in his farming youth. He did this in part so that he would be free to travel on missions among Friends as a recorded minister through Burlington Monthly Meeting. Earlier in 1746, the year he first met Pemberton,

---

[93] Ibid., 258.

[94] Vaux, *Memoirs of the Lives of Benjamin Lay and Ralph Sandiford*, 22, 34, 35; final quotation is from a PYM epistle quoted in Michener, *A Retrospect of Early Quakerism*, 45.

[95] PYM Min Bk B, pp. 416, 425, 429.

Woolman had gone on a mission, mostly of observation, journeying over three months and covering approximately 1,500 miles in the slaveholding South. On his return, he wrote his first major essay, *Some Considerations on the Keeping of Negroes,* which he withheld from publication for the next eight years.

Israel Pemberton Jr. was five years older than Woolman. He was the eldest son of Israel Sr., who was then in his nineteenth year as clerk of Philadelphia Monthly Meeting, and was a grandson of Phineas Pemberton, PYM's first named clerk. When he met Woolman, Pemberton had already completed three years of service as the clerk of the overseers of the Friends public schools in Philadelphia (in which position he continued until his death). In PYM, he had already participated in drafting the original queries by which PYM undertook to enforce the *Discipline* among its subordinate meetings; he was in a select group regularly appointed to write PYM's annual epistles to other American provincial yearly meetings and to London Yearly Meeting; and he was one of the Overseers of the Press who exercised control over works published under the auspices of the Religious Society of Friends. Israel Jr. had also followed his father's example by becoming independently wealthy as a merchant trader.

An unusual bond quickly formed between Pemberton Jr., the wealthy urbanite, and Woolman, the agrarian who renounced position and property for a life of simplicity. In 1746, Pemberton and Woolman were asked to write PYM's epistle in 1746 to the yearly meeting in Virginia, one of the colonies Woolman had visited and then written about in his unpublished *Some Considerations on the Keeping of Negroes*. Pemberton, harboring abolitionist views and finding in Woolman someone knowledgeable about slavery, embraced him as an ally. In later years, as will be seen, Pemberton would appoint Woolman to serve as an overseer of the press and also to the committee that made the first revisions to PYM's queries that had been adopted in 1743.

Embracing, then deceiving, the "nations of Indians"

From the founding of his province, Penn had intended for himself, "his heirs and successors and all the English and other Christian inhabitants . . . and all the several people of the nations of Indians" that there would be "a firm and lasting peace" and that the united peoples "shall forever hereafter be as one head and one heart and live in true friendship and amity as one people."[96] The Native Americans employed similar rich, symbolic language in addresses made at treaty negotiations when the colonists came seeking living space within Pennsylvania on lands that for ages had been the aborigines' homeland and the seat of their ancient cultures. Such language and the rituals accompanying presentations of emblematic wampum strings and belts and clothing fill the pages of the recorded treaties and deeds made by the indigenous peoples with the Europeans in search of refuge from their sufferings 'beyond the seas.' Native ideas of the friendship alliances being shaped were metaphorically expressed, as in the 1736 treaty bonding Pennsylvania and the Iroquois Confederacy, by the *Fire* to be kept "bright and burning to the end of the world" at an appointed place for councils; by the *Road* to be kept open and cleared between the nations and their council fire; and by the *Chain of Friendship* linking the parties that was to be kept free from all rust and spots, its brightness preserved "until this Earth passeth away and is no more seen."[97]

In this reaching for peace, true friendship, and amity among peoples of various cultures who were for the most part without a common language or shared customs or, of critical importance, mutual understanding about land rights and their transfer, there were likely to be differences and conflicts. Another basic difference concerned the preservation of transfer records. The English wrote and preserved documents such as treaties, deeds, minutes, and letters that the Native Americans could not read or verify, much less understand, whereas the Indians recorded essential matters through both the living memories of numerous witnesses skilled in a practiced oral tradition and through wampum memoranda.[98]

---

[96] "Articles of Agreement" with the Susquehanna Indians dated April 23, 1701, *PWP*, 4: 51.

[97] "A Treaty of Friendship held with the chiefs of the Six Nations, at Philadelphia, in September and October, 1736," as quoted in Kalter, *Benjamin Franklin*, 53. See also Kalter's discussion of similar metaphors that demonstrated that "Native Americans exercised much control over the discourse of the treaty councils, bending the British to their language. . . . It shows that the British were not impervious to Iroquois intellect." Ibid., 120–21n2. See appendix 10, which has a section discussing the alliances made by Native American nations with Pennsylvania and other American colonies.

[98] "Wampum strings and belts 'embodied' messages and terms of agreement that were formulated in tribal council, memorized, and pronounced by spokesmen

Vital and competing economic interests lay at the heart of the encounter between these disparate peoples. Life in Penn's province was founded upon such interests. For the success of their venture, Penn and his colonists needed to take possession of lands being used and occupied by the native peoples long settled on and near the basins of the Delaware and Susquehanna Rivers and their tributaries. The colonists also needed economic interaction with the Native Americans, by which colonists could obtain the animal furs and skins procured by the Lenni Lenapes, Susquehannocks, Shawnees, and other tribes.[99] For this purpose, colonial traders maintained a network of trading posts on the frontier and exchanged manufactured goods—notably guns and rum—for the natives' harvest of pelts. Therein, as well, lay many problems.

In the beginning: Penn's policy of friendship and fair dealing (1682–1712)

When Penn came into the province of Pennsylvania in 1682, he little anticipated the enormity of the challenges ahead. One supreme challenge—the need to determine the boundary lines of the province—quickly reached a crisis point and necessitated, as previously discussed, Penn's return to England within two years of his arrival. A century later, Pennsylvania (together with its Delaware counties) would become the last of America's Middle Atlantic colonies to fix its boundaries, effectively anchoring the center of the slight arc running from Long Island to the Delmarva Peninsula. The Duke of York had granted Penn this "wilderness" tract out of lands the duke had recently seized that had previously been known as New Netherland. Pennsylvania was shoehorned between other English colonies, being neighbored on the north by New York, on the east by East and

---

at treaties. Accepting the wampum meant accepting the agreement.... The strings and belts then served as records; not simply as contracts to be kept on file for reference, if necessary, but as scripts to be actively reviewed and periodically renewed by the contracting parties." Andrew Newman, *On Records: Delaware Indians, Colonists, and the Media of History and Memory* (Lincoln: University of Nebraska Press, 2012), 122.

[99] "Every spring and fall [Logan's] warehouses on Fishbourne's wharf and on Second Street bulged and stank with deerskins, elkskins, bearskins, with fox, beaver, mink, marten, raccoon, and wildcat pelts." Frederick B. Tolles, *James Logan and the Culture of Provincial America*, 90.

West Jersey across the Delaware River, and on the south by Maryland.

The first immediate issue was to find and fix the exact northern and southern borders of the new province. The Charter of Pennsylvania granted Penn on March 4, 1681, "a certain country . . . in the parts of America not yet cultivated and planted."[100] The charter then described the boundaries of this grant of land, which had an imperfect rectangular shape. It had three straight sides on the north, south, and west, while its eastern side was a navigable river, the Delaware. The eastern boundary began twelve miles north of New Castle, Delaware, and ran upriver to the line of forty-three degrees latitude north, where it turned due west and ran that line of latitude west for five degrees of longitude. The parallel southern boundary, beginning twelve miles west of New Castle, was set on forty degrees latitude north and ran west for five degrees longitude. The western boundary was a straight line connecting the western ends of the north and south boundaries.[101]

The royal description required a more exact science of land surveying than was then known. The northern and southern boundaries described in Penn's charter were incorrect and would have put his northern border at the latitude of Buffalo, Syracuse, and Amsterdam in New York and his southern limit at that of Lancaster, York, and Philadelphia. Happily, Pennsylvania's western boundary, set in the charter at present-day Pittsburgh, was close to the longitudinal mark noted in the charter. The north and south boundary uncertainties, however, were not to be fixed until 1767 with Maryland and the 1780s with New York.[102]

Penn's next land-related challenge was to locate the main areas for development from east to west and lying between the colony's uncertain northern and southern boundaries. It was in these areas that he wanted to populate his new plantation with the settlers coming over from England, Wales, Scotland, Ireland, and mainland Europe. To do so, he first needed to obtain clear and marketable 'land title' from the native 'owners.' The principle that Penn used for obtaining legally valid and marketable land titles from the native peoples was to

---

[100] Soderlund, *William Penn*, 41.

[101] Ibid., 41–42.

[102] The boundary with Maryland was surveyed between 1763 and 1767; it is the Mason-Dixon line.

never settle any lands in this province, till he had fairly purchased them of the Indians, who engaged that they would never sell any lands in this province to any other person than their brother Onas.[103]

Penn conscientiously adhered to this principle as he supervised, during his 1682–1684 visit to Pennsylvania, plans for settling and planting the lands west of the Delaware River, the colony's eastern boundary line. For that purpose, not only were lands of the native peoples on and back from the western shore of the river duly acquired, but Penn also made a legendary treaty of friendship[104] at Shackamaxon (a native village; part of its site is located in Penn Treaty Park on present-day Philadelphia's riverfront). The treaty's purpose was to secure peace and harmony between Penn, as well as his successors and fellow planters, and the Indians of the Delaware area from whom he acquired 'land title' in a series of at least ten documents, five of which are preserved.[105] These native peoples were the Lenni Lenapes who had recently experienced severe population loss due to a "grievous death toll... caused largely by disease, reduction of their food supply, and conflicts over trade or trespass with Europeans and other Indian nations."[106] Penn obtained the deeds from the Lenapes at the Falls of the Delaware (near Trenton), securing title in and to Bucks County, where he placed his own country seat at Pennsbury Manor;[107] from the Lenapes farther downriver between Neshaminy Creek and the Schuylkill River, where he settled Philadelphia as the provincial

---

[103] From the speech of Lieutenant Governor James Hamilton on August 11, 1761, at the treaty conference with Indians at Easton, Pennsylvania. Kalter, *Benjamin Franklin*, 348–49. "Onas" was the name given by the Iroquois (and "Miquon" the name given by the Lenni Lenapes) to Penn and his sons. Both these native terms meant "feather" and referred to the quill pen used by the proprietors' men at the many treaty conferences. Ibid., 407–8.

[104] *PWP*, 2:458n27. Although there is no known written treaty, a strong argument is made from period evidence that it once existed. See Jennings, *Iroquois*, 245–48.

[105] *PWP*, 2:261–69, 353–55, 404–5; *Microfilm*, 4:631; and Samuel Hazard et al., eds., *Pennsylvania Archives* (Philadelphia, 1852–), 1st series, vol. 1, pp. 95–96. See also the map of Delaware River area purchases in *PWP*, 2:491.

[106] Kalter, *Benjamin Franklin*, 12.

[107] See deeds dated July 15, 1682, and June 23, 1683, from the Falls Lenapes, *PWP*, 2:261–69, 404–5.

capital;[108] and from the Lenapes downriver into the lower counties to Duck Creek, nearer the river's mouth, which included the lands of Brandywine and Christiana Creeks.[109]

These direct contacts with the Lenapes greatly impressed Penn. Although he had written nothing about the natives in his promotional material prior to his first visit, after the Shackamaxon experience and other encounters he was filled with admiration and enthusiasm. In August 1683 Penn sent a lengthy description of the colony to the Committee of the Free Society of Traders of Pennsylvania in London (which was there printed and distributed).[110] Six of its fourteen pages were devoted to the "persons, language, manners, and government" of the native peoples, most likely the Lenapes of the Delaware Valley. Of them, he wrote:

> Their persons are generally tall, straight, well built and of singular proportion. They tread strong and clever, and mostly walk with a lofty chin. . . . Their language is lofty, yet narrow, but . . . full, and like short hand in writing, one word serves in place of three, and the rest is supplied by the understanding of the hearer. . . . I have made it my business to understand it that I might not want an interpreter on any occasion, and I must say that I know not a language spoken in Europe that has words of more sweetness or greatness in accent and emphases than theirs. . . . Of their customs and manners there is much to be said. . . . If an European come to see them, or call for lodging at their wigwam, they give him the best place and first cut and if they come to visit us, they salute us, with an *Itah* which is as much as to say Good be to you and set them down. . . . Maybe they speak not a word more, but observe all passages, if you give them anything to eat or drink, well; for they won't ask, and be it little or much, if it be with kindness, they are well pleased. . . . But in liberality they excel. Nothing is too good for their friend. Give them a fine gun, coat, or other thing, it may pass a

---

[108] These natives are referred to as the Tulpehocken Lenapes (Tulpehocken is the name of the tributary creek of the Schuylkill River where they relocated).

[109] See deed dated July 10, 1680, and its assignment dated February 21, 1683, PWP, 2:353–55; deed from Lare et al. dated October 2, 1685, in Hazard, *Pennsylvania Archives*, 1st series, vol. 1, pp. 95–96, involving the Brandywine Lenape lands.

[110] William Penn, *Letter to the Free Society of Traders* (London: Andrew Sowle, 1683).

dozen hands before it sticks. Light of heart, strong affections, but soon spent. The most merry creatures that live, feast, and dance almost perpetually. If poor one day, rich another and poor again. They never have much nor never want. Wealth circulates like the blood; all parts partake and though none shall want what another has, yet [they are] exact observers of property.[111]

At this point in his letter, Penn illustrated the liberality of the natives by describing how the purchase prices, the agreed-upon quantities of manufactured articles or "Indian goods" (see glossary) he had recently paid for the lands along the Delaware River, had been soon given away, undoubtedly in English eyes an act of improvident generosity:

Some kings have sold and others presented me four or five parcels of land. The pay or presents I made them were not hoarded by the particular owners, but the neighboring kings and their clans being present, when the goods were brought forth, the parties chiefly concerned consulted what and to whom they should give them. To every king then by hands of a person for that work appointed, is a proportion sent so sorted and folded, and with that gravity that is admirable. Then that king subdivides it in like manner among his dependents, they hardly leaving themselves an equal share with one of their subjects. And be it on such occasions at festivals, or at their common meals, the kings distribute and to themselves last. . . . They care for little because they want but little, and the reason is a little contents them. . . . In this they are revenged on us. We sweat and toil to live, their pleasure feeds them, I mean their hunting, fishing, and fowling.[112]

Then Penn addressed what was quickly becoming a foul disease among the native peoples and an evil weapon in the hands of unscrupulous colonials:

Since the Europeans came into these parts [the natives] are grown great lovers of strong liquors, rum especially, and for it exchange the richest of their skins and furs. If they are heated with liquor they are restless till they have

---

[111] Penn to the Free Society of Traders, August 16, 1683, *PWP*, 2:448–50.
[112] *PWP*, 2:450–51.

enough to sleep. That is their cry, some more and I will go to sleep. But when drunk one of the most wretched spectacles in the world, often burning and sometimes killing one another, at which times the Christians are not without danger as well.[113]

After sympathetically acknowledging the natives' beliefs in "a god and immortality without the help of metaphysics,"[114] Penn continued his letter with a description of their government under kings who succeeded to that office "but always of the mothers' side . . . that their issue may not be spurious." Every king ruled through his council made up of "all the old and wise men of his nation. . . . Nothing of moment is undertaken, be it war, peace, selling of land or traffic, without advising with them and which is more, with the young men too."[115] Continuing, Penn provided this revealing insight on how his land negotiations proceeded:

'Tis admirable to consider how absolute the kings are and yet how he [sic] moves by the breath of his people. I have had occasion to be in Council with them upon Treaties for land and to adjust the terms of trade. Their order is thus: the King sits in the middle of an half moon, and has his council . . . on each hand. . . . Having consulted and resolved their business, the King ordered one of them to speak to me. He stood up, came to me, and in the name of his King saluted me, then took me by the hand, and told me he was ordered by his king to speak to me, and that now it was not he but the King that spoke, because what he would say was the King's mind. He first prayed me to excuse them that they had not complied with me the last time. . . . It was the Indian custom to deliberate and take up much time in council before they resolved, and that if the young people, and the owners of the land had been as ready as he, I had not met with so much delay. . . . He fell to the bounds of the land they had agreed to dispose of

---

[113] *PWP*, 2:451. Penn had addressed this problem the previous year in article 17 of *The Great Law* passed by an assembly at Chester alias Upland, the 7th day December, 1682, which prohibited the sale or exchange of "any rum or brandy, or any strong liquors, at any time, to any Indian within this province." Samuel Hazard, *Annals of Pennsylvania, from the discovery of the Delaware* (Philadelphia: Hazard & Mitchell, 1850), 623–24.

[114] *PWP*, 2:451.

[115] *PWP*, 2:452.

and the price.... During the time that this person spoke not a man of them was observed to whisper, nor smile, the old grave, the young reverend in their deportment. They speak little, but fervently and with elegance. I have never seen more natural sagacity considering them without the help (I was going to say the spoil) of Tradition, and he will deserve the name of wise that outwits them in any treaty about a thing they understand.[116]

Penn concluded his account of the natives with these fateful words:

Let them have justice and you win them.... They are the worse for the Christians who have propagated their vices, and yielded them tradition for ill and not for good things. ... It were miserable indeed for us to fall under the just censure of the poor Indians' conscience, while we make profession of so far things transcending.[117]

---

[116] PWP, 2:452–53.

[117] PWP, 2:454. Historical note: John Heckewelder (1743–1823), the Moravian missionary to the Lenni Lenapes, out of his long experience living among the Native Americans of Pennsylvania and Ohio, wrote this in his "General Observations of the Indians on the White People":

The Indians believe that the Whites were made by the same Great Spirit who created them, and that he assigned to each different race of men a particular employment in this world, but not the same to all. To the whites the great Mannitto gave it in charge to till the ground and raise by cultivation the fruits of the earth; to the Indians he assigned the nobler employment of hunting, and the supreme dominion over all the rest of the animal creation.

They will not admit that the whites are superior beings. They say that the hair of their heads, their features, the various colours of their eyes, evince that they are not like themselves *Lenni Lenape,* an ORIGINAL PEOPLE, a race of men that has existed unchanged from the beginning of time; but they are a *mixed* race, and therefore a *troublesome* one; wherever they may be, the Great Spirit, knowing the wickedness of their disposition, found it necessary to give them a great Book, and taught them how to read it, that they might know and observe what he wished them to do and to abstain from. But they, the Indians, have no need of any such book to let them know the will of their Maker; they find it engraved on their own hearts; they have had sufficient discernment given to them to distinguish good from evil, and by following that guide, they are sure not to err.

It is true, they confess, that when they first saw the whites, they took them for beings of a superior kind.... It was not long, however, before they discovered their mistake, having found them an ungrateful, insatiable people, who, though the Indians had given them as much land as was

Additionally, during his first visit Penn took steps to plant and expand the colony's trading areas farther west from the Delaware, into the far-reaching valleys of the Susquehanna River and its crowning West and North Branches. The Susquehanna is like a mighty tree, the south-north trunk of which splits Pennsylvania to midpoint where it branches out into a wide-reaching canopy stretching well northward. As the longest river on America's Atlantic seaboard and the sixteenth largest river by volume in today's nation, its development promised to enrich greatly the province's economic base. There were, however, formidable problems to overcome. The branches' headwaters were within the province of New York where the government of the Duke of York, Penn's patron, had already secured the riches of the fur trade (Penn's primary objective in this scheme) through an alliance with the Iroquois Confederacy settled from New York's southern tier to the border with Canada. Control of the fur trade was centered at Albany, where pelts and hides were collected and shipped down the Hudson River to Manhattan and thence to European markets. Moreover, the mouth of the Susquehanna was in Maryland, and the proprietor of that colony was already Penn's determined antagonist in their battle over where to locate the Pennsylvania-Maryland boundary. Hanging over all else was the growing threat that local frictions would break out into open hostilities between the English and French colonial governments, each with their respective Indian allies, traders, and settlers, as populations grew, frontier settlements expanded, and economic competitors clashed. Despite all this, Penn remained optimistic.[118]

---

necessary to raise provisions for themselves and their families, and pasture for their cattle, wanted still to have more, and at last would not be contented with less than the *whole country*.

John Heckewelder, *An Account of the History, Manners, and Customs of the Indian Nations, who once inhabited Pennsylvania and the neighbouring states* (Philadelphia: Abraham Small, 1819; Miami, FL: HardPress Publishing, 2012), 187–88. Citation refers to the HardPress edition.

[118] For studies of the complex interactions of English colonists and Native Americans (and of English and French imperial interests already in conflict in North America) before and after the founding of Pennsylvania, see Francis Jennings, *The Ambiguous Iroquois Empire: The Covenant Chain Confederation of Indian Tribes with English Colonies from its Beginnings to the Lancaster Treaty of 1744* (New York: W. W. Norton, 1984) and Francis Jennings, *Empire of Fortune: Crowns, Colonies, Empire and Tribes in the Seven Years War in America* (New York: W. W. Norton, 1988).

In early August 1683, Penn empowered two commissioners to travel to 'Iroquoia' for meetings with the allies and the chiefs of the Mohawks (the eastern gatekeepers of the Five Nations of the Iroquois Confederacy who, because of their proximity to Albany, were managers of the natives' fur-trading arrangements) and of the Senecas (the westernmost of the nations).[119] The commissioners were authorized to treat "for the purchasing of the lands lying on both sides of Susquehanna River."[120] Penn's instructions coached his commissioners to "insinuate" to the "Sachems of the Mowhawk and Synacher Indians & their Alleys" that these Susquehanna lands were theirs to sell through "some Claime by Conquest, or at least that the remainder of the Susquahannahs, who are right Owners, are amongst them."[121] These Susquehannock Indians, who had once occupied the lands bounding the river whence they derived their name, were an Iroquois-speaking tribe who had lived near and at peace with their Lenape neighbors on the Delaware. Their dominance over the Susquehanna trade had ended after they lost a long war with the Iroquois Confederacy. As a result, by the 1670s most of the Susquehannocks had been pushed into Maryland and Virginia, where, after being attacked by the English during Bacon's Rebellion (1676), many accepted the invitation a year later of Sir Edmund Andros, governor of New York, to settle among and become subordinate to the Iroquois. Although some Susquehannocks returned to their original territory, the victory of claiming the lands and trade of the Susquehanna network as a spoil of conquest remained with Andros and New York.[122]

---

[119] 'Iroquoia' refers to the territory occupied by the Five Nations of the Iroquois in present-day New York's southern tier, westward from the upper Hudson River to the southeastern shore of Lake Erie. The Five Nations, from east to west, were the tribes of the Mohawks, Oneidas, Onondagas, Cayugas, and Senecas. After their defeat in the Tuscarora War (1711–1715) fought in eastern North Carolina, many Tuscarora Indians moved north and "were adopted as the Sixth Nation of the Iroquois League." Jennings, *The Ambiguous Iroquois Empire*, 297.

[120] Commission and instructions to James Graham and William Haige from Penn dated August 2, 1683, *PWP*, 2:423–24. Graham, born in Scotland, was a merchant in New York, where he arrived in 1678, after which he traded in the Delaware Valley. In 1685, he became New York's attorney general. *PWP*, 2:342n17. Haige was a Quaker merchant of London who became an extensive landowner in East and West Jersey and in Pennsylvania where he settled, serving Penn and the province in various capacities. *PWP*, 2:114n9.

[121] *PWP*, 2:423.

[122] *PWP*, 2:422.

The Mohawks' answer to Penn's offer to buy the Susquehanna River and lands was received by his commissioners, Graham and Haige, in Albany by October 4. Declaring that the river "did belong to them in ancient times" and "they did chase them [the Susquehannocks] away in the time of the war" with 120 Mohawk and thirty Onondaga warriors, they accepted the belt of wampum sent by Penn's agents and were willing "to Sell the River and Land," as were the Oneidas, Onondagas, and Cayugas. The Mohawks, further answering for themselves and the Oneidas, Onondagas, and Cayugas, stated that the Seneca nation "had nothing to do with itt, to witt with the River & Land of Susquehanne."[123]

In the meantime, the Duke of York had sent Thomas Dongan to New York as governor in the place of Andros. New York's commissioners overseeing the Iroquois fur trade at Albany had warned Dongan of the consequences to New York's economy if Penn succeeded in his ambitions in the Susquehanna region, and Dongan was also knowledgeable of the Pennsylvania-Maryland boundary dispute. He therefore instructed his Albany commissioners that it was "necessary to putt a Stopp to all proceedings in mr Penns Affaires with the Indyans untill his bounds and limits be adjusted."[124] In a letter written to Penn a month after this "stop" order, Dongan, acknowledging Penn's kindnesses when visiting him in New York, and after making diplomatically obscure references to the matter of the Five Nations of the Iroquois at Albany, informed Penn that the Iroquois had

> given me the land & pretend that they have better intrest then any others. They have all of them agreed to Give sesquehannah to me and this Government; which I have under their hands to show for it. All that I Desire of you for my own security is that you will Engage, in case his Royll Highnss be fond of their Gift, that you will save me harmless.[125]

---

[123] "The Mohawk Indians' Answer to William Haige and James Graham" dated October 4, 1683, *PWP*, 2:481–82. See also Jennings, *The Ambiguous Iroquois Empire*, 226–28.

[124] "Thomas Dongan to the Commissioners of Albany" dated September 14, 1683, *PWP*, 2:487–88.

[125] Thomas Dongan to William Penn, October 10, 1683, *PWP*, 2:488–89. See Jennings, *The Ambiguous Iroquois Empire*, 228–29.

Despite Dongan's sleight of hand, Penn did not allow his dream of expansion to die. In September and October 1683, he acquired land from the mouth of the Susquehanna upriver to the falls at Conewago Creek, between Conestoga and Paxtang.[126] Two years later, in December 1685, he had printed *A Further Account of the Province of Pennsylvania and its improvements: for the satisfaction of those that are adventurers, and enclined to be so*,[127] again declaring his intention to open up the Susquehanna for venturers seeking economic opportunity. Then in 1690 he put his project before the London public with a broadside promising "another city" on the Susquehanna where planters might have their town houses.[128] In the years that followed, this project was alternately revised and then allowed to lapse several times before Penn ordered its dissolution in 1707.[129] About 1690, he also gave the Susquehanna Indians 500 acres of land on Conestoga Creek for a settlement site later called Conestoga Indiantown.[130]

Penn's ambitions for the Susquehanna development, however, did not end with the dissolution order; they simply took another course. In January 1697 Penn had overcome Dongan's (and thereby New York's) questionable claim of title (by gift from the Iroquois) in and to the Susquehanna River and Valley by buying out the interests that had been allegedly acquired, either by gift or by trust, from the Iroquois. Penn's low payment of £100 to Dongan for releasing New York's claim to the Susquehanna lands, modestly eased Dongan's financial needs in retirement (he had been removed in 1688 as New York's governor).[131]

---

[126] See deed dated September 10, 1683, from Kekelappan and declaration dated October 18, 1683, from Machaloha (possibly a Susquehannock using a Delaware name), in *Microfilm*, 4:525, 573; Hazard, *Pennsylvania Archives*, 1st series, vol. 1, p. 67. Also see *PWP*, 2:492; Jennings, *The Ambiguous Iroquois Empire*, 225n6.

[127] This was printed in London by Andrew Sowle in 1695.

[128] William Penn, *Some proposals for a second settlement in the province of Pennsylvania* (London: Andrew Sowle, 1690). See *Microfilm*, 6:410; *PWP*, 5:367–69.

[129] William Penn to James Logan, July 8, 1707, *PWP*, 4:579n27.

[130] Kevin Kenny, *Peaceable Kingdom Lost: The Paxton Boys and the Destruction of William Penn's Holy Experiment* (New York: Oxford University Press, 2009), 12.

[131] See indenture from Dongan to William Penn dated January 12, 1697, *PWP*, 3:477–79, esp. notes 2 and 5; Jennings, *The Ambiguous Iroquois Empire*, 235.

Finally, on September 13, 1700, during his second visit to America, Penn was granted the "River Susquehanna," with all the islands therein and all the lands on both sides thereof extending to "the utmost confines of the lands which are or formerly were the Right of the People or Nation called the Susquehanna Indians or by what name soever they were called." The grantors were Widaagh, alias Orytagh, and Andaggy-junkquagh, kings or sachems of the Susquehanna Indians.[132] The grantee was "our Friend and Brother" William Penn. James Logan and four others witnessed the execution of the deed.[133]

To crown this accomplishment of his westward expansion, in April 1701 Penn and the natives of the Susquehanna region prepared their Articles of Agreement.[134] As in the lost peace treaty for the Delaware Valley made with the Lenapes at Shackamaxon, so now Penn pledged "firm and lasting peace" and "true friendship and amity as one people" with the natives then settled in the Susquehanna Valley (the Susquehannocks and the Shawnees). There were two other parties to this agreement. The first were the Conoy Indians then living on the Potomac River, whose relations with Maryland were strained and who were seeking to relocate to a refuge on the same river in Pennsylvania (reflecting the erroneous assumption that part of the Potomac flowed within Pennsylvania). The other party to the agreement was the "brother to the emperor for and in behalf of the emperor," who as principal chief of the Onondaga Indians was head of the Iroquois Confederacy.[135] These additional parties to the agreement reflect the sharply different situation facing Penn on the Susquehanna compared with the situation he had met earlier on the Delaware. Instead of negotiating with the single nation of the Lenapes with their several chiefs, here he negotiated with the Susquehannocks (former occupants of the river who had recently returned to occupy their town at Conestoga), the Shawnees (migrating from the south and west), the Conoys (seeking refuge from conflicts in Virginia and Maryland), and the central authority of the Iroquois Confederacy (which, in a time of conflict between the empires of Britain and

---

[132] This is how they were described in their deed. See also *PWP*, 4:54n2.

[133] *Microfilm*, 8:557; Hazard, *Pennsylvania Archives*, 1st series, vol. 1, pp. 133–34.

[134] See discussion above on pp. 152–53.

[135] The texts of the Articles of Agreement are in *PWP*, 4:49–55 (the quotes are from p. 51); see notes 1–5.

France, was seeking both an alternative to its constricting alliance with New York and an open river route to the native populations farther south).

Penn accomplished two additional objectives in this agreement. First, he had the "Indians of Conestoga" and their chief "absolutely ratify" and "confirm and make good" his title to "the lands lying near and about the said [Susquehanna] River" obtained in the September 13, 1700, deed from the Susquehannock chiefs.[136] Second, he settled his right to regulate commerce between Pennsylvanians and Indians by requiring that all transactions be conducted through the sole agency of traders licensed by his government "for the prevention of abuses that are too frequently put upon the said Indians in trade." The agreement expressly barred the Indians from selling their "skins, peltry, or furs or any other effects of their hunting" outside the province or through non-licensed traders. Penn promised that this regulated trade would provide the natives "with all sorts of necessary goods for their use at reasonable rates."[137]

Having thus secured from these Native Americans the gift of peace, the confirmation of his title to their former lands "upon and about the River Susquehanna," and the regulation of trade between these indigenous peoples whose ways of life were increasingly threatened by the arrival of even more "English and other Christians" into their ancient homeland, Penn gave his own solemn pledge.[138]

> ITEM the said William Penn doth hereby promise for himself, his heirs and successors, that he and they will at all times show themselves true friends and brothers to all and every of the said Indians by assisting them with the best of their advices, directions, and counsels, and will in all things just and reasonable befriend them, they behaving themselves as aforesaid and submitting to the laws of this province in all things as the English and other Christians therein do, to which they the said Indians hereby agree and oblige themselves and their posterity forever.

---

[136] This is the ninth of the ten unnumbered items in the Articles of Agreement, *PWP*, 4:53.

[137] These are the sixth and seventh items in the Articles of Agreement, *PWP*, 4:52.

[138] See the tenth item in the Articles of Agreement, *PWP*, 4:53.

Six months later, when Penn left the province for the last time, the Indians of the Susquehanna requested that there be due observance of the agreement "we have solemnly made for us and our posterity as long as the sun and the moon shall endure, one head, one mouth, and one heart."[139]

On October 27, 1701, Penn invested James Logan as his plenipotentiary with wide authority in America over the affairs of Penn Incorporated, the proprietary enterprise having as its principal purpose the sale of lands in the Delaware and Susquehanna Valleys, the legal title to which Penn had been acquiring from the Indians. Eight days later, on November 3, Penn left the shores of Pennsylvania. He was never to return, although for the next eleven years he tried, through letters written during the often stressful circumstances of his life in England, to guide and chide Logan regarding his manifold responsibilities in America. The twenty-seven-year-old Logan, who had spent only twenty-three months in Pennsylvania serving at the side of William Penn and learning his mind about the affairs of government and property, was suddenly left in charge of Penn's interests in America. Penn the principal commissioned Logan the agent with fullest praise and widest powers, as follows:

> William Penn, true and absolute Proprietary and Governor in chief of the Province of Pennsylvania and Territories thereunto belonging, to my trusty and faithful friend James Logan, Greeting:

> Reposing special trust and confidence in thy Fidelity, Ability, and Integrity know that I have constituted and appointed you . . . Secretary of the State and Government and Clerk of the Council . . . [and] Secretary of Property for the said Province and Territories.[140]

In matters of the state and Council, the Commission gave Logan "full power and authority to prepare and draw up in writing all acts of state and orders to the government." In matters of property, Logan was "to prepare and draw up all warrants and patents for lands and lots granted" by Penn or any of his four

---

[139] The text of the memorial is in *PWP*, 4:98–99 (the quote is on p. 99).

[140] The text of Penn's commission to James Logan as secretary of state, secretary of property, and clerk of council dated October 27, 1701 is recorded in the Rolls Office at Philadelphia in Patent Book A, vol. 2, pp. 156–57, *Microfilm*, 9:721.

commissioners of property, namely, Logan, Edward Shippen, Griffith Owen, and Thomas Story.[141] The Commission also gave Logan power

> to enquire into, examine, transact, and perform all and all manner of things whatsoever that relate to the granting or confirming of any lands or lots or liberties and privileges thereunto belonging from me the Proprietary of the said Province and Territories or my Commissioners appointed.[142]

For the next thirty-one years, Logan exercised his rights and duties as Penn's, and then Penn Incorporated's, plenipotentiary in America. In no other sphere of his authority did Logan act with the freedom that he exercised over land. In real property matters, he had custody of the proprietor's personal accounts, confidential records, and important papers. He authorized the issuance of warrants for preparing surveys as well as deeds. Greatly empowered through his contacts with the Native Americans during Penn's last visit in the province, he was thus perceived by tribal leaders as the living embodiment of Onas, Penn himself, the faithful governor who had paid the native peoples the fair value of their ancestral lands and then extended the hand of brotherhood to secure a shared territory in peace and harmony.[143]

And just as Penn valued Logan's fidelity and integrity, so Logan noted in a letter to Penn his own personal integrity and honesty (downplaying the depth of his religious beliefs and practices, however). Writing in 1706 amidst the ongoing battles

---

[141] See Penn's commission to the commissioners of property dated October 28, 1701, *Microfilm*, 9:751. Penn sometimes also referred to these commissioners as "commissioners of propriety"; see *PWP*, 4:118n1. For Penn's renewal of Logan's appointment as a commissioner of property dated November 9, 1711, see *PWP*, 4:710n1; for Penn's and the mortgage trustees' power of attorney to Logan and others to sell Pennsylvania lands dated November 10, 1711, see *PWP*, 4:710n2; for Penn's last will and testament of April 1712 naming Logan and others as testamentary trustees of his American lands, see *PWP*, 4:716.

[142] Penn's commission to James Logan as secretary of state, secretary of property, and clerk of council dated October 27, 1701, *Microfilm*, 9:721.

[143] According to Kalter, William Penn "continued to buy land from the Lenapes (and others). Philadelphia and the counties surrounding it emerged as a result of these sales, which became renowned for the fairness of the compensation that the Indian nations received, the clarity of the terms to which all parties had agreed, and Penn's observance of Lenape protocols of consent in land cessions." Kalter, *Benjamin Franklin*, 13. See also Jennings, *The Ambiguous Iroquois Empire*, 327.

with the antiproprietary Provincial Assembly, commenting on his fellow Quakers, Logan told Penn:

> We are weak, and I doubt [if] a very much blessed people. There is one thing I should mention of myself, viz., that travelling Friends [Quaker missionaries, many from England], if inquired of about me, will give no good account of my strictness, but if they are just they will say all I desire they should; for I am willing that all who know me should also know that I neither am, nor ever was, a strict professor [practitioner of religious teachings], and I will always make my outside appearances agree with what I really know myself to be; for I loathe hypocrisy. But I think I can defy the world to tax me with an ill thing.... If I prove not good, as I hope I shall prove honest in all its significations, religion shall never suffer by me, as it does by many a false villain.[144]

Logan's administration of land affairs (1712–1732)

Logan directly served Penn as his colonial 'eyes and ears' in governmental and proprietary matters for the seventeen years following the founder's return to England in 1701, ending with Penn's death there in 1718. As noted earlier,[145] in 1710 and 1711 the agent was in England with Penn to discuss official issues, take direct instruction, and help decide the future course of the province and of the proprietor's American interests. Their voluminous preserved correspondence for the nine years preceding that visit attests to Penn's close oversight and involvement with Logan's fiduciary labors. By the time of Logan's return home to Philadelphia in early 1712, however, Penn was unable to engage in his own affairs, leaving such matters to his wife Hannah. Further, Logan himself had returned with the resolve to begin laying the foundations for a family and for a personal fortune of his own. While Logan continued to serve the Penns in his various official duties, he now began to serve himself as well.

Logan learned well from Penn, who had long believed the fur trade with Indians in the Susquehanna region would be a possible source of his own future wealth. Penn had introduced

---

[144] James Logan to Penn, December 20, 1706, *Microfilm*, 13:026.
[145] See above, pp. 193–97.

Logan not only to the eminent merchants of Philadelphia but also to the sachems and other leaders of the Native Americans. Logan was both an official witness and recorder of the Articles of Agreement made with the Indians of the Susquehanna in April 1701. The record of those Indians' farewell tribute to Penn in October the same year is in Logan's hand.[146] In due course, Logan, the land authority and proprietary agent, began to direct his own entrepreneurial interests to the Susquehanna region and its native peoples, who were skilled in harvesting animal skins, pelts, and furs and eager to trade them for English manufactured goods.

Scholarly study of the development of the Susquehanna fur trade, and particularly of Logan's involvement in it, a study still in its early years, has been slowed by the difficulty of locating and interpreting the scattered extant record. The record was primarily created and controlled by Logan and his associates, and from its inception it was open neither to public scrutiny nor to official review. It reveals transactions pointing toward Logan's breach of his fiduciary duty of integrity, fidelity, and honesty to Penn and his sons in the administration of their land assets entrusted to his care.[147]

According to Francis Jennings, "Logan was the man who created a lucrative and lasting Indian trade in Pennsylvania and, as Joseph E. Johnson has remarked, Logan 'made a success in it because he was prepared to be as ruthless and unscrupulous as

---

[146] For provenance, see *PWP*, 4:99.

[147] The leading investigator of Logan's misconduct in his various fiduciary responsibilities has been Francis Jennings, who, in a series of articles published in learned journals beginning in 1965, sets forth his extensive research exposing Logan's actions. In his "The Indian Trade of the Susquehanna Valley," published in the *Proceedings of the American Philosophical Society*, 110 (1966): 406–24, Jennings describes the difficulty of examining the record:

> To get any considerable body of records, we are forced to rely on three major sources: the business records and private correspondence of James Logan; the official surveys, deeds, and patents relating to the lands on which the trade was conducted; and the minutes of conferences between the Indians and representatives of the provincial government. A large proportion of the total mass of these documents was penned by Logan himself; an even larger proportion was at one time or another in his keeping and subject to alterations made or directed by him. As will appear, he did not hesitate to adjust records to his purpose. Fortunately he left discrepancies, and there are just enough non-Logan sources to outline a fairly understandable picture. (p. 414)

necessary.'"[148] Jennings identified the conditions necessary for the success of that trade as a community of Indians having access to good (and protected) hunting grounds, a network of experienced traders with an ample supply of goods, and little if any competition. The object was to monopolize (or, in the term of that day, 'engross') the trade. Logan was able to build upon the foundations Penn had left behind in his care and establish his own network of trade among the natives of the Susquehanna area. His initial task was to recruit and settle his traders.

An early instance of Logan's fiduciary dishonesty in his oversight of Penn's provincial properties occurred in May 1715, when five hundred acres of Penn's proprietary "lands at the head of Pequea" Creek in Chester County were ordered by Logan to be surveyed and allotted to Joseph Cloud, one of Logan's traders. This began a pattern of appropriating Penn's lands by surveys authorized by Logan, who then allotted such lands to traders in his own network. Although no money was paid and no deeds were granted for the allotted lands, the occupier who made improvements was thereby protected in his investment and given 'squatters rights.' Jennings tracked a number of such allotments for the period 1715 to 1728; during this time, Logan allotted over seven thousand acres of Penn's lands to serve his own business purposes.[149]

Logan served his own interests in managing Penn's property in two other ways. One was to appropriate property directly to himself. Taylor's "Account of Lands in Chester County" shows that surveys were made for Logan of twelve hundred acres "at the head of Pequea" Creek in July 1713, one thousand acres "on the French Creek" in June 1715, and fourteen hundred acres "on Shickasalongoe" in June 1720.[150]

---

[148] Jennings, "The Indian Trade," 410. The Johnson quote is from Joseph E. Johnson, "A Statesman of Colonial Pennsylvania: A Study of the Private Life and Public Career of James Logan to the Year 1726" (PhD diss., Harvard University, 1942).

[149] Jennings, "The Indian Trade," 417. The table of seventeen land allotments Jennings provides makes reference (see note 54) to the archival record Jennings found for each allotment. The Cloud allotment was evidenced in the "Account of Lands in Chester County" made by the provincial surveyor general, John Taylor, aka Jacob Taylor, for Thomas Penn in 1733. See Penn family papers, 1592–1960, vol. NV-183, folio page 32, Collection 485A, HSP. The Jennings table also shows that Logan made an allotment prior to his 1710–1711 visit in England that gave his trader Peter Bizaillon in 1708 land "enough to 'build house and plant fields' . . . above Conestoga." The land was "settled by permission," undoubtedly that of James Logan.

[150] Taylor, "Account of Lands in Chester County."

Logan's other method of gaining land for himself was to grant land to a trader in debt to himself, from whom Logan would later acquire the land in satisfaction for a defaulted loan. Such is shown in a 1717 transaction at Conestoga, where Logan was settling his trader John Cartlidge near the Conestoga Indian village. On October 21, Isaac Taylor, the surveyor of Chester County (and brother of the provincial surveyor general), acting under Logan's directions, surveyed sixteen thousand acres for the Penn family's Conestoga Manor. The next day, Isaac Taylor returned to make additional surveys, one of them, according to Jennings, pursuant to Logan's "warrant for Cartlidge to settle on 300 acres of land immediately next to Conestoga village." The surveyed tract was included within Conestoga Manor, as was also the Conestoga Indian village. The commissioners of property set a value of £30 on the Cartlidge tract of raw land, but the Penns received nothing at the time for these acres, and because the records of their land holdings were private (and under Logan's control), there could be no public scrutiny. With trade goods purchased on credit from Logan, Cartlidge served as Logan's trader at Conestoga, under an ever-increasing balance of debt, until his death in 1723. Logan thereupon liquidated Cartlidge's debt to him of £612 by seizing all of his possessions, including his stock in trade and pelts purchased from the Indians, the buildings and improvements on the real property, and the land itself. When Logan moved to obtain ownership rights in the Cartlidge tract, he did so through an undisclosed agent (his brother-in-law Israel Pemberton Sr.) acting as administrator of Cartlidge's estate "for the use of" the deceased's heir who, in fact, was Logan as creditor. In 1729, Logan proceeded to sell the Cartlidge tract for £500. Somewhere along the line, the Penns belatedly received £45, the tract's original purchase price.[151]

Logan's second—and most important—fiduciary duty was to protect and defend Penn's policy of maintaining peace and friendship with the peoples of "the nations of Indians." It was his

---

[151] Jennings, "The Indian Trade," 418–19. Jennings also reports (p. 423) a similar situation in which Logan as creditor took 300 acres deeded to Peter Chartier, the son of Martin Chartier (and his Shawnee wife), another of Logan's indebted traders. In January 1718, the commissioners of property gave Peter a warrant to buy the tract on which Martin operated a trading post among the Shawnees. At Martin's death the following April, demand was made of the son for his late father's debt of £108.19.3 3/4, resulting in the conveyance of the real estate to Logan.

solemn duty not only to Penn but to the entire province that he do his best to enforce and preserve this policy, which was a keystone of Penn's holy experiment in the New World as well as an expression of Penn's own fundamental principles. It was also the basis of the colonists' security in a province where they were the aliens. In the absence of Penn and the proprietary heirs, Logan was their empowered representative and visible symbol for dealings with the native people. By the time of Penn's death in 1718, however, the special relationship that the founder had formed with the natives was beginning to suffer strains.

In September 1691, the Brandywine Lenapes complained to the proprietary land commissioners that colonists were settling on reserved native lands and had even dammed Brandywine Creek, thus ruining the fishing. The Brandywine watershed had been acquired in 1685 and was within the bounds of the largest purchase Penn ever made of Indian property fronting the western shore of Delaware waters. The purchase, extending from Duck Creek (now Smyrna River) in the lower counties upriver to Chester Creek in Pennsylvania, incorporated Christina Creek as well as the Brandywine.[152] The 1691 complaint of encroachments was resolved when more Indian goods were transferred "in full payment" of the earlier transfer (often referred to as an "extinguishment of Indian rights") and a letter was sent to the County Court at New Castle requiring that fish channels "be opened . . . which [the Indians] saw was according to their contract with the Proprietor."[153]

What the Indians' 'contract' with Penn might have meant is nowhere explained. The reference does, however, illustrate the problem of disparity occurring in these intercultural proceedings when parties foreign to each other and employing languages and legal customs not mutually understood intend in good faith to transfer land interests and to maintain records of such transfers. When any party later claims some misunderstanding, the suspicion arises that bad faith may have entered in. Such was the case with the Brandywine lands; the events were documented only through English records, if any, and the living memories of native people were lost in time. It appears that the 'contract'

---

[152] The deed dated October 2, 1685, was to Penn from Lare et al., "Indian Kings Sachemakers Right Owners . . . all along by the West Side of Delaware River and so between the said creeks backwards as far as a man can ride in two days with a horse." Hazard, *Pennsylvania Archives*, 1st series, vol. 1, pp. 95–96.

[153] See C. A. Weslager, *Red Men on the Brandywine* (Wilmington, DE: Hambleton Co., 1953), 55–56.

referred to was a formal understanding reached in or after 1685 with the proprietor, Penn, that the Brandywine Lenapes would have a reservation along the Brandywine Creek, one mile on each side, from its mouth at present-day Wilmington to its forks near Northbrook and thence along the West Branch to its headwaters at Honeybrook. The Indians claimed that their copy of the reservation document had been destroyed by fire when one of their cabins burned. The government claimed the official instrument "was not preserved in the provincial archives with the other Indian deeds."[154]

In 1705 and 1706, the commissioners of Penn's proprietary lands (Logan then being one of the four as well as secretary of the land office), hearing the further complaints of encroachment from the Brandywine Lenapes, extinguished by purchase the Indians' reservation rights from the mouth of the Brandywine Creek at the Delaware as far as Northbrook, the natives keeping the reservation above that place along the West Branch.[155]

The encroachments by colonists continued after this decision, even on the shrunken reservation. In 1725 the chief of the Brandywines addressed the Provincial Assembly, recalling Penn's settlement of a 'perpetual friendship' and his reconveyance to the natives of the reservation "a mile on each side" of the creek and protesting that "we are molested, and our lands surveyed out and settled before we can reap our corn off; and to our great injury. Brandywine Creek is so obstructed with dams that the fish cannot come up to our habitations. We desire you to take notice that we are a poor people."[156] The Assembly sent a committee of three members to advise Logan of the natives' complaints. They reported back that Logan "expressed himself in favor of the Indians." The Assembly next addressed the lieutenant governor, William Keith, on the situation, "having taken into serious consideration the fatal consequences it may be to the peace of this Province."[157] No action followed.

Then Logan as secretary of the Provincial Council wrote (or had an assistant write) a memorandum for the files entitled "Minute of the Commission on the Brandywine Indians' Complaint." The minute, found in Logan's papers, reads as a

---

[154] Ibid., 60.
[155] Ibid., 65–66.
[156] Ibid., 71–72.
[157] Ibid., 73.

civil servant's statement for the official record prepared some time after hearing an aggrieved party describe alleged wrongs. The vagueness of the date appearing on the document, "1726 or 25"—apparently a filing endorsement, being made in another hand—suggests that Logan neither took nor intended to take any action in the circumstances but needed to prepare notes that would frame the issues most favorably for his office and minimize the wrongs complained of. The minute reads, in part:

> The Brandywine Indians having for some time past complained of encroachments made on their lands on that creek which they had never sold (as they say) nor agreed to dispose of [then seven Indians are named] inhabitants on the said creek now appear and renew their complaint (by Ezekiel Harlan & Silas Prior their interpreters) setting forth [1] that they are seated on a small tract of land on the side of Brandywine which they had reserved to themselves, [2] that the English have entered upon that tract and disturb them so much that they cannot enjoy their own, [3] that they claim no land that has been sold, but this tract having never been disposed of by any of their forefathers but reserved for a settlement they desire they may enjoy it peaceably and in safety, [4] that William Penn had always protected them and promised they should be protected, but if they are thrown out of these small possession[s], having now no more left, their children must be vagabonds without any home or living, [5] that they have hitherto ever lived peaceably and have maintained a good understanding with their friends the English and earnestly desire that it may ever be continued.
>
> They complain further [6] that although they sold the lands on the creek below their settlement yet they never sold the water or creek itself for they had ever reserved the use of it for fishing, that notwithstanding that reserve, they are debarred of their usual privilege by means of two dams that have been made cross the creek below them which prevents the Rock & Shad fish from coming up as formerly, to their very great injury, and the suffering of their families whose dependence was on these fish for food during a considerable part of the year. They request therefore that these dams may be removed, and that they

may still enjoy the privilege of fishing as they had ever hitherto done before these were erected....

To which they were answered by JL. First that the Indians are in the right in saying W Penn promised that he would protect them in their dwellings and that the Council would continue the same care, and that if there were any land left they had not sold they should not be disturbed by their enemy [neighbors, squatters, or trespassers who used the Indians' lands]. That as there had always been a good understanding and friendship between WP and those that act for him and the Indians, the Council still desire the continuation of the same friendship and that small matters ought not to make a difference between friends.[158]

The provincial government still took no action. The Brandywine Lenapes complained again in June 1729, when Chief Checochinican wrote to Lieutenant Governor Keith's successor, Patrick Gordon, expressing the desire of his people to "continue in peace and love and be as one heart and soul with William Penn and his people," notwithstanding that "we are reduced to great wants and hardships."[159]

Time itself finally resolved the issue through the agency of Logan. Serving as strategist for the young new proprietors of Penn Incorporated, he outlasted, through his inaction, the Brandywine Lenapes, the last of whom departed from the area soon after 1740.[160]

Earlier, in September 1718, shortly after Penn's death in England, complaints had been first made of colonists' encroachment on other native lands. The complainant then was Sassoonan, chief of the community of Tulpehocken Lenapes, so named for their home valley and creek (the "land of the turtles") lying to the west of the Schuylkill River opposite present-day Reading. The entire inhabited native area was a part of the Great Valley of the Appalachians. The Lenapes had relocated here after the sale to Penn of their lands on the Delaware River to make

---

[158] [James Logan], "Minute of the Commission on the Brandywine Indians' Complaint," Logan family papers, 1638–1964, Folder 13, Box 11, Collection 379, HSP.

[159] Weslager, *Red Men on the Brandywine*, 89.

[160] Ibid., 92.

way for the city of brotherly love, Philadelphia.¹⁶¹ Logan intended to resolve this new complaint by making a gift or payment of some Indian goods for which, in return, he asked for and obtained from Sassoonan a quitclaim deed for the Tulpehockens' land between the east side of the Schuylkill River and the west side of the Delaware River not previously conveyed to Penn. The deed, however, did not affect the Tulpehocken watershed on the west.¹⁶² No changes occurred touching those lands until 1722, when, as a consequence of Lieutenant Governor William Keith's gratuitous invitation (possibly the result of a bribe), Palatine Germans taking refuge in New York resettled themselves in Tulpehocken. The next year, because the Palatines' livestock roamed at will through the natives' crops in unfenced fields, the Tulpehockens left the area, some moving to Shamokin at the fork of the main trunk of the Susquehanna River and its North Branch and more to the Ohio country.¹⁶³

At the time the Palatines were moving into Tulpehocken, ten thousand acres of unlocated land there were being sold. This was land given in Penn's last will to his daughter Letitia, now married to an insolvent husband who was selling his wife's assets in order to escape being sentenced to debtors' prison in England. The husband's provincial agent chose Tulpehocken as the location of the property. Although Indian property rights had not been extinguished, Logan, not wishing to alienate any of the Penns, cooperated as the survey was made and the deed executed and delivered to the purchaser of this property that could not actually be sold.¹⁶⁴ In the following years, Logan successfully temporized with the aggrieved parties. The Palatines regularly asked for and were put off with promises of deeds for the Tulpehocken lands they already possessed. Not until 1730 did Logan bend to their pressure and order surveys.¹⁶⁵ Sassoonan and the Tulpehocken Lenapes, meeting with the Provincial Council in 1728 at Philadelphia for a periodic treaty conference, when pressed to raise any concerns, did mildly

---

[161] Francis Jennings, "Incident at Tulpehocken," *Pennsylvania History* 35 (1968): 337.

[162] Ibid., 338. See *MPCP*, 3:45–47.

[163] Jennings, "Incident at Tulpehocken," 338–40. The 'Ohio country' at the time meant the watersheds of both the Ohio and its tributary, the Allegheny River.

[164] Ibid., 339–40. This land was described in Penn's last will as lands in Pennsylvania "in such places as my Trustees shall think fit." *PWP*, 4:716.

[165] Jennings, "Incident at Tulpehocken," 346–47.

acknowledge that the issue of Christians being settled "on lands that the Indians had never been paid for . . . may occasion a difference between their children and us hereafter."[166]

In the meantime, Logan's foremost ambition was to create (for investors generally and for the proprietors and himself particularly) a new investment opportunity farther up the Delaware River by opening the valleys of the Lehigh River and its subsidiaries to further land sales and settlements. The native peoples still in possession of the area were the Forks Lenapes living at the mouth of the Lehigh River where it enters the Delaware near present-day Easton. The native chiefs, however, refused to negotiate a sale unless one of the proprietors attended. Logan increased the urgency of his appeals to John, Thomas, and Richard Penn in England, stating that their direct involvement in provincial matters was becoming a critical necessity if their interests were to be protected.

Logan also initiated a strategy through which he intended to strengthen provincial control over relationships with the resident nations of Indians. Seeking to bring land matters as well as the never-ending problems with the tribes and conflicts between natives and settlers under tighter management, he embarked on a geopolitical scheme to ally the province with a regionally powerful and more influential base of native peoples than the settled and fragmented tribes that, over the years, had sought and taken refuge in the Susquehanna and Delaware regions. To this end, he made a pivot to the Iroquois Confederacy. When finally implemented, the Logan plan sounded the death knell for Penn's covenant with the natives that all peoples in the province would "forever hereafter be as one head and one heart and live in true friendship and amity as one people."[167]

In 1720, Logan had gone to Conestoga, his base of trading operations, to discuss with the resident natives the precariousness of their situation on the Susquehanna. That river was both the regular war route used by the Iroquois in their periodic forays against the southern Cherokees and Catawbas as well as the inevitable route traveled by those southern tribes

---

[166] Ibid., 342.

[167] Articles of Agreement made with the Susquehannocks and others, April 23, 1701, *PWP*, 4:51.

seeking revenge after Iroquois attacks.[168] The next year, again at Conestoga, the Pennsylvania authorities advanced a plan, conceived in Virginia, to negotiate with the Susquehanna natives and the Iroquois to set a separation boundary between the warring southern and northern Indian nations at the Potomac River as far as its source and then south along the Appalachians. The treaty conference also heard the concern of the Iroquois regarding improving trade conditions through lowering prices on traders' merchandise and raising the prices paid for the natives' furs and skins. Logan saw this as an opening to attract more native trade away from New York and to Pennsylvania.[169]

Then came an unexpected crisis that endangered Logan's trading operations (and his own future public life) and required the most diplomatic of settlements. It arose over the murder of a Seneca warrior by the brothers John and Edmond Cartlidge, Logan's principal traders at Conestoga. John Cartlidge was not only in charge of the trading station but was also a local justice of the peace and an official interpreter for the province in treaty negotiations. The murder of a warrior belonging to the Anglophobic and most warlike nation of the Iroquois Confederacy demanded satisfaction, the crime being both horrendous and provable.

Lieutenant Governor William Keith stepped into this provincial crisis. Even though he was armed with depositions against the Cartlidges given by their own indentured servants, Keith was disposed to provide Logan with protection. In the end, Keith suppressed the depositions and obtained from the Provincial Assembly a grant that was substantial enough to satisfy the Seneca chiefs for the crime. A public trial was avoided. Keith was privately rewarded with a grant allowing him to make his own settlement on land across the Susquehanna in Indian territory, the first colonist so allowed by the natives. This enraged Logan, who sought a comparable grant for himself, withdrawing his efforts only after Keith had the Cartlidges jailed for a time. Logan had reward enough in that his taking of proprietary land around Conestoga was not exposed by the Cartlidges, who were spared certain conviction if the trial had gone forward. The Senecas were rewarded by securing to the Iroquois Confederacy the opening of its Covenant Chain beyond New York to Pennsylvania and new markets there, expanding

---

[168] Jennings, *The Ambiguous Iroquois Empire*, 278–80.
[169] Ibid., 281–82.

Iroquois hegemony over the fragmented and weakened native peoples who had taken refuge in the province.[170]

The resolution of this crisis was confirmed by all five of the Iroquois Nations at the Great Treaty of 1722 held at Albany in August and September. The treaty was hosted by the governor of New York, and his counterparts from Virginia and Pennsylvania attended as participants. The natives confirmed that they would not molest [disturb] Virginia or any other English colony in North America in the future and that the great Covenant Chain, longstanding with New York, was now extended to all British provinces in America.[171] To Pennsylvania's Keith and his delegation (which included eminent Quakers Isaac Norris and Richard Hill), the Iroquois addressed words proclaiming the new oneness of the province in the Covenant Chain as if it were not a diplomatic shift but rather had existed from the founding of Pennsylvania under William Penn:

> We on our parts always have kept and forever shall keep firm peace and friendship with a good heart to all the people of Pennsylvania. . . . We are not only made one people by the Covenant Chain, but we also are people united in one head, one body, and one heart by the strongest ties of love and friendship.
>
> You desire there may be a perpetual peace and friendship between you and the Five Nations and between your children and our children and that the same may be kept as long as the mountains and rivers endure; all which we like well and on our part desire that the covenant and union made with a clean and true heart between you and us may last as long as the sun and moon shall continue to give light and we will deliver this in charge to our children that it may be kept in remembrance with their children and children's children to the latest ages and we desire that the peace and tranquility that is now established between us may be as clear as the sun shining in its lustre without any cloud or darkness and that the same may continue forever.

---

[170] Ibid., 290–92. See the section in appendix 10 that discusses the alliances made by Native American nations with Pennsylvania and other American colonies.

[171] E. B. O'Callaghan, ed., *Documents Relative to the Colonial History of the State of New York* (Albany, NY: Weed, Parsons & Co., 1855), 5:664–81.

> As to the accident of one of our friends being killed by some of your people which has happened by misfortune and against your will we say that as we are all in peace we think it hard the person who killed our friend and brother should suffer and we do in the name of all the five nations forgive that offence and desire you will likewise forgive it and that the men who did it may be released from prison and set at liberty to go whither they please and we shall esteem that as a mark of your regard and friendship for the five nations and as a further confirmation of this treaty.[172]

Thus it was that through the chance criminal agency of Logan's principal traders at Conestoga, Pennsylvania's Indian policy shifted away from the Friendship Chain established by Penn with the indigenous natives along the Delaware and Susquehanna Rivers. Instead, entry was made through the Covenant Chain into an expanding regional trading network in which the empires of Great Britain, France, and Iroquoia—as well as multiple other but fragmented Indian nations—competitively worked out the future of all the contenders. The irony was that Logan, who had sought such a policy, did not attend the meetings bringing into being the Great Treaty of 1722.[173]

In the years immediately following this regional geopolitical adjustment, the Iroquois began a strategic reorientation away from their former north-south line of engagement with the tribes of Virginia and the Carolinas and instead sought future opportunities to control the east-west axis stretching to the Ohio country and beyond into the territories drained by the Wabash and Mississippi Rivers. Many of the Lenapes, Shawnees, and others who had been displaced in Pennsylvania had already gone westward to settle in the lands around the Allegheny and Ohio Rivers.

During this post-treaty period, Logan was away from Pennsylvania (from October 1723 to July 1724) conferring with Penn's descendants in England as they awaited judicial resolution of their intrafamily dispute over William Penn's will. Finally, in 1726 the contested will was ordered into full probate,

---

[172] Ibid., 5:680.

[173] Jennings, *The Ambiguous Iroquois Empire*, 293–98. Of Logan's absence, Jennings observes, "It seems reasonable to guess that he had a hint from Keith that his presence was not desired." Ibid., 292.

thereby ensuring that Hannah Penn's sons John, Thomas, and Richard would inherit the provincial proprietorship and lands in Pennsylvania, an event marked by the almost simultaneous death of their mother. And, in the same year, Logan had the satisfaction of seeing William Keith replaced as lieutenant governor by the more compliant Patrick Gordon.

Beginning in 1727, a series of events occurred that effectively curtailed Logan's independence for the remaining six years of his oversight—and control—of proprietary land affairs. In May, Logan purchased from Chief Nutimus of the Forks Lenapes some land above Tohickon Creek, a tributary of the Delaware River, upon which he sought to build an iron mine for a personal business venture. That land, however, was part of unceded Indian property that, under Pennsylvania law, could only be transferred by the Penns after they first made a purchase of the entire property from the natives. Logan was denied a deed from the natives, who insisted that a living Penn personally come to negotiate the purchase of the entire property.[174] The need for a member of the Penn family to visit America was becoming imperative.

Then, in January 1728 Logan fell on ice outside his home on Second Street, Philadelphia, and not until a year later was the full extent of the injury diagnosed. He had sheared the femur of his left leg below the joint, and the break had become calloused and beyond repair. Logan was permanently crippled.[175]

In April 1728 the Provincial Council, to contain rising public concern and Indian disaffection over provincial-tribal problems, including mistreatment of the Brandywine and Tulpehocken Lenapes, ordered a series of treaty conferences with the natives. The meetings began in May at Conestoga, the center of Logan's trading operations, and representatives of the Conestogas, Brandywines, Conoys, and Shawnees were present. Logan attended and wrote the minutes. Another conference was held shortly after at Philadelphia with the Tulpehocken Indians. Sassoonan was the chief of these natives, who had vacated their Delaware-Schuylkill lands following the 1683 sale to Penn and relocated to Tulpehocken Creek west of the Susquehanna. Now, after unredressed encroachments upon their new land, they had uprooted themselves again. This time, some of the Tulpehockens

---

[174] Ibid., 309.

[175] Tolles, *James Logan and the Culture of Provincial America*, 146–47.

had gone to Shamokin at the Forks of the Susquehanna, where they were protected by the Iroquois. The majority of the tribe had chosen to go to the Ohio country. At the Philadelphia treaty conference, Sassoonan came from Shamokin to complain that his people had yet to be compensated for the wrongful taking of their lands by squatters. Logan, putting all the blame on former Lieutenant Governor Sir William Keith, again temporized and promised satisfaction if the Tulpehockens would keep the peace.[176]

In early 1729, the Penns were surprised to receive in England, from two sources, sufficient cash to satisfy and discharge the mortgage secured by the province of Pennsylvania. The money came from one person who was paying off the balance of his purchase price of Pennsylvania land and from another who was purchasing twenty thousand unsurveyed acres in the province once allocated for William and Springett Penn. Because the monies had not first gone into Logan's hands, he could not draw on it for purposes other than satisfying the mortgage. At last the colony would belong to John, Thomas, and Richard and be freed of the oversight of trustees (Logan being one) as protectors of the mortgage lenders' interests. This whittled away more of Logan's ability to act independently in proprietary land affairs.[177]

Further weakening his levers of control, Logan moved in November 1730 from his Philadelphia home to his country seat at Stenton in suburban Germantown, thus becoming distanced from the daily management of proprietary affairs. The next month Logan acted with vigor to order the eviction of Scotch-Irish settlers who had "possessed themselves of all [the Penn family's] Conestoga Manor." Believing the answer to their physical needs was to occupy unused acreage, these most recent frontiersmen resorted to self-help, even to defying the law by squatting on the proprietors' own lands.[178]

In recognition of Logan's long service to the proprietors and his vast experience in so many offices touching the governance of the province, on August 20, 1731, his friends on the Provincial Council appointed him the chief justice of Pennsylvania as successor to David Lloyd, Penn's longtime adversary. That Logan had no formal legal training was not deemed important.

---

[176] Jennings, *The Ambiguous Iroquois Empire*, 305–6.
[177] Jennings, "Incident at Tulpehocken," 344.
[178] Kenny, *Peaceable Kingdom Lost*, 32–33, 246n4.

His reputation for rectitude was sufficient to qualify him for the new office. He served until 1739.

Another version of Logan's 'rectitude,' however, was beginning to be heard in England from Ezekiel Harlan. He had served as an interpreter at the natives' conference with Logan in "1726 or 25" to hear their complaints about settler encroachments on their reservation on upper Brandywine Creek.[179] Harlan was a fur trader conversant in the Lenape tongue. Historian Francis Jennings comments, "It seems evident that he knew intimately, from the Indians, about Logan's own near-monopoly of the fur trade on the Susquehanna River and about Logan's embezzlement of the Penns' lands in Conestoga Manor, where Logan's trade was centered."[180] Harlan had the protection of Lieutenant Governor William Keith so long as Keith was in office. After Keith's removal, however, Harlan was punished by being charged and tried for "notorious adultery." Although the trial jury acquitted him, the judge imposed burdensome costs and some jail time.[181]

Harlan's wrath toward Logan, whom he perceived as both the author of all these property wrongs and the instigator of Harlan's personal humiliation, only smoldered the more. His opportunity for revenge came on a business trip to London in early 1731 at the time certain Tulpehocken property, once 'owned' by Penn's daughter Letitia on unceded Indian land by virtue of an irregular deed granted by Logan, was again being sold, this time to John Page, an important counselor of the Penn family.[182] Harlan began talking. He persuaded Page to retain Walter Webb, a Pennsylvania attorney—and Harlan's brother-in-law—to represent him. Page, in London, then obtained from the Penns a warrant to Logan ordering a confirmatory survey of the 'unceded' land purportedly being deeded. When Webb in Pennsylvania delivered the warrant to Logan for the resurvey of the property, Logan realized his freewheeling acts regarding land matters was coming to an end. The date of the Penns' warrant was the same as their separate letter to Logan "ordering him to

---

[179] See pp. 260–61 above.

[180] Jennings, "Incident at Tulpehocken," 340–41.

[181] Ibid.

[182] Page had been Hannah Penn's solicitor who successfully guided her to the 1726 victory in the Court of Exchequer that resulted in the admission of Penn's 1712 will to probate.

forbid all surveys under Original Rights [vested claims held by purchasers in England for unlocated Pennsylvania lands] except those warranted over the Penns' own signature."[183]

Throughout this period, Logan had continued his role as statesman in the provincial government. He was the indispensable geopolitical strategist in all matters concerning Indian affairs, especially matters that closely touched his own economic interests. On August 4, 1731, Logan, out of "his long experience and knowledge," addressed the Provincial Council at the request of Lieutenant Governor Patrick Gordon on "an affair of very great importance to the security of this colony and all its inhabitants." This was the threat of the ever-expanding claims of imperial France to lands in Pennsylvania and other English colonies, in which Logan saw the occasion for Pennsylvania to forge a treaty with the Iroquois for countering French aggrandizement as well as for delegating the management of the native peoples settled in the province. At the council meeting, Logan introduced the issue with a map of Louisiana published in a 1721 atlas that showed

> how exorbitant the French claims were on the continent of America; that by the description in the said map they claimed a great part of Carolina and Virginia, and had laid down Susquehanna as a boundary of Pennsylvania. Then he proceeded to observe that by virtue of some treaty, as they allege, the French pretend a right to all lands lying on rivers of the mouths of which they are possessed; that the River Ohio (a branch of Mississippi) comes close to those mountains which lie about 120 or 130 miles back of Susquehanna, within the boundaries of this province, as granted by the King's Letters Patent; that adjoining thereto is a fine tract of land called Allegheny, on which several Shawnee Indians had seated themselves, and that by the advices lately brought to him by several traders in those parts, it appears that the French have been using endeavors to gain over those Indians to their interest. . . . Mr. Logan then went on to represent how destructive this attempt of the French, if attended with success, may prove to the English interest on this Continent, and how deeply in its consequences it may affect this Province, and after having spoken fully on

---

[183] Jennings, "Incident at Tulpehocken," 348.

these two heads, moved that to prevent or put a stop to these designs if possible a treaty should be set on foot with the Five Nations, who have an absolute authority as well over the Shawnees as all our Indians, that by their means the Shawnees may not only be kept firm to the English interest, but likewise be induced to remove from Allegheny nearer to the English settlements, and that such a treaty becomes now the more necessary, because 'tis several years since any of those Nations have visited us, and no opportunity ought to be lost of cultivating and improving the Friendship which has always subsisted between this government and them.[184]

An occasion for "cultivating and improving the Friendship" between Iroquoia and Pennsylvania arose within days, giving the authorities in Penn's province an immediate opportunity to implement Logan's own ideas of regional geopolitical strategy.

On August 12, 1731, a memorandum appears in the records of the Provincial Council noting the grief of Sassoonan, chief of the Tulpehocken Lenapes, over his killing of his own nephew. (As noted by some scholars, this nephew was Logan's choice as Sassoonan's successor, a choice contrary to Sassoonan's will.[185]) The minutes of a Council meeting on that and the next day follow. The meeting was attended by Lieutenant Governor Gordon, Logan, and three of his fellow Council members as well as Sassoonan, Shikellamy (the resident Iroquois supervisor of the Lenapes at Tulpehocken), and Pisquetomen (Sassoonan's own choice for his successor and also his nephew). The record reflects only Sassoonan's grief over the killing during a "rum quarrel" and the urgent need to control the traders in supplying the native peoples with rum. Following this condolence meeting, the Assembly sent word to proceed with Logan's plan to "set on foot" a treaty with the Iroquois, whereupon the departing Shikellamy was charged with taking the message to the northern league (the Iroquois) and inviting them to Pennsylvania for consultations. In early December, Shikellamy brought word of acceptance from the Iroquois, along with a message from Sassoonan that he too would be there, waiting for the Iroquois chiefs "at his own house as they passed that way." Along with Shikellamy came an unnamed chief of the Cayugas as well as an

---

[184] *MPCP*, 3:402–3.
[185] See Jennings, *The Ambiguous Iroquois Empire*, 311nn5, 7.

interpreter, Conrad Weiser, a Palatine who had resettled at Tulpehocken from New York's Schoharie Valley close to the Mohawk nation, whose language he had learned. From this time forward until his death in 1760, Weiser would be Pennsylvania's principal interpreter and diplomatic liaison with the Iroquois.

Penn's sons: The Walking Purchase and a tapestry of Indian treaties (1732–1750)

On August 11, 1732, Thomas Penn arrived in Pennsylvania. Fifty years earlier, his father had set out from England on his first visit to the province. Thirty-one years earlier his father had departed from his American plantation for the last time. And, twenty-eight years earlier, the last Penn to visit Pennsylvania—the unworthy heir apparent William Jr.—entered and then abandoned the colony that he and only he, at that time, might have inherited from his father.

Thomas was a man unlike either his father or his half-brother. Strong-willed and determined, he came into the province for the purposes of attending to the business of Penn Incorporated and repairing its fortunes for the benefit of himself as well as his older brother John, owner of half of the proprietorship, and his younger brother Richard, who owned a quarter share as did Thomas. Both brothers, who remained in England, had authorized Thomas to act on behalf of all three.[186] Although Thomas only lived in Pennsylvania until 1741, even after returning to England he continued to manage all the proprietary interests until his death in 1775. John Penn, at his death in 1746, left his half share of the proprietorship to Thomas, who thereafter controlled three-quarters of the entire enterprise.

Thomas's sole purpose for spending nine years in the colony that his father had planted and struggled to improve as proprietor and governor was to take charge of the Penn family's financial fortunes in America. His immediate concern was not government; so long as competent and loyal lieutenant governors could be found to administer executive and other official affairs in Pennsylvania, he had little interest in being governor or being involved with politics or the politicians holding public offices. In sum, Thomas, John, and Richard Penn, the new proprietors, were in need of money, not only because

---

[186] Jennings, "Incident at Tulpehocken," 353n44.

they had inherited their father's debts along with his American land assets but because they had also created their own debts, being endowed with their father's tendency to live beyond his means.[187] The presence of one of the new proprietors in Pennsylvania proved to be a necessity, as Logan had long been advising, and Thomas, accepting the task, concentrated his attention with a sharp focus.

The task was daunting. Not only was it necessary to become familiar with Logan's thirty-one years of unsupervised administration of the Proprietary Land Office and its records of receipts and disbursements, of warrants for surveys and deeds, and of quieting or extinguishing Indian rights, but independent audits were needed to verify those records. More importantly, Thomas needed to master the topographical realities of the province—both the physical features of the several regions and the political constraints caused by the disputed (because unlocated) southern and northern boundary lines. As Thomas took stock, he was mindful that the proprietorship had only acquired Indian rights back from the west side of the Delaware River between Christiana Creek in the lower counties to the south and Tohickon Creek in Bucks County to the north and above the mouth of the Susquehanna back from the east side of the main branch of that river as far north as Paxtang (present-day Harrisburg). Apart from this limited area for lawful development, Thomas faced other challenges. By acquiescing in the occupation by squatters upon reserved Indian lands on two creeks, the Brandywine (a tributary of the Delaware River) and the Tulpehocken (a tributary of the Susquehanna River), the land office had helped create uncertain titles and other irregularities needing resolution. Colonists were making increasingly urgent demands for lands to settle, and chiefs of the Lenapes and other Indian nations were pressing for the fair market value of their real estate. And there was the ever-urgent need to relieve the financial straits of Penn Incorporated.

Seven days after Thomas Penn landed at Chester, Pennsylvania, representatives from the Onondaga, Cayuga, and Oneida Nations of the Iroquois arrived in Philadelphia. They had come, without Sassoonan and nearly a year after being invited,

---

[187] Francis Jennings has described the inherited and self-made debt heavily burdening the Penn family that drove the proprietors to find relief by selling provincial land, even land not freed of the Indians' ownership or 'encumbrance.' Jennings, *The Ambiguous Iroquois Empire*, 316–21.

for mutually desired consultations with their English brothers. Although a living 'Onas' (one of the sons of William Penn, who had been the first to be called Onas) had been expected in the province for many years, these chiefs only heard that one was about to appear when they were already on their way to Philadelphia. The treaty conference began on August 23 and continued until September 2. In addition to Thomas Penn, the provincial delegation included Lieutenant Governor Gordon, Logan, Isaac Norris, and three of their Provincial Council colleagues.[188]

Interpreter Conrad Weiser delivered Penn's words of greeting in praise of the parties' shared league of amity and the Friendship Chain, promising that "I shall take care to improve and strengthen and will, to the best of my power, make that Chain yet stronger and brighter."[189] Although some meetings were public, sensitive issues such as Iroquois-French relationships, disputed claims in the Ohio and Allegheny regions, and management of the Shawnees and other Indian nations were discussed only in closed meetings. The parties agreed that Weiser and Shikellamy would be their agents, speaking "our minds to each other truly and freely."[190] The "League and Chain of Friendship and Brotherhood," to last "as long as the Heavens, Sun, Moon, Stars and the Earth shall endure," was formally agreed to on behalf of the province. It was expected to be confirmed by the Iroquois Confederacy within a year. That one year, however, stretched into four.[191]

Once the treaty meetings ended, Thomas Penn had more time to examine one of the grave problems that had brought him across the Atlantic—the unknown state of affairs in the Proprietary Land Office. He scrutinized its records of receipts and disbursements, of remaining land holdings available for sale, and of the Penn family (and unceded Indian) lands warranted without authority for surveys and deeds. Ultimately, he had to assess Logan's stewardship of the fiduciary responsibilities placed upon him by the founder, his father. For Logan, this must have been a time of anxious uncertainty. That

---

[188] Minutes of the treaty conference are in *MPCP*, 3:435–52.

[189] *MPCP*, 3:436.

[190] *MPCP*, 3:449.

[191] In the intervening years, treaty conferences were held in Philadelphia with Iroquois representatives and the Conestogas in 1734 and with tribes of the Susquehanna region in 1735. See *MPCP*, 3:571–74 and 597–607, respectively.

Thomas continued to need Logan's invaluable guidance in the ongoing negotiations with the Iroquois and other Indian nations must have weighed heavily upon Thomas.

Thomas's final decision regarding Logan came on April 2, 1733, when Thomas, for himself and his brothers John and Richard, the "true and absolute Proprietaries of the Province of Pennsylvania and Counties of New Castle, Kent, and Sussex on Delaware," caused the great seal of the province to be affixed to the commission to John Georges, a 'gentleman' of Philadelphia, to be secretary of the land office and the custodian of all its records.[192] Logan suddenly lost the power to act at will and without immediate oversight in all matters concerning the Penn brothers' regional land interests granted him by their father more than thirty years earlier. Days before, on March 20, Logan had been removed as secretary of the province and clerk of the Provincial Council when Lieutenant Governor Patrick Gordon granted the commission to Robert Charles of Philadelphia.[193] Logan's removals from positions of public and proprietary trust must have been handled quietly, for they brought Logan no apparent shame or notoriety.

After receiving Thomas Penn's judgment of his fiduciary record, a record Logan had intentionally obfuscated for years, Logan seems to have probed his conscience at greater depth and reflected on humanity's call to dutiful integrity and civic virtues. The available evidence does not show Logan ever to have been an outwardly religious man. He was not known to regularly attend Friends meetings for worship, nor was he mentioned in the minutes of PYM or even those of Philadelphia Monthly Meeting, over which his brother-in-law, Israel Pemberton Sr., presided as clerk for so many years. He was, instead, a bibliophile and a scholar of vast erudition, an authority keenly interested in science and mathematics. A teacher in his early years, in his later life, in the wider world of public office and venture capitalism, Logan encouraged and helped train such

---

[192] Commission Books 1733–1809, vol. A-1, pp. 1–2, Pennsylvania State Archives, Records of the Land Office, Pennsylvania Historical and Museum Commission, Harrisburg, Pennsylvania.

[193] Patent Books, A and AA Series 1684–1781, vol. A-6, pp. 167–68, Pennsylvania State Archives, Records of the Land Office, Pennsylvania Historical and Museum Commission, Harrisburg, Pennsylvania. Although it is not stated in the record, the lieutenant governor must have been acting on instructions from the Penn brothers in removing Logan from these positions of trust in their proprietary government.

gifted leaders in the province as Benjamin Franklin, John Bartram, and Thomas Godfrey.

So it was, for his own comfort as he lived with Penn's judgment, that Logan turned to his library and pondered the classical works of wise men in former ages. Out of these reflections came his treatise *Of the Duties of Man as they may be deduced from Nature*,[194] composed between 1735 and 1737 and then lost until the 1970s (first published in 2013). The late Edwin Wolf II of the Library Company of Philadelphia, the depository of Logan's collection of almost twenty-six hundred volumes, characterized Logan's collection as "the finest library in British America" and described the treatise as "the only surviving tractate on moral philosophy written in colonial America."[195] *Of the Duties of Man* does not, however, impress the reader as the work of a tortured or even repentant soul. It strains at definitions so finely drawn as to lose the reader in abstractions and generalizations. When at last Logan arrives at a discussion of 'justice,' he observes magisterially of the reasonable man that

> he will be clearly convinced of an equality in the rights of Nature between himself and every other person he is concerned with, and from thence cannot fail of seeing with equal clearness that he ought, in all cases, to do by others, as he would desire they should do by him. To which ... if he superadded the preceding observations on the mutual dependencies of all things in Nature on each other according to their respective and reciprocal congruities, by which the good of everything consists in being supplied with what by Nature is formed to suit it, he would find it his reasonable duty to conform all his actions, and the whole tenor of his conduct, to those established laws of Nature, which he would find he was induced to set before himself as a most regular plan for his imitation; and would consider every contravention of them as an act of rebellion against that Sovereign Power, of which Nature is the handmaid, and a violation of those laws by which himself subsisted and enjoyed whatsoever

---

[194] James Logan, *Of the Duties of Man as they may be deduced from Nature*, ed. Philip Valenti (Philadelphia: Editor, 2013).

[195] *Complete Dictionary of Scientific Biography*, 2008, s.v. "Logan, James," accessed December 16, 2014, http://www.encyclopedia.com/people/history/us-history-biographies/james-logan.

was dear and valuable to him in his own estimation. And herein consists *justice,* the other of the four cardinal virtues, deservedly termed by Cicero the mistress and queen of all the rest, and was well observed by Aristotle to comprehend all the others in it, calling it the most perfect virtue as consisting in the exercise of the most perfect, for it is no other than the rendering to every power, person, and thing what properly belongs to it, very nearly to which sense it is defined in the civil law.[196]

Outside the philosopher's retreat, however, Logan remained the chief justice of the provincial supreme court until 1739. He was able to express in more direct words his righteous zeal for 'justice' when confronted with the 'degeneracy' of his day. In *The Charge delivered from the Bench to the Grand Inquest, at a court of oyer and terminer, and general jail delivery, held for the City and County of Philadelphia, 13 April 1736,* he spoke as follows:

> Let every man try his own heart, and examine whether he finds not there a concurrence with these great truths— that justice, or the giving everyone his right; benevolence, or a charitable disposition towards our neighbors, and a complacency in their welfare; fidelity in discharging trusts; compassion to the afflicted; gratitude to benefactors, all which are the immediate fruits of that, first of all the affections, love, with such like, afford a solid pleasure, and diffuse peace over the soul, and create a nobler satisfaction than all sensual gratifications whatever. . . . When we once entertain a true notion of that great and primary law by which the whole universe is supported, viz., justice, and of the reasonableness of doing to everyone as we would they should in like circumstances do to us, we should utterly abhor the thought of offering any wrong to our neighbor. To attempt to deprive him of his right, either in his estate or possession, or, what is more dear to all good men, their credit and reputation, would become detestable; and those villainous practices of calumny and scandal, that some make so free with, but are truly the scum of corrupted souls, thrown out by the acrid ferment of

---

[196] Logan, *Of the Duties of Man,* 303–4, emphasis in original.

malice, with its foundation falsehood, would appear as odiously black as the hellish source it springs from.[197]

These quotations from his philosophical treatise and his jurist's charge to the jury reveal that Logan's touchstone for justice and truth was the Golden Rule. It is doubtful whether 'everyman' for him included the Native Americans or the transported African peoples in the land or even the English poor living at the margins. But it is inconceivable he could have been ethically deaf to his praise of the "great truths" of "fidelity in discharging trusts; . . . gratitude to benefactors."

On September 20, 1734, Thomas Penn's older brother John unexpectedly returned to the province of his birth. With him were his sister Margaret Penn Freame and her husband Thomas.[198] Although John was compelled by illness to depart for England exactly one year later, his arrival in Pennsylvania set in motion the acquisition by Penn Incorporated of additional Lenape lands along the upper Delaware, an acquisition known in history as the Walking Purchase and condemned by many as a fraud committed against the native peoples. Although the Walking Purchase itself was perpetrated on a couple of late September days in 1737, the entire event, from its inception to its aftermath, spanned the years 1734 to 1762 and is in these pages referred to as the "trans-Tohickon project."

John's coming to Pennsylvania broke the logjam caused by Thomas' prudent hesitancy (only a few sales of unencumbered lands, beginning in 1729, had yet been made). The brothers set their sights on acquiring Indian territory westward from the Delaware River above the Penns' then northern limit at Tohickon Creek. By crossing into the trans-Tohickon area, they envisaged opening for development the Lehigh River Valley region above present-day Bucks County.

The Penns began negotiations for the purchase of trans-Tohickon lands with Nutimus, chief of the Forks Lenapes who occupied the area. In October 1734 the parties met at Durham, within the area where Logan already owned an iron mill on

---

[197] The text of Logan's *The Charge delivered from the Bench* is found in Armistead, *Memoirs of James Logan*, 126–27.

[198] According to Jennings, John had left England "in fearful flight from possible imprisonment for debt." Jennings, *The Ambiguous Iroquois Empire*, 320. He also provides evidence that Thomas Freame had interests in a tract of land granted him by the Penn brothers before departing for America. Ibid., 319n29.

unceded land for which he had paid Nutimus £60 in 1726.[199] The Penns failed in their first attempt with Nutimus. As was later observed by the Forks Lenapes regarding Thomas, "He keeps begging and plaguing us to give him some land and never gives us leave to treat upon anything 'til he wearies us out of our lives."[200]

Further negotiations were held in May 1735, this time at Pennsbury, where the ever-present Logan took a threatening stance that Nutimus resisted, bringing the project to a temporary but hostile stalemate. Before the meeting collapsed, however, the Penns' strategy was revealed. The brothers insisted a sale had been made of these lands to the founder, their father, many years earlier. They relied on the copy of an 'ancient deed' that Thomas Penn had brought with him from England. Truth was that the document was no deed at all and could, at best, be described only as notes for drafting a deed. It lacked any directions for boundary lines and it had neither signatures nor seals nor dates. It too, just like the original 'copy,' thereafter disappeared. As to the possible date of the instrument, the Penns waffled between 1686 when, they held, their father was in the province on his first visit and 1700. In responding to this strategy of confusion, the Lenape rebuttal, made twenty-one years later in November 1756 at Easton, came from a disinterested native, Moses Tatamy. In "a conversation" with Charles Thomson, Tatamy explained Teedyuscung's "meaning with respect to the fraud," which jolted the treaty conference then in session. In his statement, preserved by Thomson, Tatamy declared:

> [Chief] Mechkilikishi sold to Wm. Penn lands along the banks of the Delaware and the Tohickon as far as a man

---

[199] Ibid., 320–21, 330–31. Although William Penn in 1705 had issued a patent for lands above Tohickon Creek, including the site Logan later acquired, he did not guarantee these lands against Indian claims, in effect admitting they were unceded. Although Logan's payment to Nutimus quieted potential Indian claims against him for this purchase, it nonetheless remained invalid under Pennsylvania law because his grant was not from the proprietor, who alone could purchase and then dispose of native lands. *Statutes at Large of Pennsylvania from 1682–1801*, comp. James T. Mitchell and Henry Flanders (Harrisburg, PA: State Printer, 18967), 4:154–56.

[200] "Petition of Delawares Regarding the Walking Purchase, Nov. 21, 1740," in Alden T. Vaughan, ed., *Early American Indian Documents: Treaties and Laws, 1607–1789*, 20 vols. (Washington DC: University Publications of America, 1979–2005), 2:24.

could travel in one day and a half following the course of the river; there were to be two Whites and two Indians and a led horse, and as they were to walk a common days' journey, they were to stop at noon, unload their horse, eat their dinner, after that smoke a pipe and after that was done load their horse again and set forward and wherever they stopped at the end of the walk they were to draw a straight line to where the sun sets and that line was to be the boundary. Accordingly a day was fixed and as soon as the sun appeared they set out, James Yates was one of the white men. They travelled along the banks and at noon rested according to agreement. At length they arrived at Tohickon. Here a dispute arose between the Proprietor and Nutimus. The Proprietor insisted they should cross the river, Nutimus insisted they had no right, for that land on the other side was his, and Mechkilikishi had no right to sell it. The bargain was they should travel up Tohickon not cross it. The dispute grew so high that the travelers proceeded no farther. And it was agreed they should meet next year and adjust matters. In the meantime William Penn went to England and afterwards died, and also Mechkilikishi died.[201]

When John Penn returned to England for health reasons, he left Thomas to finish the trans-Tohickon project with Logan. Logan's standing improved as Thomas Penn's indispensable adviser and collaborator on Indian matters, and it was further enhanced in August 1736 when, following the death of Lieutenant Governor Patrick Gordon, Logan as eldest member of the Provincial Council was thrust into the role of chief executive of Pennsylvania pending the appointment of Gordon's successor, an appointment not made until 1738.[202] Fortune truly smiled when, in the next month, Logan welcomed chiefs of the Onondagas, Senecas, Cayugas, Oneidas, and Tuscaroras, all the nations of the Iroquois except the Mohawks, to Stenton, his home in Germantown. The chiefs had come three years later than promised to confirm the August 1732 treaty made in Philadelphia forging a new "League and Chain of Friendship and Brotherhood" between the Six Nations and Pennsylvania. Logan hosted his guests at their arrival on September 27 and at the

---

[201] Moses Tatamy's Account of Delaware Claims," ibid., 3:163.
[202] *MPCP*, 4:47–48.

opening treaty sessions held over the next two days, which were attended by Penn, Conrad Weiser, and some members of the Provincial Council.[203]

Because the August 1732 treaty proposing the new league and Friendship Chain had been made publicly in Philadelphia, it was decided that the answer of the Iroquois Confederacy should also be made publicly in Philadelphia, an outbreak of smallpox in the city notwithstanding. On October 2, 1736, at the Great Meeting House in Philadelphia, Logan presided over the treaty conference with the Iroquois chiefs. Others present included Thomas Penn, the members of the Provincial Council, the city mayor and recorder, "and a very large audience that filled the house and its galleries."[204] From the far-off seat of the Great Council, kept by the Onondagas for all the Iroquois Confederacy, the long-awaited agreement to a Friendship Chain was heard in Philadelphia, binding not only the Iroquois Confederacy and Pennsylvania but "all the English Governments and all the Indians . . . likewise the Delawares, Conoys, and the Indians living on Susquehanna, and all the other Indians who now are in League and Friendship with the Six Nations." The Iroquois also reported they had opened new relations with western tribes as requested and were calling home their own people scattered among the French.[205] The event seemed to promise a new era characterized by greatly enlarged regional unity and the creation of "one heart, one mind, and one body for one people" as first envisioned by William Penn with the Delawares and later with the native peoples of the Susquehanna. Could this greater vision become a reality?

The true reality lay in other matters either not mentioned or only alluded to in the minutes. No public treaty meetings were held after October 2, which ended with the Indian spokesman's statement that "we have nothing more to say in public; but having other matters to treat on with the Proprietor, we will

---

[203] For the minutes for this treaty (made by the secretary of the Provincial Council, Robert Charles, who had been appointed by Penn after his dismissal of Logan), see Kalter, *Benjamin Franklin*, 49–62; also *MPCP*, 4:80–95. This was the first in a series of fourteen critical treaties made by Pennsylvania with the Indian nations. The entire series was originally printed by Benjamin Franklin, who participated in some of the meetings. In 2006 the series was republished in Kalter's critical edition, which places these conferences in their wider cultural and historical settings. See Kalter, *Benjamin Franklin*.

[204] Kalter, *Benjamin Franklin*, 52.

[205] Ibid., 52–54.

enter upon them at another time."[206] Other than a meeting of the Provincial Council on October 4 noting the "necessity of dispatching the Indians of the Six Nations who being very numerous remain here at a great charge," the record is silent until October 12, when Logan informed the Council that private negotiations had just concluded between the Indians and Thomas Penn.

One of the main subjects of the private negotiations concerned Indian rights over the lands of the lower Susquehanna River. Logan's announcement concerning the settlement of that issue was stunning: the Iroquois had 'released' to the Penns "all the lands lying between the mouth of Susquehanna, and Kekachtaninius Hills [sometimes called the Blue or Kittatinny or Endless Mountains],"[207] which is a north-to-south distance nearly the length of New Jersey. Without any explanation of the Iroquoian basis for claiming ownership of that area, this cession of title in one stroke quieted all pending disputes between the Delaware natives and the Penns over the termination of Indian rights at Tulpehocken and on the Brandywine. Further, it allowed the Penns' expansion into a long-sought area that had eluded their father's reach. All of this was accomplished through a single treaty, eliminating the necessity (and cost in time and wealth) of negotiating deeds with local native chiefs as the founder had done along the Delaware. Logan's strategy had redeemed him with the proprietors, and to seal his continuing control of the situation, it was announced that Conrad Weiser and Oneida chief Shikellamy, both Logan loyalists, would henceforth be the "fit and proper persons" to act as intermediaries between Pennsylvania and Iroquoia.

On October 13 and 14, the treaty negotiations concluded with closed discussions of a variety of issues, including a request that Pennsylvania intervene on behalf of the Iroquois with Maryland and Virginia over encroachments on native lands in the Susquehanna and Shenandoah Valleys, a recent homicide, the perennial rum problem, and the abusive practices of traders with the native peoples. A key matter not mentioned in these minutes was the absence from the conference of the chiefs of the Mohawk Nation, keepers of the eastern gate of Iroquoia and of relations with New York and its fur trade. A new reality was beginning to unfold.

---

[206] Ibid., 54.
[207] Ibid., 55.

Another key matter not dealt with in the treaty minutes concerned the Penns' ongoing attempt to acquire the lands of the Lehigh and upper Delaware Valleys from Lenape chief Nutimus. Although the minutes make no mention of the trans-Tohickon project, Logan's immediate follow-up after the Iroquois left Philadelphia on their homeward journey suggests that the Confederacy had refused when asked by Logan to claim those lands by right of an earlier conquest. Logan quickly posted instructions to Weiser, who was traveling as far as Shamokin in company with the Iroquois, directing him to persuade the chiefs to "release to the Proprietors of Pennsylvania . . . all their claim and pretensions whatsoever to all the lands between Delaware and Susquehanna" and as far north as the Blue Mountain.[208] Logan assumed correctly that the Iroquois would not be concerned with the subtle English legal distinction between 'refusing' to make a baseless claim and 'releasing' a claim that was not theirs by right. The Iroquois were willing to oblige Logan, thus putting him more in their debt and obligating his assistance in their future negotiations with Maryland and Virginia over encroachments. For the Forks Lenapes, however, this legal nuance signaled the beginning of the decline of their independence and sovereignty as Pennsylvania shifted management of its native peoples to the Six Nations of the Iroquois Confederacy.

The trans-Tohickon project was driven by the Penns' financial straits, which continued unabated and led the proprietors to more extreme, even extralegal, measures. Their sales of unceded or encumbered Indian lands that had begun in 1729 continued on a growing scale; in 1735, they undertook a scheme of lottery sales, setting aside fifty-four thousand surveyed acres for the purpose. The lottery lands did not sell, however, because the public was well aware of the unreleased rights of the native peoples and of the Penns' as yet unmet responsibility to provide purchasers with clear titles. In addition, the impatient Penns had overlooked the provincial law barring lotteries. Forced to take new measures, Thomas next held a secret private lottery, selling 10,500 acres to seven individuals and managing to obscure the transfers in the official records.[209]

---

[208] Directions to Conrad Weiser, Oct. 1736, as quoted in Jennings, *The Ambiguous Iroquois Empire*, 322.

[209] See ibid., 318f, 324, 334–35, 395.

Confident of a successful outcome for the project, Logan and Thomas Penn even arranged for a trial walk for fixing the boundaries of the Walking Purchase to be performed in 1735.[210] The Iroquois assured them of ultimate success by requesting on November 19, 1736,

> our Brethren Onas and James Logan never to buy any land of our cousins, the Delawares, and others whom we treat as cousins; they are people of no virtue and . . . deal very often unjust with our friends and brethren the English. . . . They have no land remaining to them, and if they offer to sell, they have no good design.[211]

In August 1737 at Logan's Stenton estate, the final pre-walk trans-Tohickon conference was held between the proprietary party and Nutimus together with three other Lenape sachems. Although the parties did finally agree to proceed with the walk, it was an agreement tainted by intentional misrepresentations on the one hand and misplaced trust on the other. To answer the Lenapes' central question of how much Indian land the Penns were seeking, the natives were shown the sketch of a map created for the occasion by Andrew Hamilton on behalf of the proprietors, "to shew and explain to the Indians the Boundaries of the said Land, and the Course of the one and Half Day's Walk, which was to determine and fix the Extent or Head Line of that Purchase to the Northward."[212] The intentional misrepresentations lay in the sketched map, which was distorted in scale, failed to designate by name Tohickon Creek, and, as intended, misled the illiterate native chiefs into believing the "Extent or Head Line of that Purchase to the Northward" was the Tohickon and not the West Branch River Delaware [the Lehigh River] as marked. The misplaced trust of the native chiefs had been anticipated by one of them, Manawkyhickon, who, after acknowledging the earlier bonds with William Penn, said "he should be sorry if after this mutual love and friendship any thing should arise that might create the least misunderstanding."[213]

---

[210] Ibid., 334n22.

[211] Indian request of November 19, 1736, as quoted in ibid., 324.

[212] Minutes of the Council, August 24, 1737, NV-003, p. 103, ser. 9, Penn Family Papers, HSP, as quoted in Steven C. Harper, "The Map that Reveals the Deception of the 1737 Walking Purchase," *PMHB* 136 (2012): 458.

[213] Ibid., 457–58.

On September 19, 1737, the walk was begun by three men who traveled with their supply horses and Indian guides. According to historian Kevin Kenny, "The walk encircled a vast area of 1,100 square miles, or 710,000 acres—almost the size of Rhode Island—stretching from Tohickon Creek to the Kittatinny Mountains and beyond."[214] After this epic theft, the defrauded Lenapes uttered a cry of lamentation, and that cry still resonates.

Change and transition followed these events as the winners exploited their gains and the native peoples adapted to their losses. Logan, having stepped down from the executive leadership of the province in 1738 with the coming of George Thomas, the new lieutenant governor, was later further restricted in his public activities as the result of a stroke suffered in February 1740. Thomas Penn, having repaired the fortunes of Penn Incorporated by successfully concluding the trans-Tohickon project, returned to England in 1741 and managed the proprietorship from there until his death. And in the new trans-Tohickon proprietary lands encompassing the Lehigh and upper Delaware Valleys near the Forks, new settlers were humiliating and expelling the native peoples of the land.

In 1742, the Pennsylvania authorities and Iroquois chiefs met again in Philadelphia to complete the transactions of their 1736 "treaty of friendship." This second treaty conference lasted from July 2 to 12 and had the declared purpose of completing the delivery to the Iroquois of the Indian goods given in exchange for their "release of certain lands on both sides the River Susquehanna, to the southward of the Endless-Mountains, and within the limits and bounds of the King's grant of this province."[215] For some unexplained reason, the Iroquois previously had only taken possession of the Indian goods given in exchange for the eastern side of the river and had delayed taking those for the western side. Another and more critical issue for the Pennsylvanians was to sound out the Iroquois "at this critical time when we are in daily expectation of a French War" to find out whether their allegiance would be with the French or the English.[216]

---

[214] Kenny, *Peaceable Kingdom Lost*, 46. For a detailed description of how this came about, see the section in appendix 10 titled "The Walking Purchase: Descriptions of Its Boundaries and Extent Found in Deeds and Other Official Records."

[215] Kalter, *Benjamin Franklin*, 69.

[216] Ibid., 66.

William Penn's 'Holy Experiment'

In discussing an array of other issues, the official minutes, written by the clerk of the Provincial Council, make it clear that the Iroquois were addressing these English provincials with the confidence and authority of sovereign peers. An arresting example is this 1742 Iroquois protest regarding the value of their lands and encroachments by settlers:

> We know our lands are now become more valuable. The white people think we do not know their value; but we are sensible that the land is everlasting, and the few goods we receive for it are soon worn out and gone. For the future we will sell no lands but when Brother Onas is in the country; and we will know beforehand the quantity of the goods we are to receive. Besides, we are not well used with respect to the lands still unsold by us. Your people daily settle on these lands, and spoil our hunting. We must insist on your removing them, as you know they have no right to settle to the northward of [the Endless-Mountains].[217]

The provincial response rings not only with colonial paternalism and a sense of racial superiority but also gross deceit (considering the intended seventy-five-fold increase in the price of unimproved land to be charged investors by the Penns, a deal Logan tried to strike at Durham with Nutimus):[218]

> It is very true that lands are of late become more valuable: but what raises their value? Is it not entirely owing to the industry and labor used by the white people in their cultivation and improvement? Had not they come amongst you, these lands would have been of no use to you, any further than to maintain you. And is there not, now you have sold so much, enough left for all the purposes of living? What you say of the goods, that they are soon worn out, is applicable to every thing; but you know very well, that they cost a great deal [of] money, and the value of land is no more than it is worth in money.[219]

The abiding infamy of these minutes, however, lies in their record of the big-power politics by which the Penns pressured

---

[217] Ibid., 72.

[218] Jennings, *The Ambiguous Iroquois Empire*, 321.

[219] Kalter, *Benjamin Franklin*, 73.

the Iroquois to command the expulsion of the Forks Lenapes from their ancient lands on the Delaware, lands shamefully taken in the Walking Purchase. The record begins with the meeting held on the afternoon of July 9, 1742, attended by the Pennsylvanians (Lieutenant Governor George Thomas, Logan, Conrad Weiser, and some members of the Provincial Council), the Iroquois chiefs (except for the Mohawks, who did not come to Philadelphia), Tulpehocken Lenape chief Sassoonan and other Delawares, and Forks Lenape chief Nutimus and other "Forks." The sole speaker at this meeting, the lieutenant governor, reprised the "disturbance" raised by the Forks Lenapes over the lands purchased from them "above fifty-five years ago" by William Penn. He displayed as the essential documents in the case, first, "a Deed now lying on the Table" (not described but possibly a document reading "1686 Aug 28 Copy of an Indian Purchase of Lands near Delaware")[220] and, secondly, the Iroquois' request of November 19, 1736, made to Thomas Penn and Logan that they not buy any land of the Forks Lenapes as they "are people of no virtue" and "have no land remaining to them." Lieutenant Governor Thomas charged that the Forks Lenapes were still dissatisfied, having complained in writing to some provincial magistrates about the Penns "with the utmost rudeness and ill-manners." After citing demands made by the Iroquois on Pennsylvania to remove white squatters from Indian lands, Thomas concluded with a diplomatic command to the Iroquois: "We now expect from you, that you will cause these Indians to remove from the lands in the Forks of Delaware, and not give any further disturbance to the persons who are now in possession."[221]

Three days later, on July 12, the Iroquois Confederacy answered the request for its intervention in the Forks of Delaware native "disturbance." In the presence of the lieutenant governor, Logan (here making his final appearance at an Indian treaty conference), members of the Provincial Council, Conrad Weiser, chiefs of the Iroquois (including their liaison in Pennsylvania, Shikellamy), Sassoonan with others of the Tulpehocken Lenapes, Nutimus with others of the Forks Lenapes, and three Indian interpreters (one of whom was Pisquetomen, intended by Sassoonan to be his successor), the

---

[220] Jennings, *The Ambiguous Iroquois Empire*, 392.
[221] Kalter, *Benjamin Franklin*, 76–77.

judgment affirmed the 1736 treaty, meaning that Iroquoia would take charge of Pennsylvania's native peoples. Canasatego, the Iroquois speaker, assured Lieutenant Governor Thomas and the Provincial Council that, after examining the papers shown them in evidence,

> we see with our own eyes that they [the Forks Lenapes] have been a very unruly people, and are altogether in the wrong in their dealings with you. We have concluded to remove them, and oblige them to go over the River Delaware, and quit all claim to any lands on this side for the future, since they have received pay for them, and it is gone thro' their guts long ago.[222]

Then Canasatego directly addressed the Forks Lenapes, variously calling them cousins and women, all the time shaming them as subordinates:

> Cousins, Let this belt of wampum serve to chastise you. You ought to be taken by the hair of the head and shaken severely, till you recover your senses and become sober. You don't know what ground you stand on, nor what you are doing. Our Brother Onas' cause is very just and plain, and his intentions to preserve Friendship. On the other hand your cause is bad; your heart far from being upright; and you are maliciously bent to break the Chain of Friendship with our Brother Onas and his people. . . . But how came you to take upon you to sell land at all: we conquered you; we made women of you; you know you are women, and can no more sell land than women; nor is it fit you should have the power of selling lands, since you would abuse it. This land that you claim is gone through your guts; . . . But we find you are none of our blood: you act a dishonest part, not only in this but in other matters: your ears are open to slanderous reports about our brethren; you receive them with as much greediness as lewd women receive the embraces of bad men. And for all these reasons we charge you to remove instantly; we don't give you the liberty to think about it. You are women. Take the advice of a wise man. You may return to the other side of Delaware where you came from. But we do not know whether . . . you will be permitted to live there; or whether you have not swallowed that land down your

---

[222] Ibid., 79.

throats as well as the land on this side. We therefore assign you two places to go, either to Wyoming or Shamokin. You may go to either of these places, and then we shall have you more under our eye, and shall see how you behave. Don't deliberate; but remove away....

This string of wampum serves to forbid you, your children and grandchildren, to the latest posterity forever, meddling in land affairs; neither you nor any who shall descend from you, are ever hereafter to sell any land: for which purpose, you are to preserve this string, in memory of what your uncles have this day given you in charge.[223]

The Iroquois, of course, expected their quid pro quo from Pennsylvania for performing the office of shaming and alienating the Forks Lenapes. If native peoples were to police each other, then English colonies must do the same. At both the 1736 and 1742 treaty conferences held at Philadelphia, the Iroquois had requested that the provincials write on their behalf to the governors of Maryland and Virginia to compensate them for unceded Iroquois land on the Susquehanna and Shenandoah Rivers occupied by English settlers.[224] No reply having been received, by 1742 the Iroquois had become more insistent, telling the Pennsylvanians "we want to know what you have done in it" and threatening that if those in authority farther south did not make satisfaction, "we are able to do ourselves justice; and we will do it, by going to take payment ourselves."[225]

Pennsylvania's lieutenant governor, George Thomas, honored the Iroquois request and hosted the treaty conference of 1744 at Lancaster attended by commissioners from Maryland and Virginia, all of the Iroquois nations except the Mohawks, and Conrad Weiser as interpreter. Out of the discussions held between June 25 and July 4 and guided by Thomas, the Iroquois settled their claims and received satisfaction from both Maryland and Virginia in the form of Indian goods. In exchange, the natives released and deeded to those colonies their patrimony of land. As Canasatego, the Iroquois spokesman, had

---

[223] Ibid., 80–81.
[224] Ibid., 58, 59, 60, 72, 74, 77.
[225] Ibid., 72–73.

declared in answer to Maryland's earlier claim of its ownership by right after one hundred years' possession:

> Our ancestors came out of this very ground, and their children have remained here ever since. You came out of the ground in a country that lies beyond the seas, there you may have a just claim, but here you must allow us to be your elder brethren, and the lands to belong to us long before you knew any thing of them.[226]

In his concluding, and prescient, words of advice to the attending officials of the three English colonies, Canasatego stated:

> We heartily recommend union and a good agreement between you our brethren. Never disagree, but preserve a strict friendship for one another, and thereby you, as well as we, will become the stronger.
>
> Our wise forefathers established union and amity between the Five Nations; this has made us formidable; this has given us great weight and authority with our neighboring nations.
>
> We are a powerful confederacy; and by your observing the same methods our wise forefathers have taken, you will acquire fresh strength and power; therefore whatever befalls you, never fall out with one another.[227]

Three more Friendship Chain treaty conferences involving Pennsylvania and the Iroquois as well as other native peoples were held prior to 1750. Each related to King George's War (1744–1748), the third of the four colonial conflicts collectively known as the French and Indian Wars. The treaty conference of 1745 held at Albany concerned military operations in New England and Nova Scotia, whereas those of 1747 held at Philadelphia and of 1748 held at Lancaster addressed the issues of reconnecting with Lenapes and other native peoples who had left Pennsylvania to settle in the Ohio country, where French incursions were a growing threat on the western flank of the province.

At the Albany Conference, called by New York at the request of Massachusetts and Connecticut, the New England

---

[226] Ibid., 94.
[227] Ibid., 118–19.

colonies proposed that the Iroquois should be urged to declare war against the native tribes allied with France, whereupon the two Pennsylvania commissioners (one was John Kinsey, clerk of PYM) separated themselves from the other governments. The Pennsylvanians refused to be drawn into a declaration of war, observing that "it was necessary the legislature of each government should be consulted before the Indians were put on declaring war; that it would be very mischievous to all the colonies, as it would be a means of drawing the war nearer on their borders."[228] In any event, the Iroquois declared themselves neutral in the war, refusing to be the warriors in a conflict between England and France. No doubt they also remembered Canasatego's earlier advice that "strength and power" come through "union and amity.'"

The treaty held at Philadelphia on three days in November 1747, arose out of an unexpected visit to the Provincial Council by "warriors living at Ohio . . . and the rest of the warriors of the Six Nations."[229] The region of the Ohio River and its tributary the Allegheny had become the refuge for many of Pennsylvania's younger Lenapes who had been displaced by colonists settling around the Forks of the Delaware and in the Tulpehocken and Brandywine areas. By relocating to scattered exilic communities among local native settlements in the west, these Ohio warriors had removed themselves from the immediate control of the chiefs and elders of the Iroquois Confederacy at Onondaga. Although the Confederacy had heeded the English request that the natives remain neutral, believing the war would be fought at sea, it was now clear that the French and their Indian allies, in the words of an Ohio warrior,

> had begun the war on the land in the Indian countries, and had done a great deal of mischief to the English, and [the English] now desired their brethren, the Indians, would take up the hatchet against the French, and likewise prevail with their allies to do the same. The old men at Onondaga, however, refused to do this, and would adhere to the neutrality. . . . At last the young Indians, the warriors and captains, consulted together and resolved to take up the English hatchet against the will of their old

---

[228] Ibid., 125.
[229] Ibid., 142.

people, and to lay their old people aside, as of no use but in time of peace.[230]

The Ohio warriors then stated they were in need of "better weapons, such as will knock the French down," observed that "we put a great deal of fire under our kettle . . . (meaning they carried the war on briskly)," and pointedly asked "how comes it to pass, that the English, who brought us into the war, will not fight themselves?" The warriors added, we "desire you would put more fire under your kettle."[231]

The Council's considered response came after it had called upon Conrad Weiser to advise it regarding the "particular history of these Indians, their real disposition towards us, and their future designs" and dispatched him with the Council's secretary to brief James Logan and learn "Mr. Logan's sentiments about what might be proper to be said to the Indians."[232] This being done and the Secretary having taken Logan's "sentiments in writing, and on them formed the plan of an answer," the Council (of which Logan's son William was a member) prepared its reply to the Ohio warriors. The Council approved their taking up the English hatchet and encouraged them to live united with each other and to understand that the English fire would soon again be ablaze. Indian goods were provided, some then and more in the spring when Weiser would distribute them "at Ohio . . . and about the Lake Erie."[233]

The Lancaster treaty, made in July 1748 just as a cessation of arms between England and France was being reported, was concerned with admitting the Twightwee (Miami) Nation into the Friendship Chain linking Iroquoia and Pennsylvania and their respective tribal and colonial allies. The Twightwees, sponsored by "some chiefs of the Six Nations at Ohio," were settled on the Wabash, a tributary of the Ohio River. Their admission to the Chain was meant to strengthen the regional alliance, which was facing French military and commercial challenges farther west and north in the Upper Mississippi Valley and Great Lakes regions.[234] Indeed, as William Logan and

---

[230] Ibid., 143.
[231] Ibid., 143–44.
[232] Ibid., 144.
[233] Ibid., 146.
[234] See ibid., 149–59.

his three fellow commissioners reported to the Provincial Council in their minutes of the conferences,

> It is manifest, that if these Indians [the Twightwees] and their allies prove faithful to the English, the French will be deprived of the most convenient and nearest communication with their forts on the Mississippi ... and that there will be nothing to interrupt an intercourse between this province and that great river.[235]

Within his own lifetime, James Logan's vision of treaty alliances for the promotion of mutual defense and the expansion of trade networks among the native peoples had become a reality that was embraced by his son's generation and by the young native warrior leaders in the Ohio country and farther west. It was not, however, the vision of peace and amity with all indigenous peoples that William Penn had embraced.

The Lancaster treaty also addressed the problem of the Shawnees, who confessed they had been "misled" and "deceived" by the French into serving the enemy's interests and had thus abandoned their English allegiance. Through the intercessions of the Ohio Iroquois, the Shawnees asked to be restored to the Friendship Chain. Although forgiven their defection to the French, the formalized restoration of the Shawnees to the Chain was conditioned on their future behavior.[236]

The state of the holy experiment on the eve of its reform

In May 1750, John Kinsey died, thus creating a vacuum at the end of a long period of institutional stagnation in the leadership of PYM. After serving twenty consecutive years as clerk (which had been immediately preceded by the nineteen years of Isaac Norris's clerkship), Kinsey's death befell yearly meeting at a time when strong, courageous leadership was critically necessary if Penn's vision of a holy experiment was to be preserved, much less refreshed and renewed. His death, just as that of Norris, disclosed a basic weakness in the Religious Society of Friends of this era—its preoccupation with enacting and then revising and constantly enforcing a code of discipline for its own members while tolerating and even ignoring horrendous issues in the

---

[235] Ibid., 157.
[236] Ibid., 157–58.

wider community, particularly the plight of enslaved Africans and the estrangement of native peoples. This weakness was reinforced by an unfortunate practice that had evolved of uniting the offices of speaker of the Provincial Assembly and of the clerk of PYM in one person (Norris held both offices in 1712 and 1720 and Kinsey in every year from 1739 until his death eleven years later; see appendix 11). Such 'politician-clerks' appeared to be potent symbols of a united church and state, symbols that were especially misleading in a province founded as a refuge for religious dissenters and nonconformists suffering for their faith in the Old World and expecting to find the freedom of religion and liberty of conscience that Penn had promised as the cornerstone of his holy experiment in the New World.

As with Norris before him (who, among his many business ventures, had traded in slaves), Kinsey suffered a serious defect of character—in his case, a failure of honesty—that was not discovered until after his death. Sometime attorney general, then chief justice of Pennsylvania as well as speaker of its Assembly, Kinsey had also served by appointment from 1738 until his life's end as the principal commissioner of Pennsylvania's General Loan Office. In administering the affairs of Kinsey's estate, it was found that during his service in the Loan Office he had misappropriated to himself more than £3,000.[237]

Regarding the state of the holy experiment at the conclusion of Kinsey's PYM clerkship, the founding principles of freedom of religion and liberty of conscience continued to be vigorous and strong. Waves of settlers in flight from the endless wars and hardships in their homelands were crossing the Atlantic from Europe to take up new lives in the growing communities and on the fertile lands of Pennsylvania. Although there was much intolerance in the contentious political life of the province, there was peace in matters of religious faith and practice as Quakers, Presbyterians, Lutherans, Moravians, Mennonites, Amish, Dunkers, Anglicans, Roman Catholics, and others breathed the generous spirit of toleration.

Toleration of other peoples' religious beliefs, however, did not extend to toleration of people of all races, especially races with dramatic cultural differences from the Eurocentric colonists of the day. The enslavement of Africans and the practice of selling them into the American market as tools of labor to be

---

[237] Edwin P. Bronner, "The Disgrace of John Kinsey, Quaker Politician," *PMHB* 75 (1951): 407, 410.

traded like any other commodity was met with only a small voice of protest from a few brave souls in PYM under Norris and Kinsey. The theft of land from the native peoples, a gross betrayal of William Penn's founding principles and a key provocation undermining the maintenance of peace in the province, was ignored entirely by PYM except for the occasional cautionary advice about restricting the Indians' supply of rum and encouraging traders to use honest business practices with the natives.

Education of the youth in Penn's province remained a constant principle among Friends. The Friends Public School in Philadelphia was established by Philadelphia Monthly Meeting in 1689, and its charter was confirmed by William Penn just before his final departure from the province in 1701. To this day, its mission to provide for the education and instruction of the local youth, with a special care and concern for the poor, has continued. Supervision of the Philadelphia Friends schools was a special interest of Israel Pemberton Jr., who was appointed in 1742 as one of the "overseers of the public school founded in Philadelphia" and served as its clerk from 1743 until his death in 1779. In 1746, PYM widened its horizons for the education of youth by advising all its monthly meetings "to encourage and assist each other in the settlement and support of schools."[238]

Though disregarded by PYM when first made, a serious proposal was put forward in 1741 to prevent pacifist Quakers from serving in the Provincial Assembly. This was one means of separating the church from the state when a legislator in civil government held a conscientious position inimical to the needs of the state. The proposal came from James Logan, who, as an influential geopolitical strategist, could rightly say of himself,

> I have been longer and more deeply engrossed in the affairs of government, and I believe I may safely say, have considered the nature of it more closely than any man besides in the province.[239]

In light of his experience and authority, Logan penned a closely argued letter to PYM proposing that

---

[238] Michener, *A Retrospect of Early Quakerism*, 244.

[239] "A letter from James Logan to the Society of Friends, on the subject of their opposition in the Legislature to all means for the defence of the Colony, September 22, 1741," in *Collections of the Historical Society of Pennsylvania* (Philadelphia: Historical Society of Pennsylvania, 1851), 1:36.

> all such, who for conscience sake cannot join in any law for self-defense, should not only decline standing [as] candidates at the ensuing election of representatives themselves, but also advise all others who are equally scrupulous to do the same.[240]

Logan's conclusion arose out of his premise that

> being sensible that as government is absolutely necessary amongst mankind, so, though all government, as I had clearly seen long before, is founded on force, there must be some proper persons to administer it.[241]

Acknowledging that he had "ever condemned offensive war" but was in "support of the lawfulness of self-defense," Logan based his 'separation' proposal on the reasonableness of Quakers "amassing wealth according to our practice, to a degree that may tempt others to invade it, [therefore] it has always appeared to me to be full as justifiable to use means to defend it when got, as to acquire it." Logan concluded from this that "all civil government as well as military is founded on force, and therefore the Friends as such in the strictness of their principles, ought in no manner to engage in it."[242] Logan's separation proposal to PYM was referred to a committee, which found that since it related to the civil and military affairs of the government, it was "unfit to be read in this meeting."[243]

Nine years later, another separation issue arose. The prime positions of speaker of the Provincial Assembly and clerk of PYM had been united in the person of John Kinsey for eleven years at the time of his death in 1750. Succession to those offices now required the Assembly and PYM to make prudent decisions regarding whether it was better to continue such an appearance of symbiosis between church and state in Pennsylvania or to select separate leaders.

Separation was the way forward in calling the new generation to take up these positions of authority and power. The Provincial Assembly elected as its new speaker Isaac Norris II. The son and namesake of William Penn's close confidant as well as the son-in-law of James Logan, the younger Norris had

---

[240] Ibid., 40–41.
[241] Ibid., 36.
[242] Ibid., 37.
[243] PYM Min Bk B, p. 425.

served in the Assembly all but two years from 1734 until his 1750 election to the speakership, an office he held for all but one year thereafter until 1764.

In PYM, the mantle of leadership fell on Israel Pemberton Jr., as richly endowed for service in his office as young Norris was in his. Pemberton was the grandson of Phineas Pemberton, the first named clerk of PYM. He was the son of Israel Sr., who was clerk of Philadelphia Monthly Meeting from 1728 until his death in 1754. Israel Jr. served as clerk of the overseers of the Friends Public Schools in Philadelphia from 1743 until his death in 1779. Part of his birthright heritage may have been the awareness that James Harrison, his maternal great-grandfather, was the Friend to whom Penn wrote the August 1681 letter observing that by God's "kind providence" Pennsylvania "may be set up to the nations . . . for such an holy experiment." Well educated, successful enough in his merchant ventures to become a man of great wealth, he was a natural leader not only in his faith community but in the wider community. However, his one year of service (1750) in the Assembly just after his father had completed nineteen years (1731–1749) in that body was sufficient to give him his fill of civil government and political life.

Although a self-portrait of Pemberton in his own words has not been found, some sense of the inner strength of the man who was to become the reformer of PYM may be glimpsed in an April 1749 letter written by thirty-four-year-old Israel to his brother James. Speaking of "that habit and disposition of mind which is acceptable to God and good men," he observed:

> Humility, the first step to true honor, is the foundation of it, it being as I conceive impossible to be really sensible of the infinite power and goodness of the Almighty without remembering our own weakness and unworthiness of the multitude of favors and blessings conferred upon us by the dispensation of his providence, for which we are incapable of making any adequate returns, yet we are at times convinced that the grateful remembrance and acknowledgment thereof by a right improvement of the powers and qualifications given us will be accepted and that the sincerity of our endeavors therein will be rewarded with immediate assistance and ability to discharge the duties of the station allotted us, and thus often the love and unity of good men is maintained and increased, for though they may not have frequent

conversation or acquaintance with each other, yet their minds being assured that they are engaged in the same cause, in which they are mutually concerned, this begets a nearness and concern for each other which is not partial or selfish, and therefore not subject to the uncertainty which attends the common friendships of mankind, and I have sometimes been sensible of so much strength and benefit from such an intercourse of spirits, even of those with whom I have had little personal converse, that I confess I know scarce anything temporal more to be coveted than the friendship and regard of good men, for the advantages are too great to be expressed and like the flowings of a stream are constantly increasing by the confluence of others, until they at last emerge into the ocean, which is neither fathomed or bounded.

Such thoughts have afforded me pleasant reflections, but this is the first time I have ever expressed them in this manner and I am now in doubt whether I shall not yet keep them to myself. . . . Though I have now unexpectedly scribbled so much, it is in common a hard task to me to undertake it.[244]

Pemberton's leadership was demonstrated in the determinedness of his actions and the choices he made in finding associates to work with him in major causes. He gave a sign of his boldness in February 1750, three months before the sudden end of the Kinsey era, when, as clerk of the Overseers of the Schools, he led his colleagues in replacing James Logan as a fellow overseer because Logan "for sometime past by several fits of the palsy [has been] rendered quite incapable of any further service as an Overseer, without any prospect of his recovery, and as he sometime before his being so indisposed expressed his declining the trust, as he could not give his attendance, it is therefore concluded to choose another in his place."[245] Not stated was that Logan was one of the initial overseers, having undertaken his 'trust' at the Overseers of the Schools' first meeting held in 1712. Neither was it stated that Logan, who was

---

[244] Israel Pemberton Jr. to James Pemberton, April 29, 1749, Pemberton family correspondence, 1740–1787, vol. 1, pp. 129–30, Collection 1355, HSP. For a more complete version of the letter, see appendix 7.

[245] Minutes of the Overseers of the Philadelphia Friends Public School Meetings 1712–1790, MS Collection 1115, p. 86, Haverford College Quaker Collection, Haverford College, Haverford, Pennsylvania.

Pemberton's uncle, had not attended a meeting since May 1730. The reasons given—his failing health and nonattendance—were not new and had long been overlooked out of respect, one must presume, for this public eminence who had served Penn himself and whose betrayal of the founder's trust had never been revealed. But Pemberton, his nephew, and others knew of Logan's betrayal and could no longer tolerate his retaining this position of public trust because the issues of enslavement and ethnic cleansing (that being Logan's own policy) were emerging in the next generation that these new men were to lead. Primarily, Logan's removal was a potent sign of the new generation's ascension, a generation without fear of bold action and dynamic change in the service of Truth.

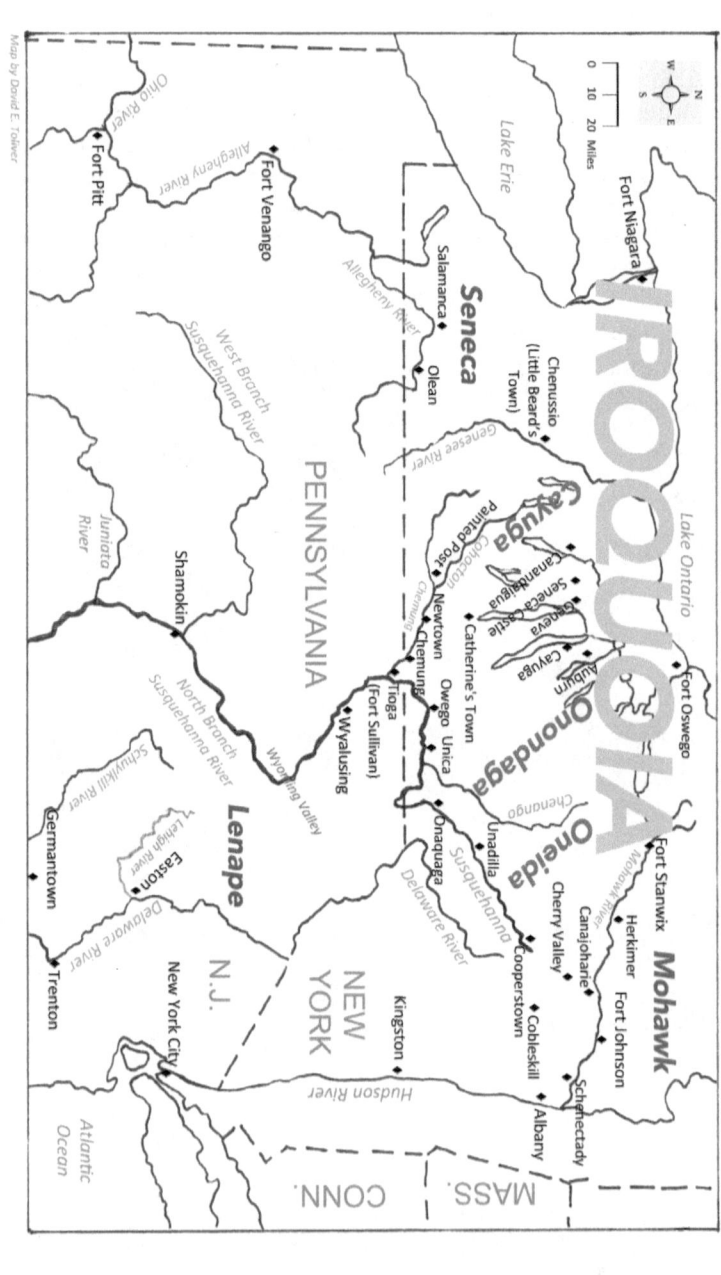

CHAPTER 4

ENDING THE HOLY EXPERIMENT: QUAKER TRUTH IN PENNSYLVANIA AT THE CLOSE OF AMERICA'S COLONIAL AGE (1750–1781)

By 1750, Penn's holy experiment, then in its seventieth year, was near crisis. Born of the sufferings endured in the British Isles and elsewhere by those 'in scorn called Quakers,' many of the sufferers had come into Pennsylvania and, with their newly made wealth, plunged other people into grievous sufferings—Native Americans uprooted from their lands and enslaved laborers carried out of Africa to transform a "wilderness" into a fruitful province. The trajectories of these new sufferings to 1750 are traced in the previous chapter. The outcome was shaped during the PYM clerkships of Israel Pemberton Jr. (from 1750 to 1759) and his brother James (from 1761 to 1781, except for 1767 and 1777).

Condemning the inhumanity of enslavement (1750–1781)

The bond formed between Israel Pemberton Jr. and John Woolman at the 1746 sessions of PYM lasted the rest of their lives. It was a bond begun and sustained in mutual commitment to the truths revealed by the inner light of their consciences, urging them to cast out the works of darkness that they viewed as corrupting the social order of their time. Living in different stations of society—one enjoying wealth and privilege, the other preferring austere simplicity—the men first made common cause in their fight against the inhumanity of enslavement. At the time of their meeting, Woolman had recently completed his initial missionary journey of 1,500 miles in three months into the southern slave-owning colonies, where he had witnessed (in contrast to the occasional bondaged African farm hand or house servant he was used to seeing in the Philadelphia environs) large labor forces of enslaved Africans overseen by taskmasters and tilling vast fields, as well as the favored few who were raised to serve the families of the plantation owners in their mansions.

After returning home and before attending PYM, Woolman wrote (and may have shown to Pemberton) what, at its publication eight years later, would be his first major work, the essay *Some Considerations on the Keeping of Negroes*. Both Woolman and Pemberton certainly shared "a Christian benevolence towards our inferiors [disadvantaged]," of which Woolman wrote:

> If we do not consider these things aright, but through a stupid indolence conceive views of interest separate from the general good of the great brotherhood, and in pursuance thereof treat our inferiors with rigor, to increase our wealth and gain riches for our children, what then shall we do when God rises up; and when he visits, what shall we answer him? Did not he that made us make them, and "did not one fashion us in the womb?" (Job 31:14).[1]

Based on his personal experience, Woolman was well qualified for his appointment that year to help Pemberton write PYM's annual epistle to Virginia Yearly Meeting.

The next year, Woolman went on a similar journey (lasting four months and covering 1,650 miles), this time to New York's Long Island and New England, where he witnessed the far reach of the slave trade into the northern colonies. Later that year, he was asked to assist Richard Smith Jr. of Burlington in writing PYM's annual epistle to Rhode Island Yearly Meeting.

In most of the other years after 1746 and until 1754, Woolman made missionary journeys nearer home in New Jersey, Maryland, and Pennsylvania, areas where slavery was practiced. In all those years, he continued to assist in writing epistles to other yearly meetings.[2] Meanwhile, he patiently awaited the time when *Some Considerations on the Keeping of Negroes* could be printed within the constraints of the Friends' *Book of Discipline*. Although Woolman was fixed in his opposition to enslavement, he was equally resolved not to risk losing his right to proclaim that conviction among Quakers by suffering the fate of being disowned or otherwise silenced, a fate that PYM, beginning in 1716, had laid on Quaker abolitionists William Southersby, John Farmer, Ralph Sandiford, and Benjamin Lay. Woolman would not allow his work

---

[1] John Woolman, *John Woolman and the Affairs of Truth: The Journalist's Essays, Epistles, and Ephemera*, ed. James Proud (San Francisco: Inner Light Books, 2010), 12.

[2] See ibid., 241–42, 244, tables 1 and 2.

to be printed without the approval of the PYM Overseers of the Press.

After taking hold of PYM's reins in September 1750, Pemberton began his preparations for advancing the anti-enslavement cause. The first move came in 1752 when six new Overseers of the Press were appointed to fill the vacancies created by death, retirement, and advanced age. This was the single largest group of additions made to that body since 1743, the year that Pemberton and Isaac Norris II, sons and heirs of two of Philadelphia's leading international traders, had been appointed along with five weighty leaders who were not only prominent in business but were also elders in service to government and Quaker meetings in both Pennsylvania and New Jersey. The new men chosen in 1752 were all born between 1705 and 1722 and thus were near contemporaries of Pemberton, and they reflected a wide range of vocational skills and avocational interests. Samuel Preston Moore was not only a physician but a sometime treasurer of Pennsylvania. Samuel Smith was not only a merchant trader but also the author of a history of colonial New Jersey. Mordecai Yarnall was a minister who began his ministry in Chester County, the seat of corporate protest for many years against PYM's pusillanimous stand on the problem of enslavement. Anthony Benezet was the son of well-to-do Huguenot émigrés who had fled religious persecution in France; his extended family had connections with prominent European linen merchants. Benezet and Pemberton lived close to each other near Chestnut and Third Streets in Philadelphia, were fellow members of Philadelphia Monthly Meeting, and, most significantly, were joined in the cause of educating poor children.[3] Several months after Pemberton was appointed one of the overseers of the schools, he presented to his colleagues Benezet's proposals "to teach writing, arithmetic, accounts and the French language" and to give instruction to an additional "fifteen poor children." Through Pemberton's patronage, Benezet began his career at the William Penn Charter School in January 1743, where in later years he established a school for girls and another for "Black People."

---

[3] See Maurice Jackson, *Let This Voice Be Heard: Anthony Benezet, Father of Atlantic Abolitionism* (Philadelphia: University of Pennsylvania Press, 2009), 21–24.

William Penn's 'Holy Experiment'

PYM 1754: The axial moment in Atlantic abolitionism

One of Pemberton's next moves in the anti-enslavement cause came on January 25, 1754, when Benezet rose in a regular meeting for business of Philadelphia Monthly Meeting to express his concern for "making that Rule of our Discipline respecting the importation of Negroes or the purchasing of them after imported more public, together with some reasons to discourage that practice."[4] Undoubtedly Pemberton had planned beforehand for this expression of concern, not only with Benezet but with his father Israel Sr., clerk of Philadelphia Monthly Meeting since December 1727. Tragically, however, some days before the January meeting, Israel Sr. had been stricken ill while attending a funeral. His death on January 19 denied the meeting the benefit of his mature guidance in the discussion.[5] (And, at the February meeting, his son Israel Jr. declined the request to succeed his father in the clerkship.) An insight into Israel Sr.'s position on enslavement, and particularly on his sense of responsibility for a slave he owned, is revealed in the following passage in his last will and testament dated December 17, 1751, its nine pages written in his own hand:

> As my negro Betty hath lived with me many years, her mistress did some years since make her an offer of her freedom, which she then refused to accept of, rather choosing to continue with us, and as she is now further advanced in years, it is not likely that she would be able to maintain herself long if she should now have the like offer made to her again; therefore it is my mind and desire, that she should continue with her mistress or some of my children, but if my wife declines letting her live with her, and not any of my children are inclined she should live with them, then it is my mind and will that she have a room or some convenient place, provided for her and put upon some business, that she may be earning something toward a livelihood, and in case it appears she is not able to support herself, that then she should be supplied with such things as may be convenient and necessary, for the

---

[4] Philadelphia Monthly Meeting Minute Book, 25 1st mo 1754, p. 291, Haverford College Quaker Collection, Haverford College, Haverford, Pennsylvania.

[5] Pemberton, "The Annals of the Pemberton Family," 46.

making her life as comfortable to her, as the infirmities of old age will admit of, out of my estate, not letting her want the necessarys or conveniencys of life, suitable for a person in [her] circumstances, she having in her younger years, approved herself a good servant, therefore I leave it as a charge to you my children, not to neglect taking the necessary care of her, more especially if she should live until old age.[6]

The response to Benezet's proposal at the January 25 meeting of Philadelphia Monthly Meeting was positive, and out of it came an enlarged deliberative forum to explore the way ahead for ending enslavement among Quakers. A committee of eight members (including Benezet) was appointed to prepare a "more public" rule of discipline on the enslavement issue "to be laid before our next meeting in order for publication."[7] All but two of the chosen eight were Overseers of the Press, in whose hands also lay the future of Woolman's essay. By the next meeting of Philadelphia Monthly Meeting, the committee had produced an "essay of an Epistle of Advice and Caution against the buying of Negroes and to such Friends who have any of them," which, after discussion, was recommitted to the committee "to review and make such alterations and additions as they, having heard the sense of the meeting, shall think necessary."[8] The committee's work was continued monthly thereafter until July 26, when the meeting, after "maturely considering" the revised "Epistle of Advice and Caution," referred it to Philadelphia Quarterly Meeting for its consideration.[9]

This proposed epistle adopted by the monthly meeting testified against the importation and purchasing of "Negroes and other slaves." Because, as observed, the number of those in bondage was increasing, the Quaker advice and judgment was in need of being renewed and made more public as a rule of discipline. Friends owning inherited enslaved persons were urged

---

[6] Last Will and Testament of Israel Pemberton Sr., Probate No. 97 1754, p. 8, Philadelphia County Register of Wills Office, City Hall, Philadelphia, Pennsylvania.

[7] Philadelphia Monthly Meeting Minute Book, 25 1st mo 1754, p. 291, Haverford College Quaker Collection, Haverford College, Haverford, Pennsylvania.

[8] Ibid., 294.

[9] Ibid., 306.

to consider them as souls held in trust. Further, owners were to consider it their duty to give freedom to such souls as were deemed properly instructed. Not addressed, however, were the problems of 'slaves' already owned or yet to be received by inheritance or gift. As will become apparent, 1754 was but a gradual step, the beginning of a stirring that eventually led to abolition.

On August 5, Philadelphia Quarterly Meeting gave Philadelphia Monthly Meeting's proposal "solid consideration" and ordered the eighteen representatives from Philadelphia Quarterly Meeting to PYM to "lay before" the parent body at its September 14 to 19 meeting the paper on the purchasing of slaves, noting that "we think something of the kind published by order of the Yearly Meeting may be of general service."[10] Of Philadelphia Quarterly Meeting's eighteen representatives to yearly meeting, four at the time were also members of the Overseers of the Press, and another—Pemberton's brother John—became a member in 1756.

Pemberton had carefully planned the January to September course of this paper against enslavement from Philadelphia Monthly Meeting through Philadelphia Quarterly Meeting to PYM. Upon its first reading in PYM, the minutes note that the paper from Philadelphia Quarterly Meeting was "in substance approved." Fourteen members of PYM were then appointed to be a committee "to review and consider it and make such alterations as they may judge necessary" for further consideration by the entire body on the following day. The next day, September 18, "the Friends appointed to consider the Epistle of Advice and Caution . . . report they have perused and approve of it," and thereupon the Overseers of the Press were ordered to take charge of its printing and distribution among the quarterly and monthly meetings as twelve named persons "may think expedient and that those Friends sign it on behalf of the meeting."[11]

On examination of the PYM minutes, however, there is an unexplained difference between the membership of the fourteen-person initial committee of review and the next day's twelve-person committee that approved and signed the final work, newly titled *An Epistle of Caution and Advice, Concerning the Buying*

---

[10] Philadelphia Quarterly Meeting Minute Book, 5 8th mo 1754, pp. 178–80, Haverford College Quaker Collection, Haverford College, Haverford, Pennsylvania.

[11] PYM Min Bk C, pp. 45–46.

and Keeping of Slaves. The next day, the committee consisted of seven members of the original committee plus five new members. This suggests serious self-examination among at least seven of the initial committee members, a concern that Pemberton's careful planning must have long considered possible. In addition, of all the PYM appointees, none had served on the committee examining the question in Philadelphia Quarterly Meeting, and only one, John Smith, had served on the Philadelphia Monthly Meeting committee. It thus appears that Pemberton had planned for as many Friends as possible to be engaged in deliberating this testimony opposing enslavement, the first of its kind among higher church councils in the colonies.

The final work that emerged from this labor of many hearts and minds between January 25 and September 19 brought resolution to PYM's "disunity with the importation and purchasing of negroes and other slaves." Of the brutality of the seizure of men, women, and children in their native lands, the published work stated:

> How then can we who have been concerned to publish the Gospel of universal love and peace among mankind, be so inconsistent with ourselves, as to purchase such who are prisoners of war, and thereby encourage this antichristian practice? And more especially as many of these poor creatures are stolen away, parents from children, and children from parents, and others who were in good circumstances in their native country, inhumanly torn from what they esteemed a happy situation, and compelled to toil in a state of slavery, too often extremely cruel! What dreadful scenes of murder and cruelty those barbarous ravages must occasion in these unhappy people's country are too obvious to mention. Let us make their case our own, and consider what we should think, and how we should feel, were we in their circumstances. Remember our blessed Redeemer's positive command, "to do unto others as we would have them do unto us;" and that "with what measure we mete, it shall be measured to us again."[12]

Of the brutality of the slaves' treatment in the land of their captivity, the committee wrote:

---

[12] PYM, *An epistle of caution and advice, concerning the buying and keeping of slaves* (Philadelphia: James Chattin, 1754), 3–4.

> And it is obvious, that the future welfare of those poor slaves who are now in bondage is generally too much disregarded by those who keep them. If their daily task of labor be but fulfilled little else perhaps is thought of. Nay, even that which in others would be looked upon with horror and detestation is little regarded in them by their masters, such as the frequent separation of husbands from wives and wives from husbands. . . . How fearful then ought we to be of engaging in what hath so natural a tendency to lessen our humanity and of suffering ourselves to be enured to the exercise of hard and cruel measures, lest thereby we in any degree lose our tender and feeling sense of the miseries of our fellow creatures, and become worse than those who have not believed?
>
> And, dear Friends, you who by inheritance have slaves born in your families, we beseech you to consider them as souls committed to your trust, whom the Lord will require at your hand, and who, as well as you, are made partakers of the Spirit of Grace, and called to be heirs of salvation.[13]

This concern for the inherited "slaves born in your families" placed a godly trust upon the masters to treat them not only with familial regard but as equals in their entitlement to God's salvation and mercy. It was a grave charge, but it still fell far short of giving them their freedom.

Although neither Woolman nor Benezet are recorded as being directly engaged in the last days of composition of the 1754 epistle against enslavement, Pemberton gave them quiet recognition by appointing them to write that year's annual epistle to Virginia Yearly Meeting, the same body to which Woolman and Pemberton had written the epistle of 1746, the year of Woolman's first southern missionary journey. The 1754 message to Virginia Yearly Meeting makes no direct reference to the enslavement issue then before PYM but, in the typical exhortatory style of these messages, lifts up as truth that God's tender mercies extend to all God's creation and that God protects God's own. The epistle, drafted in Woolman's hand and appearing to be in his voice, includes these words:

---

[13] Ibid., 5–6.

Ending the Holy Experiment 1750–1781

Truth is a treasure of the greatest worth that no earthly consideration can be too great to purchase it. And if we through a steadfast adhering to it advance so far as to be heirs of the promise of God "to dwell in us and walk with us, if he be our God and we his people" our fruits will be such as become his family—meekness and gentleness and a calm resignation to his will. If from an evidence so certain we find our building is on the sure foundation, though we may be tried with sore afflictions and sufferings, yet he who is the God of our life is omnipotent and with safety we may commit our cause to him.

For as we believe from the strongest evidence that his tender mercies extend to all his works and that his providence is continually over us; that he administers to each individual in such sort as is agreeable to his wisdom and goodness and answerable to the depth of his judgments which to us are unsearchable, as he is all-powerful and needs not the help of man, our most ardent supplications are that we may ever be preserved from seeking to helps whose foundations are on weakness, but in the steady performance of our respective duties look unto the Lord and lean on that arm which is able to support us.[14]

At last, PYM had begun to purge itself of the shameful testimony that tolerated enslavement, a sad remnant of the Norris and Kinsey clerkships, and had adopted and published its *An Epistle of Caution and Advice, Concerning the Buying and Keeping of Slaves*. The same year also saw the publication, finally approved by the Overseers of the Press, of Woolman's *Some Considerations on the Keeping of Negroes*. Both works were printed and sold by James Chattin, PYM's official printer.

On the personal level, for Pemberton, Woolman, and Benezet the momentous year of axial change in Atlantic abolitionism was especially difficult. For Pemberton, the untimely death of his father in early January had meant the heavy loss not only of a parent but also of a wise adviser, one experienced in church leadership. For Woolman, the year brought joy at the birth and,

---

[14] 1754 Epistle from PYM to Virginia Yearly Meeting, PYM Miscellaneous Records, Box 46, Document #22 of 1754, Call #D2.5 (1754–1759), Haverford College Quaker Collection, Haverford College, Haverford, Pennsylvania.

after two months, grief at the death of his only son. That death on September 30, eleven days after the historic meeting of PYM ended, was a cross of sorrow about which he never wrote. For Benezet, the year included facing the challenge of voluntarily leaving secure employment with the Penn Charter School and launching his own girls' school.

Becoming clear of "holding mankind as slaves"

For those engaged in the cause of ending the enslavement of all under the care and discipline of PYM, the publication of the testimony concerning buying and keeping slaves meant the struggle had only begun. In 1755, PYM revised its tenth query, first adopted in 1743, so that it now asked whether Friends were both "clear of importing or buying slaves" and were using "those well which they are possessed of by inheritance, or otherwise, endeavoring to train them up in the principles of the Christian religion." Yearly meeting further directed overseers to report any "transgressors" who violated the 1754 rule of discipline so that monthly meetings might direct them "in the wisdom of truth."[15]

In 1756, Pemberton strengthened the Overseers of the Press by adding eight new members whose abolitionist views he well knew. These men included his brothers James and John Pemberton, their cousin William Logan, the eminent Quaker missionary John Churchman of Chester County, Churchman's brother-in-law and fellow minister William Brown, and John Woolman.[16] Because of the urgent human needs for relief and assistance arising on Pennsylvania's frontiers in this time of the French and Indian War, that year PYM created a new subsidiary body, the Meeting for Sufferings, and placed the Overseers of the Press under its jurisdiction. James Pemberton served as clerk of the new meeting. In the meantime, strengthened by PYM's moral resolve in opposition to enslavement, Woolman resumed his missionary journeys to more distant Quaker provinces, traveling to Long Island in New York in 1756 and the next year returning, after more than a decade's absence, to Maryland, Virginia, and North Carolina.

A significant shift was made in 1758 when PYM, citing "a unanimous concern prevailing, to put a stop to the increase of the practice of importing, buying, selling, or keeping slaves for term

---

[15] PYM Min Bk C, p. 72.
[16] Ibid., 87.

Ending the Holy Experiment 1750–1781

of life," and identifying with the present "desolating calamities of war and bloodshed, so that many of our fellow-subjects are now suffering in captivity," was led to propose that Quakers owning slaves "set them at liberty, making a Christian provision for them, according to age, &c."[17] A carrot and a stick accompanied this proposed emancipation. The carrot was friendly persuasion to voluntarily "set . . . at liberty" any slaves owned by Friends, the persuaders being John Woolman, John Churchman, John Scarborough, John Sykes, and Daniel Stanton, who were appointed by PYM to "visit and treat with all such Friends who have any slaves." The stick was that if "any professing with us should persist to vindicate it [i.e., enslavement], and be concerned in importing, selling, or purchasing slaves," then they should be disowned by refusing their presence in meetings for discipline, by denying them employment "in the affairs of Truth," and by refusing both their contributions for poor relief and their "other services."[18]

In 1760 Woolman made his second missionary journey into New England, where he attended various meetings, including those at Narraganset, Newport, Boston, and Nantucket. He was gone from home just one week shy of four months. In his *Journal* account of his time around Newport, where he attended yearly meeting, he wrote:

> The great number of slaves in these parts and the continuance of that trade from there to Guinea made [a] deep impression on me, and my cries were often put up to my Father in secret that he would enable me to discharge my duty faithfully in such way as he might be pleased to point out to me.[19]

At Newport, he "understood that a large number of slaves were imported from Africa and then on sale by a member of our Society. . . . I had many cogitations and was sorely distressed."[20] He considered either having Friends petition the Rhode Island legislature to oppose the importation of slaves or addressing the House of Assembly himself. In the end, he drafted a petition to

---

[17] Ibid., 121.

[18] Ibid. See Jean R. Soderlund, *Quakers and Slavery: A Divided Spirit* (Princeton, NJ: Princeton University Press, 1988), 87–111.

[19] John Woolman, *The Journal and Major Essays of John Woolman*, ed. Phillips P. Moulton (Richmond, IN: Friends United Press, 1971), 108.

[20] Ibid., 109.

the legislature, had it discussed by Friends, and left it with them to proceed with as they might decide.

In 1757 and 1760, Woolman made lengthy missionary journeys back to the southern and northern colonies that he had first visited in 1746 and 1747, and he now was prepared, thanks to his years of travel as well as his close engagement with Pemberton and others in PYM's abolition movement, to write his second major essay against enslavement. Entitled *Considerations on Keeping Negroes: Recommended to the Professors of Christianity of every Denomination. Part Second*, it was approved by the Overseers of the Press and printed in 1762. The printing was at Woolman's own expense rather than that of PYM because Woolman was concerned that Friends (especially those who owned slaves) should not involuntarily pay for "books being spread amongst a people where many of the slaves are learned [taught] to read, and especially not at their [the slave owners'] expense."[21] As in the earlier essay, Woolman makes rich use of biblical citations, but he now adds quotations from firsthand accounts found in contemporary works descriptive of the African slave coasts and the evil trade. The intensity of Woolman's prophetic sorrow over that trade is palpable in the essay's final words:

> Negroes are our fellow creatures and their present condition among us requires our serious consideration. We know not the time when those scales in which mountains are weighed may turn. The parent of mankind is gracious. His care is over his smallest creatures. . . . He turns the channels of power, humbles the most haughty people, and gives deliverance to the oppressed at such periods as are consistent with his infinite justice and goodness. And wherever gain is preferred to equity, and wrong things publicly encouraged, to the degree that wickedness takes root and spreads wide among the inhabitants of a country, there is real cause for sorrow to all such whose love to mankind stands on a true principle and wisely consider the end and event of things.[22]

Woolman's 1762 essay was not only the distilled wisdom reflecting his missions to America's principal slave-owning colonies. It was also, perhaps unconsciously, his tribute honoring

---

[21] Ibid., 117–18.
[22] Woolman, *John Woolman and the Affairs of Truth*, 60–61.

Israel Pemberton Jr.'s leadership of the anti-enslavement cause, given after the 1760 closure of his service as PYM clerk. While Israel continued as clerk of the Overseers of the Schools for the rest of his life, the responsibility for PYM now passed to his brother James.

The plight of the enslaved was again addressed by PYM in 1774 when Bucks Quarterly Meeting sought advice regarding members who gave slaves to others "without any other consideration but clearing their estates of any future encumbrance, the Negro remaining in the state of slavery the same as before."[23] This practice often resulted in the bondage of the enslaved continuing "beyond the time limited by law or custom for white persons." After study, it was concluded that monthly meetings should judge, in such instances of prolonged or disparate terms of service, what was "reasonable and necessary for the restoring such slave to his or her natural and just right to liberty."[24] PYM also directed its subsidiary quarterly and monthly meetings to prevail upon Friends detaining slaves in bondage "to release from captivity such slaves as shall be found suitable for liberty," to assist those Friends "honestly and religiously concerned for their own relief and the essential benefit of the negro," and to see to the "instruction and learning" of young slaves "to qualify them for the enjoyment of the liberty intended."[25]

Gradualism and friendly persuasion had finally run their course among the Quakers of PYM by September 1776 when, two months after America's Declaration of Independence from British domination was proclaimed, PYM rid its own body of the cancer of enslavement. The yearly meeting held:

> Under the calming influence of pure love we do with great unanimity give it as our sense and judgment, that Quarterly and Monthly Meetings should still speedily unite in a farther close labor with all such as are slaveholders, and have any right of membership with us, and where any members continue to reject the advice of their brethren, and refuse to execute proper instruments of writing, for releasing from a state of slavery such as are in their power, or to whom they have any claim, whether

---

[23] PYM Min Bk C, p. 307.
[24] Ibid., 314–15.
[25] Ibid., 315.

arrived to full age, or in their minority, and no hopes of the continuance of Friends' labor being profitable to them, that Monthly Meetings, after having discharged a Christian duty to such should testify their disunion with them.[26]

The yearly meeting also evidenced its ongoing concern for the well-being of former slaves by amending the slavery query as follows:

> Are Friends clear of importing, purchasing, disposing of, or holding mankind as slaves; and do they use those well who are set free, and are necessarily under their care, and not in circumstances through nonage [youth] or incapacity to minister to their own necessities; and are they careful to educate and encourage them in a religious and virtuous life?[27]

In 1778 the following message was given, evidencing PYM's continuing attention to the conditions of life for the newly freed and at last acknowledging the slaves' 'hard toil' in helping to transform Pennsylvania's forests into productive farmland:

> It is recommended to Friends in their Quarterly and Monthly Meetings, seriously and attentively to consider the circumstances of these poor people, and the obligation we are under to discharge a religious duty to them . . . and to advise them in respect to their engagements in worldly concerns, as occasion offers. . . . We of the present generation are under strong obligations to manifest our concern and care for the offspring of these people, who by their labor have greatly contributed towards promoting the cultivation of several of these colonies, under the afflicting disadvantage of enduring a hard bondage, and many among us enjoying the benefit of their toil.[28]

In 1780, the Pennsylvania Assembly, under the new 1776 Constitution of the Commonwealth of Pennsylvania, passed the Act for the Gradual Abolition of Slavery. This law, which barred importing any more slaves into Pennsylvania, mandated the annual registration of slaves already present and gave freedom at

---

[26] Ibid., 354.
[27] Ibid.
[28] Ibid., 404.

birth to all children born in Pennsylvania notwithstanding the condition or race of their parents. This early attempt among American civil authorities to advance the cause of abolition was the work of a unicameral legislative body in a government from which PYM had urged Quakers to withdraw all participation.

In 1781, James Pemberton served his final year as clerk of PYM, a position he had held for eighteen of the past twenty years. The PYM minutes for 1781 make no mention of this. Perhaps it was a mark of Quaker modesty and of avoiding noting personal and corporate feelings in the public record. It is, however, a tribute to Pemberton's effective leadership during such difficult years of trying to rid the yearly meeting of the cancer of enslavement that the following words were placed in the year's epistle to London Yearly Meeting:

> And though we are generally clear of holding our fellow men in bondage yet a concern for the oppressed Africans and their descendants and to promote their spiritual and temporal well-being weightily remains as a duty indispensably claiming our religious attention. These people have had a deep share in this day of public calamity.[29]

James Pemberton resumed a leading role in the anti-enslavement cause when, in 1787, he joined with Benjamin Franklin and other civic leaders in Philadelphia to reorganize the Pennsylvania Society for Promoting the Abolition of Slavery, the Relief of Free Negroes Unlawfully Held in Bondage, and for Improving the Condition of the African Race. At the death of Franklin in 1790, Pemberton succeeded him as president.[30]

---

[29] Philadelphia Yearly Meeting of the Religious Society of Friends (Quakers), Minute Book 1780–1798, p. 40, Haverford College Quaker Collection, Haverford College, Haverford, Pennsylvania. "This day of public calamity" is a reference to the American Revolution, which did not end until the month after this letter with the British capitulation at Yorktown. In 1777–1778, Philadelphia had been occupied by the British while its Quaker leadership was held in exile in Virginia; and in 1779, the war had shattered life in the Susquehanna River areas of northeastern Pennsylvania.

[30] See *An historical memoir of the Pennsylvania Society for Promoting the Abolition of Slavery, the relief of free negroes unlawfully held in bondage, and for improving the condition of the African race*, comp. Edward Needles (Philadelphia: Merrihew and Thompson, 1848), 38.

William Penn's 'Holy Experiment'

Disaffection among Pennsylvania's "One People":
The French and Indian War (1756–1763)

The newborn colony that William Penn entered in 1682 had become, by the mid-1750s, a cockpit of war between the empires of France and Great Britain, with regions in Pennsylvania's western parts being claimed by the colonies of Virginia and Connecticut and with frontier lands being stealthily 'settled' by European colonists in search of new lives and opportunities on the American frontier. Amid all these dynamic forces and energies newly loosed on the soil and waterways of Pennsylvania were the Native Americans, the indigenous peoples to whom Penn had pledged "forever hereafter [to] be as one head and one heart and live in true friendship and amity as one people." It was a pledge he kept in his lifetime but one that his heirs and agents thereafter dishonored due to their greed.[31]

It is an irony of fate that the leading defenders of what William Penn once in writing named a 'holy experiment' were the three generations born to James Harrison to whom that writing had been addressed. And it is a great misfortune that Penn's own sons included betrayers rather than defenders of his work. Phineas Pemberton, the son-in-law of James Harrison, presided with integrity over PYM as its first named clerk. Phineas's son Israel Sr. was wisely entrusted with the clerkship of Philadelphia Monthly Meeting from December 29, 1729, to January 19, 1754. His oldest son, Israel Jr., undertook the clerkship of PYM and the defense of the holy experiment in the difficult decade beginning in 1750.

For many years there had been concern in PYM for the well-being of the Native Americans in the province, but the scope of its godly admonitions had been limited to promoting religious instruction and being concerned about the problems brought on

---

[31] The complex background of the first half of this period is well set out in Jennings, *Empire of Fortune*. That work begins with an account of William, the Duke of Cumberland, George II's younger son, as the victor in the 1745 battle of Culloden, which brought to an end the attempt of the Highland Scottish clans to place a Stuart—James II's grandson, Bonnie Prince Charlie—back on the British throne. In this, his sole victory, Cumberland mercilessly destroyed Scots warriors, armed only with swords and spears, with the superior power of English cannons, thus earning his reputation in history as 'Butcher' Cumberland. It was this man who directed from London the British Crown's military strategy in the early years of America's French and Indian War, sending favorites to America as commanders in the field, where they often engaged in brutal tactics of war.

by the availability of rum and other strong liquors. Not to the church but to the state (and the proprietors of Pennsylvania) belonged the core issues of the use and occupation of the land and of how the colonists and natives were to live together "in true friendship and amity as one people," the very problems mortally threatening the experiment in the 1750s. In the face of another looming transatlantic imperial war, of vague boundary descriptions in royal territorial grants that were contested among the colonies, and of colonists occupying unceded Indian lands, Israel Pemberton Jr. was forced to labor outside the structures of the Religious Society of Friends to protect the Native American peoples befriended by Penn who were then being victimized.

The decade of the 1750s began with potent signs of change. The removal for unstated reasons in February 1750 of James Logan as an overseer of the Philadelphia Friends Public School by Israel Jr., who was both the overseers' clerk and Logan's nephew, is a significant marker of the rise of the new generation. The death shortly thereafter of John Kinsey, clerk of PYM, followed by the discovery of his embezzlement in one of his several public offices, shook public confidence in the stability and integrity of the Religious Society of Friends in Pennsylvania. The marriage in August 1751 of Thomas Penn to Lady Juliana Fermor, fourth daughter of Thomas, the first Earl of Pomfret, and an Anglican, marked the end of the principal proprietor's nominal ties to the Religious Society of Friends. Penn, who owned three-quarters of the proprietorship of Pennsylvania, thereafter was regular in attending worship services in parishes of the established Church of England.[32] Logan's death on October 31, 1751, signaled the end of his generation. And the English world itself seemed to give universal recognition to momentous change on September 2, 1752, on which date the modern Gregorian calendar replaced the ancient Julian calendar.

---

[32] As early as 1743, Penn had written to Lieutenant Governor Thomas that "I felt obliged to solicit the ministry against the Quakers, or at least I stated that I did not hold their opinions concerning defence. I no longer continue the little distinction of dress." Thomas Penn to Lieutenant Governor George Thomas, 1743, as quoted in Jenkins, *The Family of William Penn*, 145.

From dispossessing and expelling the Lenapes to rending the Friendship Chain: The opening hostilities

War came to Pennsylvania at the Battle of Jumonville Glen, which took place on May 28, 1754, between Virginia militiamen and French forces. At issue was France's attempt to gain control over the wealth of the Ohio country lying on Pennsylvania's western border. This epitomized the complex external influences now set afoot in William Penn's plantation of peace. After two more years of scattered armed unrest, the Jumonville incident finally led Great Britain in May 1756 to declare war against France. The war during America's colonial period was fought not only in America (between imperial troops with their respective colonial and Native American allies) but also in Europe and in Britain's and France's possessions elsewhere. It is best known as the Seven Years' War (measured from the opening war declaration in 1756 to the concluding peace treaty at Paris in 1763).[33]

The preliminaries to Jumonville were long in the making. Probably the most critical factor had been the displacement of the Lenapes away from the Delaware Valley—out of their homelands on the Brandywine, on the Schuylkill and the Tulpehocken, from Shackamaxon and the adjacent tracts comprising Penn's site for Philadelphia, and upriver to the Falls, and even farther to the Forks of the Delaware—into the west, either to the nearer Shamokin settlement or Wyoming Valley on the Susquehanna or beyond the Allegheny Range to the more distant Ohio country. On the Ohio and its tributaries, the displaced Lenapes found other exiles—eastern Shawnees, Susquehannocks, and Mingos, as well as those from western tribes such as Miamis and Wyandots. And all these exiles, in Francis Jennings's words, "maneuvered frantically to avoid being crushed between the expanding

---

[33] This was the fourth and last of the conflicts in North America between France and Britain during America's colonial period. These conflicts were collectively known as the French and Indian Wars, a name signifying that France and its Indian allies were the enemies of Britain and its Indian allies. The chart below gives the American and European names for the four French and Indian Wars in North America, as well as the treaties that concluded them.

Years	American Name	European Name	Treaty of
1688–1697	King William's	Grand Alliance	Ryswick
1702–1713	Queen Anne's	Spanish Succession	Utrecht
1744–1748	King George's	Austrian Succession	Aix-la-Chapelle
1756–1763	French and Indian	Seven Years'	Paris

Ending the Holy Experiment 1750–1781

powers"[34] of France and Britain, themselves maneuvering to capture the resources and rich trade of the Ohio country. Where the Lenape exiles went, the traders followed, both French and English.

As previously noted, young warriors from the Delaware basin self-exiled westward into the Ohio country and, acting independently of the Iroquois council at Onondaga, presented themselves for a treaty conference in Philadelphia in November 1747, expressing their desire to take up the English hatchet and asking for "better weapons, such as will knock the French down."[35] They were well received by Pennsylvania's Provincial Council. Also noted was the Lancaster treaty conference of July 1748 held by Ohio chiefs of the Iroquois, Lenapes, Shawnees, Nanticokes, and Miamis with four Pennsylvania commissioners (one being William Logan). They met for the purpose of admitting the Miamis, a western tribe seated on the Wabash River, a tributary of the Ohio, into Pennsylvania's Friendship Chain, thereby strengthening the regional alliance as it faced encroaching French military and commercial challenges.[36]

Another critical factor leading up to the skirmish at Jumonville had its origin on March 16, 1749, when George II granted the Ohio Company of Virginia two hundred thousand acres near the Forks of the Ohio. The Ohio Company was a partnership organized by Virginians to speculate in western lands and to promote colonization beyond the Alleghenies. The company claimed that the original royal charter ran Virginia's western boundary line to the Pacific Ocean. The 1749 grant also provided that if one hundred families were settled by the company within seven years and if a fort were constructed and quartered by troops for the settlers' protection, then a further three hundred thousand acres would be granted. Expedited approval by the king in council was facilitated by an influential tobacco merchant in London, the Quaker John Hanbury. Implementing the Ohio Company project, however, awakened many fears. To the French, the undertaking was belligerent. To the Ohio Indians, it represented another provocative European

---

[34] Jennings, *Empire of Fortune*, 23

[35] See p. 292 above. See also the treaty minutes in Kalter, *Benjamin Franklin*, 142–48.

[36] See pp. 292–93 above. See also the treaty minutes in Kalter, *Benjamin Franklin*, 149–59.

encroachment. For Pennsylvania's proprietors it was a violation of the province's charter from Charles II.[37]

In May 1752, commissioners came from Virginia to Logstown on the Ohio River (seventeen miles above present-day Pittsburgh, opposite Aliquippa) for a treaty conference with the Ohio Indians. Three of the Virginians had been commissioned by the governor, but only one of them was concerned for the Ohio Company's interests; the other two served possible competitors. The company sent its own agent for protection. In addition, the Virginians chose as their interpreter Andrew Montour, who had been sent as an observer on behalf of Pennsylvania but for a bribe redirected his allegiance. Pennsylvania was not officially represented. Uniting the Virginia representatives and agents was their intention of obtaining "an Indian quitclaim to the Ohio lands."[38] Obstructing that goal were the claims of imperial France, of the Iroquois Confederation, and of the Lenapes who had been driven to an Ohio exile through successive dispossessions from their eastern homelands in Penn's province. At Logstown, the Ohio Lenapes and their newly created chief, Shingas, were recognized in their own right as participants in the treaty conference, thus overthrowing their shameful subordination to the Iroquois imposed at the time of their expulsion from the Forks of the Delaware just ten years earlier. This was an assertion of independence that Tanaghrisson, Iroquoia's liaison to the Ohio Indians, had to accept.

Bribery was also employed to obtain the desired "Indian quitclaim to the Ohio lands" that the Virginians needed to meet the Crown's conditions for being granted an additional three hundred thousand acres. In exchange for money and land given by the Virginians to Montour and for enhancing the reputation of Tanaghrisson, the Virginians received from the Mingos (the Ohio Iroquois) their "Consent and Confirmation" to the rights granted in the Lancaster Treaty of 1744, together with their further consent to "a settlement or settlements of British subjects on the southern or eastern parts of the river Ohio . . . [further promising] that the said settlement or settlements shall be unmolested by us, and that we will, as far as our power, assist and protect the British

---

[37] See Jennings, *Empire of Fortune*, 8–13. For more on John Hanley, see Jacob M. Price, "The Great Quaker Business Families of Eighteenth-Century London," in *The World of William Penn*, ed. Richard S. Dunn and Mary Maples Dunn (Philadelphia: University of Pennsylvania, 1986), 379–80.

[38] Jennings, *Empire of Fortune*, 37–38.

Ending the Holy Experiment 1750–1781

subjects there inhabiting."[39] The Mingos, although Iroquoian, could not speak for the Onondaga Council. Nor could they speak for the Ohio Lenapes, who, though present at the treaty, were kept in the dark by the secrecy purchased with bribery. And because they were not able to read the official minutes and other documents prepared in English, the Lenapes could verify nothing they were being told. The Ohio Lenapes now experienced the deceit so often practiced on their brethren, the eastern Lenapes, by the English and their Indian collaborators.

During the time the Logstown conferees were commencing their deliberations, a new governor general, Marquis Duquesne, arrived to take charge of New France and to restore its control of the Great Lakes region through the Ohio Valley to the Mississippi and thence south to the Gulf of Mexico. English settlers and those trading with them were to be kept out of the Ohio country and held on the eastern side of the Alleghenies. Lines of communication between Montreal and New Orleans were to be fortified and maintained. Thus, shortly after Duquesne's arrival, plans were set in motion for constructing a series of forts at Presque Isle (today's Erie, Pennsylvania) on Lake Erie, at Venango on the Allegheny River, at Monongahela Forks (today's Pittsburgh), and at Logstown and Beaver Creek, both on the Ohio River. Inevitably, the Ohio Indians protested. In September 1753, Tanaghrisson led some of his Mingo warriors to Presque Isle, where he tried unsuccessfully to order the French to cease all fort building. His colleague Scarouady, the Iroquois liaison to the Ohio Shawnees, took ninety-eight Indians from the Ohio country—Shawnees, Wyandots, Miamis, and Lenapes—for treaty conferences with the Virginians at Winchester and with the Pennsylvanians at Carlisle. The party of Ohio Lenapes included their "royal family": the paramount chief Shingas and his three brothers, Beaver King, Delaware George, and Pisquetomen (the latter had been Sassoonan's choice as his successor but was successfully blocked by James Logan).

The Indian party led by Scarouady conferred at Carlisle in late September and early October 1753 with the three treaty commissioners appointed by Pennsylvania's lieutenant governor, James Hamilton. The commissioners were Richard Peters, secretary of both the Provincial Council and the Proprietary Land Office, the preeminent positions of public and fiduciary

---

[39] Ibid., 43.

responsibility formerly held by James Logan; Isaac Norris II, speaker of the Provincial Assembly; and Benjamin Franklin, then in his third one-year term as a member of the Assembly. The commissioners received from the Indians disturbing news "on the State of Affairs at Ohio," specifically, "of the march of a large French army to the heads of Ohio, with intent to take possession of that country."[40] The Ohio Lenapes at Venango had been "alarmed" [disturbed], and they had invoked an established native custom and given formal notice to the French commander to proceed no farther than Niagara. When this was disregarded, a second notice was given the French as their army approached Venango. The French responded that although they intended "no hurt" to the Indians, they had come to build forts at Venango, the Monongahela Forks, Logstown, and Beaver Creek and to dispatch the English from "all the land and waters on this side Allegheny Hills [which] are mine, on the other side theirs."[41]

The Indian response, decided upon by the Iroquois, Lenapes, and Shawnees of Ohio who directed that the third and final formal notice be given, informed the French that their advancing army was itself a breach of the peace made with the Indians, who now "forbid you . . . I tell you, in plain words, you must go off this land. . . . It is true, you are a strong body, and ours is but weak, yet we are not afraid of you. We forbid you to come any further; turn back to the place from whence you came." Scarouady concluded his report of these events by explaining the significance of the three warning messages: "The Great Being who lives above, has ordered us to send three messages of peace before we make war."[42] While Scarouady with his party of ninety-eight Indians from the Ohio country had been holding these treaty conferences at Winchester and at Carlisle, Tanaghrisson with his warriors had a third meeting with the French. Word came to Carlisle that the French commander had received the third message of peace "in a very contemptuous manner."[43]

Then, the customary ceremony of condolence was held for the deaths of some of the chiefs and principal men of the Ohio

---

[40] Kalter, *Benjamin Franklin*, 161. The minutes of the treaty conference served as the report of the Pennsylvania Indian Commissioners to Lieutenant Governor Hamilton. Ibid., 160–80.

[41] Ibid., 161–62. The Allegheny Hills (or Mountains) rise in west-central Pennsylvania and continue to the southwest through western Maryland, ending in eastern West Virginia.

[42] Ibid., 162–63.

[43] Ibid., 164.

Ending the Holy Experiment 1750–1781

Miamis, Shawnees, and Lenapes and of all the "good old wise men" of the Wyandots, during which spiritual powers were invoked so that, figuratively, the bloodied seats of the mourners were wiped clean and set in order, the bones of their warriors carefully wrapped and the graves of their wise men covered, and all tears wiped from the eyes of the sorrowful so that they could see the sun. After the traditional meeting and condolence gifts of Indian goods and money had been presented by the Pennsylvanians, the business of the Carlisle treaty conference could finally commence.[44] That business, the French invasion toward the Ohio country, Scarouady "supposed," had been undertaken to counter the intention of the Ohio Company of Virginia to build a fort at the Forks of the Ohio, thereby opening up the western lands to Virginia's settlements and ensuring the Ohio Company's monopolization of the western trade. In restrained language, he then said:

> We desire that Pennsylvania and Virginia would at present forbear settling on our lands, over the Allegheny Hills. We advise you rather to call your people back on this side the Hills, lest damage should be done, and you think ill of us. . . . Let none of your people settle beyond where they are now; nor on the Juniata lands, till the affair is settled between us and the French.[45]

The Pennsylvanians gave no answer to this, the foremost concern of Scarouady's delegation. Although they were careful to respond to the other items of concern raised by the Ohioans, the Pennsylvanians were silent regarding settlements on unceded native lands. Another important issue for the natives involved the English traders, specifically that there were too many of them, their prices were excessive, and their merchandise "scarce anything but rum and flour. They bring little powder and lead. . . . The rum ruins us."[46] The complaint was heard, but the Pennsylvanians did nothing to remedy the problem. Even the additional Indian goods intended to be given to the Ohioans in their present need and danger were withheld. Sending them at the time was deemed to "be too great a risk, considering the present disorder things are in at Ohio." Instead they were "committed . . .

---

[44] Ibid., 165–68.
[45] Ibid., 169.
[46] Ibid., 169–70.

William Penn's 'Holy Experiment'

to the care of your friend George Croghan," whose traders had alarmed the conference about the risk. What became of the goods Croghan took into his care for the Ohio Indians remains unknown.

The issue over the merchandise sold by the traders—too little lead and powder, too much rum—has prompted significant commentary. As to lead and powder, a modern scholar has noted that "this failure by the British traders to supply arms to the Ohio region became a major problem for the British, and may indeed have led to unnecessary casualties in the Seven Years' War. Had the Ohio Indians been able to present a more formidable opposition to French forces, they likely would not have turned against the British in 1755."[47]

A singular commentary was made by Pennsylvania's three Indian commissioners at the treaty conference who volunteered their own opinion on traders and rum in concluding their official account to the lieutenant governor:

> In justice to these Indians, and the promises we made them, we cannot close our Report, without taking notice, that the quantities of strong liquors sold to these Indians in the places of their residence, and during their hunting seasons, from all parts of the counties over Susquehanna, have increased of late to an inconceivable degree, so as to keep these poor Indians continually under the force of liquor, that they are hereby become dissolute, enfeebled and indolent when sober, and untractable and mischievous in their liquor, always quarreling, and often murdering one another: that the traders are under no bonds, nor give any security for their observance of the laws, and their good behavior; and by their own intemperance, unfair dealings, and irregularities, will, it is to be feared, entirely estrange the affections of the Indians from the English; deprive them of their natural strength and activity, and oblige them either to abandon their country, or submit to any terms, be they ever so unreasonable, from the French. These truths, may it please the Governor, are of so interesting a nature, that we shall stand excused in recommending in the most earnest manner, the deplorable state of these Indians, and the heavy discouragements under which our

---

[47] Ibid., 179n9.

commerce with them at present labors, to the Governor's most serious consideration, that some good and speedy remedies may be provided, before it is too late.[48]

Of course, nothing was done to heed the natives' requests to control the traders. The consequence of Pennsylvania's allowing such unregulated business malpractice was described six years later by Charles Thomson in his *An Enquiry into the Causes of the Alienation of the Delaware and Shawanese Indians from the British Interest*, as follows:

> Had this been complied with, the English might easily have engrossed [monopolized] the trade, and secured the affections, of many of the Indian nations; whereas, by neglecting this, and suffering a parcel of banditti, under the character of traders, to run up and down from one Indian town to another, cheating and debauching the Indians, we have given them an ill opinion of our religion and manners, and lost their esteem and friendship.[49]

The time for preserving peace was running out. On October 31, 1753, twenty-one-year-old George Washington, on behalf of Robert Dinwiddie, the lieutenant governor of Virginia, left Williamsburg on a fruitless diplomatic mission. He carried a letter to the French at Fort LeBoeuf on the Allegheny River declaring that the "lands upon the river Ohio, in the western parts of the colony of Virginia are . . . notoriously known to be the property of the crown of Great Britain."[50] By late November he had arrived at Lenape chief Shingas's village at the Forks of the Ohio, where Virginia and France each intended to build a fort to prevent the other from taking control of the Ohio country. Shingas accompanied Washington for a short distance to Logstown, where he left him with other native guards. When Washington eventually arrived at Fort LeBoeuf, he had only four Mingos with him. The French entertained him but quickly dismissed his message and mission. The oncoming winter was severe,

---

[48] Ibid., 177.

[49] Thomson, *An Enquiry*, 75.

[50] George Washington, *The Journal of Major George Washington, sent by the Hon. Robert Dinwiddie, Esq; His Majesty's Lieutenant-Governor, and commander-in-chief of Virginia, to the Commandant of the French Forces on Ohio. To which are added, the Governor's letter, and a translation of the French officer's answer* (Williamsburg, VA: printed by William Hunter, 1754; facsimile ed., Colonial Williamsburg Foundation, 1959), 25.

necessitating the return of many of the French personnel to Montreal. "Through the depths of winter, the Indians starved in despair, seeking consolation in almost perpetual drunkenness."[51] And what had happened to the much-needed goods the Pennsylvanians had given the Indians but entrusted to Croghan to protect on their behalf?

In January 1754, Washington reported to Dinwiddie and was ordered, with a small force of Virginians, back to the Forks of the Ohio, where the building of Fort Prince George was begun on February 17. The natives then occupying the lands at the Forks, as noted, were the Ohio Lenapes, who seemed indifferent to the Virginia project, even declining to hunt game for the colonials.[52] Occupation of the site ended for the Virginians on April 18 when a superior French force arrived, demanding and receiving a capitulation. After selling their carpentry tools to the French, Washington's small force marched away and the French began to replace the work of the Virginians with the formidable Fort Duquesne.

Upon receiving news of this loss, Governor Dinwiddie obtained an appropriation from the legislature for raising troops who were placed under the command of Washington, newly promoted to the rank of lieutenant colonel. The force was immediately sent to the west to engage the French at the gateway to the Ohio country. The Battle of Jumonville Glen, the first skirmish of the French and Indian War (not formally declared for another two years), had been fought on May 28, 1754.[53] The aftermath of Jumonville, in which the death of the French commander in ambush was afterwards called by his nation an assassination, was French vengefulness. Washington asked his advisor Tanaghrisson to provide Ohio Lenapes for assistance. Although an assorted group of natives did come, the Lenapes among them soon left, refusing to believe Washington's promises that the battle was to put them in possession of their own lands and offended that Washington's orders came through Tanaghrisson, Iroquoia's liaison to the Ohioans, not through Shingas, their own chief whom the Virginians had recognized at the treaty of Logstown.

Washington belatedly found a defensive location for his troops at the Great Meadows (present-day Farmington, about ten

---

[51] Jennings, *Empire of Fortune*, 64.

[52] Ibid., 65.

[53] See p. 318 above.

miles southeast of Jumonville Glen), where his men hastily erected a defensive work in open space that they named Fort Necessity. By the time Washington had to face battle, all the Indians, including Tanaghrisson, also known as the Half King, had abandoned the Virginia militiamen. As Tanaghrisson later explained, Washington

> would by no means take advice from the Indians; that he lay at one place from one full moon to the other and made no fortifications at all, but that little thing upon the meadow, where he thought the French would come up to him in open field; that had he taken the Half King's advice and made such fortifications as the Half King advised him to make he would certainly have beat the French off; that the French had acted as great cowards, and the English as fools in that engagement; that he (the Half King) had carried off his wife and children, so did other Indians before the battle begun, because Col. Washington would never listen to them, but was always driving them on to fight by his directions.[54]

The engagement at Fort Necessity was soon over. The superior number of French surrounded "the little thing upon the meadow," demanded and received its capitulation, and Washington and his militia departed the site on July 4.

Strains in British-Native American relations, such as the events at the Forks of the Ohio and Jumonville Glen, occurring at a time of increasing tensions between Britain and France, were now pressing the higher authorities to find and implement a strategy for securing Britain's interests in its American colonies. In London, the Board of Trade had already received notice of yet another serious problem in America. On June 16, 1753, Hendrick, a Mohawk chief, had informed the New York Provincial Council that because of the natives' unredressed "grievances about our lands . . . the Covenant Chain of our forefathers was like to be broken, and brother you tell us that we shall be redressed at Albany, but we know them so well, we will not trust to them, for they are no people but devils, so we rather desire that you'll say, nothing shall be done for us. . . . So brother you are not to expect to hear of me any more, and brother we desire to hear no more of

---

[54] Tanaghrisson's speech is reported in Weiser's journal, *MPCP*, 6:151–52.

you."[55] This particular issue was over Kayaderossera, a favorite hunting land of the Mohawks that was alleged to have been conveyed in one of the largest patents granted in New York's colonial period. (Today the area takes in much of Saratoga County and parts of Warren, Montgomery, and Fulton Counties.) An Indian deed may have been given in 1703, but it was never produced, nor were settlements made for many years. Despite their repeated charges of fraud, the Mohawks received no redress until 1771.[56]

The gravity of Chief Hendrick's declaration moved the Board of Trade in London to order the American colonies to hold a conference with the Iroquois in New York under the direction of its governor for the purpose of delivering a present of money to the Iroquois Nation and "for burying the hatchet, and for renewing the Covenant Chain with them."[57] To New York only, London expressed the concern that its special relationship with the Mohawks had been allowed to fail "without any measures taken to bring them to temper, or to redress their complaints."[58] Specific instructions to New York also included the warning

> to take care that all the provinces be (if practicable) comprised in one general treaty to be made in his majesty's name, it appearing to us that the practice of each province making a separate treaty for itself in its own name is very improper and may be attended with great inconveniency to his majesty's service.[59]

In addition, an order of the king in council directed the American provinces to aid each other in case of an invasion.[60]

In compliance with London's insistence, representatives from the American provinces of Connecticut, Maryland, Massachusetts, New Hampshire, New York, Pennsylvania, and

---

[55] Conference minutes, New York, June 16, 1753, in E. B. O'Callaghan, ed., *Documents Relative to the Colonial History of the State of New York* (Albany, NY: Weed, Parsons and Co., 1855), 6:788.

[56] Georgiana C. Nammack, *Fraud, Politics, and the Dispossession of the Indians: The Iroquoisland Frontier in the Colonial Period* (Norman: University of Oklahoma Press, 1969), 53–57.

[57] *MPCP*, 5:711–12; Fernow and O'Callaghan, *Documents Relative to the Colonial History of the State of New York*, 6:800–802.

[58] Fernow and O'Callaghan, *Documents Relative to the Colonial History of the State of New York*, 6:800.

[59] Ibid., 6:801.

[60] Ibid., 6:794–95.

Ending the Holy Experiment 1750–1781

Rhode Island met together at Albany between June 14 and July 11 in 1754. The royal governor of New York, James De Lancey, not only summoned the congress but also presided over it as the only governor present. He also assigned his own council members to be the New York delegation rather than allow the legislature to appoint commissioners. Representatives of New Jersey and Virginia did not attend. The only Indians present were from the tribes resident at Iroquoia. Pennsylvania's commissioners, as at Carlisle in 1753, were Richard Peters, a confidant of Thomas Penn; Isaac Norris II, speaker of the Assembly; and Benjamin Franklin, whose interest and involvement in Pennsylvania's Indian affairs continued to grow. A new commissioner was added: Thomas Penn's nephew John, whose father Richard was the third son of William and Hannah Penn to survive his parents' deaths. John Penn had been sent by his uncle Thomas from England to Pennsylvania in 1752 to assist in the government and to become knowledgeable about the office of the lieutenant governor. It was an office Thomas hoped that John Penn would one day occupy.

In its public business, the Albany Congress succeeded in appearing to preserve the Covenant Chain among the Iroquois Nations and New York together with its allied sister colonies and in making some amends with the Mohawks, Iroquoia's eastern gatekeeper and liaison with New York. Several observers noted the perfunctory approval given the Chain's renewal by the Iroquois present.[61] The other important matter publicly discussed involved the issue of the colonies giving mutual assistance to each other "in case of any invasion," as directed by the Crown's order. Rather than confine themselves to aid and assistance in times of emergency, Benjamin Franklin shepherded through the congress a proposal for a union of the colonies that was adopted by the commissioners but then found no favor either in the provincial legislatures or at the Board of Trade in London. The resolution of the Mohawk grievance that was to have been disposed of publicly by the congress was arranged by New York's Governor De Lancey to be dealt with by the New York delegates and the Mohawks in private sessions, out of the hearing of the other delegations.

In its non-public business, the Albany Congress helped to advance the ambition motivating several of the delegations and others who were there—the acquisition of more Indian land. The delegates were already aware of the Mohawk land grievance

---

[61] See Jennings, *Empire of Fortune*, 99.

against New York, and they learned of the recent ill-fated engagements between Virginia and the French at Jumonville Glen and Fort Necessity. At the same time, another audacious plan—to acquire unceded Indian lands in the Wyoming Valley of Pennsylvania's Susquehanna River—was acted on by delegates from Connecticut who were vying with agents of Thomas Penn. On July 6, Penn's agent Conrad Weiser obtained a deed from the Mohawks granting the Penn proprietorship nearly all the Indians' unceded land remaining within Pennsylvania's charter boundaries.[62] A few days later, the Susquehanna Company of Connecticut obtained its own deed,[63] signed by some of the same Indians as before, granting that company land in the Wyoming Valley, an area now home to members of some of the Lenape tribes displaced from lands along the Delaware River and its tributaries. In addition, Shawnees and others were present in the Wyoming area, together with Moravians who were laboring to create a Christian mission for the newly resettled natives.

Meanwhile, the reaction in England to the news from Jumonville Glen and Fort Necessity was bellicose. The Duke of Cumberland, the youngest son of George II and the victor at Culloden, was now sitting in the government and influencing its geopolitical strategies. Resolved that French interests in North America must be restricted, the duke appointed one of his protégés, Major General Edward Braddock, as commander-in-chief of British forces in America. On February 19, 1755, Braddock arrived in Virginia, having been duly instructed by his superiors in London as to military strategy in America. The line of French defensive installations blocking British interests was to be neutralized, beginning with the Fortress of Louisbourg at the mouth of the Gulf of St. Lawrence and continuing to Fort Oswego east of Lake Ontario, Fort Niagara at the west end of Lake Ontario, Fort St. Frédéric (Crown Point, New York) at the north end of Lake George, and Fort Duquesne at the Forks of the Ohio. Braddock himself commanded the expedition to Fort Duquesne. The wars and the armies of the European imperialists had now come to William Penn's plantation of peace.

---

[62] Deed dated July 6, 1754, from Iroquois chiefs of the Mohawk, Oneida, Onondaga, Cayuga, Seneca, and Tuscarora Nations to Thomas Penn and Richard Penn, proprietaries, *MPCP*, 6:119–23.

[63] Deed dated July 11, 1754, from Indians of the Six Nations to the Susquehanna Company, *The Susquehanna Company Papers,* ed. Julian P. Boyd, vol. 1 (Ithaca, NY: Cornell University Press, 1962), 101–21.

Braddock's approach to Fort Duquesne began with his decision to build a military road for moving his army of twenty-two hundred men (in two regiments—one from Ireland and the other colonial militia) with all the requisite equipment, supplies, horses, and carriages across the mountainous terrain lying ahead. With Benjamin Franklin's assistance in solving logistical problems, Braddock advanced to Fort Cumberland, Maryland, where, as arranged, his strength was increased by fifty Mingo warriors who had escaped from the Ohio region to shelter at Carlisle with the trader and sometime Pennsylvania agent George Croghan. The warriors arrived at Cumberland with their families, thereby so disrupting life at the fort that on May 20 Braddock ordered all wives and children out of the camp. In the end, only nine of the warriors remained. All the warriors, however, had the opportunity to judge Braddock's leadership. As reported by Scarouady, the Mingos found Braddock to be filled with "pride and ignorance . . . he looked upon us as dogs, and would never hear anything what was said to him. We often endeavoured to advise him and to tell him of the danger he was in with his soldiers; but he never appeared pleased with us, and that was the reason that a great many of our warriors left him and would not be under his command."[64]

Further evidence of Braddock's disregard, if not contempt, for Native Americans was provided by Shingas, chief of the Ohio Lenapes, who related an interview he and five other Ohioan chiefs had in May with Braddock, then in need of Indian allies after the Mingos' defection. When asked what Braddock "intended to do with the land if he could drive the French and their Indians away," the general replied that

> the English should inhabit and inherit the land, on which Shingas asked General Braddock whether the Indians that were friends to the English might not be permitted to live and trade among the English and have hunting ground sufficient to support themselves and families as they had no where to flee to but into the hands of the French and their Indians who were their enemies (that is Shingas' enemies). On which General Braddock said that no savage should inherit the land.

[64] *MPCP*, 6:589.

After conferring overnight and informing their people, the chiefs returned to the interview in the morning, repeated their questions, and received the same answers. At this point, Shingas and the other chiefs answered that if they might not have liberty to live on the land they would not fight for it, to which General Braddock answered that he did not need their help and had no doubt he would drive the French and their Indians away.[65]

Thus disposed, Braddock went into battle. The army left Fort Cumberland on May 29, but it traveled at such a frustratingly slow pace that Braddock divided the force in half. He burdened the rear with cannons and supply wagons; he led the forward flying column himself, hoping the more quickly to gain Fort Duquesne and end the campaign. On July 9, Braddock with about fourteen hundred men crossed the Monongahela River, less than ten miles from the Fort. An advance guard had already come out from the fort made up of 218 French marines and Canadian militiamen and 637 Indians. Suddenly the opposing forces met and engaged in the Battle of the Monongahela (sometimes called the Battle of the Wilderness). The British succeeded in killing the commander of the French advance, but they could not overcome the prowess of the Indians fighting in that party, who, from the heights above and the woods lining the road on which Braddock's men held their ranks, wrought a terrible destruction on the British force. For more than two hours the British fought grimly, but when Braddock was mortally wounded, his forces lost heart and fled their ground. Braddock died on July 13 and his surviving men, routed from the battle, found their way through Philadelphia to Albany. The number of killed and wounded on each side reveals the fatal folly of Braddock's scorn for Indian assistance when waging war on their lands and using their strategies. Of the British, 456 were killed and 421 wounded (and 558 were safe); of the French, 28 were killed and probably the same number wounded; and of the French Indians, 11 were killed and 29 wounded.[66]

---

[65] Charles Stuart, "The Captivity of Charles Stuart, 1755–57," ed. Beverly W. Bond Jr., *Mississippi Valley Historical Review* 13 (1926–1927): 63. This is the firsthand account of a Great Cove resident who was taken captive October 29, 1755, by Indians under Lenape chief Shingas, who spared Stuart from the death sentence agreed on by the warriors' council. Ibid., 61–62.

[66] See Jennings, *Empire of Fortune*, 158n58. Although it is not known how many of the French and their Indian allies were safe, Jennings reports that the

Ending the Holy Experiment 1750–1781

Braddock's defeat sealed French control over the eastern entryway into the Ohio country at Fort Duquesne. It also ended any hopes of neutrality in the imperial contest for the Indians residing in the Ohio country. Shingas, chief of the Ohio Lenapes, recorded that "after the French had ruined Braddock's army they immediately compelled the Indians to join them and let them know that if they refused they would immediately cut them off, on which the Indians joined the French for their own safety."[67] The Ohio Lenapes, however, first sent a delegation to Philadelphia for a treaty with Pennsylvania, promising

> in the strongest terms that if their brethren the English (especially those of Pennsylvania) will give them their hatchet they would make use of it, and would join with their uncles [the Iroquois] against the French. So we assure you by this belt of wampum that we will gather all our allies to assist the English in another expedition. One word of yours will bring the Delawares to join you.[68]

Robert Hunter Morris, then lieutenant governor of Pennsylvania, referred the proposal to the Iroquois council at Onondaga, but the Ohio Lenapes no longer had the luxury either of delay or of risking others' timidity and procrastination. Shingas's record continued:

> On their returning home from Philadelphia without meeting with the necessary encouragement the Indians agreed to come out with the French and their Indians in parties to destroy the English settlements. . . . Captain Jacobs, King Shingas, Captain John Peter and Captain Will a Delaware chief were sent out by the French commander at Fort Duquesne against Pennsylvania and accordingly they went out, dividing themselves into two parties, one of which under Captain Jacobs went against the Canallaway, and the other party under Shingas with the two other chiefs, Captain John Peter and Captain Will fell upon the Great Cove. Thus began the war between the English and the Indians.[69]

---

total number of combatants in the English army was "twice the size" of the French army. Ibid., 158.

[67] Stuart, "The Captivity of Charles Stuart," 64.

[68] August 22, 1755, *MPCP*, 6:589–90.

[69] Stuart, "The Captivity of Charles Stuart," 64.

Penn's experiment in creating a new society inclusive of Native Americans and Europeans, "forever hereafter [to] be as one head and one heart and [to] live in true friendship and amity as one people," came to a sudden and brutal climax on Saturday, November 1, 1755, when a war party of Lenapes and Shawnees from the Ohio country led by Shingas entered the Great Cove (in present-day Fulton County) and massacred many of its inhabitants. This area had been purchased by the Penns from the Iroquois Nation at the Albany Congress through a deed extinguishing Indian rights in the lands west of the Susquehanna River to the western charter boundary of Pennsylvania.[70] It came years after squatters, mostly Scotch-Irish immigrants driven out of Lancaster and York Counties by the settled German colonists, had moved west and taken actual possession of then unceded lands. In May 1750, Richard Peters had complied with a direction from the Penns to expel the intruders. Joined by local magistrates, representatives of the Iroquois Nation (among them a Mohawk chief), and interpreters, Peters and party went to various sites, including the Great Cove, where they conducted legal proceedings, symbolically burned some cabins of no value, and pressed the usurpers to vacate the Indian lands. The result was continued Indian forbearance of the status quo under the Penns, who, in league with the Iroquois council at Onondaga, had demonstrated a good faith effort to control the squatter problem.[71]

After more than thirty years of provincial temporizing regarding complaints of sharp proprietary land practices and settler encroachments, the Native Americans' patience was finally exhausted. The fury was ignited in southwestern Pennsylvania with Braddock's defeat on July 9, 1755, the rout that occurred just one year after the Penns' purchase of the area. Local historians described the vengeance, with some melodrama, as follows:

> The fires of savage warfare, long since kindled, blazed forth anew, and spread rapidly, leaving death and desolation in their train. The Indians entered upon a wild career of carnage. Madness seemed to possess them and they literally reveled in blood. Throughout the frontiers of Pennsylvania their warcry sounded; many fair valleys

---

[70] See note 62 on p. 330 above.

[71] *History of Bedford, Somerset, and Fulton Counties, Pennsylvania: with illustrations and biographical sketches of some of its pioneers and prominent men* (Chicago: Waterman, Watkins, & Co., 1884), chap. 79.

were laid waste, hundreds of homes made desolate; victims of the scalping-knife were numbered by scores; and captivity, worse than death, became the fate of many more. There is scarcely a valley in all the mountain region of the state then occupied by the whites which was not the scene of fiendish atrocities.[72]

The avenged, who had suffered wrongs beyond endurance, no longer were seen by colonists as welcoming, generous people. Now they were known as 'savages.'

The intercessions of peacemakers: Pemberton and friends

As discussed above, the collective spiritual energy of PYM between the first and ninth months of 1754 had been concentrated on discerning God's Truth regarding the widespread acceptance of enslavement in American life. After years of temporizing, the yearly meeting moved from complaisance to a testimony proclaiming that the holding of another human being in lifelong servitude is evil. This was the beginning of a trans-Atlantic emancipation movement that would in time lead to breaking the manacles of legalized bondage. This decisive and bold testimony was in large measure due to the initiative and effective leadership of Israel Pemberton, then in his fifth year as clerk of PYM. While the yearly meeting labored to come to unity on justice for the enslaved, the peace of Pennsylvania was being threatened by an imperial conflict that eventually led to the alienation of the province's native peoples. Not until 1755 would Pemberton and the other followers of William Penn's founding peace testimony begin grappling with the issue of justice for the Indians.

Today, more than 235 years after his death, Pemberton remains relatively unknown. Although he was a man of major achievements within Quaker institutions, the official record of how those achievements were wrought is slim. And despite his being personally bold and decisive in action, Pemberton wrote so little about himself that it is necessary to take his measure by reading what others penned to and said of him, especially at times of crisis in his life.

At the juncture, in late 1754, of the bold initiative Friends under his leadership had taken in PYM to abolish enslavement

---

[72] Ibid., 595-96.

and, in early 1755, of the need to preserve the Quaker peace testimony as war loomed in western Pennsylvania, Pemberton uncharacteristically took time away from home and his personal and public responsibilities to accompany Samuel Fothergill, an English Quaker and traveling minister, on a mission journey through the American South from Virginia to South Carolina. The bond between the Pemberton and Fothergill families had been formed in Jamaica in 1708 when Israel Sr., who was there on a business trip, met the English Quaker preacher and farmer John Fothergill Sr., who was there on a missionary journey.[73] The strong friendship between the men continued between their children. In July of 1754, Israel Jr. floated an inquiry through a mutual friend whether Fothergill would accept Pemberton's hospitality while in Philadelphia and would allow Pemberton to accompany him on part of his journey. Pemberton's diffident offer was passed on to Fothergill through his sister, who quoted these words from Pemberton:

> ... the reverence I have for his worthy father's memory ... . the wish I have of engaging his company to my house, determined me to salute him with a few lines, and even offer to attend him through the adjacent provinces ... [but] some doubt arises, whether such a proposal would or may be agreeable.[74]

Fothergill accepted the offer and arrived in the American colonies, just above Wilmington, on September 24. That evening he began his stay at Pemberton's home in Philadelphia, "where I met a kind reception."[75] He had arrived five days after the close of the historic yearly meeting. On this mission, which lasted into 1756, Fothergill was traveling with certificates from several meetings in England, including his home monthly meeting at Hardshaw (where Phineas Pemberton had been "an early and active member")[76] and the London Yearly Meeting of Ministering Friends. After several days in Philadelphia in the Pemberton home, Fothergill made his first outing, into the Pennsylvania backwoods as far as the Susquehanna. After a brief return to

---

[73] Pemberton, "The Annals of the Pemberton Family," 45.

[74] Ann Fothergill to her brother Samuel, 7th mo 23 day 1754, quoting an earlier letter from Israel Pemberton to William Brown, in Samuel Fothergill, *Memoirs of the life and gospel labours of Samuel Fothergill* ..., ed. George Crosfield (London: W. and F. G. Cash, 1857), 147–48.

[75] Samuel Fothergill, *Memoirs*, 151.

[76] Ibid., 160.

Philadelphia on November 7, he set out into the American South. Approximately one month later, in Virginia, Pemberton joined the mission and remained with Fothergill until the two returned to Philadelphia in mid-April 1755, having reached their southernmost point at Charleston, South Carolina. Fothergill, in a letter to his wife from Philadelphia dated April 15, gave her news of his "safe return in good health, to this place, where I am arrived," and then the following detached commentary on the threat of war hanging over the land, a threat that was, without doubt, greatly troubling to Pemberton:

> The vessels of the earth seem smiting one against another; but I am not dismayed by any appearance of danger, nor drawn from my quiet habitation, in the power of endless strength, to meddle at all.[77]

What this journey with Fothergill meant for Pemberton is beyond our knowing, but the tentative manner in which Pemberton offered the hospitality of his home and then gave such a generous amount of his time suggests a man of bold vision yet inner insecurity. George Crosfield, who shepherded Fothergill's *Memoirs* into print, writing almost a century later said of Pemberton that he was a man of "clear and sound judgment, yet of a quick and ardent temperament, against which he had often to contend, but he was enabled to yield in good measure to the subduing and regulating power of Truth."[78] On the other hand, Fothergill's own cool and distant comment in a letter to his own wife that "my companion, Israel Pemberton, is agreeable and helpful in various respects, and [I] hope he will receive some profit from this journey"[79] might sound to a modern ear as ungrateful and condescending

Two other letters, both addressed to Pemberton, give insight probably as much into their authors as into Pemberton, who was then journeying through the heartland of the evil confronted by PYM in 1754. The first letter, dated January 11, 1755, while Pemberton was traveling with Fothergill, was written by Pemberton's cousin William Logan, who commented:

---

[77] Ibid., 178, 179.
[78] Ibid., 161.
[79] Samuel Fothergill to his wife, 2nd mo. 13, 1755, ibid., 174.

> I often think of thee, and sincerely hope thou mayest be made fully sensible how greatly thou art favored in being a companion to so worthy and truly valuable a friend . . . and be thereby refreshed and revived to a sense of thy duty to thy Maker. Thou hast been under great and frequent visitations, my dear cousin. . . . and I have sometimes thought that no person has had greater advantages from their youth up than thou hast, by the frequent private sittings with friends in your family. . . . The good advice dropped by friends at such times, extraordinary example of worthy pious parents, together . . . with the frequent visitations and awakenings of a gracious and kind Providence. How many hungry souls would think themselves highly favored with some of the smallest of these crumbs. . . . I think, my dear cousin, thy present situation seems to crown all, therefore neglect not to comply with whatever may be made known to thee as a duty to thy Maker, obey his still small voice in thy heart, remember his frequent and tender callings to thee, and endeavor to overcome thy natural dispositions, set a constant guard upon them, and bring thy will to be entirely subject to that of thy Heavenly Father, who has greatly blest and endowed thee with natural abilities and qualifications to be of great service in Church and State.[80]

The tone of this letter from the thirty-eight-year-old Logan to the forty-year-old Pemberton sounds strangely exhortatory in the present day. Here may also be an air of condescension masking jealousy. The hint of faultfinding regarding "thy natural dispositions" hardly squares with the peaceful and conciliatory language of the recently prepared epistle and essay cautioning against enslavement, both of which were guided through PYM and into print under Pemberton's quiet administrative hand.

The second letter was written by Fothergill to Pemberton on June 23, 1755, after they had parted in Philadelphia and Fothergill had continued his mission on into New England. He wrote:

> I have often, dear Israel, remembered thee in a distinguished manner, being sensible the Lord of all power and wisdom would clothe with eminent

---

[80] William Logan to Israel Pemberton Jr., 1st mo 11th da 1755, vol. 2, pp. 65–66, Pemberton Family Correspondence 1740–1787, Collection 1355, HSP.

qualifications for his service, in this thy day, in which the Church has on her sable weeds, and her priests are in bitterness. . . . O that thy spirit might be more and more seasoned and bowed with and by that power which alone sanctifies our all to God, and doeth his work and service. I have seen thee, dear friend, in the hidden conflict, and the struggle between the two opposite powers, and have sympathized with and for thee, when thou hast been bruised and hurt by the prevalence of that which stands as an armed man in thy way to rest. I am sensible of thy secret bemoaning at times, when loss hath been sustained, and the renewal of holy reaches for thy help and recovery. I earnestly wish thee, as well as for myself, the thorough subjection of all within us to that abasing, humbling hand, who prepares instruments for his service from the dust of Zion, and ordains praise out of the mouths of babes and sucklings. In the spreading of tender love, I could lay my hands under thy feet, if necessary, that thou might receive strength to reign in the Lamb's dominion over all which diminishes that excellent service thou might grow up in, for the revival and strengthening of the Lord's cause in thy generation.[81]

In Pemberton's coming struggle to find justice for the indigenous peoples of Pennsylvania, he would, indeed, become "bruised and hurt," and there would be "loss" for him to "sustain." That central struggle would be surrounded by multiple other conflicts, especially those between the proprietors' self-interest and the Quakers' principles, between two competing imperial powers, and between the mother country's need to control her colonies and the colonists' reach toward independence. Amid these issues, Pemberton and friends labored to hold to the rock of the Quaker peace testimony.

As preparations were made for the murderous and desolating butchery of war, that peace testimony was heard again. Even though PYM had no direct role in the government and Quaker influence in administering the province was much less than it had once been, the 1755 General Spring Meeting of Ministers and Elders of PYM addressed an epistle "To Friends on the Continent of America," written by John Woolman, that stated in part:

---

[81] Samuel Fothergill, *Memoirs*, 192–93.

And now dear Friends, with respect to the commotions and stirrings of the powers of the earth at this time near us, we are desirous that none of us may be moved thereat; "But repose ourselves in the munition of that rock that all these shakings shall not move, even in the knowledge and feeling of the eternal power of God keeping us subjectly given up to his heavenly will, and feel it daily to mortify that which remains in any of us which is of this world: For the worldly part in any, is the changeable part, and that is up and down, full and empty, joyful and sorrowful, as things go well or ill in this world; for as the Truth is but one, and many are made partakers of its spirit, so the world is but one, and many are made partakers of the spirit of it, and so many as do partake of it, so many will be straitened and perplexed with it; but they who are single to the Truth, waiting daily to feel the life and virtue of it in their hearts, these shall rejoice in the midst of adversity," and have to experience with the prophet, that, *Although the fig tree shall not blossom, neither shall fruit be in the vines, the labor of the olive shall fail, and the fields shall yield no meat, the flock shall be cut off from the fold, and there shall be no herd in the stalls, yet will they rejoice in the LORD, and joy in the GOD of their salvation* (Hab. 3:17, 18).[82]

The disinterest of Penn Incorporated in anything concerning Pennsylvania other than its own investment properties and revenues, its powers and privileges, and its exemption from taxes was now patently obvious to the provincials, especially to the leaders in business, government, and the professions. Since the death of John Penn in 1746, three-quarters of the proprietorship had been owned, and the entirety controlled, by his brother Thomas. The remaining quarter was owned by their brother Richard. Although John had remained a member of the Religious Society of Friends throughout his life, Thomas had severed his nominal connection to the Quakers by the time of his marriage in August 1751 to Lady Juliana Fermor, a daughter of the Earl of Pomfret, whose family was Anglican. Just as Thomas had ceased to be a member of his father's Quaker meeting, mirroring William Penn's journey away from his own father's Anglican faith, he

---

[82] The text is in Woolman, *John Woolman and the Affairs of Truth*, 18; the internal quotation is from Stephen Crisp (1628–1692), "An Epistle to Friends concerning the present and succeeding times" (London: 1666), 22.

demonstrated that he had ceased to hold his father's, or the Quaker community's, principles of toleration, peace, and love of humanity.

As Thomas Penn distanced himself from Quakers during this period of increasing unrest in the province, his practical and immediate concern was with the opposition of those Friends who blocked his will in the Assembly.[83] To eliminate Quakers from the Assembly, he used several strategies, one being to urge, through the agency of William Smith, an Anglican clergyman and anti-Quaker activist, that Parliament enact a mandatory test oath for all persons elected to the Provincial Assembly. Smith wrote an anonymous polemic designed to spread contempt for Quakers, who he said were unconcerned about defending the province. This was printed in London in early 1755.[84]

Persecution over oath-taking had a painful history among Quakers, so concern over Smith's pro-proprietary rant was raised in Philadelphia Quarterly Meeting, prompting the meeting to request counsel and intervention in its epistle of May 5, 1755, to the Meeting for Sufferings in London. The epistle was signed by Pemberton and seven others, and it stated the critical issue as follows:

> On an impartial and calm review of the transactions of the government it will appear that in divers instances the Proprietaries and their deputies have extended their prerogatives and obtained concessions from the people, some with their consent, others by custom, and thereby made a large addition of power and treasure which the people did not originally intend to part with, but while the fundamental of our constitution remained unattacked and there appeared no design to enervate the principles on which it was established we thought it most prudent to submit to smaller inconveniences. We now think our circumstances are such that we have abundant cause to complain that the most unwearied endeavors are and have sometime past been used and various artifices attempted to wrest from us our most valuable privileges and the conduct and language of those whose duty it is to

---

[83] See generally Jennings, *Empire of Fortune*, 224–32.

[84] [William Smith], *A brief state of the province of Pennsylvania* (London: 1755).

protect us in the enjoyment thereof fully convince us of the pernicious tendency of their designs.[85]

Concerning defense appropriations ("supplies") and Friends' scruples regarding war, they wrote:

> We consider that in the present situation of public affairs the exigencies being great the supplies must be proportioned thereto and we only desire that as we cannot be concerned in the preparations of war, we may be permitted to serve the government by raising money and contributing towards the public exigencies by such methods and in such manner as past experience has assured us are least burdensome to the industrious poor and most consistent with our religious and civil rights and liberties and which our present Proprietaries when one of them was personally present consented to and approved and to which no reasonable or just objection hath ever since been made.[86]

To preserve William Penn's founding principle of liberty of conscience, the Pennsylvanians asked that the London Meeting for Sufferings intervene on their behalf with the proprietors.

> One point we have therefore in view by laying our case so fully before you is that as there are some among you whose stations and circumstances will entitle them to a free conference with our Proprietaries, we earnestly desire your engaging such in this necessary service. The attempt must be allowed to be laudable and if it succeeds undoubtedly rewardable; the making of peace having a blessing annexed to it by the author of every blessing.[87]

As requested, the London Meeting for Sufferings appointed several Friends to meet with the proprietors to discuss the concerns of Philadelphia Quarterly Meeting. In answer, Thomas Penn gave assurances that the proprietors "had no intention of the abridging the inhabitants of the Province of Pennsylvania, either Friends or others, of any rights or privileges to which they

---

[85] Epistle dated May 5, 1755, from Philadelphia Quarterly Meeting to Meeting for Sufferings in London, Philadelphia Yearly Meeting for Sufferings Minutes 1756–1775, 11–19 (quote is on p. 13), Haverford College Quaker Collection, Haverford College, Haverford, Pennsylvania.

[86] Ibid., 16.

[87] Ibid., 17.

are by charter entitled, and that if the inhabitants of the province apprehend they have any just cause of complaint it shall when made known to them be duly considered and redressed."[88] Although not deceived by these gracious words, London advised Philadelphia that without moderation and mutual respect, "what side soever prevails in this contest both must be sufferers, as a public discussion here will most probably end in subjecting the Charter and whole Frame of Government to alterations, by which the Proprietaries and the country may be affected to their prejudice. . . . This in our opinion is the only effectual means to prevent the subversion of a constitution which has done so much credit to the benevolent Founder and to those who have since had so considerable a share in its administration."[89]

Pemberton, meanwhile, believed Thomas Penn might be brought to a different mind after he received a letter dated July 8, 1755, from John Fothergill, who was an older brother of Samuel and a London physician (one of his patients was Thomas Penn), horticulturist, clerk of London Yearly Meeting in the years 1749, 1764, and 1779, and longstanding Pemberton family friend. The day after hearing Philadelphia Quarterly Meeting's May epistle read in the London Meeting for Sufferings, Fothergill wrote to Pemberton. He first noted that reports of the worsening prospects of England losing in the armed conflict on Pennsylvania's western frontier led to a

> torrent of perfidious reflections that are poured out and propagated industriously by a set of men who, because they have once used us extremely ill, think the best way to prove that in making martyrs of some of our ancestors they did right, is to continue the inveterate enemy, in secret at least, of those they have so evilly mistreated through every generation.[90]

Astutely identifying "the inveterate enemy" (England's established church with which Pennsylvania's principal

---

[88] Meeting for Sufferings London to Philadelphia Quarterly Meeting, October 3, 1755, in Philadelphia Yearly Meeting for Sufferings Minutes 1756–1775, pp. 19–20, Haverford College Quaker Collection, Haverford College, Haverford, Pennsylvania.

[89] Ibid., 21.

[90] John Fothergill to Israel Pemberton, July 8, 1755, in Fothergill, John Fothergill, *Chain of Friendship: Selected letters of Dr. John Fothergill of London, 1735–1780* (Cambridge: Belknap Press of Harvard University Press, 1971), 158.

proprietor was now aligned), Fothergill went on to take the measure of Thomas Penn and to propose a path toward resolving the threat of the abolition of Pennsylvania's constitutional rights of religious freedom and liberty of conscience. He wrote:

> The Proprietor is reserved, tenacious and inflexible, yet there is one person who I believe can influence him. . . . The person I mean is the President of the Privy Council.[91]

The president of the Privy Council from 1751 until his death was the Earl of Granville, born John Carteret (1690–1763). He was also Thomas Penn's brother-in-law since both their wives were daughters of the Earl of Pomfret.

The threat to Pennsylvania's constitution, however, had not yet run its course. The October elections to the Assembly dealt a major defeat to the proprietary interests, the electorate again giving Quakers a majority.[92] Because of this, in November William Smith, charged by Penn with the anti-Quaker project in Philadelphia, petitioned the king to ask relief for a defenseless province that was being denied defense preparations by a pacifist legislature.

When, on March 17, 1755, the trustees of the newly chartered College of Philadelphia elected Smith the first provost of the institution, they also accepted the resignation of Charles Thomson, the Latin tutor in the companion Academy and Charitable School in the Province of Pennsylvania.[93] The Academy, which had opened in Philadelphia in 1751 to provide boys with a secondary education, had been founded by Benjamin Franklin. Thomson was born to Scotch-Irish parents in Ireland but had been orphaned after the deaths of his mother in Ireland and of his father on the Atlantic voyage while he was bringing his young sons to America. The impoverished, orphaned boys were separated in the colonies; Charles was cared for in Delaware and educated in Pennsylvania. He began teaching Latin in the Academy at its opening but resigned the position on the coming of Smith. The following September 27, he was employed by the Quaker overseers of the schools as master of the Latin School. Pemberton, ever alert to discovering new talent to assist in his causes (such as Woolman and Benezet for the enslavement issue), found in Thomson an intelligent inquirer into Indian affairs who

---

[91] Ibid., 159.

[92] See Jennings, *Empire of Fortune*, 231–32.

[93] Ibid., 232n26.

over the next months researched all Indian treaties and deeds held in the provincial offices. Thereafter, Thomson became a participant with Pemberton in Indian treaty conferences and proved to be a bridge between Pemberton and Franklin in their evolving common efforts to obtain justice for the Indians.

Within weeks of the Great Cove massacre of November 1, 1755, the human suffering caused by the war in another theater of operations—the battle for the Louisbourg naval base on Cape Breton—presented itself on Philadelphia's Delaware waterfront. Three ships had arrived there holding 454 people forcibly removed by the British from Acadia (the present-day Canadian provinces of Nova Scotia, New Brunswick, and Prince Edward Island). The ships were secured and maintained as prisons, holding their human cargo for the coming months. These Acadian refugees were descended from French colonists who had settled in the Atlantic maritime region of Canada in the seventeenth century. Subjected to British rule since 1710 and refusing to take unconditional oaths of allegiance to Britain, during the French and Indian War the Acadians were presumed to be disloyal, and consequently between 1755 and 1764 approximately 11,500 persons were distributed among the American colonies in the Great Expulsion, or *Le Grand Dérangement*. Pennsylvania's lieutenant governor posted guards to prevent any of those imprisoned on the three ships from coming ashore. Pennsylvania's Assembly provided them with some assistance as well as protection. Quaker Anthony Benezet (born in France to Huguenot parents) visited them in confinement aboard ship and raised contributions for their relief. The Penns did nothing.[94]

Just as 1755 was considered a terrible year in Pennsylvania's colonial history, so 1756 was a year not only of living with conflict and war but also of examining their root causes. Residents of the province experienced the fear of living on the frontier; the near immobilization of the proprietary, executive, and legislative functions of the provincial government; the ineffectual results of British defense strategies and colonial administration; and the consequences of not redressing the grievances of the native peoples displaced from lands that the planters and settlers had illegally acquired while professing friendship.[95]

---

[94] See *MPCP*, 6:712–13, 729–30, 751; Jennings, *Empire of Fortune*, 246–47; Jackson, *Let This Voice Be Heard*, 25–27.

[95] For more information, see Jennings, *Empire of Fortune*, 251–81.

And William Smith's petition to the king for redress from the pacifist Assembly advanced in London, where the provincial chief justice, William Allen, who was a supporter of the petition, had arranged for its presentation to the Privy Council. By early March 1756 an oath bill—providing that all those elected to colonial assemblies prior to serving must have "duly and solemnly taken such oaths, upon the holy evangelists as by the laws and statutes of this kingdom . . . to qualify any person to sit or vote in the House of Commons for this kingdom"[96]—had been approved in the Privy Council with the support of the Board of Trade. (Either unknown or disregarded in those bodies was the fact that the Pennsylvania Assembly had been funding defense measures with generous grants, although they were appropriated "to the king's use.")

On March 16, 1756, John Fothergill wrote to Pemberton of a proposed solution to this threatened undoing of religious freedom and liberty of conscience in Pennsylvania:

> A person of high rank, a steady friend to the Society [the Religious Society of Friends], . . . was desirous of communicating his opinion and advice to the Society on the present situation of your affairs; a deputation accordingly waited upon him consisting of the following Friends, viz., J[ohn] Hanbury, Silvanus Bevan, Peter Collinson, Thomas How, John Hunt, myself, with Peter Andrews and Edmund Peckover, who both happened to be then in town.
>
> He told us that he discovered a general prepossession against us as a people both here and in America, that many seemed disposed to give in to the most violent counsels, . . . and that no measures could be proposed to either House so disadvantageous to us but what would probably be passed, or at least be strenuously supported.
>
> [He said] that nevertheless himself and a few more, from motives of justice and regard to those who had been the principal means of raising the colony to its present flourishing condition, were in some hopes that this torrent of violence might be a little [abated?] and that they would much rather that we ourselves if possible

---

[96] Ibid., 234.

should apply a remedy than that those should do it who seemed inclined to the severest [actions].

That as it seemed much more eligible, our Friends should at present decline accepting seats in the Assembly of their own accord [rather] than be totally excluded forever from a possibility of sitting there, which would certainly be the case was there a majority of our profession in the next assembly.

It was our unanimous opinion that the advice was the best that then occurred, and undertook to present the state of affairs to you in the strongest light we could, and in some respects took upon us to answer for your compliance, who we imagined were by this time sufficiently weary of your stations on various accounts.[97]

Fothergill, reflecting on the dynamic witness and shared principles of international Quakerism when under threat, wrote:

I need not now advise how to act. I may be mistaken in thinking so, but I apprehend it is not only the Society but the Province itself are obliged to us, and to those who have powerfully assisted us, in preventing a fatal blow to your constitution, which ends only in fixing one point which has been a matter of debate, but not an essential. Remember that our credit is pledged for you. We are daily told we shall repent of the pains we have taken—it's in your breasts whether we shall or not.[98]

Fothergill's next letter to Pemberton, that of April 3, 1756, brought the welcome news that an oath bill recently laid before Parliament was likely not to be voted upon if Friends "for the present should decline sitting in the Assembly." The influence of the president of the Privy Council had been obtained within the government and, by extension, with the proprietors.

Had it not been for Lord Granville's interposition . . . you would ere this time have been incapacitated (I mean

---

[97] John Fothergill to Israel Pemberton Jr., March 16, 1756, in John Fothergill, *Chain of Friendship*, 175–76. Fothergill identified the "person of high rank" as Thomas Villiers (1709–1786), a member of Parliament from Tamworth and soon to be made the first Baron Hyde and, later, Earl of Clarendon. Ibid., 178n4. For more on John Hanbury, see the discussion above on p. 319.

[98] Ibid., 176.

Friends) from ever sitting in any Assembly in America. This nobleman very early communicated to our Friend John Hanbury the temper of the people in power, the views they seemed to entertain, the endeavors he has used to prevent so violent a remedy, and gave him his opinion what seemed most proper to be done under the present circumstances and repeated it to several Friends who at J. Hanbury's request waited upon him on this occasion. The purport was that he thought it much better for us, and for the colony likewise, that those of our Society for the present should decline sitting in the Assembly, rather than be forced out by an Act of Parliament from hence, which was already framed and would be carried, if endeavors were not used by application to persons in power.[99]

After this, parliamentary consideration of the oath bill ceased. The pledged honor of the London Quakers was upheld when, in late June, six new Pennsylvania assemblymen were seated to fill the vacancies created by the formal resignations of James Pemberton and five of his Quaker colleagues because "many of our constituents seem of opinion that the present situation of public affairs call upon us for services in a military way, which, from a conviction of judgment . . . we cannot comply with."[100] And Thomas Penn apparently was reconciled to his brother-in-law, for he named his second surviving son, born in 1761, Granville Penn.

On April 14, 1756, the French and Indian War was formally initiated in Pennsylvania by lieutenant governor Robert Hunter Morris's "Proclamation of War against the Delawares," which he issued on his sole authority.[101] This was done despite his receipt two days earlier of *The Humble Address of some of the People called Quakers, residing in the city of Philadelphia, on behalf of themselves and many others*.[102] This address, a plea written in anticipation of Morris's imminent move, was signed by Israel Pemberton Jr. and five colleagues active in PYM and its working committees: Samuel Powell, Anthony Morris III, John Reynell, Samuel Preston Moore, and John Smith. These pacifist Quakers were pleading for the peace that William Penn had established.

---

[99] John Fothergill to Israel Pemberton Jr., April 3, 1756, ibid., 179.
[100] Hazard, *Pennsylvania Archives*, Eighth Series, 5:4087, 4245–50.
[101] See text in *MPCP*, 7:88–90.
[102] See text in *MPCP*, 84–86.

On April 13, Governor Morris struck fear in the hearts of members of the Provincial Council when he warned that "a great body of the inhabitants of the back counties" was intending a march on Philadelphia from Lancaster to press for war. Morris was then advised by the Council and several members of the Assembly to issue the war proclamation, and he did so the next day. It included a barbaric provision for scalp bounties that had different rates for the head hair of Indian men, women, and children. (Five weeks later, on May 17, Britain would declare war against France just as John Campbell, fourth Earl of Loudoun, was leaving London on his way to America, chosen by the Duke of Cumberland as the next commander in chief of all British troops and forces in North America.)

The war proclamation galvanized Pemberton. Through him, the Quakers delivered an address to the Assembly pleading for peace. He also conferred with Conrad Weiser (at that time ardent for peace), who recommended that William Locquies, a Lenape, be sent as a peace messenger to the Lenapes at Wyoming. Pemberton facilitated that plan, even personally conferring with Morris to obtain his consent. On April 19 Pemberton hosted a dinner in his Philadelphia home attended by fourteen Indians, foremost of whom was Scarouady, liaison of the Iroquois Nation to the Ohio Shawnees; more than ten pacifist Quakers, including Pemberton's wife Mary, his brother James, and Anthony Benezet; and, as translators, Weiser, Montour, and Daniel Clause, the deputy of William Johnson. The event, held with Morris's approval, raised such hopes for re-establishing Penn's harmony with the natives that the group was enlarged and held further meetings on April 21 and 23, resulting in the decisions to send Native American messengers to the Lenapes and have Scarouady report to Iroquoia.[103] Thus began the ambitious endeavors of Pemberton and his colleagues to heal the grievous breach in William Penn's holy experiment and restore the lost peace with the natives of the area.

---

[103] Theodore Thayer, "The Friendly Association," *PMHB* 67 (1943): 358–60; "Substance of an occasional conversation with several Indians after dinner at Israel Pemberton's, Philadelphia, 19 April 1756," ms., PYM Indian Commission Collection 1250, sheet 103 A–D, Haverford College Quaker Collection, Haverford College, Haverford, Pennsylvania; *MPCP*, 7:204–20; Jennings, *Empire of Fortune*, 269–70; Kenny, *Peaceable Kingdom Lost*, 84.

Teedyuscung at Easton:
An American Tragedy in Six Acts

Prologue

The mission to restore peace unfolded like a Greek tragedy, beginning with a prologue. For the instruction of the messengers to the Lenapes internally exiled from lands on and about the Delaware River westward to the Susquehanna River's Wyoming Valley, Pemberton, the manager of the peacemakers, diplomatically deferred to Morris, the warmaker answerable to Sir William Johnson. Johnson, who once had been New York's Indian agent but now served as Britain's superintendent of Indian affairs in the northern colonies, was angry because his own Indian policy had been crossed by Morris's proclamation against the Lenapes.[104] The messengers were Jagrea (a Mohawk and Scarouady's son-in-law), Newcastle (a Seneca and Quaker), and William Locquies. The message of the Iroquois Nation, in the words framed by Morris and given the bearers on April 26, advised the Lenapes to lay down the hatchet and surrender their English prisoners. For their compliance, the Iroquois would "persuade the English not to prosecute the war, but to accept fair, just and honorable terms."[105] Morris added his own word that he was "for peace," as were the descendants of those who had come over with William Penn. "All those are extremely desirous to interpose with the government, to receive the submission of the Delawares, and to overlook what is past, and establish for the future a firm and lasting agreement, peace and affection between us."[106] On May 31, 1756, the messengers returned to Philadelphia and delivered verbatim to "the governor and people of Pennsylvania" three answers, all compliant, received from the Lenapes and their associated tribes on the Susquehanna. They

---

[104] Benjamin Franklin's printing of the treaties made between Pennsylvania and its native peoples from 1736 to 1762 prefaces the treaties of 1756 with minutes of the conferences held in Philadelphia on April 26 instructing the messengers and on May 31 receiving the Lenapes' answers, as well as minutes of the Provincial Council at its June 8 meeting confirming agreement with the Lenapes regarding mutual commitments prior to a formal treaty conference. See Kalter, *Benjamin Franklin*, 181–87.

[105] Ibid., 182.

[106] Ibid.

reported the words of Teedyuscung, "a Delaware chief," who gave the principal answer of the Lenapes:

> Brother Onas, and the people of Pennsylvania, We rejoice to hear from you, and that you are willing to renew the old good understanding, and that you call to mind the first treaties of friendship made by Onas, our great friend, deceased, with our forefathers, when himself and his people first came over here. We take hold of these treaties with both our hands, and desire you will do the same, that a good understanding and true friendship may be re-established. Let us both take hold of these treaties with all our strength, we beseech you; we on our side will certainly do it.
>
> Brother Onas, What you said to us we took to heart, and it entered into our heart; and we speak to you from our heart; and we will deal honestly with you in every respect.
>
> Brother Onas, We desire you will look upon us with eyes of mercy. We are a very poor people; our wives and children are almost naked. We are void of understanding, and destitute of the necessaries of life. Pity us.

On June 8, Pennsylvania made its reply to the Lenapes and other Indians on the Susquehanna. The reply was announced by Lieutenant Governor Morris in the presence of several Provincial Council members; Richard Peters (secretary of both the province and the Proprietary Land Office and both a member and the clerk of the Council, thus making him the principal American agent of the proprietors who were at the center of, but made no appearance in, the unfolding drama); Conrad Weiser, the Indian agent for the province; and Jagrea and Newcastle, two of the three messengers. Welcoming the Indians' professions of friendship and good intentions and the confirmation of existing treaties, Morris called for "a public convention" or treaty conference and kindled "a council fire at the house of Conrad Weiser" at Tulpehocken, the Indians "always at liberty to name another [place]." At that council "all prisoners taken on both sides shall be delivered up" and the government will bring "a sufficiency of clothes and provisions" to relieve the Indians' distress. Further, because the Indians had laid down the hatchet, the messengers were to bear the Proclamation for Suspension of Hostilities, effective for thirty days, issued by Morris. Finally, Morris announced that at the request of Scarouady and other Iroquois, Pennsylvania would build a fort at Shamokin (the Forks of the Susquehanna) for the "protection of our friendly Indians, their wives and children."[107]

Following this prologue but before opening the first treaty conference, two outside events occurred, each important for peace. During June, James Pemberton and five other pacifist Quakers resigned their seats in the Provincial Assembly to make way for defense-minded legislators, thus keeping faith with John Fothergill and other Friends in London. And on July 22, Israel Pemberton led a large meeting of Friends to raise funds for work on behalf of the Indians. The success of the appeal led to the formal organization on December 1 that year of the Friendly Association for Regaining and Preserving Peace with the Indians by Pacific Measures.[108] The peace-making efforts of the Friendly Association began immediately after the July 22 meeting.

Easton 1

The action of the central drama was set not at Conrad Weiser's house at Tulpehocken but at the Forks of the Delaware. The location was chosen by the Lenapes and their allies, who had long called it "the Place at the Forks." In 1739 the 'place' had been given the new name of 'Easton,' and in 1752 Easton was made the seat of the new county of Northampton. Both these new names had dark connections to the grievances about to be exposed in the treaty negotiations, for they were chosen by Thomas Penn to honor his wife and her family whose estate was at Easton Neston in Northamptonshire, England. The Walking Purchase, which encompassed Northampton and other counties, had been plotted and perpetrated against the Forks Lenapes near the new Easton, and the fraud was exposed at the treaty conference of Easton 2.[109]

---

[107] Ibid., 185–87.

[108] Thayer, "The Friendly Association," 362, 364.

[109] The following table shows (1) the six treaty conferences held at Easton from 1756 to 1762 between Pennsylvania and the Lenapes and other Native American peoples, (2) the conference dates, and (3) the pages in Kalter where the Franklin text of each may be found for Easton 1 through 5 and in Johnson of the hearing record sent to the Crown following Easton 6:

Easton 1	(July 28–31, 1756)	Kalter, 187–99
Easton 2	(November 8–17, 1756)	Kalter, 199–225
Easton 3	(July 25–August 6, 1757)	Kalter, 255–89
Easton 4	(October 7–20, 1758)	Kalter, 290–333
Easton 5	(August 3–12, 1761)	Kalter, 334–57

Ending the Holy Experiment 1750–1781

Presiding at Easton 1 was Morris, in his last weeks as Pennsylvania's lieutenant governor. He was attended by Richard Peters, James Logan's son William, other Council members, three Indian commissioners from the Assembly, and Conrad Weiser as "interpreter for the Six Nations." The natives present were "Teedyuscung and fourteen other chiefs" as well as three "interpreters for the Delawares." Also attending was a "large company, consisting of officers of the Royal American Regiment, and of the provincial forces; magistrates and freeholders of this and neighboring provinces; and about forty citizens of the city of Philadelphia, chiefly of the people called Quakers." The military presence was intended to relieve Morris's fears for his own safety.

The foremost Quaker present was Israel Pemberton, prepared to spend what was necessary to assist the natives out of funds he himself had contributed to and collected from Quakers as a result of the July 22 meeting. On July 25 he arrived in Easton and, with three colleagues, waited on Morris at his lodgings to pay their respects. It was then that

> we first saw Teedyuscung who on our coming immediately expressed his regard for and confidence in the Quakers. We afterwards called and shook hands with him at his lodgings . . . now he saw [the Quakers] he felt [satisfaction] to the point of his heart and should not say anything to the governor unless the Quakers were present. To avoid offense we did not stay five minutes with him.* . . .
>
> * Soon after coming to town we were informed that the governor had given orders that no person should speak with the Indians, and a guard was set near their lodgings to prevent it.[110]

Easton 6   (June 18–28, 1762)   Johnson, 3:760–91, 794–818, 837–52

Sources: Kalter, *Benjamin Franklin*; William Johnson, *The Papers of Sir William Johnson* (Albany: University of the State of New York, Division of Archives and History, 1921).

[110] "Friendly Association Minutes, 1755–1757," p. 12a, Collection #AM 525, HSP. This important manuscript documents the Quaker presence and involvement in the first three Easton conferences, which was minimized in the treaty texts printed by Franklin and republished in Kalter, *Benjamin Franklin*. The same cited page also shows that on July 23–24, 1756, a wagon load of Indian goods and about twenty Quakers were, by Morris's misdirection, at Bethlehem while Morris, Teedyuscung, and others were at Easton.

The minutes kept by the Quakers also disclose that they were informed by Newcastle on July 26 that Teedyuscung and his party were now sober but "had been drinking intemperately several days before." Further, the Quakers learned that when Newcastle and Pumpshear (his interpreter) were questioned by Morris in some matters they had previously discussed with Pemberton, they referred Morris to Pemberton,

> with which the governor appeared highly displeased and charged Pumpshear to inform said Pemberton and by that means all the Quakers in town, that he should treat them as his Majesty's enemies if they held any conferences with the Indians on any matter relating to the government, and that he had strictly charged the same to be observed by all persons whatsoever on his first coming.[111]

The next day Morris went fishing, the Indians were drinking, forty or so Quakers were now present, and Conrad Weiser had at last arrived. Thus, the stage was set for the first act.

On July 28 the conference opened. After a few words of welcome, Morris said the messengers had not returned answers from the Indians to some of his words of invitation. Immediately, Teedyuscung took center stage and began answering with authority, first reminding all that he had been waiting at Easton "several days, smoking my pipe with patience, expecting to meet you here." He pointed out there were ten Indian nations present,[112] all "authorizing me to treat with you, and what I do they will all confirm." He warned against self-appointed chiefs, or kings, of the Indians who had "wild and irregular way[s] of doing business," such as out of the public eye and "in the bushes." He assured his hearers that "there are only two kings appointed to transact public business, of which I am one." He concluded with a challenge to "the English, and particularly the Governor of Pennsylvania":

> Be strong; look round you; enable us to engage every Indian Nation we can; put the means into our hands; be sure [to] perform every promise you have made to us; in particular do not pinch matters neither with us or other

---

[111] Ibid., p. 12b.

[112] Members of five tribes from the Iroquois League (the Tuscaroras were absent) were present, along with Lenapes, Wename, Munsey, Mawhickon, and Nanticokes. See Kalter, *Benjamin Franklin*, 255; Thomson, *An Enquiry*, 84.

Indians; we will help you; but we are poor, and you are rich; make us strong, and we will use our strength for you; and, besides this, what you do, do quickly; the times are dangerous; they will not admit of delay. . . . Do it effectually, and do it with all possible dispatch.[113]

Morris concluded that day's meeting by promising to consider with his Council what Teedyuscung had said and to answer when ready.

The conference resumed the next day, and again the Quakers were in attendance "by crowding ourselves in" and "kept minutes of most that was said, though the hasty and inconsiderate method in which the Indians' answers were received, rendered it impracticable to be as exact as the importance of the occasion and subject required."[114] Morris laid bare the quandary the province professed to be in:

When our back inhabitants were attacked last fall, we at first were at a loss to know from whence the blow came; and were much surprised when we were informed that it was given by our old friends and neighbors the cousins of our brethren the Six Nations; we wondered at it; and the more so, as we had not, to our knowledge, given them any just cause of offence.[115]

Morris continued his feigned ignorance of what had caused the Great Cove massacre by reciting that although Pennsylvania had been ready to "revenge the injury we had received," it had deferred to the Six Nations as they took control over their "nephews" the Lenapes through the good offices of William Johnson. He concluded by noting that "your whole people" are invited to the council fire, "the greater the number that shall come, the more acceptable it will be to me . . . but then you must bring with you also all the prisoners you have taken during these disturbances." Then, to fill Teedyuscung with pride and raise him to a distinctive status, Morris declared:

Great works require strong hands and many; this is a good and a great one, the work of peace. . . . I therefore desire your assistance for Pennsylvania in this matter;

---

[113] Kalter, *Benjamin Franklin*, 189–90.
[114] "Friendly Association Minutes," p. 13b.
[115] Kalter, *Benjamin Franklin*, 190.

having great influence with many who live far distant from us, you are esteemed, and will be heard; we therefore choose you as agent and counselor for this province; engage in it heartily. You ought to do it; you owe it to the country in which you were born; you owe it to your brethren the English; you owe it to your uncles the Six Nations; you owe it to your own people over which you preside.[116]

Teedyuscung, without conferring with his advisers and colleagues, responded immediately to Morris. He declared that he had received the invitation to this treaty just as the Iroquois League was removing the shame it had imposed on the Lenapes at the 1742 Treaty of Philadelphia. Lifting up a large belt, he said:

> This belt denotes that the Six Nations by their chiefs have lately renewed their Covenant Chains with us; formerly we were accounted women, and employed only in women's business; but now they have made men of us, and as such we are now come to this treaty. Having this authority as a man to make peace, I have it in my hand. . . . This belt holds together ten nations; we are in the middle between the French and English; look at it. There are but two chiefs of the ten nations; they are now looking on, and their attention is fixed, to see who are disposed really for peace . . . see the dangerous circumstances I am in; strong men on both sides; hatchets on both sides; whoever does incline to peace, him will I join.[117]

That evening Teedyuscung and a son were the guests of Morris at dinner.

On the third day of the treaty, July 30, the business was entirely ceremonial. Morris delivered the Indian goods, noting that "a part of this present was given by the people called Quakers

---

[116] Ibid., 192.

[117] Ibid., 192–93. Charles Thomson, who was assisting Pemberton and acting as secretary to Teedyuscung at the Easton treaties, kept his own notes of these proceedings and used them in *An Enquiry into the Causes of the Alienation of the Delaware and Shawanese Indians from the British Interest*, printed in London in 1759, of which Thomson was the unnamed author. At this point in the speech, Thomson records Teedyuscung saying, contradicting the words given him by Richard Peters in the above quoted official text, that "whoever was willing to guarantee these lands to the Indians, him they would join; but whoever would not comply with these terms of peace, the ten nations would join against him and strike him." Thomson, *An Enquiry*, 96.

... as a particular testimony of their regard and affection for the Indians, and their earnest desire to promote the good work of peace in which we are now engaged."[118] Teedyuscung returned thanks and pledged anew his best efforts to promote peace as he visited "all the Indians far and near" to encourage them to come to the enlarged treaty to be held at Easton in several months. He entered two serious reservations about his mission, however, saying he had neither influence with the Ohio Indians nor control over the French Indians from Ohio who might make mischief on the east side of the Susquehanna.

The treaty ended with a dinner provided by the province, after which the Quakers took their leave, Teedyuscung parting with them "in a very affectionate manner." The minutes, however, continue with a meeting of Morris and his Council to determine whether the belt Teedyuscung had given Morris should be kept or returned. Weiser was stumped and brought in Newcastle, the messenger (and Quaker Seneca), who advised that, it being of "great consequence," the Iroquois belt Teedyuscung had handed to Morris should be preserved with the Council wampum and that another of comparable value designed and presented to Teedyuscung the next morning. Indian women were called in to make the great belt overnight. The official minutes next record that Teedyuscung, "who was very irregular in his visits, as well as in his discourses, bolted all of a sudden into the room, and with a high tone of voice" addressed Morris:

> Brother, I desire all that I have said, and you have said to one another, may be taken down aright; some speak in the dark; do not let us do so; let all be clear and known. What is the reason the governor holds councils so close in his hands, and by candle light? . . . What is the reason the governor makes him a woman, meaning, Why does he confer with Indians without sending for him, to be present and hear what was said?[119]

Morris answered that "he holds councils on a hill; has no secrets; never sits in swamps, but speaks his mind openly to the world. . . . The women were sent for to make a belt, not to council." Teedyuscung "seemed well pleased" and parted, saying darkly, "He that won't make peace must die."

---

[118] Kalter, *Benjamin Franklin*, 194.
[119] Ibid., 196.

On July 31, Morris met with his Council, Weiser, Teedyuscung, and Newcastle. First, Weiser asked Newcastle to report any messages the Lenapes had received from the Iroquois Nation before coming to Easton. The Council heard this:

> Cousins, the Delaware Indians, you will remember that you are our women; our forefathers made you so, and put a petticoat on you, and charged you to be true to us, and lie with no other man; but of late you have suffered the string that tied your petticoat to be cut loose by the French, and you lay with them, and so became a common bawd . . . but notwithstanding this, we have still an esteem for you, and as you have thrown off the cover of your modesty, and become stark naked, which is a shame for a woman, you must be made a man; and we now give you a little power, but it will be some time till you shall be a complete man. . . .
>
> Cousins, the English and French fight for our lands; let us be strong, and lay our hands to it, and defend it; in the mean time turn your eyes and ears to us, and the English, our brethren, and you will live as well as we do.[120]

Morris then presented to Newcastle and Teedyuscung the new "belt now making," prayed for "a speedy and honorable peace, and a return of the offices of love and friendship between the Indians and their brethren the English," and declared both Newcastle and Teedyuscung to be agents for the province, giving "them authority to do the public business together." Thus ended Easton 1.

Easton 2

Easton 2 opened one hundred days later, on November 8. There were important cast changes. In the place of Morris as lieutenant governor of Pennsylvania (and, thus, the attending 'Onas') was William Denny, recommended to Thomas Penn by the Duke of Cumberland after the removal of Morris for his preemptive war declaration to the Lenapes as well as his scalp bounties. Two new Indian commissioners from the Assembly attended, Benjamin Franklin and William Masters, who was a colleague of Franklin and a trustee of the Academy of

---

[120] Ibid., 197.

Philadelphia. Teedyuscung was now minuted as the "Delaware king, Speaker of the Six Nations," attended not by other Indian chiefs as before but by "Delaware Indians, Shawanese, Mohiccons." As at Easton 1, there were officers of the provincial forces and the Royal American regiment and "a number of gentlemen and freeholders from the several counties and from the city of Philadelphia." Those from Philadelphia were "chiefly of the people called Quakers" according to Charles Thomson, who had come to Easton with Israel Pemberton.[121]

The conference, by agreement, was begun by Teedyuscung, who referred to the earlier treaty and to the pains he had been through to accomplish his mission of bringing Indians "far and near" for an enlarged peace conference, asserting that he had been "true and faithful to my promises." Then, "in conformity to an ancient and good custom established among our ancestors," he proceeded to open the eyes and ears of all present and to "remove all obstructions out of your throats." Finally, he dismissed "some [unidentified] bad reports" that had "lately been spread, which deserve to be no more minded than the whistling of birds." Whereupon he said he was done, and sat down. The curt manner of this mercurial Lenape king may have been triggered by Denny marching "from his lodging to the place of conference, guarded by a party of the Royal Americans in the front and on the flanks, and a detachment of Colonel Weiser's provincials, in sub-divisions, in the rear, with colors flying, drums beating, and music playing, which order was always observed in going to the place of conference."[122] Denny, too, responded very briefly, thanking Teedyuscung for his speech, dismissing idle reports as the "chirping of birds," and quickly reciprocating the ritual of opening eyes and ears and "particularly the passage from your heart to your mouth, that in what you have to say to this government they may both concur, nor the mouth utter anything but what is first conceived in the heart. And I promise you openness and sincerity in everything I shall speak." The first day of Easton 2 had an early ending. (The Quaker records alone disclose that Provincial Secretary Peters requested Charles Thomson "to assist in taking

---

[121] Thomson, *An Enquiry*, 99; "Friendly Association Minutes," 23b.

[122] All quoted matter for the November 8 meeting is from Kalter, *Benjamin Franklin*, 199–201. Kalter notes that the Lenapes placed high value on free speech and that the display of arms at treaty negotiations might have appeared to—or been intended to—threaten that speech. Ibid., 224n6.

minutes, which he complied with, and continued to do so, until the conclusion of the treaty."[123])

The second day was brevity itself. Teedyuscung made the only recorded speech, and in it he simply repeated his earlier message, saying pointedly to Denny that what William Penn had

> said to the Indians is fresh in our minds and memory, and I believe it is in yours. The Indians and Governor Penn agreed well together; this we all remember, and it was not a small matter that would then have separated us. And now, as you fill the same station he did in this province, it is in your power to act the same part.[124]

Although the conference did not convene on November 10 and 11 because of concerns among Indian warriors in the area regarding Teedyuscung's safety, separate meetings of the several parties were held and Council minutes were kept for November 10 and 12. Of significance are the minutes of the Council meeting on the tenth, which considered what answer Denny should make to Teedyuscung's speech. The minutes conclude with this: "At a meeting of the Governor and Commissioners, it was mentioned, that the Indians had surmised as if injustice had been done them in land affairs, the governor therefore added to his answer a paragraph, putting the question in plain terms."[125] The comment itself is important, as shall soon be seen, and undoubtedly was included because Franklin was present as a commissioner and, being also the editor and printer of the treaty minutes, had the opportunity to maintain a fairer and more complete record.

The conference resumed in the afternoon of November 12 with Denny's answer to Teedyuscung given in a gentler tone than anything yet heard. His words seemed to come from a genuine need to know the truth.

> I throw a large log into the council fire, that it may blaze up to the heavens, and spread the blessings of peace far and wide. . . .

> You was pleased to tell me the other day, that the league of friendship made by your forefathers was as yet fresh in your memory; you said that it was made so strong that a

---

[123] Samuel Parrish, *Some Chapters in the History of the Friendly Association for Regaining and Preserving Peace with the Indians by Pacific Measures* (Philadelphia: Friends Historical Association, 1877), 30.

[124] Kalter, *Benjamin Franklin*, 202.

[125] Ibid., 203.

small thing would not easily break it. As we are now met together, at a council fire, kindled by us both, and have promised on both sides to be free and open to one another, I must ask you, how that league of friendship came to be broken? Have we, the governor or people of Pennsylvania, done you any kind of injury? If you think we have, you should be honest, and tell us your hearts. You should have made complaints before you struck us, for so it was agreed in our ancient league.... Speak your mind plainly on this head, and tell us if you have any just cause of complaint, what it is.[126]

Denny told Teedyuscung to take "full time to consider" his answer as it was "a matter of consequence."

The answer came the next day. Teedyuscung opened with an extensive ritual for healing the wounds opened by the distress and confusion of the war between the parties and then recounted receiving at Wyoming the governor's messenger, who accused him of attacking the English, and reported the futility of his denials. Next, he protested that "the King of England, and of France, have settled or wrought this land, so as to coop us up as if in a pen. Our foolish and ignorant young men, when they saw the proceeding of this enemy, and the things that were told them, believed them, and were persuaded ... to strike our brethren the English," a reference to the French-influenced Ohio Lenapes over whom Teedyuscung had no control. Evidencing his great difficulty in speaking the complete truth to power, he added:

> but this is not the principal cause; some things that have passed in former times, both in this and other governments, were not well pleasing to the Indians; indeed, they thought them wrong; but as I said before, they were not the principal cause.... Now, brother, I have told you the truth, as you desired me, and also the uneasiness of my mind, because I verily believe it was our duty to go to the very bottom, be it as bad as it will.[127]

But Denny persisted, realizing that Teedyuscung, who he said "had mentioned grievances received by the Indians from this and other governments," was not at the "very bottom." Abandoning with a passion his reticence and uneasiness, the Lenape king said:

---

[126] Ibid., 205.
[127] Ibid., 207.

> This very ground that is under me (striking it with his foot) was my land and inheritance, and is taken from me by fraud; when I say this ground, I mean all the land lying between Tohiccon Creek and Wyoming, on the River Susquehanna. . . . When I have sold lands fairly, I look upon them to be really sold. A bargain is a bargain. Though I have sometimes had nothing for the lands I have sold but broken pipes, or such trifles. . . . The Proprietaries, who have purchased their lands from us cheap, have sold them too dear to poor people, and the Indians have suffered for it. . . . Although you have purchased our lands from our forefathers on so reasonable terms, yet now at length you will not allow us to cut a little wood to make a fire; nay, hinder us from hunting, the only means left us of getting our livelihood.[128]

Next, Denny asked Teedyuscung "what he meant by fraud and forgery"[129] and was told:

> When one man had formerly liberty to purchase lands, and he took a deed from the Indians for it, and then dies, if, after his death his children forge a deed like the true one, with the same Indian names to it, and thereby take lands from the Indians which they never sold—this is fraud. Also, when one king has lands beyond the river, and another has lands on this side, both bounded by rivers, creeks and springs, which cannot be moved, and the Proprietaries, greedy to purchase lands, buy of one king what belongs to the other—this likewise is fraud.[130]

Denny asked whether Teedyuscung had been so used, and received the final answer:

> Yes;—I have been served so in this province. All the land extending from Tohiccon, over the Great Mountain, to Wyoming, has been taken from me by fraud; for when I had agreed to sell the land to the old Proprietary by the course of the river, the young Proprietaries came and got

---

[128] Ibid., 208–9.

[129] According to Thomson, Teedyuscung said the ground was "taken from me by fraud and forgery." Thomson, *An Enquiry*, 100.

[130] Ibid., 100–101; also Kalter, *Benjamin Franklin*, 209.

it run by a straight course by the compass, and by that means took in double the quantity intended to be sold. . . .

I have told you the truth, and have opened my mind fully. I did not intend to speak thus, but I have done it at this time, at your request . . . you should look into your own hearts, and consider what is right, and that do.[131]

The next day, November 14, Denny held a Provincial Council meeting with the two members present at Easton 2—William Logan and Richard Peters, each associated, one by birth and the other by official succession, with a key perpetrator of the fraud alleged by Teedyuscung. The minutes record Conrad Weiser's participation in the meeting with the councilors.

When Denny asked Weiser, the adviser present with the most direct knowledge of these problems, about "the foundation of the complaint . . . as to the frauds," Weiser temporized, saying that "few or none of the Delawares present, as he could recollect, originally owned any of these lands, or any land in this province; that if any injury was done, it was done to others, who were either dead or gone, some to the Ohio, some to other places." He had "heard" that the lands had been sold to William Penn and paid for by him. Thomas and John Penn had renewed their father's agreement and again settled the "limits" in person with the resident Indians "and, accordingly, a line was soon after run by Indians and surveyors." He reported that later, when the Lenapes complained, "a Great Council of the Six Nations, held at Philadelphia in the Year 1743" examined the deeds by the Lenapes to the Proprietaries and, after hearings, "declared the complaints of . . . the Delawares to be unreasonable, and were very angry with them for complaining without cause."[132] Peters confirmed what Weiser had said, having "heard things to the same effect." Since

---

[131] Kalter, *Benjamin Franklin*, 209–10. Thomson gives the first paragraph quoted here but not the one following. Instead, Thomson writes: "It may be deemed foreign to the purpose to mention the opposition that was made by Secretary Peters and C. Weiser to the asking the Indians the cause of their uneasiness, and how the Secretary threw down his pen, and declared he would take no minutes when the King came to complain of the Proprietaries." Thomson, *An Enquiry*, 101. At this point, according to Parrish, "Charles Thomson, was requested by the Governor, to record all that passed, which, it is asserted, he did with great precision." Parrish, *History of the Friendly Association*, 34.

[132] Kalter, *Benjamin Franklin*, 210–11. Thomson's *An Enquiry* makes no reference to a 1743 council meeting of the Iroquois in Philadelphia, nor has any been found in *MPCP*.

the relevant papers were in Philadelphia, Denny "proposed to let the Indians know, that as to the particular grievances they had mentioned, they should be thoroughly examined into, well considered, and, if justly founded, amply redressed as quickly as the nature of the business would admit."[133]

The same minutes for November 14 show that Denny then conferred (presumably separately and apart) with the Indian commissioners, in which he heard the opinion of Benjamin Franklin and his three colleagues that "such promises had been frequently made the Indians by governors of other provinces, and not performed, and these people might consider them as now made with a design to evade giving them redress. . . . It would be better, whether the claim was just or unjust, to offer them immediate satisfaction . . . judging this would effectually remove all their uneasiness."[134]

On November 15 all parties met again in conference to hear Denny's reply to the fraud and forgery charge. Having no documentary evidence to read and study and no experts present with immediate knowledge of the facts willing to advise him, he was without guidance and, hence, left to improvise and keep avenues open without making a judgment but yet giving some satisfaction. Following preliminary remarks, he told Teedyuscung:

> Brother, I am but lately come among you; the grievances you mention are of old date. If former Indian kings have, as you say, sometimes sold more land than they had a right to sell, in so doing they injured us, and we, as well as you, have cause to complain of them. . . . Moreover, many people, both English and Indians, concerned in the former purchases of lands, are now dead; and as you do not understand writings and records, it may be hard for me to satisfy you of the truth, though my predecessors dealt ever so uprightly; therefore, to show our sincere desire to heal the present differences, and live in eternal peace with you our brethren, tell me what will satisfy you for the injustice you suppose has been done you in the purchase of lands in this province; and if it be in my

---

[133] Ibid., 211.
[134] Ibid.

power, you shall have immediate satisfaction, whether it be justly due you or not.[135]

Changing the rules of this global game, Denny then announced that because the British Crown had given the general management of all Indian affairs in this part of America to Sir William Johnson as general agent, it would be necessary for Teedyuscung and a deputation of his chief men to go to Johnson's council fire on the Mohawk River in New York to present their case and "take advice as to your future conduct." To conclude, he presented the Indians with a quantity of goods, necessities for the coming cold season, noting that "a large part of them is given by the people called Quakers."

Teedyuscung answered the next day, November 15. After explaining that nurturing the growth of peace is like nurturing seeds of corn from planting to harvest, he declined to consider the question of damages due those Indians wronged by the claimed land fraud. He noted that "there are many more concerned in this matter, not now present; and though many who have suffered are now in the grave, yet their descendants feel the weight, and the more now for the time they have waited."[136] He asked for "Liberty to all Persons and Friends to search into these matters" and promised to return in the spring "with as great a force of Indians as I can get, to your satisfaction." Then, reflecting the counsel he was receiving from Pemberton, Thomson, and other advisers, he made his own unexpected, game-changing request:

> I think it prudent, in order to prevent misunderstandings, that I should be furnished with a copy of what is done, as well in the conferences held here last summer as at this time; for though I am not able to read, yet others may; it will be a great satisfaction to have it in my power to show to others what has passed between this government and me. What is committed to writing will not easily be lost, and will be of great use to all, and better regarded; and I would have the names and seals of all that have been concerned in transacting this business put to it.[137]

---

[135] Ibid., 213–14.

[136] Ibid., 217.

[137] Ibid., 218. See also Parrish, who recorded, "He urged that Friends might have liberty to examine into their complaints, and asked for a copy of the minutes of the treaty." Parrish, *History of the Friendly Association*, 39.

This ended the formal meetings of Easton 2, but Franklin included two additional entries. Each involved Franklin and his fellow Indian commissioners. In connection with the November 17 Council meeting of Denny, Logan, and Peters with Weiser, the commissioners advised Denny to fix a sum in satisfaction of the claimed damages. Weiser in private then asked Teedyuscung if this was agreeable and heard again the answer that the Lenape king had no such power, "the people to whom the land belonged being absent." It would have to await his return next spring. Then, the Council being opened to the Indians and all others, Denny confirmed the continuing appointment of Teedyuscung "as the counselor and agent of this province." He also invited all friendly Indians to move near the provincial fort at Shamokin, where they would find a store of goods and safe habitation. Most importantly, Denny acknowledged that "peace is now settled between us by the assistance of the Most High." Teedyuscung also spoke in favor of the peace "now settled, and implored the assistance of the Most High to bring it to perfection." The treaty conference ended on the sad news of Newcastle's death in Philadelphia from smallpox.[138]

The second additional entry, extracted from the minutes of the Pennsylvania House of Representatives of January 29, 1757, is a paper presented to the House by Franklin and his three fellow Indian commissioners after they had reviewed the official minutes of Easton 2 kept by Secretary Peters. They noted in the paper:

> We think it necessary to observe to the House, that we conceive the warmth and earnestness with which they [the Indians] insisted on the wrongs that had been done them in the purchases of land, are much too faintly expressed in this account of the conference. That we were not present at the palliating hearsay accounts of the Walking Purchase said to be given the governor by Mr. Weiser and Mr. Peters . . . though, by the concluding paragraphs . . . it may seem as if we were. But we well remember, that the transaction of that Walk at Easton was universally given up as unfair, and not to be defended, even the Secretary [Peters], though he did say, that he believed satisfaction was afterwards made the Indians, and that this was the only instance in which any foundation of complaint had ever been given them, yet

---

[138] All quotations from the November 17 meeting are from Kalter, *Benjamin Franklin*, 219–21.

this he allowed was (in his own words) unworthy of any government.[139]

In the spring of 1757, the time appointed by Teedyuscung for the gathering of Indians personally concerned in the award of damages for the land fraud, another treaty opened. It met at Harris's Ferry (now Harrisburg) on the Susquehanna. Representatives of all six tribes of the Iroquois Nation came to this treaty, as well as Nanticokes, Lenapes, and Conestogas. Those gathered were initially presided over by George Croghan, the Irish-born former trader in Ohio who was now William Johnson's deputy agent in Indian affairs. By April 7, the conference site had been relocated to Lancaster, where Denny and his party arrived on May 9. The treaty conference, opened at last by Denny on May 12, was attended by his Council, the speaker, and a committee of the Assembly, magistrates of Lancaster "with a great number of other gentlemen," interpreters (Weiser served for the province), and Indian deputies.

These Lancaster meetings ended on May 20—without Teedyuscung making an appearance. On April 20 those at Lancaster heard he was "so long detained on the way by the scarcity of provisions" that Denny had supplies sent to him.[140] On May 9 it was reported he told messengers at Tioga, "You have been at a great deal of trouble in sending messages to us . . . but the persons you employed are young warriors, and not counselors, therefore unfit for such business; likewise the belts you have sent, in comparison, are no more than strings; but if you will send to call us together, and send proper belts, and wise men to take us by the hand, we will come down and give you a meeting."[141] Then, on May 19 the conference heard the Mohawk chief Little Abraham, a speaker for the Iroquois Nation. After relating that the Lenapes had been given lands "to plant and hunt on at Wyoming and Juniata, on Susquehanna," he complained

---

[139] Ibid., 221–22.

[140] Ibid., 231.

[141] Ibid., 235; see also Thomson, *An Enquiry*, 105–6. Thomson also reports that at an Iroquois-Lenape meeting at Otsaningo, "the Delawares had thrown off their dependence, and they would no longer acknowledge any but the Senecas as their uncles and superiors" (p. 107). This realignment probably was in recognition of the move of the Lenape Nation's prominent warriors from the east to the Ohio country and their resulting proximity to the Senecas, who lived at the western gate to the Iroquois Nation. Teedyuscung, who had been a Lenape chief in the Jerseys before relocating to the Forks of the Delaware, was sure to have acquiesced to this.

against the Crown and province by telling Johnson (who was not present) and Denny (who was):

> But you, covetous of land, made plantations there, and spoiled their hunting grounds; they then complained to us, and we looked over those lands, and found their complaints to be true.[142]

The final formal meeting was held on May 20. The Indians remained for the distribution of the customary presents the following day, and their chiefs met yet again with Denny on May 22 to hear his gracious message that was sent to Teedyuscung:

> I do by this belt of wampum invite you to come down as soon as it will suit your convenience, and leave it to you to bring with you your uncles, the Senecas . . . to open your hearts to us your brethren; and if it shall appear that you have been defrauded of your lands, or received any other injuries from this province, I do promise you shall receive satisfaction. . . . Your brother Onas, in England . . . acquaints me he is willing to have the injuries complained of fully heard and settled as soon as possible.[143]

The native peoples then returned home to plant their crops.

Two weeks prior to Easton 3's opening, a committee of Pemberton and four others was appointed by the Friendly Association, which had been contributing to the needs of the Indians and the peace effort since the previous July 22, to meet with Denny to receive "the continuance of his approbation of our attendance as heretofore."[144] Instead, they received this strongly written denial of their request, a denial that evidenced the extent of the Penn brothers' opposition to the Quakers and their reach into the highest levels of the British government to achieve their purposes.

> The Proprietaries have acquainted me [Denny], that the Earl of Halifax has communicated to them, with very strong expressions of dissatisfaction, a treaty held with the Indians at Philadelphia, by the people called Quakers, which his Lordship was pleased to think the most extraordinary procedure he had ever seen in persons who are on the same footing only, with all others of the King's

---

[142] Kalter, *Benjamin Franklin*, 244; Thomson, *An Enquiry*, 108.
[143] Kalter, *Benjamin Franklin*, 250; Thomson, *An Enquiry*, 110.
[144] Parrish, *History of the Friendly Association*, 69.

private subjects, to presume to treat with *Foreign Princes*; and further, that as the suffering any one part of the King's subjects, whether of different profession of religion, or however else distinguished, to treat, or act as mediators between a province in which they live, and any independent people, is the highest invasion of his Majesty's Prerogative Royal, and of the worst consequence, as it must tend to divide the King's subjects into different parties and interests.... The Proprietaries, therefore, have directed me not to suffer these people or any other body or particular Society in Pennsylvania, to concern themselves in any treaty with the Indians, or on any pretense to suffer presents from such persons to be given to the Indians.... It would be prudent in you to decline going in a body, your attendance at treaties as a distinct Society, having given great offence to the ministry.[145]

In response, Pemberton and his fellow committee members wrote a memorial[146] to Denny on behalf of the Friendly Association, but the lieutenant governor "peremptorily refused to reason with them upon the subject."[147] The Friendly Association minute book only has blank pages where the account of the proceedings of Easton 3 should be entered. The extant record of the treaty conferences is in the official minutes printed by Franklin (and made for Croghan) as well as the notes kept by Richard Peters for the Penns and by Charles Thomson for Teedyuscung.

Easton 3

The third treaty conference at Easton began on July 25, 1757. There, finally, appeared "Teedyuscung, King of the Delawares, living on Susquehanna, who is empowered by the ten following nations, viz. Lenape, Wename, Munsey, Mawhickon, Tiawco, or

---

[145] Ibid., 69–70. The "Earl of Halifax" reference is to George Montague-Dunk (1716–1771), 2nd Earl of Halifax and president of the Board of Trade and Plantations from 1748 to 1761. The "treaty held with the Indians at Philadelphia" is a reference to Pemberton's dinner party to discuss peace that was held for the Indians and others in his home on April 19, 1756, to which lieutenant governor Morris had given his prior consent.

[146] Samuel Hazard, ed., *Hazard's Register of Pennsylvania*, 16 vols. (Philadelphia: Wm. F. Geddes, 1831–1835), 5:359–62.

[147] Parrish, *History of the Friendly Association*, 74.

Nanticokes, and the Senecas, Onondagas, Cayugas, Oneidas, and Mohawks, to settle all differences subsisting between them and their brethren the English."[148] So reads the opening paragraph of the conference minutes prepared for Croghan, which Franklin chose to print.[149] William Denny presided on July 25, and those present were members of his Council (including William Logan); Isaac Norris II, the Assembly speaker, with five Assembly members, four of whom were the Indian commissioners (Franklin was no longer a commissioner, having gone to London in June pursuant to his January appointment as the Assembly's agent to negotiate with the Penns over provincial matters); interpreters; Indians ("about three hundred men, women, and children"); and "a number of gentlemen of the city of Philadelphia, and others, inhabitants of this province."[150]

The Quakers must have heeded Denny's admonition because their presence is scarcely noted at Easton 3 in the official minutes.[151] Thomson did attend, however, and was recognized as clerk to take minutes for Teedyuscung. His notes reveal much more about the dynamics of Easton 3 than do the official Croghan minutes, which were written for the benefit of Johnson and the Crown. Thomson reveals that the first four conference days were spent resolving Teedyuscung's request to Denny that he should appoint his own secretary in case of another incident in which a clerk would "throw down his pen, and declare he would not take minutes when complaints were made against the Proprietors."[152] Denny refused and was supported by Croghan, who invoked the authority of Johnson. But Teedyuscung would not relent, coming "to believe there was a design to lead him on blindfold, and in the dark, or to take advantage of his ignorance."[153] Teedyuscung's request, supported by his council at home, became a demand and a condition of his continuing the treaty, whereupon Denny relented. The first meeting, as recorded in the official minutes, began on July 25 with Thomson being called to the table as the appointed clerk to take minutes for Teedyuscung.[154]

---

[148] Kalter, *Benjamin Franklin*, 255.

[149] Ibid., 287–88n1.

[150] Ibid., 256.

[151] Ibid., 272, 282.

[152] Thomson, *An Enquiry*, 110.

[153] Ibid., 111.

[154] Kalter, *Benjamin Franklin*, 256; Thomson, *An Enquiry*, 112.

Ending the Holy Experiment 1750–1781

Parts of Teedyuscung's earliest speech seem "dark and confused," a characterization used in both the official minutes and Thomson's notes, which Thomson explains resulted from "four or five days" of Teedyuscung's being "kept almost continually drunk ... more especially as the interpreter, at the time the speech was delivered, was dozed with liquor and want of sleep." Thereafter, "by the interposition of his council," the Lenape king was "restrained from liquor."[155] Yet, even while so impaired, Teedyuscung carefully laid the foundation of his cause. He requested the production of the "writings and deeds by which you [the Penns] hold the land, and let them be read in public and examined, that it may be fully known from what Indians you have bought the lands you hold, and how far your purchases extend, that copies of the whole may be laid before King George."[156]

Teedyuscung asserted that the Lenapes intended to settle at Wyoming on the Susquehanna and wanted boundaries to be fixed between the Indians and others, with prohibitions against any sales by the Indians or purchases by others, so that we may "have a certain country fixed for our own use and the use of our children for ever."[157]

And he desired instructors for his people in building houses at Wyoming and in making "necessaries"; in the Christian religion; and in reading and writing. In addition, he asked for the establishment of fair trade "between us" and for the appointment of honest, competent traders.[158]

When told that, notwithstanding earlier understandings, he must again present his case, this time before Sir William Johnson at Mount Johnson on the Mohawk River in Iroquoia for final determination, he refused, insisting that he would present his reasons in a speech prepared in his own council and read to the treaty conferees, "to follow the example of the governor." When Teedyuscung came to the treaty gathering with his speech, Denny and Croghan successfully blocked it being read, insisting the Lenape king must deliver it from memory, no doubt a test of his sobriety. Noting their inconsistency in denying him "the privilege they had taken themselves," Teedyuscung declared he would not go to Sir William Johnson because he did not know him. Further,

---

[155] Thomson, *An Enquiry*, 114.
[156] Kalter, *Benjamin Franklin*, 265; Thomson, *An Enquiry*, 115.
[157] Kalter, *Benjamin Franklin*, 265; Thomson, *An Enquiry*, 115–16.
[158] Kalter, *Benjamin Franklin*, 265; Thomson, *An Enquiry*, 116.

he argued, Johnson was settled among the Iroquois, "who had been instrumental to this misunderstanding, by the manner in which they had heretofore treated them [the Lenapes], and by selling lands in this province, and, lastly, because deferring matters might again embroil us in war."[159]

Faced with the strengthened determination and improving negotiating skills of this native leader, Thomson notes that Denny embarked upon a devious plot to withhold the truth on the crucial issue of land titles by scheming to produce for the Lenapes an incomplete set of deeds.

> The Governor, finding that Teedyuscung was not to be put off, resolved in appearance to comply with his request [for deeds]. But as it was agreed not to deliver up all the deeds, and as this might give umbrage to the Indians, Mr. Weiser and Mr. Croghan were privately sent to practice [to scheme] with the King, and to get him to be content with the delivery of a part, alleging that the whole of the deeds was not brought up, but such only as were necessary, and relating to his complaint and the late purchases. Part of two days being spent in these practices, and the Indians in the mean time plied with liquor, the Governor met the Indians, and having assigned some late orders from the King's ministers as the cause of his referring Teedyuscung to Sir William Johnson, he told him, that as he so earnestly desired to see the deeds for the lands, mentioned in the last treaty, he had brought them with him, and would give Teedyuscung copies of them agreeable to his request. Hereupon some deeds being laid upon the table, the Governor desired that all further debates and altercations concerning lands might rest till they should be fully examined and looked into by Sir William Johnson, in order to be transmitted to the King for his royal determination. When Teedyuscung was made sensible that the deeds were delivered, without examining to see what deeds they were, he immediately, in the name of the ten nations, solemnly concluded a peace. The reading [of] the deeds was put off till next day.[160]

---

[159] Thomson, *An Enquiry*, 117–18.
[160] Ibid., 118–19.

The first reader undoubtedly was Charles Thomson, the orphaned Presbyterian and classics scholar who for the past year had been serving as head of the Friends Latin School in Philadelphia and as Pemberton's expert on the treaties, deeds, and other documents relating to the Indians found in the accessible public records of Pennsylvania. He tersely commented:

> Upon examination, it was found very few deeds were delivered, and those not sufficient to throw full light into the matters in dispute, which showed there was no design of doing justice, or of making a full and candid inquiry into the complaints of the Indians.[161]

With particularity, Thomson noted that an important deed of 1718 had been withheld.[162] As the anonymous editor of *An Enquiry into the Causes of the Alienation of the Delaware and Shawanese Indians from the British Interest*, referring to himself in the third person, he wrote:

> Mr. Thomson, who was Teedyuscung's Secretary, having, before he knew there was any intention of nominating him to take minutes, had an opportunity of reading the treaty in 1728, and seeing there the stress that was laid on the deed of 1718, and considering farther that the Governor, as being but lately arrived, might be unacquainted with that matter, thought he could not, consistent with his duty, do less than inform the Governor there was such a deed. This he did by a letter which he delivered into the Governor's own hands. This, however, had not the desired effect, for the next day, when the deeds were again produced, that of 1718 was still wanting. The Proprietary's agents, it seems, had laid the plan, and it was necessary to prosecute that at all adventures, let the consequence be what it would. . . . As a just determination could not be given while papers and deeds of such importance were withheld, and as the lives of many of his Majesty's subjects, and the alliance of many Indian Nations depended upon a just determination, it was not to be imagined that the Governor

---

[161] Ibid., 119.

[162] From Thomson's list of thirteen deeds found in the public records, it appears the 1718 deed was that made by Sassoonan "and his six counselors, to William Penn, their deed of confirmation of all former sales of lands from Duck Creek to the mountains on this side Lechay." Thomson, *An Enquiry*, 125–28.

would join in deceiving the King and his Council in a matter of so great consequence.[163]

Teedyuscung, who was unable to read, assumed that all relevant deeds and papers had been delivered as requested, and he asked that copies be made and delivered to Isaac Norris and the Assembly for examination and then forwarded to King George, where he trusted justice would be done.[164]

Here, after peace was declared between Pennsylvania and Teedyuscung's Lenapes, even though the land fraud issue remained unresolved, Thomson ended both his notes on Easton 3 and the text of his *Enquiry*.[165] He concluded prophetically:

> We have already experienced the cruelties of an Indian war, and there are more instances than one to show they are capable of being our most useful friends, or most dangerous enemies. And whether, for the future, they are to be the one or the other, seems now to be in our own power. How long matters will rest so, or whether, if the present opportunity be neglected, such another will ever return, is altogether uncertain. It becomes men of wisdom and prudence to leave nothing to chance where reason can decide.[166]

Between the close of the Easton 3 treaty conference in August 1757 and the opening of Easton 4 in October 1758, the geopolitical situation in Britain had been so altered that it caused significant change in Britain's management of the French and Indian War in Pennsylvania. In September 1757, Cumberland was disgraced by a military capitulation in continental Europe and forced to resign from the government, then under the leadership of William Pitt the Elder. In furtherance of Pitt's more assertive North American policy, chiefly carried out through the

---

[163] Ibid., 119–21.

[164] Ibid., 121.

[165] The *Enquiry* then took on a life of its own. A manuscript copy was brought to London by John Hunt, an English Quaker and friend of John Fothergill, who had been sent by London Yearly Meeting to Pennsylvania in 1756 to investigate the very issues being raised at Easton 3. Upon Hunt's return to London with the manuscript, it was first shown to Lord Granville and thereafter to Benjamin Franklin, who had it printed in London in 1759 with important addenda, as discussed below. See *The Journal and Essays of John Woolman*, ed. Amelia Mott Gummere (New York: Macmillan Co., 1922), 511; Jennings, *Empire of Fortune*, 381; Kalter, *Benjamin Franklin*, 36.

[166] Thomson, *An Enquiry*, 122.

appointment of more qualified commanders in the field, the following December John Forbes was made brigadier general and given charge of the expedition to take Fort Duquesne. In the succeeding months of preparation, Forbes, requiring intelligence about French force strength and defensive arrangements at the Forks of the Ohio, "under pressure of necessity . . . blasted through the obstructionism of [Sir William] Johnson and Penn's men" to get word to Pennsylvania's estranged native peoples in the Ohio country. He did so by uniting in common cause with Israel Pemberton, who had previously made futile attempts to bring the Ohio Indians into the treaty process.[167]

The geopolitical situation among the native peoples both in Pennsylvania and in the adjacent English colonies was also undergoing change, a change in part prompted by the reluctance of the Iroquois to ally themselves with Forbes in his preparations. The refusal of the northern confederacy led Forbes to ask their ancient enemies in the south, the Cherokees and Catawbas, to send warriors into Pennsylvania to aid in the coming campaign to dislodge the French from Fort Duquesne. Those warriors came forth in large numbers but proved so unruly that they disbanded themselves even before the expedition could set out. The search for warriors to assist the English turned again to regaining the allegiance of the Ohio Indians. Forbes and Pemberton agreed this could only be achieved by working through Teedyuscung at Wyoming to get messages to the Ohio Indians to join in a peace treaty. The resistance of Penn's agents—Denny, Peters, Weiser—to such a peace mission was overcome, and in June 1758 Thomson and Christian Frederick Post, a Moravian missionary who had lived with the Lenapes for seventeen years and "married twice among them,"[168] met with Teedyuscung near Wyoming and secured his acceptance of the proposal to call for a peace treaty.[169]

The treaty conference was held at Philadelphia on July 8–12. Attending were Denny; Peters; Pemberton with Friendly Association colleagues; the lieutenant governor of New Jersey; and Teedyuscung, speaking on behalf of Indians from the Shawnees, Lenapes, Mahicans, and two "Alleghenyans" who were also present.[170] The latter were chiefs of the Ohio Lenapes,

---

[167] Jennings, *Empire of Fortune*, 375, 384.
[168] Thomson, *An Enquiry*, 129.
[169] Jennings, *Empire of Fortune*, 384.
[170] Ibid., 385–88.

Keekyuscung and Pisquetomen, the same Pisquetomen who had been chief Sassoonan's chosen successor at Tulpehocken but, after being rejected by James Logan, had relocated to Ohio, there to escape the interference and manipulation of the Penns and their agents in matters of land, trade, and rum, the instruments of ruin to the native peoples' way of life. Ironically, it had been Pisquetomen's younger brother Shingas, Logan's "acceptable" successor to Sassoonan, who commanded at Great Cove during the massacre. In consequence of the Philadelphia treaty, Pisquetomen and Keekyuscung led Post on a perilous but successful journey to and from the Ohio country between July 15 and September 20, 1758, to both secure the allegiance of the Indians at the Forks of the Ohio and obtain information on the French military situation. Charles Thomson had volunteered to join the party but was barred by Denny, who feared he would spread word of the fraud charge regarding the Walking Purchase.[171]

Easton 4

Easton 4 took place between October 7 and 26, 1758. The notable personnel change on the English side was the readmission of the Quakers, the reported attendance including a number of citizens from Philadelphia "chiefly of the people called Quakers."[172] The Indian representation was large (about five hundred persons), being the "chief sachems and warriors" of the Six Nations of Iroquoia, the Lenapes, Nanticokes and Conoys, Tuteloes, Chugnuts, Munsies (or Minisinks), Mohickons, and Wapings. No secretary was named, but presumably Peters, present with other members of the Provincial Council, kept the official minutes. Charles Thomson was also there keeping notes, "setting down nothing but what I heard or saw myself, or received from good authority. The intimacy I had with several of the Indians, and the confidence they have been pleased to repose in me, gave me an opportunity of being acquainted with what passed at the private council."[173]

---

[171] Post's journal of this journey "from Philadelphia to the Ohio on a message from the government of Pennsylvania to the Delaware, Shawanese and Mingo Indians settled there, and formerly in alliance with the English" is an addendum in Thomson, *An Enquiry*, 130–71. Also see Jennings, *Empire of Fortune*, 388–96.

[172] Kalter, *Benjamin Franklin*, 291.

[173] Thomson, *An Enquiry*, 172. Thomson's notes, published as an addendum entitled "Extract of a letter from Philadelphia, dated Dec. 10, 1758" (pp. 172–82),

Thomson reports that, after the first day in which the usual compliments were exchanged, the second and third days of the treaty were spent by the Indians "in close consultations among themselves. The place of their meeting at Croghan's." He then explains the political purpose of the 'close consultations':

> The reason of the Indians meeting at [Croghan's] house is ... he treats them with liquor, and gives out he himself is an Indian. The subject in debate these two days is whether what Teedyuscung has done shall stand, or they are to begin anew? The grand thing aimed at by our Proprietary managers is to get Teedyuscung to retract the charge of fraud and forgery. In order to gain this point the Senecas and Six Nations are privately treated with and prompted to undo what has been done, in order, as is pretended, to establish their own authority and gain the credit of the peace. Teedyuscung and his people absolutely refuse to retract anything they have said. ... The debates were warm. At length it is agreed that everything already transacted between Teedyuscung and the English shall stand.[174]

The attempt to vilify Teedyuscung and thereby invalidate his charge of fraud and forgery against the proprietors is one of the themes running throughout Easton 4. Generously supplied with liquor by those trying to discredit him, Teedyuscung sometimes appeared at meetings in a drunken state. Thompson reports that one day the Lenape chief came into a meeting drunk, demanding that Denny read aloud a peace letter from the Ohio Indians recently brought to Easton by messengers. Judging him "too drunk to do business," Secretary Peters told the chief it would be read another time. Later in the same meeting, Isaac Norris raised an issue about the Wyoming lands and was told by an aide to

---

are used here because of their succinctness and interpretive commentary. The letter is anonymously written as is also the one following, entitled "Extract of a letter from one of the Friendly Association in Philadelphia, dated December 11, 1758," undoubtedly by Israel Pemberton Jr. Ibid., 183–84. These two letters, along with "The Journal of Christian Frederick Post, in his journey from Philadelphia to the Ohio, on a message from the government of Pennsylvania to the Delaware, Shawanese and Mingo Indians settled there, and formerly in alliance with the English" (Thomson, *An Enquiry*, 130–71), were included in Franklin's printing of the *Enquiry* in London.

[174] Ibid., 173.

Teedyuscung that he "was too drunk to enter upon that matter now."[175]

The attack upon Teedyuscung was also carried out in complaints that he was an upstart, a self-proclaimed "great man" and "chief of Ten Nations."[176] The originator of this complaint was Nichas, the Mohawk chief who was both the father-in-law of Croghan and an important ally of Croghan's boss William Johnson, whose own authority among the Iroquois was principally derived from his tight bond with the Mohawk Nation. Teedyuscung's principle supporter at Easton 4 was Tagashata, chief of the Senecas, the keepers of the western door to Iroquoia and rivals within the confederation of the Mohawks, keepers of the eastern door. The rivalry behind this Seneca-Mohawk dynamic was occasioned by the political-economic-demographic shift away from the north-south axis of the nearby Indian lands, overseen by the Mohawks along the Susquehanna and Shenandoah Valleys, and toward the east-west axis guarded by the Senecas extending into the Ohio country and beyond to the Mississippi basin.

Failing to create dissension among the Indians, Croghan tried to make mischief by spreading a rumor that Isaac Norris, the speaker of the Assembly, together with others, including "New England people," was purchasing lands at or near Wyoming. This was the area Teedyuscung intended for a permanent home for the eastern Lenapes. Appalled at the prospect and at Croghan's assurances that he had "the power in him . . . to set that affair right," Teedyuscung declared "that if this should prove true, neither he nor any other Indians, would settle on these lands, but would resent the injury."[177]

About one week into the treaty conference, the peace message from the Ohio Indians was received at Easton from the hands of Pisquetomen and Thomas Hickman, a warrior. They had returned from Ohio with Christian Frederick Post, who had left them at Harris's Ferry to report to General Forbes on the French defensive arrangements at Fort Duquesne.[178] Pisquetomen had been appointed peace messenger to the Ohio Indians at the Philadelphia Treaty, and before reading the letter from Ohio, he

---

[175] Ibid., 175–76.

[176] Kalter, *Benjamin Franklin*, 304.

[177] Thomson, *An Enquiry*, 176–77. See also Kalter, *Benjamin Franklin*, 315.

[178] Thomson, *An Enquiry*, 175. For a sanitized account of how the letter came to Easton and for the text of the letter itself, see Kalter, *Benjamin Franklin*, 301–3.

recalled that he had been "employed" for the mission by Denny, Teedyuscung, and Israel Pemberton and, in Ohio, had been charged by the chiefs there to shake hands with his "employers" and to deliver to each a string of wampum. Pisquetomen thereupon discharged his ceremonial duty and concluded by saying that "you gentlemen, who are head men, sent Frederick Post with me, desiring me to take and carry him in my bosom there, and when I came there, to introduce him to the public Council; I did this, and have brought him back safe again."[179] Thereupon, the letter from the Ohio Indians was read. In it they expressed their longing for the peace and friendship "we had formerly" and asked to receive the agreement settling the new peace which, upon finding that "everything is well done, so that I can send it to the nations of my color, they will all join to it, and we all will hold it fast." It was signed by fifteen captains and counselors, and the first named were Beaver King, Shingas, Delaware George, and Pisquetomen, the brothers of the Lenni Lenape royal family.

After hearing this letter read, Nichas "with great vehemence" stirred up the "great man" complaint against Teedyuscung. It is likely he found the appropriate incentive for attack in the unexpected recognition given the eastern Lenape chief by Pisquetomen, and he doubtless chose the moment to show Pisquetomen that Teedyuscung was not the Lenape leader whom all of the paramount chiefs in Iroquoia would accept or even respect. It may also have been a Mohawk cry of outrage that a great leader of the Lenni Lenape would honor an eastern Lenape upstart. The moment was so embarrassing that Weiser, when ordered by Denny to interpret, declined, asking that Andrew Montour do so instead but in private.[180] "The Governors, Councils, and Commissioners" held a conference with the chiefs of the Iroquois Nation two days later and heard the natives' complaints against Teedyuscung that, in the end, were without consequence. His standing and the charge of fraud and forgery remained firm.

Teedyuscung had other supporters at Easton 4. Several days later, after both Nichas, a speaker of the senior (advisory) Iroquois chiefs, and Denny's counterpart from New Jersey, Francis Bernard, had finished their remarks, Thomas King, an

---

[179] Kalter, *Benjamin Franklin*, 301–2.
[180] Ibid., 303.

Oneida chief and the speaker for the younger (warrior) Iroquois, Lenape, and Minisink Indians, delivered an indictment of the English. To explain "the true cause of the bitterness of our hearts," he cited five provocations that had led to the war then being waged. They involved the English mistreatment of Shawnee warriors in South Carolina and of Seneca warriors in Virginia; the failure of Virginia and Pennsylvania to provide defense or supplies when notified of the French incursion into the Ohio country; and the seizure of Indian lands in New Jersey by "the English settling so fast" that the Minisinks were "pushed back, and could not tell what lands belonged to them. . . . Our nephews, when they sold the land, did not propose to deprive themselves of hunting the wild deer, or using a stick of wood, when they should have occasion." Without mentioning the Walking Purchase, Thomas King named as the fifth cause of war the Penns' most recent Pennsylvania land grab.[181] It had occurred "in the bushes" at the Albany Congress in 1754, was legalized in a release executed by chiefs of the Iroquois, and covered lands from the west side of the Susquehanna to the western bounds of the province and from a creek (Kayanondinhag) entering the Susquehanna at its New York border in the north as far south as the Maryland border.[182] The payment made for this vast tract of Pennsylvania from the Susquehanna River to the western boundary of the province was compensation only for the lands under occupation. Thomas King then said:

> We acknowledge to have received payment for those parts that were settled, but for the other part that we have not received payment for, that we reclaim. Our warriors, or hunters, when they heard we had sold such a large tract, disapproved our conduct in council; so now we acquaint you, that we are determined not to confirm any more, than such lands as the consideration was paid for, and were settled; tho' included in the deed, they are our hunting grounds, and we desire the request may be granted.[183]

In his response, Denny promised to release the lands so reclaimed. He also took up, finally, Teedyuscung's persistent claim that the Walking Purchase was a fraud with regard to the

---

[181] Ibid., 309–12.

[182] Thomson, *An Enquiry*, 127.

[183] Kalter, *Benjamin Franklin*, 312.

lands "between Tohiccon Creek and the Kittochtinny Hills." Denny attempted to confuse this simple claim by raising doubt about the original ownership and then throwing the issue of who was entitled to convey lands west of the Delaware River back to the Iroquois and Lenape Indians to resolve between themselves. He did so with these disingenuous words: "The Proprietaries are desirous to do strict justice to all the Indians, but it cannot be supposed they can know in which of you the right was vested."[184] It was a futile attempt to invoke once more James Logan's discredited and cruel policy of subordinating the Lenapes to the Iroquois so as to unburden the Pennsylvania government of an unwanted responsibility.

Teedyuscung next repeated his claim in a special meeting of the Iroquois and Lenapes held on October 21 and reported in the official minutes of Easton 4. Some members of the Provincial Council, the Indian commissioners from the Assembly, and Pemberton and other Quakers were invited to be present "at the particular request of the Delawares."[185] After making his statement, support came from an Iroquois, a Cayuga chief named Tokaaion, who affirmed Teedyuscung with these words:

> I thank you for your openness and honesty on this occasion, freely to declare the truth. We wish our brethren the English, naming the governors of Pennsylvania, Virginia, Carolina and Jersey, were so honest and precise.
>
> They have called us down to this council fire, which was kindled for council affairs, to renew treaties of friendship, and brighten the chain of friendship. But here we must hear a dispute about land, and our time is taken up, but they don't come to the chief point.
>
> The English first began to do mischief; we told them so. They only thanked us for our openness and advice, and said they would take care for the future, but healed no wounds. In short, when they speak to us, they do it with a shorter belt or string than that which we spoke to them with; tho' they can make wampum, and we cannot.

---

[184] Ibid., 316.
[185] Ibid., 321.

They ought not thus to treat with Indians on council affairs. Several of our strong belts are lost in their hands entirely. I fear they only speak from their mouth, and not from their heart.[186]

The business of Easton 4 was concluded with the departure on October 21 of Pisquetomen carrying the treaty conference answer to the Ohio Indians and with the distribution on October 23 of the Indian goods together with a promise, solicited by Teedyuscung, that King George's adjudication of the Walking Purchase dispute would be communicated to him as soon as it was known. According to Thomson's notes, the final event of Easton 4 was a public entertainment given to the Indians. It was held on a Tuesday, most likely October 25.[187] At this gathering, the Indians signed new deeds related to their reclaiming of lands acquired by the proprietors in their 1754 Albany deed, lying west of the Susquehanna but remaining unoccupied (as described in the official minutes).[188] The following account of the transaction by Thomson varies greatly from the official minutes and is, in itself, a grim record of yet another Penn land fraud.

> On Tuesday a public entertainment was given to the Indians, and in the evening the chiefs were called together by R. Peters and C. Weiser. Hitherto the Indians, 'tho several times pressed to it, had deferred giving an answer to the proposal made on behalf of the Proprietors to release back to the Indians the lands of the purchase of 1754, west of the Allegheny Mountains, provided the Indians would confirm to them the residue of that purchase. But the deeds being drawn up agreeable to what the Proprietors proposed, it now remained to persuade the Indians to sign them as drawn. And tonight 'tis said that is done. I wish this may not be a foundation of fresh uneasiness. In public council they declared they would confirm no more of that land than what was settled

---

[186] Ibid., 322.

[187] The official minutes of Easton 4 printed by Franklin (see Kalter, *Benjamin Franklin*) date each of the several conferences and side meetings. In contrast, Thomson's notes for this treaty (*An Enquiry*, 172–82), contained in a letter sent presumably to the Friendly Association, frequently only name the day of the week for each session. Where he does attempt the exact date, it is sometimes incorrect, hence requiring that Thomson be correlated with, and corrected to, Kalter in fixing the dates of specific events.

[188] See p. 380 above.

in the year 1754, for which only they had received the consideration; but all the rest they reclaimed. Yet now by the deed as drawn, ten times, nay I may say twenty times as much land is conveyed as was then settled. For the English settlements in 1754 extended but a little way up the Juniata and Sherman's Creek, whereas the present grant reaches to the Allegheny Mountains. May not the warriors to whom the lands have been granted for hunting grounds disapprove this grant as they did before, and maintain their right by force of arms? I wish this fear may be groundless. Besides, I could have wished that another time than the close of an entertainment had been chosen for executing the deeds, considering the Indians' fondness for liquor.[189]

A notable success, aided by the labors at Easton 4, was achieved one month later on November 25 when General Forbes took possession of Fort Duquesne. It had been abandoned the previous day by its French defenders, who were in sore need of the warriors of the Ohio Lenapes, now reconciled to the English through the Pemberton strategy adopted by Forbes. To honor the victory and the war's leading architect in the British government, William Pitt the Elder, the strategic location at the Forks of the Ohio was renamed Pittsburgh.

With western Pennsylvania thus secured to the British interest by the end of 1758 and a way into the Ohio country safely opened, the proprietors and their agents in the province had no immediate need to engage in further treaties with the Indians, nor did they want to be burdened with the costs of such treaties. Relative peace seemed to be restored, and Indian-provincial relations were quiet. Early in 1759, however, Benjamin Franklin, as the Pennsylvania Assembly's agent in London, on behalf of the Assembly petitioned the Privy Council for an adjudication of Teedyuscung's claim of fraud in the Walking Purchase. The Council referred the matter to the Board of Trade, which responded in June with a recommendation that Sir William Johnson be instructed to hear the parties' testimony, examine the evidence, and make a report to the government in London. The Privy Council accepted the advice and sent the dispute back to

---

[189] Thomson, *An Enquiry*, 182.

America for Johnson to resolve.[190] This is how the province kept Denny's word to Teedyuscung that his complaint would be submitted directly to King George!

At the end of 1759, Teedyuscung arrived in Philadelphia on business, bringing invitations for his attendance at a treaty to be held at Pittsburgh in the spring of 1760. Pemberton, who in September 1759 had resigned as clerk of PYM after ten years of distinguished service in American Quakerism's preeminent position, tried without success to have the treaty site relocated to Philadelphia. His plan was to gather all the Indians formerly living along both sides of the Delaware River for the purpose of having them declare their independence of the Iroquois and elect Teedyuscung their paramount chief. In addition, he intended that they would as a body refuse to allow Sir William Johnson to hear and decide their claims.[191] Pemberton's plan failed. In March 1760, Teedyuscung received Johnson's note asking him to name a time and place for a hearing on his claim. Evidencing his own animosity toward Johnson, the Lenape chief angrily refused Sir William's intervention and told the bearer of the message, Pennsylvania's Lieutenant Governor Hamilton, that he, Hamilton, could hold the hearing.[192]

Teedyuscung went to Pittsburgh, accompanied by Christian Frederick Post and others, carrying peace belts from the provincial government and outfitted for the occasion by a £50 grant from the Friendly Association.[193] His presence was a disaster.

> Teedyuscung's conduct at Pittsburgh was such as soon to divest him of any influence he may have had on coming. He was drunk from morning till night, while the belts and strings provided him by the Friendly Association soon adorned the squaws for whom he had taken a fancy. His fellow Delawares of the Ohio treated him with the utmost disdain. Now that his Quaker advisers were not present, Richard Peters declared, Teedyuscung had shown himself

---

[190] Theodore Thayer, *Israel Pemberton: King of the Quakers* (Philadelphia: Historical Society of Pennsylvania, 1943), 177–78.

[191] Ibid., 178.

[192] Ibid.

[193] Within days of making this grant, the minute book of the Friendly Association comes to an end. Parrish, *History of the Friendly Association*, 117.

in his true character—'a senseless, low, drunken wretch.'[194]

Two major geopolitical changes in the wider Atlantic world occurred later in 1760. The end of the French and Indian War came with the fall of Montreal to Britain in September. And the death of George II in October brought to Britain's throne his twenty-two-year-old grandson, George III, who, seeking to purge corruption and arrogant ministers from his government, first needed to free himself from the undue influence of others.

Easton 5

Pennsylvania did not hold another Indian treaty conference until Easton 5. According to Theodore Thayer, "In July 1761, nearly five hundred Lenapes, Iroquois, and subsidiary Indians appeared at Easton and sent notice to Philadelphia that they had arrived for a treaty. Governor Hamilton professed not to know why they had come; he had not called them and no one else had a right to do so. He was certain that Israel Pemberton was at the bottom of it, but now they were here he dared not refuse to treat with his uninvited guests."[195]

The parties gathered for a week in August 1761, nearly three years after Easton 4, with some important changes in the participants. William Denny was no longer lieutenant governor, having been replaced by James Hamilton in 1759.[196] Conrad Weiser had died in 1760, and his son Samuel was named his successor as interpreter and liaison to the Iroquois on the recommendation of their speaker, Seneca George. No chief

---

[194] Thayer, *Israel Pemberton*, 178; see also Parrish, *History of the Friendly Association*, 116–17. The Provincial Council's (1) instructions to Christian Frederick Post for escorting Teedyuscung to "the Ohio treaty" and (2) memorandum that Post and his party had returned from "the great Indian Council ... held by the Western Indians over the Ohio" and had delivered the "Journal of their Travels and Proceedings" for deposit with the Council papers are contained in its minutes at *MPCP*, 8:469–72 and 491, respectively. The Council minutes do not, however, otherwise record anything related to the proceedings of the Pittsburgh Treaty conference. Nor is it mentioned in Kalter, *Benjamin Franklin*.

[195] Thayer, *Israel Pemberton*, 179.

[196] Denny was removed as lieutenant governor by Thomas Penn in 1759 for violating his instructions to prevent the Assembly from taxing proprietary lands in the province. Hamilton, who was being reappointed to the office he had previously held from 1748 to 1754, was a supporter of the Penns and the developer of the town of Lancaster, which he laid out on William Penn's grid plan for Philadelphia. Kenny, *Peaceable Kingdom Lost*, 35.

"sachems and warriors" of either the Mohawks or Senecas made appearances, according to the minutes of the unnamed secretary (undoubtedly Peters). Charles Thomson, whose *Enquiry into the causes of the alienation* was by now in print and circulating among government ministers and others in London and beyond, was not present, but Israel Pemberton, unmentioned in the minutes, certainly was.

The principal business of the conference was Teedyuscung's long-standing unfulfilled request for a deed to the reservation at Wyoming in western Pennsylvania. Inasmuch as the Iroquois had so far withheld any document that, according to the English land law and custom then prevailing in the province, would secure the Lenapes in their own land, Teedyuscung was now forced to consider the need to "get up and leave it" for his peoples' sake and that of their children and grandchildren.[197] In answer, an Iroquois speaker referred to the problem of "straggling Indians," unauthorized and dishonest natives who sold land they did not own. In turn, Hamilton said that such a fraudulent sale had been made by four Iroquois to "a great number of people from Connecticut" who had moved near the Wyoming area "against my Will and Consent" and would not remove themselves. He advised the Iroquois to send the native 'sellers' "into the Great Council at Onondaga, reprove them for their conduct, and cancel their deeds."[198]

Teedyuscung responded to this evasion by reminding the Iroquois that he and his people had removed to Wyoming at their direction and due to the promise of a permanent homeland that, if now lost, would benefit neither Lenapes nor Iroquois. To Hamilton, he renewed the expectation that "you will pay us for the lands we have been complaining about," meaning the Walking Purchase fraud case referred to King George, of which "I have not heard you say anything about it since."[199]

The conferees also heard a new Indian complaint against William Johnson's administration of native affairs. There were as well the oft-repeated concerns over the increasing poverty among the tribes, the ready availability of liquor, and the harsh practices of traders.[200]

---

[197] Kalter, *Benjamin Franklin*, 340.
[198] Ibid., 346–47, 349.
[199] Ibid., 353–54.
[200] Ibid., 344–46.

Easton 6

The final act of the Teedyuscung tragedy was played out at Easton from June 18 to 28, 1762. Although styled a 'treaty' by its presiding officer, it was, in fact, a semi-judicial hearing held before an authority predisposed by his powerful nature and his singular office to dislike both Teedyuscung and his Quaker supporters. The business now at Easton 6 was "the proceeding . . . into the complaint of the Delaware Indians against the Proprietors of Pennsylvania for defrauding them of their lands."[201] Conducting the proceeding was Sir William Johnson, attended by his assistant George Croghan and Pennsylvania's lieutenant governor James Hamilton. Representing the proprietors of Pennsylvania, Thomas and Richard Penn, as proprietary commissioners were Richard Peters (the provincial secretary) and Benjamin Chew (the provincial attorney general). Representing the Lenapes was Teedyuscung, attended by a delegation of "sachems and warriors" of the eastern Lenapes as well as allied "Mohiccons and Opings." Present also were eight members acting as a committee of the Provincial Assembly along with "a great many gentlemen, inhabitants of Philadelphia, and other parts of the Province of Pennsylvania,"[202] among them Israel Pemberton.

The Easton proceeding originated in the petition of February 1759 filed with the Crown by Benjamin Franklin as the Assembly's agent in London, which resulted in the order of the king in council issued on August 29 directing Johnson to "examine thoroughly" the Lenape Indians' complaint of land fraud. The delay of nearly three years in holding the hearing was formally attributed by Johnson to Teedyuscung, "who thought proper to put off the meeting." The five-day delay, from June 13 to 18, in getting down to business at Easton was reported by Johnson as due to "the Indians being until that day drunk."[203]

The contest of wills between Johnson and Teedyuscung began in earnest the second day of the hearings when Teedyuscung asked for his own clerk "to take down what I may

---

[201] These treaty proceedings were not printed by Franklin and hence are not included in Kalter, *Benjamin Franklin*. They can be found in Johnson, *The Papers of Sir William Johnson*, 3:760–91, 794–818, 837–52.

[202] Ibid., 3:761.

[203] Ibid., 3:838.

have occasion to say."[204] Johnson called the request unprecedented; the Lenape chief persisted for the sake of providing his grandchildren with a record of the event. In the end, Johnson prevailed, "surprised at [Teedyuscung] showing any diffidence [distrust] of the Secretary, who was a sworn officer."[205]

Defeated but unphased, Teedyuscung next asked that he be shown any deeds for the lands, which Johnson answered with a barrage of six questions, effectively putting Teedyuscung the complainant in the role of the defendant. Johnson, asking where the lands lay, demanded a legal description. After giving the boundaries of the disputed territory, Teedyuscung continued:

> Some years ago, Nutimus (then chief of the Delawares) made some complaint to Mr. James Logan, now deceased, who told Nutimus it would not be worth his while to trouble himself about the lands. "If you do," said he, "you'll make the big trees and logs, and great rocks and stones tumble down into our road"; and added, he did not value Nutimus, but looked upon him as the little finger of his left hand; but that he himself was a great, big man, at the same time stretching out his arms. Mr. Logan added, "that nobody dared to write anything wrong, for if anyone writes anything out of his own head, we hang him."[206]

Asked when and where this had occurred, Teedyuscung said it had taken place at the Pennsbury meeting (May 1735) between Logan and Nutimus that was attended by the Penn brothers, himself, and others. Teedyuscung rested his case by observing that "what Mr. Logan said to Nutimus has made me travel greatly, and take much pains for six years (and I am almost tired) in order to make up the breach occasioned by Mr. Logan's words."[207] Teedyuscung's present active role and his earlier witnessing of critical events touching on the disputed Walking Purchase become clearer in light of his written statement, submitted to Johnson on June 24, that he received his knowledge not from "any white man" (Johnson believed throughout that the Quakers were directing and coaching the Indians for their own purposes)

---

[204] Ibid., 3:766.

[205] Ibid. The minutes of the Easton 6 proceeding were signed by "Witham Marsh, Secretary for Indian Affairs." See ibid., 3:791.

[206] Ibid., 3:767.

[207] Ibid.

but from Nutimus "when he gave me his place of chief man of the Delawares."[208] When Johnson finally asked Teedyuscung whether this was "the whole of his charge about the lands against the proprietaries," the Lenape chief said it was, desiring Johnson "to consider of what he had said, and when he had considered to bring out the deeds."[209]

The proprietary commissioners presented their answer to the charge against the Penns on June 21. The clerk read aloud their written statement together with "several deeds, original letters, affidavits, affirmations, and other papers" to Johnson, Teedyuscung, and others in attendance, plus "a great number of auditors, both whites and Indians." Although the minutes of the hearing fail to report the substantive arguments, Johnson's report to the Lords of Trade explains the Penns' case at length.[210] Immediately following, Johnson sent one of Croghan's assistants "to let Teedyuscung and the other Indians know . . . what had been read on behalf of the proprietaries" and that Johnson had received their "several proofs and papers," which he would carefully peruse and duly consider. Hasty by nature and ever ready to be accommodating in the cause of peace, Teedyuscung, according to the minutes, replied that "what had been read was very satisfactory to him and the Indians; for they very well understood the purport or meaning of what had been read."[211]

By the next day the Lenape chief, when directed to reply to the Penns' answer to the complaint, forcefully contradicted his own accommodating words of the previous meeting, telling Johnson:

> Brother; Please to hear what I am going to say. What passed yesterday neither I nor my people understood it, as no one interpreted what was said.[212]

After expanding on the injustices that he and others perceived were afoot, Teedyuscung then handed Johnson a "paper," signed by himself and eight other Indians, formally complaining of the arbitrariness and inequities in the proceeding:

---

[208] Ibid., 3:778.
[209] Ibid., 3:768.
[210] Ibid., 3:768–69, 839–45.
[211] Ibid., 3:769.
[212] Ibid., 3:770.

> Brother Johnson: You promised to see justice done, but when you refused to let me have a clerk, I began to fear you intended to do as George Croghan did when we were here five years since. King George has ordered you to hear me and all the Indians fully. But how do you think I can make answer at once to as many papers as your Clerk was four hours reading, in a language I do not understand, and which have not been interpreted to me? I expect to have all those papers delivered to me, that I may have time to consider them, and if you refuse this, I and all the Indians shall see you do not intend to do justice, and we shall complain to King George, who we are sure is our friend and ... we know the King will do us justice.[213]

Johnson stood on his dignity, on his professed intention to do justice, on his belief someone "put it in [Teedyuscung's] head" to make such complaints, and on the contradiction in the Lenape's words of satisfaction the previous day and of dissatisfaction that day, appealing to the memories of "everyone who was present" then and now who would have heard Teedyuscung declare "he understood [yesterday's] proceeding well, and was very well satisfied with what had been done."[214]

At this point Israel Pemberton, "one of the heads of the Quaker Society, stood up, and speaking aloud with great warmth and indecency, contradicted Sir William." The minutes report the following:

> Since Sir William had appealed to the by-standers for the truth of this matter, he [Israel Pemberton] thought himself obliged to declare that Teedyuscung said no such thing, and that the minutes were not fairly taken, that many material things which Teedyuscung had said were altogether omitted, and other things misrepresented; that it was unjust and unreasonable to call on Teedyuscung to answer a number of title deeds and proofs produced yesterday on the part of the Proprietaries, which took up three hours and an half in reading, especially as they were wrote in English, not one sentence of which Teedyuscung understood to his certain knowledge, and he had known him for many years; that the lives of the inhabitants, and the peace and welfare of the province were concerned in

---

[213] Ibid., 3:771.
[214] Ibid., 3:772.

having this matter fully heard, and that if Sir William would not do them justice, they would not suffer the matter to rest here, but would complain home, where he did not doubt of being heard and redressed.[215]

This launched a verbal duel between Johnson and Pemberton.

> Sir William then asked Israel Pemberton, "what right he had to interpose in this matter, and said that, he was, by the Royal Order, to hear the complaints of the Indians, and the Proprietaries' defense, and that no other person had any right to intermeddle. . . ."—Israel insolently answered "that, he was a freeman, and had as much right to speak as the Governor. That it was unjust to deny Teedyuscung a clerk, which was his natural right.—That he had as much right to appoint a clerk, as Sir William." . . . Sir William then observed that, "He plainly saw through what channel Teedyuscung conducted his business, and had taken notice that he was constantly nursed and entertained at Pemberton's, or at the lodgings of the Committee of Assembly": to which Israel replied, that Teedyuscung was as much with Sir William, as with him.[216]

The sparring with Johnson continued as three of the assemblymen in attendance voiced their concerns about the fairness of the proceeding. Joseph Fox "warmly" stated that Teedyuscung "did not understand a word of what was read yesterday, nor did he say that he understood it." Joseph Galloway announced the assemblymen had made a written request to Sir William for "a copy of the state of the Proprietaries' title . . . which he had not granted them," to which Johnson then replied that "he did not think it right to give any copy of the proceedings, lest they should be in everybody's hands, before he could make his report to His Majesty." Then Fox and Galloway, joined by John Hughes, reminded Johnson that their appointment by the Assembly was for the purpose of seeing justice done, for upon it depended the peace of the province.[217]

The encounter ended when Pemberton jumped in again, reminding his hearers of the King's "paternal regard and affection

---

[215] Ibid., 3:772–73.
[216] Ibid., 3:773.
[217] Ibid., 3:773–74.

for the Indians," and Johnson decried "the mischiefs of any person's interposing but the King's Agent in Indian Affairs," for which, he said, he had the opinion of the "King's Ministers." Pemberton countered that "he had the opinion of the ablest man in America on that point."[218] Unable to quiet the hearing, Johnson ended the day's conference. Afterwards, at his lodgings, the Assembly committeemen presented to Johnson their written reply to the defense of the proprietors given by Peters and Chew the previous day in which they corrected its omissions and misrepresentations.[219]

On June 24, the conference resumed with the reading of a long paper addressed to Johnson dealing with title issues. It was prepared by Teedyuscung, signed by eight other Indians, and made part of the official minutes. In it Teedyuscung again requested "copies of the papers, which you know is my right; and if I can have them, I will, with the assistance of the Assemblymen, who are now here, give you such further answer, as I may think proper; but I do not think your wanting to do things in the dark looks well."[220]

Peters and Chew, the proprietary commissioners in the case, gave written rebuttals to the papers of the assemblymen and of Teedyuscung.[221] As the dispute increased in complexity, a paramount problem emerged in the rebuttals: there were unknown, unrecorded deeds of critical importance to the case that were not available to anyone but the proprietors. These deeds were unknown even to Charles Thomson, who in 1756 had made a diligent search for them and in 1759 had printed in his *Enquiry* a schedule of all relevant and available treaty minutes and deeds. Missing from the *Enquiry*, and not otherwise known until the Peters and Chew rebuttal to the assemblymen, were deeds dated "1682" (without day and month); June 30, 1685; September 7, 1732; and August 20, 1733. Also missing was the deed dated 28th day 6th month 1686, the one that gave rise to the Walking Purchase. In their rebuttal, Peters and Chew revealed the history of this essential document:

---

[218] Ibid., 3:774–75.

[219] Ibid., 3:794–99. Of serious concern was unproduced documentary evidence, including an unrecorded deed of 1732, certain requested but denied Provincial Council minutes, and Peters and Chew's statement of their case. Ibid., 795–96 and 798, respectively. Peters and Chews' response to the assemblymen's paper is on pp. 799–811.

[220] Ibid., 3:781.

[221] Ibid., 3:799–811 and 812–18, respectively.

> The original deed of 1686 . . . was soon after [its execution] lost or mislaid, and Thomas Holme who made that purchase and was possessed of that deed dying in 1694, and that deed having never been seen to our knowledge by any person who survived him, it is impossible that it could be shown and read to Sassoonan in the year 1718. The truth is there was no vestige of the said deed until Thomas Penn Esquire, one of the present Proprietaries, came from England in the year 1732 and happened to bring with him among his father's papers the said ancient copy of this deed, which was the occasion of the several meetings, with the chiefs who claimed the lands now in dispute, at Durham, Pennsbury and at last at Philadelphia, where the sachems whose ancestors had formerly owned the lands in question, in the most solemn and deliberate manner, as mentioned in our former state[ment], ratified and confirmed the sale made by their said ancestors after had they received undeniable proof of the fairness of the first purchase.[222]

Proving the validity of a 1686 Indian deed supposedly made, retained, and then lost or mislaid by Penn's surveyor general who died in 1694/95, "and that deed having never been seen to our knowledge by any person who survived him," seems an impossible evidentiary task. And to prove a lost original of such importance by an alleged copy requires the highest standards of authentication of the copy. That "there was no vestige of the said deed until Thomas Penn . . . happened to bring with him among his father's papers the said ancient copy of this deed" on his 1732 arrival in America puts the case on very dubious grounds, at best. The most qualified authority on the "ancient copy" of this deed was Charles Thomson, who described it in his schedule of deeds included with the *Enquiry*:

> A paper said to be a copy of a deed, dated 28th of 6th month 1686 and endorsed, Copy of the last Indian purchase. To give it some credit, it has been confidently asserted, that the said endorsement is of the hand-writing of William Penn; but on its being produced at Easton, and examined, it appeared clearly, and was confirmed by the Secretary and several others acquainted with Mr. Penn's

---

[222] Ibid., 3:806.

hand-writing, not to be his, nor indeed is it like it. Its chief mark of credit is, that it appears to be an ancient paper. But there is no certificate of its being a copy, nor was it ever recorded. As the name of Joseph Wood is put as one of the evidences, and as a person of that name declared at Pennsbury 1734, he was present at an Indian Treaty in 1686, and it is not known there was any other of the name, it seems extraordinary, if this be a genuine copy, that he was not then called upon to make some proof of it.[223]

Thomson then concludes his 1759 remarks regarding the Indian deeds he had examined with this complaint against the proprietors for not producing many other deeds:

There is a considerable number of Indian deeds in the hands of the Secretary for Lands purchased at several times, and particularly for the lands on the branches of Schuylkill above Tulpehocken, purchased in 1732 and 1733, which it was particularly desired might be produced, but they will neither record nor produce them. There is reason to believe the said last mentioned deed would particularly militate against the subsequent proceedings from 1733 to 1737.[224]

Left unsaid was that the withholding of deeds from the public record (as in the Walking Purchase) rendered the just resolution of title questions impossible, thus leaving the validity of many titles derived from the Indians through the Penns uncertain.

The June 18 session of Easton 6 was dominated by Teedyuscung, who delivered his third and final paper addressed to Johnson. This time, he was the only signer. The paper read:

At a treaty held about six years ago [Easton 2] I made a complaint against the Proprietaries, and charged them with depriving us of our lands by forgery and fraud, which we did at a time when we were just come from the French, by whom we were very much incensed against our brothers the English. This matter was afterwards, by our mutual consent, referred to the great King George over the water, who directed you, brother, to inquire into

---

[223] *Thomson, An Enquiry*, 127–28.
[224] Ibid., 128.

the circumstances of the case and make a report to him that he might do what was just therein.

You have taken the trouble to come here for this purpose, and many days have been spent in this affair. It now appears by sundry old writings and papers, which have been shown by the Proprietary Commissioners and read at this conference, that the said charge of forgery was a mistake, into which mistake we were led by the accounts we had received from our ancestors concerning the land sold by Mayhkerrick-kisho, Sayhoppey, and Taugh-haughsy, to old William Penn, in the year 1686.

As to the Walk, the Proprietary Commissioners insist that it was reasonably performed, but we think otherwise, which difference in opinion may happen without either of us being bad men. But this is a matter that brethren ought not to differ about. Wherefore, being desirous of living in peace and friendship with our brothers the Proprietaries and the good people of Pennsylvania, we bury under ground all controversies about land, and are ready, such of us as are here, to sign a release for all the lands in dispute, and will endeavor to persuade the rest of our brethren, who are concerned, to sign the same.[225]

It is unknown whether Teedyuscung's abandonment of the Indian claim resulted from his perception that Johnson's impatience reflected his hostility to the case as well as to the Lenapes and their Quaker and Assembly supporters. Johnson's attitude throughout—evidenced in his repeated denials of Teedyuscung's requests for a clerk/secretary; for copies of all relevant deeds, minutes, and other papers at issue; and for adequate time alone with counsel to scrutinize, for content and authenticity, these technical, foreign-language documents—all but certainly spelled defeat for the Lenapes. Also unknown is whether the hearings were but a charade to cover an "in the bushes" financial deal already agreed on for settling a case the Indians never could be allowed to win. In the end, Teedyuscung accepted with some grace that his cause was lost. It was lost because all the power lay with the British, who would not suffer any jurisprudence and sovereignty other than their own to prevail in such a colonial setting. Altogether avoided in this tortured dispute

---

[225] Johnson, *The Papers of Sir William Johnson*, 3:786.

was the profound challenge of finding and doing justice in the resolution of conflicts among peoples with differing cultures, customs, and laws.

Epilogue

The settlement of the Indian claim accepted by Teedyuscung at Easton 6 for the eastern Lenapes was ratified by the Ohio (or Allegheny) Lenapes and other "northern and western Indians" at a treaty conference held at Lancaster from August 11–28, 1762.[226] Presiding was Pennsylvania's lieutenant governor and Lancaster's leading citizen, James Hamilton. The Ohio Lenapes were led by their peace chief, Beaver, accompanied by other chiefs and warriors. The eastern Lenapes were led by Teedyuscung, who had with him about 175 persons. Of the Iroquois, only the Mohawks were absent. Also present were chiefs of the Shawanese and of three western nations—the Kickapoe, Wawachtanies, and Twightwee. With Hamilton were William Logan, Peters, and Chew from the Provincial Council. Observing the proceedings were members of the Provincial Assembly, and among the "number of gentlemen from Philadelphia" was Israel Pemberton.

On August 18, Hamilton, addressing Beaver as paramount chief of the Ohio Lenapes, informed him in detail of the claim of fraud made by Teedyuscung for "about six years" regarding the Walking Purchase and of the recent settlement of that claim agreed upon at Easton 6. When asked whether the release of the claim against the proprietors was satisfactory—the forgery and fraud charges in regard to the Walking Purchase were dropped by the Wyoming and Ohio Lenapes, who received gifts of money and goods—Beaver, after briefly consulting with his colleagues, responded:

> I must acknowledge I know nothing about the lands upon the Delaware, and I have no concern with lands upon that river. We know nothing of the Delawares' claim to them. I have no claim myself, nor any of my people. I suppose there may be some spots or pieces of land in some parts of the province that the Delawares claim, but neither I nor any of my people know anything of them. As to what you and our brother Teedyuscung have done, if you are both pleased, I am pleased with it. As to my part, I want

---

[226] The Lancaster treaty minutes are in Kalter, *Benjamin Franklin*, 358–405. These are the last Indian treaty minutes Franklin printed.

to say nothing about land affairs; what I have at heart, and what I came down about, is to confirm our friendship, and make a lasting peace, so as our children and grandchildren may live together in everlasting peace, after we are dead.[227]

Whereupon Teedyuscung, silent until then in this treaty record, a record presumably prepared by Peters for William Johnson, said to Hamilton:

Before all these Allegheny Indians here present, I do now assure you that I am ready and willing to sign a release to all the lands we have been disputing about, as I told you I would at Easton, and desire no more may be ever said or heard of them hereafter.[228]

Hamilton concluded these exchanges by announcing that, pursuant to the Penns' direction, presents would be made to the Lenapes in their names. On August 22 the presents were delivered, increased by "an addition of equal value" made by "the good people of this province," meaning the Quakers. Witnessed by Pemberton and several colleagues from the Friendly Association, along with Logan, Peters, Chew, some assemblymen, and many Indians, Beaver, as chief of the Lenape Nation at Allegheny, received for his people £100 "in milled dollars" and goods valued at £600, and Teedyuscung, as chief of the Lenape Nation at Wyoming, received for his people £100 "in milled dollars" and goods valued at £400.[229]

Although the Lancaster Treaty seemingly brought peace between the proprietaries of Pennsylvania and the Lenape Indians of Wyoming and of Allegheny, there were forebodings of

---

[227] Kalter, *Benjamin Franklin*, 374. The disingenuous words in the first three sentences of the quotation are undoubtedly an invention of Secretary Peters, for the words of the native peoples throughout these Franklin-Kalter treaties seem credible. It is an irony of history that Beaver, a chief of the Ohio Lenapes, whose people included some of those displaced in 1742 from the Forks of the Delaware as a result of the Walking Purchase, was making peace in 1762 to conclude a conflict that had commenced in 1755 when his brother Shingas led the Lenape warriors in the Great Cove massacre. The peace process was facilitated by their elder brother Pisquetomen, once the chosen successor as paramount Lenape chief to Sassoonan until his appointment was subverted by James Logan, thereby aggravating the Lenape alienation. For an account of this "Royal Family of the Delawares," see Francis Jennings, "The Delaware Interregnum," *PMHB*, 89 (1965): 174–98.

[228] Kalter, *Benjamin Franklin*, Ibid.

[229] Ibid., 375, 383–85.

future land problems. Thomas King, an Oneida chief, looking past the historical moment into the future, addressed the presiding colonial authority, Hamilton:

> You are always longing after my land, from the east to the west; . . . I desire you will not covet it anymore; you will serve me as you have done our cousins the Delawares; you have got all their land from them; all the land hereabouts belonged to them once, and you have got it all.[230]

And it was Hamilton and Thomas King who drew attention to the festering concern that "a number of people from Connecticut" had settled near the Wyoming Valley, claiming title under a purchase from some Iroquois Indians that was made without the consent of the Onondaga Council, which rendered the land under occupation 'stolen.' Thomas King insisted the land at issue was owned by the Lenapes. Hamilton asked for all the Six Nations in council to advise him.[231] Iroquoia was silent.

The next year began in peace. In February 1763 the French and Indian War was ended by the Treaty of Paris. For Britain in North America, this meant taking from France all the territory of Canada east of the Mississippi. For America's Atlantic colonies, it meant being separated from the ongoing geopolitical competition of European imperial powers. For Pennsylvania, however, the peace was but a pause before more blood was shed.

In April, settlers of Connecticut's Susquehanna Company came to Wyoming in force and ended the Lenapes' occupation of the area. Teedyuscung was burned alive in his cabin.[232] Then, in May, Pontiac's War (1763–1766) began at Fort Detroit, the culmination of Indian resentment and frustration at the hands of the British who, having prevailed over the French, had now become contemptuous of the Native Americans. Instead of withdrawing troops, as promised, the British had increased garrisons; and instead of continuing presents of food and other necessary subsistence supplies, including ammunition for hunting, they cut off all such necessities both to economize and to

---

[230] Ibid., 381.

[231] Ibid., 396–97.

[232] Jennings, *Empire of Fortune*, 436; Paul A. W. Wallace, *Indians in Pennsylvania*, 2nd ed. (Harrisburg: Pennsylvania Historical and Museum Commission, 1981), 158; Anthony F. C. Wallace, *King of the Delawares: Teedyuscung, 1700–1763* (Philadelphia: University of Pennsylvania Press, 1949), 258–61.

teach the natives how to fend for themselves. This marked the beginning of ethnic cleansing.

As these events worked their devastation among Pennsylvania's native peoples, the seizure of whose lands was the goal of the ever-encroaching colonists, Quaker concern for the Indians was heightened. As early as August 1761, John Woolman had noted in his *Journal* that he had "many years felt love in my heart toward the natives of this land who dwell far back in the wilderness."[233] Now, with that wilderness made perilous, Woolman decided to journey to visit "those natives who lived on the east branch of the river Susquehanna at an Indian town called Wyalusing, about two hundred miles from Philadelphia."[234] In early June 1763, he set out from Burlington, New Jersey, escorted by Israel and John Pemberton. Israel parted with him the next morning, but John kept him company to Bethlehem. As he entered more deeply into the wilderness and the danger surrounding him, Woolman meditated on Truth as he knew it:

> The sun appearing, we set forward, and as I rode over the barren hills my meditations were on the alterations of the circumstances of the natives of this land since the coming in of the English. The lands near the sea are conveniently situated for fishing. The lands near the rivers, where the tides flow, and some above, are in many places fertile and not mountainous, while the running of the tides makes passing up and down easy with any kind of traffic. Those natives have in some places, for trifling considerations, sold their inheritance so favorably situated, and in other places been driven back by superior force, so that in many places, as their way of clothing themselves is now altered from what it was and they far remote from us, they have to pass over mountains, swamps, and barren deserts, where travelling is very troublesome, in bringing their skins and furs to trade with us. . . .
>
> And in this lonely journey I did this day greatly bewail the spreading of a wrong spirit, believing that the prosperous, convenient situation of the English requires a constant attention to divine love and wisdom, to guide and support us in a way answerable to the will of that good, gracious,

---

[233] Woolman, *Journal and Major Essays*, 122.
[234] Ibid.

and almighty Being who hath an equal regard to all mankind. And here luxury and covetousness, with the numerous oppressions and other evils attending them, appeared very afflicting to me, and I felt in that which is immutable that the seeds of great calamity and desolation are sown and growing fast on this continent. Nor have I words sufficient to set forth that longing I then felt that we who are placed along the coast, and have tasted the love and goodness of God, might arise in his strength and like faithful messengers labor to check the growth of these seeds, that they may not ripen to the ruin of our posterity.[235]

But the work of ruin went forward. Senecas and Lenapes had been drawn into Pontiac's War, the Senecas besieging Fort Niagara and taking the forts—at Presque Isle, LeBoeuf, and Venango—on the Venango Path, the Indian route from Lake Erie (at present-day Erie, Pennsylvania) to the Ohio River (at present-day Pittsburgh), while the Lenapes besieged Fort Pitt. There, on June 24, at a parley in the fort where smallpox had broken out earlier that month, the commander at Fort Pitt presented the Lenape chiefs with blankets from the fort's hospital known to be infected with smallpox. Soon after, as Jennings notes, "An epidemic raged among the Delawares, after which some familiar chiefs appear no more in any account: Great Chief Shingas, for example, and his brother Pisquetomen."[236]

In October, Thomas Penn tightened the proprietors' control over their province by setting in place as lieutenant governor his nephew John Penn. Succeeding James Hamilton in the office, the young John arrived in Philadelphia with his brother Richard Jr. These young sons of Richard Sr., who owned one-quarter of the proprietorship, arrived as dutiful nephews who undoubtedly would be more malleable to the will of their uncle Thomas than the experienced colonist Hamilton or his professional predecessors had been. They had also come to begin their apprenticeships as the next generation of chief executives for Penn Incorporated.

---

[235] Ibid., 128–29.

[236] Jennings, *Empire of Fortune*, 447–48. As Jennings also notes: "An account book for the same month bears the item, 'To sundries got to replace in kind those which were taken from people in the hospital to convey the small pox to the Indians,' listing two blankets and two handkerchiefs." Ibid., 447n26.

Ending the Holy Experiment 1750–1781

Then, in the final days of 1763, came the year's climactic atrocity. As if directed by some law commanding historical symmetry, the remnant of the Native Americans on the lower Susquehanna—those to whom William Penn in 1701 had pledged "forever hereafter [to] be as one head and one heart and live in true friendship and amity as one people"—were massacred by fifty-seven Scotch-Irish Presbyterian frontiersmen from upriver Paxton (today's Harrisburg). Just as the remnant of the eastern Lenapes had been violently driven out of the Wyoming Valley earlier in the year, now the Susquehanna-Conestoga Indians living at Conestoga Indiantown, a protected reserve close to the Penns' own Conestoga Manor, were put to death. On December 14, the "Paxton Boys" killed the six Conestogas they found at Indiantown. On the 27th, the murderers returned and slaughtered the fourteen Indians who had been away from home on the 14th. This time, however, the bloody work was accomplished in the Lancaster public workhouse where the Indians had been placed in order to be protected by the colonial authorities.[237]

There were universal cries of outrage, but no effectual actions were taken. The newly arrived lieutenant governor, John Penn, issued two proclamations commanding that the perpetrators be brought to justice, but none were apprehended. Although the murderers were known and collectively reviled, not one of them was punished. Benjamin Franklin, then back in the province for a two-year interlude in his service as the Assembly's agent in England, memorialized the lives of the martyred Christian native people and recorded the judgment of history on the Paxton Boys in his *A narrative of the late massacres: in Lancaster County, of a number of Indians, friends of this province, by persons unknown. With some observations on the same.*[238] Noting that "the faith of this government has been frequently given to those Indians;—but that did not avail them with people who despise government," Franklin wrote:

> We pretend to be Christians, and, from the superior light we enjoy, ought to exceed *Heathens, Turks, Saracens, Moors, Negroes* and *Indians,* in the knowledge and practice of what is right.[239]

---

[237] See Kenny, *Peaceable Kingdom Lost,* 135–43.

[238] Benjamin Franklin, *A narrative of the late massacres . . .* (Philadelphia: Anthony Armbruster, 1764).

[239] Ibid., 13–14, emphasis in original.

Describing examples of the "sacred rites of hospitality" found among the other peoples he had named, Franklin concluded that the murdered Conestogas

> would have been safe in any part of the known world,— except in the neighborhood of the Christian white savages of Pecktang [Paxton] and Donegall!
>
> O ye unhappy perpetrators of this horrid wickedness! Reflect a moment on the mischief ye have done, the disgrace ye have brought on your country, on your religion, and your Bible, on your families and children! Think on the destruction of your captivated country-folks (now among the wild Indians) which probably may follow, in resentment of your barbarity! Think on the wrath of the United Five Nations, hitherto our friends, but now provoked by your murdering one of their tribes, in danger of becoming our bitter enemies. Think of the mild and good government you have so audaciously insulted; the laws of your King, your Country, and your God, that you have broken; the infamous death that hangs over your heads:—For justice though slow, will come at last.—All good people everywhere detest your actions.—You have imbrued [drenched] your hands in innocent blood; how will you make them clean?—The dying shrieks and groans of the murdered, will often sound in your ears. Their spectres will sometimes attend you, and affright even your innocent children! —Fly where you will, your consciences will go with you. Talking in your sleep shall betray you, in the delirium of a fever you yourselves shall make your own wickedness known.[240]

But the Paxton Boys were not yet a spent, much less repentant, force. In early February of 1764, over five hundred of them were headed toward Philadelphia, there to murder Indians from Bethlehem who had been converted to Christianity by Moravian missionaries and were now under the province's protection from the savage Scots-Irish coming for them out of Pennsylvania's frontier country. John Penn, noting in his December 22, 1763, proclamation that the Indians were in Philadelphia "for their better security . . . where provision is made

---

[240] Ibid., 27–28.

for them at the public expense," strictly forbade their being molested or injured.[241] When news of the approaching menace reached Philadelphia, the residents, including many Quakers, prepared to defend themselves with arms. Israel Pemberton was known to be a special target of the Paxton Boys, and he left the city after being urged to do so.[242] On February 7, the Paxton Boys were met outside the city by Franklin, who had with him the speaker of the Assembly, the provincial attorney general, the mayor of Philadelphia, and provincial councilor William Logan.[243] The march ended in Germantown, where the rebels agreed to submit their grievances and demands for redress to the Assembly. Franklin, anticipating this threat of further atrocities against peaceable Christian Indians, had already put in print his condemnation of the would-be assassins in words that must have served him well in bringing them to lay down their arms at Germantown, thus saving the city from bloodshed.

> Unmanly men! who are not ashamed to come with weapons against the unarmed, to use the sword against women, and the bayonet against young children; and who have already given such bloody proofs of their inhumanity and cruelty. Let us rouse ourselves, for shame, and redeem the honor of our province from the contempt of its neighbors; let all good men join heartily and unanimously in support of the laws, and in strengthening the hands of government; that justice may be done, the wicked punished, and the innocent protected; otherwise we can, as a people, expect no blessing from heaven, there will be no security for our persons or properties; anarchy and confusion will prevail over all, and violence, without judgment, dispose of every thing.[244]

With this pacification of the Paxton savages by Franklin, who was acting to preserve innocent Lenape Indians cared for by Moravian missionaries and protected by the Assembly, William Penn's experiment in planting a province, secure in the peaceful

---

[241] Ibid., 7–8.

[242] Thayer, *Israel Pemberton*, 188–89.

[243] Kenny, *Peaceable Kingdom Lost*, 162.

[244] Franklin, *A narrative of the late massacres*, 29.

coexistence of all its people and embracing their many diversities of origin, race, religion, and culture, only paused in its unwinding. Its peace testimony had failed the peoples' need for self-defense, and its pledge of unity and amity with the native peoples had been undone by the removal of the Indians from their ancestral lands by sons of William Penn, the founder. Thus, two fundamental principles of the holy experiment were fatally weakened. New leadership was emerging in the public life of Pennsylvania, but it came neither from the Penns nor from the Friends but from the Assembly and from new, rising, talented men like Franklin.

Separation and revolution: End times (1764–1781)

By 1764, the dynamics of change driving Britain's colonies in North America toward separation from their mother country's interests had been at work in Pennsylvania for some time. As its centenary year approached, the colony, planted by William Penn as a refuge for dissenters from state churches as well as for those seeking liberty of conscience, was a magnet drawing many away from Europe to America's ever westward-thrusting colonial frontier. It was inevitable that Pennsylvania's population growth, won against formidable obstacles, would cause conflicts within the colony and bring on its own dynamics of change that challenged even William Penn's founding vision.

The religious freedom enjoyed by the Quakers in Pennsylvania was practiced as an ordered faith grounded in the Christian testimonies and sufferings of George Fox and his followers, testimonies embodied in the spirit of the holy experiment and carried out in the lives of the members of the Religious Society of Friends. Even when the Society adjusted and righted the experiment through the agency of PYM and its clerks, as in its awakening to the evils of slavery, it did so through unity in the Spirit and self-education. Contention and factionalism were antithetical to the faith.

As already noted, in 1760, after serving as clerk of PYM for ten years, Israel Pemberton Jr. had stepped down from that office. During his ten years of service, he had skillfully built up support for the anti-slavery cause within PYM. PYM had given the Atlantic world the first such corporate Quaker abolition testimony in 1754 with the adoption of *An Epistle of Caution and Advice, Concerning the Buying and Keeping of Slaves* and with the permission of the Overseers of the Press to publish Woolman's

Some Considerations on the Keeping of Negroes.[245] In 1760, Pemberton was still engaged in a major cause, that of supporting the Lenape Indians in seeking justice for the wrongful taking of their lands through the Walking Purchase carried out by the proprietors of Pennsylvania. Concerned by the Lenapes' growing poverty brought on by their removal from those lands and by their need of strategic support in treaty negotiations with the proprietors, Pemberton had organized the Friendly Association among Quaker supporters but outside the formal structures of PYM. Pemberton and members of the Friendly Association labored hard at the Easton treaty conferences to support Teedyuscung, the eastern Lenape chief, in his tribal claims against the Penns and their agents. By the time the six treaty conferences ended with a face-saving formal victory for the proprietors and some monetary satisfaction for the Lenapes, half of which was contributed by the Friendly Association for humanitarian purposes, Pemberton, although continuing as clerk of the overseers of the Philadelphia Friends Public School until his death in 1779, had left his leadership role among Pennsylvania's Quakers. The mantle of the PYM clerkship that he had worn with energy and vision then passed to his brother James, who served as clerk for all but two years (1767 and 1777) between 1761 and 1781.

During the disastrous year of 1763, the eastern Lenapes were expelled from the Wyoming Valley on the north branch of the Susquehanna River and into the Ohio country (a calamity that had begun when Teedyuscung was burned alive in his Wyoming home) and the Paxton Boys massacred the remnant of the Conestoga Indians on the lower Susquehanna in Lancaster County. In that same year, as mentioned above, a direct descendant of William Penn arrived in Pennsylvania. Thirty-four-year-old John Penn, grandson of the founder and son of Richard Penn Sr., who owned one-quarter interest in the proprietorship, had come to take up the executive authority in the province and to serve as lieutenant governor at the pleasure of Thomas Penn, his uncle who owned the remaining three-quarters interest in the proprietorship.

This young man, sometimes referred to as John Penn the Governor, had for many years been under the watchful eye of his

---

[245] See above, pp. 304–10.

uncle Thomas.[246] Until the birth in 1760 of his first son to survive childhood (later known as John the Writer), Thomas protected this nephew as the apparent successor to the principal proprietary share of Pennsylvania. When John at age seventeen made a secret and unfortunate marriage that his family opposed, his uncle Thomas sent him to Geneva with a tutor but without the bride. Upon his return from Geneva, John was sent alone to Philadelphia as a student of the local politics, serving the lieutenant governor, James Hamilton, and attending meetings of the Council with Richard Peters and William Allen, among others, as well as of the Albany Congress of 1754 alongside Isaac Norris and Benjamin Franklin. Called back to England when Thomas became concerned about his nephew's "extravagant expenses," John continued in the family land enterprise. At last, in 1763, he was rewarded by being appointed the lieutenant governor of Pennsylvania. Thomas had decided John was ready to take on the responsibility of quasi-viceroy in the province for Penn Incorporated and thus gave him the opportunity to manage what at least should someday be the one-quarter interest now owned by John's father Richard, if not the three-quarter interest likely to be passed on from Thomas to his underage son.

The new lieutenant governor embraced life in Pennsylvania and, except for absences necessitated by war and business, lived out the remainder of his years there. In that, he was unique among the Penns. In 1766 he married Anne Allen,[247] the daughter of William Allen, who was a wealthy merchant, the chief justice of Pennsylvania, and a Penn family familiar and supporter, with landholdings (a result of the Walking Purchase) in the Lehigh Valley. At his father's death in 1771, John and his family returned to England to deal with estate concerns and with John's new one-quarter proprietary interest inherited from his father. He was succeeded as lieutenant governor in Pennsylvania by his brother Richard Jr., but when Thomas became so dissatisfied with Richard's administration that he removed him in 1773, he ordered John back to Philadelphia to serve as viceroy again. John Penn's

---

[246] This John Penn was sometimes referred to as "the Governor" to distinguish him from his uncle John Penn "the American," who was the oldest son of William and Hannah Callowhill Penn and the second chief proprietor of Pennsylvania, as well as from John Penn "of Stoke" or "the Writer," the elder son of Thomas Penn, the fourth and last chief proprietor of Pennsylvania.

[247] Whether John's earlier marriage was terminated by death or otherwise is not known; "the light on that episode is very imperfect." Jenkins, *The Family of William Penn*, 188.

service ended in 1776, one year after Thomas's death, when a convention, presided over by Franklin, adopted a new constitution for Pennsylvania providing for a supreme executive council and a unicameral legislature. This constitution effectively abolished William Penn's charter and terminated proprietary government in the province.

In 1777, as British forces advanced on Philadelphia, John Penn was held under house arrest in the city until he signed a statement that he would not harm the revolutionary cause. He was then exiled to a New Jersey estate of his wife's family until July 1778, when it was safe to return to Philadelphia, at which time he and all residents were required to take a loyalty oath to the commonwealth. Having already lost his office in government, in November 1779 he also lost his share in the proprietorship's 24 million acres of unsold lands in Pennsylvania when the Assembly passed "An Act for vesting the estates of the late Proprietaries of Pennsylvania in this Commonwealth." He and his cousin John Penn of Stoke were eventually paid £130,000 for the confiscation, a fraction of the real value of the land. Later they jointly made a successful claim in Parliament and won a total annuity for life of £4,000. During the time of shepherding the claim through Parliament, John Penn lived in England. Upon returning to his home in Lansdowne outside Philadelphia, John Penn, the last colonial governor of the province, enjoyed a quiet and peaceful retirement with his family until his death in 1795. He was buried at Christ Church, Philadelphia, the only one of the province's proprietors to make his final resting place in Pennsylvania.[248]

By the time PYM sat for its annual meeting in September 1760, Israel Pemberton had ended his responsibilities as its clerk. During his service, this influential body of Friends had issued its historic testimonies against the evils of slavery. However, it was in the capacity of private citizen and Quaker leader in 1756 and later that Pemberton, joined by many Friends, had been engaged in the cause of assisting the Lenapes in their struggle with the proprietors at the Easton treaties over the claimed wrongful taking of native lands in the Walking Purchase. It was a contest no one won, not even the proprietors, whose assets held in the Proprietary Land Office were confiscated in 1779. But the settlement of that dispute in 1762 and the tragic massacres of 1763 so reduced citizen Pemberton's ability to offer aid and

---

[248] Ibid., 188–92.

assistance to the native peoples that he was ultimately diminished in his own energies and in his once commanding influence in Philadelphia public life.

In many of the years following Israel Pemberton's leadership of PYM, that institution appeared to be turning inward. During James Pemberton's clerkship lasting nineteen of the years between 1761 and 1781 (others taking the office in 1767 and 1777), PYM was mostly focused on such matters as maintaining and codifying its discipline, enforcing the performance of duties, keeping up meeting attendance, condemning lotteries and excessive alcohol consumption, and educating youth. In 1762, for example, Pemberton recorded in the PYM minutes his intention of collecting and alphabetizing the rules of discipline and the interpretive advices that later meetings had added.[249] When the occasion was urgent, however, problems facing the holy experiment were addressed. The 1762 epistle from PYM to London Yearly Meeting noted "the controversies . . . respecting [Indian] lands" and voiced the concerned albeit helpless "attention and care of many Friends, that the fruits of life among the [Indian] nations of this land may be rightly cherished in a manner suitable to their weak states."[250] In its 1763 epistle to London Yearly Meeting, referring to the "distressed state of our frontier settlements," PYM cited approvingly the royal order in council of 1761 "forbidding any settlements made or continued on any lands not purchased of the Indians."[251]

As threats of force and civil unrest were increasingly heard in the fractured province, PYM began to give voice to the Quakers' venerable peace testimony. In its 1764 epistle to London Yearly Meeting, written seven months after the Paxton Boys marched on Philadelphia, PYM noted that some Quakers "deviated from our peace principles and bore arms in the late commotion." It reported that the monthly meetings were investigating all such violations and taking appropriate action. The unrest had led to a decision in the Assembly to petition the king to annul the proprietary charter and put in place a royal government. On that issue, PYM chose to remain "still and quiet" while asking the London Quakers "to interpose with your influence for securing our liberties and privileges."[252]

---

[249] PYM Min Bk C, p. 173.
[250] Ibid., 174.
[251] Ibid., 188–89.
[252] Ibid., 204.

Ending the Holy Experiment 1750–1781

In the final years before the American Revolution, Quaker pacifism drew growing condemnation from other American colonies as many citizens became increasingly resolved to remove all British overlordship. In 1774 PYM sent an epistle "to Friends in these and the adjacent provinces" touching on Quaker sufferings and rights and liberties, civil and religious. Recalling the sacrifices for the sake of conscience made by the early Quakers, the Friends gathered in Philadelphia wrote:

> Let us carefully guard against being drawn into the vindication of [our sufferings, rights, and liberties], or seeking redress by any measures which are not consistent with our religious profession and principles nor with the Christian patience manifested by our ancestors in such times of trial; and we fervently desire all may impartially consider whether we have manifested that firmness in our love to the cause of Truth and universal righteousness which is required of us.[253]

The same meeting was reminded of the debt to the king "for our religious liberty" and of the loyalty and fidelity owed to the Crown. To counter the growing war spirit, all were cautioned against committing fraud "in customs or duties" and advised to "submit to just administration" and avoid the "violence of parties."[254]

In 1775 PYM adopted anti-war resolutions that included the disownment of members taking up arms. Those Friends who scrupled against even engaging in financial transactions "issued expressly for the purpose of carrying on the war" were exhorted not to "censure in their minds" those who did not share that view. This was so that "nothing is done through strife and contention, but [rather] that they act from a clear conviction of Truth in their own minds; showing forth, by their meekness, humility, and patient suffering, that they are followers of the Prince of Peace."[255]

Two months after the Declaration of Independence was signed in Philadelphia, PYM again ventured boldly into the public arena with its peace testimonies. The yearly meeting of 1776 sent out an epistle to the monthly and quarterly meetings "in these and the adjacent provinces" ordering Friends to cease serving in

---

[253] Ibid., 366.
[254] Ibid., 366–67.
[255] Michener, *A Retrospect of Early Quakerism*, 300.

public offices of any kind, either of profit or trust, "it now appearing to us that the power and authority . . . are founded and supported on the spirit of wars and fightings."[256] Its epistle to London Yearly Meeting that year gave expression to the gospel foundation of the testimony:

> Jesus taught that wrath, contention, wars and fighting are unlawful; meekness, patience, and universal love to mankind will be rewarded with peace.[257]

There was a price to be paid for this boldness. On August 28, 1777, the Continental Congress meeting in Philadelphia recommended to the executive authorities that it was

> necessary for the public safety at this time, when a British army has landed in Maryland, with a professed design of enslaving this free country, and is now advancing toward this city, as a principal object of hostility, that dangerous persons be accordingly secured.[258]

The document named forty-one "dangerous persons." In response, a warrant to law officers was issued on August 31 by the Supreme Executive Council of Pennsylvania for the seizure and securing of Israel, James, and John Pemberton along with thirty-eight other citizens. The reason given was that these were persons "who have in their general conduct and conversation evinced a disposition inimical to the cause of America."[259] Following their arrest, the prisoners were exiled to Winchester, Virginia, where they were held until March of the following year, at which time the Continental Congress ordered their return to custodial authorities in Pennsylvania. There, in April, the Supreme Executive Council, as directed by the Assembly, authorized their discharge. While the sufferings for faith endured by Quakers in England were being repeated in the New World, concerned Friends attending the 1777 yearly meeting sent a commission to the contending generals, Howe and Washington, to address the "calumnies" being cast upon Quakers. They also prepared and widely circulated a printed testimony explaining how "we are led

---

[256] Ibid., 356

[257] Ibid., 360.

[258] Thomas Gilpin, *Exiles in Virginia: With Observations on the Conduct of the Society of Friends during the Revolutionary War* (Bowie, MD: Heritage Books, 2003), 71–72.

[259] Ibid.

out of all wars and fightings by the principle of grace and truth."[260]

Some of those who came home from Winchester did not long survive the rigors—including an unnamed epidemic—they had endured in the Virginia exile. One of the earliest to fall was Israel Pemberton Jr., who in exile had written to his wife Mary (the clerk of PYM's Women's Meeting from 1760 to 1777), "I am become a poor weak, old man."[261] When at last he returned home in March 1778, he found Mary herself nearing death (she died in October of that year). He also found that his personal wealth and estates had sunk in value during the banishment. His own death on April 22, 1779,[262] at the age of sixty-four years, ended his thirty-four years of service as clerk of the overseers of the Philadelphia Friends Public School, one of the lasting institutional successes of Penn's experiment.

James Pemberton continued in office as clerk of PYM until his successor was appointed at the yearly meeting held in 1782, one hundred years after the commencement of Penn's 'holy experiment.' William Penn had named the experiment in his letter dated August 25, 1681, to James Harrison, Pemberton's great-grandfather, and the experiment had been well served through Harrison's succeeding generations by Phineas, Israel Jr., and finally James Pemberton as clerks of PYM; by Israel Sr. as clerk of Philadelphia Monthly Meeting; and by Mary as clerk of PYM's Women's Meeting. As the last of these guardian clerks serving the founder's noble ideals, James had presided over a provincial institution preeminent in both church and state. Even though the concerns of PYM in the last years of James Pemberton's clerkship addressed not only the ongoing parochial matters of maintaining Quaker discipline but the wider labors for ending slavery, assisting those newly emancipated in finding real freedom, and preserving the peace testimony in time of war, there were already evident signs of the beginnings of a new age in a new nation being forged in a new strength. New people of ability and skill were now emerging as the new leaders. Of these, none was more gifted or talented than Benjamin Franklin.

Franklin's extraordinary rise through business, public office, and civic philanthropy into renown as a statesman,

---

[260] PYM Min Bk C, p. 383.
[261] Quoted in Thayer, *Israel Pemberton*, 230.
[262] Ibid., 231–33.

founding father, scientist, inventor, and even educational pioneer is legendary. Beginning in 1752 with his service in the Assembly, where, as already noted, he closely involved himself in Indian affairs by advocating fairness for the Native Americans and resistance to the hostile policies of the Penns, his services so closely tracked the paths of the holy experiment that it seems today that it came under his charge. The last years of the Pembertons' distinguished clerkships coincided with the rise of Franklin's influence. That change was clearly signaled in February 1764 when Franklin, just home from five years in London as the agent representing the Assembly in its relations with the Penns, met the Paxton Boys outside Philadelphia and defused their threatened attack on the center city while Israel Pemberton was escaping that city in fear of his life.

Franklin's influence in the affairs of Philadelphia, of Pennsylvania, of the American colonies in revolt against Britain, and of the United States of America at its founding played a large role in the nation's history. His influence seemingly was felt everywhere, even though much of Franklin's time was spent in Europe on official business. The first of his three foreign appointments sent him to England, where, from 1757 to 1762, he served as Assembly agent vis-à-vis the Penns. Briefly back in Philadelphia in 1763 and 1764, he confronted the Paxton Boys in their murderous march on the city, wrote and printed an account of their infamous massacre of innocent Indians in Lancaster County, led the antiproprietary party in the Assembly, was elected Assembly speaker, called for a royal government, and was defeated for re-election to the Assembly but then returned to England as the Assembly's agent. His second service to the Assembly in London lasted from 1764 to 1775, in which time he opposed the Crown's short-lived Stamp Act of 1765 and the successor Townshend Acts and so distinguished himself that Georgia, New Jersey, and Massachusetts appointed him agent in London to represent each of them to the Crown.

Upon returning to Philadelphia, where he stayed from May 1775 to December 1776, Franklin was quickly appointed by the Assembly as its delegate to the Second Continental Congress and then by the Congress as a member of its Committee of Five charged with drafting the Declaration of Independence. At the conclusion of that work, Franklin was made the president of the Pennsylvania constitutional convention, convened for the purpose of writing and adopting a state constitution to replace its prerevolutionary charter. In Pennsylvania, that meant William

Penn's handiwork in constitutional law was to be superseded—including his formulation of the primary principles of the holy experiment: freedom of religion and liberty of conscience. In addition, the Pennsylvania constitutional convention took the first of the two formal actions that terminated the Penns' rights of overlordship in their New World colony.

The Pennsylvania convention under Franklin's presidency assembled at Philadelphia on July 15 and completed its charge on September 28, 1776. As with William Penn's several frames of government then being swept into history's archives, the new 1776 "Constitution of the Commonwealth of Pennsylvania" was composed of two parts: Chapter I titled "A Declaration of the Rights of the Inhabitants of the State of Pennsylvania," consisting of sixteen articles, and Chapter II titled "Plan or Frame of Government," consisting of forty-seven sections.[263] This constitution was not required to be submitted to the voters for ratification, and it became effective upon its proclamation. The Frame of the Government provided for a unicameral legislature and a collective executive, sealing the closure of both the Penns' rule and the Crown's oversight from across the Atlantic.

The declaration of rights sets out the specific "natural," "inherent," and "inalienable" rights of Pennsylvania's inhabitants. Second only to the first declaration that "all men are born equally free and independent" with rights for "enjoying and defending life and liberty, acquiring and protecting property, and pursuing and obtaining happiness and safety" was the "natural and unalienable" "right to worship Almighty God according to the dictates of [their] own consciences and understanding." Those dictates, however, could just as well defend the *right not to worship,* thus significantly altering Penn's declaration in the 1701 Charter of Privileges that

> no person or persons inhabiting in this province . . . who shall confess and acknowledge one almighty God, the creator, upholder, and ruler of the world and profess him or themselves obliged to live quietly under the civil government, shall be in any case molested or prejudiced

---

[263] *The First Laws of the Commonwealth of Pennsylvania,* comp. John B. Cushing (Wilmington, DE: M. Glazier, 1984), vii–xxi. This is a facsimile reprint of *The acts of the General Assembly of the Commonwealth of Pennsylvania* (Philadelphia: Francis Bailey, 1782).

in his or their person or estate because of his or their conscientious persuasion or practice.[264]

This 1776 declaration of rights, lifting up the preeminent rights of all men as "born equally free and independent," gave men the right to worship or not as they saw fit. In sharp contrast, Penn in 1701 lifted up as the preeminent truth that "Almighty God [is] the only Lord of Conscience, Father of Lights and Spirits, and the Author as well as object of all divine knowledge, faith and worship, who only can enlighten the mind and persuade and convince the understandings of people," thus allowing diversity of expression only within the duty of God's people to worship God. Penn, in effect, made the protection of freedom of religion available to those who "confessed and acknowledged one God," not to non-believers. In 1776, Franklin and the other 'new' leaders in Pennsylvania set aside Penn's concept of the reign of God in the governance of Pennsylvania and replaced it with what they viewed as the rights of man.

There were other significant differences between Penn's declaration of 1701 and that of Franklin's convention in 1776. Penn's declaration protected "persons" rather than "men" and premised their right to freedom of religion on their obligation to live quietly under the civil government. Further, Penn expressly limited the right to serve in the executive or legislative branches of government to those persons "who also profess to believe in Jesus Christ the savior of the world," but the 1776 declaration limited the right of any man not to be unjustly "deprived or abridged of any civil right" because of religion if he "acknowledges the being of a God." The 1776 declaration of rights thus broadened the protection of freedom of religion to cover not only Christians, who were protected by Penn's 1701 declaration of rights, but all who believed in "a God."

As already seen, PYM's reaction to this constitutional change came at its annual meeting, which began on the day the declaration of rights was proclaimed. In an epistle to its quarterly and monthly meetings, PYM urged that Friends withdraw from being active in civil government and from continuing "in public offices of any kind."[265]

---

[264] For the complete text of the Charter of Privileges, see *PWP*, 4:104–10 (quotation is from p. 106).

[265] PYM Min Bk C, p. 356.

Ending the Holy Experiment 1750–1781

The second of the two formal actions taken by the revolutionary government in Pennsylvania terminating the proprietorship of that American colony was finalized on November 27, 1779, when the Assembly enacted a sweeping law "vesting the estates of the late Proprietaries of Pennsylvania in this Commonwealth."[266] Section 5 of the act vested every right held "in or to the soil and land" of Pennsylvania on July 4, 1776, by the proprietors (who on that date were Thomas Penn's son known as John of Stoke or John the Writer, who owned three-quarters of the proprietorship, and Richard Penn's son known as John the Governor, who owned the other quarter) "in the commonwealth of Pennsylvania, for the use and benefit of the citizens thereof." Any and all claims or rights whatsoever that the Penns might have had under the royal charter of Charles II were repealed, and the soil and lands now vested in the commonwealth were held subject to the disposal of the legislature (section 6). Provisions were made to confirm all titles granted by or derived from the proprietors before July 4, 1776 (section 7) as well as all lands and estates that, prior to July 4, 1776, were possessed by or else were the private entitlements of the proprietors, including the proprietary manors (section 8). All former powers of the proprietors were repealed (section 11), and all persons then possessing any land office records were ordered to deliver them on demand, subject to a penalty (section 16). Remembering "the enterprising spirit which distinguished the founder of Pennsylvania, and mindful of the expectations and dependence of his descendants on the propriety thereof," the Assembly, "desirous to manifest . . . their liberality," authorized the payment of £130,000 "to the devisees and legatees of Thomas Penn and Richard Penn . . . and to the widow . . . of the said Thomas Penn" (sections 12 and 13).

The "devisees and legatees of Thomas Penn and Richard Penn" were John of Stoke and John the Governor, respectively. The two Johns found the award not "liberal" enough, however. Indeed, it was a modest amount for the approximately 24 million acres of unsold land in Pennsylvania now passing from them as the proprietors into the ownership of the commonwealth. By

---

[266] *An Act for vesting the estates of the late proprietaries of Pennsylvania in this commonwealth*, Chap. CXXXIX [of the Acts of the General Assembly], in *The First Laws of the Commonwealth of Pennsylvania*, 258–63. The Act was attested by the speaker of the Assembly, Thomas Paine, another 'new' man of the age (and the son of a Quaker father).

1789, the commonwealth had received £825,000 for the sale of part of the lands.[267] That same year, seeking further compensation, the two Penn cousins returned to England, where they successfully petitioned Parliament for relief from the underpayment. The relief was an annual grant of £4,000 in perpetuity.[268]

The Revolutionary War in Pennsylvania: The Philadelphia Campaign (1777–1778)

The grim reality in Philadelphia and Pennsylvania during the last years of the holy experiment was that the peace of Penn's province was rapidly fading. In its place, pervading all life in the commonwealth, came first the threat of war and then war itself.

The most difficult years in Philadelphia were 1777 and 1778, when the virtual capital of the new nation and its seaboard geographic center was first under siege and then occupation by the British. The occupation lasted until the invaders voluntarily evacuated in mid-1778. In an attempt to disrupt the work of the Continental Congress at its seat, the British began an advance on Philadelphia from the south, making an amphibious landing on the Elk River in the northeastern area of Chesapeake Bay near Head of Elk (modern Elkton, Maryland) on August 25, 1777. As the invaders under General Sir William Howe made an overland advance north toward Philadelphia they successfully skirmished with units of George Washington's Continental Army in the battles of Brandywine (September 11), of the Clouds (at Warren Tavern near Malvern on September 16), and of Paoli (September 20). Entering Philadelphia on September 26, General Howe divided his force, leaving some three thousand men in the city and placing about nine thousand troops in Germantown to protect the western approaches to Penn's 'city of brotherly love' from Washington's forces then in the area. Believing he had the advantage, Washington engaged the British in the Battle of Germantown on October 4 with a force of eleven thousand men,

---

[267] Lorett Treese, *The Storm Gathering: The Penn Family and the American Revolution* (University Park: Pennsylvania State University Press, 1992), 188–91; Richard S. Rodney, "The End of the Penns' Claim to Delaware, 1789–1814," *PMHB* 61 (1937): 182–203.

[268] Ibid., 199.

Ending the Holy Experiment 1750–1781

but a heavy morning fog so upset his strategy that the valiant attempt of the Continentals ended in yet another defeat.[269]

Washington remained in the area with his army during the weeks after the defeat at Germantown. Persevering in his campaign to dislodge the British in Philadelphia, he secured an entrenched site just beyond Germantown in White Marsh Township near Wissahickon Creek, enabling him to observe British troop movements in the region. Howe, determined to wipe out before winter the threat posed by Washington and his forces, attacked the Americans on December 4 and continued skirmishing until the 8th. Washington successfully defended his position, and this Battle of White Marsh (or Edge Hill) resolved nothing. On the 10th, Washington's council decided to move to winter quarters west of the Schuylkill River and sent out advance patrols for that purpose. One patrol met and skirmished with a British foraging party on December 11 in the Battle of Matson's Ford (now Conshohocken). By the 12th, however, the Americans were safely across the river, and by the 19th they had reached their winter encampment at Valley Forge. In the meantime, from September 26 to November 16 the British, in order to secure for their troops a line of supply on the Delaware River, engaged in a successful siege of Fort Mifflin on Mud Island lying in the river just below the city.[270]

The next year's campaign season brought additional setbacks for Washington's forces. On May 1, 1778, at Hatboro, some four hundred Pennsylvania militiamen—engaged in patrolling the area north of Philadelphia between the Schuylkill and Delaware Rivers in order to prevent loyalist farmers in the area from taking their goods into the city market as well as to protect local patriots from British harassment—were caught unawares at daybreak at the Crooked Billet Inn, where some were lodging. The Battle of Crooked Billet reduced the patriot forces by twenty-six lives and further diminished their strength by eight wounded and fifty-

---

[269] See Robert Middlekauff, *The Glorious Cause: The American Revolution, 1763–1789* (New York: Oxford University Press, 1982), 384–95; Don Higginbotham, *The War of American Independence: Military Attitudes, Policies, and Practice, 1763–1789* (New York: Macmillan, 1971), 181–88; Douglas Southall Freeman, *George Washington: A Biography*, vol. 4 (New York: C. Scribner's Sons, 1951), 467–519; Thomas J. McGuire, *The Philadelphia Campaign, Vol. 1: Brandywine and the Fall of Philadelphia* (Mechanicsburg, PA: Stackpole Books, 2006).

[270] Thomas J. McGuire, *The Philadelphia Campaign, Vol. 2: Germantown and the Roads to Valley Forge* (Mechanicsburg, PA: Stackpole Books, 2007).

eight captured men. And at the May 20 Battle of Barren Hill (now Lafayette Hill), Washington, informed of a coming British withdrawal from Philadelphia, sent Lafayette with a force of 2,200 men to reconnoiter British troop movements. Caught in a trap by sixteen thousand men of the enemy, Lafayette slipped away unscathed.

The war elsewhere, however, had already taken a dramatic turn in America's favor. On October 17, 1777, thirteen days after Washington's brave but unsuccessful engagement at Germantown, an American force under General Horatio Gates forced the surrender of a British invasion army under General John Burgoyne advancing southward from Montreal through the Champlain Valley toward Albany and the Hudson River, intending to capture that city and control the river. This American success at the Battles of Saratoga (September 19 and October 7, 1777) and the valiant fight of Washington's men at Germantown gave resolve to the French intention to aid the Americans. On February 6, 1778, France recognized the United States of America as an independent nation, and the two entered into both a Treaty of Alliance and a Treaty of Amity and Commerce. In consequence, on March 17 Britain declared war on France, giving its ancient enemy opportunity to recoup some of the territorial losses it had suffered in America at the end of the recent French and Indian War.

By June 1778, the British command and strategy in America had changed. Howe, whose plans for Burgoyne's thwarted Albany attack miscarried in part because of his own inaction, resigned his command and sailed for England on May 24. His successor, General Sir Henry Clinton, as ordered, evacuated Philadelphia in June and relocated his forces to assist in the defense of New York City. Also in June, a commission led by the Earl of Carlisle came to Philadelphia from England to present peace proposals to the Continental Congress. Negotiations could not even begin, however, because the Americans insisted that either their independence must be recognized or the British forces withdrawn from the states as a precondition for meeting.

The Revolutionary War in Pennsylvania: Iroquoia and the Sullivan Expedition (1778–1779)

Even before Philadelphia was rid of the British, the war had appeared on the wilderness frontier of Pennsylvania. Beginning in the spring of 1778, the British put into effect plans for making

Ending the Holy Experiment 1750–1781

preemptive attacks in the state's backcountry to keep patriot settlers and vengeful French interests out of those areas. The planners were the American loyalist John Butler, long associated with Sir William Johnson; Mohawk chief Joseph Brant; and Seneca chiefs Sayenqueraghta and Cornplanter. Their strategy was to recruit both colonists and Native Americans who were loyal to the Crown to carry out raids on settlements along the Allegheny River, the North and West Branches of the Susquehanna River, and the Mohawk River.

The intention of the Treaty of Stanwix in 1768 between Britain and the Iroquois Nations had been to adjust the boundary line between native lands and the British colonies first set in the Royal Proclamation of 1763. Included in the treaty were provisions for resolving certain land matters between the Native Americans and the Penn proprietors. Those provisions involved a so-called New Purchase that led to conflict along the West Branch of the Susquehanna, the settlers insisting that their new western line crossed the river at Pine Creek (near the modern Jersey Shore) and the Senecas with their allies and the colonial authorities insisting that the line was drawn at Lycoming Creek (near modern Williamsport) farther to the east. The land between the disputed two western lines was known as the Fair Play area and was self-governed by three commissioners elected by the resident settlers, who were deemed squatters by the Indians and colonial authorities. Here on the West Branch, Seneca and allied Cayuga and Lenape warriors, concerned to protect their homeland claims in the disputed area, opened a theater of war in early 1778. Settlements were raided on May 16 at Bald Creek (today's Lock Haven), then later at Loyalsock Creek (today's Montoursville), and still later at Pine Creek. A string of primitive forts and fortified houses was prepared along the West Branch, but local militias and the state did not provide effective protection. Finally, after further raids made on June 10 had struck settlers on both the Loyalsock and Lycoming Creeks, local authorities ordered the mass evacuation of the West Branch valley. All was abandoned, including small forts and fortified houses, as the refugees escaped on foot and raft down the West Branch to Muncy, some going farther downriver to Fort Augusta at Shamokin (today's Sunbury) near the confluence of the Susquehanna's West and North Branches. Despite the terrible losses suffered in this Big Runaway, as it was later known, some of the uprooted settlers later returned to rebuild their lives.

Other massacres were carried out in the backcountry in furtherance of the British war plans. On July 3, Butler joined with the Senecas in attacking the Wyoming Valley on the North Branch of the Susquehanna. He reported success to his superior on July 8, noting that

> in this action were taken 227 scalps and only five prisoners. . . . In this incursion we have taken and destroyed eight palisaded forts, and burned about one thousand dwelling homes, all their mills, etc. . . . But what gives us the sincerest satisfaction is . . . that in the destruction of this settlement not a single person has been hurt of the inhabitants, but such as were in arms, to those indeed the Indians gave no quarter.[271]

While the Senecas harried the Susquehanna areas, the British strategy of waging guerilla warfare against patriot settlements was being carried out in the valleys of New York's Mohawk River and the upper North Branch of the Susquehanna by Joseph Brant's Mohawk Indians and their native allies. On May 30, they destroyed the settlement at Cobleskill in Schoharie County (the area from which Palatine German refugees had relocated in 1722 to Pennsylvania's Tulpehocken valley). Then, on September 17 at the German Flatts (present-day Herkimer), Brant and his force of Mohawks with allied Iroquois warriors and loyalist troops destroyed sixty-three homes and some mills, drove off or killed all the livestock, and left 719 people homeless. On November 11, at Cherry Valley in Otsego County, Seneca and Mohawk warriors with British and loyalist troops attacked the unprepared fort and village. The Senecas targeted non-combatant inhabitants, resulting in thirty being killed and another thirty being taken captive. These killings of civilians were committed to avenge both the accusations, denied by the Senecas, of their brutality at the Battle of Wyoming and the Americans' destruction between October 6 and 10 of the nearby Mohawk towns at Unadilla and Onaquaga.

The patriot response to the loyalists' frontier guerilla warfare was belated, and the option of striking further blows remained with the British and their allies through the spring and summer of 1778. Not until September 24 did the patriots undertake

---

[271] Copy of letter from Major John Butler to Lieutenant Colonel Bolton, Lacuwanack, July 8, 1778, Frederick Haldimand Papers, Additional Manuscripts No. 21,760, folios 31–34, British Library, http://revwar75.com/battles/primarydocs/wiom1778.htm.

retaliatory strikes against Iroquois villages in the North Branch of the Susquehanna. This was at the initiative of Pennsylvanian Thomas Hartley, who led his own newly raised Additional Continental Regiment. During his two-week campaign, nine to twelve Seneca, Lenape, and Mingo villages were burned in Pennsylvania and New York, including those at Tioga, Chemung, and Catherine's Town (at the southern end of Watkin's Glen).

Although the War Board of the Continental Congress on June 10 had called for an expeditionary force to engage those Iroquois Nations that were pro-British, namely, the Onondagas, Mohawks, Senecas, and Cayugas, no immediate action was taken. Not until March 6, 1779, was George Washington prepared to tap a willing general within his command worthy of accepting the leadership of an expeditionary army into Iroquois country. Washington gave the command to John Sullivan, a New Hampshire delegate to the Continental Congress who was familiar to Washington as a commander in the recent battles of Brandywine and Germantown as well as in earlier engagements. Washington's orders to Sullivan from "Head-Quarters 31 May 1779" made the mission brutally clear:

> The Expedition you are appointed to command is to be directed against the hostile tribes of the Six Nations of Indians, with their associates and adherents. The immediate objects are the total destruction and devastation of their settlements, and the capture of as many prisoners of every age and sex as possible. It will be essential to ruin their crops now in the ground and prevent their planting more....
>
> I would recommend that some post in the center of the Indian Country should be occupied with all expedition, with a sufficient quantity of provision; whence parties should be detached to lay waste all the settlements around, with instructions to do it in the most effectual manner, that the country may not be merely overrun but destroyed.... But you will not by any means listen to any overture of peace before the total ruin of their settlements is effected.... Our future security will be in their inability to injure us and in the terror with which the severity of

the chastisement they receive will inspire them. Peace without this would be fallacious and temporary.[272]

Washington's plan had been for the army of the Sullivan Expedition to total five thousand men organized in fifteen regiments. Due to casualties, illness, desertion, and under-enrollment, however, the Expedition at full strength never exceeded four thousand men in arms. As instructed, Sullivan had gathered his main force at Easton, and on June 18 he began moving it toward the Wyoming Valley in the North Branch of the Susquehanna, presumably following an upriver route along the Lehigh. The troops remained in the Wyoming Valley from June 23 to July 31 awaiting provisions and supplies and then made their way up the North Branch to Tioga (now Athens, Pennsylvania) at the forks of that river and the Chemung. After their August 11 arrival, construction began on Fort Sullivan, the temporary "post in the center of Indian Country," as commanded by Washington in his May 31 orders to Sullivan.

The rest of Sullivan's main force was put under the command of his deputy officer, General James Clinton of New York, who, as directed by Washington, in mid-June led his men west from Schenectady, New York. After marching through the Mohawk River Valley to Canajoharie, they portaged south to Otsego Lake, the source of the North Branch, there to await Sullivan's command for Clinton to bring his force to Tioga. After encamping on June 20 at the south end of the lake (now Cooperstown, New York), Clinton dammed and raised the level of Otsego, later destroying the dam and flooding the downriver areas.[273] On August 7, Clinton, upon receiving Sullivan's order, began his march to Tioga, destroying all Indian villages along the way.

The expeditionary force totaling almost thirty-five hundred men was at last united on August 22 at Fort Sullivan. Seven days later it proceeded up the Chemung River into the central western New York territories of Iroquoia. On August 29, the Expedition achieved a significant victory at the Battle of Newtown, its only major engagement. On Sullivan's men went, scorching the earth as far as Chenussio (near modern Geneseo, New York), a principal

---

[272] George Washington, *The Writings of George Washington from the Original Manuscript Sources, 1745–1799*, 39 vols., ed. John C. Fitzpatrick (Washington, DC: U. S. Government Printing Office, 1931–1944), 15:189–92.

[273] See the introduction to *The Pioneers, or the Sources of the Susquehanna; A Descriptive Tale*, the first to be published of James Fennimore Cooper's five novels known as the Leatherstocking Tales.

Ending the Holy Experiment 1750–1781

Seneca town. In his report on the expedition, Sullivan described the devastation inflicted there on September 15 as follows:

> We reached the Castle, which consisted of 128 houses, mostly large and elegant. The town was beautifully situated, almost encircled with a cleared flat, which extended for a number of miles, covered by the most extensive fields of corn, and every kind of vegetables that can be conceived. The whole army was immediately engaged in destroying the crops. The corn was collected and burned in houses and kilns, so the enemy might not reap the least advantage from it, which method we have pursued in every other place. . . . After having destroyed this town, beyond which I was informed there was no settlement, and destroyed all their houses and crops in that quarter, the army having been advancing seventeen days . . . and the Cayuga country being as yet unpenetrated, I thought it necessary to return as soon as possible in order to effect the destruction of the settlements in that quarter. The army therefore began its march to Kanadasaga [also known as Seneca Castle; near today's Geneva, New York].[274]

By the end of September, this army had returned to Fort Sullivan, which it soon abandoned to move on to its winter quarters at Morristown, New Jersey.

In addition to Sullivan's campaign, between August 11 and September 14 another expedition had been ravaging Seneca villages and crops up the Allegheny River from Fort Pitt as far as today's Salamanca, New York. Led by General Daniel Brodhead, commander of the Western Department of the army, the force of about six hundred men met little resistance, finding that most of the Seneca warriors living in the Allegheny area had gone eastward to help resist the Sullivan Expedition. Washington's plan for the two expeditions to join and advance on Fort Niagara was not carried out.

The devastations inflicted on the Iroquois by the Expeditions of Sullivan and Brodhead were compounded by the severity of the winter that followed. Made refugees in their wasted homelands,

---

[274] "Major Gen. Sullivan's Official Report," in *Journals of the Military Expedition of Major General John Sullivan against the Six Nations of Indians in 1779 with Records of Centennial Celebrations,* ed. Frederick Cook (Auburn, NY: Peck & Thompson Printers, 1887), 301–2.

many of the native Iroquois starved or froze to death. Although raids by the British and their Indian allies upon regional frontier families continued intermittently until the war's end, these expeditions across Iroquoia broke its power and its way of life. Iroquoia was now being ethnically cleansed, many of its peoples distressed and cast out of their homelands.

Thus ended James Logan's sophisticated geopolitical strategy of bonding Pennsylvania with the Iroquois Nations in a bright Friendship Chain, a strategy that was subverted at its inception and employed to drive out of the Delaware and lower Susquehanna Rivers the indigenous peoples William Penn had embraced at the beginning of his holy experiment. Now, in this savage campaign season of 1799, the broken Friendship Chain symbolized the climactic failure of the experiment. The peace of Pennsylvania was destroyed, and most of the native peoples were expelled from the region.

+ + +

Lest any think the holy experiment in Pennsylvania was but a failed dream, it should be acknowledged that, even in our own day, many of William Penn's founding principles continue to have wide influence. The heritage from the founder and his worthy successors continues in the Friends' schools, some established during William Penn's lifetime in Philadelphia and others springing forth as the Quaker witness spread through America and beyond. The seeds for emancipating slaves and abolishing the practice of involuntary servitude were cultivated within the structures of the Religious Society of Friends in Pennsylvania and New Jersey before being spread along the Atlantic seaboard and into the wider Western world. And the radical 'first cause' of the entire experiment—religious toleration and freedom of conscience—even in Penn's lifetime had become so widely accepted as to appear to be self-evident truth.

The great failures of the holy experiment—the forsaking of the covenant friendship with the indigenous people and the waging of war to secure control of the land—in hindsight now seem inevitable. The utopian task of planting a 'new world' in a wilderness fell to venturers and planters, many of whom had suffered under abusive state authority and inequitable social and economic conditions in the 'old world.' They were not saints, yet the founder wanted to establish a saintly society. It was a daunting task, his time was limited, an ocean separated his

Ending the Holy Experiment 1750–1781

province from the mother country, and Penn needed to be in both places at the same time. Overwhelmed by details until rendered mentally incapable of continuing to conduct his experiment, Penn failed to train his successors or even supervise his principal associates. But he did attempt the holy experiment; he sought a way that others may yet find.

The peace William Penn sought to plant in the colony named to honor his father, a man of war, which was lost through acts of his own sons and others, is memorialized at a Quaker site on a beautiful ridge above the Brandywine Valley. Within a walled area of the Birmingham Friends Meetinghouse burial ground is a peace garden. There, behind a large marker, is the common grave of colonial and British soldiers, "those who fell in this vicinity" on September 11, 1777, during the Battle of Brandywine. There also are thirteen stones set in the ground, arranged elliptically, each stone engraved with words from the past and reflecting on peace. The central stone has words of Penn offering a truthful epitaph upon the experiment he launched:

> A good end cannot sanctify evil means; nor must we ever do evil, that good may come of it. . . . Let us then try what love will do.[275]

---

[275] William Penn, *Some Fruits of Solitude in Reflections & Maxims*, introduction by Edmund Gosse (New York: Scott-Thaw Co., 1903), 102–3.

APPENDIX 1

Glossary

Note: The texts of the parliamentary acts referred to in this appendix, except for the years 1642–1660, may be found in *The Statutes of the Realm . . . from original records and authentic manuscripts*, 10 vols. (London: 1810–1828); those from 1642 to 1660 may be found in C. H. Firth and R. S. Rait, eds., *Acts and Ordinances of the Interregnum*, 3 vols. (London: H. M. Stationery Office, 1911).

abjure—to renounce an allegiance upon oath, to formally repudiate or disavow.
Act of Uniformity—See under Clarendon Code.
alderman—an associate to the chief civil magistrate of a corporate town or city.
assizes—periodic sittings of Court of King's Bench judges riding in seven circuits in England and Wales; heard the most serious cases referred by county courts of Quarter Sessions.
bailiff—officer under a sheriff.
bale-dock—an enclosed space occupied by prisoners in a criminal court.
Blasphemy Act (*Acts and Ordinances* [1650])—legislated punishment in England of "atheistical, blasphemous and execrable opinions derogatory to the honour of God and destructive to human society."
Board of Trade—also known as the Lords of Trade and Plantations. In the first half of the eighteenth century the Board was a committee of the Privy Council that regulated and managed the crown's trading networks among its colonies.
Chain of Friendship—See Friendship Chain.
Clarendon Code:
    Act of Uniformity (14 Car. II, c. 4 [1662])—mandated use of the Anglican Book of Common Prayer in worship services in England.
    Conventicle Act (16 Car. II, c. 4 [1664]; amended, 22 Car. II, c. 1 [1670])—prohibited meetings for unauthorized worship of five or more persons not of the same household in England.
    Corporation Act (13 Car. II, stat. 2, c. 1, [1661])—excluded nonconformists from public office in England.
    Five Mile Act (17 Car. II, c. 2 [1665])—forbade non-conformist ministers from coming within five miles of incorporated towns or from teaching in schools in England.
close prison—solitary confinement.
close prisoner—a prisoner in solitary confinement.

Appendix 1: Glossary

constable—officer appointed to keep peace in an assigned district.
Conventicle Act—See under Clarendon Code.
convincement—among early Quakers, a powerful and personal in-breaking of God; occurred when an individual submitted him or herself to an examination of their spiritual condition under the auspices of the divine light of Christ within. When the individual acknowledged where they had fallen short in their faith and behavior, they were "convicted" ("sanctified," in other Christian traditions).
Corporation Act—See under Clarendon Code.
Court of Assize—Crown circuit court holding semi-annual jury trials in England and Wales. See also assizes.
Court of Chancery—a superior court of record with jurisdiction in questions of law and equity.
Court of Common Pleas—an English court with jurisdiction over civil actions.
Court of Exchequer—a superior court of record with jurisdiction in questions of law and revenue.
Court of King's Bench—in the seventeenth century, an English national court of record that heard criminal cases and matters that concerned the monarch.
Court of Oyer and Terminer—an English court for the examination and trial of criminals.
Court of Quarter Sessions—an English quarterly court, primarily for criminal trials.
Covenant Chain—alliance between the Iroquois Nation and New York and other colonies. See appendix 10 for more information.
distress of goods—the act of seizing property to compel payment of a fine, judgement, etc.
epistle—a pastoral letter from a yearly or quarterly or monthly meeting to other bodies of Friends regarding matters of faith and practice of mutual concern; early in Quaker history, individual Quaker leaders wrote pastoral letters.
Five Mile Act—See under Clarendon Code.
Frame of the Government— the name given in 1682 by William Penn to the first constitution of Pennsylvania and given thereafter to the succeeding constitutions of 1683, 1696, and 1701 until replaced by the constitution of 1776, which was prepared by the convention presided over by Benjamin Franklin.
Friendship Chain—1701 agreement of friendship and amity between William Penn and the tribes of the Susquehanna River; may have been similar to an agreement, now lost, made by Penn with the Lenni Lenapes on the western shore of the Delaware River in 1682–1683; both agreements were made for the purpose of securing peace in Pennsylvania.

gaol—a place of incarceration for those awaiting disposition of criminal charges or serving short sentences; a jail.

General Assembly—See Provincial Assembly.

habeas corpus—order directing an official to produce a prisoner in court.

House of Correction—built in England after 1601 for commitment and forced labor of vagrants, beggars, and others.

Indian goods— English manufactured goods, the stock-in-trade used by the traders in bartering with the Native Americans. In exchange, usually for animal pelts, were many machine- or handmade mass-produced wares such as "needles and thread, scarlet coats and beaver hats, brass kettles and tobacco pipes, blankets and hoes, mittens and fish hooks, scissors and mirrors."[1] Rifles, powder, lead, and rum would also be available, along with other necessities of life. Such necessities were often presented to the indigenous peoples at the conclusion of treaty conferences, especially when their living conditions worsened or as winter approached.[2]

indictment—formal accusation that a person has committed a crime.

Iroquois League—The confederation of the Seneca, Cayuga, Onondaga, Oneida, and Mohawk Nations located in the southern tier of New York. In 1722, these Five Nations, upon adopting the Tuscaroras, became the Six Nations. See appendix 10 for more information.

justice of the peace—judge who hears and decides in prosecutions of lesser criminal charges; magistrate.

letters patent—government grant, by a recorded instrument, of an exclusive right.

magistrate—a public civil officer invested with some part of the executive, legislative, or judicial power under statute or basic law.

Meeting for Sufferings—a standing committee created in October 1675 under the auspices of London Yearly Meeting by Friends in London concerned with the sufferings of Quakers then under persecution for violating the religious conformity laws; a similar body was created by Philadelphia Yearly Meeting in 1756 for providing relief and assistance during the French and Indian War.

meeting house—the structure within which a monthly meeting of the Religious Society of Friends gathers for worship or business or other purposes.

mittimus—in criminal practice, a warrant of commitment to prison.

---

[1] James H. Merrell, *Into the American Woods: Negotiators on the Pennsylvania Frontier* (New York: W. W. Norton & Co., 1999), 257.

[2] Kalter, *Benjamin Franklin*, 215.

Appendix 1: Glossary

monthly meeting—a Quaker congregation, generally gathering weekly for worship and once a month for business; in some instances, a number of smaller groups, sometimes called preparative meetings, that gather together monthly to conduct business.

Oath of Abjuration—enacted in 1655 during Oliver Cromwell's protectorate, in which the oath-giver renounces "the pope's supremacy and authority over the Catholic Church in general, and over my self in particular." For the full text, see appendix 2.

Oath of Allegiance—enacted in 1605 during reign of James I, in which the oath-giver declares "I will bear faith and true allegiance to his majesty" and "will defend to the utmost of my power, against all conspiracies." For the full text, see appendix 2.

Oath of Supremacy—enacted in 1558 during reign of Elizabeth I, in which the oath-giver "does utterly testify and declare in my conscience, that the king's highness is the only supreme governor of this realm." For the full text, see appendix 2.

opening—an inspired human perception (or revelation) of divine will or Truth.

Overseers of the Press—in the eighteenth-century, these were the managers of the Friends' print media (ministry) within their jurisdiction; the overseers acted as censors of Quaker publications that might stir contention or occasion a breach of unity among Friends.

Overseers of the Schools—the board of managers that had oversight of the Friends schools in Philadelphia as chartered by William Penn.

oyer—request in court that a written instrument in litigation be read.

Penn Incorporated—author's term for the Penn family's business enterprise in Pennsylvania.

praemunire—prohibition against claiming or maintaining papal or other foreign jurisdiction or supremacy in England.

Privy Council (sometimes *king,* or *queen, in council*)—a body of advisers to the sovereign whose members were senior officials experienced in military, civil, judicial, ecclesiastical, economic, legislative, and diplomatic affairs, who were entrusted with executive oversight in the management of government; with the rise of parliament over royal pre-eminence it evolved into the modern cabinet.

professor—a person who avows something that he or she does not truly believe or practice.

proprietary, proprietor—an owner, as of a colony, with the power of governing.

prorogue—to end a session of the English Parliament without dissolving it, by an order of the Crown.

Provincial Assembly (sometimes General Assembly)—the legislative branch of Pennsylvania's government that consisted of the Assembly and the Provincial Council under the Frame of the Government of 1682; upon the adoption of the Frame of 1683, this was made the sole legislative chamber.

Provincial Council—a chamber of the legislative branch of Pennsylvania's colonial government under the Frame of 1682, which thereafter was made a council of advice to the chief executive.

Quaker Act (13 & 14 Car. II, c. 1. [1662])—English act "for preventing mischiefs and dangers that may arise by certain persons called Quakers and others refusing to take lawful oaths."

Quarter Sessions—See Court of Quarter Sessions.

quarterly meeting—the joint quarter-yearly meeting of a number of Quaker monthly meetings in a district.

query——a question (or questions) based on Quaker practices and testimonies for use by individuals and groups to examine their lives and actions and spiritual condition, both as individuals and as a community.

recusant—one who separates from the church established by law.

remand—returning either a case to a lower court or a prisoner to detention.

sheriff—the officer of a county representing the superior royal or national executive and administrative power.

tender consciences—persons with deep moral and spiritual feelings seeking lives of faithful adherence to God's word and will; a 'liberty to tender consciences' was promised by Charles II in his Declaration of Breda on the eve of the Restoration.

Test Act (25 Car. II, c. 2 [1672]; amended, 30 Car. II, stat. 2 [1678])—required all in English civil or military office to take oaths of allegiance and supremacy and subscribe to a declaration denying transubstantiation.

Townshend Acts—a series of British measures passed beginning in 1767; adopted to pay the salaries of colonial governors and judges, enforce trade regulations, and establish Parliament's right to tax the American colonies.

Truth, the—for Quakers, the mystery of God's being and purposes as revealed in the creation, salvation, and sanctification of the world and made manifest in human affairs through social justice, peace, and equity; in a profound and living sense, Truth and God are synonymous.

Valiant Sixty—early leaders and missionaries of the Religious Society of Friends active in the nationwide spread of the movement; numbering more than sixty, many were from northern England where they had been inspired by George Fox's preaching in 1652; they used Margaret Fell's home, Swarthmoor Hall, as their base.

Appendix 1: Glossary

warrant—the writ of a constituted authority ordering an official to deliver a named party to that authority.
yearly meeting—the annual meeting for business of all quarterly meetings of Friends in a certain geographic area.

APPENDIX 2

The Statutory Oaths Demanded of Early Quakers in England

The Oath of Supremacy[1]
(1 Eliz. I, c. 1 [1558])[2]

I, *A.B.* do utterly testify and declare in my conscience, that the king's highness is the only supreme governor of this realm, and of all other his highnesses' dominions and countries, as well in all spiritual and ecclesiastical things or causes, as temporal. And that no foreign prince, prelate, state or potentate hath or ought to have any jurisdiction, power, superiority, pre-eminence or authority, ecclesiastical or spiritual, within this realm. And therefore I do utterly renounce and forsake all foreign jurisdictions, powers, superiorities and authorities, and do promise that from henceforth I shall bear faith and true allegiance to the king's highness, his heirs and lawful successors, and to my power shall assist and defend all jurisdictions, privileges, pre-eminences and authorities granted, or belonging to the king's highness, his heirs and successors, or united and annexed to the imperial crown of this realm. So help me God, and by the contents of this book.

The Oath of Allegiance[3]
(3 Jac. I, c. 4 [1605])[4]

(I) I, *A.B.* do truly and sincerely acknowledge, profess, testify and declare before God and the world,

(a) that our sovereign lord King James is lawful and rightful king of this realm, and of all other his majesty's dominions and countries, and

---

[1] Besse, *Sufferings of the People Called Quakers*, 1:viii–ix. The author has modernized the capitalization and punctuation of the text. This text may also be found in *The Statutes of the Realm*, 4:352.

[2] The Oath of Supremacy was enacted upon Elizabeth's accession in 1558.

[3] Besse, *Sufferings of the People Called Quakers*, 1:ix–x. The author has modernized the capitalization and punctuation of the text and inserted the roman numerals, lower case letters, and formatting to mark the structure and for ease of reading. This text may also be found in *Statutes of the Realm*, 4:1074.

[4] This is from the Popish Recusants Act, enacted in the third year of James I's reign after discovery of the Gunpowder Plot on November 4, 1605; proclaimed law June 22, 1606.

Appendix 2: Statutory Oaths

(b) that the Pope, neither of himself, nor by any authority of the church or See of Rome, or by any other means with any other, hath any power or authority to depose the king, or to dispose of any of his majesty's kingdoms or dominions, or to authorize any foreign prince to invade or to annoy him or his countries, or to discharge any of his subjects from their allegiance and obedience to his majesty, or to give licence or leave to any of them to bear arms, raise tumults, or to offer any violence or hurt to his majesty's royal person or government, or to any of his subjects within his majesty's dominions.

(II) Also I do swear from my heart, that notwithstanding any declaration, or sentence of excommunication, or deprivation, made or granted, or to be made or granted by the Pope or his successors or by any authority derived, or pretended to be derived, from him or his See, against the said king, his heirs or successors, or any absolution of the said subjects from their obedience, I

(a) will bear faith and true allegiance to his majesty, his heirs and successors, and him and them will defend to the utmost of my power, against all conspiracies and attempts whatsoever which shall be made against his or their persons, their crown and dignity, by reason or color of any such sentence or declaration or otherwise. And

(b) will do my best endeavor to disclose and make known unto his majesty, his heirs and successors, all treasons and traitorous conspiracies which I shall know or hear of to be against him or any of them. And I do farther swear, that I

(c) do from my heart abhor, detest and abjure, as impious and heretical, that damnable doctrine and position, that princes which be excommunicated or deprived by the Pope, may be deposed or murdered by their subjects or any other whatsoever. And I do believe, and in my conscience am resolved, that

(d) neither the Pope, nor any other person whatsoever, hath power to absolve me of this Oath, or any part thereof, which I acknowledge by good and full authority to be lawfully administered to me, and do renounce all pardons and dispensations to the contrary.

(III) And all these things I do plainly and sincerely acknowledge and swear according to the express words by me spoken, and according to the plain and common sense and understanding of the same words, without any equivocation or mental evasion, or secret reservation whatsoever.

(IV) And I do make this recognition and acknowledgement heartily, willingly, and truly, upon the true faith of a Christian. So help me God.

The Oath of Abjuration[5]
[1655; 1657][6]

I, *A.B.*, do abjure and renounce the pope's supremacy and authority over the Catholic Church in general, and over my self in particular; and I do believe the Church of Rome is not the true church; and that there is not any transubstantiation in the sacrament of the Lord's Supper, or in the elements of bread and wine, after consecration thereof, by any person whatsoever.

And I do also believe that there is not any purgatory; and that the consecrated host, crucifixes, or images ought not to be worshipped, neither that any worship is due unto any of them; and I also believe that salvation cannot be merited by works; and I do sincerely testify and declare that the pope, neither of himself, nor by any authority of the Church or See of Rome, or by any other means with any other, has any power or authority to depose the chief magistrate of these nations, or to dispose of any of the countries or territories thereunto belonging, or to authorize any foreign prince or state to invade or annoy him or them, or to discharge any of the people of these nations from their obedience to the chief magistrate; or to give license or leave to any of the said people to bear arms, raise tumults, or to offer any violence or hurt to the person of the chief magistrate, or to the state or government of these nations, or to any of the people thereof.

And I do further swear that I do from my heart abhor, detest and abjure this damnable doctrine and position, that princes, rulers, or governors which be excommunicated or deprived by the pope, may by virtue of such excommunication or deprivation be killed, murdered, or deposed from their rule or government, or any outrage or violence done unto

---

[5] Firth and Rait, *Acts and Ordinances* 2:1171. The author has modernized the capitalization and punctuation of the text and formatted it to mark the structure and improve ease of reading.

[6] Parliament nullified (with the protector's assent on June 26, 1657) the ordinance imposing the Oath of Abjuration that had become effective on April 26, 1655 (see Fox, *Journal*, 220), along with other acts and ordinances made or passed between April 20, 1653, and September 1656, as being "made without the consent of the people assembled in Parliament, which is not according to the fundamental laws of the nation, and the rights of the people" (Firth and Rait, *Acts and Ordinances*, 3:xxiii). The nullified ordinance was, however, simultaneously replaced by *An Act for convicting, discovering and repressing of Popish Recusants* (ibid., 2:1170–71), which prescribed the Oath of Abjuration quoted above.

Appendix 2: Statutory Oaths

them by the people that are under them, or by any other whatsoever upon such pretence.

And I do further swear that I do believe that the pope, or Bishop of Rome, has no authority, power, or jurisdiction whatsoever, within England, Scotland, and Ireland, or any or either of them, or the dominion or territories belonging to them, or any or either of them. And all doctrines in affirmation of the said points, I do abjure and renounce, without any equivocation, mental reservation, or secret evasion whatsoever, taking the words by me spoken according to the common and usual meaning of them. And I do believe no power derived from the pope or Church of Rome or any other person can absolve me from this my oath. And I do renounce all pardons and dispensations to the contrary. So help me God.

The Oath Forswearing Taking Arms against the King or Making Any Alteration of Government in Church or State[7]
(17 Car. II, c. 2 [1665])[8]

I, A.B., do swear that it is not lawful upon any pretense whatsoever, to take arms against the King, and that I do abhor that traitorous position of taking arms by his authority against his person, or against those that are commissioned by him in pursuance of such commissions; and that I will not at any time endeavor any alteration of government either in Church or State.

The Declaration Denying Transubstantiation[9]
(25 Car. II c. 2 [1672])[10]

I, N, do declare that I do believe that there is not any transubstantiation in the sacrament of the Lord's Supper, or in the elements of the bread and wine, at or after the consecration thereof by any person whatsoever.

---

[7] Besse, *Sufferings of the People Called Quakers*, 1:xxi. The author has modernized the capitalization and punctuation of the text. This text may also be found in *Statutes of the Realm*, 5:575.

[8] This oath is from the Five Mile Act (1665), which was the fourth and final statute of the Clarendon Code.

[9] *The Statutes of the Realm*, 5:784.

[10] From the Test Act of 1673 (the regnal year 1672 is based on the Old Style, or Julian, calendar).

APPENDIX 3

Glossary of Religious Sects Referred to in Chapter 1

Arians—sixteenth-century reformers who adhered to an anti-Trinitarian belief that Jesus the Son was created by and hence inferior to God the Father.

Baptists—reformers who believed in the baptism of conscious believers as a rule for church membership (following Mennonite and other Anabaptist teachings). John Bunyan (1628–1688), author of *Pilgrim's Progress* and a contemporary of George Fox, was a leading English Baptist.

Brownists—English dissenters who, following Robert Browne (born ca. 1550), tried to set up a congregational church separate from the established Church of England. They went into exile in the Netherlands in 1581.

Calvinists—followers of the French reformer John Calvin (1509–1564) who held to the theological system set forth principally in his *Institutes*, a work influential among many non-Lutheran Reformed churches.

Congregationalists—See *Independents*.

Episcopal men—Fox's term, presumably referring to adherents of the Church of England in contradistinction to Puritans (a term Fox did not use).

Familists—a sect founded by the German mystic Henry Nicholis (ca. 1501–ca. 1580) that taught loving service to others, quietism, and sympathy and tenderness for promoting moral and spiritual improvement. Its followers objected to bearing arms and taking oaths, denied the doctrine of the Trinity, and repudiated infant baptism. Also known as Family of Love and Familia Caritatis.

Fifth Monarchy Men—an English sect generally supporting Oliver Cromwell and active from 1649 to 1661, the period from the end of the Civil War until shortly after the beginning of the Restoration. Its believers sought to bring in the Fifth Monarchy (Dan. 2:44) in succession to the earlier, and fallen, first four world empires—Babylonian, Median, Persian, and Greek—under the thousand-year reign of Christ and his saints (Rev. 20:4).

Appendix 3: Glossary of Religious Sects

Independents—Christians who maintained the independence or autonomy of the congregation; another term for *Congregationalists*.

Jesuits—members of the Society of Jesus, the order founded by St. Ignatius of Loyola (1491 or 1495–1556) and formally approved by Pope Paul III in 1540.

Lollards—followers of John Wycliffe who sought the reform of Christianity through giving people access to the Bible in their native language and eliminating corrupt practices and non-scriptural doctrines of the Roman Catholics. The movement was active until the English Reformation.

Lutherans—followers of Martin Luther (1483–1546), whose chief teachings held that the scriptures are the sole rule of faith and that humans are justified by faith alone (*sola fide*).

Muggletonians—a sect founded in 1651 by Lodowicke Muggleton (1609–1698) and his cousin John Reeve (1608–1658), who held they were the two witnesses of God anticipated in Revelation 11:3–6. They denied Trinitarianism, condemned prayer and preaching, and taught that matter is eternal and reason the devil's creation.

Papists—Fox's term for followers of the Church of Rome; Roman Catholics.

Presbyterians—those who believe in governance of the church congregation by its elders, as modeled by the first Christian churches in Palestine (Acts 11:30, 14:23, and 15:22).

Puritans—members of a religious reform movement that urged the further purification of the Church of England by the removal of all scriptural excesses and abuses.

Ranters—a nonconformist dissenting group that, while denying the authority of the scriptures, theological doctrines, and the ministry, believed Christians were freed by grace from obedience to the law of Moses as well as other restraints.

Seekers—dissenting Puritans who, starting in the 1620s, were inspired by the preaching of Bartholomew Legate (ca. 1575–1612) and his brothers Thomas and Walter. They embraced Bible study and anticlericalism, avoided credal formulations, and promoted broad religious toleration within a pluralistic society. Their silent waiting in worship for Christ to establish his true church was one of several ways in which they were forerunners of Quakerism. A number of Seekers in time became convinced Friends. Also known as Legatine Arians and the Scattered Flock.

Socinians—followers of Fausto Paolo Sozzini (in Latin, Faustus Socinus; 1539–1604), an Italian reformer who denied the divinity of Christ. His teachings were influential in the Minor Reformed Church of Poland and in the Unitarian Church of Transylvania, whence they eventually came into England.

APPENDIX 4

Phineas Pemberton's Prefatory Epistle in the First Philadelphia Yearly Meeting Minute Book, ca. 1700

Source: PYM Min Bk B, pp. A–D.

An Epistle
Being a short testimony of the Lord's goodness to us
in the settlement of ourselves in these parts of the world,
and an account of the first setting up of our Yearly Meeting.

Dear Friends:

It hath pleased God in his infinite goodness and good providence to give us his people who were and are in scorn called Quakers a lot and inheritance in this new and remote and formerly to us unknown part of the world now called America, into which desert and wilderness he hath called, drawn, and allured many of us, and here hath given us of the comforts of his house, and abundantly blessed us by pouring down of his mercies upon us both inwardly and outwardly. What the Lord hath done for us since he first called us from our native land we cannot well demonstrate; but when we call to remembrance his kind and gentle dealings, the care he had over us in making way for our coming, his safe conducting us by sea and land, his providing for us, and preserving of us when here, I know that I have many witnesses who when they look back at those things, and about us, what he hath done, and is daily doing for us, our hearts are greatly engaged to love, serve, fear, and obey him, and to praise and reverence his great and worthy name; and greater mercies hath yet in store for all those that in faithfulness persevere unto the end. Wherefore let us be encouraged to hold on our way, and you that may succeed in his service be not slack-handed, negligent, or backward in the performance of your duty to the Lord, but be zealously concerned for the glory of his name, and the propagation of his Truth upon earth, that his blessings may be multiplied upon you, as upon your fathers and predecessors. And be not high-minded or puffed up with those mercies which the Lord hath bestowed upon them, and so to you; but remember we were a despised people in our native land, accounted of by the world as scarce worthy to have a name or place therein, daily liable to their reproach, under great sufferings by long and tedious imprisonments sometimes to the loss of life, banishment, spoil of goods, beatings, mockings, and threatenings, so that we had not been a people at this day, had not the Lord stood by us, and preserved us, but none of these things were done unto us because of our evil deeds, but because of the exercise of our tender consciences towards our God, and he encouraged us and blessed us so that we underwent all these things cheerfully, having faith towards him, and our dependence upon him, and we experimentally know that he never yet failed us, nor will fail his faithful ones, but is a God near at hand, full of mercy, compassion, and loving kindness.

Therefore for your encouragement in his work was I drawn forth to salute you with this short Epistle in the beginning of this book, desiring that you may lay hold of Truth, and steadfastly walk in the way thereof, confirming of your forefathers' testimony to the glory of the Lord who called them, whereby you may obtain the like blessings they have; but if you trample under foot their testimony and sufferings, and grow careless, slothful, and negligent in his work and service, it will prove heavy, and too heavy to be borne in the day of account.

About the year 1676, the province of West Jersey was purchased by divers of our friends, and in the year 1677, several proprietors and adventurers came over to these parts, and settled themselves and families, and as more friends came in, monthly meetings were set up for the better ordering the affairs of the church according to the good order used amongst us in our native land, that the transgressions of transgressors might be brought to condemnation, and the shame of their guilt set upon their heads, and our holy profession kept clear of scandal and reproach that might be brought thereon by the evil conversation of any who made profession thereof, and walked not accordingly therein. And as the people increased and came into the province, it was agreed that there should be a General or Yearly Meeting held annually by Friends of the provinces of East and West Jersey and places adjacent.

But afterwards it pleased the Lord to allot the province of Pennsylvania in the year 1681 to our valuable friend William Penn whereby our portions of land and inheritance in these parts were greatly enlarged, many friends becoming purchasers under him, so that by the latter end of the year 1682 considerable settlements were made in the said province and divers meetings established, and in a short time monthly, quarterly, and yearly meetings, were appointed in that province. Yearly Meetings in both the said provinces were held distinct until the year (1685 or 1683) when friends well knowing that the interest of Truth, and the prosperity thereof, was labored for by its friends and followers in both the said provinces and that by uniting the said two meetings together they might thereby be the more strengthened in carrying on the affairs of the church, it was agreed therefore that the said yearly meetings should become one meeting to be held, one year at Burlington in West New Jersey, and the other at Philadelphia in Pennsylvania and so annually to continue in that course.

The proceedings of which said yearly meetings, from their first being set up in Burlington hereafter follow in this book in their order; so

Appendix 4: Phineas Pimberton's Epistle

many of them as are now to be had, having been kept until now in loose papers.

This from a friend to Truth, and a lover of all those that sincerely love it.

                Phineas Pemberton

Wrote in or about the year 1700 and finding it among the early papers of our Yearly Meeting, and it appearing as an intended introduction to the book of minutes which the author was directed to collect in order to be transcribed which by his decease was prevented, but was many years after performed by his son (my father Israel Pemberton) I have therefore now transcribed the said Epistle as worthy to be preserved.

Philad 3 mo 13 1781   James Pemberton

APPENDIX 5

Penn's Disposition of His Proprietary Interests in the Province under His Several Last Wills and Testaments

William Penn wrote at least five last wills and testaments, four of which are preserved. Whether there were other wills is not now known. The following briefly traces the sequence of the five known wills and their provisions for the disposition of Penn's interests in America.

A. **Will prior to Penn's 1682 voyage to Pennsylvania,** made in England sometime before Penn's 1682 voyage to Pennsylvania, as he stated in the initial provision of his 1684 will, which was the first such document to survive ("I confirm and ratify all of the matter of my last will made in England").[1] Although neither the date nor the terms of this will are known, their provision for the succession of Penn's proprietary interests in his province may be deduced from his next will.

B. **Will of August 6, 1684,** made in Philadelphia before Penn's return to England.[2] This document confirms and ratifies the prior (lost) will and grants specific lots in Philadelphia and extensive acreage elsewhere in the province to family members as well as cash annuities out of his quitrents.[3] In addition, it provides fifty thousand acres for distribution among "poor families" in the country and ten thousand acres each to support a school and a hospital in Philadelphia County. To "all my servants I had before I came and that came with me," Penn gave 200 acres each. Since this 1684 will made no provision for Penn's interests as proprietary and governor, those interests can only be presumed to have already been settled in the pre-voyage will (see A), herein ratified, in favor of his son Springett, here mentioned but once: "I give to my dear wife [Gulielma] the enjoyment of Pennsbury til my son Springett is of age, then to him and his for a Manor."[4]

C. **Will of October 30, 1701,** made in New Castle in the province of Delaware before returning to England.[5] This 1701 will is the first Penn made following the deaths of Gulielma and Springett, his marriage to Hannah Callowhill, and the birth of their first child, John Penn. In it, he

---

[1] *PWP*, 2:585.

[2] *PWP*, 2:585–87.

[3] This 1684 instrument is more in the nature of a codicil or amendment rather than a will, although it is called a will.

[4] *PWP*, 2: 585.

[5] *PWP*, 4:112–15.

Appendix 5: William Penn's Wills and Testaments

acknowledged that his property in England and Ireland as well as in America was encumbered by debt. He made distributions of property on both sides of the Atlantic and among the living children of his two marriages, including another child Hannah was then expecting. Most significantly, Penn gave all "my estate in America . . . the Province of Pennsylvania and Counties annexed" to his son William Jr., "to him and his heirs forever, as proprietary and governor."[6] He did, however, grant his one-tenth share in Salem, West Jersey, to his and Hannah's son John.

D. **Will of October 20, 1705**, made in England, along with a codicil dated August 21, 1707.[7] As a consequence of William Jr.'s troubles while in Pennsylvania and his subsequent renunciation of Quakerism in 1705, Penn executed this will that reduced his son's proprietary interests in Pennsylvania from the entirety (under the 1701 will) to "two-thirds of my Pennsylvanian estate," with the title of "chief proprietary" on condition that William Jr. share with his half-siblings the Irish estates inherited by Penn from his own father, the admiral. If, however, William Jr. refused to so share "by act of parliament or otherwise," then only one third of Pennsylvania was to be his.

E. **Will of ca. April 6, May 27, 1712**, made in England.[8] During this year when he was increasingly enfeebled by strokes, Penn made his final will. In the first provision, he cut William Jr. out of his estate, noting that his eldest son was well provided for by a settlement of his mother's and Penn's father's estates. He gave the government of the province and territories of Pennsylvania to three English noblemen as trustees to sell to the Crown "or any other person." All of his lands and rents in America he gave to six English trustees (his wife, father-in-law, sister, and three others) together with five Philadelphia trustees (Samuel Carpenter, Isaac Norris, James Logan, and two others) to sell whatever was necessary to pay his debts, to convey ten thousand acres each to William Jr.'s three young children and his own daughter Letitia, and to distribute the rest among "my children which I have by my present wife." He made Hannah the sole executrix of the estate.[9]

---

[6] *PWP*, 4:112.
[7] *PWP*, 4:394–96.
[8] *PWP*, 4:715–19.
[9] *PWP*, 4:716.

APPENDIX 6

Opinion of Sir Edward Northey, Counsel to Hannah Penn, in Penn v. Penn (December 11, 1719)

Note: This is Northey's legal analysis of the basic facts in the case of Penn v. Penn as presented to him in a letter from Hannah Penn's solicitors. In the original, Northey's answers are in dark ink, inserted after each of the questions, and in a hand other than that of the question writer. Northey's responses to the questions are in bold below; the square brackets in the bolded answers indicate words that are difficult to read in the manuscript. Source: Penn-Forbes papers 1644–1744, vol. 1, p. 31, Collection 485C, HSP.

1 – Since the Powers of Government are expressly named in the Patent but not in the Deed of Mortgage; whether general words (all royalties, franchises, duties, jurisdictions, liberties, privileges, powers and all the estate, right, title, and interest therein, and all charters, patents, grants, deeds and writings concerning the premises) do effectually include the same in the mortgage? For it was so apprehended when the agreement was made for the sale of the government to the Queen and the then Attorney General [who at the time of the sale in 1712 was Northey himself] advised that the mortgagees should join with Mr. Penn in the conveyance.

I am of opinion the mortgage includes as well the powers of government as the lands and it was [reason] it should be [seen] that the whole might [join] together.

2 – If the Government were effectually passed together with the propriety in the land to the mortgagees; whether if this sale be perfected, or any other made, the mortgage shall not be discharged out of the money arising therefrom? even though the heir should be thought to stand entitled to the rest, by reason of the omission in the Will by not making any particular appointment of that money.

I am of opinion the Testator's contract if executed, makes the money contracted for part of Mr. Penn's personal estate, and it will be applied to satisfy the mortgage; besides the interest of the powers of government being in the mortgagees they will not nor can be compelled to surrender these powers without having their mortgage debt satisfied out of the purchase money; and the remainder of the money will belong to the Executrix for the performance of the Testator's Will.

3 – If the devise of the Government to the Lords, as it now stands in the Will, be not sufficient to exclude the heir; whether the contract which

Appendix 6: Opinion of Sir Edward Northey

the Testator made after the executing his Will shall not be deemed an effectual sale of the government and the £66,000 remaining unpaid be taken as a debt due to the personal estate, and consequently pass as such to the Executrix? Or whether (if the government not being sufficiently conveyed by the Testator) the conveyance must be perfected by William Penn the heir, he shall have the residue of the money or the Executrix and devisees?

> **I am of opinion the devise to the lands in the Will excludes the heir from any pretence and that Will being proved against the heirs in Chancery and the contract with the government being executed, the overplus of the money beyond what as severed by the mortgage will belong to the Executrix as personal estate, for the contract when executed will be the same as if it had been executed in the Testator's life.**

4 – If the devise to the Lords be good; Whether, because there is no express direction to the Lords how they shall dispose of the money arising from the sale of government, the heir will be entitled to the whole, without any remedy left for the Executrix and her children; notwithstanding that it appears evidently that the intent of the Testator was wholly to exclude him?

> **I am of opinion the contract made by Mr. Penn, and his Will enabling the Lords to execute it, the heir is not further concerned, but when the contract is executed, it will be the contract that Mr. Penn made, and thereby the produce of it will be personal estate and belong to the Executrix. The want of direction how to dispose of the money arising on the sale is not material, for the consequence of it is the [rest] of the money being for Mr. Penn, as it is, it will belong to his Executrix yet a question may be made whether though the Executrix take the overplus as Executrix, yet she will not be obliged to distribute it among herself and all Mr. Penn's children as money undisposed of by the Testator, he having reserved it to a future disposition, which he did not make.**

Edw Northey
Dec 11th 1719

APPENDIX 7

Israel Pemberton Jr.'s Letter of April 29, 1749, to His Brother James

Source: Pemberton family correspondence, 1740–1787, vol. 1, pp. 128–30, Collection 1355, HSP.

Dear brother,

... And it would be more agreeable to me to be able to communicate something of another kind, that might be instructive and useful and evince the sincerity and ardency of my affection and friendship, but this I find is not in my power to command, yet I cannot attribute my incapacity to a deficiency of that love I find some of my friends seem constantly ready to express. True friendship appears to me to be of a sacred original and I deem it safest to be cautious of speaking or writing much concerning it, unless that principle, which qualifies for performing our duty, is sensibly active in our minds, and whenever that prevails we shall be enabled to express ourselves with some degree of evidence of the spring and purpose of our hearts; such, I am convinced, was thy disposition when thou wrote thy letter to me soon after thy arrival; the satisfactory account of your agreeable passage, safe arrival, etc. were sufficient to render it very acceptable, but the comfort and real pleasure it afforded to observe the grateful sentiments and good resolutions thy mind was then filled with I can more sensibly feel than express; as our good friend John Evans observed upon reading it, he found it warmed him much, which I the more freely mention as I hope it may tend to excite the more ardent desire to attain and preserve that habit and disposition of mind which is acceptable to God and good men. May this be thy constant care and endeavor is my hearty prayer! for I cannot ask or think of anything better so far as I have experienced it. Humility, the first step to true honor, is the foundation of it, it being as I conceive impossible to be really sensible of the infinite power and goodness of the Almighty without remembering our own weakness and unworthiness of the multitude of favors and blessings conferred upon us by the dispensation of his Providence, for which we are incapable of making any adequate returns, yet we are at times convinced that the grateful remembrance and acknowledgment thereof by a right improvement of the powers and qualifications given us will be accepted and that the sincerity of our endeavors therein will be rewarded with immediate assistance and ability to discharge the duties of the station allotted us, and thus often the love and unity of good men is maintained and increased, for though they may not have frequent conversation or acquaintance with each other, yet their minds being assured that they are engaged in the same cause, in which they are mutually concerned, this begets a nearness and concern for each other which is not partial or selfish, and therefore not subject to the uncertainty which attends the

Appendix 7: Israel Pemberton Jr.'s Letter

common friendships of mankind, and I have sometimes been sensible of so much strength and benefit from such an intercourse of spirits, even of those with whom I have had little personal converse, that I confess I know scarce anything temporal more to be coveted than the friendship and regard of good men, for the advantages thereof are too great to be expressed and like the flowings of a stream are constantly increasing by the confluence of others, until they at last emerge into the ocean, which is neither fathomed or bounded. Such thoughts have often afforded me pleasant reflections, but this is the first time I have ever expressed them in this manner and I am now in doubt whether I shall not yet keep them to myself, for I have no apprehension thou needs any incentive to seek the knowledge of such men, as thou hast always preferred it, and I am sensible I may be justly charged with a neglect of some I have ever esteemed and valued much; but I know I have been more weak than willful therein, for though I have now unexpectedly scribbled so much, it is in common a hard task to me to undertake it; and I must beg thee to endeavor if thou hears any complaints of me, to convince my friends of the honesty of my intentions to pay them with interest when I am able.
...

      Thy loving brother
      Isr: Pemberton Junr

APPENDIX 8

Chronology of Events

1384
John Wycliffe's death at Lutterworth (Leicestershire)

1428
Wycliffe's ashes cast into River Swift

1624
July: George Fox born at Drayton in the Clay (Leicestershire)

1625
James I dies (r. 1603–1625); Charles I ascends throne (r. 1625–1649)

1628
James Harrison born near Kendal (Westmorland)

1642
Battle of Edgehill; Charles I relocates royal seat to Oxford

1643
George Fox begins journey of spiritual exercises and trials at Lutterworth; returns home the following year

1644
Battle of Marston Moor; Battle of Newbury
October 14: William Penn born in London

1645
New Model Army; Self-Denying Ordinance; Leicester captured and plundered; Battle of Naseby

1646
First Civil War ends when Oxford surrenders to Parliament
George Fox begins journey of 'openings' and further trials; returns home the following year

1648
August 17: Battle of Preston
December: Pride's Purge of Parliament
George Fox begins his first national mission (which ends in 1657)

Appendix 8: Chronology of Events

1649
January 30: Charles I beheaded; republican Commonwealth proclaimed

George Fox's first imprisonment, at Nottingham, for disturbing the peace; held "a pretty long time"

1650
George Fox's second imprisonment, at Derby; sentenced to six months for blasphemy but held an additional 23 weeks for refusing both a captaincy and enlistment in the parliamentary army

Phineas Pemberton born at Wigan (Lancashire)

1651
Battle of Worcester

1652
George Fox has vision on Pendle Hill (Lancashire) of "a great people to be gathered" to the Lord, later realized in the mission of the Valiant Sixty

June: Fox preaches on Firbank Fell (Westmorland) to about one thousand Seekers, convincing many of the Truth

June: Fox's first visit to Swarthmoor Hall (Lancashire), the home of Judge Thomas and Margaret Fell

1653
George Fox's third imprisonment, at Carlisle, for blasphemy; held seven weeks

December 15-16: creation of the Protectorate and end of the Commonwealth of England, Scotland, and Ireland; Oliver Cromwell installed as lord protector

1655
January: Oliver Cromwell dissolves first Protectorate Parliament; military rule by major generals

George Fox arrested near Leicester, meets Oliver Cromwell for the first time

James Harrison goes on preaching mission in Scotland

Oath of Abjuration imposed

1656
George Fox's fourth imprisonment, at Launceston (Cornwall), for disturbing the peace, refusing to take Oath of Abjuration, etc.; held more than eight months; meets Oliver Cromwell for the second time

1657
May 25: *Instrument of Government* repealed by *Humble Petition and Advice*; Oliver Cromwell declines offer of Crown
Fox completes his first national mission, meets Oliver Cromwell for the third time, travels into Wales and Scotland

1658
Fox begins his second national mission (ending in 1660), meets Oliver Cromwell for the fourth time
September 3: Cromwell dies; succeeded by son Richard as lord protector
October 8: Thomas Fell, Margaret Fell's husband, dies at Swarthmoor

1659
May 25: Protectorate ends and Commonwealth resumes

1660
Charles II, after issuing Declaration of Breda while in exile, returns to England and the restored monarchy
George Fox completes his second national mission; fifth imprisonment, June to October, at Lancaster, for disturbing the peace and being an enemy to the king; is released on king's warrant
James Harrison imprisoned in Shrewsbury prison for two months

1662
George Fox begins his third national mission (ending in 1663), interrupted in September by his sixth imprisonment, at Leicester, for refusing Oath of Allegiance; held for one month

1663
James Harrison imprisoned at Worcester

1664
George Fox's seventh imprisonment, at Lancaster but transferred to Scarborough Castle (Yorkshire), for refusing Oath of Allegiance; held from January 12, 1664, to September 1, 1666, when released on king's order
Margaret Fell's first imprisonment, for refusing oath; held until 1668, when released on order of king and council
Charles II grants James, Duke of York, the provinces of New York and New Jersey but not the western bank of the Delaware River
James Harrison imprisoned at Chester Castle (1664–1666)

1665
Great Plague of London
Phineas Pemberton leaves home in Wigan for apprenticeship in Manchester (Lancashire)

Appendix 8: Chronology of Events

1666
William Penn sent to Ireland by his father as agent to secure family land titles and negotiate leases
September 1: Fox's seventh imprisonment ends, released from Scarborough Castle by order of king
September 2: Great Fire of London
Fox begins his fourth national mission, which ends in 1670

1667
August–October: William Penn convinced by Thomas Loe at Cork to accept Quaker principles
November 3: Penn's first arrest, at Cork; ordered home to London by father

1668
William Penn and his father become estranged
October 6: death of Thomas Loe, Penn's Quaker mentor
December 16: Penn imprisoned in Tower of London for writing a "Blasphemous Booke"

1669
July 28: William Penn released from Tower of London and delivered to his father
May–August: George Fox makes his only journey to Ireland
September: Penn in Ireland for second time as father's business agent; en route meets Fox in Bristol
October 27: Fox marries Margaret Fell at Bristol

1670
Phineas Pemberton imprisoned in Lancaster Castle for over nineteen weeks
Fox ends his fourth national mission; writes epistle to every quarterly meeting about apprenticeship program for children of poor Friends; arrested at London meeting; temporarily loses hearing and sight
Margaret Fox's second imprisonment
August 14: William Penn's third arrest; Penn-Mead trial; Penn held at Newgate Prison, London, ca. four weeks
September 16: death of Admiral Sir William Penn, father of William Penn

1671
February 5: William Penn's fourth arrest; held at Newgate Prison, London, six months
April 4: Margaret Fox released from second imprisonment

William Penn's 'Holy Experiment'

August 13: George Fox begins first international mission, traveling to Barbados, where he arrives October 3; Penn and others accompany Fox from London to his ship at Gravesend

August–October: Penn makes first missionary journey to the Netherlands and Germany

1672

January 8: George Fox leaves Barbados for Jamaica, where he arrives January 18

March 8: Fox leaves Jamaica for voyage to West River, Maryland, arriving April 23

April 4: William Penn marries Gulielma Springett

Phineas Pemberton's apprenticeship in Manchester ends and he sets up trade in Bolton

1673

May 21: George Fox leaves Maryland for England

June 28: Fox arrives in Bristol, England, ending first international mission; William Penn and wife at Bristol to welcome Fox home; Fox later visits Penns at Rickmansworth (Hertfordshire)

December 17: Fox's eighth imprisonment, at Worcester, for refusing Oaths of Allegiance and Supremacy; held until February 11, 1675

1675

January: William Penn arbitrates Byllynge and Fenwick land dispute in West Jersey

February 11: George Fox's eighth (and last) imprisonment ends

1676

July–September: Penn oversees partition of East and West Jersey as well as settlement of West Jersey

1677

July–October: George Fox, William Penn, Robert Barclay, and others go on mission to the Netherlands and Germany

Phineas Pemberton marries Phoebe, daughter of James Harrison, at Hardshaw Monthly Meeting (Lancashire)

1678

September: Titus Oates's fictitious Popish Plot revealed, sets nation in turmoil

Fox begins second of two long working sojourns at Swarthmoor

1679

January: Charles II dissolves the Cavalier Parliament

February: first general election since 1661, but the new body (known as the first Exclusion Parliament) is quickly dissolved by Charles for

Appendix 8: Chronology of Events

its attempt to exclude the Duke of York from the succession; another election held in summer

1680
March: George Fox ends nineteen-month working sojourn at Swarthmoor
[May?]: William Penn petitions Charles II for a colony in America

1681
March 4: Charter of Pennsylvania granted by Charles II to William Penn
Summer: Penn drafts Fundamental Constitutions of Pennsylvania
August 25: Penn writes to James Harrison appointing him a Pennsylvania land agent and referring to the 'holy experiment' in Pennsylvania

1682
April 25: William Penn signs his first Frame of the Government
May 5: Penn signs his Laws Agreed upon in England
August 24: Penn gives Philip Ford a mortgage on three hundred thousand acres in the province of Pennsylvania
August 31: Penn sails aboard the *Welcome* from Deal (Kent) for America
September 5: James Harrison and Phineas Pemberton with families sail from Liverpool for America aboard the *Submission*
October 28: William Penn arrives at New Castle, Delaware, on the *Welcome*
October 30: Harrison and Pemberton arrive with their families at Choptank, Maryland

1683
January 9: Philadelphia Monthly Meeting of Friends established
April: Samuel Carpenter arrives in Philadelphia from Barbados; becomes an influential merchant, serving in various public offices
August: Thomas Lloyd arrives in Philadelphia from Wales; appointed by William Penn as keeper of the seal and master of the rolls
September 4: Burlington Yearly Meeting appoints William Penn, James Harrison, and four others to promote American yearly meeting of Friends

1684
March: Lord Baltimore has fort built at Christiana Bridge (Delaware)
July: William Penn appoints James Harrison steward of Pennsbury
August 6: William Penn assigns his executive authority during his upcoming absence in England to the Provincial Council; Thomas Lloyd named council president
August 18: William Penn sails on the *Endeavour* from Lewes (Delaware) for England, seeking to resolve boundary issue with Maryland

William Penn's 'Holy Experiment'

October 3: William Penn arrives in England at Worthing (Sussex) for meetings with Charles II and Duke of York

1685

February 6: death of Charles II (r. 1660–1685); James II ascends throne (r. 1685–1688)

February 20: birth of Israel Pemberton Sr.

June 10: William Penn gives Philip Ford an additional mortgage on provincial property

November: Crown resolves Delaware boundary dispute in William Penn's favor

1686

March 9, 15: royal decree pardoning William Penn and suspending legal proceedings against all Friends for violations under the religious conformity laws

June–August: William Penn journeys to the Netherlands and Germany publicly on Friends' concerns, privately to confer on the king's matters of state with his son-in-law, William of Orange

1687

February 1: William Penn reassigns provincial executive authority to Thomas Lloyd, Nicholas Moore, James Claypoole, Robert Turner, and John Eccle

April: James II issues Declaration of Indulgence

April 11: William Penn gives Philip Ford additional mortgage on Pennsylvania

August–September: William Penn goes with James II on official journey in central England

October: James Harrison dies

1688

April: King William's War (1688–1697), begins in colonies

July 12: William Penn reassigns provincial executive authority to John Blackwell, a Puritan with service in Cromwell's army, as deputy governor

November: Glorious Revolution begins as William of Orange (husband of Mary, the elder daughter of James II) lands at Brixham (Devonshire) at the head of a large army

December: James flees from England to France; Penn is arrested and questioned and posts bail

1689

February 27: first warrant issued for William Penn's arrest on suspicion of treason

Appendix 8: Chronology of Events

May 24: Parliament passes Act of Toleration granting freedom of religion to nonconformists who pledge to Oaths of Allegiance and Supremacy and reject transubstantiation

June: second warrant issued for Penn who is arrested, released, then again arrested as Jacobite plotter; finally discharged in November

August 12: Penn reassigns executive authority to the Pennsylvania Provincial Council, which elects Thomas Lloyd its president

December 16: Parliament enacts Bill of Rights, a statutory restatement of the Declaration of Rights, by which it invites William III and Mary II to become joint sovereigns of England with limited powers

1690

August 1: William Penn enters prison for one month on Crown charge of conspiring to commit high treason

September 2: Penn leases province of Pennsylvania and lower counties (Delaware) to Philip Ford

November: treason charge against Penn dismissed by order of the Court of King's Bench

1691

January 13: death of George Fox, in London; William Penn attends funeral; committal at Friends' Burial Ground near Bunhill Fields

February 5: another Crown proclamation issued to arrest Penn for high treason; Penn goes into seclusion

March: Provincial Council elects Thomas Lloyd the lieutenant governor, whereupon the members of the lower counties (Delaware) secede

1692

September: PYM resolves doctrinal dispute between followers of Quaker minister George Keith and 'orthodox' members led by Thomas Lloyd; PYM disowns Keith

October: William Penn loses governorship to Benjamin Fletcher, governor of New York, who was commissioned by William and Mary to take over governorship of Pennsylvania

1693

William Penn's *An Essay Towards the Present and Future Peace of Europe* published

Isaac Norris moves to Philadelphia from Jamaica and becomes a strong ally of Penn

May: Penn's *Some Fruits of Solitude: in Reflections and Maxims relating to the Conduct of Human Life* published

November: William III grants Penn his freedom and Privy Council acquits him of treason charges

William Penn's 'Holy Experiment'

1694
February 23: death of Gulielma Penn after a long illness
August 9: Queen in Council restores provincial government to William Penn with William Markham as lieutenant governor, ending Fletcher's governorship
December 28: Mary II dies (r. 1689–1694)

1695
William Penn remains in England engaged as Quaker leader and author; makes ministerial tours with son Springett; attends London Yearly Meeting where George Keith is disowned; begins soliciting subscriptions for Susquehanna settlement

1696
March 5: William Penn marries Hannah Callowhill; new Navigation Act tightens Crown control of trading
April 10: Penn's eldest son, Springett, dies at Lewes (Sussex)
May: William III appoints Board of Trade to supervise trade and colonial administration
September 23: Phineas Pemberton becomes clerk of PYM
September 29: Penn transfers to Philip Ford legal ownership of province of Pennsylvania and lower counties (Delaware)
November: General Assembly enacts new Frame of the Government, thus challenging Penn's powers

1697
January: William Penn leases Susquehanna Valley for one thousand years
March 12: Remonstrance of Philadelphians to Penn
April 1: Ford grants governing powers in province for ten years to Penn and his agents William Markham, Samuel Carpenter, and three others

1698
Summer: William Penn in Ireland on personal business and Quaker matters

1699
September 3: William Penn returns to America, sailing from Isle of Wight aboard the *Canterbury*
December 3: Penn arrives at Philadelphia accompanied by new secretary, James Logan, who in time becomes Penn's principal American agent

1700
January 28: birth of John Penn, William Penn's only American-born child

Appendix 8: Chronology of Events

February: Penn removes William Markham, Anthony Morris, and David Lloyd (attorney general) from their offices on orders of the Board of Trade; Lloyd becomes leader of resistance to both Penn and the Crown as the province is increasingly politicized
Summer: Penn withdraws to Pennsbury, absenting himself from governance and politics
September: Penn attends PYM

1701

Parliament determines royal succession by Act of Settlement and considers proposals for ending colonial proprietary governments
September: William Penn attends PYM and writes epistle to its quarterly and monthly meetings
October 25: Penn grants and confirms charter to Friends' public school in Philadelphia
October 28: Penn accepts new Charter of Privileges as provincial constitution (with unicameral legislature)
November 3: Penn sails for England; lodges in London

1702

January 8: death of Philip Ford
March 1: death of Phineas Pemberton
March 8: death of William III (r. 1689–1702); Anne ascends the throne (r. 1702–1714)
March 9: birth of William Penn's son Thomas
Queen Anne's War (1702–1713), second of four French and Indian colonial wars, begins, bringing on an economic depression

1703

April 26: death of lieutenant governor Andrew Hamilton
May: Penn offers to negotiate transfer of the provincial government to the Crown
July 6: Penn petitions the Crown to approve John Evans as lieutenant governor
August 30: birth of William and Hannah Penn's daughter Hannah Margarita

1704

February: arrival in America of John Evans, an Anglican from Wales, as new lieutenant governor, together with William Penn's son and agent, William Jr., who quits and sails for England in November
September: PYM adopts first *Book of Discipline*
November 7: birth of Penn's daughter Margaret
Separation of the Pennsylvania and Delaware assemblies ends union between Penn's province and lower counties

1705
January: William Penn resumes negotiating sale of provincial government to the Crown

October 4: Philip Ford's estate commences probate proceedings to enforce its claim against Penn; landowners in Pennsylvania disquieted

1706
January 17: birth of William and Hannah Penn's son Richard

July 22: Treaty of Union between England and Scotland leading to Acts of Union passed by parliaments of England (1706) and of Scotland (1707), creating Great Britain

1707
February: Provincial Assembly votes impeachment articles against James Logan

February 26: birth of William and Hannah Penn's son Dennis

November: Penn's home at Warminghurst sold

1708
January–September/October: William Penn committed to debtors' prison in London for adjudicated debt owed to the Fords

February: death of William and Hannah Penn's daughter Hannah Margarita

May: dismissal of John Evans and appointment of Charles Gookin as provincial lieutenant governor (approved by Crown in July)

September 5: birth of William and Hannah Penn's daughter Hannah

October: Penn settles Ford estate's claim for £7,600, of which £6,600 is borrowed from, and secured by mortgage to, thirty-eight Friends, nine of whom are made the trustees of Pennsylvania

1709
January 24: death of William and Hannah Penn's daughter Hannah

December 3: James Logan, protected by Gookin from David Lloyd's arrest warrant, departs the province for England, where he stays for two years

1710
William Penn settles his family at Ruscombe (Berkshire)

March: James Logan arrives in England to consult with Penn

July 31: Penn renews negotiations with the Crown to sell his proprietary government of Pennsylvania

1711
September: Isaac Norris becomes clerk of PYM

December: James Logan sails for Pennsylvania

Appendix 8: Chronology of Events

1712
March 22: James Logan arrives in Pennsylvania
April: William Penn suffers first apoplectic stroke
April, June: deaths of Hannah Penn's parents
September 9: Penn receives part payment on sale of the provincial government to the Crown
October 4: Penn suffers second stroke at Bristol
December: Penn suffers third, and incapacitating, stroke at home

1713
Hannah Penn begins managing proprietary affairs

1714
April 10: death of Samuel Carpenter in Philadelphia
August 1: death of Anne (r. 1702–1714) before Parliament concurs on surrender of Pennsylvania government; George I, the Elector of Hanover, comes to the throne (r. 1714–1727)
December 9: James Logan marries Sarah Read, sister of Israel Pemberton Sr.'s wife

1715
May: birth of Israel Pemberton Jr.

1716
November: William Keith commissioned as provincial lieutenant governor in place of Charles Gookin

1718
July 30: death of William Penn at Ruscombe (Berkshire) at the age of seventy-four
August 5: Penn buried at Jordans (Buckinghamshire)
September: Penn's 1712 will filed for probate in Prerogative Court, London
September: Lenapes complain of colonists' encroachments on native lands in the Tulpehocken area
September: John Farmer, English abolitionist, refused unity by PYM

1719
September: PYM's first revision of 1704 *Book of Discipline*
December: Advisory opinion letter of Sir Edward Northey on admissibility of William Penn's 1712 will to probate

1720
June: death of William Penn Jr.

1721

October: Hannah Penn files suit in Court of Exchequer to resolve 1712 will dispute
November or December: Hannah Penn suffers a stroke

1722

April: Israel Pemberton Sr. appointed a schools overseer
September: Great Treaty of Albany between Pennsylvania, Iroquois Confederacy, and others to extend Covenant Chain
death of Dennis Penn
Lenapes begin to vacate Tulpehocken lands as colonists encroach

1723

August: birth of James Pemberton
October: James Logan sails to England on *London Hope* to consult with the Penns

1724

May: Hannah, John, Thomas, and Springett Penn sign deed giving James Logan five thousand acres near Susquehanna River; Logan leaves England and arrives home July 16 with Hannah Penn's instructions to Lieutenant Governor Keith, which are ignored

1725

Lenapes make formal complaint in Assembly of encroachments on their Brandywine reservation
November 17: Petition of Hannah Penn and Springett Penn to king to appoint Patrick Gordon lieutenant governor

1726

January 7: Hannah Penn signs second deed of appointment apportioning proprietary shares to her sons
February 9: revival of Penn v. Penn in Court of Exchequer
June 22: Patrick Gordon in Philadelphia to succeed William Keith as lieutenant governor
September: Israel Pemberton Sr. begins attending PYM
December 13: Court of Exchequer admits William Penn's 1712 will to probate, making effective Hannah Penn's January 7, 1726, appointment of the proprietary interest in Pennsylvania to sons John (half interest) and Thomas and Richard (quarter interest each).
December 20: death of Hannah Penn

1727

May: James Logan buys Lenape land at Durham north of Tohickon Creek
June: death of George I; accession of George II

Appendix 8: Chronology of Events

November: birth of John Pemberton
December 29: Israel Pemberton Sr. appointed clerk of Philadelphia Monthly Meeting

1728
January: James Logan permanently crippled in a fall
Pennsylvania mortgage paid off by Penn Incorporated

1729
September: Isaac Norris I retires after nineteen years as PYM clerk; John Kinsey appointed as successor with Israel Pemberton Sr. as assistant

1730
September: John Kinsey begins his twenty years of service as clerk of PYM
November: Logan moves to his country seat at Stenton in Germantown
Ralph Sandiford's abolitionist *The Mystery of Iniquity* printed

1731
April: death of David Lloyd, chief justice of Pennsylvania
August: James Logan appointed chief justice
September: Ralph Sandiford disowned by PYM for anti-slavery views
October: Israel Pemberton Sr. serves first of nineteen consecutive annual terms in Pennsylvania Assembly
December: Ulster squatters removed from the Penns' Conestoga Manor

1732
August 11: Thomas Penn arrives in the province (remaining until 1741)
August–September: Treaty at Philadelphia with Iroquois to discuss French relations.

1733
March: death of Ralph Sandiford
March 20: James Logan replaced as secretary of province and clerk of Provincial Council
April 2: Logan replaced as secretary of the Proprietary Land Office

1734
September 20: John Penn arrives in the province, remains one year
September 25: Philadelphia meeting with Oneida and Conestoga chiefs
October: John and Thomas Penn and James Logan confer with Lenape chief Nutimus at Durham to buy trans-Tohickon lands

1735
May: John and Thomas Penn and James Logan confer with Nutimus at Pennsbury to buy trans-Tohickon lands
June 4: death of Isaac Norris I
August: Philadelphia meeting with Conestoga and Shawnee tribes; renewal of Friendship Chain
September 20: John Penn returns to England

1736
April: James Logan's *Charge delivered from the bench to the Grand Inquest* printed
August: death of Lieutenant Governor Patrick Gordon; Logan, as Provincial Council president, becomes temporary chief executive
September–October: Treaty of Philadelphia with the Iroquois confirms August 1732 treaty and brings Iroquoia into the Friendship Chain; the Iroquois release to the Penns all lands of the lower Susquehanna below Blue Mountain

1737
Israel Pemberton Jr. begins career in international trade
August: James Logan arranges Walking Purchase with Lenape chiefs at Stenton
September 19-20: Walking Purchase executed
Benjamin Lay's abolitionist *All slave-keepers that keep the innocent in bondage* printed

1738
George Thomas appointed lieutenant governor; resigns 1747
September: Benjamin Lay disowned by PYM for anti-slavery views

1739
September: PYM issues peace advisory not "to join with such as may be for making warlike preparations, offensive or defensive"
James Logan resigns as chief justice of Pennsylvania

1740
February: James Logan suffers a stroke

1741
August: Thomas Penn departs Pennsylvania for England
September: James Logan in letter to PYM warns that Friends don't belong in government if their principles prohibit defense

1742
July: Treaty of Philadelphia, principally involving the Iroquois, Susquehanna, and Lenape nations, results in the latter's expulsion from the Forks of the Delaware region

Appendix 8: Chronology of Events

August: Israel Pemberton Jr. appointed an overseer of the schools

1743
August: Israel Pemberton Jr. appointed clerk of the Overseers of the Schools
September: PYM prepares queries to subordinate meetings, with Israel Pemberton Jr. a member of drafting committee

1744
May: King George's War begins in Nova Scotia (ends in 1748)
June–July: Treaty of Lancaster

1745
October: Albany Conference
October: Israel Pemberton Sr., in his fifteenth year of Pennsylvania Assembly service, elected to but declines speakership

1746
April–May: Israel Pemberton Sr. asks for successor as clerk of Philadelphia Monthly Meeting; requested by meeting to continue in office; assisted by Israel Pemberton Jr.
June: death of Sarah Pemberton, wife of Israel Pemberton Jr.
September: PYM urges monthly meetings to establish schools
October 25: death of chief proprietor John Penn in England; his share of province of Pennsylvania left to brother Thomas, the third chief proprietor
October: Israel Pemberton Jr. and John Woolman begin their collaborations in PYM

1747
September: PYM additions to 1719 edition of *Book of Discipline* sent to quarterly meetings
November: Treaty of Philadelphia with Ohio Indians
December: Israel Pemberton Jr. marries Mary Jordan
Lieutenant Governor George Thomas resigns

1748
July: Treaty of Lancaster
October 18: King George's War ends

1749
October: Israel Pemberton Sr. serves last of nineteen consecutive years in Pennsylvania Assembly

1750
February: James Logan removed as a schools overseer

May 11: death of PYM clerk John Kinsey
Kinsey embezzlement exposed
September: Israel Pemberton Jr. appointed clerk of PYM

1751

August 22: Thomas Penn marries Lady Juliana Fermor, fourth daughter of Thomas, first Earl of Pomfret
October 14: Benjamin Franklin's first election to the Pennsylvania Assembly
October 31: death of James Logan

1752

May–July: Logstown Treaty between Ohio Indians and Virginia
Summer: John Penn (the Governor) first comes to Pennsylvania
September 2: Gregorian calendar becomes effective in Britain and its dominions
September: appointment of six new members, including Anthony Benezet, to PYM Overseers of the Press

1753

September: PYM adopts Gregorian calendar
October: Carlisle treaty with Indians concerning French incursion at heads of Ohio River

1754

January 19: death of Israel Pemberton Sr.
January: Philadelphia Monthly Meeting hears Benezet urge stronger discipline against slavery, appoints a committee
February: Philadelphia Monthly Meeting appoints John Smith clerk after Israel Pemberton Jr. declines to serve
March 24: James Pemberton succeeds father as an overseer of the schools
April 18: French drive British from Forks of Ohio River, then construct Fort Duquesne
May 28: first skirmish leading to French and Indian War (1754–1763) at Battle of Jumonville Glen in western Pennsylvania
June–July: Albany Congress of seven American colonies discusses improving Indian relations amid growing French threat; Franklin presents a proposal for a union of the colonies
July 4: George Washington surrenders Fort Necessity to the French
August–September: Duke of Cumberland nominates Edward Braddock to be commander of the British forces in America
September: PYM adopts *Epistle of Caution and Advice*; Overseers of the Press approve and print Woolman's *Considerations on Keeping Negroes*
December–April: Israel Pemberton Jr. accompanies Samuel Fothergill on preaching mission in American South

Appendix 8: Chronology of Events

1755
William Smith's anti-Quaker tract *A Brief State* printed in England
February: Major General Edward Braddock arrives in Virginia
March: Woolman's peace epistle issued by PYM's Meeting of Ministers and Elders
May 5: Philadelphia Quarterly Meeting sends epistle to Meeting for Sufferings in London regarding threatened abridgement of liberties by proprietors
ca. May: Braddock orders George Croghan's Indians out of his camp; spurns offer of help from Lenapes in coming campaign
July 9: Braddock's army routed at Battle of the Wilderness in western Pennsylvania near Fort Duquesne
August: Lenapes' offer of help in battle to Pennsylvania referred by lieutenant governor to Iroquoia
September: Charles Thomson employed by the Overseers of the Schools as master of Friends Latin School in Philadelphia
Autumn: John Penn returns to England
October: Assembly elections return Quaker majority
November 1: settlers massacred at Great Cove (Fulton County, Pennsylvania) by Lenapes, Mingos, and Shawnees under chief Shingas
November: William Smith's petition to the Privy Council that the oath for colonial legislative office be required
November: Acadian refugees arrive in Philadelphia

1756
January–March: Oath bill in Parliament lobbied against by English Quakers John Hanbury, John Fothergill, and others; through Earl Granville the bill dies and English Quakers pledge that Pennsylvania pacifist Quaker assemblymen will withdraw from office during hostilities
April 12: "Humble Address" of Israel Pemberton Jr. and five other pacifist Quakers to Pennsylvania Lieutenant Governor Morris
April 14: Morris declares war on Lenapes and allies; scalp bounties established
April 19: Israel Pemberton Jr. holds dinner party with Indians and pacifists
May 17: Britain declares war against France; Lord Loudoun sails to America as commander in chief of military forces
June: James Pemberton and five other pacifist Quakers resign from the Pennsylvania Assembly
July: first Easton treaty with Teedyuscung and other Indians
July 22: Israel Pemberton Jr. leads general meeting of Quakers for promoting and funding peace with the Indians
September: PYM creates Meeting for Sufferings; eight new members (including Woolman, William Logan, John Churchman, James

Pemberton, and John Pemberton) appointed PYM Overseers of the Press
October: Benjamin Franklin leads Assembly's antiproprietary party
November: second Easton treaty with Indians; Teedyuscung charges fraud in the Walking Purchase; Israel Pemberton Jr., Benjamin Franklin, and Charles Thomson attend
December 1: "The Friendly Association for regaining and preserving peace with the Indians by Pacific Measures" is founded
December: William Pitt the Elder becomes leader of British ministry, adopts new American policy

1757

January: Benjamin Franklin appointed Pennsylvania Assembly agent in London to deal with the proprietors; departs in June and stays abroad until 1762
March–May: Lancaster treaty with Indians; Teedyuscung stays away
July–August: third Easton treaty with Indians
August: Lord Loudoun abandons siege of Louisbourg; French forces capture and destroy Fort William Henry, and massacres follow
September 8: Duke of Cumberland forced to resign as captain general of British armies
September: Friendly Association address to Lieutenant Governor Denny
December: Brigadier General John Forbes given command of expedition to retake Fort Duquesne

1758

January: Quaker John Hunt returns to England, bringing with him Charles Thomson's *An enquiry into the causes of the alienation of the Delaware and Shawanese Indians from the British interest*, which is circulated among government officials
May: Israel Pemberton Jr. and John Forbes begin cooperation
July 15–September 20: Christian Frederick Post's first journey to Ohio Indians
October 7–26: fourth Easton treaty with Indians; Lenapes and Iroquois renew Covenant Chain
October 21: Post sets out on second journey to Ohio Indians with Easton message
November 25: Fort Duquesne, ruined by French occupants on previous day, taken by British under Forbes and renamed Pittsburgh

1759

February: Benjamin Franklin presents petition to Privy Council to investigate Teedyuscung's fraud complaint and Thomas Penn and Richard Penn Sr.'s conduct of Indian affairs
March: Franklin arranges London printing of Thomson's *Enquiry into the causes of the alienation*
July: Pennsylvania Assembly seizes the Penns' Land Office records

Appendix 8: Chronology of Events

August: The king in council refers Walking Purchase fraud claim to Sir William Johnson for examination
September: Quebec capitulates to British forces
September: John Woolman's peace epistle issued by PYM, addressed to its quarterly and monthly meetings; Israel Pemberton Jr. resigns as PYM clerk

1760
April: Final entry in minute book of Friendly Association
Spring: Pittsburgh treaty of western Indians, attended by Teedyuscung
September: British capture Montreal, ending French and Indian War
October 25: death of George II; ascension of George III

1761
August: fifth Easton treaty with Indians
September: James Pemberton elected clerk of PYM, serves until 1781 (except in 1767 and 1777)
October 5: William Pitt resigns ministry

1762
May: Susquehanna Company of Connecticut sends settlers into Wyoming Valley
June 18–28: sixth Easton treaty, a proceeding held by Sir William Johnson to examine Teedyuscung's claim of fraud and forgery in the Walking Purchase, which results in settlement of the dispute
August: Lancaster treaty with western and northern Indians
September: PYM revises its *Book of Discipline*
November: Benjamin Franklin returns to Philadelphia at end of first mission in England

1763
February: Paris Treaty ends America's French and Indian War; France cedes Canada east of the Mississippi River to Britain
April 19: arsonists burn out the Lenapes at Wyoming, Teedyuscung killed
May: Pontiac's War (1763–1766) begins at Fort Detroit, forces include Lenapes
June: John Woolman journeys to visit Native Americans at Wyalusing
July: British at Fort Pitt give smallpox-infected blankets to the Lenapes
October 4: boundary between English colonies and Indians set along crest of the Alleghenies from New York to Georgia by proclamation of the British Board of Trade
October: John Penn (with his brother Richard Jr.; both are sons of William Penn's son Richard Sr.) arrives as lieutenant governor after his uncle Thomas Penn removes James Hamilton
October 31: Pontiac lifts siege of Fort Detroit

December 14, 27: Paxton Boys massacre six Conestoga Indians at Conestoga Indiantown and fourteen more in Lancaster workhouse

1764

January–February: Benjamin Franklin's *Narrative of the late massacres, in Lancaster County* printed

February: over 500 Paxton Boys march on Philadelphia to murder Lenapes under Moravian care; Benjamin Franklin and others pacify them at Germantown

March 24: Pennsylvania Assembly resolves to ask for royal government

April: Iroquois attack eastern Lenapes during Pontiac's War

May: Franklin, leader of antiproprietary party in Assembly, elected speaker and serves until October, when he is defeated for re-election after calling for royal government

July: Pennsylvania declares war on Lenape and Shawnee Indians

September: PYM opposes taking arms, even in defense

October: Assembly votes to send Franklin on second mission to Britain to present petition for a change of government; he serves until 1775

November: Privy Council dismisses Pennsylvania's petition for royal government

1765

March 22: Stamp Act given royal assent; taxes levied on documents (including newspapers and legal and commercial papers used in the American colonies) for the support of British troops stationed there after the French and Indian War

1766

March 18: Stamp Act repealed following colonial protests

May 31: Lieutenant governor John Penn marries Anne Allen, daughter of Chief Justice William Allen

July 25: Treaty at Fort Ontario ends Pontiac's War

1767

June 29: first of the five Townshend Acts passed

1768

September: British seize Boston

November 5: first treaty with Indians at Fort Stanwix relocates the 1763 Proclamation Boundary with Indians farther west into Ohio country; the Penns pay the Iroquois for all unceded land in Pennsylvania

1769

April 20: Chief Pontiac murdered

Pennamite-Yankee War (1769–1799) begins when Connecticut settlers enter the Wyoming Valley under claim of a royal grant

Appendix 8: Chronology of Events

1771
February 4: death of Richard Penn Sr. in England
May: John Penn (the Governor) returns to England as successor to his father's one-quarter share in the Pennsylvania proprietorship
October: Richard Penn Jr. becomes lieutenant governor in place of his brother

1772
May: Lieutenant Governor Richard Penn weds Mary, daughter of assemblyman and Philadelphia merchant William Masters
September: Philadelphia Monthly Meeting divided, creating Philadelphia Monthly Meeting for the Northern District and Philadelphia Monthly Meeting for the Southern District. The original monthly meeting was thereafter sometimes known as the Middle District.
October: death of John Woolman while on mission in England

1773
August 30: John Penn (the Governor) returns to Pennsylvania as lieutenant governor in place of his brother Richard; remains until his death in February 1795
December: Boston Tea Party

1774
September 5–October 26: first Continental Congress
September: PYM directs disownment of any member owning or dealing in slaves

1775
March 21: death of Thomas Penn
March 21: Franklin ends second English mission; arrives in Philadelphia May 5
April 14: Pennsylvania Abolition Society founded
April 19: opening battles of American Revolution at Lexington and Concord
May: second Continental Congress (sits until 1781)
Summer: Richard Penn leaves Pennsylvania to live in England
September: PYM approves resolutions disowning members not emancipating their slaves as well as those engaging in war

1776
July 4: Continental Congress votes for Declaration of Independence
September 28: Constitution of Pennsylvania, adopted by Convention and signed by its president, Benjamin Franklin, replaces Penn's charter; proprietary government terminated

September: PYM epistle to monthly meetings and quarterly meetings "in these and the adjacent provinces" calling for Friends "to withdraw from being active in civil government"
December 21: Franklin arrives in Paris as American envoy; seeks French aid; serves until 1785

1777

September 26: Philadelphia captured by British forces; Congress flees to Lancaster, then York
September: Philadelphia Quaker leadership and others exiled to Winchester, Virginia, as persons having "evinced a disposition inimical to the cause of America"
Winter: George Washington's army encamps at Valley Forge

1778

February 6: Treaty of Alliance signed by France and America
April: end of Winchester exile for Pembertons and other Quakers; Pennsylvania imposes loyalty oath on all residents; those refusing are to suffer property confiscation
June 18: British evacuate Philadelphia

1779

January: Benjamin Franklin made sole minister plenipotentiary to France
April 22: death of Israel Pemberton Jr.
Summer: General John Sullivan campaigns to break Iroquois control of northeastern Pennsylvania
July: James Pemberton appointed clerk and John Pemberton appointed member of the Overseers of the Schools
November 27: Assembly passes "An Act for vesting the estates of the late Proprietaries of Pennsylvania in this Commonwealth," taking 24 million acres of unsold lands for £130,000

1780

March 2: Act for the Gradual Abolition of Slavery passed by Pennsylvania Assembly

1781

March: second Continental Congress becomes Congress under Articles of Confederation
September: James Pemberton resigns as clerk of PYM
October 19: capitulation of British at Yorktown ends American Revolution and leads to Treaty of Paris, September 3, 1783

1784

October: the Iroquois cede claims to Pennsylvania lands at second Treaty of Stanwix

APPENDIX 9

Biographical Information on Europeans

Allen, William [1704–1780]: Penn loyalist; chief justice of province of Pennsylvania 1750–1774; founder of Allentown; father-in-law of lieutenant governor John Penn, one of the last two proprietors of Pennsylvania

Aubrey, Letitia Penn [1678–1746]: daughter of William and Gulielma Penn

Audland, John [1630–1664]: early Quaker minister, convinced by Fox at Firbank Fell; one of the Valiant Sixty

Benezet, Anthony [1713–1784]: French-born Huguenot, became a Quaker in England, came to Philadelphia at age eighteen, where he taught for many years at Friends Public School; active in the antislavery cause

Brodhead, Daniel [1736–1809]: army general appointed by George Washington to command the expedition that in summer 1779 destroyed the power of the Seneca tribe on the Allegheny River in western New York and Pennsylvania

Burrough, Edward [1634–1662]: early Quaker leader, itinerant preacher, and martyr; one of the Valiant Sixty, he engaged John Bunyan in a pamphlet debate; was arrested for holding a meeting and confined in Newgate Prison, London, where he died

Carpenter, Samuel [1649–1714]: born in England; after the murder of his father and his convincement as a Quaker, he relocated to Barbados and prospered as a merchant; in 1683 he arrived in Pennsylvania, becoming prominent in business and government

Churchman, John [1705–1775]: Quaker minister in Chester County who traveled extensively on missions in the American colonies and Europe

Croghan, George [ca. 1718–1782]: son-in-law of Nichas, Mohawk chief; Irish-born Indian trader in the Ohio country 1744–1753; William Johnson's deputy from 1756 to the early 1770s

Cumberland, Prince William Augustus, Duke of [1721–1765]: third son of George II; victor at Battle of Culloden 1745

Duquesne de Menneville, Michel-Ange; Marquis Duquesne [ca. 1700–1778]: French governor general of New France 1752–1755

Evans, John [ca. 1678–ca. 1743]: Welsh Anglican; lieutenant governor

Fell, Margaret—see Fox, Margaret

Fell, Thomas [1598–1658]: Member of Parliament; vice-chancellor, duchy of Lancaster; Puritan; offered George Fox the hospitality of his home

Forbes, John [1707–1759]: British general who captured Fort Duquesne in November 1758 and renamed it Pittsburgh

Ford, Philip [ca. 1631–1702]: William Penn's steward and business manager from 1669 until his death in 1702

Fothergill, John [1712–1780]: English Quaker, physician, and botanist

Fothergill, Samuel [1715–1772]: English Quaker minister who missionized in America 1754–1756

Fox, George [1624–1691]: founder of Religious Society of Friends (Quakers)

Fox, Margaret [1614–1702]: widow of Thomas Fell; married George Fox in 1669; known as the "mother of Quakerism"; one of the Valiant Sixty, she provided in her home, Swarthmoor Hall, an administrative and communications center for Friends

Franklin, Benjamin [1706–1790]: member of the Pennsylvania Assembly 1751–1763; attended Indian treaty conferences in 1753, 1754, and 1756; Assembly representative in London 1757–1762, and then 1764-1775; published a series of Pennsylvania Indian treaties 1736–1762; wrote *A narrative of the late massacres in Lancaster County* (1764)

Freame, Margaret Penn [1704–1751]: daughter of William and Hannah Penn

Granville, Earl, born John Carteret [1690–1763]: president of the Privy Council 1751–1763; Thomas Penn's brother-in-law

Hamilton, James [1710–1783]: lieutenant governor of Pennsylvania 1748–1754, 1759–1763

Hanbury, John [1700–1758]: London Quaker; leading tobacco merchant; London agent for William and Mary College

Harrison, James [ca. 1628–1687]: father of Phoebe, the first wife of Phineas Pemberton and mother of Israel Sr.; a provincial land agent for William Penn; member of the first Provincial Council; first steward of Pennsbury

Hill, Richard [1673–1729]: born in Maryland, arrived in Philadelphia in 1700; merchant, ship captain; son-in-law of Thomas Lloyd

Holme, Thomas [1624–1695]: appointed by Penn as surveyor general of Pennsylvania in 1682

Howgill, Francis [1618–1669]: early Quaker minister, convinced by Fox at Firbank Fell; one of the Valiant Sixty

Johnson, Sir William [ca. 1715–1774]: Britain's sole agent and superintendent of Indian affairs for the Northern District of America, 1756–1774; presiding officer at Easton 6 in June 1762

Keith, George [ca.1639–1716]: Scottish born Presbyterian who became a convinced Quaker; while in Philadelphia as schoolmaster he led a separation of 'Christian' Quakers; following disownment by PYM he became an Anglican priest

Kinsey, John [1693–1750]: Clerk of PYM 1730–1749; speaker of the Provincial Assembly 1739–1750; Pennsylvania's attorney general 1739–1741 and chief justice 1743–1750

Appendix 9: Europeans

Lloyd, David [1656–1731]: Pennsylvania's first attorney general and its chief justice 1718–1731; member of the Assembly and its speaker thirteen years between 1694 and 1725; became an opponent of Penn and led the antiproprietary faction

Lloyd, Thomas [1640–1694]: supporter and official under Penn until they broke in the late 1680s when Lloyd joined and later led antiproprietary interests

Loe, Thomas [d. 1668]: English Quaker, 'the apostle of Ireland,' convinced 1654; became a minister in 1657, often traveling to Ireland, where he convinced William Penn in 1667

Logan, James [1674–1751]: Irish-born Quaker, in 1699 came to Philadelphia with William Penn as Penn's secretary, over the years becoming his principal representative in Pennsylvania; in 1714 married Sarah Read, sister of Israel Pemberton Sr.'s wife Rachel

Logan, William [1717–1776]: son of James; Israel Pemberton Jr.'s first cousin; served on Provincial Council 1747–1775

Markham, William [ca. 1635–1704]: William Penn's cousin and deputy governor 1681–1682 and 1693–1699

Morris, Anthony [1654–1721]: London-born Quaker brewer; active in provincial government and schools; clerk of PYM 1704 and 1710

Morris, Anthony III [1682–1763]: brought from London to Philadelphia as an infant; merchant, civic official, and major landowner

Norris, Isaac, I [1671–1735]: born in London; moved to Jamaica in 1678, where in 1692 his family died after an earthquake; moved to Philadelphia; successful Quaker merchant; served in provincial offices and as clerk of PYM 1711–1729

Norris, Isaac, II [1701–1766]: married Sarah, daughter of James Logan; speaker of the Provincial Assembly 1750–1758, 1760–1764

Owen, Griffith [1647–1718]: born in Wales; arrived in Philadelphia 1684; physician, Quaker minister; served in provincial government; clerk of PYM in 1702

Pemberton, Israel, Jr. [1715–1779]: clerk of PYM 1750–1759; clerk of overseers of the Philadelphia Public School 1743–1779; member of Provincial Assembly in 1750

Pemberton, Israel, Sr. [1685–1754]: in 1710 married Rachel Read, whose sister later married James Logan; clerk of Philadelphia Monthly Meeting 1727–1754; member of Provincial Assembly 1731–1749; father of Israel Pemberton Jr., James Pemberton, and John Pemberton

Pemberton, James [1723–1809]: clerk of PYM 1761–1766, 1768–1776, and 1778–1781; member of the Provincial Assembly 1755 and 1765–1769

Pemberton, John [1727–1795]: public Quaker minister

Pemberton, Mary Jordan [1704–1778]: second wife of Israel Jr.; clerk of Philadelphia Yearly Women's Meeting 1760–1777

Pemberton, Phineas [1650–1702]: clerk of PYM 1696–1701; speaker of the Provincial Assembly 1698; father of Israel Pemberton Sr.
Penn, Dennis [1707–1722]: son of William and Hannah Penn
Penn, Gulielma Maria Springett [1644–1694], William Penn's first wife; mother of Springett Penn, Letitia Penn Aubrey, and William Penn Jr.
Penn, Hannah Margaret Callowhill [1671–1726]: William Penn's second wife; mother of John Penn "the American," Thomas Penn, Margaret Penn Freame, Richard Penn Sr., and Dennis Penn
Penn, John, "of Stoke" or "the Writer" [1760–1834]: son of Thomas Penn
Penn, John, "the American" [1700–1746]: son of William and Hannah Penn
Penn, John, "the Governor" [1729–1795]: son of Richard Penn Sr.
Penn, Richard, Jr. [1735–1811]: son of Richard Penn Sr.
Penn, Richard, Sr. [1706–1771]: son of William and Hannah Penn
Penn, Springett [1674–1696]: son of William and Gulielma Penn
Penn, Springett, II [1701-1731]: son of William Penn Jr.; successor to his father's unsuccessful claim to the proprietorship of Pennsylvania
Penn, Thomas [1702–1775]: son of William and Hannah Penn
Penn, Sir William [1621–1670]: British admiral; father of William Penn
Penn, William [1644–1718]: founder and proprietor of Pennsylvania; father (by first wife Gulielma) of Springett Penn, Letitia Penn Aubrey, and William Penn Jr.; father (by second wife Hannah) of John Penn "the American," Thomas Penn, Margaret Penn Freame, Richard Penn Sr., and Dennis Penn
Penn, William, Jr. [1681–1720]: son of William and Gulielma Penn
Peters, Richard [1704–1776]: attorney, civil servant, Anglican minister; secretary of the Provincial Council and the Proprietary Land Office 1743–1760
Pitt, William, the Elder [1707–1778]: leader of the British cabinet from 1756 to 1761
Post, Christian Frederick [1710–1785]: Moravian missionary to Native Americans; messenger to Ohio country for Easton 4
Proud, Robert [1728–1813]: historian of colonial Pennsylvania
Pusey, Caleb [ca. 1651–1726/7]: born in Berks, England; moved to the province of Pennsylvania near Chester in 1682; active in government; clerk of PYM 1702
Reynell, John [1708–1784]: born and educated in England; came to Philadelphia in 1728; successful international merchant; leading Quaker and philanthropist; last president of the Friendly Association
Smith, John [1722–1771]: son of Richard Smith; married Hannah, daughter of James Logan; merchant trader, founder of Pennsylvania Hospital, member of the Provincial Assembly, member of the King's Council in New Jersey, clerk of PYM in 1760

Appendix 9: Europeans

Smith, Samuel [1720–1776]: son of Richard Smith; historian of colonial New Jersey and of colonial Pennsylvania; merchant trader; secretary of the King's Council and treasurer of West Jersey province

Smith, William [1727–1803]: Anglican clergyman and anti-Quaker activist; author of *A brief state of the province of Pennsylvania*

Sullivan, John [1740–1795]: army general appointed by George Washington to command the expedition that in summer 1779 destroyed the Iroquois power in western New York

Thomson, Charles [1729–1824]: born in Ireland; came to America as an orphan; educated in Pennsylvania; in 1755 became master of the Friends School, Philadelphia; in November 1756 brought by Pemberton to Easton 2, where he served as a secretary of the conference; in 1759 his *Enquiry into the Alienation of the Delaware and Shawanese Indians* was printed; served as secretary of the Continental Congress 1774–1789

Weiser, Conrad [1696–1760]: Palatine German who settled in Schoharie Valley; learned to speak Mohawk; relocated in 1723 to Tulpehocken; interpreter and liaison for the Penns to the Iroquois

Whitehead, George [ca. 1636–1723]: Quaker; strong advocate for national policy of toleration

Woolman, John [1720–1772]: New Jersey farmer; Quaker minister and author; friend and colleague of Israel Pemberton Jr. in the reform of PYM; died in England on a missionary journey

Wycliffe, John [1328–1384]: theologian and critic of the established church; translator of the Bible that sparked what became the Protestant Reformation; ended his days as pastor of the church at Lutterworth where Fox began his spiritual pilgrimage

APPENDIX 10

Native Americans: Nations and Leaders, Alliance Systems, and the Walking Purchase

Nations and Leaders

Iroquois (or Five Nations)

The "people of the longhouse" were known to themselves as the Haudenosaunee, to the French as the Iroquois, and to the British as the Five Nations (the nations being the Mohawks, Oneidas, Onondagas, Cayugas, and Senecas). They occupied lands in present-day New York between Canada and Pennsylvania westward from the upper Hudson River toward Lake Erie. After 1722, with the adoption of the Tuscaroras, the Iroquois League (sometimes Confederacy or Nation) became the Six Nations.

Brant, Joseph (Mohawk) [1743–1807]: chief; allied with William Johnson, his sister's common-law husband, to attack colonists on the Pennsylvania-New York frontier during the American Revolution

Canasatego (Onondaga) [d. 1750]: treaty speaker for Iroquois League, possibly a chief

Jagrea (Mohawk) [d. 1758]: a Pennsylvania peace messenger prior to Easton 1

Cornplanter (Seneca) [ca. 1732–1836]: Iroquois war chief; allied with William Johnson during the American Revolution; signed the Treaty of Stanwix

King, Thomas (Oneida): speaker at Easton 4

Newcastle (Seneca) [d. 1756]: Quaker; represented the Iroquois Nation at Easton 1, at which he was appointed joint agent for Pennsylvania with Teedyuscung; died of smallpox in Philadelphia

Nichas (Mohawk): chief; father-in-law of George Croghan; tried to diminish the authority of Teedyuscung at Easton 4

Sayenqueraghta (Seneca) [ca. 1707–1786]: Iroquois war chief; allied with William Johnson during the American Revolution

Shikellamy (Oneida) [d. 1747]: captured French national adopted by the Oneidas; liaison at Shamokin between the Iroquois League and the Shawnees; aided James Logan and Conrad Weiser in the Friendship Chain

Appendix 10: Native Americans

Lenni Lenape

Also widely known by the British as the Delawares, the name means "original people" and refers to the Native Americans who occupied the Delaware and Schuylkill Rivers drainage systems in Pennsylvania as well as riverine lands in New Jersey and Delaware. Generally referred to herein as Lenapes, occasionally as Delawares.

Locquies, William: a peace messenger for Pennsylvania before Easton 1

Moses Tatamy [b. late seventeenth century–d. 1761]: Lenape chief, born near Cranberry, New Jersey; provincial interpreter and messenger; settled on a 300-acred tract near Easton on Tatamy's (now Bush Kill) Creek.

Nutimus: chief at Forks of the Delaware; his land was allegedly stolen in the Walking Purchase

Pisquetomen: Sassoonan's chosen successor as chief at Tulpehocken but rejected by James Logan; relocated to Ohio from Shamokin

Sassoonan (aka Olumapies) [d. 1747]: chief at Tulpehocken

Teedyuscung [d. 1763]: rose as a chief in New Jersey and became principal leader of eastern Lenapes and other tribes at the Easton treaties; later settled in the Wyoming Valley of Pennsylvania, where he was assassinated by settlers from Connecticut

Susquehannocks

Tribes on lands within the Susquehanna River system, also known as Minquas or Conestogas, the Nanticokes and the Conoys or Ganawese or Piscataways from Maryland, and the Shawnees.

Ohio Indians

Commingled tribes of various Indian nations that settled on lands around the Ohio River and its tributaries. Some of the tribes were indigenous to those lands (e.g., the Miamis [Twightwees], Wabash, and Wyandots); others were displaced or otherwise self-relocated (e.g., Shawnees, Lenapes [Delawares], Mingos [Iroquoian Senecas and Cayugas], Nanticokes).

Beaver King (Lenape) [aka Beaver, Tamaqua]: chief

Delaware George (Lenape) [aka Nenatchehan]: an Ohio warrior and brother of Pisquetomen, Beaver King, and Shingas

Keekyuscung (Lenape): chief

Scarouady (Oneida): Iroquois liaison to the Ohio Shawnees after Shikellamy

Shingas (Lenape): chief 1752–1763; nephew of Sassoonan

Tanaghrisson (Seneca) [aka Half King]: Iroquois liaison to the Ohio Indians

William Penn's 'Holy Experiment'

Teedyuscung's Five Tribes

By Easton 4, Teedyuscung had established himself as the head of five tribes. In addition to the named (eastern) Lenapes, he commanded the Wename, Munseys, Mawhickons (Mohiccons), and Wapingers (Wapings).

Alliance Systems Made by Native American Nations with Pennsylvania and Other American Colonies

According to Iroquois legend and scholarly opinion, by ca. 1150 CE a Great Peace[1] was achieved among the Mohawk, Oneida, Onondaga, Cayuga, and Seneca Nations when they bonded together to form the *Iroquois League*. This league grew into a regional authority reaching beyond its own territories to other tribes and to European traders, adventurers, planters, and officials who were arriving in the Hudson, Delaware, and Susquehanna River Valleys as those areas were increasingly coming under Iroquois hegemony.

The term *Covenant Chain*, used in reference to the alliance and treaty system developed by the Iroquois with its European neighbors and with Native Americans outside the Iroquois League, began to evolve in the 1670s. According to a recent history of the state of New York,

> The term Covenant Chain entered the written record around 1677, shortly after the English had regained control of New York from the Dutch. Prior to that date, the Iroquois had made treaties with Dutch traders and officials but had not used the term. At a council in 1659 between the Mohawk and Dutch, official reference was made to a 1643 treaty in which the Mohawk claimed that they had metaphorically bound themselves to the Dutch by an 'iron chain.' By the late 1670s the term Covenant Chain was increasingly used to convey that sense of alliance. At meetings in Albany and various Iroquois villages, participants renewed alliances, claiming that they came to 'polish' the chain. In later Iroquois oral traditions, Iroquois leaders expressed how their relationships with Europeans grew in significance by describing how their alliances had gone from one bound by 'rope' to one linked by a 'chain of silver.'[2]

In 1677, the silver Covenant Chain was formally instituted by the Iroquois (with strong Mohawk urging) and New York, forming an alliance with Massachusetts, Connecticut, Maryland, and Virginia.

Pennsylvania at its founding instituted its own alliance system with the indigenous peoples of the colony. In 1701, William Penn entered into an agreement of friendship and amity with the tribes of the Susquehanna, thereby creating a *Friendship Chain*. That chain, intended to secure peace along the Susquehanna River, was preceded, according to legend and tradition, by Penn's treaty of peace made during 1683–1684 with the Lenni Lenapes who were settled on lands west of the Delaware River. While

---

[1] Kalter, *Benjamin Franklin*, 4–7.

[2] José António Brandão, "Covenant Chain," in *The Encyclopedia of New York State*, ed. Peter Eisenstadt (Syracuse, NY: Syracuse University Press, 2005), 416.

Appendix 10: Native Americans

preserving the Friendship Chain, in 1722 Pennsylvania joined the Covenant Chain with New York and the Iroquois League at the Great Treaty of Albany. And in 1736 at the Treaty of Philadelphia it joined with Iroquoia in their "League and Chain of Friendship and Brotherhood," to expand its geopolitical influence and to have access to some of the backcountry fur trade long dominated by New York.

In 1753, the Mohawks declared the Covenant Chain broken after claiming that their nation had been defrauded of land. Although the Covenant Chain was renewed (as ordered by the British government) at the 1754 Albany Congress, it was finally destroyed in 1779 following the Sullivan Expedition's sweep through Iroquoia that burned its villages and fields and uprooted the people and their way of life.

The Walking Purchase: Descriptions of Its Boundaries and Extent Found in Deeds and Other Official Records

The Walking Purchase is the name history has given to the scheme used by William Penn's son Thomas, acting for himself and his brothers John and Richard, to acquire a vast tract of Native American land in the areas of the Lehigh and upper Delaware Rivers in Pennsylvania in 1737. The brothers' purpose was to satisfy the land hunger of investors and colonists seeking opportunities in the growing province, particularly in the area of the valley of the Lehigh River, a western tributary of the Delaware River along which Easton, Bethlehem, and Allentown are now situated. Another, and more pressing, purpose of the Penns was to raise funds to meet the demands of their creditors.

Set out below are descriptions found in the relevant deeds and other documents related to William Penn's land acquisitions and negotiations in the Delaware River area above Philadelphia. Here also are those documents related to his sons' claims to the Lehigh Valley lands taken in the Walking Purchase of 1737 and to the vigorous protests made by or on behalf of the Lenni Lenapes who claimed the rightful ownership. All of the footnotes in this section, including those within quotations from documents, have been added by the author.

July 15, 1682—William Penn's land purchase above Neshaminy Creek:[3] In July 1682, William Penn obtained from the Lenni Lenapes a deed for lands lying on the west side of the Delaware River beginning at Neshaminy Creek thence upriver to some point beyond the Falls of the Delaware. That "point" is now difficult if not impossible to locate, it being described in the deed as a "corner marked Spruce Tree, with the letter P at the foot of a mountain." Had it been a more fixed point, such as a creek, the deed would have so stated. Beyond that point the Indian lands were unceded and remained in the ownership and under the control of the Lenapes, although some irregular non-Indian possession was taken prior to the Walking Purchase, including an area held by James Logan at Durham. The description of the 1682 purchase, known as the Pennsbury tract, begins midpoint on the tract's eastern boundary at the Falls of the Delaware, which is between modern Morrisville, Pennsylvania, and Trenton, New Jersey.

---

[3] Deed from the Delaware Indians [July 15, 1682], *PWP*, 2:261–63.

Beginning at a certain white oak in the land now in the tenure of John Wood & by him called the Gray stones over against the Falls of Delaware River, and so

> from thence up by the [Delaware] riverside to a **corner**[4] marked **Spruce Tree**, with the letter P at the foot of a mountain and
> from the said corner marked spruce tree **along** by **the ledge or foot of the mountains [West North] West to a corner white oak marked with the letter P standing by the Indian Path that leads to an Indian town** named **Playwicky**[5] and near the head of a creek called Towsissink,[6] and
> **from thence westward to** the creek called **Neshammonyes** [Neshaminy] **Creek,**[7] and
> [from thence] along by the said Neshammonyes Creek unto the River Delaware, alias Maksrich Kitton,[8] and
> [from thence] so bounded by the said main river to the first [mentioned] white oak in John Woods Land.
> And all those islands . . . [Matinicunck, Sepassincks, and Orecktons] etc.

June 23, 1683—William Penn's land purchase between Pennypack and Neshaminy Creeks:[9] In June 1683, Penn acquired his second deed for Lenape land on the upper Delaware River. It was for land adjacent to the western or downriver side of the Pennsbury tract, simply described as the land "betwixt Pemapeck [Pennypack] & Neshamineh [Neshaminy] Creeks and all along upon Neshaminy Creek." Rather than fixing a description by landmarks inland from the Delaware River of the land "betwixt" these two creeks, the deed (undoubtedly prepared by Penn's draftsmen) recited only that it was for lands "backward of the same and to run two days journey with an horse up into the country as the said river doeth go." This vague description invited controversy when a similar formula was used later for the Walking Purchase.

Post-1683—William Penn's negotiations for lands above the Pennsbury tract: Prior to the 1732 arrival of Thomas Penn in Pennsylvania, no claim or record had been made that William Penn had conducted or completed any further land transactions with the Lenapes for territory above the upriver line described in the July 1682 deed. That changed when Thomas came to Philadelphia asserting that his father had personally involved himself in proceedings to purchase lands up the Delaware River beyond his 1682 acquisition. The evidence Thomas offered was a paper brought from England that he alleged he had discovered there among his father's records. He also alleged it was the copy of a 1686 deed, notwithstanding it had neither signatures, nor the required seals of the signatories, nor a

---

[4] The bolded text in this description is duplicated in the same word order in the Walking Purchase confirmation and quitclaim deed of August 1737, discussed below.

[5] See George P. Donehoo, *A History of the Indian Villages and Place Names in Pennsylvania* (Harrisburg, PA: 1928; repr. Lewisburg, PA: Wennawood Publishing, 2006), 157.

[6] Not found in Donehoo, *A History of the Indian Villages*.

[7] Donehoo, *A History of the Indian Villages,* 127–28.

[8] Ibid., 53–54.

[9] Deed from the Delaware Indians [23 June 1683], *PWP*, 2:404.

Appendix 10: Native Americans

description of the property being conveyed. At best, in the judgment of Francis Jennings, it was an incomplete draft that, like the claimed original, has since disappeared.[10]

Doubts of this paper's authenticity mount when one recalls that Penn was not even in America between September 1684 and December 1699. Further, Charles Thomson, the authority on Penn Incorporated deeds, studied "a paper said to be a copy of a deed, dated 28th of 6th month [August] 1686, and indorsed, Copy of the last Indian Purchase."[11] Although some asserted it was in the handwriting of William Penn, when "produced at Easton, and examined, it appeared clearly, and was certified by the Secretary and several others acquainted with Mr. Penn's handwriting, not to be his, nor is it indeed like it. Its chief mark of credit is, that it appears to be an ancient paper. But there is no certificate of its being a copy, nor was it ever recorded."[12] Whatever this paper was, it has disappeared and the alleged original has never been seen since. It is not among the documents held in the Pennsylvania State Archives. In the end, we are left with the editorial judgment of Donald H. Kent, writing in *Early American Indian Documents* as ". . . not recorded. Wanting and immaterial."[13] In spite of its dubious if not fraudulent evidentiary value, the alleged copy of a 1686 deed was accepted as a source of title by reference to it both in the deed of 1737 and in the determination of Sir William Johnson in favor of the Penns settling their Walking Purchase title at Easton 6 as discussed below.

Some light was shed in November 1756, however, regarding a theretofore unknown and hence undocumented event in which William Penn tried to extend his Pennsbury tract up the Delaware to and beyond the banks of Tohickon Creek,[14] but there is no record of this attempt resulting in any agreement or deed. During the 1756 proceedings at Easton 2, when Teedyuscung first made the Lenapes' charge of land fraud against the Penn proprietorship, Moses Tatamy, a Lenape chief and convert to Christianity who was an interpreter and messenger for Pennsylvania's provincial government, dictated to Charles Thomson this account regarding the Lenape claim to the lands beyond Tohickon:

> Mechkilikishi possessed all the lands below Tohicon [Tohickon Creek] as far as Pitcock's Fall.[15] From Tohicon to the Lehi [Lehigh River][16] belonged to Neutimus [Nutimus] in right of his grandfather Tishexkum, and beyond belonged to several chiefs.

---

[10] Jennings, *The Ambiguous Iroquois Empire*, 332.

[11] Charles Thomson, *An Enquiry into the Causes of the Alienation*, 127–28.

[12] Ibid., 127.

[13] Vaughan, *Early American Indian Documents*, 1:80.

[14] Donehoo, *A History of the Indian Villages*, 229.

[15] Pitcock's Fall or Falls, later called Well's Falls, is now known as Lambertville Falls. From Tatamy's account, it appears to have been the upriver limit of William Penn's Pennsbury Tract, Mechkilikishi having retained ownership of his lands on the Delaware River from Pitcock's Fall up to Tohickon Creek. Pitcock's Fall can be accessed from Pennsylvania Route 32 bordering the Delaware River and is about halfway between Washington Crossing and New Hope, Pennsylvania.

[16] See Donehoo, *A History of the Indian Villages*, 89–90.

William Penn's 'Holy Experiment'

. . . Mechkilikishi had at several times sold to William Penn the land where Philadelphia stands and up along the River Delaware to a spruce tree a little below the Falls of Pitcock's now called Well's Falls. But William Penn still wanted to purchase more, and when Mechkilikishi came to sell him the rest of his lands, there were several chiefs from the Forks [at the meeting of the Delaware and Lehigh rivers, near the site of Easton].[17] Being asked whether it was a treaty he said no it was only a private Bargain and Sale between Mechkilikishi and William Penn, and the several chiefs from the Forks were invited by Mechkilikishi to be witnesses, besides he wanted to sell his lands with their consent, that they afterwards might suffer him to hunt on their lands. At that time Mechkilikishi sold[18] to William Penn lands along the banks of Delaware and the Tohicon as far as a man could travel in one day and a half following the course of the river [Tohicon]; there were to be 2 Whites and 2 Indians and a led horse, and as they were to walk a common days journey, they were to stop at noon, unload their horse, eat their dinner, after that smoke a pipe and after that was done load their horse again and set forward. Wherever they stopped at the end of the walk they were to draw a straight line to where the sun sets and that line was to be the boundary. Accordingly a day was fixed and as soon as the sun appeared they set out. . . . They travelled along the banks and at noon rested according to agreement. At length they arrived at Tohicon. Here a dispute arose between the Proprietor and Neutimus. The Proprietor insisted they should cross the river, Neutimus insisted they had no right, for that land on the other side was his, and consequently Mechkilikishi had no right to sell it. The bargain was they should travel up Tohicon, not cross it. The dispute grew so high that the travelers proceeded no farther. And it was agreed they should meet next year and adjust matters. In the meantime William Penn went to England and afterwards died and also Mechkilikishi died. Afterwards the Young Proprietors, sons of William Penn came over, and the matter was again renewed.[19]

At Easton 4 in October 1758, yet another account was given of William Penn's intention to extend his property beyond the Delaware River boundary set in the July 1682 deed. This account was given by Weshaykanikon (alias Amos) to "J. G."[20] Based on what "he heard his father say," he stated:

William Penn having made purchase of the Indians which extended up the river as far as a spruce tree a little below John Pillcocks

---

[17] Ibid., 56–57.

[18] Rather than "sold," Mechkilikishi seems only to have agreed to sell his property upon mutually satisfactory terms. He could not sell land that he did not own beyond the Tohickon, but when William Penn insisted on walking off land across that creek, the terms of the sale were put in dispute, thus requiring further 'adjustment' before it could be consummated.

[19] "Moses Tatamy's Account of Delaware Claims," in Vaughan, *Early American Indian Documents*, 3:163–64.

[20] "Weshaykanikon's Account of the Walking Purchase of 1686," in Vaughan, *Early American Indian Documents*, 1:81. J. G. was possibly Joseph Galloway, a member of the provincial governor's council, attending Easton 4. Kalter, *Benjamin Franklin*, 291.

Appendix 10: Native Americans

[probably Pitcock's], and some distance above Taxseesksung,[21] and being about to remove to England, was desirous to know how much farther a day and an half's walk would extend, which he talked of purchasing of the Indians, procured one James Yeates a tall man living about Newton to make the trail, who began in company with W. Penn and some white men and Indians at the spruce tree aforesaid and walked up the river to the mouth of Tohicon and thence up the same to that branch thereof which stretches over the nearest to Cosshohoppion[22] and from the head of that branch across the lands to Cosshohoppon,[23] and down the same a small distance when it was twelve o'clock the second day when they stopped, and marked three large white oaks on the west side of the creek from whence he understood the intended purchase was to be bounded westerly by a line run to the south sun till it fell in with the line of some former purchase. After this he says Penn went to England, but without making the Indians any pay for the lands which they expected at his return.[24]

October 25, 1736—Deed of Release from the chiefs of the Iroquois to the proprietors of Pennsylvania:[25] In early September 1736 a breakthrough event in the Penns' scheme to possess the valleys of the Lehigh and upper Delaware Rivers occurred when, without appointment (a not unusual event), approximately twenty chiefs of the tribes of the Iroquois Nations appeared in Philadelphia. They came to accept belatedly the offer of a league of friendship made to them at Philadelphia in 1732. Now, at this new Treaty of Philadelphia, held between September 28 and October 14,[26] the Iroquois chiefs and Thomas Penn, with his Provincial Council under James Logan's presidency, joined together in making "the firmest League of Friendship" and became "as one people." Additionally, the Penns were granted a sweeping transfer of unceded Native American lands in Pennsylvania for, on October 11, 1736, the Iroquois "released" to them

> all our right, claim, and pretensions whatsoever, to all and every the lands on both sides of the River Susquehanna, from the mouth thereof as far Northward or up the said river as that Ridge of hills called the Tyoninhackta or Endless Mountains, Westward to the setting of the sun, and Eastward to the furthest springs of the waters running into the said river.[27]

In this single stroke, the Penns advanced their geopolitical strategy of acquiring more land within the province while simultaneously passing off to the Iroquois the paramount control over the Lenni Lenapes.

But the Penns wanted more than just the Susquehanna lands as granted in the October 11 deed of release, so on October 25 a correction deed of release was

---

[21] Not found in Donehoo, *A History of the Indian Villages.*

[22] Not found in Donehoo, *A History of the Indian Villages.*

[23] Not found in Donehoo, *A History of the Indian Villages.*

[24] "Weshaykanikon's Account of the Walking Purchase of 1686," in Vaughan, *Early American Indian Documents,* 1:81.

[25] Vaughan, *Early American Indian Documents,* 1:443–44.

[26] Kalter, *Benjamin Franklin,* 49–62.

[27] Vaughan, *Early American Indian Documents,* 1:443–44.

signed by twenty-one chiefs of the Six Nations of the Iroquois declaring that "our true intent and meaning" in the earlier deed had been to release

> all our right, claim and pretensions whatsoever, to all and every the lands lying within the bounds and limits of the government of Pennsylvania, beginning Eastward on the River Delaware, as far Northward as the said Ridge or Chain of Endless Mountains as they cross the country of Pennsylvania, from Eastward and to the West.[28]

August 24, 1737—Walking Purchase Treaty:[29] The day before four Lenape chiefs executed the so-called Walking Purchase confirmation and quit-claim deed, "a great number of those Indians, with several of their chiefs and ancient men,"[30] met with Thomas Penn and six members of the Provincial Council and its president James Logan. Andrew Hamilton and William Allen were also present. Thomas recalled for the Council his prior meetings with the Lenapes at Durham (October 1734) and Pennsbury (May 1735) on the subject of those lands described as "lying in the county of Bucks, which, though formerly fully and absolutely released by the Indians, then inhabiting those parts, to his Father, yet they had of late made some claim to them."[31] Now in the presence of the Indians, portions of the Pennsbury minutes were read and interpreted as well as deeds dated August 28, 1680, and July 15, 1682. The Lenapes requested time to consider what they had heard, and the meeting was adjourned to the afternoon. Upon its resumption, Manawkyhickon, their spokesperson, although not a chief of any Lenape tribe near the Delaware River, recalled the mutual love and friendship that William Penn and "all the Indians" had enjoyed, observing the necessity of now avoiding any misunderstanding among them.

The Provincial Council minutes report Manawkyhickon next stated that while "the Proprietor knows well how the Lines mentioned in the deed [of 1680] . . . are to run" the Indians "do not fully understand them."[32] (The alleged 1680 deed is even more problematical than the alleged 1686 deed. Not only does it predate by more than six months the grant on March 4, 1681 of the Pennsylvania Charter given by Charles II to William Penn and by more than twenty-six months Penn's first arrival in Pennsylvania, there is no record or mention of such a deed in Thomson and it is not to be found either in the State Archives or in *Early American Indian Documents*). As the Council minutes note, "Hereupon, a draught was made and . . . explained to the Indians."[33] One scholar of this moment in Walking Purchase history has described how the Lenapes were shown a map, sketched for the occasion by Andrew Hamilton, a Penn confidant, to evidence the boundaries of the land being acquired but falsely representing the area as being south, not north, of Tohickon Creek.[34] After the Lenapes considered the 1680 deed and Hamilton's sketched map, Manawkyhickon stated they were "sufficiently convinced" of their truth and of the earlier sale of the lands at issue to William Penn, and had "no objection" to

---

[28] Ibid.

[29] "Council with the Delawares at Philadelphia [Aug. 24, 1737]," in Vaughan, *Early American Indian Documents*, 1:455–57.

[30] Ibid., 455.

[31] Ibid.

[32] Ibid., 456.

[33] Ibid.

[34] See Steven C. Harper, "The Map That Reveals the Deception of the Walking Purchase," *PMHB*, 136:457–60.

Appendix 10: Native Americans

confirming the prior sale, requesting only that the resident Lenapes "may be permitted to remain on their present settlements and Plantations, though within that purchase, without being molested. In answer to which, the assurances that were given on this head at Pennsbury, were repeated and confirmed to them."[35]

August 25, 1737—Walking Purchase confirmation and quitclaim deed:[36] The provisions of the Walking Purchase deed were agreed upon at the prior day's treaty, and the instrument itself was executed by the four Lenape chiefs, including Nutimus, and witnessed the next day. Its direction that the Walk should be carried out was accomplished the following September 19 and 20. The description in the 1737 deed is based on the spurious 1686 deed, and both deeds borrow the beginning course found in the 1682 Pennsbury tract deed but follow it not with a return to the Delaware via the Neshaminy but with a day and a half's walk further west "to the utmost extent" from the western terminus of the Neshaminy, thence to the Delaware River and south to the place of beginning. The 1737 description reads:

> Beginning upon a line formerly laid out from a **corner**[37] **spruce tree** by the River Delaware, about Makeerickkitton,[38] and
> from thence running **along the ledge or foot of the Mountains, West North West to a corner white oak marked with the letter P, standing by the Indian path that leadeth to an Indian town** called **Playwickey**, and
> **from thence** extending **westward to Neshameney Creek**,
> *from which said line the said tract or tracts thereby granted doth extend itself back into the woods as far as a man can go in one day and a half, and bounded on the westerly side with the Neshameny, or the most westerly branch thereof, so far as the said branch doth extend, and*
> *from thence by line to the utmost extent of the said one day and a half's journey,* and
> from thence to the aforesaid River Delaware, and
> from thence *down*[39] the several courses of the said River to the first mentioned spruce tree.

The text of the Walking Purchase confirmation and quitclaim deed concluded with the date, the marks of the four Lenape grantors, and then this declaration:

---

[35] Vaughan, *Early American Indian Documents*, 1:456–57.

[36] Walking Purchase deed, in Hazard et al., *Pennsylvania Archives*, first series, vol. 1, pp. 541–43.

[37] The bolded text in this description is duplicated in the same word order in the deed to William Penn from Delaware sachems on July 15, 1682, described above. Historical note: The italicized text, however, was not in the July 1682 deed. It was instead in the spurious 1686 deed (quoted in Vaughan, *Early American Indian Documents*, 1:80), which was undoubtedly an invention of the Penns, who ordered their draftsman to insert the italicized text in the Walking Purchase deed, thereby greatly enlarging the territory.

[38] See Donehoo, *A History of the Indian Villages*, 53–54.

[39] This single insertion in the 1682 deed template resulted in the final course of the description in the Walking Purchase deed being *down*, not *up*, the Delaware River as it had been in the 1682 deed.

The above deed being read and explained to all the Indians at this Treaty, the following persons, on behalf of themselves and all the other Indians now present, have agreed to sign or put their names to the same as witnesses, in token of their free and full consent to what the above named [four grantors] have signed and sealed.

Twelve Indians put their marks with their names on this declaration.

Finally, in satisfaction of the customs of English law for transferring land, there was an additional declaration—"Sealed, Subscribed, and Delivered in the presence of us"—followed by the signatures of fifteen witnesses. Each of these witnesses was loyal to the Penns, and all had somehow supervised and managed, or been otherwise interested in, both the details of the transaction and the appearance of fully complying with its legal formalities. The witnesses were Thomas Freame (husband of the Penns' sister Margaret), Richard Assheton and Thomas Griffitt (members of the governor's Provincial Council), Robert Charles (sometime clerk of Provincial Council and secretary of the province), John Georges (sometime secretary of Thomas Penn and clerk of the Proprietary Land Office), James Logan and his son William, Edward Shippen III (business partner of James Logan), James LeTort (a trader in James Logan's fur network), James Steel Jr. and his father (who had been Logan's associate in the Proprietary Land Office and later managed the Walking Purchase rehearsal), Andrew Hamilton[40] (sometime provincial attorney general) and his son James Hamilton (sometime provincial lieutenant governor and brother-in-law of William Allen), Bearefoot Brunson (the provincial Indian interpreter at this treaty), and William Allen (provincial chief justice from 1751 to 1774, the brother-in-law of James Hamilton, the father-in-law of John Penn the Governor, and the purchaser in 1735 of a 5,000-acre tract in the Lehigh Valley that today includes Allentown, the city that he founded).

After it was executed and delivered to the Penns, the deed remained out of public view until it was recorded in the Office for Recording of Deeds for the City and County of Philadelphia on May 8, 1741.[41] The following August, Thomas Penn left Pennsylvania forever and returned to England, becoming the majority proprietor of Pennsylvania upon the death of his brother John in 1746.

In the years following the 'Walk,' it became the source of controversy between the Lenapes and the province. About twenty years later, William Allen found it necessary to protect his personal investment with this memorandum, which was filed in the Office for Recording Deeds in Philadelphia:[42]

> BE IT REMEMBERED, that on the twenty third of 7ber, Anno Domini 1757, before me, William Allen, Esquire, Chief Justice of the Province of Pennsylvania, personally appeared James Hamilton, of the City of Philadelphia, Esqr., and made oath on the holy evangelists, that, after the above written deed had, as above mentioned, been read and explained to the several Indians present, the same was, on or about the day of the date thereof, signed and sealed by the four Delaware sachems or chiefs, all above named, viz., Manawhyhickon, Lappawinzoe, Teeshacomin, and Nootamis, severally and respectively,

---

[40] Ca. 1676-1741, no known relationship to the PA Lt. Governor 1701-3.

[41] Philadelphia Deed Book G, Vol. 1, 282–83.

[42] Recorded on November 9, 1757, in Philadelphia Deed Book G, Vol. 1, 411.

Appendix 10: Native Americans

in presence of this deponent, the said William Allen, and the several other witnesses whose names are there above subscribed, and also of the several other Indians who have thereto set their marks to signify their approbation of, and assent to the said deed. And that the name James Hamilton, subscribed thereto, and above, is the proper handwriting of this deponent. And I, the said William Allen, do also certify that the said deed was executed, as aforesaid, in my presence, and that the name Will. Allen, subscribed as a witness thereto, is my own proper handwriting. Witness my hand and seal, the said twenty third day of September, 1757.

William Allen, Chief Justice

November 21, 1740—Protesting the Walking Purchase—the Petition of the Lenni Lenapes:[43] Over three years after the walk was made, the Lenapes gave notice to "all magistrates of Pennsylvania" of what they termed "the great wrong we receive in our lands," a wrong suffered when "about 100 families settled on it."[44] The settlers claimed that Thomas Penn had sold them the land. The Lenapes stated their position thus:

> [It is] very strange that T. Penn should sell him that which was never his for we never sold him this land. The case was this. That when we were with Penn to treat as usual with his father, he keep begging and plagueing us to give him some land and never gives us leave to treat upon any thing till he wearies us out of our lives. . . . If he lets us alone we will let him alone. The lands we do own to be ours, begin at the mouth of Tohickon,[45] runs up along the said branch to the head springs, thence up with a strait line to Patquating,[46] thence up with a straight line to the Blue Mountain,[47] thence to a place called Mohaining,[48] thence along a mountain called Neshameek,[49] thence along the Great Swamp[50] to a branch of Delaware River, so along Delaware River to the place where it first began. All this is our own land.[51]

This petition ends with the request that Thomas Penn remove the settlers "in peace" so that the Lenapes will not be troubled to drive them off, "for the land we will hold fast with both our hands not in privately but in open view of all the country and all our friends and relations," naming the eastern Indians and the tribes of the Iroquois and of others in the region. In conclusion, the assistance of the Pennsylvania magistrates was requested.[52] No assistance was given the Lenapes from any quarter. Rather,

---

[43] "Petition of Delawares Regarding the Walking Purchase," in Vaughan, *Early American Indian Documents*, 2:24.

[44] Ibid.

[45] This is the first reference to Tohickon Creek in the official documents of this Walking Purchase record.

[46] Not found in Donehoo, *A History of the Indian Villages*.

[47] See Donehoo, *A History of the Indian Villages,* 84–85 ("Kittatinny").

[48] Not found in Donehoo, *A History of the Indian Villages*.

[49] A mountain in the Kittatinny range.

[50] Not found in Vaughan, *Early American Indian Documents*.

[51] Vaughan, *Early American Indian Documents*, 2:24.

[52] Ibid.

at the treaty held in Philadelphia in July 1742, the Iroquois, as directed by the authorities of Pennsylvania, shamed the Lenapes and ordered them out of the Forks of the Delaware and the Lehigh Valley and back to New Jersey or to either Shamokin[53] or Wyoming on the Susquehanna River.

November 8–17, 1756—Moses Tatamy's Account of Lenni Lenape claims:[54] Tatamy's account, discussed above in connection with William Penn's unsuccessful attempt to acquire lands beyond Tohickon Creek before returning to England, also mentions that Penn's sons in 1737 brought a Lenape chief, Monochkihikon (sometimes Manawkyhickon), from west of the Susquehanna River to sign the Walking Purchase deed with Nutimus and two others in July 1742. Tatamy claimed this chief only "pretended" to rights to "any lands on this side Wyoming."[55]

1756–1762—Teedyuscung's descriptions at the Easton treaties of land lost in the Walk: Beginning with Easton 2 (November 1756), when he first made his charge of the Penns' land fraud in the Walking Purchase, Teedyuscung described the area referred to in various ways and in sweeping terms. He said at Easton 2 that it comprised "all the land lying between Tohickon Creek and Wyomings[56] on the River Susquehanna"[57] and "all the land extending from Tohickon over the Great Mountain to Wyoming";[58] at Easton 4 (October 1758), it was "the land that lies between Tohickon Creek and the Kittochtinny Hills";[59] and at Easton 5 (August 1761), it was the lands "betwixt the Mountains and Tohickon Creek."[60] At Easton 6 (June 1762), in testimony before Sir William Johnson, he seems to have been more carefully prepared and so delineated the territory lost as being from Easton up the River Delaware to Samuel Dupuy's at the Gap[61]; to the Kittatiny Hills, or Blue Mountains, and along the top of those mountains to Allimingey;[62] thence to Mackcungee;[63] thence to Shammony;[64] thence across to Delaware River at Pitcock's Creek; and thence to Easton.[65]

1928—George P. Donehoo's description of the Walking Purchase:[66] Although not part of the official record, the following early-twentieth-century description of the Walk may aid the twenty-first century reader to better understand some of the courses taken by the eighteenth-century

---

[53] See Donehoo, *A History of the Indian Villages*, 186–90.

[54] Vaughan, *Early American Indian Documents*, 3:163–64.

[55] Ibid., 3:163.

[56] This is referring to Pennsylvania's Wyoming Valley. See Donehoo, *A History of the Indian Villages*, 259–63

[57] See Kalter, *Benjamin Franklin*, 208.

[58] Ibid., 209–10.

[59] Ibid., 322.

[60] Ibid., 354.

[61] See Donehoo, *A History of the Indian Villages*, 57.

[62] Not found in Donehoo, *A History of the Indian Villages*. in

[63] Present Emmaus. See Donehoo, *A History of the Indian Villages*, 100.

[64] Not found in Donehoo, *A History of the Indian Villages*.

[65] Johnson, *The Papers of Sir William Johnson*, 3:767.

[66] Donehoo, *A History of the Indian Villages*, 246.

Appendix 10: Native Americans

walkers. The preceding deeds and other descriptions of the landmarks and courses of the Walk contain many place names and reference points that are lost to our collective modern memory. This 1928 description, given by George Donehoo, a former secretary of the Pennsylvania Historical Commission as well as former state librarian, is prefaced by a statement that these were the lands purchased by William Penn and deeded to him by the Indians on August 28, 1686. Though this is not evidence that such a deed existed, it at least provides an intelligible description of the land taken by Penn's sons. Donehoo states that the Walk started on September 19, 1737, at Wrightstown,

> going in a northerly course, along the old Durham Road to Durham Creek, and from there in a westerly direction, and at about 2 o'clock they forded the Lehigh about half a mile below Bethlehem, and from thence in a northwest course through present Bethlehem, and passed on through the northeast angle of Hanover Township, into Allen Township, and stopped at sunset at the site of Howell's Mill, on the Hockendauqua, where they passed the night of the 19th of Sept. This was the site of an old Indian village, at which Tishekunk lived. The next morning the walkers continued the "walk," crossing the mountains near the Lehigh Water Gap, and finishing the walk, after having covered about 60 or 65 miles. From the point where this walk was finished a line was drawn, parallel to the line of the previous purchase of 1749,[67] to near the mouth of the Lackawaxen.[68] This purchase contained about 1,200 square miles, including in its limits the upper part of the present Bucks County, nine-tenths of Northampton County, a large part of Carbon County, and about a fourth of Monroe and Pike Counties. This land included the greater part of the Minisinks, the habitat of the Munsee clan of the Delawares.[69]

---

[67] Donehoo, *A History of the Indian Villages*, 69. The reference to the "previous purchase of 1749" refers to the August 1749 Release of the Chiefs of the Six Nations of lands between the Kittochtinny Mountains and Maghoinoy on Susquehanna, and the said mountains and Lechawachsein on Delaware. Thomson, *An Enquiry into the Alienation*, 126–27.

[68] The mouth of Lackawaxen Creek is on the west side of the Delaware River at present-day Lackawaxen in Pike County, approximately sixty miles north-northeast of Palmerton.

[69] See Donehoo, *A History of the Indian Villages*, 84–85.

William Penn's 'Holy Experiment'

APPENDIX 11

Church and State Leadership in Colonial Pennsylvania (1682–1781)

The provincial executives of Pennsylvania listed below include the proprietor (William Penn), lieutenant governors (e.g., Thomas Lloyd, Markham, Carpenter, Evans, Gookin, John Penn), presidents of the Provincial Council (e.g., Logan), and a crown-appointed governor who administered from New York (Fletcher). In 1776, the Penns' proprietary and executive governing rights ended. William Penn's final colonial charter, the 1701 Charter of Privileges, was abolished when the Constitution of Pennsylvania was adopted.

Philadelphia Yearly Meeting was established September 15, 1685, by union with Burlington Yearly Meeting to form a yearly meeting for Friends of "Pennsylvania, East and West Jerseys, and of the Adjacent Provinces." The name of the clerk was first recorded in 1696. The last year in which a member of the Pemberton family clerked Philadelphia Yearly Meeting was 1781.

Sources: The list of speakers of the General Assembly is based on *Pennsylvania Archives, Eighth Series, Volumes I and II* (Harrisburg: np, 1931). The list of clerks of Philadelphia Yearly Meeting is taken from the Minute Books of Philadelphia Yearly Meeting (PYM Min Bk A–D). It is also found in John M. Moore, ed., *Friends in the Delaware Valley: Philadelphia Yearly Meeting 1681–1981* (Haverford, PA: Friends Historical Association, 1981), 258.

Year	Provincial Executive	General Assembly (Speaker)	Philadelphia Yearly Meeting (Clerk)
1682	William Penn	Nicholas Moore	
1683	William Penn	Thomas Winn; John Songhurst	
1684	Thomas Lloyd	Nicholas More	
1685	Thomas Lloyd	John White	
1686	Thomas Lloyd	John White	
1687	Thomas Lloyd	John White	
1688	Thomas Lloyd	John White	
1689	John Blackwell	Arthur Cook	
1690	Thomas Lloyd	Joseph Growdon	
1691	William Markham	*No record*	
1692	William Markham	William Clark	
1693	Benj Fletcher; Wm Markham	Joseph Growdon	
1694	Samuel Carpenter	David Lloyd	

Appendix 11: Leadership in Colonial Pennsylvania

Year	Provincial Executive	General Assembly (Speaker)	Philadelphia Yearly Meeting (Clerk)
1695	Samuel Carpenter	Edward Shippen	
1696	Samuel Carpenter	John Simcock	Phineas Pemberton
1697	Samuel Carpenter	John Blunston	Phineas Pemberton
1698	Samuel Carpenter	Phineas Pemberton	Phineas Pemberton
1699	William Penn	John Blunston	Phineas Pemberton
1700	William Penn	John Blunston; Joseph Growdon	Phineas Pemberton
1701	Andrew Hamilton	Joseph Growdon	Phineas Pemberton
1702	Andrew Hamilton	Meeting prorogued; no minutes	Griffith Owen
1703	Andrew Hamilton; Edward Shippen	David Lloyd	*No appointment minuted*
1704	John Evans	David Lloyd	Caleb Pusey and Anthony Morris
1705	John Evans	Joseph Growdon	
1706	John Evans	David Lloyd	
1707	John Evans	David Lloyd	
1708	John Evans	David Lloyd	
1709	Charles Gookin	David Lloyd	
1710	Charles Gookin	Richard Hill	Anthony Morris
1711	Charles Gookin	Richard Hill	Isaac Norris I
1712	Charles Gookin	Isaac Norris I	Isaac Norris I
1713	Charles Gookin	Joseph Growdon	Isaac Norris I
1714	Charles Gookin	David Lloyd	Isaac Norris I
1715	Charles Gookin	Joseph Growdon	Isaac Norris I
1716	Charles Gookin	Richard Hill	Isaac Norris I
1717	William Keith	William Trent	Isaac Norris I
1718	William Keith	Jonathan Dickinson	Isaac Norris I
1719	William Keith	William Trent	Isaac Norris I
1720	William Keith	Isaac Norris I	Isaac Norris I
1721	William Keith	Jeremiah Langhorne	Isaac Norris I
1722	William Keith	Joseph Growdon	Isaac Norris I
1723	William Keith	David Lloyd	Isaac Norris I
1724	William Keith	William Biles	Isaac Norris I
1725	William Keith	David Lloyd	Isaac Norris I
1726	William Keith; Patrick Gordon	David Lloyd	Isaac Norris I
1727	Patrick Gordon	David Lloyd	Isaac Norris I
1728	Patrick Gordon	David Lloyd	Isaac Norris I
1729	Patrick Gordon	Andrew Hamilton	Isaac Norris I
1730	Patrick Gordon	Andrew Hamilton	John Kinsey
1731	Patrick Gordon	Andrew Hamilton	John Kinsey
1732	Patrick Gordon	Andrew Hamilton	John Kinsey
1733	Patrick Gordon	Jeremiah Langhorne	John Kinsey
1734	Patrick Gordon	Andrew Hamilton	John Kinsey
1735	Patrick Gordon	Andrew Hamilton	John Kinsey
1736	Patrick Gordon; James Logan	Andrew Hamilton	John Kinsey
1737	James Logan	Andrew Hamilton	John Kinsey
1738	George Thomas	Andrew Hamilton	John Kinsey

William Penn's 'Holy Experiment'

Year	Provincial Executive	General Assembly (Speaker)	Philadelphia Yearly Meeting (Clerk)
1739	George Thomas	John Kinsey	John Kinsey
1740	George Thomas	John Kinsey	John Kinsey
1741	George Thomas	John Kinsey	John Kinsey
1742	George Thomas	John Kinsey	John Kinsey
1743	George Thomas	John Kinsey	John Kinsey
1744	George Thomas	John Kinsey	John Kinsey
1745	George Thomas	John Wright; John Kinsey	John Kinsey
1746	George Thomas	John Kinsey	John Kinsey
1747	George Thomas; Anthony Palmer	John Kinsey	John Kinsey
1748	James Hamilton	John Kinsey	John Kinsey
1749	James Hamilton	John Kinsey	John Kinsey
1750	James Hamilton	Isaac Norris II	Israel Pemberton Jr.
1751	James Hamilton	Isaac Norris II	Israel Pemberton Jr.
1752	James Hamilton	Isaac Norris II	Israel Pemberton Jr.
1753	James Hamilton	Isaac Norris II	Israel Pemberton Jr.
1754	James Hamilton; Robert Hunter Morris	Isaac Norris II	Israel Pemberton Jr.
1755	Robert Hunter Morris	Isaac Norris II	Israel Pemberton Jr.
1756	Robert Hunter Morris; William Denny	Isaac Norris II	Israel Pemberton Jr.
1757	William Denny	Isaac Norris II Thomas Leech	Israel Pemberton Jr.
1758	William Denny	Isaac Norris II Thomas Leech	Israel Pemberton Jr.
1759	William Denny; James Hamilton	Joseph Fox	Israel Pemberton Jr.
1760	James Hamilton	Isaac Norris II	John Smith
1761	James Hamilton	Isaac Norris II	James Pemberton
1762	James Hamilton	Isaac Norris II	James Pemberton
1763	James Hamilton; John Penn	Isaac Norris II	James Pemberton
1764	John Penn	Isaac Norris II	James Pemberton
1765	John Penn	Joseph Fox	James Pemberton
1766	John Penn	Joseph Galloway	James Pemberton
1767	John Penn	Joseph Galloway	George Churchman
1768	John Penn	Joseph Galloway	James Pemberton
1769	John Penn	Joseph Galloway	James Pemberton
1770	John Penn	Joseph Galloway	James Pemberton
1771	John Penn; Richard Penn Jr.	Joseph Galloway	James Pemberton
1772	Richard Penn Jr.	Joseph Galloway	James Pemberton
1773	Richard Penn Jr.	Joseph Galloway	James Pemberton
1774	Richard Penn Jr.	Joseph Galloway	James Pemberton
1775	Richard Penn Jr.	Edward Biddle	James Pemberton
1776	Richard Penn Jr.; John Penn	John Morton	James Pemberton
1777			Isaac Jackson
1778			James Pemberton

Appendix 11: Leadership in Colonial Pennsylvania

Year	Provincial Executive	General Assembly (Speaker)	Philadelphia Yearly Meeting (Clerk)
1779			James Pemberton
1780			James Pemberton
1781			James Pemberton

Bibliography and Abbreviations

Abbreviations Used in Footnotes

HSP	Historical Society of Pennsylvania, Philadelphia.
Microfilm	The Papers of William Penn, 14 reels and guide (microfilm, 1975), Historical Society of Pennsylvania, Philadelphia. References are to reels and frames.
MPCP	State of Pennsylvania. *Minutes of the Provincial Council of Pennsylvania, from the Organization to the Termination of the Proprietary Government*, 17 vols. (Harrisburg, PA: 1851–1860).
PMHB	*The Pennsylvania Magazine of History and Biography.*
PWP	Mary Maples Dunn and Richard S. Dunn, *The Papers of William Penn*, 5 vols. (Philadelphia: University of Pennsylvania Press, 1981–1987).
PYM Min Bk A	Philadelphia Yearly Meeting of the Religious Society of Friends (Quakers), Minute Book 1681–1710. Haverford College Quaker Collection, Haverford College, Haverford, Pennsylvania.
PYM Min Bk B	Philadelphia Yearly Meeting of the Religious Society of Friends (Quakers), Minute Book 1681–1746. Haverford College Quaker Collection, Haverford College, Haverford, Pennsylvania.
PYM Min Bk C	Philadelphia Yearly Meeting of the Religious Society of Friends (Quakers), Minute Book 1747–1779. Haverford College Quaker Collection, Haverford College, Haverford, Pennsylvania.
PYM Min Bk D	Philadelphia Yearly Meeting of the Religious Society of Friends (Quakers), Minute Book 1780–1798. Haverford College Quaker Collection, Haverford College, Haverford, Pennsylvania.

Select Bibliography

American Council of Learned Societies. *Dictionary of American Biography*, 20 vols. New York: Scribners, 1928–1936.

Armistead, Wilson. *Memoirs of James Logan: A Distinguished Scholar and Christian Legislator*. London: C. Gilpin, 1851.

Besse, Joseph. *A Collection of the Sufferings of the People Called Quakers*. 2 vols. London: Luke Hinde, 1753.

Brown, George Williams. *Historical Sketches, chiefly relating to the early settlement of Friends at Falls, in Bucks County, Pennsylvania*. Philadelphia: J. P. Murphy, 1882.

Collier, Jeremy. *An Ecclesiastical History of Great Britain*. Edited by Francis Barham. 9 vols. London: Wm. Straker, 1840.

"The Convincement of William Penn." *Journal of Friends Historical Society* 32 (1935): 22–26.

Donehoo, George P. *A History of the Indian Villages and Place Names in Pennsylvania*. Harrisburg, PA, 1928; repr. Lewisburg, PA: Wennawood Publishing, 2006.

Drinker, Sophie Hutchinson. *Hannah Penn and the Proprietorship of Pennsylvania*. Philadelphia: The National Society of the Colonial Dames of America in the Commonwealth of Pennsylvania, 1958.

"Friendly Association Minutes, 1755–1757." Collection #AM 525, Historical Society of Pennsylvania, Philadelphia, Pennsylvania.

"John Farmer." *The Friend* 28 (1855): 316–17.

Fernow, Bethold, and E. B. O'Callaghan, eds. *Documents Relative to the Colonial History of the State of New York*. 15 vols. Albany, NY: Weed, Parsons and Co., 1853–1887.

The First Laws of the Commonwealth of Pennsylvania. Compiled by John B. Cushing. Wilmington, DE: M. Glazier, 1984.

Firth, C. H., and R. S. Rait. *Acts and Ordinances of the Interregnum*. Edited by C. H. Firth and R. S. Rait. 3 vols. London: H. M. Stationery Office, 1911.

Fothergill, John. *Chain of Friendship: Selected Letters of Dr. John Fothergill of London, 1735-1780.* Cambridge: Belknap Press of Harvard University Press, 1971.

Fothergill, Samuel. *Memoirs of the life and gospel labours of Samuel Fothergill, with selections from his correspondence: also an account of the life and travels of his father, John Fothergill, and notices of some of his descendants.* Edited by George Crosfield. London: W. and F. G. Cash, 1857.

Fox, George. *The Journal of George Fox with an Epilogue by Henry J. Cadbury and an Introduction by Geoffrey F. Nuttall.* Edited by John L. Nickalls. Philadelphia: Religious Society of Friends, 1997.

Foxe, John. *The Book of Martyrs.* Edited and abridged by G. A. Williamson. Boston: Little, Brown & Co., 1965.

Franklin, Benjamin. *A narrative of the late massacres . . .* Philadelphia: Anthony Armbruster.

Hazard, Samuel, et al., eds. *Pennsylvania Archives.* 119 vols. in 9 series. Philadelphia and Harrisburg, 1852—).

Jackson, Maurice. *Let This Voice Be Heard: Anthony Benezet, Father of Atlantic Abolitionism.* Philadelphia: University of Pennsylvania Press, 2009.

Jenkins, Howard M. *The Family of William Penn, Founder of Pennsylvania: Ancestry and Descendants.* London: Hadley Bros., 1899.

Jennings, Francis. *The Ambiguous Iroquois Empire: The Covenant Chain Confederation of Indian Tribes with English Colonies from Its Beginnings to the Lancaster Treaty of 1744.* New York: W. W. Norton, 1984.

_____. *Empire of Fortune: Crowns, Colonies, Empire and Tribes in the Seven Years War in America.* New York: W. W. Norton, 1988.

_____. "Incident at Tulpehocken." *Pennsylvania History* 35 (1968): 335–55.

_____. "The Indian Trade of the Susquehanna Valley." *Proceedings of the American Philosophical Society* 110 (1966): 406–24.

Bibliography

Johnson, William. *The Papers of Sir William Johnson.* Albany: University of the State of New York, Division of Archives and History, 1921.

Jordan, John W., ed. *Colonial Families of Philadelphia.* Edited by John W. Jordan. 2 vols. New York: Lewis Publishing, 1911.

Kalter, Susan, ed. *Benjamin Franklin, Pennsylvania, and the First Nations: The Treaties of 1736–62.* Urbana: University of Illinois Press, 2006.

Kenny, Kevin. *Peaceable Kingdom Lost: The Paxton Boys and the Destruction of William Penn's Holy Experiment.* New York: Oxford University Press, 2009.

Logan, James. *Of the Duties of Man as they may be deduced from Nature.* Edited by Philip Valenti. Philadelphia: Editor, 2013.

The Manuscripts of the House of Lords, 1695–1697. London: 1903.

The Manuscripts of the House of Lords, 1699–1702. London, 1908.

Marietta, Jack D. *The Reformation of American Quakerism, 1748–1783.* Philadelphia: University of Pennsylvania Press, 1984.

Michener, Ezra. *A Retrospect of Early Quakerism; being extracts from the Records of Philadelphia Yearly Meeting and the meetings composing it.* Philadelphia: T. Ellwood Zell, 1860.

Nash, Gary. *Quakers and Politics: Pennsylvania, 1681–1726.* Boston: Northeastern University Press, 1993.

Parrish, Samuel. *Some Chapters in the History of the Friendly Association for Regaining and Preserving Peace with the Indians by Pacific Measures.* Philadelphia: Friends Historical Association, 1877.

"A Partial List of the Families who resided in Bucks County, Pennsylvania, prior to 1687, with the date of their arrival." *The Pennsylvania Magazine of History and Biography* 9 (1885): 23–33.

Pemberton, John. "The Annals of the Pemberton Family." In *Friends' Miscellany,* edited by John and Isaac Comly, vol. 7, 1–48. Philadelphia: William Sharpless, printer, 1831–1839.

Penn family papers, 1592–1960, Series VIII, NV-079. Collection 485A. Historical Society of Pennsylvania, Philadelphia, Pennsylvania.

Penney, Norman, ed. *"The First Publishers of Truth": Being early records (now first printed) of the introduction of Quakerism into the counties of England and Wales.* London: Headley Brothers, 1907.

Proud, Robert. *The History of Pennsylvania in North America, from the Original Institution and Settlement of that Province under the first Proprietor and Governor William Penn, in 1681, till after the Year 1742.* 2 vols. Philadelphia: Z. Poulson, 1797.

Root, Winfred Trexler. *The Relations of Pennsylvania with the British Government, 1696–1765.* New York: D. Appleton, 1912.

Soderlund, Jean R., ed. *William Penn and the Founding of Pennsylvania 1680–1684: A Documentary History.* Philadelphia: University of Pennsylvania Press, 1983.

The Statutes of the Realm . . . from original records and authentic manuscripts. 10 vols. London: 1810–1828.

Stephen, Leslie, and Sydney Lee, eds. *The Dictionary of National Biography: From the Earliest (1921–1922) Times to 1900.* 22 vols. London: Oxford University Press, 1921–22.

Stuart, Charles. "The Captivity of Charles Stuart, 1755–57." Edited by Beverly W. Bond Jr. *Mississippi Valley Historical Review* 13 (1926–1927): 58–81.

Taylor, John. "Account of Lands in Chester County." Penn family papers, 1592–1960, vol. NV-183, folio page 32. Collection 485A. Historical Society of Pennsylvania, Philadelphia, Pennsylvania.

Thayer, Theodore. "The Friendly Association." *The Pennsylvania Magazine of History and Biography* 67 (1943): 356–76.

———. *Israel Pemberton: King of the Quakers.* Philadelphia: Historical Society of Pennsylvania, 1943.

[Thomson, Charles]. *An Enquiry into the Causes of the Alienation of the Delaware and Shawanese Indians from the British Interest* [1759]. St. Claire Shores, MI: Scholarly Press, 1970.

Tolles, Frederick B. *James Logan and the Culture of Provincial America*. Edited by Oscar Handlin. Boston: Little, Brown, 1957.

Trevelyan, G. M. *History of England*. London: Longmans, Green & Co., 1926.

Vaughan, Alden T., ed. *Early American Indian Documents: Treaties and Laws, 1607–1789*. 20 vols. Washington DC: University Publications of America, 1979–2005.

Vaux, Roberts. *Memoirs of the Lives of Benjamin Lay and Ralph Sandiford: Two of the Earliest Public Advocates for the Emancipation of the Enslaved Africans*. London: William Phillips, 1816.

Votes and Proceedings of the House of Representatives of the Province of Pennsylvania, Dec. 4, 1682–August 6, 1726, Volumes 1–3. Philadelphia: B. Franklin and D. Hall, 1752–1754.

Weslager, C. A. *Red Men on the Brandywine*. Wilmington, DE: Hambleton Co., 1953.

"William Southeby." *The Friend* 28 (1855): 293, 301–2, 309–10.

Woolman, John. *John Woolman and the Affairs of Truth: The Journalist's Essays, Epistles, and Ephemera*. Edited by James Proud. San Francisco: Inner Light Books, 2010.

―――. *The Journal and Major Essays of John Woolman*. Edited by Phillips P. Moulton. Richmond, IN: Friends United Press, 1971.

Zimmerman, Albright G. "James Logan, Proprietary Agent." *The Pennsylvania Magazine of History and Biography* 78 (1954): 143–76.

Index

Abd-ar-Rahman III, ii–iii
abolition of slavery. *See* slavery
abolitionists. *See* slavery
Academy of Saumur (France), 44
Acadia (Canada), 345, 465
Acadians. *See* Acadia
Act for the Gradual Abolition of
 Slavery (Pennsylvania; 1780),
 314, 470
Act of Uniformity (1662), 91, 426
Africans. *See* slavery
Albany, Great Treaty of (1722),
 265–66, 460, 479
Albany Conference (1745), 290–91,
 463
Albany Congress (1754), 328–30,
 334, 380, 406, 464, 479
Allen, Anne, 406, 468
Allen, William, 346, 406, 468, 471,
 484, 486–87
American Revolution, iv, vi–vii,
 109, 167, 197, 315n29, 409,
 416–25, 469–70, 476
Andros, Sir Edmund, 106, 247, 248
Anglicans, 12, 70n206, 155, 178,
 186, 294
anti-enslavement cause. *See* slavery
anti-slavery cause. *See* slavery
Archbishop of Canterbury, 4, 210
Areopagitica, 7–8
Arians, 12, 436, 438
Articles of Agreement (Indians of
 Susquehanna area; 1701), 152,
 238n96, 250–51, 255, 263n167
Ashoka, ii–iii
assizes, 13, 18, 23, 31, 33, 92, 426,
 427
Atlantic abolitionism. *See* slavery
Audland, John, 16, 471
Baptists, 12, 70n206, 436
Barbados, 39, 42, 160, 234, 452–
 53, 471
Barclay, Robert, 71, 95n267, 127,
 133, 452
Battle of Brandywine, 416, 421, 425
Battle of Germantown, 416–18, 421
Battle of Jumonville Glen, 318,
 326–27, 330, 464
Battle of Lowestoft, 85, 89
Battle of the Monongahela, 332,
 465

Battle of the Wilderness. *See* Battle
 of the Monongahela
Battle of Wyoming, 420
Beaver, 321, 379, 396–97, 477
Beaver King. *See* Beaver
Benezet, Anthony, 303–5, 308–10,
 344, 345, 349, 464, 471
Berkeley, John Lord, 42, 64–65
Besse, Joseph, iv, 82
Black Death, iv, 2
Blackwell, John, 129, 130, 133, 454,
 491
Blasphemy Act (1650), 14, 17, 41,
 426
Board of Trade, 182, 346, 383, 426,
 456, 457
 Iroquois and, 327–29
 William Penn and, 85, 138,
 140–50, 159, 163–70
Book of Common Prayer, 41, 91,
 426
books of discipline (Philadelphia
 Yearly Meeting)
 (1704), 172, 173, 224, 457
 (1719), 173, 181, 200, 202, 232,
 302, 459
Braddock, General Edward, 330–
 34, 464, 465
Brandywine Creek and Valley
 (Pennsylvania and Delaware),
 vin6, 242, 258–60, 269, 273,
 282, 291, 318, 425, 460
Brandywine Lenapes. *See* Lenapes
Brant, Joseph, 419–20, 476
Breda. *See* Declaration of Breda
"Brief Account of the Rise and
 Progress of the People Called
 Quakers, A" (1694), 127
Brown, William, 310, 336n74
Brownists, 12, 436
Bucks County (Pennsylvania), ,
 241, 273, 278, 484, 489. *See
 also* Grove Place; Pennsbury
 Manor
 administration of, 112–13,
 134–35, 158–59
 Harrisons and Pembertons
 settle in, 101, 111, 135–36,
 161
 Penn's manor in, 117, 148

Index

Bucks (Pennsylvania) Quarterly Meeting, 132, 133n109, 136, 232, 313
Burlington (New Jersey) Monthly Meeting, 131, 236
Burlington (New Jersey) Quarterly Meeting, 232, 236
Burlington Yearly Meeting, 116–117, 131, 440, 453, 490
Burnyeat, John, 127
Burrough, Edward, 40, 471
Byllynge, Edward, 65–68, 452
Cadbury, Henry, 35n123, 83
Callowhill, Hannah, 137, 406n246, 442, 456. *See also* Penn, Hannah
Callowhill, Thomas, 190, 192, 193n285, 205, 212n17
Calvinists, 12, 436
Canasatego, 288, 289, 290, 291, 476
Carolinas,
   French claims in, 270
   South Carolina, 380
   travels of George Fox in, 42–43
   travels of John Woolman in, 310
   travels of Samuel Fothergill in, 336–37
   tribes of the, 266
   yearly meetings, 131,
Carpenter, Samuel, 160, 173, 194, 453, 459, 471
   business ventures of, 118, 161, 184n260, 221–22, 224
   Ford mortgage, 188, 190, 456
   Friends Public School and, 133n107, 153
   public offices, 118, 142, 161, 490–91
   William Penn and, 169, 173, 179, 185, 190, 443, 456
Carteret, Sir George, 42, 64, 66
Carteret, John (Earl of Granville), 344, 347, 348, 374n165, 465, 472
Cartlidge, John, 257, 264
Catawbas, 263, 375
Cayugas. *See also* Iroquois
   Iroquois League and, 271, 273, 280, 370, 428, 476, 477
   Revolutionary War and, 419, 421, 423
   speech of Tokaaion at Easton 4, 381–82

William Penn and, 247n119, 248
Chain of Friendship
   conferences during King George's War, 290–93
   general, 266, 381, 424, 427, 462, 476
   Pennsylvania, with Susquehannocks, 152, 478–79; with Iroquois, 280–81, 483; with Lenapes, 288; with Miamis, 319
   protocols, 238, 274
Charles I, 8, 89, 105, 164n194, 448–49
Charles II, 15, 119, 122, 452, 454
   becoming king, 25–26, 36
   concern for Quaker sufferings and, 40, 71, 430
   George Fox and, 32, 201
   land grant to James, Duke of York, and, 106, 450
   land grant to William Penn and, i, 83–92, 148, 150, 165, 214, 415, 453, 484
   plantation trade and, 140n126, 140
   plot against, 74
   return from exile, 43, 89, 450
Charles, Robert, 275, 281n203, 486
Charter of Liberties (1682, 1683), 95, 114, 151n155
Charter of Pennsylvania (1681), 87, 240, 453
Charter of Privileges (1701)
   David Lloyd and, 170, 192, 193, 194
   enactment of, 150–51, 457
   freedom of conscience and religion in, 151, 199–200
   replaced by Constitution of Pennsylvania (1776), 413–14, 490
   separation of lower counties and, 169
   signing of, 154
Charter of Property (1701), 150
Charter or Fundamental Laws of West Jersey (1676). *See* Jersey, West
Cherokees, 263, 375
Chesapeake Bay, 110, 152, 416
Chester Quarterly Meeting, 181, 200, 228–29, 231, 232, 234
Chugnuts, 376

Church of England, 41, 91, 169
  affirmations, 177–80
  George Fox's condemnation of, 12–13, 436
  George Keith and, 134
  jurisdiction over English estates, 209–10
  Penn family commitment to, 44, 317
Churchman, John, 310, 311, 465, 471
Clarendon Code, 41, 54, 61, 71–72, 91, 426–27, 435n8
Clarke, William, 115, 117
Clement, Simon, 211, 213n
Clinton, General James, 422
Collection of the Sufferings of the People called Quakers, A (1753), iv, 62
Collection of the Works of William Penn, A (1726), 62
Committee of Five. *See* Declaration of Independence
Commonwealth (English), i, 11–12, 19, 26, 35, 140, 449–50
Commonwealth of Pennsylvania (1776), 134, 314, 407, 413, 415–16, 470
Conestoga (Pennsylvania; also known as Conestoga Village, Conestoga Indiantown, and Conestoga Indian Village)
  gift of land to Susquehanna Indians, 249
  James Logan and, 256n149, 257, 263–66, 268, 269
  Paxton Boys at Conestoga, 401–2, 468
  William Penn and, 172, 249, 250–51
Conestoga Indians, 249, 250–51, 477
  meetings in Philadelphia, 461, 462
  murder of by Paxton Boys, 401–2, 405, 468
  treaty conferences with, 267, 274n191, 367
Conestoga Manor, 257, 268–69, 401, 461
Conoys (also known as Ganawese and Piscataways), 250, 267, 281, 376, 478
Constitution of the Commonwealth of Pennsylvania (1776), 314, 407, 412–14, 427, 469, 490

Continental Congress, 410, 412, 416, 418, 469–70, 475
Conventicle Act, 38, 41, 45, 54, 62, 71, 72, 426–27
Convention Parliament, 123
Cornplanter, 419, 476
Corporation Act of 1661, 41, 91, 426–27
Council at Rome, 5
Council of Constance, 5, 6
Council of State (Pennsylvania), 154, 160, 161
County Palatine of Durham, 164
Court of Chancery, 65, 115, 189, 190, 211, 213, 427
Court of Common Pleas, 58n183, 84, 189, 427
Court of Exchequer, 188, 217, 219–20, 269n182, 427, 460
Court of King's Bench, 18, 28, 33–34, 125, 426, 427, 455
Court of Quarter Sessions, 29, 54, 427, 430
Covenant Chain, 427, 460, 478–79
  preservation of, 327–29, 356, 466
  with Pennsylvania, 264–66
Croghan, George, 471
  as deputy agent in Indian affairs, 367, 369–72, 377–78, 387, 390, 476
  as trader, 324, 326, 331, 465
Cromwell, Oliver
  as lord protector of England, 19, 41, 429, 449–50
  George Fox and, 20–26, 449–50
  military campaigns of, 11
  Sir William Penn and, 43
Cromwell, Richard, 25, 450
De Lancey, James, 329
Declaration of Breda (1660), 26–27, 31, 40–41, 71, 88, 90–92, 430, 450. *See also* Declarations of Indulgence
Declaration of Independence (1776), 313, 409, 412, 469
Declarations of Indulgence (1660, 1662, 1672, 1687), 40, 71, 72, 91, 120–21, 454. *See also* Declaration of Breda
Delaware (also known as lower counties)
  assembly of, 172
  conveyance of to Philip Ford, 188, 455, 456

Index

conveyance of to William Penn, 87, 106–7, 114, 116, 150, 214, 240, 258, 273
military actions in, 175–76
proprietary powers in, 139, 148, 150, 166, 169
union with and separation from Pennsylvania, 106–7, 108, 108n9, 113, 129–30, 149n150, 151, 155, 169, 455, 457
Delaware Bay, 105, 107, 147
Delaware George, 321, 379, 477
Delaware River and Valley
acquisition of lands along, 107, 115–16, 241–43, 261–63, 273, 278–80, 381, 450, 479–89
during the American Revolution, 417
Falls of the, 101, 111, 115, 135, 148, 241, 479
Forks of the, 285, 287, 291, 318–20, 352, 367n141, 397n227, 477, 482, 488
Indians living along, vin6, 152, 241–43, 241n105, 291, 318, 330, 350, 384, 424, 478
Lenapes in, 242–45, 250, 267, 283, 285, 318
William Penn's arrival in, 105, 117
Delawares. *See* Lenapes
Denny, William
Easton 2 and, 358–69
Easton 3 and, 369–76
Easton 4 and, 377–85
Dinwiddie, Robert, 325–26
Dongan, Thomas, 152, 248–49
Dublin (Pennsylvania) Monthly Meeting, 225
Duke of Cumberland, 316n31, 330, 349, 358, 374, 464, 466, 471
Earl of Pomfret, 317, 340, 344, 464
eastern Lenapes. *See* Lenapes
Easton (Pennsylvania), 263, 422, 477, 479, 482, 488
Easton treaty conferences, 350–52, 352n109
Easton 1, 352–58, 465, 476
Easton 2, 279, 358–68, 466, 475, 481, 488
Easton 3, 369–74, 466
Easton 4, 376–83, 466, 474, 476, 478, 482n20, 488

Easton 5, 241n103, 385–86, 467, 488
Easton 6, 387–97, 467, 472, 481, 488
Easton (all), vi, 405, 407, 477
Edict of Nantes, 44
Ellwood, Thomas, 127
Endless Mountains (also known as Blue and Kittatinny Mountains), 282–83, 285, 286, 462, 483–84, 488, 489. *See also* Kekachtaninius Mountains; Kittochtinny Hills
England. *See also* Charles II; English Civil War; Glorious Revolution; James II; Mary II; Parliament
George Fox's travels in, 12–26, 28–39
William Penn returns to from Pennsylvania, iv, v
Wycliffe and, 2, 7
English Civil War, i, iv, 8–10, 448
Enquiry into the Causes of the Alienation of the Delaware and Shawanese Indians, An (1759), vin8, 325, 356n117, 373, 374n165, 386, 393, 394nn223,224, 466, 481nn11,12
enslavement. *See* slavery
Epistle General to the people of God called Quakers, An (1689), 124
Epistle of Caution and Advice, Concerning the Buying and Keeping of Slaves, An (1754), 306–7, 309, 404, 464
Essay towards the present and future peace of Europe, An (1693), 201, 455
Evans, John, 168–73, 183–84, 457, 458, 471, 492
James Logan and, 176, 192
Exhortation and caution to Friends concerning buying or keeping of Negroes, An (1693), 226
Falls Lenapes. *See* Lenapes
Falls (Pennsylvania) Monthly Meeting, 112, 131, 136, 157
Falls of the Delaware. *See* Delaware River and Valley
Familists, 12, 436
Farmer, John, 230, 230nn73–74, 302, 459

503

Fell, Judge Thomas, 17, 28, 34, 449, 450, 471
Fell, Margaret. *See also* Fox, Margaret
  arrest of, 82, 450
  marriage to George Fox, 37–38, 52, 64, 82, 451
  speaking on behalf of George Fox, 28, 34
  Swarthmoor Hall and, 17, 30, 430, 449, 472
Fell, Rachel, 64, 83
Fell, Susannah, 83
Fenny Drayton (England), 1
Fenwick, John, 65, 107n6, 452
Fermor, Lady Juliana, 317, 340, 464
Fifth Monarchy Men, 12, 45, 436
Firbank Fell, 16–17, 449, 471–72
First Publishers of Truth, 17, 127
Five Mile Act, 41, 61, 72, 91, 426, 427, 435n8
Five Nations of the Iroquois. *See* Iroquois
Fletcher, Benjamin, 130, 147, 148, 455, 456, 490–91
Forbes, General John, 375, 378, 383, 466, 472
Ford, Bridget, 84, 102, 188–89, 189n272, 458
Ford, Philip, 80, 158, 453–58, 472
  William Penn's debt to, 84, 101, 137, 159, 181, 186–90
Forks Lenapes. *See* Lenapes
Forks of the Delaware. *See* Delaware River
Forks of the Ohio. *See* Ohio River
Forks of the Susquehanna. *See* Susquehanna River
Fort Cumberland, 331, 332
Fort Detroit, 398, 467
Fort Duquesne, 326, 330–33, 375, 378, 383, 464–66, 472
Fort LeBoeuf, 325
Fort Prince George, 326
Fothergill, Dr. John, vii, 343–44, 346–48, 352, 465, 472
Fothergill, Samuel, 336–39, 343, 464, 472
Fox, George, 81–83, 125–27, 448–53, 455, 472
  arrests, imprisonments, and trials, iv, 13–35, 40, 68, 449–52
  friendship with William Penn, 52, 63–64, 70–71, 74, 451–52

Journal of George Fox, The, iv, 35, 42–43, 44, 127
  journeys and missions of, iv, 1, 11–40, 42–43, 70–71, 74, 98, 227, 448, 450–52
  life prior to 1648, 1–2, 7–10, 448
  marriage to Margaret Fell, 37–38, 52, 451
  on swearing oaths, 22, 26, 29–30, 41
  'openings' to and preaching of, 9–10, 448
  writings of, 76–78, 201
Fox, Joseph, 391, 494
Fox, Margaret, 42, 64, 82–83, 472. *See also* Fell, Margaret
  arrests of, 38, 83, 451
  speaking on behalf of George Fox, 34
Frame of Government of the Province of Pennsylvania
  (of 1682), 95–96, 108, 113, 199, 427, 430, 453
  (of 1683), 96, 109, 113–14, 147–48, 150, 154, 427, 430
  (of 1696), 148, 149n146, 199–200, 343, 427
Franklin, Benjamin, 276, 345, 370, 406, 411–14, 427, 464, 466–70, 472
  as Indian treaty commissioner at Carlisle (1753), 322; at Albany (1754), 329, 406; at Easton 2 (1756), 358, 360, 364, 366, 369
  as Pennsylvania Assembly agent in London, 370, 383, 387
  as president of Pennsylvania constitutional convention (1776), 407, 412–14, 427
  condemnation of the Paxton Boys, 401–4, 468
  during the French and Indian War, 331, 345
  involvement of in anti-slavery movement, 234, 315
  Philadelphia Academy and Charitable School and, 344
Freame, Margaret Penn, 198, 278, 457, 472, 486
Freame, Thomas, 278, 486
Free Society of Traders, 109, 242–45
freedom of religion. *See* religious freedom

Index

French and Indian War, vi, 316–35, 345, 374–76, 464
  end of the war, 385, 398, 418, 467
  proclamation of war (1756), 348–49
  Quaker relief efforts and, 310, 428
French and Indian Wars, 290, 318n33
Friendly Association, vi, vin8, 353n110
  founding of, 352, 466
  Indian treaty conferences and, 353n110, 368–69, 375, 384, 397
  Israel Pemberton Jr. and, 405
Friends. *See* Religious Society of Friends
Friends public schools. *See* schools (Quaker)
Friendship Chain. *See* Chain of Friendship
Galloway, Joseph, 391, 482n20, 494–95
Ganawese. *See* Conoys
General Meeting of Friends (Cornwall and Devonshire), 35
General Yearly Meeting (American colonies), 116–17, 131
General Yearly Meeting of Friends (England), 25
George I, 180, 181, 459, 460
George II, 316n, 319, 330, 374, 385, 460, 467, 471
  Teedyuscung's complaint and, 382, 384
George III, 385, 386, 390, 394, 467
Georges, John, 275, 486
Germantown (Pennsylvania)
  during the American Revolution, 416–18, 421
  James Logan's home in, 268, 280, 461
  Paxton Boys in, 403, 468
Germantown (Pennsylvania) Monthly Meeting, 132, 200, 225
Germany
  Quaker missions to (1671), 63, 68, 93, 452
  Quaker missions to (1677), 68, 70–71, 74, 83, 93, 133, 452
  William Penn's journey to the Netherlands and Germany (1686), 120, 454

Glorious Revolution of 1688, 12, 122, 123, 454
Golden Rule, the, 226, 229, 278
Gookin, Charles, 172–78, 180, 198, 458–59, 490, 492
Gordon, Patrick, 219, 280, 462, 492–93
  commissioning as lieutenant governor of Pennsylvania, 209n9, 267, 460
  Indians and, 261, 270–71
  removal of James Logan from office, 275
Gracechurch Street (London), 53, 189
Great Council (of the Onondaga), 281, 319, 333, 334, 363, 386
Great Cove massacre, 332n65, 333–34, 345, 355, 376, 397n227, 465
Great Fire of London, 32, 85, 451
Great Lakes, 292, 321
Great Plague of London, 31, 85, 450
Gregorian calendar, viii, 317, 464
Grove Place, 111–12, 135–37, 161
Gunpowder Plot, 29, 432n4
Hamilton, Andrew (colonial governor), 154, 158, 167–68, 183, 457, 491
Hamilton, Andrew (Penn family adviser and father of James), 284, 484, 486, 492–93
Hamilton, James, 321, 472, 493–94
  Easton 4 and, 384
  Easton 5 and, 385–86
  Easton 6 and, 387
  John Penn the Governor and, 400, 406, 467
  Walking Purchase and, 396–98, 486–87
Hanbury, John, 319, 346, 348, 465, 472
Harlan, Ezekiel, 260, 269
Harrison, James, 97, 135–36, 316, 448, 452, 453, 454, 472. *See also* holy experiment of William Penn
  as guardian of Springett Penn, 118
  as member of the provincial government, 113–18, 161
  as steward of Pennsbury, 117, 135
  in England and Scotland, 98–100, 449, 450

involvement in Quaker
matters, 131, 453
relocation to Pennsylvania, 101,
109–12, 453
Hill, Richard, 169, 173, 194, 265,
472, 492
Holme, Thomas, 108, 115, 118, 136,
393, 472
Holy Communion, 41, 91
holy experiment of William Penn,
i–vi, 97, 199, 224, 258, 293–
94, 411–12, 424–425
laying down of, ii, vi, 301, 316,
404, 412–13, 416
William Penn's 1681 letter to
James Harrison, i–iii, 97,
199, 297, 411, 453
House of Assembly (Rhode Island),
311
House of Commons, 11, 62, 72, 74,
163, 346
House of Correction, 14, 428
House of Lords, 11, 139, 142, 144,
146, 159, 163
Howe, General Sir William, 416
Howgill, Francis, 16, 472
Huguenot, 44, 303, 345, 471
Hus, John, 5–7
Independents, 12, 436–37
"Indian goods." *See* trade with
Indians
Innocency with Her Open Face, 51
Instrument of Government
(England), 19, 24–25, 450
Ireland
George Fox's concern for, 24,
37
Quakers in, 62, 71, 93
Springett Penn (William Jr.'s
son), in, 208, 220
trade regulations affecting, 140
Sir William Penn's property in,
43–44, 47, 52, 66, 72, 86–
87, 451
William Penn and property in,
79–80, 187, 442–43, 456
Iroquois, vi, 247n119, 334–35, 427,
428, 460–62, 466, 468, 470,
475–79, 483, 487. *See also*
Cayugas; Covenant Chain;
French and Indian War; Great
Treaty of Albany; Mingos;
Mohawks; Oneidas;
Onondagas; Senecas; Treaties
of Philadelphia (1732, 1736);
Tuscaroras

American Revolution and,
420–24
Easton treaty conferences and,
350, 352, 356–58,
363n132, 367, 367n141,
372, 375, 378–81, 384–86,
396, 398, 466
French and Indian War and,
319–22, 328–29, 333–34,
349
James Logan and, 263–66,
268, 270–72
Ohio Iroquois, 293
Pennsylvania's Friendship
Chain and, 273–75, 280–
91
treaty language of, 238,
238n97
Treaty of Stanwix (1768) and,
419
William Penn and, 152, 246–
50
Iroquois Confederacy. *See* Iroquois
Iroquois League. *See* Iroquois
Iroquois Nations. *See* Iroquois
Jacobites, 122–24, 455
Jagrea, 350–51, 477
Jamaica, 39, 42, 186, 222, 336,
452, 455, 474
James I, 29, 41, 64, 140, 429, 432,
448
James II, 119, 123, 454. *See also*
James, Duke of York
concern for toleration of
dissenters, 119–21, 454
friendship with William Penn,
119, 121, 124, 454
Glorious Revolution and, 122–
23
James, Duke of York, 119. *See also*
James II
friendship with Admiral Penn
and William Penn, 76, 85,
88–89, 108, 119
fur trade and, 246, 248
land grants in the colonies and,
41, 64, 88, 105–6, 108,
148, 150, 166, 214, 239,
450
Popish Plot and, 74
Jennings, Francis, 255–57,
255n147, 269, 318, 400,
400n236, 481
Jersey, East. *See also* New Jersey
land grants in, 42
William Penn and, 95, 117,
187–88

Index

Jersey, East and West. *See also* New Jersey
  proprietorship of, 139
  Quaker meetings in, 116, 131–32, 155–56, 440
Jersey, West. *See also* New Jersey
  Charter or Fundamental Laws of (1676), 67–70
  land grants in, 42
  proprietorship of, 64
  sale of land in, 66–70, 81
  William Penn and, 93, 105, 107, 115, 117, 187–88, 443, 452
Jesuits, 80, 437
Johnson, Sir William, 350, 352–53n109, 419, 467, 472, 476, 481
  Easton 1 and, 355
  Easton 2 and, 365, 367, 368
  Easton 3 and, 370, 371–72, 375
  Easton 4 and, 378, 383–84
  Easton 5 and, 386
  Easton 6 and, 387–92, 394–95, 488
Journal of John Woolman, The, 311, 399
Julian calendar, viii, 318
Keekyuscung, 376, 478
Keith, George, 132–34, 137, 226–27, 455, 456, 472
Keith, William, 180, 269, 459, 460, 492
  Hannah Penn and, 198, 209n9, 218–19, 267
  Indians and, 259, 262, 264–65, 268
Keithian controversy. *See* Keith, George
Kekachtaninius Mountains, 282. *See also* Endless Mountains; Kittochtinny Hills
Kent (Delaware), 106, 106n3, 116, 169, 275,
Kent (England), 11, 106n3
  Hannah Penn's lands in, 79–80, 81, 84
  Quaker missions in, 36, 64
  William Penn sails for America from, 101, 453
Kickapoe, 396
King George. *See* George II, George III
King George's War, 290, 318n33, 463
King of the Delawares. *See* Teedyuscung

King William's War, 127, 130, 318n33, 454
King, Thomas, 380, 398, 476
Kinsey, John, 472, 493
  as Assembly speaker, 294, 296
  as clerk of Philadelphia Yearly Meeting, 231–32, 235, 293, 296, 309, 461, 464
  as Indian commissioner, 291
  misappropriation of Pennsylvania's General Loan Office funds and, 294–95, 317, 464
Kittochtinny Hills, 381, 489n67, 488. *See also* Endless Mountains; Kekachtaninius Mountains
Lancaster Castle, 27, 31, 82, 99, 451
Lancaster (England). See also Lancaster Castle
  Quaker missions in, 16
  Quaker sufferings in, 27–28, 30, 31, 38, 82–83, 99, 450, 451
  Thomas Fell as chancellor of, 17, 471,
Lancaster (Pennsylvania; city and county of). *See also* Lancaster treaties
  during the American Revolution, 470
  as boundary of Pennsylvania, 240
  backcountry unrest in, 349
  Paxton Boys in, 401, 405, 412, 468
  settlement of, 334, 385n196
Lancaster treaties
  (1744), 289, 320, 463
  (1748), 290, 292–93, 319, 463
  (1757), 367, 466
  (1762), 396, 397, 467
Langhorne, Richard, 80–81
Lay, Benjamin, 233–36, 302, 462
Le Grande Derangement, 345
Lehigh River and Valley (Pennsylvania)
  development of by William Penn's sons, 263, 278, 283–85
  during the American Revolution, 422
  Walking Purchase and, 406, 479, 481–83, 486, 488–89
Lehnmann, Philip, 118
Lenapes, in1, vin6, 245n117, 247, 272–92, 350–400, 461, 462,

507

477. *See also* Covenant Chain; Easton treaty conferences; Teedyuscung; trans-Tohickon project; Treaties of Lancaster (1748); Treaties of Philadelphia (1742, 1747) Walking Purchase
conflicts with settlers and, 401, 403, 465, 467, 468
during the American Revolution, 419, 421
fur trade and, 239
Brandywine Lenapes, vin6, 242, 258–61, 267, 460
Delawares, vi, 281, 333, 358, 359, 363, 367n141, 384, 387, 396
displacement of, 266, 291, 318–27, 330, 459, 460, 462
eastern Lenapes, 321, 378, 379, 387, 396, 401, 405, 468, 477, 478
Falls Lenapes, vin6, 241
Forks Lenapes, vin6, 263, 267, 278–80, 283–85, 287–89, 352
Ohio Lenapes, 266, 290, 291, 320–323, 326, 331–34, 361, 376, 383, 396–97, 477
Quakers and, 317, 349, 407
settlers' demands for lands of, 105, 273, 419, 459, 460
Tulpehocken Lenapes, 242n108, 261–63, 267, 271, 287, 459, 460
William Penn and, 241–45, 250–51, 253n143, 427, 478
Lenni Lenapes. *See* Lenapes
liberty of conscience. *See also* Declaration of Breda (1660), religious freedom
Charles II and, 26, 41, 71
George Fox and, 26
in Pennsylvania after William Penn's death, 294, 342, 344, 346–47, 413
in *The Concessions* of West Jersey, 70
Oliver Cromwell and, 12, 19–20, 41
William Penn's convictions on, I, ii, 46, 62, 71–72, 119, 124, 404
William Penn's holy experiment and, 62, 66, 163–64, 179–80, 182, 199, 294

Lloyd, David, 457, 458, 461, 473, 491–92
as attorney general of Pennsylvania, 144, 146
as chief justice of Pennsylvania, 233, 268
as opponent of William Penn, 150, 170–72, 192, 194, 457
Friends Public School and, 153
James Logan and, 192, 194, 458
Lloyd, Thomas, 118, 125, 126, 129, 133nn107,108, 223, 453, 454, 455, 473, 490–91
Locquies, William, 349, 350, 477
Loe, Thomas, 44–45, 49–51, 451, 473
Logan, James, 138, 221–22, 223, 250, 459, 460, 461, 462, 464, 473, 483, 486, 493
as American agent for William Penn, 154, 159–60, 170, 180, 191–98, 250, 252–72, 424, 443, 456, 458, 459, 460, 483
as chief justice of Pennsylvania, 277–78, 462
as dealer in Indian trade goods, skins, and furs, 222, 239n99, 254–57, 293
attempts to impeach, arrest, etc., 171, 176–77, 194, 458
Charles Gookin and, 174–76, 180
Easton treaty conferences and, 388
family life of, 181, 196–97, 222, 459
fiduciary dishonesty of, v, 255–72, 273–75, 275–89
Hannah Penn and, 197–98, 202, 205–9, 212–13, 217–20
John Evans and, 168–69
Lenapes and, 321, 376, 381, 388, 460, 461, 462, 477, 479, 484, 486
library of, 196, 199, 276–77
Philadelphia Treaty of 1747, 291–92
Philadelphia Yearly Meeting and, 295–96, 462
replacement as an overseer of the schools, 298–99, 317, 463

Index

Thomas Penn and brothers and, 221, 273–75, 280–85, 287
William Penn Jr. and, 183–86
Logan, William, 337–38, 465, 473, 486
   as an Assembly member, 353
   as an overseer of the press, 310
   Indians and, 292, 319, 363, 366, 370, 396, 397, 486
   Paxton Boys and, 403
Lollard Conclusion of 1394, 7
Lollards, iv, 4, 12, 437
London (England), 27, 32, 85, 122, 450, 451
   Benjamin Franklin in, 370, 383, 387, 412, 466, 472
   George Fox imprisoned and tried in, 28, 33–38, 451, 452
   George Fox working and dying in, 21, 24, 25, 70, 82, 83, 125, 201, 455
   Hannah Penn in, 208, 209–10, 212, 217, 218
   James Logan in, 193, 196–97, 218
   William Penn imprisoned in, 50–63, 84, 119, 451, 458
   William Penn Jr. in, 182, 185
   William Penn living and working in, 43–44, 46, 47, 66–68, 70, 72, 73, 113, 116, 125, 128, 160, 163, 192, 205, 212, 448, 456, 457
London Meeting for Sufferings, 342–44, 428, 465
London Yearly Meeting, 343, 428
   disownment of George Keith by, 133–34, 456
   Philadelphia Yearly Meeting epistles to, 134, 228–29, 237, 315, 408, 410
   slavery and, 228–29, 232–33, 315
   sufferings of Quakers and, 121
   William Penn and, 73, 117, 131
Lord Baltimore, 88, 164n194, 453
   patent for Maryland granted to, 105
   William and Hannah Penn's boundary disputes with, 106, 109, 114–16, 117, 119–20, 218
Lords of Trade, 88, 108, 115, 120, 140, 141, 389, 426
Louis XIV, 74, 127
lower counties. *See* Delaware
Loyal Parliament, 122
Lutherans, 12, 294, 437
Lutterworth, 1–2, 5, 6, 448, 475
Magna Carta of 1215, 29, 56
Mahicans, 375
Manawkyhickon, 284, 484, 488
Markham, William, 116, 150–51, 188, 473
   as deputy governor of Pennsylvania, 107–8, 108n9, 130, 142, 143–44, 146, 148–49, 456, 457, 490–91
Mary II. *See* Queen Mary II
Maryland
   Board of Trade and, 142, 144, 145
   boundary disputes related to, 92, 109, 116, 119–20, 198, 217, 218, 240, 246, 248, 453
   Charles Gookin and, 174, 175
   during the American Revolution, 410, 416
   George Fox in, 43, 227, 452
   grant to Lord Baltimore of, 64, 86–88, 105–6
   Harrisons' and Pembertons' arrival in, 109–11, 453
   Indians and, 152, 247, 250, 282–83, 289–90, 328, 331, 380, 477, 478
   John Woolman in, 302, 310
Mason-Dixon survey, 109, 240n102
Masters, William, 358, 469
Mawhickon, 354n112, 369, 478
Mead, William, 53–58, 61, 72, 95, 451
Meeting for Sufferings. *See* London Meeting for Sufferings; Philadelphia Meeting for Sufferings
Miamis (also known as Twightwees), 292, 293, 318, 319, 321, 323, 396, 477
Milton, John, 7–8
Mingos, 318, 320, 321, 325, 331, 465, 477. *See also* Iroquois
Minisinks, 376, 380, 489
Minute of the Commission on the Brandywine Indians' Complaint, 259–61
Mohawks, 247n119, 428, 476, 478–79. *See also* Iroquois

Albany Congress and, 327–30
American Revolution and,
  419–21
Conrad Weiser and, 272, 475
Easton treaty conferences and,
  370, 378, 379, 386, 396
sales of land of, 247–48, 329–
  30
treaty negotiations with, 280,
  282, 287, 289
Mohickons, 376
Monck, General George, 90
Monongahela Forks, 321, 322
Moore, Samuel Preston, 303, 348
Moravians, 294, 330
Morgan, Cadwalader, 227
Morris, Anthony, 473
  as clerk of Philadelphia Yearly
    Meeting, 132, 172, 173, 492
  as justice of the peace, 144,
    146, 457
  Friends Public School and, 153
Morris, Robert Hunter, 333, 348–
  49, 350–51, 352–58, 369n145,
  465, 494
Muggletonians, 12, 70n206, 437
Munseys (also referred to as
  Munsies), 354n112, 369, 376,
  478
My Irish Journal, 52, 80
Mystery of Iniquity, The, 232, 233,
  461
Nanticokes, 319, 354n112, 367, 370,
  376, 477
Navigation Acts, 139–45
negroes. *See* slavery
Neshaminy Creek, 241, 479, 480,
  485
Netherlands. *See also* Declaration
  of Breda, 42, 43
  Quaker missions to (1671), 63,
    68, 452
  Quaker missions to (1677), 68,
    70–71, 74, 83, 133, 452
  Royal Charles and, 89
  William III and, 128
  William Penn's journey to
    (1686), 120, 454
New Castle (Delaware), 169, 240,
  275. *See also* lower counties
  (Delaware)
  county court in, 258
  fort near Christiana Creek, 116
  James Harrison and Phineas
    Pemberton in, 111
  John Evans and, 169, 172

James Logan sails for England
  from, 193
William Penn in, 105–7, 149,
  154, 442, 453
New England, 175, 378
  Albany Conference (1745) and,
    290–91
  Quaker missions in, 230,
    230n73, 302, 311, 338
  sufferings and persecutions of
    Quakers in, 39–40, 75, 136
  yearly meeting for, 116–17, 131
New Jersey, vii, 64, 86. *See also*
  Jersey, East; Jersey, East and
  West; Jersey, West
  Benjamin Franklin and, 412
  division into East and West
    Jersey, 66, 452
  Indians and, 329, 367n141,
    375, 380, 477, 488
  Israel Pemberton Sr., and, 181
  John Kinsey and, 231
  John Penn the Governor and,
    407
  John Woolman and, 302, 399,
    475
  land grants in, 42, 450
  Quaker meetings in, 232, 303,
    424, 440, 490
  William Penn and, 70
New Model Army, 9, 10, 11, 14, 15,
  25, 448
New Testament, 7, 29
New York. *See also* Albany
  Congress; Iroquois; Mohawks;
  Senecas
  Benjamin Fletcher and, 130,
    455, 490
  boundaries of, 86, 133, 239–
    40, 467
  Covenant Chain and, 264–65,
    427, 478–79
  government of, 130,
  Indians and, 152, 247, 247n119,
    251, 282, 327–30, 350,
    365, 380, 428, 476
  John Woolman's missions in,
    302, 310
  land grant of to the Duke of
    York, 64, 88, 450
  military concerns in, 130, 148,
    201–2, 290, 418, 420–24,
    471, 475
  Palatine Germans, 262, 272
  Pennsylvania and, 107, 246
  William Penn and, 92, 105,
    106n2, 108, 111, 248–49

Index

trade and, 142, 264
Newcastle (Seneca), 350, 351, 354, 357–58, 366, 476
Newgate Prison (London), 189n277
  George Keith imprisoned in, 133
  William Penn imprisoned in, 53, 58–59, 61–63, 72, 81, 451
Nichas, 378, 379, 471, 476
No Cross, No Crown, 50–51, 101
nonconformists, iv, 12. *See also* freedom of religion
  Charles II and, 91
  James II and, 121
  laws against, 24, 41, 71, 426
  laws protecting, 40–41, 71, 455
  Penn and, 62–63, 70n206, 72, 76, 88, 294
Norris, Isaac I, 181, 222–24, 462, 473
  abolition of slavery and, 181, 224–25, 228–31, 293–95, 309
  as a politician, 181, 223, 492
  as an overseer of the press, 173
  as clerk of Philadelphia Yearly Meeting, 181, 224–31, 235, 293–95, 458, 461, 492
  business interests of, 177, 181, 184n260, 185, 193, 222
  Indians and, 265, 274
  James Logan and, 196, 221
  William Penn and, 169, 173, 177–80, 190, 194, 202, 221, 443, 455
Norris, Isaac, II, 181, 473
  as a politician, 296–97, 322, 329, 370, 374, 378, 406, 493–94
  as an overseer of the press, 303
  James Logan and, 222
Norristown, 223. *See also* Williamstadt
North Carolina. *See* Carolinas
Northey, Sir Edward, 211, 214–16, 444–45, 459
Nutimus, 477, 481, 485
  James Logan and, 267
  Walking Purchase and, 278–80, 279n199, 283, 284, 286–87, 388–89, 461–62, 488
Oath of Abjuration, 21–23, 29–30, 41, 429, 434–35, 449

Oath of Allegiance, 29–30, 91, 429, 432–34
  George Fox and, 29–31, 33–34, 450
  Quakers and, 45, 72–73, 82
Oath of Supremacy, 29–30, 33, 41, 71, 91, 429 432
Of the Duties of Man as they may be deduced from Nature, 276
"Ohio country," vi, 262n163
  control over trade and resources of, 293, 318–19, 321–23, 325–26, 333, 334, 375–76, 378, 380, 383, 468
  Iroquois and, 266
  Lenapes (includes Tulpehockens) in, vin6, 262, 267–68, 290, 367n141, 405
Ohio Indians, 477. *See also* Lenapes; Miamis; Mingos; Nanticokes; Shawnees; treaties of Philadelphia (1747); Wyandots
  negotiations with, 319–20, 357, 375, 377, 378–79, 382, 463, 464, 466
  the French and, 321, 322–24
Ohio Lenapes. *See* Lenapes
Ohio River
  control over trade and resources of, 323–27, 330, 375–76, 383
  Indian settlements on, 266, 291, 292, 400, 477
  Indian treaties regarding, 320
  the French and, 319–21, 464
Old Bailey (London), 53, 189
Onas. 241n103, 253, 274, 284, 286, 288, 351, 358, 368. *See* Penn, William
Oneidas, 247n119, 428, 476, 477, 478 *See also* Iroquois
  negotiations with, 248, 273, 280, 282, 370, 380, 398
Onondaga (New York), 291, 319, 333, 334, 386
Onondaga Council, 250, 281, 291, 319, 321, 333, 334, 386, 398
Onondagas, 152, 247n119, 428, 476, 478. *See also* Iroquois; Onondaga Council
  American Revolution and, 421
  negotiations with, 273, 280–81, 370

William Penn and, 248
Overseers of the Press, 173,
    173n227, 429
  abolition-related writings and,
    229, 234, 305–6, 309, 310,
    312, 404–5, 464
  Israel Pemberton Jr. and, 237,
    303, 464
  John Woolman and, 303, 464,
    466
Overseers of the Schools, 429. *See
    also* schools (Quaker)
  Charles Thomson and, 344,
    465
  Israel Pemberton Jr. and, 237,
    295, 298, 303, 313, 317,
    405, 411, 463, 473
Owen, Griffith, 169, 172, 173, 179,
    232, 253, 473, 491
Oxford Parliament, 122
Oxford University, 2, 3, 4, 5, 6, 44
pacifism. *See* peace
Page, John, 211, 213–14, 269,
    269n182
Palatine Germans, 262, 272, 420,
    475
Palatinate, 164
Parliament, 429, 455, 458
  Charles II and, 26–27, 71–72,
    89, 90–92, 452
  controlling England's colonial
    trade, 140, 144, 146, 159,
    430, 457
  English military and, 7–9, 11,
    25, 448, 449
  George Fox and, 13, 15, 19, 22,
    24, 27
  Oliver Cromwell and, 19, 24
  Pennsylvania's charter and,
    407, 416, 457, 459
  proposed oath bill, 341, 347–
    48, 465
  royal succession and, 162
  "Rump," the, 11, 14, 25
  statutes harmful to Quakers,
    14, 22, 30, 41, 62–63, 71–
    72, 74–78, 120–23, 455
  William Penn and, 62–63, 71–
    73, 182, 191
Pastorius, Francis Daniel, 161
Paxtang, 249, 273
Paxton Boys, 401, 402, 403, 405,
    408, 412, 468
peace. *See also* holy experiment of
    William Penn
  George Fox on, 13, 15, 20, 26,
    27, 33–34, 76, 78
  Iroquois and, 265–66, 478
  James Logan on, 277
  Margaret Fell on, 28
  peace testimony (Quaker), 184,
    339–40, 408–11
  religious freedom and, 40, 41,
    45, 90, 199–200,
  William Penn's experiment in,
    i–iv, 95, 152, 199, 201–2,
    237–38, 241, 250–51,
    403–4, 424–25
  William Penn on, 63, 127–28,
    155–56
peace testimony (Quaker). *See*
    peace
Pearson, Anthony, 18–19
Pemberton, Israel, Jr., ii, vii, x, 237,
    297–98, 335–39, 412, 459,
    463, 464, 470, 473
  abolitionist cause and, vi, 303–
    10, 312–13, 335, 404–5
  aiding Indians during French
    and Indian War, 317, 335,
    339, 344–45, 348–50, 352,
    405, 407
  American Revolution and, vi
  arrest of, 410–11, 470
  as a merchant trader, 237, 297,
    462
  Easton treaty conferences
    (general), 350, 352, 405,
    407–8, 465
  Easton 1, 352, 353, 354, 465
  Easton 2, 359, 365, 368–69,
    466, 475
  Easton 3, 373, 375
  Easton 4, 377n173, 379, 381,
    383–84
  Easton 5, 385–86
  Easton 6, 387, 390–92
  John Woolman and, 236–37,
    301–2, 312–13, 399, 463,
    475
  letter to James Pemberton
    from, 297–98, 446–47
  mission trip with Samuel
    Fothergill, 336–39
  overseers of the schools and,
    vii, 275, 295, 297, 298–99,
    303, 405, 407, 463
  Paxton Boys and, 403
  services to Philadelphia Yearly
    Meeting, ii, 297, 301, 316,
    384, 404, 463, 464, 467,
    493–94
  threats to religious freedom
    and, 341–48, 465

Index

Treaty of Lancaster (1762) and, 396–97
Pemberton, Israel, Sr., ii, 161–62, 181, 199, 237, 257, 297, 304, 336, 411, 441, 454, 459, 460, 461, 463, 464, 472, 473
   as clerk of Philadelphia Monthly Meeting, 275, 316, 459, 461, 463
   Philadelphia Yearly Meeting and, 231, 461
Pemberton, James, 310, 349, 460, 464, 465–66, 473
   arrest of, 410, 470
   Pennsylvania Society for Promoting the Abolition of Slavery and, 315
   resignation from Provincial Assembly, 347–48, 352, 465
   services to Philadelphia Yearly Meeting, ii, vi, 301, 315, 408, 411, 441, 446–47, 467, 470, 494–95
Pemberton, John, 306, 310, 399, 410, 461, 466, 470, 473
Pemberton, Mary, 349, 411, 463, 473
Pemberton, Phineas, 135–37, 158–60, 162, 237, 297, 336, 457, 472, 474, 491
   arrival in America, 101, 109–12, 453
   homes in Bucks County, 117, 135, 137
   in England, 98–101, 449, 450, 451, 452, 453
   Philadelphia Yearly Meeting and, ii, 132, 134, 136, 155–57, 162, 172, 224, 297, 316, 411, 456, 474, 491
   public office of in Pennsylvania, 112–13, 134–35, 136, 154, 491
Pendle Hill, 16, 449
Penington, Isaac, 43, 51, 63, 70, 79, 80, 187
Penington, Mary, 42–43, 63, 79, 102
"Penn Incorporated," 191, 340, 429, 461
   Hannah Penn and, 205, 219
   James Logan and, 191, 198, 218, 219, 252–53, 261
   John Penn ("the American") and, 278

John Penn ("the Governor"), 400, 406
Richard Penn Jr. and, 400
Richard Penn Sr. and, 340
Thomas Penn and, 272–73, 278, 285, 340, 400, 406
William Penn Jr. and, 191
Penn proprietorship. *See* proprietorship of Pennsylvania
Penn Treaty Park, x, 241
Penn, Dennis (son of William Penn), 198, 206n3, 212, 217n30, 218, 219, 458, 460, 474
Penn, Gulielma (first wife of William Penn), 43, 79–80, 83–84, 102–3, 188, 211, 442, 471, 474. *See also* Springett, Gulielma
   children of, 182, 203
   illness and death, 126, 137, 456
   life with William Penn, 119, 126
   marriage to William Penn, 50, 63, 70, 79, 80, 452
Penn, Hannah (second wife of William Penn), 205, 221, 457–59, 472, 474. *See also* Callowhill, Hannah
   friendship with James Logan, 197, 206
   life with William Penn, 147, 157, 163, 186, 197
   management of Penn family affairs, 198, 202, 205–9, 254, 329, 459, 460
   marriage to William Penn, 137, 138, 452, 456
   William Penn's will and, 197, 202–3, 209–20, 266–67, 442–43, 444–45, 460
Penn, John (son of William Penn, sometimes referred to as "the American"), 340, 406n246, 442, 456, 460, 461, 462, 463, 474
   as a child, 138, 147–48, 198, 206n, 208–9
   Pennsylvania proprietorship, inheritance and management of, 203, 212, 212n17, 217n30, 218, 219, 220, 221, 263, 266–67, 268, 272, 275, 340
   trans-Tohickon project and, 278–80, 363, 479

513

Penn, John (son of Richard, grandson of William Penn, sometimes referred to as "the Governor"), 405–7, 406n246, 464, 465, 468, 471, 474, 486
  compensation of for unsold lands in Pennsylvania, 407, 415–16
  government of Pennsylvania and, 329, 400–3, 405–7, 467, 469, 486, 490, 494–95
Penn, John (son of Thomas Penn, sometimes referred to as "the Writer" or "of Stoke"), 406nn246,247, 407, 415–16, 474
Penn, Letitia (daughter of William Penn; also known as Letitia Penn Aubrey), 209n9, 471, 474
  as a child, 79, 83, 102
  in Pennsylvania, 138, 206
  inheritance from William Penn, 215, 217, 262, 269, 443
Penn, Lady Margaret (mother of William Penn), 79, 86–7, 102
Penn, Mary Jones (wife of William Penn Jr.), 206–9, 206n3, 207n4, 209n9
Penn, Richard (son of William Penn), 469, 474
  and his sons, 329, 400, 405, 415, 467
  as a child, 198, 458
  Pennsylvania proprietorship, inheritance of, 203, 212, 219, 220, 223, 266–67, 272–73, 340, 406, 460
  Pennsylvania proprietorship, management of, 263, 268, 275, 387
  trans-Tohickon project and, 368, 387, 466, 479
Penn, Richard, Jr. (son of Richard Penn), 400, 406, 467, 469, 474, 494–95
Penn, Springett (son of William Penn), 474
  as a child, 79, 102
  as heir to William Penn, 118, 191, 442
  death of, 137, 182, 456
  William Penn and, 128, 137, 268, 456
Penn, Springett (son of William Penn Jr.), 474

Hannah Penn and, 206n3, 207n4, 208, 209n9, 460
William Penn estate litigation, 217–20
Penn, Thomas (son of William Penn), 415, 461, 464, 469, 474
  as a child, 163, 198, 206n, 208, 209n9, 457
  complaint of Hannah Penn and, 217n30
  Easton treaty conferences and, 352, 358
  Indian affairs and, 329, 330, 466
  James Logan and, 218, 220, 221, 256n149, 263, 461, 462
  Pennsylvania proprietorship, inheritance of, 203, 212, 219, 220, 263, 266–67, 340, 463
  Pennsylvania proprietorship, management of, 221, 263, 268, 272–75, 400, 405–7, 461, 462, 467
  Religious Society of Friends and, 317, 340–41, 342–44, 346–48
  representatives in Pennsylvania and, 329–30, 385n196
  trans-Tohickon project and, 278–87, 330, 363, 368, 387, 393–94, 461–62, 466, 479
Penn, Sir William (father of William Penn), 63, 474
  military career of, 43, 50, 71, 85
  proprietorship of Pennsylvania granted in memory of, 84–90
  relationship with William Penn, 43–47, 52–54, 58–60
  William Penn as heir of and executor of will of, 80, 81, 84
Penn, William, i–iv, 43, 424–25, 474, 448, 451–59
  as "Onas," 241, 241n103, 253, 274, 284, 286, 288, 351, 358, 368
  end of proprietary government of, 407, 412–14, 427, 490
  estates and debts of, 79–81, 101–2, 117–18, 158–59,

Index

181–82, 186–93, 211–16, 221–22, 442–45
family of, 43, 102–3, 137, 138, 182–86, 202–3, 205–6
land grant from Charles II, 83–92
Lenapes and, 279–80, 284, 287, 360, 363, 395, 427, 478–85, 489
Pennsylvania, government of, 93–96, 106–9, 113–19, 128–31, 137, 142–54, 160–61, 163–80, 193–202, 491
Pennsylvania, selling land in, 97,
policy with Indians, 228, 237–54, 316, 403–4, 424, 427
Religious Society of Friends and, 38, 44–45, 70–76, 126–28, 131–32, 155–57, 440
slavery and, 228, 424
sufferings as a Quaker in England, 43–64, 119–22, 124–26
West Jersey and, 64–70
mentioned, 207, 209, 223, 224, 232, 295, 296, 299, 335, 340, 342, 350, 385n196, 411
Penn, William, Jr. (son of William Penn), 474
as a child, 79, 84, 92, 102, 168
as heir apparent to Pennsylvania proprietorship, 158, 163, 174, 182–86, 191–92, 202–3, 223, 272, 443
decline and death of, 198, 203, 457, 459
Ford debt and, 189
Hannah Penn and, 206–9, 210–17, 219, 444–45
Penn-Mead trial, 53–58, 60, 72, 94, 451
Pennsbury Manor, 241, 442, 453, 457, 472
as part of William Penn's purchase of Pennsbury tract, 479, 480, 481, 481n15, 485
leasing of from Philip Ford, 187
site of negotiations with Indians, 279, 388, 393, 394, 462, 484, 485
William Penn Jr. and, 183–84

William Penn, James Harrison, and, 117, 135, 136, 147–48, 154
Pennsylvania Assembly (also known as General Assembly, Provincial Assembly, and House of Representatives), 112, 430, 490–95
antiproprietary partisanship, 194–95, 219, 253–54, 344, 466, 468
Benjamin Franklin, 401, 403–4, 411–12, 464, 466, 468, 472
Charles Gookin, 174–80, 492
Charter of Privileges, 148–51
David Lloyd, 194, 473, 491, 492
Easton treaty conferences, 353, 358, 367, 370, 374, 378, 381, 383, 387, 391–92, 395, 396, 397
establishment of, 93, 96, 108
Frame of Government, 108, 113–14, 199, 202, 456
French and Indian War and, 322, 329, 345
Iroquois and, 264
Isaac Norris I and, 181, 223, 492
Israel Pemberton Sr. and, 461, 463
Israel Pemberton Jr., James Pemberton, and John Pemberton and, 410, 493–95
James Logan and, 192, 458, 493
John Evans and, 170–72, 492
John Kinsey and, 231, 493
Lenapes and, 259, 271, 403–4, 460
oath-taking and, 341, 346–48, 352, 465
Phineas Pemberton and, 135, 136, 491
rejection of charter for Free Society of Traders in Pennsylvania by, 109
separation of church and state and, 294, 295–97, 465
slavery and, 228, 314–15, 470
trade policies of, 109, 145
vesting unsold proprietary lands in the Commonwealth and, 407, 415–16, 470

515

Pennsylvania Society for
    Promoting the Abolition of
    Slavery, 315
Peters, Richard, 321, 329, 334, 406,
    474
  Easton 1 and, 353, 356n117
  Easton 2 and, 359–60, 363,
    363n131, 366, 369
  Easton 3 and, 375
  Easton 4 and, 376, 377, 382,
    384–85,
  Easton 5 and, 386
  Easton 6 and, 387, 392
  Easton treaty conferences
    (general) and, 351, 396–97
Philadelphia, ii, 107–8, 241–42,
    470
  as site of meetings with
    Indians, 152, 241, 262–63,
    319, 333, 349, 350n104,
    368, 369n145, 384
  as site of yearly meetings
    (Quaker), 131
  business community in, 181,
    221–22
  Continental Congress in, 410,
    412
  disease in, 139
  displacement of Indians for,
    261–62, 318
  early settlers of, 111, 136
  John Penn (the Governor) in,
    407
  John Evans in, 172
  Isaac Norris I in, 223
  Paxton Boys' march on, 402–3,
    408, 412, 468
  Philadelphia Campaign during
    the American Revolution,
    416–18
  slavery in, 232, 301, 315
  William Penn's city lot in, 187
Philadelphia Meeting for
    Sufferings, 310, 428, 465
Philadelphia Monthly Meeting,
    453, 469
  clerks of, 237, 297, 304, 316,
    411, 461, 463, 464
  debates over slavery, 227–28,
    229, 304–7, 464
  establishment of Friends
    Public School by, 153, 200,
    295
  William Penn and, 151–52
Philadelphia Quarterly Meeting,
    225–26, 227, 232, 305–7, 341–
    43, 465

Philadelphia treaties. *See* Treaties
    of Philadelphia
Philadelphia Yearly Meeting
    (PYM), 132, 490. *See also*
    Overseers of the Press;
    Overseers of the Schools
  aid to Indians from, vi, 295,
    316–17, 335, 348–49, 384–
    85, 405, 407–8
  American Revolution and, vi,
    408–11, 414
  Anthony Morris as clerk of,
    132, 172, 473, 492
  books of discipline of, 172–73,
    181, 200–01, 202, 224–25,
    310, 457, 459, 463, 467
  Caleb Pusey as clerk of, 172,
    232, 474, 492
  clerkship of, 132, 172, 296, 316,
    490–95
  debates over slavery by, 132,
    181, 224–37, 294–95, 301–
    15, 335, 338, 404–5, 461,
    462, 464, 469
  disownment of members of,
    133–34, 302, 455, 461,
    462, 469, 472
  epistles of, 134, 155–56, 202,
    229, 237, 308–9, 408,
    439–41, 465, 467
  establishment of Friends
    Public School by, 132
  Griffith Owen as clerk of, 172,
    232, 473, 491
  Isaac Norris I as clerk of, 181,
    222–31, 235, 293–95, 458,
    461, 473, 492
  Israel Pemberton Jr. as clerk
    of, vi, 297–99, 301, 316,
    384, 464, 467, 473, 475,
    493–94
  James Pemberton as clerk of,
    vi, 315, 408, 411, 467, 470,
    473, 494–95
  John Kinsey as clerk of, 231–
    35, 291, 293–94, 296, 461,
    464, 472, 493
  John Smith as clerk of, 474,
    494
  Meeting for Sufferings of, 310,
    428, 465
  minute books of, v, vi, 160n182
  pacifism and, 468
  Phineas Pemberton as clerk of,
    134–35, 136, 155–56, 162,
    297, 316, 456, 474, 491
  Robert Proud and, vii–viii

Index

schools and, 463
separation of church and state and, 295–97, 462, 470
William Penn and, 457
Women's Meeting and, 411, 473
Piscataways. *See* Conoys
Pisquetomen, 271, 287, 321, 376, 378–79, 382,397n227, 400, 477
Pitt the Elder, William, 374, 383, 466, 467, 474
Pittsburgh (Pennsylvania), 240, 320, 321, 383, 384, 400, 466, 467, 472
Pontiac's War, 398, 400, 467, 468
Popish Plot, 74–75, 81, 84, 452
Popish Recusants Act of 1605, 29, 432–34
Post, Christian Frederick, 375, 377n173, 378, 384, 385n194, 466, 474
Potomac River, 152, 250, 264
praemunire, 31, 33, 34, 35, 38, 40, 54, 82, 83, 429
Prerogative Court, 188, 210–11, 459
Presbyterians, 11, 12, 49, 295, 437
primogeniture, 211, 212n18, 216, 217
Privy Council, 429
  Board of Trade and, 85, 88, 140–41, 164–65, 426
  consideration of an oath bill by, 344, 346, 347–48, 465
  Earl Granville and, 344, 472
  Maryland boundary dispute and, 114–15, 119, 120
  Pennsylvania Assembly petitions for royal government, 468
  Walking Purchase and, 383–84, 466
  William Penn and, 50, 52, 81, 108, 164
  William Penn charged with treason and, 124, 128, 130, 137, 455
  William Penn's petition for royal charter and, 84–85, 88
Proclamation of War against the Delawares (1756), 348
Proprietary Land Office, v, 273, 274, 321, 351, 407, 461, 474, 486

proprietorship of Pennsylvania, 429. *See also* Hannah Penn; John Penn ("the American"); Richard Penn; Thomas Penn; trans-Tohickon project; William Penn; William Penn Jr.
  absences of proprietors and, 118–19, 128–30, 161, 205–6, 254, 285, 351
  antiproprietary movement and, 170–71, 192, 194–95
  debts of William Penn and, 101, 181, 214–16, 219–20, 272–73, 283
  engagement in colonial government by, 400
  England's proposal to divest colonial proprietors of power to govern and, 139, 143–47, 159, 196
  Hannah Penn's sons and, 267–68, 317
  Indians and, 330, 483
  Quaker principles and, 339, 340
  sale of the provincial government and, 163, 167, 215–16, 407, 415–16
  Walking Purchase and, 387, 405
  William Penn Jr. and, 168
proprietorship of West Jersey, 64, 65–66
Protectorate, 1, 21, 25, 30, 35, 449, 450
Proud, Robert, vii–viii, 474
Provincial Assembly. *See* Pennsylvania Assembly
Provincial Council of Pennsylvania, 430
  Easton treaty conferences and, 350n104, 351, 363, 376, 381, 385n194, 392n219, 396, 486
  Frame of Government and, 96, 107–8, 113–14, 118, 148, 154
  education and, 153, 200
  Friendship Chain and, 280–81
  Iroquois and, 270, 274, 281–82, 286–88, 291, 293, 321, 319, 483
  Isaac Norris I and, 177, 223
  James Logan and, 268, 270, 275, 280, 461, 462

517

Lenapes and, 259, 262, 267, 271, 321, 484, 486
Paxton Boys and, 403
Phineas Pemberton and, 135
war declaration and, 349
William Penn and, 129, 149, 453, 455
William Southersby and, 228
Puritans, 12, 436, 437
Pusey, Caleb, 172–73, 232, 474, 492
PYM. *See* Philadelphia Yearly Meeting
Quaker Act (1662), 28, 30, 41, 91, 430
Quakers Act (1695), 177

Quaker principles, 30, 61, 231, 451
Quakers. *See* Religious Society of Friends
Queen Anne
   affirmation act and, 178–80
   Fords' petition to, 189–90
   Religious Society of Friends and, 164
   succession to the throne and, 158, 162
   William Penn and, 166–67, 168, 170, 196, 198, 214–15, 457, 459
Queen Anne's War, 161n185, 175, 184, 193, 222, 224, 318n33, 457
Queen Mary II, 122, 123, 125, 130, 159, 162, 455, 456
Randolph, Edward, 139, 141–44
Ranters, 12, 437
religious freedom. *See also* holy experiment of William Penn; liberty of conscience; religious toleration
   in England, 12, 71, 84, 455
   in West Jersey, 68–70
   Pennsylvania as a haven of, i, ii, 151, 164, 182, 199–200, 294, 344, 346–47, 404, 413–14
religious toleration. *See also* liberty of conscience; religious freedom
   in England, 26–27, 40, 72, 73, 75–76, 90–92, 119–21, 123, 437
   in Pennsylvania, ii, 94–95, 220, 294, 424
   William Penn and, 44
Religious Society of Friends (Quakers). *See also* books of discipline, Fox, George; Friendly Association; holy experiment of William Penn; London Yearly Meeting; Overseers of the Press; Overseers of the Schools; peace; Penn, William; Philadelphia Monthly Meeting; Philadelphia Yearly Meeting; schools (Quaker); slavery
   establishment of in colonies other than Pennsylvania, 39–40, 41–42, 70–71, 116–17, 131–32
   establishment of in Pennsylvania, 112, 131–32, 151, 202, 404, 439–41, 490
   founding of in England, 1, 9–11, 16–17, 35, 37n126
Republic of the United Netherlands, 41
Restoration, the
   George Fox and, 13, 27, 32, 36
   Charles II and, 36, 40, 71, 140, 430
   Sir William Penn and, 43
   sufferings of Quakers during, i, 13, 26–27, 32, 74, 132
   William Penn and, 201
Revelation to John (book of the Bible), 2–3, 8n24, 31–32, 32n113
Revolutionary War. *See* American Revolution
Rhode Island, 42, 78, 285, 311, 329
Rhode Island Yearly Meeting, 230, 302
Rickmansworth, 64, 79, 452
"rights of man," 232, 414
Roman Catholics,
   in England, 5, 12, 21, 30, 74, 80–81, 429, 434–35, 437
   in Pennsylvania, 227, 294
   James II and, 119–22
Royal Charles, 71, 88–89, 166
Royal Navy, 43, 91
Royal Proclamation of 1763, 419
Royalists, 9, 11, 28, 43
"Rump" Parliament. *See* Parliament
Sandiford, Ralph, 232–34, 302, 461
Sandy Foundation Shaken, The, 49, 50, 51
Sassoonan, 477

Index

complaints about enroachments on native lands, 261–63, 267–68
successor of, 271, 287, 321, 376, 477
William Penn and, 373n162, 393
Sayenqueraghta, 419, 476
Scarborough Castle, 31–32, 450, 451
Scarouady, 321–23, 331, 349, 350, 352, 477
schools (Quaker). *See also* Overseers of the Schools
Friends Latin School, 344, 373, 465
Friends Public School, vii, 132, 133, 153–54, 161, 200, 237, 295, 297, 317, 405, 411
George Fox and the establishment of, 37
William Penn and, 164
William Penn Charter School, 303
Schuylkill River
Indian lands near, 241, 261–62, 267, 318, 394, 417, 477
Williamstadt manor near, 185, 223
Scotch-Irish settlers, 268, 334, 401
Second Anglo-Dutch War, 85, 89
Second Continental Congress, 412, 469, 470
Second-Day's Morning Meeting (London), 233n81
Seed of God, 38, 125
Seekers, 12, 17, 437, 449
Senecas, 476, 477. *See also* Iroquois
Iroquois League, 428, 478
military campaigns of, 400, 419–23, 471
murder of a Seneca warrior, 264–66
treaty conferences with, 247, 248, 280, 330n62, 350, 357, 368, 370, 377, 378, 380, 386
Serious Expostulation with the inhabitants of Pennsylvania, A (1710), 195
Seven Years' War, 318, 324
Shackamaxon, x, 241, 250, 318
Shamokin (Pennsylvania), Conrad Weiser and, 283

provincial fort at, 352, 366, 419, 476
Tulpehocken Lenapes' relocation to, 262, 268, 289, 318, 477, 488
Shawanese. *See* Shawnees
Shawnees (also known as Shawanese), 468, 476, 477
displacements and relocations of, 152, 250, 266, 318, 330
Easton treaty conferences and, 359, 373, 380, 396
fur trade and, 239, 325
James Logan and, 257n151, 271
participation in Great Cove massacre, 334, 465
Thomas Penn and, 274
treaty conferences with, 267, 293, 319, 321–23, 349, 375, 462
Shenandoah Valley, 282, 289, 378
Shikellamy, 271, 274, 282, 287, 476, 477
Shingas, 477
Easton treaty conferences and, 379, 400
French and Indian War and, 320, 321, 325, 326, 331–33
Great Cove massacre and, 334–35, 376, 465
Shippen, Edward, 153, 169, 179, 194, 253, 486, 491
Simcock, John, 116, 118, 149n146, 491
slave trade. *See* slavery
slavery, 424
abolition principles for Pennsylvania and West Jersey, ii, 69
Chester Quarterly Meeting's condemnation of, 181, 200, 228–30, 231, 234
in Barbados, 160, 234
Philadelphia Yearly Meeting's adoption of abolitionism, 225–31, 232–37, 299, 301–15, 335, 404–5, 407, 411, 464, 469, 470
Philadelphia Yearly Meeting's temporizing on, 132, 136, 200–1, 224–26, 231–32, 236, 293–95, 461, 462
Quaker abolitionists and, 225–37, 301–15, 404–5, 459, 461, 462, 464

519

Quaker books of discipline on, 200–01, 231–32
religious education of slaves, 151–52
William Penn and, 155
Smith, Samuel, vii, 303, 475
Smith, William, 341, 344, 346, 465, 475
Socinians, 12, 70n206, 438
Some Considerations on the Keeping of Negroes, 237, 302, 309, 405
Some Fruits of Solitude, 128, 425n275, 455
Some Proposals for a Second Settlement in the Province of Pennsylvania, 126, 249n128
South Carolina. *See* Carolinas
Southersby, William, 227–30, 302
Springett, Gulielma, 43, 50, 63, 70, 79, 452. *See also* Penn, Gulielma
Springett, Herbert, 211, 214, 215
Springett, Sir William, 43, 79
Stamp Act (1765), 412, 468
Starling, Sir Samuel, 53, 54, 60
Story, Thomas, 210, 253
Supreme Executive Council of Pennsylvania, 407, 410
Susquehanna Company of Connecticut, 330, 398, 467
Susquehanna River and Valley. *See also* Wyoming Valley
  colonial ruination of Indians in, 318, 324, 405
  during the American Revolution, 419–24
  Easton treaty conferences and, 350–51, 357, 362, 367, 369, 371, 378, 380, 382
  Forks of the Susquehanna and, 268, 352
  James Logan and, 218, 254–56, 262, 263–64, 266, 269, 270, 273, 460
  negotiations with Indians regarding, 274n191, 281–83, 285, 289, 330, 334, 427, 462, 467, 478, 483–84, 488
  William Penn's development of, 120, 126, 137, 152–53, 239, 246–52, 456
Susquehannocks, 477. *See also* Friendship Chain, Paxton Boys
  massacre of by Paxton Boys, 401, 405

negotiations regarding lands of, 152–53, 247–52, 263–64, 281–83, 462, 477
  relocation to Susquehanna River, 152, 318
  trade with colonists, 239, 254–56, 264
  William Penn and, 156
Swarthmoor Hall,
  as administrative center for Quakers, 17, 430, 472
  George Fox at, 17, 27, 30, 35, 76, 81–83, 449, 452, 453
  Thomas Fell dies at, 450
Tanaghrisson, 320, 321, 322, 326–27, 477
Tatamy, Moses, 279–80, 477, 481, 481n15, 488
Taylor, Christopher, 112–13, 115, 117
Teedyuscung, 477, 478. *See also* Easton treaty conferences; Walking Purchase
  as negotiator at Easton treaty conferences, 351, 353–97, 405, 465, 466, 467, 476, 488
  complaint about the Walking Purchase of, 279, 466, 481, 488
  murder of, 398, 405, 467
"tender conscience," 12, 26, 31, 40–41, 71, 90, 430, 440.
Test Act of 1673, 41, 71, 72, 74, 91, 121, 430, 435
Test Act of 1678, 74, 121, 430
Thomas, George, 285, 287, 289, 317n32, 462, 463, 493
Thomas, first Earl of Pomfret. *See* Earl of Pomfret
Thomson, Charles, 344–45, 465, 475
  as author of *Enquiry into the Causes of the Alienation of the Delaware and Shawanese Indians, An*, vin8, 325, 386, 466
  Easton 1 and, 356n117
  Easton 2 and, 279, 359–60, 363n131, 365, 369, 466
  Easton 3 and, 370–76
  Easton 4 and, 376–77, 382
  Easton 6 and, 392–94
  Walking Purchase and, 481, 484
Tiawco, 369

Index

To Friends in America, concerning their Negroes and Indians, 78
Tohickon Creek (also known as Tohiccon Creek), 267, 273, 278, 279–80, 279n199, 284, 285, 362, 381, 460, 481, 482n18, 484, 487, 487n45, 488. *See also* trans-Tohickon project,
Toleration Act (1689), 123
Tories, 75
Tower of London, 46–47, 50, 51, 52, 53, 60, 62, 451
Townshend Acts, 412, 430, 468
trade with Indians
　abuses of by European traders, 153, 241, 256, 264, 271, 282, 295, 323–25, 371, 376, 381–82, 478–79
　"Indian goods" and, 239, 285, 289, 292, 323, 356–57, 382, 428
　James Logan and, 222, 254–57, 293
trans-Tohickon project, 278–80, 283–85, 461–62, 481–83. *See also* Tohickon Creek
treaties of Philadelphia
　(1728), 267–68
　(1732), 274, 281
　(1736), 238, 281–83, 288, 462, 479, 480, 483
　(1742), 285–89, 356, 463
　(1743), 363, 363n132
　(1747), 291–92, 319, 463
　(1758), 375, 379
treaties of Stanwix
　(1768), 419, 468
　(1784), 470
treaties with Indians. *See* names of treaties and of tribes
Treaty of Alliance (1778), 418, 470
Treaty of Amity and Commerce (1778), 418
Treaty of Carlisle (Pennsylvania; 1753), 321–25, 329, 331, 464
Treaty of Paris (1763), 318n33, 398, 467, 470
Trenton, 223, 241, 479
Truth, iii, 337, 430
　early Quakers' understanding of, 16–17, 39, 98, 429
　George Fox's understanding of, 10–14, 21, 25, 29, 30, 34, 76–78, 82, 116, 233n81
　John Woolman's understanding of, 399

Margaret Fox and, 82
Philadelphia Yearly Meeting's understanding of, 131n102, 155, 172n225, 173n227, 301, 308–9, 340, 409, 410–11, 439–41
slavery and, 200, 225, 229, 230, 233, 234, 310, 311
William Penn's understanding of, i, iii, 48, 65, 94, 97, 101, 124, 157–58, 185, 186, 199
truths. *See* Truth
Tulpehocken Valley (Pennsylvania)
　Chief Sassoonan and, 271–72, 477
　Conrad Weiser and, 351–52, 475
　displacement of Lenapes from, 262, 267, 268, 291, 318, 459, 460
　Iroquois land release and, 282
　missing land deeds and, 394
　Palatine Germans resettling in, 262–63, 269, 273, 420
Tulpehocken Lenapes. *See* Lenapes
Turner, Robert, 117, 128, 454
Tuscaroras, 247n119, 280, 330n62, 354n112, 428, 476. *See also* Iroquois
Tuteloes, 376
Twelve Mile Circle, 106
Twightwees. *See* Miamis
Twysden, Judge Thomas, 31
Uniformity Act of 1662, 41, 91, 426
Upland (Chester), 108, 111, 115, 131, 244n113
Upper Mississippi Valley, 292
Valiant Sixty, 17, 430, 449, 471, 472
Virginia
　claims by to Pennsylvania lands, 316
　displacement of Indians, 247, 250
　exile of "dangerous" Quakers to, vi, 315n29, 410–11, 470
　in the French and Indian War, 318–23, 325–27, 329, 330, 380, 465
　Quakers in, 132, 237, 310, 336–37, 410–11, 470
　treaties with Indians and, 264–65, 266, 270, 282, 283, 289, 381, 464
Virginia Yearly Meeting, 302, 308
Walking Purchase, the, 479–89. *See also* Easton treaty

521

conferences; trans-Tohickon project
   execution of, (1737), 272, 278, 284–85, 286–87, 462, 479–89
   fraud charge regarding, 352, 366, 376, 380–83, 386, 388, 392–93, 394, 396, 405, 406, 407, 466–67, 477
Wapings, 376, 478
War of the Spanish Succession, 173, 193, 318n33
Warminghurst (England),
   as home of William Penn and family, 79, 83–84, 102, 126, 183, 185
   sale of, 186, 208, 458
Washington, George, 325–27, 410, 416–18, 421–23, 424, 464, 470, 471, 475
Wawachtanies, 396
Weiser, Conrad, 475, 476
   as Pennsylvania government's interpreter and agent with Iroquois, 272, 274, 281, 282–83, 287, 289, 292, 330, 349, 351
   Easton treaty conferences and, 352–54, 357–58, 359, 363, 363n131, 366–67, 372, 375, 379, 382, 385
Welcome, 101, 105–6, 453
Wename, 354n112, 369, 478
Westminster Hall, 28, 65
Whigs, 75
Whitehead, George, 49, 62, 475
William III and Mary II, 122, 123, 130, 159, 455
William III, 127, 128, 140–41, 140n126, 158, 162, 455, 456, 457
William of Orange, 120–22, 454
William Penn Charter School. *See* Schools (Quaker)
Williams, Roger, 78
Williamstadt, 185, 223. *See also* Norristown
Woolman, John, 236–37, 475
   as a member of Overseers of the Press, 310, 465–66
   infant son of, 309–10
   mission travels of, 236–37, 301–2, 310, 311–12, 399–400, 467, 469
   writings of, 237, 301–3, 305, 308–9, 312–13, 339–40, 404–5, 464, 465, 467
writ of habeas corpus, 28, 33, 34, 58n183, 428
Wyandots, 318, 321, 323, 477
Wycliffe, John, iv, 1–7, 12, 437, 448, 475
Wycliffe Bible, 3
Wyoming Valley (Pennsylvania). *See also* Walking Purchase
   displacement of Indians to, 289, 318, 350, 371, 477, 488
   during the American Revolution, 420, 422
   during the French and Indian War, 349
   Easton treaty conferences and, 361–62, 367, 375, 378, 386, 405
   expulsion of Indians from, 398, 401, 467
   occupation of land in by Connecticut settlers, 330, 378, 386, 398, 467, 468
Yardley, William, 98, 111, 112
Yorkshire, 16, 18, 31, 32, 36, 450

Also available from Inner Light Books

A Guide to Faithfulness Groups
By Marcelle Martin
    ISBN 978-1-7328239-4-5 (hardcover)
    ISBN 978-1-7328239-5-2 (paperback)
    ISBN 978-1-7328239-6-9 (eBook) $10

A Word from the Lost
By David Lewis
    ISBN 978-1-7328239-7-6 (hardcover)
    ISBN 978-1-7328239-8-3 (paperback)
    ISBN 978-1-7328239-9-0 (eBook)

In the Stillness
Poems, prayers, reflections
by Elizabeth Mills
    ISBN 978-1-7328239-0-7 (hardcover)
    ISBN 978-1-7328239-1-4 (paperback)
    ISBN 978-1-7328239-2-1 (eBook)

Walk Humbly, Serve Boldly
Modern Quakers as Everyday Prophets
by Margery Post Abbott
    ISBN 978-0-9998332-6-1 (hardcover)
    ISBN 978-0-9998332-7-8 (paperback)
    ISBN 978-0-9998332-8-5 (eBook)

Primitive Quakerism Revived
by Paul Buckley
    ISBN 978-0-9998332-2-3 (hardcover)
    ISBN 978-0-9998332-3-0 (paperback)
    ISBN 978-0-9998332-5-4 (eBook)

Primitive Christianity Revived
by William Penn
Translated into Modern English by Paul Buckley
    ISBN 978-0-9998332-0-9 (hardcover)
    ISBN 978-0-9998332-1-6 (paperback)
    ISBN 978-0-9998332-4-7 (eBook)

Jesus, Christ and Servant of God
Meditations on the Gospel According to John
by David Johnson
    ISBN 978-0-9970604-6-1 (hardcover)
    ISBN 978-0-9970604-7-8 (paperback)
    ISBN 978-0-9970604-8-5 (eBook)

The Anti-War
by Douglas Gwyn
    ISBN 978-0-9970604-3-0 (hardcover)
    ISBN 978-0-9970604-4-7 (paperback)
    ISBN 978-0-9970604-5-4 (eBook)

Our Life Is Love, the Quaker Spiritual Journey
by Marcelle Martin
    ISBN 978-0-9970604-0-9 (hardcover)
    ISBN 978-0-9970604-1-6 (paperback)
    ISBN 978-0-9970604-2-3 (eBook)

A Quaker Prayer Life
by David Johnson
    ISBN 978-0-9834980-5-6 (hardcover)
    ISBN 978-0-9834980-6-3 (paperback)
    ISBN 978-0-9834980-7-0 (eBook))

The Essential Elias Hicks
by Paul Buckley
    ISBN 978-0-9834980-8-7 (hardcover)
    ISBN 978-0-9834980-9-4 (paperback)
    ISBN 978-0-9970604-9-2 (eBook)

The Journal of Elias Hicks
edited by Paul Buckley
    ISBN 978-0-9797110-4-6 (hardcover)
    ISBN 978-0-9797110-5-3 (paperback)

Dear Friend: The Letters and Essays of Elias Hicks
edited by Paul Buckley
    ISBN 978-0-9834980-0-1 (hardcover)
    ISBN 978-0-9834980-1-8 (paperback)

The Early Quakers and 'the Kingdom of God'
by Gerard Guiton
    ISBN 978-0-9834980-2-5 (hardcover)
    ISBN 978-0-9834980-3-2 (paperback)
    ISBN 978-0-9834980-4-9 (eBook)

John Woolman and the Affairs of Truth
edited by James Proud
    ISBN 978-0-9797110-6-0 (hardcover)
    ISBN 978-0-9797110-7-7 (paperback)

Cousin Ann's Stories for Children by Ann Preston
edited by Richard Beards
illustrated by Stevie French
    ISBN 978-0-9797110-8-4 (hardcover),
    ISBN 978-0-9797110-9-1 (paperback)

Counsel to the Christian-Traveller: also Meditations and Experiences
by William Shewen
    ISBN 978-0-9797110-0-8 (hardcover)
    ISBN 978-0-9797110-1-5 (paperback)

www.ingramcontent.com/pod-product-compliance
Lightning Source LLC
Chambersburg PA
CBHW021147230426
43667CB00006B/287